Communications
in Computer and Information Science   1957

Rationale

The CCIS series is devoted to the publication of proceedings of computer science conferences. Its aim is to efficiently disseminate original research results in informatics in printed and electronic form. While the focus is on publication of peer-reviewed full papers presenting mature work, inclusion of reviewed short papers reporting on work in progress is welcome, too. Besides globally relevant meetings with internationally representative program committees guaranteeing a strict peer-reviewing and paper selection process, conferences run by societies or of high regional or national relevance are also considered for publication.

Topics

The topical scope of CCIS spans the entire spectrum of informatics ranging from foundational topics in the theory of computing to information and communications science and technology and a broad variety of interdisciplinary application fields.

Information for Volume Editors and Authors

Publication in CCIS is free of charge. No royalties are paid, however, we offer registered conference participants temporary free access to the online version of the conference proceedings on SpringerLink (http://link.springer.com) by means of an http referrer from the conference website and/or a number of complimentary printed copies, as specified in the official acceptance email of the event.

CCIS proceedings can be published in time for distribution at conferences or as postproceedings, and delivered in the form of printed books and/or electronically as USBs and/or e-content licenses for accessing proceedings at SpringerLink. Furthermore, CCIS proceedings are included in the CCIS electronic book series hosted in the SpringerLink digital library at http://link.springer.com/bookseries/7899. Conferences publishing in CCIS are allowed to use Online Conference Service (OCS) for managing the whole proceedings lifecycle (from submission and reviewing to preparing for publication) free of charge.

Publication process

The language of publication is exclusively English. Authors publishing in CCIS have to sign the Springer CCIS copyright transfer form, however, they are free to use their material published in CCIS for substantially changed, more elaborate subsequent publications elsewhere. For the preparation of the camera-ready papers/files, authors have to strictly adhere to the Springer CCIS Authors' Instructions and are strongly encouraged to use the CCIS LaTeX style files or templates.

Abstracting/Indexing

CCIS is abstracted/indexed in DBLP, Google Scholar, EI-Compendex, Mathematical Reviews, SCImago, Scopus. CCIS volumes are also submitted for the inclusion in ISI Proceedings.

How to start

To start the evaluation of your proposal for inclusion in the CCIS series, please send an e-mail to ccis@springer.com.

Constantine Stephanidis · Margherita Antona ·
Stavroula Ntoa · Gavriel Salvendy
Editors

HCI International 2023 – Late Breaking Posters

25th International Conference on Human-Computer Interaction
HCII 2023, Copenhagen, Denmark, July 23–28, 2023
Proceedings, Part I

Editors
Constantine Stephanidis
University of Crete and Foundation for
Research and Technology – Hellas (FORTH)
Heraklion, Crete, Greece

Margherita Antona
Foundation for Research and Technology
Hellas (FORTH)
Heraklion, Crete, Greece

Stavroula Ntoa
Foundation for Research and Technology
Hellas (FORTH)
Heraklion, Crete, Greece

Gavriel Salvendy
University of Central Florida
Orlando, FL, USA

ISSN 1865-0929   ISSN 1865-0937 (electronic)
Communications in Computer and Information Science
ISBN 978-3-031-49211-2   ISBN 978-3-031-49212-9 (eBook)
https://doi.org/10.1007/978-3-031-49212-9

This Springer imprint is published by the registered company Springer Nature Switzerland AG
The registered company address is: Gewerbestrasse 11, 6330 Cham, Switzerland

Paper in this product is recyclable.

Foreword

Human-computer interaction (HCI) is acquiring an ever-increasing scientific and industrial importance, as well as having more impact on people's everyday lives, as an ever-growing number of human activities are progressively moving from the physical to the digital world. This process, which has been ongoing for some time now, was further accelerated during the acute period of the COVID-19 pandemic. The HCI International (HCII) conference series, held annually, aims to respond to the compelling need to advance the exchange of knowledge and research and development efforts on the human aspects of design and use of computing systems.

The 25th International Conference on Human-Computer Interaction, HCI International 2023 (HCII 2023), was held in the emerging post-pandemic era as a 'hybrid' event at the AC Bella Sky Hotel and Bella Center, Copenhagen, Denmark, during July 23–28, 2023. It incorporated the 21 thematic areas and affiliated conferences listed below.

A total of 7472 individuals from academia, research institutes, industry, and government agencies from 85 countries submitted contributions, and 1578 papers and 396 posters were included in the volumes of the proceedings that were published just before the start of the conference. Additionally, 267 papers and 133 posters were included in the volumes of the proceedings published after the conference, as "Late Breaking Work". The contributions thoroughly cover the entire field of human-computer interaction, addressing major advances in knowledge and effective use of computers in a variety of application areas. These papers provide academics, researchers, engineers, scientists, practitioners and students with state-of-the-art information on the most recent advances in HCI. The volumes constituting the full set of the HCII 2023 conference proceedings are listed on the following pages.

I would like to thank the Program Board Chairs and the members of the Program Boards of all thematic areas and affiliated conferences for their contribution towards the high scientific quality and overall success of the HCI International 2023 conference. Their manifold support in terms of paper reviewing (single-blind review process, with a minimum of two reviews per submission), session organization and their willingness to act as goodwill ambassadors for the conference is most highly appreciated.

This conference would not have been possible without the continuous and unwavering support and advice of Gavriel Salvendy, founder, General Chair Emeritus, and Scientific Advisor. For his outstanding efforts, I would like to express my sincere appreciation to Abbas Moallem, Communications Chair and Editor of HCI International News.

July 2023   Constantine Stephanidis

HCI International 2023 Thematic Areas and Affiliated Conferences

Thematic Areas

- HCI: Human-Computer Interaction
- HIMI: Human Interface and the Management of Information

Affiliated Conferences

- EPCE: 20th International Conference on Engineering Psychology and Cognitive Ergonomics
- AC: 17th International Conference on Augmented Cognition
- UAHCI: 17th International Conference on Universal Access in Human-Computer Interaction
- CCD: 15th International Conference on Cross-Cultural Design
- SCSM: 15th International Conference on Social Computing and Social Media
- VAMR: 15th International Conference on Virtual, Augmented and Mixed Reality
- DHM: 14th International Conference on Digital Human Modeling and Applications in Health, Safety, Ergonomics and Risk Management
- DUXU: 12th International Conference on Design, User Experience and Usability
- C&C: 11th International Conference on Culture and Computing
- DAPI: 11th International Conference on Distributed, Ambient and Pervasive Interactions
- HCIBGO: 10th International Conference on HCI in Business, Government and Organizations
- LCT: 10th International Conference on Learning and Collaboration Technologies
- ITAP: 9th International Conference on Human Aspects of IT for the Aged Population
- AIS: 5th International Conference on Adaptive Instructional Systems
- HCI-CPT: 5th International Conference on HCI for Cybersecurity, Privacy and Trust
- HCI-Games: 5th International Conference on HCI in Games
- MobiTAS: 5th International Conference on HCI in Mobility, Transport and Automotive Systems
- AI-HCI: 4th International Conference on Artificial Intelligence in HCI
- MOBILE: 4th International Conference on Design, Operation and Evaluation of Mobile Communications

HCI International 2023 Thematic Areas and Affiliated Conferences

Thematic Areas

- HCI: Human-Computer Interaction
- HIMI: Human Interface and the Management of Information

Affiliated Conferences

Conference Proceedings – Full List of Volumes

1. LNCS 14011, Human-Computer Interaction: Part I, edited by Masaaki Kurosu and Ayako Hashizume
2. LNCS 14012, Human-Computer Interaction: Part II, edited by Masaaki Kurosu and Ayako Hashizume
3. LNCS 14013, Human-Computer Interaction: Part III, edited by Masaaki Kurosu and Ayako Hashizume
4. LNCS 14014, Human-Computer Interaction: Part IV, edited by Masaaki Kurosu and Ayako Hashizume
5. LNCS 14015, Human Interface and the Management of Information: Part I, edited by Hirohiko Mori and Yumi Asahi
6. LNCS 14016, Human Interface and the Management of Information: Part II, edited by Hirohiko Mori and Yumi Asahi
7. LNAI 14017, Engineering Psychology and Cognitive Ergonomics: Part I, edited by Don Harris and Wen-Chin Li
8. LNAI 14018, Engineering Psychology and Cognitive Ergonomics: Part II, edited by Don Harris and Wen-Chin Li
9. LNAI 14019, Augmented Cognition, edited by Dylan D. Schmorrow and Cali M. Fidopiastis
10. LNCS 14020, Universal Access in Human-Computer Interaction: Part I, edited by Margherita Antona and Constantine Stephanidis
11. LNCS 14021, Universal Access in Human-Computer Interaction: Part II, edited by Margherita Antona and Constantine Stephanidis
12. LNCS 14022, Cross-Cultural Design: Part I, edited by Pei-Luen Patrick Rau
13. LNCS 14023, Cross-Cultural Design: Part II, edited by Pei-Luen Patrick Rau
14. LNCS 14024, Cross-Cultural Design: Part III, edited by Pei-Luen Patrick Rau
15. LNCS 14025, Social Computing and Social Media: Part I, edited by Adela Coman and Simona Vasilache
16. LNCS 14026, Social Computing and Social Media: Part II, edited by Adela Coman and Simona Vasilache
17. LNCS 14027, Virtual, Augmented and Mixed Reality, edited by Jessie Y.C. Chen and Gino Fragomeni
18. LNCS 14028, Digital Human Modeling and Applications in Health, Safety, Ergonomics and Risk Management: Part I, edited by Vincent G. Duffy
19. LNCS 14029, Digital Human Modeling and Applications in Health, Safety, Ergonomics and Risk Management: Part II, edited by Vincent G. Duffy
20. LNCS 14030, Design, User Experience, and Usability: Part I, edited by Aaron Marcus, Elizabeth Rosenzweig and Marcelo Soares
21. LNCS 14031, Design, User Experience, and Usability: Part II, edited by Aaron Marcus, Elizabeth Rosenzweig and Marcelo Soares
22. LNCS 14032, Design, User Experience, and Usability: Part III, edited by Aaron Marcus, Elizabeth Rosenzweig and Marcelo Soares

48. LNCS 14054, HCI International 2023 - Late Breaking Papers: Part I, edited by Masaaki Kurosu, Ayako Hashizume, Aaron Marcus, Elizabeth Rosenzweig, Marcelo Soares, Don Harris, Wen-Chin Li, Dylan D. Schmorrow, Cali M. Fidopiastis, and Pei-Luen Patrick Rau
49. LNCS 14055, HCI International 2023 - Late Breaking Papers: Part II, edited by Qin Gao, Jia Zhou, Vincent G. Duffy, Margherita Antona, and Constantine Stephanidis
50. LNCS 14056, HCI International 2023 - Late Breaking Papers: Part III, edited by Hirohiko Mori, Yumi Asahi, Adela Coman, Simona Vasilache, and Matthias Rauterberg
51. LNCS 14057, HCI International 2023 - Late Breaking Papers: Part IV, edited by Vincent G. Duffy, Heidi Krömker, Norbert A. Streitz, and Shin'ichi Konomi
52. LNCS 14058, HCI International 2023 - Late Breaking Papers: Part V, edited by Jessie Y. C. Chen, Gino Fragomeni, and Xiaowen Fang
53. LNCS 14059, HCI International 2023 - Late Breaking Papers: Part VI, edited by Helmut Degen, Stavroula Ntoa, and Abbas Moallem
54. LNCS 14060, HCI International 2023 - Late Breaking Papers: Part VII, edited by Panayiotis Zaphiris, Andri Ioannou, Robert A. Sottilare, Jessica Schwarz, Fiona Fui-Hoon Nah, Keng Siau, June Wei, and Gavriel Salvendy
55. CCIS 1957, HCI International 2023 - Late Breaking Posters: Part I, edited by Constantine Stephanidis, Margherita Antona, Stavroula Ntoa, and Gavriel Salvendy
56. CCIS 1958, HCI International 2023 - Late Breaking Posters: Part II, edited by Constantine Stephanidis, Margherita Antona, Stavroula Ntoa, and Gavriel Salvendy

https://2023.hci.international/proceedings

25th International Conference on Human-Computer Interaction (HCII 2023)

The full list with the Program Board Chairs and the members of the Program Boards of all thematic areas and affiliated conferences of HCII2023 is available online at:

http://www.hci.international/board-members-2023.php

HCI International 2024 Conference

The 26th International Conference on Human-Computer Interaction, HCI International 2024, will be held jointly with the affiliated conferences at the Washington Hilton Hotel, Washington, DC, USA, June 29 – July 4, 2024. It will cover a broad spectrum of themes related to Human-Computer Interaction, including theoretical issues, methods, tools, processes, and case studies in HCI design, as well as novel interaction techniques, interfaces, and applications. The proceedings will be published by Springer. More information will be made available on the conference website: http://2024.hci.international/.

General Chair
Prof. Constantine Stephanidis
University of Crete and ICS-FORTH
Heraklion, Crete, Greece
Email: general_chair@2024.hci.international

https://2024.hci.international/

Contents – Part I

Accessibility, Usability, and UX Design

HCI in Education and Collaborative Learning

HCI for Health and Well-Being

User Experience Design for Cultural Heritage

Contents – Part II

Interaction with Robots and Intelligent Agents

**Designing Immersive Experiences in Extended Reality and the
Metaverse**

HCI in Mobility and Aviation

Case Studies in HCI

HCI Theory and Practice

Components and Events Identification Challenges and Practices in Interactive Prototypes Construction: A Field Study in a Design Course

Andrea Alessandrini[✉]

University of Urbino, Via A. Saffi, 2, 61029 Urbino, Italy
andaleo@gmail.com

Abstract. Prototyping technologies are crucial for sustaining an iterative prototype process that is efficient and adaptable. For designers, building, programming, and troubleshooting an interactive prototypes' electronic connections, communications, and computing system's components continues to be a challenging task. This fieldwork study explores, describes, and analyses the practices, tools, and technologies used by design students in the construction of interactive prototypes on a university course. The research investigation reviews the interactive prototypes and presents and analyses excerpts of interviews with students. Our findings shed light on the socio-technical factors that influence the choice of digital components. The study describes the types of digital connections and communications among prototype components and the practices adopted by design students to build them. Last, our results show that practices to identify components and users' interactions were based on sophisticated time- or event-based strategies. Finally, the implications of the findings of the study are discussed.

Keywords: Interactivity · Design · Education · Prototyping Tools · Practices

1 Introduction

Prototyping methods and tools are essential means to support designers in exploring and programming the prototype design space [8]. In recent years, many market-available prototyping platforms have become available for designers to construct interactive prototypes rapidly in a way that was unimaginable a few years ago. For example, a study explored the design challenges, issues, and limitations for designers and researchers in constructing Internet of Things systems using existing prototyping tools [2].

Debugging software and hardware physical digital prototypes is a very complex activity. According to recent research, design students use simple hardware components (e.g., buttons) to scaffold the development of their prototype online data exchange with the Internet [4]. The difficulty in prototyping comes from several factors. For example, software and hardware processes during debugging are invisible and require higher cognitive efforts for programmers or designers [3, 7]. A recent empirical study on physical computing tasks shows that circuit problems cause more failure than program problems and 80% of failures are due to missing wiring, independent from the designer's expertise [5]. Other debugging strategies on various software and components assembly programmers used several methods to visualize processes flows, for example, using several print statements on their prototype codes [6].

Despite all these important studies, there is still little understanding of prototyping practices in physical-digital interactive prototyping. Expanding the research topic will advance the development of enhanced design tools which are effortlessly integrable into real design practices and contexts [1]. In this study, we present the results of a fieldwork study that investigated how design students constructed interactive prototypes in a final-year university design course. The study examined the prototypes, the technologies used, and student practices to understand how designers build interactive products.

2 Methodology

In this section, we describe the study context, the research methods, and the data analysis method conducted with design students in a final (fourth) year course on design at the Design Department at the University of Dundee (United Kingdom). Students produce individual design outcomes for their own chosen project brief, drawing on the knowledge and skills they have developed throughout the program. They have access to a faculty workshop, a digital fabrication lab, and an IT suite. They get support from design studio specialists and workshop technicians.

The students have regular deliverables and assignments over two semesters. The class is organized as a studio where each student has their area, sharing their learning experience in the same studio space. The course was composed of product design (PD) and interaction design (IxD) students. Both interaction and product design students have a shared class on Arduino and Processing during their second year. The students' projects were very varied and broad, covering a large range of community and individual needs and desires. The technologies and tools used for implementing the projects were numerous and specific. In general, the more popular technologies and tools for prototypes were Arduino, Processing programming language, basic sensors and actuators, and HTML5 & CSS.

During the study, we used semi-structured interviews with students and prototype analyses. We contacted the fifty-seven students via e-mail, nineteen of whom agreed to be interviewed. The participants ranged in age from 23 to 27 years; eleven were male and eight were female. They had an average of two to three years of experience in building interactive prototypes. All interviews were video-recorded with the participants' permission, and the researchers took written notes. The semi-structured interviews were conducted in the design studio. After we concluded the data-gathering process, we begin to elaborate on the collected data. We highlighted all the data which contain information about the technologies, the tools, and the practices used to construct the prototypes. We conducted data analysis focusing on thematic coding. We moved from descriptive to more theoretical levels leading to a saturation of the material insight and interpretation. In the next section, we will elaborate on the study results.

3   Prototyping Interaction Practices

In the fieldwork study, we observed that the design students used a broad and rich range of practices for connecting components and for overcoming technical problems that emerged during the prototype development. Recognising, detecting, and identifying objects, data streams, and devices were crucial for the design students when developing interactions. The students employed a variety of techniques to recognise digital hardware components, or to shorten their ID addresses.

A student was able to transfer two data streams from two objects to one item at the same frequency. To distinguish between the two signals, she applied a time-delay-based technique, and was able to work around the fact that radio frequency data links are typically utilised to construct one-to-one connections, and the receiver cannot discern and identify between two transmitters. To detect which objects are delivering data to the receiver, the student used a simple and efficient method. However, this time identification approach may be difficult to implement due to the need to define the ideal time threshold without sacrificing the user experience.

Design students employed a practice to simplify the identification of prototype digital components. A student was working on a project to help gym users track their progress and goals. To distinguish between the use of different weights, track exercises, and identify individuals, the prototype has radio frequency identification (RFID) tags and readers. The student simplified RFID addresses to make prototypes simpler and improve tag recognition. This simplification technique made it easier for the student to work with simplified RFID tags that can be easily transmitted via the serial communication interface to a computer (Fig. 1).

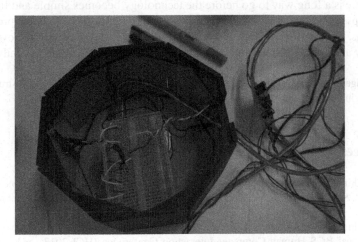

Fig. 1. An advanced prototype utilising a breadboard circuitry.

4 Discussion

The purpose of this fieldwork study was to explore the issues and practises that design students encountered when building interactive prototypes in a final-year university design course. The fieldwork combines prototype analysis with semi-structured interviews. Recognising, detecting, and identifying objects, data streams, and devices is critical when building interactive prototypes. Based on conventional tools and technology, the students used simple but effective techniques to distinguish between incoming signals. Handling interaction events is a critical challenge for prototype development. According to the end user development literature, events handling and multithreading are difficult for non-expert programmers such as design students to implement [9]. Our findings may point to the need for new prototyping tools to help design students comprehend, explore, and integrate event handling and multithreading functionalities while building interactive prototypes.

Our research demonstrates that prototyping interaction is a creative activity that necessitates tinkering and design-thinking skills, yet most tools do not completely support those processes today. Designing tools necessitates a different approach than engineering. It is critical in design to soften technology in order to shape the user's experience by making it rapid, inventive, and simple. Despite the limits of this study due to the limited sample size, we believe that our findings may lead to fascinating new lines of research on this topic beyond the scope of this study.

5 Conclusion

Even if there is a long way to go before the technology becomes simple and fully intelligible, steps are being taken in the direction of the full realisation of simple prototyping interactions. This will provide users with the necessary level of control over digital technology and enable it to become an important part of design students' daily life.

Acknowledgements. We would like to thank all of the design students and instructors that participated in our field study research.

References

1. Alessandrini, A.: A study of students engaged in electronic circuit wiring in an undergraduate course. J. Sci. Educ. Technol. **32**(1), 78–95 (2023). https://doi.org/10.1007/s10956-022-09994-9
2. Alessandrini, A.: End–user construction mechanisms for the Internet of Things. In: 27th International BCS Human Computer Interaction Conference (HCI 2013), vol. 27, pp. 1–6 (2013)
3. Alessandrini, A.: How an undergraduate group of design students solved wiring errors during the prototyping of an interactive. Artifact (2022). https://doi.org/10.1145/3552327.3552345
4. Alessandrini, A.: Practices, technologies, and challenges of constructing and programming physical interactive prototypes. In: Kurosu, M. (ed.) HCI 2015. LNCS, vol. 9169, pp. 132–142. Springer, Cham (2015). https://doi.org/10.1007/978-3-319-20901-2_12

5. Booth, T., et al.: Crossed wires: investigating the problems of end-user developers in a physical computing task. In: Proceedings of the 2016 CHI Conference on Human Factors in Computing Systems, pp. 3485–3497 Association for Computing Machinery, New York, NY, USA (2016). https://doi.org/10.1145/2858036.2858533
6. Brandt, J. et al.: Opportunistic programming: how rapid ideation and prototyping occur in practice. In: Proceedings of the 4th International Workshop on End-user Software Engineering, pp. 1–5 (2008)
7. Détienne, F.: Software Design-Cognitive Aspect. Springer, London (2001)
8. Hartmann, B., et al.: Reflective physical prototyping through integrated design, test, and analysis. In: Proceedings of the 19th Annual ACM Symposium on User Interface Software and Technology, pp. 299–308 (2006)
9. Ko, A.J., et al.: six learning barriers in end-user programming systems. In: Proceedings of the 2004 IEEE Symposium on Visual Languages - Human Centric Computing, pp. 199–206 IEEE Computer Society, USA (2004). https://doi.org/10.1109/VLHCC.2004.47

How Do NATO Members Define Cyber Operations?

Marko Arik(✉) 🔟

Tallinn University of Technology, Tallinn, Estonia
marko.arik@taltech.ee

Abstract. This paper presents a systematic mapping study of NATO member states prominent in the cyber domain, and their interpretation of cyber terminology. NATO nations currently participate in a range of cyber exercises, but there is no unified conceptual framework for accepted cyberspace definitions to ensure interoperability. There is therefore a requirement for a common understanding of how member states define cyber operations.

This study seeks to determine if the doctrinal publications of NATO member states can answer the research question - How do NATO members define cyber operations?

The Systematic Mapping Study aims to provide a broad overview of the research area to provide evidence on the topic and its quantity.

60 national doctrinal publications were reviewed from 12 prominent NATO nations. Of these, ten defined cyber operations in a similar manner providing coherency in understanding the concepts involved. This provides a basis for successful cyber operations and exercises.

Keywords: NATO cyber operations definitions · Systematic Mapping Study · Literature Review

1 Introduction

The conceptual development of national cyberspace operations has evolved with the introduction of new technologies and techniques to exploit their capabilities. To a large extent, definitions and doctrines have reflected how individual states have embraced this new environment leading to a broad spectrum of different terminologies. NATO's recognition of cyberspace as a domain of operations in 2016 has led to the need for a common understanding of how it's members will engage in this new environment. This requirement has been accelerated by a growing interest in offensive cyber operations (OCO), which is expressed by the creation of cyber commands, branches, or services within their armed forces [2]. Training and exercising are conducted by the NATO-affiliated Cooperative Cyber Defence Centre of Excellence (CCDCOE) in Tallinn, which hosts the annual Exercise Crossed Swords[1]. Crossed Swords is an annual technical red teaming cyber

---

[1] https://ccdcoe.org/exercises/crossed-swords/

C. Stephanidis et al. (Eds.): HCII 2023, CCIS 1957, pp. 8–14, 2024.
https://doi.org/10.1007/978-3-031-49212-9_2

exercise training penetration tester, digital forensics experts and situational awareness experts. Crossed Swords has evolved from a straightforward technical training workshop to an exercise involving leadership training for the command element, legal aspects, and joint cyber-kinetic operations [3]. This exercise brings together participants from over 21 countries, including NATO and non-NATO member states, which jointly plan and carry out a range of offensive cyber activities. In planning and executing cyberspace operations, it is especially important that human-computer interactions begin communication with commonly understood concepts.

This article gives an overview of the range of definitions and types of cyber operations used among NATO's prominent cyber countries.

The reviewed doctrinal[2] publications of NATO member states provide an overview of how each nation defines their cyber operations by mapping their cyber operations terminology. Since 2016 NATO Joint Publications have released a series of publications on cyber operations and terminology. These are meant for NATO member states and form the basis for combined cyber operations. This review is focused on identifying if NATO member states follow this established doctrine. If it is not so, it then examines how their cyber operations terminology is defined.

2 Methods

A Systematic Mapping Study was conducted during this research following the steps of Guidelines for performing Systematic Literature Reviews in Software Engineering by Barbara Kitchenham [4]. These comprise the following 7 stages:

1) Identify the scope of research.
2) Formulate the research questions of the review.
3) Carry out mapping of the doctrinal cyber publications of selected NATO member states.
4) Analyse the data needed to answer the research question.
5) Extract data from the chosen doctrinal publications.
6) Summarise and analyse the study results.
7) Prepare a report on the results.

2.1 Scope of the Research

NATO has 31 [4] member states, and the doctrinal publications of the most prominent cyber countries were analysed in this Systematic Mapping Study. The choice of nations that were selected was based on the National Cyber Power Index 2020 [5]. These were the United States, United Kingdom, Netherlands, France, Germany, Canada, Spain, Sweden, Estonia, Turkey, Lithuania, and Italy. Although these were identified as the NATO nations with the greatest involvement in cyber operations, it should be noted that not all NATO members possess cyber capabilities. This further influenced the choice of national publications that were examined. This study was limited to publicly available sources and no nationally classified material was included.

---

[2] Doctrinal publications are considered as governmental, official publications concerning doctrines.

2.2 Validation

To determine the validity of the doctrinal publications of the selected NATO member states, national representatives were consulted. This was to determine whether their doctrinal publications needed to be more comprehensive and to verify the currency of the sources. For example, two national representatives Italy working at the NATO CCDCOE were interviewed who confirmed the validity of the of the sources identified. Conversely, the accuracy of the Spanish cyber definitions was determined to be inadequate due to inconclusive literature and the national representative being unable to provide confirmation of the currency of the publications.

3   Results

The doctrinal publications of the selected NATO member states were analysed with Fig. 1 indicating the distribution of the publications and whether cyber operations were defined.

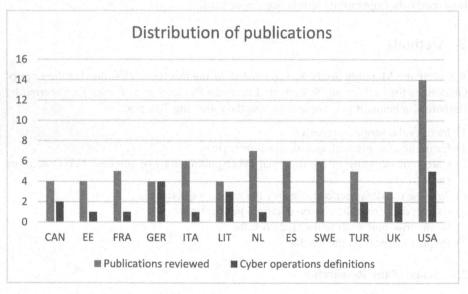

Fig. 1. Distribution of NATO cyber operations doctrinal publications

3.1 Temporal View of Publications

The year of publication of the national doctrinal publications that were examined is presented in Table 1 REF _Ref138149000 \h * MERGEFORMAT Publication date of NATO cyber operations doctrinal publications. The majority of the publications (15) were published in 2018, which relates to ~26% of the 56 publications. This was followed by 2020, when 11 publications were published, which formed ~ 19% of the total. No trend was identified from the data of publication date.

Table 1. Publication date of NATO cyber operations doctrinal publications

Year	CAN	EE	FRA	GER	ITA	LIT	NL	ES	SWE	TUR	GB	USA
2013					1							
2014						1						
2015					1	1						1
2016				1				1	1	1	2	1
2017		1	2		1	1		1				1
2018	1	1	1			1	2			1	1	2
2019	2	2			1		2	1				1
2020	2				1		1	3	1	1		2
2021	1		1	1	1							1
2022		1		1	1		1				1	
2023												1

3.2 Data Sources

Three main agencies were identified as the authors of the doctrine used by NATO nations These are presented in Table 2 Data source of NATO cyber operations doctrinal publications by the following sources: GOV - National governmental publication, MIL – Armed Forces publication and CCDCOE – The NATO CCDCOE publications.

Table 2. Data source of NATO cyber operations doctrinal publications

	Data sources		
	GOV	MIL	CCDCOE
CAN	6	-	-
EE	5	-	-
FRA	5	-	-
GER	1	1	1
ITA	6	-	1
LIT	3	-	1
NL	6	-	-
ES	5	-	1
SWE	1	1	-
TUR	2	-	1
UK	4	-	-
USA	8	2	-

The results of this research are shown in Table 3 Results, which indicates how prominent NATO member states define and classify their cyber operations. These are divided into defensive, offensive and intelligence cyber operations with the US having an additional category of Department of Defense Information Networks (DODIN).

Table 3. Results

	Defensive	Offensive	Intelligence Operations	Cybersecurity	DODIN
CAN		X		X	
EE	X	X		X	
FRA	X	X	X	X	
GER	X	X		X	
ITA	X	X	X	X	
LIT				X	
NL	X	X	X	X	
ES	X	X	X	X	
SWE	X	X	X	X	
TUR	X	X		X	
UK	X	X	X	X	
USA	X	X	X	X	X

4   Analysis

This article utilised an effective methodology to analyse selected NATO states' doctrinal publications to determine how they define cyber operations. Ten out of twelve states recognise and define defensive cyberspace operations. Eleven out of twelve recognise and define offensive cyberspace operations. In addition, seven out of twelve recognise intelligence operations in cyberspace. All the member states recognise cybersecurity. Exclusively, the United States has its Department of Defense Information Networks (DODIN) operations. The DODIN operations can be considered as a key terrain for the U.S. cyberspace. Key terrain in cyberspace is analogous to key terrain in a physical domain, in that access to or control of it affords any combatant a position of marked advantage [6].

From these results, it can be seen that these nations define their cyberspace operations to align with their own unique national cyber capabilities and requirements.

Furthermore, it can be seen that there is no agreed format or procedure on publishing and updating the cyberspace definitions across member states. The definitions are published according to individual timescales and are not related to each other. It was also found that the publications were not always easy to identify, and some were out of date with regards to current NATO doctrine. This work identified a widespread weakness regarding the common understating of the cyberspace operations.

Overall, the study showed that allied member states have their own unique cyberspace definitions. This can lead to one member state understanding key aspects the cyberspace and its operations significantly differently from other member states.

5 Discussions and Conclusions

From this short investigation it can be concluded that there is a need for a single institution to maintain a common database of cyberspace terminology for NATO member nations. This central body should ensure that NATO member states align their cyberspace definitions and that they are recorded in an up-to-date database.

NATO's understanding of cyberspace activities needs to be clear and unambiguous to avoid issues from national publications being written in different languages to avoid issues with translation.

Scope of Cyber operations of the member states fulfils defensive, offensive or intelligence purposes with the United States adding a unique DODIN category. All of the nation's recognise cybersecurity. From most doctrinal publications, the essence of cyber operations could be identified, but not the degree of detail that can provide a comparable definition.

In order to establish common cyberspace activities and corresponding terms it is recommended that member states collaborate more to adopt common definitions.

NATO collaborative cyber defence and offensive exercises are increasing in complexity and sophistication. A common understating of cyberspace activities and their specific definitions is key to the success of these events and ensuring that operators from different nations can successfully work together.

Finally, a future study is proposed to investigate semantics and human-computer interaction in cyberspace doctrinal terms. [7].

Acknowledgments. Dr Adrian Nicholas Venables and Dr Rain Ottis from Taltech University.

References

1. Arik, M., Venables, A., Ottis, R.: Planning cyberspace operations: exercise crossed swords case study. J. Inf. Warfare **21**, 74 (2022)
2. CCDCOE, "Crossed Swords," The NATO Cooperative Cyber Defence Centre of Excellence (2023). [Online]. https://ccdcoe.org/exercises/crossed-swords/. Accessed 15 June 2023
3. Kitchenham, B.: Guidelines for performing systematic literature reviews in software engineering. IEEE Softw. Newcastle (2007)
4. NATO, NATO member countries (2023). https://www.nato.int/cps/en/natohq/topics_52044.htm. Accessed 21 June 2023
5. Belfer Center for Science and International Affairs John F. Kennedy School of Government, "National Cyber Power Index 2020 (2020). https://www.belfercenter.org/publication/national-cyber-power-index-2020. Accessed 15 June 2023

6. U.S. Air Force, "Air Force Doctrine Publication 3–12 - Cyberspace Operations," (2023). https://www.doctrine.af.mil/Doctrine-Publications/AFDP-3-12-Cyberspace-Ops/
7. I. H. D. C. Julia Voo, "National Cyber Power Index 2022," Belfer Center, Cambridge (2022)
8. K. A. L. Kaska Julgeolekuasutuste roll küberjulgeoleku tagamisel ja seda mõjutavad suundumused rahvusvahelises õiguses 2020. https://juridica.ee/article.php?uri=2020_2_julgeolekuasutuste_roll_k_berjulgeoleku_tagamisel_ja_seda_m_jutavad_suundumused_rahvusvahelis
9. Andrew, E.O.: HUMAN COMPUTER SYMBIOSIS (2016). https://arxiv.org/pdf/1601.04066.pdf. Accessed 21 June 2023

New Trends Based on 4.0 Technologies for the Study of Juvenile Crime: A Bibliometric Study

Marlene Ballesta[1]([✉]), Sonia Duran[2], and Alfredo Perez-Caballero[3]

[1] Institución Universitaria de Barranquilla, 18 Street # ##39-100, Soledad, Colombia
mballestas@unibarranquilla.edu.co
[2] Universidad Metropolitana de Barranquilla, 76 Street #42-78, Barranquilla, Colombia
[3] Universidad Libre de Colombia, 177 Street 30 #20, Cartagena, Colombia

Abstract. The present study is directed towards identifying the new scientific trends based on 4.0 technologies for the study of juvenile crime in the Scopus database. For the development of this research, a descriptive and quantitative method is proposed, based on bibliometric tools that allow to effectively measure the scientific production of the variables juvenile crime and technology 4.0 within the Scopus database. This process then requires the approach of a search equation that covers the crucial elements of the study, resulting in the following command: (TITLE-ABS-KEY ("Youth in conflict with the law") OR TITLE-ABS-KEY ("Juvenile delinquency") OR TITLE-ABS-KEY (youth AND crime) OR TITLE-ABS-KEY (underprivileged AND youth) AND TITLE-ABS-KEY (big AND data) OR TITLE-ABS-KEY (data AND mining) OR TITLE-ABS-KEY (4.0) OR TITLE-ABS-KEY (intelligent AND systems) OR TITLE-ABS-KEY (machine AND learning) OR TITLE-ABS-KEY (artificial AND intelligence) OR TITLE-ABS-KEY (iot) OR TITLE-ABS-KEY ("internet of things")). From an initial search, a total of 85 documents published between 2011 and 2023 are observed, of which more than 58,8% have been submitted from 2020 to date. The leaders in terms of publication in the area are University of Pittsburgh and King Khalid University with five publications each.

Keywords: Juvenile delinquency · youth crime · industry 4.0

1 Introduction

Juvenile crime is considered one of the most important problems of today, where there is a high level of difficulty in achieving a true reintegration of those who enter the penal system from an early age. This results in the application of various techniques and tools focused on the study of this problem, so that effective prevention and management mechanisms can be counted on for cases of crime in children and adolescents, who in many cases are the result of a series of environmental conditions, which result in the performance of acts of vandalism and criminality [1].

© The Author(s), under exclusive license to Springer Nature Switzerland AG 2024
C. Stephanidis et al. (Eds.): HCII 2023, CCIS 1957, pp. 15–21, 2024.
https://doi.org/10.1007/978-3-031-49212-9_3

Children and teenagers who engage in criminal activity frequently become entangled in a complex web of environmental factors that encourage them to commit crimes and vandalize property [2]. The study of this phenomenon necessitates a multidisciplinary approach that incorporates social, psychological, economic, and technological perspectives due to the complexity of the factors that contribute to juvenile crime [3]. At the same time, the Fourth Industrial Revolution's emergence in recent years has opened up new possibilities for comprehending and addressing the problems brought on by juvenile delinquency. Industry 4.0 technologies, distinguished by their connectivity, automation, and data-driven capabilities, hold enormous potential to revolutionize how we understand, prevent, and address juvenile crime [4].

Giving some examples of this, there can be created predictive models that predict the likelihood of future criminal behavior among youth at risk thanks to the integration of artificial intelligence (AI) and machine learning algorithms [5]. These models offer insights into the potential pathways leading to criminality by taking into account a number of variables, including socioeconomic factors, family dynamics, educational background, and peer influences. Interventions can be tailored to each person's unique needs by identifying those who are most likely to engage in delinquent behavior. This could reroute their trajectory in the direction of successful outcomes [6].

It is therefore important to take advantage of 4.0 technologies to be able to study and support the generation of real solutions to this problem. In this sense, carrying out an exercise of scientific observation allows us to understand for sure how the state of the art is within this relevant theme. From this, the present study is directed towards identifying the new scientific trends based on 4.0 technologies for the study of juvenile crime in the Scopus database.

Priceless insights can be gained and aid in the creation of useful, evidence-based interventions by utilizing the power of cutting-edge technological tools [7]. To determine the current state of the art within this important domain, it is therefore crucial to conduct a rigorous scientific observation, understanding 4.0 technologies can give access to a wealth of cutting-edge tools that significantly improve the comprehension of juvenile crime dynamics [8]. Advanced data analytics, for instance, enables the scientific community to draw important patterns and correlations from sizable datasets, illuminating the underlying causes of juvenile delinquency [9].

This data-driven approach enables researchers and decision-makers to create targeted interventions, early warning systems, and preventive measures that can successfully reduce the risk of juvenile involvement in criminal activities [10], and is the final result this investigation heads to: a bibliometric review that bring the first stone for the construction of feasible solutions for juvenile crime through 4.0 technologies.

2   Materials and Methods

For the development of this research, a descriptive and quantitative method is proposed, based on bibliometric tools that allow to effectively measure the scientific production of the variables [11, 12], which in this case are juvenile crime and technology 4.0, within the Scopus database. This process then requires the approach of a search equation that covers the crucial elements of the study, resulting in the following command:

(TITLE-ABS-KEY ("Youth in conflict with the law") OR TITLE-ABS-KEY ("Juvenile delinquency") OR TITLE-ABS-KEY (youth AND crime) OR TITLE-ABS-KEY (underprivileged AND youth) AND TITLE-ABS-KEY (big AND data) OR TITLE-ABS-KEY (data AND mining) OR TITLE-ABS-KEY (4.0) OR TITLE-ABS-KEY (intelligent AND systems) OR TITLE-ABS-KEY (machine AND learning) OR TITLE-ABS-KEY (artificial AND intelligence) OR TITLE-ABS-KEY (iot) OR TITLE-ABS-KEY ("internet of things")).

3   Results

Below are the results of the bibliometric review process carried out in the Scopus database based on the search equation explained in the methodology (Fig. 1):

Fig. 1. Main data obtained from scopus

The previous figure shows the general results available in Scopus related to the use of 4.0 technologies for the study and analysis of crime in young people, being able to observe in the first instance that the stipulated time range was between 2011 and 2023, because the temporal concordance between the analyzed products and the use and rise of said technologies is considered a key criterion.

In this way, it is evident how there are a total of 293 authors present in 85 documents published in 81 sources with a significant growth of 3.44%, which is in accordance with the concentration of scientific production in the area of 58.8% between 2020 and 2023. The can be observed more clearly in the following figure related to annual production (Fig. 2):

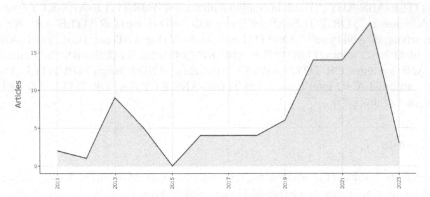

Fig. 2. Annual production of the knowledge area

In this sense, within the area of knowledge studied related to new technologies 4.0 for the study of juvenile crime, it is possible to recognize a series of institutions that appear as protagonists in terms of scientific production, generating relevant contributions in the deepening and documentation of development of these new technologies (Table 1):

Table 1. Most relevant affiliations

Affiliation	Articles
Arizona State University	9
Universiti Kebangsaan Malaysia	7
Mit Media Lab	5
Temple University	5
University Of Western Australia	5
Utrecht University	5
Birla Institute Of Technology	4
Children's Hospital Of Pittsburgh Of University Of Pittsburgh Medical Center	4
Jiangsu University	4
Minia University	4
University of Texas Health Science Center Houston	4

Said table shown above shows institutions such as Arizona State University with nine publications, which is internationally recognized for its area of criminology, followed by Universiti Kebangsaan Malaysia with seven publications and an international trajectory in the field of criminology studies. On the other hand, institutions such as Mit Media Lab, Temple University, University of Western Australia and Utrecht University with five contributions each can also be mentioned.

In terms of scientific production by author, it is observed how Lotka's law explains the recurring participation of researchers within the study area; allowing to show a low concentration of researchers who constantly generate contributions as part of their reported lines of research (Table 2):

Table 2. Lotka law

Documents written	N. of Authors	Proportion of Authors
1	276	0,942
2	9	0,031
3	6	0,02
5	2	0,007

Finally, with respect to the keywords of the articles studied, it is observed how the nodes make up a total of three four clusters: the first related to general terminology and identification of the actors as crime victims. Sex difference, among others; the second associated with technologies where terms such as big data, data mining, learning systems, NLP, computer crime, among others, are displayed. In turn, there are two less frequent clusters with terms such as psychology or juvenile crime (Fig. 3):

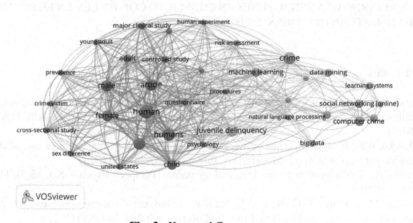

Fig. 3. Keyword Co-occurrence

4   Discussion and Conclusions

From the results described in the previous section, the annual scientific production in relation to technology 4.0 and juvenile crime has experienced a clear growth in the period between 2015 and 2022, reaching a maximum of nineteen (19) publications in the latter anus. In turn, in the total timeline studied (2011:2023) a total of eighty-one (81) sources derived from eighty-five (85) documents have been identified. In relation to the authors, a total of two hundred and ninety-three (293) authors have been identified, of which once (11) they published specifically and the rest were co-authors, totaling an average of 3.79 co-authors per document, each one of them. Which cited by other works an average of 11.44 times.

It can be concluded then that, based on the awareness that technology is crucial to advance the understanding of juvenile delinquency and develop effective emergencies, scientific research has shown a growing and sustained interest in this regard [13]. By leveraging advanced data analytics, artificial intelligence, machine learning, and virtual reality simulations, deeper insights into the complex dynamics of youth crime can be gained.

These recent technologies are innovative means of identifying people at risk, predicting future criminal behavior, and designing targets to redirect their paths toward positive social integration [14]. That is why the present study and the systematic analysis of the Scopus database developed through it, is intended to serve as a diagnosis of the latest scientific trends and provide a comprehensive vision of the transformative role of 4.0 technologies in the study of juvenile delinquency.

Acknowledgement. The authors thanks Ministerio de Ciencia, Tecnología e Innovación from Colombia and the Institución Universitaria de Barranquilla for funding this product under the project "DESARROLLO DE UN SISTEMA INTELIGENTE MULTIPARAMÉTRICO PARA EL RECONOCIMIENTO DE PATRONES ASOCIADOS A DISFUNCIONES. NEUROCOGNITIVAS EN JÓVENES EN CONFLICTO CON LA LEY EN EL DEPARTAMENTO DEL ATLÁNTICO" BPIN: 2020000100006.

References

1. Ettah, A.A., Daru, E.R.: Social skills training and violent crimes among juvenile delinquent adolescents, the case of borstal institute of Buea. Int. J. Trend in Sci. Res. Dev. 3(5), 315–321 (2019)
2. Maseko, W.F.: How youth crime is affected by drug abuse and mental health–a case study of Kawale policing area. Int. J. Modern Dev. Eng. Sci. 2(3), 11–26 (2023)
3. Orben, A.: The sisyphean cycle of technology panics. Perspect. Psychol. Sci. 15(5), 1143–1157 (2020)
4. Samper, M.G., Florez, D.G., Borre, J.R., Ramirez, J.: Industry 4.0 for sustainable supply chain management: drivers and barriers. Procedia Comput. Sci. 203, 644–650 (2022)
5. Fonseka, T.M., Bhat, V., Kennedy, S.H.: The utility of artificial intelligence in suicide risk prediction and the management of suicidal behaviors. Aust. N. Z. J. Psychiatry 53(10), 954–964 (2019)
6. Ragan, D.T., Osgood, D.W., Kreager, D.A.: Impulsivity, peers, and delinquency: a dynamic social network approach. J. Quant. Criminol. 39, 1–34 (2022)
7. Lin, N.: Research on the influence of the internet on teenagers' psychology and behavior. In: 7th International Conference on Humanities and Social Science Research (ICHSSR 2021), pp. 996–1000. Atlantis Press (2021)
8. Jaitman, L.: Frontiers in the economics of crime: lessons for Latin America and the Caribbean. Lat. Am. Econ. Rev. 28(1), 1–36 (2019). https://doi.org/10.1186/s40503-019-0081-5

9. Saxena, K., Shukla, P.: Clustering technique for crime rate prediction and warning to users in big data environment. In: 2023 2nd International Conference for Innovation in Technology (INOCON), pp. 1–7. IEEE (2023)
10. Sutton, C.E., Monaghan, M., Case, S., Greenhalgh, J., Wright, J.: Contextualising youth justice interventions: making the case for realist synthesis. Sustainability **14**(2), 854 (2022)
11. Niebles-Nunez, W., Ramirez, J., Garcia-Tirado, J.: International trade between Colombia and Asia in the framework of logistics processes: a bibliometric review. J. Distrib. Sci. **20**(10), 39–50 (2022)
12. Castro, A.J., Zanello, L., Lizcano, J., Daza, A.: USR as a tool for meeting the SDGs: a systematic review. IEEE Revista Iberoamericana de Tecnologías del Aprendizaje (2022)
13. McGloin, J.M., Thomas, K.J.: Peer influence and delinquency. Ann. Rev. Criminol. **2**, 241–264 (2019)
14. Holstein, K., Doroudi, S.: Equity and artificial intelligence in education: will" aied" amplify or alleviate inequities in education?. arXiv preprint arXiv:2104.12920 (2021)

Older Adults Decision-Making During the COVID-19 Infodemic

DeeDee Bennett-Gayle(✉) and Xiaojun Yuan

College of Emergency Preparedness, Cyber Security and Homeland Security University at Albany, State University of New York, 1400 Washington Avenue, Albany, NY 12222, USA
dmbennett@albany.edu

Abstract. The coronavirus pandemic has exposed the reality disaster researchers have known all along, pre-existing inequities in society often cause extraordinary harm to previously marginalized segments of the population. During this pandemic, there are significant physical and even deadly risks for specific portions of the population, such as older adults and those with pre-existing health conditions. Meanwhile, the mixed messaging on social networks and the Web, which is composed of information and misinformation causes the so-called "infodemic." The infodemic and the coronavirus pandemic present challenges to older adults in their decision-making. Risk communication includes the perception of risk and the exchange of real-time information, advice, and opinions between experts and people facing threats to their health, economic or social well-being. This research surveyed older adults to explore the factors that impact decision-making in response to communications disseminated to them about COVID-19 by operationalizing the Protective Action Decision-Making Model. The research questions investigate associations between behavioral changes, trust, and demographic characteristics of the respondent. Results indicate that trust in stakeholders, the state where the respondent resides, demographic characteristics, and prior disaster experience correlate with older adults' behavioral change measured by staying indoors, wearing gloves, and wearing masks.

Keywords: COVID-19 · Decision-making · Older Adults · Infodemic · Trust

1 Introduction

At the start of the pandemic, health officials warned that specific populations were more at risk for infection to the virus, including older adults (Shahid et al. 2020). The World Health Organization (WHO) disseminated information about the risks for individuals over 60 years of age and those with co-morbidities. By March of 2020, the Centers for Disease Control and Prevention (CDC) reported that older adults were represented in 31% of the infections, 45% of the hospitalizations, 53% of the Intensive Care Unit (ICU) admissions, and 80% of the deaths (CDC, 2020). The adoption of public health measures during COVID included masking in public places and physical distancing (in general approximately 6 feet). These measures varied among various populations and over the course of the pandemic (Benham et al. 2021, Sutton et al. 2020). The differences in decision-making can be attributed to cultural concerns, demographics, awareness, health literacy, risk perception, message fatigue, and trust, among others (Pakkari and Okan 2020, Sutton et al. 2020, Benham et al. 2021).

Trust has been previously researched as a significant indicator of individual behavioral change (Zhao et al 2020; Hughes and Chauhan 2015; Appleby-Arnold et al. 2019; Liu, et al., 2021). Trust can relate to the stakeholder perception (referring to the individual or organization disseminating the message), threat perception (referring to how one feels about the risk and potential problems due to contracting the virus), or protective action perceptions (referring to the efficacy of mitigating efforts, such as wearing a mask). Lack of trust during the pandemic has been connected to misinformation creating an infodemic. Because of the unregulated user-generated content on social networks, mixed messages with information and misinformation occupied the Internet (Garrett, 2020; Zarocostas, 2020; Xie, et al., 2020). Since misinformation was distributed on the Internet from the COVID-19 pandemic (Ma, Vervoort and Luc, 2020), and thus, in turn, led to the so-called "information epidemic." Lin (2020) pointed out that "the politicization of the pandemic, aided by the infodemic and the media establishment, had been on full display since the start of this national crisis." According to the misinformation "campaigns" via the infodemic about Covid-19, most of the American public reported that social media and the Trump administration were the major sources for misinformation (Jones, 2020).

The mixed messaging surrounding mask usage may have also led to mistrust (Ho and Huang 2021, Shelus et al. 2020). The protracted length of the pandemic also took a toll on decision-making, leading to potential message fatigue (Sutton et al 2020). Several studies examined the potential link between message fatigue and decision-making regarding the use of masks (Ball and Wozniak 2021), social distancing (Seiter and Curran 2021, Chou and Budenz 2020), and vaccination (Chou and Budenz 2020). Message fatigue and mistrust were barriers to appropriate decision-making regarding personal protective action during the pandemic.

Modeling decision-making during crisis situations often includes risk behavior, demographics, trust in and credibility of the information, and willingness to make certain hazard adjustments. Hazard adjustments may be deciding whether to evacuate, how and when to prepare, or making financial decisions. One decision-making model for modeling individual behavior often for various disasters is the Protective Action Decision-Making Model (Lindell and Perry, 2003).

This research explores the factors of trust that impact decision-making by older adults through the communications disseminated to them about COVID-19 by operationalizing the Protective Action Decision-Making Model (PADM). The survey was funded through the SUNY (State University of New York) SEED COVID-19 funding, award # COVID202053.

2   Literature Review

Disaster research has exposed challenges in crisis and emergency communications, including cultural concerns of varying demographics (Crouse 2008). These concerns are often mirrored for pandemic and infectious disease communications (Crouse 2008). For example, research on emergency communications from past disasters expose concerns related to cultural social connections in a hurricane (Eisenman et al. 2007), demographics during the recovery from a tornado (Nejat et al. 2018), and accessibility and awareness for people with disabilities (LaForce et al. 2015; Bennett et al. 2018). For public health messaging, specifically, researchers have also highlighted the importance of culture (Kreuter and McClure 2004), considered the disparities among different demographics (Brankston et al. 2021) and have challenges in expanding awareness and accessibility about public health and social determinants of health (Niederdeppe et al. 2008). During the COVID pandemic, officials struggled with culturally competent messaging that effectively led to appropriate protective action, such as with the mask mandates (Ho and Huang 2021; Martinelli et al. 2021).

Decision-making during COVID was influenced by several other factors, as well. Health literacy, trust, and COVID perceptions are among the more common influences. COVID perceptions can influence decision-making for social distancing, avoiding crowded areas, increased handwashing, and wearing a mask (Schiffer, O'Dea, and Saucier 2021). Though older adults wore masks more often than other age groups, in the study by Haischer and colleagues, 57% of older adults wore a mask and only 41% of individuals prior to mask mandates wore one (2020). Regarding trust in health information, Yuan and White (2012) carried out a user experiment to compare the health information behaviors of general users with medical professionals and found that trust is a key factor in users' selection of websites to search for health-related information.

The PADM has been used to understand individual decision-making in response to disaster related communications and messaging (Mayhorn 2005, Lindell and Perry, 2004, Lindell and Perry 2011). The PADM is multistage and uses six factors that influence decision-making to environmental hazards. The six factors are environmental cues, social cues, message receipt, receiver characteristics, information sources, and channel access & preference (Lindell and Perry 2011). The model also includes perceptions of threats (such as severity or risk due to COVID-19), perception of the hazard adjustment (use of a mask or effectiveness of social distancing), and perception of the social stakeholders (those in decision-making authority to enforce adoption of hazard adjustment) (Lindell and Perry, 2011).

In this paper, we examine how older adults make decision-making at the beginning of the pandemic, and how trust plays a role in their decision-making processes using the PADM model as a guide. We focused on behavioral change in terms of wearing masks, wearing gloves, and staying indoors more often than usual. At the beginning of the pandemic, among the preparedness measures suggested were to invest in personal protective equipment to mitigate the spread of the virus, this initially included gloves and medical masks for healthcare and community settings (WHO, 2020). Though later changed to focus only on healthcare settings, the public readily used gloves for necessary errands outside of the home (Khubchandi, Saiki, and Kandiah 2020). Khubchandi, Saiki, and Kandiah (2020) found significant correlations between demographic characteristics and the use of both masks and gloves. To address our goal, we investigate the following research questions (RQs).

RQ1: Does trust in stakeholders relate to behavioral change?

RQ2: Does the state in which the respondent resides correlate with behavioral change?

RQ3: Were there demographic characteristics that correlated with behavioral change?

RQ4: Does prior disaster experience relate to behavioral change?

3 Methods

We collected the data in late spring of 2020. The survey was chosen in this study because it is the most reasonable and convenient method to collect data when the global pandemic started, while most people were required to stay at home. The survey was conducted over a 3-month period using Qualtrics, 182 individuals responded. It was sent out to various older adult listservs in and outside of the University at Albany, SUNY. Respondents were given the opportunity to receive an incentive for participating, through entering a raffle for one of 20 Amazon gift cards worth $50. Winners were randomly selected.

As this study focused on stakeholder, threat, and protective action perceptions, Table 1 lists survey questions and variables that were used in the data analysis to analyze behavioral change. As shown, several factors were considered to identify receiver characteristics (or demographics) of the respondents. Also considered was previous exposure to disasters including other infectious disease outbreaks. Furthermore, behavioral change was considered as decisions to stay indoors, wear a mask, or wear gloves.

4 Results

In the following section information about the respondents in the survey is presented highlighting the significant correlations to behavioral response due to messages received about COVID-19. The study primarily included older adults (75%, n = 141). Several respondents indicated they were a caregiver to someone over the age of 65, 18% (n = 32). However, as noted in Table 2, this indicates that 9 individuals answered the survey who were not eligible for this study, as such they were not included in the study.

The demographics of the respondents show that including caregivers provides valuable information about multigenerational housing, whereas most older adults who responded reported that they lived in a dyad (with a spouse). As expected, most of the caregivers and many of the older adults were women. The demographics information also shows that there was a skewed representation of respondents with most having a graduate degree or making over $100K annually. While the race may appear skewed, according to the census data, approximately 72% of the US population is White.

Approximately 40% of the respondents are from New York, 7% were from Florida, over 6% were from New Jersey, and 6% were from Maryland. The survey reached two-thirds of the states in the nation, with 18 states not represented.

4.1 Protective Action Perception

In response to which necessary precautions have been taken to protect themselves from COVID-19, 29% respondents chose to wear masks when in the presence of others, and

27% decide to stay indoors more than usual. At least 13% of respondents also chose to wear gloves.

Over 97% of older adult respondents changed their behavior because of the pandemic response. Nearly 131 respondents have begun to wear a mask when in the presence of others and 125 respondents have stayed indoors more than usual. However, the reasoning behind their use of a mask is not what is reported through most governors or the world health organization (WHO, 2020).

In the response to the survey, however, 78% of older adult respondents use masks to protect themselves and others. Only 14% of older adult respondents indicated the mask was used as means to protect others. Half of the respondents (43%) indicated that they began to use masks as requested by their governors, if requested.

Most respondents decide to take necessary actions when the governor of the state issued a stay-at-home order (42.44%), and when COVID-19 was declared as a pandemic by WHO (20.93%). However, from a separate question, majority of the older adult respondents indicated they learned of COVID-19 after news reports about the outbreak in Wuhan China (72%). We performed Pearson's Chi-squared test on the relationship between respondents' pandemic knowledge and their behavior change but did not find any significant result.

4.2 Stakeholder Perception

The perception one has of the organization or individual disseminating the message may influence their willingness to take protective action or make behavioral changes as a response to the pandemic. When asked about the most trusted individuals or organizations, by far, most of the respondents' trust messages sent through CDC (23%), State Governor Briefings (20%), and the World Health Organizations (19%). For those who selected 'other,' responses ranged from employer, PubMed, science magazine, Stansberry Research reports, Dr. Fauci, Dr. Birx, specific shows on TV, and doctors interviewed on news shows.

We performed Pearson's Chi-squared test on the relationship between behavioral response with stakeholder perception and found significant relationships. Though most of our respondents indicated that they changed their behavior due to the pandemic, once probed for specifics, there were differences in types of change.

There were significant relationships found between trust international, national, state, and local government entities. Significant relationships were found between trust in WHO and the decision to stay indoors ($X^2 = 13.98$, p < .001), wear masks ($X^2 = 26.91$, p < .001), to wear gloves ($X^2 = 5.69$, p = .017). Additional relationships were found between trust in the CDC and the decision to stay indoors ($X^2 = 24.21$, p < .001), wear masks ($X^2 = 34.86$, p < .001). Trust in the state governor was also significantly correlated with the decision to stay indoors ($X^2 = 14.52$, p < .001), wear masks ($X^2 = 27.57$, p < .001), and use gloves ($X^2 = 3.84$, p = .050). Trust in the local mayor led to one significant behavioral change finding, which was to stay indoors more ($X^2 = 5.08$, p = .024).

Furthermore, there were no significant relationships found between trust in the US President, news anchors, primary care physicians, or family and friends with decision to make behavioral changes in response to COVID-19.

4.3 Receiver Characteristics

Previous disaster and public health studies have emphasized the importance of the demographics of the message receiver on their willingness or ability to take behavioral changes. We performed Pearson's Chi-squared test on the relationship between behavioral response with receiver characteristics and found significant relationships, see Table 8. Not all receiver characteristics resulted in significant relationships.

The decision to wear masks was significantly related to the income level of the respondent ($X^2 = 22,19$, p = .024), where the actual count was higher than the expected for income ranges \$49,999k and below, as well as \$100k and above. Similarly, the decision to wear gloves was significantly related to the race/ethnicity of the respondent ($X^2 = 13.15$, p = .022), where the actual count was higher than expected for African American/Black and Hispanic/Latino respondents.

4.4 Situational Factors

There were situational factors to consider, as well. Though most of our respondents were from the New York area, the survey reached 32 states. The guidance provided during the pandemic varied by state, and therefore, we performed Pearson's Chi-squared test on the relationship between behavioral response with the state in which the respondents were located and found significant relationships.

There was a significant association between the decision to wear masks and the location in which the respondent resided (p = .038), where the expected count was lower than the actual count in every state except California, Maryland, New York, Virginia, and Washington.

4.5 Previous Disaster Experience

Nearly 38% of older adults and 29% of caregivers have had previous disaster experience and 45% of older adults and 42% of caregivers have had family or friends who were survivors of a disaster. Among the disasters listed, infectious disease outbreak was listed as the fourth, after winter weather, hurricane, and flooding. Approximately 19 respondents selected 'other' their responses were, terrorism (specifically 9/11), great depression, California wildfires, and war.

It is worth mentioning that about 41.86% of respondents reported that a close family member or friend had been previously impacted by disasters. About 43.6% of respondents had not. The Pearson's Chi-squared test shows that the respondents' previous disaster experience had a significant impact on their behavior change ($X^2 = 153.07$, df = 9, p < 0.01).

5 Discussion

Trust in Stakeholders vs. Behavioral Change. Pearson's Chi-squared test showed that there were significant relationships between trust international, national, state, and local government entities. Significant relationships were found between trust in WHO and the decision to stay indoors, wear masks, and to wear gloves. Furthermore, there were no significant relationships found between trust in the US President, news anchors, primary care physicians, or family and friends with decision to make behavioral changes in response to COVID-19.

Pearson's Chi-squared test found significant relationships between trust in the CDC and the decision to stay indoors, and wear masks. Trust in the state governor was also significantly correlated with the decision to stay indoors, wear masks, and use gloves. Trust in the local mayor led to one significant behavioral change finding, which was to stay indoors more. A majority of respondents decided to take necessary actions when the governor of the state issued a stay-at-home order and when COVID-19 was declared as a pandemic by WHO. Of note, several indicated that they listened to a state governor, not necessarily their own. For example, respondents from other states indicated that they followed the press briefings of the New York State governor. Trust and credibility are often key in receipt of emergency or warning messages and one's interest in taking appropriate protective action. This finding confirms to the results from Yuan and White (2012) that in dealing with health and well-being related questions or issues, people trust the authorized websites, government websites, and professionals' suggestions. This idea should be explored further, as all government entities were not trusted equally. The characteristics of the emergency messages from authorized organizations should be explored so the trustful contents can be given to older adults in time.

The State in Which the Respondent Resides vs. Behavioral Change. Pearson's Chi-squared test indicated that there was a significant relationship between the decision to wear masks and the location in which the respondent resided, where the expected count was lower than the actual count in every state except California, Maryland, New York, Virginia, and Washington. This result may be attributable to the findings related to trust in stakeholders and behavioral change, as aforementioned in RQ1. During the infodemic, misinformation was spread by the Trump administration (Lin 2020; Jones 2020; Germani and Biller-Andorno 2021) causing governors to provide dedicated state-level guidance. The mixed information potentially provided at federal and state levels may contribute to the significant associations found between behavioral change and the state in which the respondent resides. Again, this may also be related to how government agencies and individuals were not trusted equally, necessitating some to follow guidelines from a different state.

Demographic (or Receiver Characteristics) vs. Behavioral Change. Pearson's Chi-squared test indicated that the decision to wear masks was significantly related to the income level of the respondents; the decision to wear gloves was significantly related to the race/ethnicity of the respondent. However, there was a skewed representation of respondents with most having a graduate degree or making over $100K annually. Also, a significant amount of our respondents are White women. These findings are consistent with many others regarding behavioral changes during the pandemic based on race/ethnicity, gender, and income (Hearne and Niño 2021; Haischer et al. 2020; Weill et al. 2020).

Prior Disaster Experience vs. Behavioral Change. Respondents' prior disaster experience had a significant impact on their behavior change. The more experience they had, the more likely they would take necessary protective action as early as possible. Our findings coincide with Johnson and Mayorga's (2021) results in that information participants received from the authorities were trusted and led to protective actions. This may be attributed to the difference of the targeted respondents. Our study only focused on older adults who might have gained enough knowledge from their prior life and disaster experience which in turn can lead to their taking protective actions at appropriate times in emergency situations.

As far as taking protective action nearly all respondents (97%) changed their behavior in some way following receipt of public health messaging. However, 30% began to wear a mask and 27% stayed indoors more than usual. Those that did wear a mask may have misunderstood the purpose for wearing the mask. Furthermore, over the course of the pandemic, the researchers have observed differences in how the mask is worn by the public. This leads us to more questions regarding exposure, attention, and comprehension, and time, which were not included in this survey. It may be interesting in future research to examine how cultural bias or knowledge of infectious disease could affect the behavioral changes of older adults, as well as their perception of wearing masks. The time of the protracted pandemic is not a factor currently considered in the PADM; however, many have begun to question the attention and exposure of the public to emergency messages over the continuance of this pandemic (and potential second wave). As highlighted in the PADM model, there is a predecision process, which relates to threat perception, protective action perception and stakeholder perceptions.

Limitations. As a traditional survey, this study is restricted by the limited number of respondents, and a limited number of questions. As aforementioned, there was a skewed representation of respondents with most having a graduate degree or making over $100K annually. In addition, a significant amount of our respondents are White women. These factors may restrict the generalization of the results of this study. Despite these limitations, this study contributes to the body of knowledge of understanding older adults' decision-making process at the beginning of COVID-19 pandemic and identifying social factors affecting such process.

6 Conclusion

This study investigated the social factors affecting older adults' decision-making process at the beginning of the global pandemic, and how trust plays a role in the decision-making process. There were significant relationships between stakeholder perception and the behavioral change, which indicates the important influence stakeholders have in the decision-making process in response to emergency situations. Therefore, to contribute to the global discovery from the COVID-19 pandemic, it is critical for professionals gain trust in communities by including stakeholders and supporting their scientific insights and depoliticizing the influence of politicians on the public. This survey was a pilot to examine the receipt of disaster messaging and to collect preliminary data on older adults' protective actions in response to COVID-19. The long-term goal of this research is to better understand and model risk perception, and preparedness and response activities among older adults to strengthen resiliency among them.

References

Shahid, Z., et al.: COVID-19 and older adults: what we know. J. Am. Geriatr. Soc. **68**(5), 926–929 (2020)

World Health Organization. (2020). Rational use of personal protective equipment for coronavirus disease (COVID-19): interim guidance, 27 February 2020 (No. WHO/2019-nCov/IPCPPE_use/2020.1). World Health Organization

Centers for Disease Control and Prevention. Severe Outcomes Among Patients with Coronavirus Disease 2019 (COVID-19)—United States, February 12–March 16, 2020. https://www.cdc.gov/mmwr/volumes/69/wr/mm6912e2.htm. Accessed March 26 2020

Benham, J.L., et al.: Attitudes, current behaviours and barriers to public health measures that reduce COVID-19 transmission: a qualitative study to inform public health messaging. PLoS ONE **16**(2), e0246941 (2021)

Sutton, J., et al.: Longitudinal risk communication: a research agenda for communicating in a pandemic. Health Secur. J. **19**(4), 370–378 (2020). DOI: https://doi.org/10.1089/hs.2020.0161 https://www.liebertpub.com/doi/full/10.1089/hs.2020.0161

Paakkari, L., Okan, O.: COVID-19: health literacy is an underestimated problem. Lancet. Public Health **5**(5), e249 (2020)

Zhao, E., Wu, Q., Crimmins, E.M., Ailshire, J.A.: Media trust and infection mitigating behaviours during the COVID-19 pandemic in the USA. BMJ Glob. Health **5**(10), e003323 (2020)

Hughes, A.L., Chauhan, A.: Online media as a means to affect public trust in emergency responders. In: ISCRAM (2015)

Appleby-Arnold, S., Brockdorff, N., Fallou, L., Bossu, R.: Truth, trust, and civic duty: cultural factors in citizens' perceptions of mobile phone apps and social media in disasters. J. Contingencies Crisis Manage. **27**(4), 293–305 (2019)

Liu, Y., Qin, Z., Ye, Z., Zhang, X., Meng, F.: Explaining trust and consequences of COVID-19 rumors on social media: a SOR perspective (2021)

Garrett, L.: COVID-19: the medium is the message. Lancet **395**(10228), 942–943 (2020)

Zarocostas, J.: How to fight an infodemic. Lancet **395**(10225), 676 (2020)

Xie, B., et al.: Global health crises are also information crises: a call to action. J. Am. Soc. Inf. Sci. **71**(12), 1419–1423 (2020)

Ma, X., Vervoort, D., Luc, J.G.Y.: When misinformation goes viral: access to evidence-based information in the COVID-19 pandemic. J. Globe Health Sci. **2**(1), e13 (2020). https://doi.org/10.35500/jghs.2020.2.e13Accessed 23 Feb 2021 pISSN 2671–6925·eISSN 2671–6933

Jones, J.: Americans struggle to navigate COVID-19 "infodemic". Gallup Poll (2020). https://news.gallup.com/poll/310409/americans-struggle-navigatecovid-infodemic.aspx

Ho, A., Huang, V.: Unmasking the ethics of public health messaging in a pandemic. J. Bioethical Inquiry **18**, 1–11 (2021)

Shelus, V.S., et al.: Motivations and barriers for the use of face coverings during the COVID-19 pandemic: messaging insights from focus groups. Int. J. Environ. Res. Public Health **17**(24), 9298 (2020)

Ball, H., Wozniak, T.R.: Why Do some Americans resist COVID-19 prevention behavior? An analysis of issue importance, message fatigue, and reactance regarding COVID-19 messaging. Health Commun. **37**(14), 1–8 (2021)

Seiter, J.S., Curran, T.: Social-distancing fatigue during the COVID-19 pandemic: a mediation analysis of cognitive flexibility, fatigue, depression, and adherence to CDC guidelines. Commun. Res. Rep. **38**(1), 68–78 (2021)

Lindell, M.K., Perry, R.W.: The protective action decision model: theoretical modifications and additional evidence. Risk Anal. Int. J. **32**(4), 616–632 (2012)

Crouse Quinn, S.: Crisis and emergency risk communication in a pandemic: a model for building capacity and resilience of minority communities. Health Promot. Pract. **9**(4_suppl), 18S–25S (2008)

Eisenman, D.P., Cordasco, K.M., Asch, S., Golden, J.F., Glik, D.: Disaster planning and risk communication with vulnerable communities: lessons from Hurricane Katrina. Am. J. Public Health, **97**(Supplement_1), S109–S115 (2007)

Nejat, A., Binder, S.B., Greer, A., Jamali, M.: Demographics and the dynamics of recovery: a latent class analysis of disaster recovery priorities after the 2013 Moore, Oklahoma Tornado. Int. J. Mass Emergencies Disasters **36**(1), 23–51 (2018)

LaForce, S., Bennett, D.M., Linden, M., Touzet, C., Mitchell, H.: Optimizing accessibility of wireless emergency alerts: 2015 survey findings. J. Technol. Persons with Disabil. (2016)

Bennett, D., Laforce, S., Touzet, C., Chiodo, K.: American sign language & emergency alerts: the relationship between language, disability, and accessible emergency messaging. Int. J. Mass Emerg. Disasters **36**(1), 71–87 (2018)

Kreuter, M.W., McClure, S.M.: The role of culture in health communication. Annu. Rev. Public Health **25**, 439–455 (2004)

Brankston, G., et al.: Socio-demographic disparities in knowledge, practices, and ability to comply with COVID-19 public health measures in Canada. Can. J. Public Health **112**(3), 363–375 (2021)

Niederdeppe, J., Bu, Q.L., Borah, P., Kindig, D.A., Robert, S.A.: Message design strategies to raise public awareness of social determinants of health and population health disparities. Milbank Q. **86**(3), 481–513 (2008)

Martinelli, L., et al.: Face masks during the COVID-19 pandemic: a simple protection tool with many meanings. Front. Public Health, 947 (2021)

Schiffer, A.A., O'Dea, C.J., Saucier, D.A.: Moral decision-making and support for safety procedures amid the COVID-19 pandemic. Personality Individ. Differ. **175**, 110714 (2021)

Haischer, M.H., et al.: Who is wearing a mask? Gender-, age-, and location-related differences during the COVID-19 pandemic. PLoS ONE **15**(10), e0240785 (2020)

Yuan, X.J., White, R.: Building the trail best traveled: effects of domain knowledge on web search trailblazing. In: Proceedings of the ACM SIGCHI Conference on Human Factors in Computing Systems (CHI 2012). Austin, Texas, USA, May 2012 (2012)

Mayhorn, C.B.: Cognitive aging and the processing of hazard information and disaster warnings. Nat. Hazard. Rev. **6**(4), 165–170 (2005)

Khubchandani, J., Saiki, D., Kandiah, J.: Masks, gloves, and the COVID-19 pandemic: rapid assessment of public behaviors in the United States. Epidemiologia **1**(1), 16–22 (2020)

Germani, F., Biller-Andorno, N.: The anti-vaccination infodemic on social media: A behavioral analysis. The anti-vaccination infodemic on social media: A behavioral analysis (plos.org) (2021)

Hearne, B.N., Niño, M.D.: Understanding how race, ethnicity, and gender shape mask-wearing adherence during the COVID-19 pandemic: evidence from the COVID impact survey. J. Racial Ethnic Health Disparities (2021). https://doi.org/10.1007/s40615-020-00941-1

Weill, J.A., Stigler, M., Deschenes, O., Springborn, M.R.: Social distancing responses to COVID-19 emergency declarations strongly differentiated by income. Proc. Natl. Acad. Sci. **117**(33), 19658–19660 (2020)

Johnson, B.B., Mayorga, M.: Americans' early behavioral responses to COVID-19. Human Ecol. Risk Assess. Int. J. **27**, 1–14 (2021)

Automated Nonverbal Cue Detection in Political-Debate Videos: An Optimized RNN-LSTM Approach

Yanru Jiang[✉] [iD]

Department of Communication, University of California Los Angeles, Los Angeles, CA 90095, USA
yanrujiang@g.ucla.edu

Abstract. This study proposes a computational-video-analysis pipeline using OpenPose for keypoint detection, the RNN-LSTM network for constructing 12 gesture classifiers, and data augmentation and epoch early-stopping techniques for performance optimization. Through the measurement of accuracy, precision, recall, and F1 scores, this study compares three approaches (the vanilla approach, data-augmentation approach, and epoch-optimization approach), which gradually increase the model performance for all gesture features. The study suggests that a combination of data augmentation and epoch early-stopping techniques can effectively solve the imbalanced dataset problem faced by customized datasets and substantially increase the accuracy and F1 scores by 10–20%, achieving a satisfying accuracy of 70%–90% for most gesture detections.

Keywords: Computer Vision · Gesture Detection · Video Analysis

1 Introduction

Using facial and body landmarks to detect gestures and facial expressions in videos has been a well-explored application in the field of computer vision. However, previous work tends to utilize videos drawn from staged performances or movie clips rather than samples of actual gestures from real-life situations, which is known as naturalistic data. In comparison, naturalistic gesture and facial expression data pose a more realistic, albeit more challenging, recognition task for deep learning networks [1, 2]. Recently, some studies have been utilizing interview clips from athletes for naturalistic data curation [3], although the video quality varies. In this demo paper, I offer political speeches (specifically presidential debates from US general elections curated by C-SPAN) as a source of well-standardized short clips for non-verbal cue detection.

Presidential debates constitute one of the most important election-campaign activities in the United States, attracting a broad audience and providing a significant breadth of information on candidates [4, 5]. Due to their often-televised format, debates allow voters to evaluate not only candidates' positions on issues and rhetorical strategies, but also their nonverbal cues [6]. Political debates thus provide strong evidence for assessing

C. Stephanidis et al. (Eds.): HCII 2023, CCIS 1957, pp. 32–40, 2024.
https://doi.org/10.1007/978-3-031-49212-9_5

how candidates' communication styles affect voters' perceptions and decision making [7].

In the past, most political-debate studies have employed manual content-annotating analysis to detect nonverbal cues, an expensive and time-consuming approach subject to researchers' cognitive bias [8]. With recent advances in computer vision, a machine-learning approach to analyzing visual inputs, computational social scientists have begun to apply automated coding to study multimodal communication in televised debates [8]. Research of this type has tended to directly apply image-based tools to estimate emotions in debate videos [7]. This approach could lead to substantive bias and inaccuracy because videos comprise sequential data (sequences of body movement) rather than unordered images [8].

To avoid such bias, this study first replicates the video-analysis pipeline in [8], which employs recurrent neural network (RNN), a type of neural network with cyclic connection (which is commonly used for analyzing sequential data such as time-series and natural language processing), to sequential-image data for building video classifiers. This study further explores the possibility of using *data augmentation* and *epoch optimization* to enhance classifier performance.

2 Methods and Results

This study employed an OpenPose API to first extract low-level features (including facial and body keypoints) and then used RNN-LSTM models to detect gestures and facial expressions in debate videos based on sequential keypoint data [8]. Additionally, it emphasizes the use of video augmentation and epoch optimization to enhance model performance. Lastly, the model performances of the three approaches are compared based on multiple performance measures.

2.1 Data Collection

This study uses video annotation from [8] and the dataset from [4], which contains manual labeling of 21 gestures and facial expressions from the first 2016 Presidential Debate between Donald Trump and Hillary Clinton. Among the 21 gestures, 12 were selected for this demo paper as they provide relatively more balanced distributions between the positive and negative cases. These gestures and facial expressions include *Look at, Brush off, Disagreement, Look into, Eyebrow movement, Angry face, Happy face, Neutral face, Affinity gesture, Defiance gesture, Agentic gesture, Interrupt*. The annotation was performed on the C-SPAN split-screen version of the televised debate (see Fig. 1) because it standardizes the human annotation as well as the computer-vision processing in the following steps. The 90-min C-SPAN debate video was split into 530 chunks based on 10-s intervals using FFmpeg, an open-source video-processing and handling API that offers a command-line version, in which each chunk is associated with the presence of each gesture or facial expression for Trump and Clinton, respectively. The choice of using 10-s intervals as the units of analysis was due to human-cognition limit of identifying the presence of certain gestures within a short timeframe, rather than the technical restriction of the RNN-LSTM approach. Overall, the dataset includes 530 data points for 24 gestures and facial expressions (12 gesture features for each candidate).

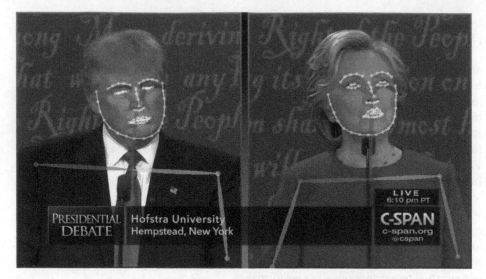

Fig. 1. C-SPAN split screen with facial and body keypoints

2.2 Feature Extraction

Previous studies have explored the possibility of using sequential key-point-movement data rather than the sequential imagery frames for video classification [3, 8]. The advantages of the use of keypoint data are twofold: (1) it effectively saves the computing power of running deep-learning models on hour-long videos in which each second of the video could contain 15–40 frames, and (2) it provides better interpretability and understandability because the gesture and facial-expression detection can be operationalized as a sequential movement in body and facial keypoints across frames rather than any convoluted or abstract information that might be detected at the imagery-frame level.

This study uses OpenPose, a multi-person computer-vision system that can jointly detect human body, hand, facial, and foot keypoints for sequential keypoint movement extraction (see Image 2) [9]. While multiple APIs offer the body and facial-keypoints-extraction function [3, 10], OpenPose was selected due to its capacity to simultaneous extract body and facial keypoints, which makes it easier to track people across frames. In total, 25 body keypoints and 70 facial keypoints were extracted for each frame using OpenPose. This study used all facial keypoints but only 11 body key-points. Fourteen body keypoints were excluded from following processing because the C-SPAN debate videos mainly featured candidates' upper bodies. When the keypoint is not shown in frames, OpenPose either generates an estimated keypoint location or assigns a zero value to the keypoints that cannot be detected, leading to an inaccurate representa-tion of body movements.

Keypoint data are stored in the following format: [x0, y0, c0, x1, y1, c1...], in which (x, y) represents the coordinate of each keypoint and c indicates the confidence score of each keypoint-coordinate prediction. The confidence score was excluded in the following processing steps. As the debate video was 30 frames per second, each input size for the RNN model was 162 (81 keypoints × 2) times 300 (30 fps × 10 s).

Due to its functional limit, OpenPose does not track people across frames automatically. In other words, the output of the keypoint dictionary does not always follow the same sequential order, even if the target person does not change locations during the entire video. A common approach to tracking target person is using bounding box to sequentially link keypoint data of individuals whose head keypoints (or other body key-points) move within the area of the bounding box. Because there were only two candidates in the selected debate video and they always stayed on the same side of the frame, this study used a naïve approach, assuming that the keypoint data on the left side of the frame always belonged to Trump, and those on the right side belonged to Clinton.

2.3 RNN-LSTM

As RNN is commonly used for sequential data, it tackles the challenge in computational video analysis that videos are composed by frames/ images with sequential orders. In particular, movements in each frame are de-pendent on movements in previous frames. Thus, directly applying the image-analysis tools to a bag of frames with the assumption that the order is irrelevant could bias the video-analysis results. RNN, as an iterative function that takes the input sequence and internal state from the last timestep (t–1) to predict the current timestep (t), updates its state as follows:

$$h_t = f(x_{t-1}, h_{t-1}) \quad t \in \{0, 1, 2, \ldots T - 1\} \tag{1}$$

While RNN could leverage the context between elements by maintaining its internal state during processing of the entire sequence, its vanilla model faces the vanishing-gradient problem during the model training [11, 12]. Long short-term memory (LSTM), the function f in the model above, introduces an additional state variable, the cell state, which maintains "specific information that needs to be kept while processing the whole sequence and controls when the information needs to be updated" (p. 4054) [8]. Consequentially, LSTM effectively reduces the vanishing-gradient problem encountered by RNN [12]. The LSTM is particularly useful when the input data have a long dependency, which is a feature of the input data in this study—a 300-timestep sequence input.

To test the performance of the RNN-LSTM model, this study started with the vanilla architecture and gradually added complexity to tune the model. Specifically, the vanilla model contains one RNN-LSTM layer to process sequential input and capture the sequential information and a fully connected layer for the binary-output classification. Both input dimensions and hidden dimensions were set to 162, as there were 82 keypoints, and each keypoint had a (x, y) coordinate. The number of layers was set to three as the model contains an input layer, a single hidden layer, and a standard feedforward output layer. The output category was set to two because each model detected the presence of certain gestures or facial expression.

2.4 Model Fine-Tuning

This study compares the model performances of three approaches: the vanilla RNN-LSTM approach, the data-augmentation approach, and the epoch-optimization approach.

Vanilla RNN-LSTM. Because adding more neural-network layers did not effectively improve the model performance, the vanilla RNN model was used as the baseline approach. In total, 20% of shuffled annotated samples were used for the test data, and the remaining data were further split into 80% training data and 20% validation data. Empirically, Adam optimizer was observed to perform better than SGD optimizer in this study.

The number of epochs indicates the times an entire dataset has been passed forward and backward through the neural network. As the number of epochs increased, the training performance shifted from underfitting to optimum to overfitting. The default number of epochs was set to 10 for all classifiers to avoid potential overfitting.

Data Augmentation. One major issue in constructing customized datasets in social-science research is that most content-based data tend to be heavily imbalanced, with much more negative cases than positive ones. The most common approach in computer vision is data augmentation, in which researchers can transform the minority label through image rotation, reflection, cropping, and color adjustment [13]. These transformation techniques can alleviate the imbalance issue and enhance the generalizability of the neural network because it artificially expands the training-data space. However, while the transformation techniques in image processes have been well established, video transformation is still underexplored. Rather than transforming video samples, this study simply up-sampled the minority label by randomly duplicating its data samples for training and validation datasets. The performance on test data was evaluated on a pre-augmented dataset to ensure a fair comparison and realistic representation of the models' performances. The default number of epochs was set to 10 for all classifiers.

Epoch Optimization. In addition to data augmentation, this study adopted an early-stopping approach to optimize the number of epochs [14]. Specifically, it chose a sufficient number of epochs (n = 25) to train the network, detected the epoch choice with the highest validation accuracy, and reran the model with the selected epoch number for the test data.

2.5 Results

Vanilla Approach. The vanilla approach does not perform any data augmentation, and the number of epochs was set to 10 for all gestures. This approach directly applied the RNN-LSTM to 12 gestures and facial expressions by Trump and Clinton, of which half were heavily imbalanced (minority label less than 20% of the entire data).

The results in Table 1 indicate that almost all the heavily imbalanced nonverbal cues with much more negative cases were predicted as zero for all the data points. Even if these gestures received high accuracy scores, this was due to the all-zero prediction rather than the satisfying model performance. Accordingly, most of these imbalanced gestures received zero or inapplicable recall, precision, and F1 scores. Additionally, Clinton was observed to have more imbalanced data and tended to receive more all-zero predictions than Trump.

Data-Augmentation Approach. The data-augmentation approach addresses the imbalanced-dataset problem by oversampling the minority labels to generate relatively balanced training and validation datasets. All the epochs were set to 10. Table 2 indicates that the data augmentation effectively solved the all-zero prediction issue for both Trump and Clinton and reduced the asymmetry between Trump and Clinton's results. Although the heavily imbalanced gestures tended to have lower accuracy and F1 scores than the other gestures, there was a substantial improvement in all performance metrics for both Trump and Clinton.

Early-Stopping Approach. In this approach, epoch early stopping was performed in addition to the data augmentation to illustrate the best possible performance that can be achieved for the pipeline proposed. Because of the epoch optimization, the accuracy and F1 scores of all the gestures were further increased. Most of the classifiers stopped updating after 11–20 epochs (Table 3).

Table 1. Model performance of the vanilla approach for gesture detection.

Gestures	Pos	Acc	R	P	F1	Pos	Acc	R	P	F1
	Trump					Clinton				
Look at	0.64	81.13	0.92	0.83	0.87	0.51	70.75	0.40	1	0.58
Brush off	0.08	93.40	0			0.13	87.74	0		
Disagree	0.71	78.30	1	0.78	0.88	0.10	92.45	0		
Look into	0.80	82.08	1	0.82	0.90	0.68	83.96	0.96	0.82	0.88
Eyebrow	0.91	87.74	1	0.88	0.93	0.33	69.81	0.09	0.75	0.16
Angry	0.58	77.36	0.81	0.78	0.79	0.13	86.79	0		
Happy	0.09	89.62	0			0.51	46.23	1	0.46	0.63
Neutral	0.29	68.87	0.24	0.50	0.33	0.02	100			
Interrupt	0.04	95.28	0			0.35	69.81	0		
Affinity	0.03	99.06	0			0.07	95.28	0		
Defiance	0.33	76.42	0.21	0.75	0.32	0.10	90.57	0		
Agentic	0.61	68.87	0.59	0.84	0.69	0.49	54.72	0.14	1	0.25

* *Pos = positive cases of each gesture; Acc = accuracy; R = recall; P = precision*

Table 2. Model performance of the data augmentation approach for gesture detection.

Gestures	Aug	Acc	R	P	F1	Aug	Acc	R	P	F1
	Trump					Clinton				
Look at	534	83.96	0.93	0.85	0.89	426	81.13	0.83	0.83	0.83
Brush off	772	31.13	0.67	0.05	0.10	740	68.87	0.62	0.22	0.33
Disagree	598	62.26	0.48	0.97	0.64	764	91.51	0		
Look into	682	52.83	0.42	0.95	0.58	568	50	0.32	0.92	0.48
Eyebrow	772	52.83	0.51	0.96	0.67	568	64.15	0.88	0.46	0.60
Angry	484	67.92	0.53	0.95	0.68	738	85.85	0.43	0.46	0.44
Happy	768	53.77	0.57	0.08	0.14	432	59.43	0.83	0.56	0.67
Neutral	598	71.70	0.70	0.50	0.58	832	60.38	1	0.02	0.05
Interrupt	812	77.36	0.40	0.09	0.14	568	57.55	0.47	0.48	0.47
Affinity	824	66.04	0.40	0.06	0.10	798	49.06	1	0.16	0.27
Defiance	564	67.92	0.83	0.51	0.63	758	33.02	1	0.09	0.16
Agentic	512	76.42	0.72	0.89	0.80	434	75.47	0.92	0.69	0.79

* *Aug = post-augmentation sample size; Acc = accuracy; R = recall; P = precision*

Table 3. Model performance of the early stopping approach for gesture detection.

Gestures	Ep	Acc	R	P	F1	Ep	Acc	R	P	F1
	Trump					Clinton				
Look at	20	89.62	0.94	0.89	0.91	10	84.91	0.83	0.89	0.86
Brush off	23	80.19	0.33	0.24	0.28	18	67.92	0.58	0.19	0.29
Disagree	15	79.25	0.74	0.95	0.83	7	39.62	0.91	0.14	0.24
Look into	21	75.47	0.74	0.94	0.83	9	81.13	0.80	0.92	0.86
Eyebrow	9	73.58	0.73	0.97	0.84	14	63.21	0.82	0.50	0.62
Angry	19	87.74	0.86	0.93	0.89	8	62.26	0.94	0.30	0.46
Happy	23	75.47	0.22	0.10	0.13	13	55.66	0.59	0.49	0.53
Neutral	25	76.42	0.76	0.64	0.70	24	86.79		0.00	
Interrupt	24	95.28	0.00	0.00		11	43.40	0.71	0.30	0.42
Affinity	14	78.30	1.00	0.04	0.08	22	82.08	0.73	0.33	0.46
Defiance	19	74.53	0.68	0.55	0.61	14	55.66	0.71	0.10	0.18
Agentic	14	89.62	0.86	0.97	0.91	23	78.30	0.71	0.82	0.76

* *Ep = early stopping epoch; Acc = accuracy; R = recall; P = precision*

3   Conclusion

This demo paper details a gesture detection pipeline that is inspired by the approach in [8], which utilizes the RNN-LSTM for analyzing sequential keypoint movement data. This study compares three approaches (the vanilla RNN-LSTM approach, the data-augmentation approach, and the epoch-optimization approach), all of which gradually increased the model performance for all the gesture features. The latter approach demonstrates that even with only 530 annotated samples with half of the gesture features being heavily imbalanced, the RNN still achieved a satisfying accuracy and F1 score, varying from 70%–90%, for most of the gestures through data augmentation and epoch early stopping. Overall, this study illustrates the better possible performance that can be achieved for a customized non-standardized dataset and a RNN video-classification pipeline that was built from scratch.

3.1   Limitations and Future Research

This research has several limitations. Although it explored the possibility of data augmentation through up-sampling minority labels and effectively enhanced the model performance, the simple duplication of videos is not as advantageous as data transformation, which is an established technique in image analysis. While the data transformation and augmentation were still underexplored in the computational video analysis, future research could explore more innovative video transformation that can simultaneously improve the model generalizability and solve the imbalanced-dataset problem. Secondly, this study utilized a customized dataset for training gesture and facial-expression classifiers in a political debate. However, manual annotation for model training and building is viewed as costly in terms of human labor, time usage, and computing resources. While several off-the-shelf datasets and models have been developed for upper-body gesture-and-emotion recognition, future studies could explore the performances of these models and datasets in comparison with the current study's approach in terms of accuracy, efficiency, and interpretability.

3.2   Data and Code Availability

https://github.com/JoyceJiang73/OpenPose-RNN-LSTM-PoliticalDebate/blob/main/OpenPose_LSTM_PresidentialDebate.ipynb.

References

1. Zeng, Z., Pantic, M., Roisman, G.I., Huang, T.S.: A survey of affect recognition methods. In: Proceedings of the Ninth International Conference on Multimodal Interfaces - ICMI 2007 (2007). https://doi.org/10.1145/1322192.1322216
2. D'mello, S.K., Kory, J.: A review and meta-analysis of multimodal affect detection systems. ACM Comput. Surv. (CSUR), **47**(3), 1–36 (2015). https://doi.org/10.1145/2682899
3. Liu, X., Shi, H., Chen, H., Yu, Z., Li, X., Zhao, G.: iMiGUE: an identity-free video dataset for micro-gesture understanding and emotion analysis. In: Proceedings of the IEEE/CVF Conference on Computer Vision and Pattern Recognition, pp. 10631–10642 (2021)

4. Bucy, E.P., et al.: Performing populism: Trump's transgressive debate style and the dynamics of Twitter response. New Media Soc. **22**, 634–658 (2020)

5. Bucy, E.P., Gong, Z.H.: Image bite analysis of presidential debates. Exploring C-SPAN Arch. 45–76 (2015). https://doi.org/10.2307/j.ctv15wxr41.7

6. Grabe, M.E., Bucy, E.P.: Image Bite politics: News and the Visual Framing of Elections. Oxford University Press, Oxford (2009)

7. Boussalis, C., Coan, T., Holman, M., Müller, S.: Gender, candidate emotional expression, and voter reactions during televised debates (2020). https://doi.org/10.31235/osf.io/4kqgr

8. Joo, J., Bucy, E., Seidel, C.: Computational communication science| automated coding of televised leader displays: detecting nonverbal political behavior with computer vision and deep learning. Int. J. Commun. **13**, 23 (2019). https://ijoc.org/index.php/ijoc/article/view/10725

9. Cao, Z., Hidalgo, G., Simon, T., Wei, S., Sheikh, Y.: OpenPose: realtime multi-person 2D pose estimation using part affinity fields. IEEE Trans. Pattern Anal. Mach. Intell. **43**, 172–186 (2021)

10. Ranganathan, H., Chakraborty, S., Panchanathan, S.: Multimodal emotion recognition using deep learning architectures. In: IEEE Winter Conference on Applications of Computer Vision, pp. 1–9. IEEE (2016)

11. Dupond, S.: A thorough review on the current advance of neural network structures. Annu. Rev. Control. **14**, 200–230 (2019)

12. Sherstinsky, A.: Fundamentals of recurrent neural network (RNN) and long short-term memory (LSTM) network. Physica D **404**, 132306 (2020). https://doi.org/10.1016/j.physd.2019.132306

13. Shorten, C., Khoshgoftaar, T.M.: A survey on image data augmentation for deep learning. J. Big Data **6**, 60 (2019). https://doi.org/10.1186/s40537-019-0197-0

14. Prechelt, L.: Early stopping - but when? In: Orr, G.B., Müller, K.-R. (eds.) Neural Networks: Tricks of the Trade. LNCS, vol. 1524, pp. 55–69. Springer, Heidelberg (1998). https://doi.org/10.1007/3-540-49430-8_3

Analyzing Smart Cities Governance Publications Using CiteSpace: Integration of Organizational Strategy and Human Resources for Sustainable Urban Development

Herman Lawelai[1,2](✉) 📵 and Achmad Nurmandi[1] 📵

[1] Doctoral Program of Government Affairs and Administration, Jusuf Kalla School of Government, Universitas Muhammadiyah Yogyakarta, Brawijaya Street, Yogyakarta City 55183, Indonesia
herman.lawelai.psc22@mail.umy.ac.id

[2] Department of Government Studies, Universitas Muhammadiyah Buton, Betoambari Street, Baubau City 93724, Indonesia

Abstract. This study aims to investigate the dominant themes in publications related to smart cities governance and the integration of organizational strategies and human resources for sustainable urban development. The study employs bibliometric analysis using CiteSpace software to collect articles related to Smart Cities Governance and sustainable urban development from the Scopus database. The data collected is processed using CiteSpace software to generate visualizations and analyze research trends and topic development in the field of Smart Cities Governance. The results of the study identified 10 clusters, with the largest cluster being "underground space," with 55 members and a silhouette value of 0.837 by LLR, smart cities by LSI, and knowledge management (3.09) by MI. The analysis showed that the use of underground space can be a solution to overcome the land constraints faced by large cities, as discussed in Goel, RK's work, which is the most cited article in this cluster. The most cited nodes in this cluster are "smart city," "sustainable development," and "urban development," indicating that sustainable Smart Cities development is a significant concern in research related to this cluster. The network analysis formed in the research clusters can provide useful information for experts and decision-makers in developing sustainable smart cities by considering the use of underground space as a solution to overcome land constraints. These findings are expected to guide experts and decision-makers in considering the use of underground space as one of the options in developing sustainable smart cities and overcoming the land constraints faced by large cities.

Keywords: Smart Cities · Development · Decision-Makers

1 Introduction

Rapid urban growth has created major challenges for urban governance in an effective and sustainable way [1–5]. In response to this challenge, the concept of smart cities has been adopted by various governments across the world as a promising approach [6–8].

C. Stephanidis et al. (Eds.): HCII 2023, CCIS 1957, pp. 41–48, 2024.
https://doi.org/10.1007/978-3-031-49212-9_6

Smart cities integrate information and communication technologies (ICT) to improve efficiency, quality of life, and urban progress [9, 10]. But the implementation of smart cities does not only involve technological aspects; it also requires smart policies and good governance [11].

Smart cities governance involves governments and institutions managing and regulating smart city development, focusing on evaluation indicators, data collection, cross-sector coordination, and decision-making for efficient, sustainable development [12, 13]. Citizens are increasingly involved in policy making, and blockchain technology is explored for data collection and processing [14–16].

Smart transportation policy is one of the key aspects of developing sustainable smart cities. Smart transport policy involves the use of ICT to improve the efficiency and sustainability of urban transport, including efficient public transport, smart parking systems, multimodal transport integration, and app-based transport services [17, 18].

Although research on transport policy has been conducted by previous researchers, there is still a lack of understanding of how this research has affected sustainable urban development. Therefore, this study aims to quantify the impact of smart city governance research on sustainable urban development. To achieve this goal, we use CiteSpace, an application that can help identify the impact of research through quotation analysis.

Through the integration of organizational strategies and human resources, this research is expected to provide a deeper understanding of the impact of smart city governance research on sustainable urban development. Mapping relevant literature based on keywords, this research will provide valuable insights for policymakers and practitioners in formulating smart and sustainable urban policies and strategies. Thus, this research has high urgency as it provides an important contribution to understanding the impact of smart city governance research on sustainable urban development.

2 Research Method

The study evaluates literature using the Scopus database, analyzing articles from 201 documents. It uses API calls to find papers with TITLE-ABS-KEY (Smart Cities Governance) AND TITLE-ABS-KEY (Sustainable Urban Development) AND PUBYEAR > 2012 AND PUBYEAR < 2023 AND (LIMIT-TO (PUBSTAGE, "final")) AND (LIMIT-TO (LANGUAGE, "English")) AND (LIMIT-TO (SRCTYPE, "j")).

The emerging field of visualises scientific knowledge using social network analysis and trend analysis [19], with software developed for science mapping [20, 21]. The research uses in-depth studies to explain and understand smart city governance patterns towards sustainable urban development, as indexed by Scopus. The research used analytical methods to evaluate Scopus database search results and analyse them using CiteSpace [22].

CiteSpace is a popular and leading Java-based software used to create colour maps from bibliographic data and visualise and dig out the instructive meanings of those maps [23, 24]. In this study, we analysed co-citation research documents on smart city governance and sustainable urban development. Co-citation analysis can reveal important keywords in papers as well as topics and concepts that tend to cross research areas [25]. In addition, a keyword-based explosion detection analysis is used to identify research limits among current publications.

3 Results and Discussion

From the results of analysis using CiteSpace, the research found ten clusters that describe key topics in smart city governance research, as shown in Fig. 1. These findings provide in-depth insight into smart city governance research trends. Through cluster analysis, the research identifies and groups together interrelated topics that provide a better understanding of the conceptual framework used in this research. The subsequent co-cited analysis provides additional information on topics that are trending by identifying the most frequently quoted publications together.

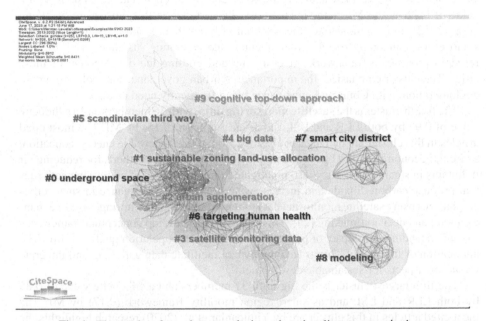

Fig. 1. The results of our cluster analysis are based on literature co-citations.

Figure 1 shows that the **underground space** cluster is the largest cluster has 55 members and a silhouette value of 0.837 by LLR, smart cities by LSI, and knowledge management (3.09) by MI. The most cited articles in this cluster are by Goel's (2015) research highlights India's urban living challenges due to population growth surpassing development. To address this, underground facilities have been implemented in developed countries. India has the potential to utilize underground space, offering additional space and natural protection [26]. Smart city governance research focuses on the use of underground space in urban development, emphasizing intelligent cities and sustainable urban development. To achieve sustainable development, cities must integrate organizational strategies, involve stakeholders, and leverage skilled human resources. By combining effective strategies and skilled human resources, cities can optimize the use of underground space for better urban interests.

The second largest cluster is the **sustainable zoning land-use allocation**, with 46 members and a silhouette value of 0.756 by LLR, smart cities by LSI, and app (0.68) by MI. The most cited articles in this cluster are by Hammad et al. (2019) proposes mathematical frameworks to enhance sustainability in smart city decisions related to zoning, land use allocation, and facility location. The framework optimizes land use, new building locations, and infrastructure investment, considering social, economic, and environmental aspects. It also considers traffic impact through optimized traffic allocation to existing networks [27]. This research focuses on sustainable smart city development by optimizing decisions related to zoning, land use allocation, and facility location, considering social, economic, and environmental aspects.

The third largest cluster **urban agglomeration** has 42 members and a silhouette value of 0.762 by the LLR and LSI methods, and as an open data ecosystem with a value of 0.72 by the MI method. The most cited articles in this cluster are by Wong et al. (2022) study demonstrates the potential of blockchain technology in sustainable smart cities, enhancing social, environmental, and economic sustainability [28]. The research proposes a framework for designing and guiding the development of these cities. The cluster emphasizes the importance of urban governance and policy in urban agglomeration, with China and governance being frequently cited as topics.

The fourth cluster is the **satellite monitoring data**, with 36 members and a silhouette value of 0.92 by both LLR and LSI, and as air pollution (0.15) by MI. The most cited articles in this cluster are by Dincă et al. (2022) found that renewable energy, education, a circular economy, and EU government policies are effective methods for reducing air pollutants in smart cities. They also highlighted the importance of addressing activities that produce carbon dioxide and increase water pollution. Governance in smart cities emphasizes using satellite monitoring data for environmental monitoring, resource management, and decision-making [29]. This data can help develop conceptual frameworks for understanding the impact of policies and projects on population quality of life. The application of Internet of Things technology can facilitate data gathering and integrate urban life aspects for sustainable development.

The fifth largest cluster is the **big data** 31 members and a silhouette value of 0.85 by both LLR and LSI, and as smart region mobility framework (0.17) by MI. The most cited articles in this cluster are by Yigitcanlar et al. (2020) research highlights the emerging field of artificial intelligence (AI) in smart cities, focusing on technologies, algorithms, and applications. AI impacts business efficiency, data analysis, education, energy, environment, health, land use, security, transportation, and urban management [30]. Governance emphasizes sustainable land management and zoning approaches, with AI being discussed and evaluated for its contributions and risks. AI applications should be carefully considered to maximize benefits while minimizing risks.

The sixth largest cluster is the **scandinavian third way**, with 24 members and a silhouette value of 0.831 by LLR, smart city by LSI, and scientific literature (0.28) by MI. The most cited articles in this cluster are by Baraniewicz-Kotasiska (2022), which highlights the Scandinavian region's cooperation and political decision-making in influencing the development of Aarhus, Denmark's smart city. The city government adopted the Scandinavian third-way approach, implementing smart city activities and creating a modern city management model [31]. This research emphasises the importance of sustainable urban planning and development in the development of sustainable smart cities.

The seventh largest cluster is **targeting human health**, with 23 members and a silhouette value of 0.861 by LLR, smart city by LSI, and app (0.27) by MI. The most cited articles in this cluster are by Buttazzoni et al. (2020), who found that smart cities aim to improve public health but often overlook the importance of equality in interventions. Common characteristics of equality include residence, socio-economic status, social capital, and personal characteristics, while employment, gender, religion, race, ethnicity, culture, language, and education are less addressed. Existing assessments lack robust evaluation designs and commercially available technologies [32]. Research in this cluster focuses on incorporating and analysing equality considerations in health interventions to improve public health and well-being in smart cities.

The eighth cluster is the **smart city district**, 13 members and a silhouette value of 0.974 by LLR, smart energy systems for smart city districts: case study reininghaus district by LSI, and smart cities (0.04) by MI. The most cited articles in this cluster are by Maier (2016), which shows that a decentralised system with low-temperature waste heat and decentralised heat pumps in a building group is the most financially and ecologically viable solution to supply new buildings [33]. Therefore, research in this cluster focuses on approaches to the development of smart and sustainable energy systems by considering the use of renewable energy sources and energy efficiency in the context of smart city development.

The ninth largest cluster is the **modeling**, with 12 members and a silhouette value of 1 by LLR, insight by LSI, and smart cities (0.03) by MI. The most cited articles in this cluster are by Faber et al. (2018), whose research resulted in a visual analytical system (VAS) designed to collect, combine, and map data about the business ecosystem in the context of smart cities [34]. In sustainable smart city development, research in this cluster focuses on approaches that advance collaboration, innovation, and proactive management in the business ecosystem formed around smart city initiatives.

The ten largest cluster is the **cognitive top-down approach**, with 9 members and a silhouette value of 0.873 by LLR, self-sustainable smart cities by LSI, and smart cities (0.03) by MI. The most cited articles in this cluster are by Bai et al. (2022), whose research concluded that the Healthy Cities initiative in China should align with national and global strategic agendas like Healthy China 2030 and the SDGs by providing an inclusive governance framework for coherent cross-sectoral programmes. This requires utilising best practises and expanding assessment efforts to ensure systematic population health improvements [35]. The research cluster focuses on sustainable smart city development to improve population health.

4   Conclusion

The results of this study conclude that sustainable smart cities require organizational strategies, stakeholder involvement, and skilled human resources. Optimizing underground space and zoning, land use allocation, and facility location is crucial for sustainable development, considering social, economic, and environmental aspects. This study suggests a framework for planning and guiding urban development in agglomerations, emphasizing urban governance and policy. Conceptual frameworks help understand the impact of policies and projects on the quality of life of the population. IoT applications facilitate data collection and integration of urban life aspects for sustainable development. Governance emphasizes sustainable land management and zoning approaches, with AI being evaluated for its contributions and risks. AI applications should be carefully considered to maximize benefits while minimizing risks. Health interventions should be equal to improving public health in smart cities. Sustainable energy systems should be developed using renewable energy sources and energy efficiency. Collaboration, innovation, and proactive management are essential in the business ecosystem for sustainable smart city initiatives.

References

1. Rustiadi, E., Pravitasari, A.E., Setiawan, Y., Mulya, S.P., Pribadi, D.O., Tsutsumida, N.: Impact of continuous Jakarta megacity urban expansion on the formation of the Jakarta-Bandung conurbation over the rice farm regions. Cities **111**, 103000 (2021). https://doi.org/10.1016/j.cities.2020.103000
2. Song, Y., de Jong, M., Stead, D.: Bypassing institutional barriers: New types of transit-oriented development in China. Cities **113**, 103177 (2021). https://doi.org/10.1016/j.cities.2021.103177
3. Awolorinke, A.C., Takyi, S.A., Amponsah, O.: Insouciant , powerless or helpless : an assessment of the factors that contribute to the non-compliance with the regulations that protect ecologically sensitive areas in the Greater Kumasi Metropolis," Urban Gov.,pp. 1–9 (2023). https://doi.org/10.1016/j.ugj.2023.03.004
4. Dame, J., Schmidt, S., Müller, J., Nüsser, M.: Urbanisation and socio-ecological challenges in high mountain towns: Insights from Leh (Ladakh), India. Landscape Urban Plan. **189**, 189–199 (2019). https://doi.org/10.1016/j.landurbplan.2019.04.017
5. Gaubatz, P., Hanink, D.: Learning from Taiyuan: Chinese cities as urban sustainability laboratories. Geogr. Sustain. **1**(2), 118–126 (2020). https://doi.org/10.1016/j.geosus.2020.06.004
6. Zhang, S.: Public participation in the Geoweb era: defining a typology for geo-participation in local governments. Cities **85**, 38–50 (2019). https://doi.org/10.1016/j.cities.2018.12.004
7. Huovila, A., Bosch, P., Airaksinen, M.: Comparative analysis of standardized indicators for smart sustainable cities: what indicators and standards to use and when? Cities **89**, 141–153 (2019). https://doi.org/10.1016/j.cities.2019.01.029
8. Hujran, O., Al-Debei, M.M., Al-Adwan, A.S., Alarabiat, A., Altarawneh, N.: Examining the antecedents and outcomes of smart government usage: an integrated model. Gov. Inf. Q. **40**(1), 101783 (2023). https://doi.org/10.1016/j.giq.2022.101783
9. Tomor, Z., Przeybilovicz, E., Leleux, C.: Smart governance in institutional context: an in-depth analysis of Glasgow, Utrecht, and Curitiba. Cities **114**, 103195 (2021). https://doi.org/10.1016/j.cities.2021.103195
10. Praharaj, S., Han, J.H., Hawken, S.: "Urban innovation through policy integration: critical perspectives from 100 smart cities mission in India", City. Cult. Soc. **12**, 35–43 (2018). https://doi.org/10.1016/j.ccs.2017.06.004
11. Ullah, F., Qayyum, S., Thaheem, M.J., Al-Turjman, F., Sepasgozar, S.M.: Risk management in sustainable smart cities governance: A TOE framework. Technol. Forecast. Soc. Change **167**, 120743 (2021). https://doi.org/10.1016/j.techfore.2021.120743
12. Hsu, W.-L., Qiao, M., Xu, H., Zhang, C., Liu, H.-L., Shiau, Y.-C.: Smart city governance evaluation in the era of internet of things: an empirical analysis of Jiangsu, China. Sustainability **13**(24), 13606 (2021). https://doi.org/10.3390/su132413606

13. Laurini, R.: A primer of knowledge management for smart city governance. Land Use Policy **111**, 104832 (2021). https://doi.org/10.1016/j.landusepol.2020.104832
14. Bai, Y., Hu, Q., Seo, S.H., Kang, K., Lee, J.J.: Public participation consortium blockchain for smart city governance. IEEE Internet Things J. **9**(3), 2094–2108 (2022). https://doi.org/10.1109/JIOT.2021.3091151
15. Alsaid, L.A.Z.A.: Performance measurement in smart city governance: a case study of an Egyptian city council. J. Account. Emerg. Econ. **11**(3), 395–430 (2021). https://doi.org/10.1108/JAEE-09-2020-0244
16. Fonseca, D., Sanchez-Sepulveda, M., Necchi, S., Peña, E.: Towards smart city governance. Case study: IMPROVING the interpretation of quantitative traffic measurement data through citizen participation. Sensors, **21**(16), 5321 (2021). https://doi.org/10.3390/s21165321
17. Wang, M., Zhou, T., Wang, D.: Tracking the evolution processes of smart cities in China by assessing performance and efficiency. Technol. Soc. **63**, 101353 (2020). https://doi.org/10.1016/j.techsoc.2020.101353
18. Zhang, D., Pee, L.G., Pan, S.L., Cui, L.: Big data analytics, resource orchestration, and digital sustainability: a case study of smart city development. Gov. Inf. Q. **39**(1), 101626 (2022). https://doi.org/10.1016/j.giq.2021.101626
19. Lawelai, H., Sadat, A., Suherman, A., Agustiyara, A., Nurmandi, A.: Trend analysis of public enthusiasm for COVID-19 vaccines on social media. Stud. Media Commun. **10**(2), 105–114 (2022). https://doi.org/10.11114/smc.v10i2.5603
20. Lawelai, H., Iswanto, I., Raharja, N.M.: Use of artificial intelligence in public services : a bibliometric analysis and visualization. TEM J. **12**(2), 798–807 (2023). https://doi.org/10.18421/TEM122
21. Nurmandi, A., Kurniawan, D., Salahudin, M.: A meta-analysis of big data security: how the government formulates a model of public information and security assurance into big data In: Stephanidis, C., Antona, M., Ntoa, S. (eds.) HCI International 2021- Late Breaking Posters. HCII 2021. Communications in Computer and Information Science, vol. 1499, pp. 472–479. Springer, Cham (2021).https://doi.org/10.1007/978-3-030-90179-0_60
22. Chen, C., Song, M.: Visualizing a field of research: a methodology of systematic scientometric reviews. PLoS ONE **14**(10), e0223994 (2019). https://doi.org/10.1371/journal.pone.0223994
23. Chen, C.: A glimpse of the first eight months of the COVID-19 literature on microsoft academic graph: themes, citation contexts, and uncertainties. Front. Res. Metrics Anal. **5**(December), 1–15 (2020). https://doi.org/10.3389/frma.2020.607286
24. Chen, C.: Science mapping: a systematic review of the literature. J. Data Inf. Sci. **2**(2), 1–40 (2017). https://doi.org/10.1515/jdis-2017-0006
25. Liu, X.: Full-text citation analysis : a new method to enhance. J. Am. Soc. Inf. Sci. Technol. **64**(July), 1852–1863 (2013). https://doi.org/10.1002/asi
26. Goel, R.K.: Use of underground space for the development of cities in India. Water Energy Int. **58RNI**(9), 41–45 (2015)
27. Hammad, A.W., Akbarnezhad, A., Haddad, A., Vazquez, E.G.: Sustainable zoning, land-use allocation and facility location optimisation in smart cities. Energies **12**(7), 1318 (2019). https://doi.org/10.3390/en12071318
28. Wong, P.F., Chia, F.C., Kiu, M.S., Lou, E.C.W.: Potential integration of blockchain technology into smart sustainable city (SSC) developments: a systematic review. Smart Sustain. Built Environ. **11**(3), 559–574 (2022). https://doi.org/10.1108/SASBE-09-2020-0140
29. Dincă, G., Milan, A.A., Andronic, M.L., Pasztori, A.M., Dincă, D.: Does circular economy contribute to smart cities' sustainable development? Int. J. Environ. Res. Public Health **19**(13), 7627 (2022). https://doi.org/10.3390/ijerph19137627
30. Yigitcanlar, T., Desouza, K., Butler, L., Roozkhosh, F.: Contributions and risks of artificial intelligence (AI) in building smarter cities: insights from a systematic review of the literature. Energies **13**(6), 1473 (2020). https://doi.org/10.3390/en13061473

31. Baraniewicz-Kotasińska, S.: The Scandinavian third way as a proposal for sustainable smart city development—a case study of Aarhus city. Sustainability **14**(6), 3495 (2022). https://doi.org/10.3390/su14063495
32. Buttazzoni, A., Veenhof, M., Minaker, L.: Smart city and high-tech urban interventions targeting human health: an equity-focused systematic review. Int. J. Environ. Res. Public Health **17**(7), 2325 (2020). https://doi.org/10.3390/ijerph17072325
33. Maier, S.: Smart energy systems for smart city districts: case study Reininghaus district. Energy, Sustain. Soc. **6**(1), 1–20 (2016). https://doi.org/10.1186/s13705-016-0085-9
34. Faber, A., Rehm, S.V., Hernandez-Mendez, A., Matthes, F.: Modeling and visualizing smart city mobility business ecosystems: insights from a case study. Information **9**(11), 270 (2018). https://doi.org/10.3390/info9110270
35. Bai, Y., et al.: Healthy cities initiative in China: progress, challenges, and the way forward. Lancet Reg. Heal. - West. Pac. **27**, 100539 (2022). https://doi.org/10.1016/j.lanwpc.2022.100539

Biocompatible Electric Muscle Stimulation Pads with Enhanced Skin Adhesion for Stable Signal Transmission During Varied Physical Movements

Chang Kee Lee[✉], Chang Gyu Lee, Jungmin Yun, Ohung Kwon, and Dae Young Lim

Korea Institute of Industrial Technology, Ansan 15588, Gyeonggi-Do, Korea
withs@kitech.re.kr

Abstract. This paper introduces a novel approach for designing and fabricating biocompatible and efficient electric muscle stimulation (EMS) pads. The EMS pads are composed of a CNF-CNT composite material dispersed in pure water, exhibiting both electrical conductivity and non-toxic properties. The CNF-CNT ink is spray-coated onto a urethane film and hot-melted using the hot-stamping process, resulting in a thin, flexible, and adhesive EMS electrode that is resistant to external deformation. By possessing high adhesion to human skin, the proposed EMS electrodes overcome the constraints of existing dry electrodes, thereby enabling the stable transmission of EMS signals even during varied physical movements during exercise. The proposed approach holds significant potential for wearable technology design, particularly for enhancing the user experience of fitness clothing and wearable technology for rehabilitation and physical therapy. Furthermore, this technology can be integrated with augmented reality (AR) to provide real-time feedback to users during exercise, thereby improving the overall workout experience.

Keywords: EMS · Skin adhesion · Flexible thin pad

1 Introduction

Electrical muscle stimulation (EMS) is a highly effective and commonly used therapeutic technique involving electrical impulses to induce muscle contraction for therapeutic purposes. It's essential to understand the importance of certain factors to ensure the successful application of EMS, such as the proper utilization of paired electrodes and adherence of EMS pads to the skin. These factors significantly determine treatment outcomes and are critical for optimizing therapy efficacy and patient comfort.

To effectively transmit electrical current in EMS devices, it's important to strategically place electrodes on the skin's surface in proximity to target muscles [1]. This establishes a closed electrical circuit that allows for optimal electrical conductivity. Additionally, using EMS pads that adhere well prevents movement or displacement during muscle stimulation and enhances the comfort and safety of individuals undergoing therapy.

C. Stephanidis et al. (Eds.): HCII 2023, CCIS 1957, pp. 49–54, 2024.
https://doi.org/10.1007/978-3-031-49212-9_7

EMS devices use paired electrodes to serve multiple important functions. One electrode acts as the active electrode that delivers electrical impulses, while the other acts as the return electrode that sends the current back to the device. This configuration allows for precise and controlled stimulation of specific muscles. Additionally, this setup promotes coordinated muscle activation by directing the current through the muscle fibers, resulting in synchronized contractions and improved muscle recruitment.

It's important to ensure that EMS pads stick correctly to the skin to get the best results from your treatment. When the pads stick well, they create a strong and steady connection between the electrodes and the skin. This helps the electrical signals pass through smoothly and effectively, crucial for getting the most out of therapy. Good adhesion also keeps the pads in place during muscle contractions to stimulate the correct muscles accurately and consistently [2]. Plus, it helps feel more comfortable and safer by reducing the risk of skin irritation or accidental detachment of the pads.

We have developed a new type of electric muscle stimulation pad that is safe for use on the body. These pads are made from a flexible and conductive biopolymer composite, which makes them comfortable to wear and won't cause any skin irritation or allergic reactions. Our pads also have a vinylated silica-nanobead surface that improves contact and reduces resistance, making them perfect for use during physical activities. The backing layer is also thin and stretchable, allowing the pads to fit comfortably on the body. In this paper, we evaluate the performance of our innovative pads in terms of EMS signal quality during physical movement scenarios, including running.

2   Experiment

2.1   Preparation of EMS Pad

Figure 1 shows a process of manufacturing a cellulose nanofiber-based EMS pad having excellent skin adhesion. We used a multi-spray coater with a hollow cone nozzle and air dispenser from Hantech in Daejeon, Korea, to spray the samples. The sprayed samples were left to dry at room temperature for 24 h before analysis. We used a polyurethane (PU) film as the substrate and vinylated silica nanobead as the skin adhesion surface to create the hot stamping samples.

2.2   Characterization of EMS Signal

Based on our evaluation, the EMS strength perceived by the EMS pad tester during running was initially set to a scale of 1–5. To determine the variation in EMS strength, the EMS strength was measured using a KEYSIGHT DSOX1204A oscilloscope according to the adhesion of the EMS pad. We maintained the running speed at 12 km/h to maintain consistency. We measured the EMS stimulation strength after approximately 5 min of running when the individual's heart rate reached 70% to 85% of their maximum heart rate. It's important to note that when differentiating between jogging and running, heart rate zones are more pertinent than speed alone. Specifically, exercise intensity within the 60–70% range of the maximum heart rate is classified as jogging, while exercise intensity within the 70–85% range of the maximum heart rate corresponds to running.

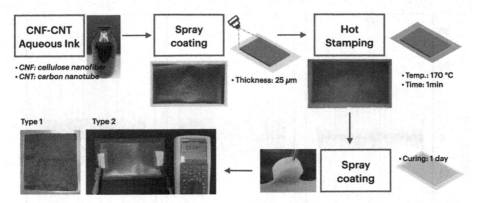

Fig. 1. The fabrication process of an EMS pad. There are two types of EMS electrodes: Type 1 is a dry electrode that lacks adhesion, while Type 2 has an adhesive surface

3   Results and Discussion

The configuration of EMS signals is known to vary according to the specific purpose of the device. A fundamental element in this regard is stimulus frequency, which governs the rate at which electrical impulses are administered to the muscles. Typically, EMS signals encompass a carrier frequency and a modulating stimulus frequency [3]. The carrier frequency serves as the continuous base frequency of the signal and exhibits variation based on the device's design. Conversely, the modulating stimulus frequency regulates the contraction speed of the muscles by modulating the intensity of the electrical impulses. This parameter is critical in eliciting targeted muscle responses during the stimulation process. The selection of an appropriate stimulus frequency in EMS depends on the desired therapeutic objectives and specific muscle outcomes. Different frequencies yield distinct physiological effects and selectively target specific muscle fibers. Lower frequencies, typically below 10 Hz, find application in promoting muscle relaxation and aiding in recovery processes, whereas higher frequencies, ranging from 20 Hz to several hundred Hz, are commonly employed to enhance muscle strength and endurance [4]. Additionally, EMS signals may incorporate additional adjustable parameters, including pulse width, amplitude, and waveform shape. These parameters offer the flexibility to customize the treatment regimen to suit individual tolerance levels and specific treatment objectives.

In this study, Fig. 2 shows the EMS application strength based on the skin adhesion of the EMS pad. The EMS signal used was a carrier frequency of 60 Hz and a modulating stimulus frequency of 20 Hz. Generally, EMS control devices adjust the EMS input strength in relation to the impedance between the EMS electrode and the skin to maintain a consistent EMS strength. This ensures the user experiences the same level of EMS stimulation each time. As indicated in Fig. 2 (B) and (C), an increase in skin adhesion of the EMS pad results in an improvement in modulating stimulus frequency strength without altering the carrier frequency. Amplitude in EMS signals refers to the intensity or strength of the carrier frequency, which serves as the base frequency of the electrical signal. A large amplitude indicates a higher intensity of the electrical current

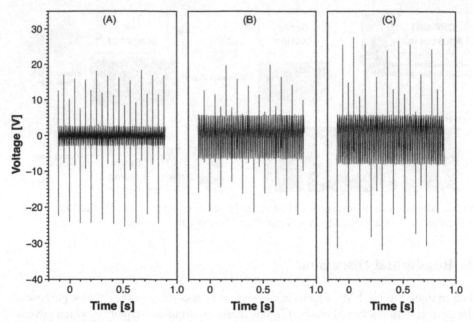

Fig. 2. EMS signal characteristics according to EMS skin adhesion. (A) is the pure output signal waveform of the EMS signal controller, and (B) and (C) are signal characteristics through type 1 and type 2 EMS pads in Fig. 1, respectively

associated with the carrier frequency, resulting in a stronger and more pronounced signal applied to the muscles during EMS. This leads to robust and intense muscle contractions. Conversely, a small amplitude signifies a lower intensity of the electrical current, yielding a milder and less pronounced signal delivered to the muscles. Consequently, EMS signals with a smaller amplitude may induce less intense muscle contractions.

As depicted by Fig. 3, the skin adhesion of EMS pads significantly impacts the applied EMS signal while running. When comparing EMS pads with weak skin adhesion (red) to those with solid adhesion (black), it is evident that the carrier frequency amplitude increased by approximately 43%, accompanied by sporadic variations in the strength of modulating stimulus frequency that prompts muscle contraction. In this study, the high adhesion of the EMS pad means that the resistance between the skin and the EMS pad is lowered. In other words, it can be seen that it is the same as the effect of improving electrical conductivity.

The effect of the carrier frequency amplitude on the EMS signal depends on the electrical conductivity of the EMS pad. The pad's electrical conductivity significantly impacts the efficiency of transferring current from the pad to the skin and basal muscles. If the EMS pad exhibits high electrical conductivity, it shows excellent current conductivity. Therefore, even if the carrier frequency amplitude is small, the current can be effectively transmitted to the muscles. High electrical conductivity facilitates efficient current transmission and adequate muscle stimulation and contraction. Conversely, if the EMS pad has a relatively low electrical conductivity, the carrier frequency may need to be large to obtain the desired muscle stimulation. A lower conductivity reduces the

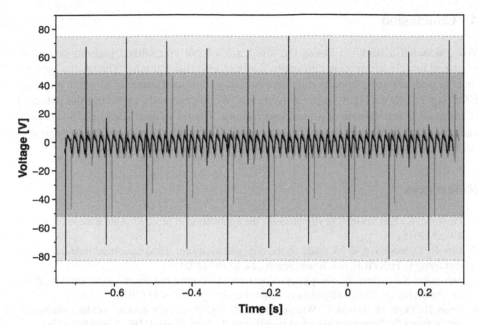

Fig. 3. Skin adhesion effect of EMS pad during exercise. The red line is type 1 without adhesion and the black line is EMS signal characteristics of type 2 with adhesion (Color figure online)

efficiency of EMS devices because higher amplitudes must be used to compensate for the reduced efficiency of current transmission.

Unstable skin contact with EMS pads can have various implications for the EMS signal, including frequency and intensity. The following effects may arise:

- Signal dispersion: Unstable skin contact can cause uneven electrical signal distribution across the skin surface. Gaps or poor contact between EMS pads and the skin can result in a higher resistance, leading to inconsistent or diminished electrical signal delivery to the targeted muscles.
- Increased impedance: Unstable skin contact raises the overall impedance of the electrical circuit. This impedes the efficient transmission of the electrical current, reducing its intensity or requiring higher voltage settings to achieve the desired stimulation level.
- Inaccurate intensity control: Inconsistent or intermittent skin contact disrupts the accuracy of intensity control during EMS. Fluctuations in skin contact can result in deviations between the intended and perceived intensity of the EMS signal, making it challenging to achieve consistent and precise stimulation.
- Potential discomfort or skin irritation: Unstable skin contact can cause discomfort or skin irritation. Insufficient contact may increase friction or rubbing between the pads and the skin during muscle contractions, resulting in discomfort or skin abrasion. Moreover, localized pressure points or concentrated current delivery due to unstable contact can cause skin irritation or discomfort in specific areas.

4   Conclusion

We conducted a study to assess the efficiency of our specialized pads in providing electrical muscle stimulation during physical exercises like running. The results indicate that our pads are exceptionally reliable, providing consistent stimulation while reducing EMS signal loss during dynamic movements. We are currently exploring the potential of our pads in rehabilitation, fitness, and gaming. Thanks to their stable EMS signaling and enhanced skin adhesion, our biocompatible EMS pads present intriguing prospects for EMS applications.

References

1. Pavlović, R.: Electro-muscle stimulation - the application in practice. Acta Kinesiologica **10**, 49–55 (2016)
2. Eun-Ji, Y., Joo-Yong, K.: A Study on the high sensitivity electrical muscle stimulation (EMS) pad using E-TEXTILE. Sci. Emot. Sensib. **24**, 81–90 (2021)
3. Sebastian, Z., Joshua, B.: Frequency-dependent reaction of the triceps surae muscle of the mouse during electromyostimulation. Front. Physiol. **11**, 150–155 (2020)
4. Evan, R., Piotr, M., David, F.: Wide-pulse-width, high-frequency neuromuscular stimulation: implications for functional electrical stimulation. J. Appl. Physiol. **101**, 228–240 (2006)

A Proposal for Complementary Use of Readiness Potential and NIRS in BMI Development

An Attempt of Assessment Using Hybrid 1DCNN-BiLSTM

Puwadej Leelasiri[1], Fumitaka Aki[2], Tatsuhiro Kimura[3], Hiroshi Ohshima[2], and Kiyoyuki Yamazaki[2(✉)]

[1] Department of Biomedical Engineering, Graduate School of Engineering, Tokai University, Tokyo, Japan

[2] Department of Biomedical Engineering, School of Engineering, Tokai University, Tokyo, Japan
ymzkkyyk@gmail.com

[3] Department of Human Information Engineering, School of Humanities and Science, Tokyo, Japan

Abstract. The purpose of this study is to develop a novel Brain Machine Interface (BMI) algorithm using near-infrared spectroscopy (NIRS) to supplement data on readiness potential (RP) obtained from electroencephalography (EEG) in order to recognize human motions. Congenital and acquired disabilities make it impossible to live comfortably as an able-bodied person. BMI assists people with disabilities in moving prosthetics, computer operations, etc. Our recent research has shown that the hybrid 1DCNN-BiLSTM algorithm, which combines two deep learning algorithms, can more correctly identify between left- and right-handed motions than EEG when total hemoglobin is monitored by NIRS. This is due to the fact that brain waves come in a variety of unique waveforms, such as RP. EEG has a weakness of external and internal noise. NIRS, on the other hand, is more noise-resistant than EEG, despite it lacking the precise indicators of activity readiness that EEG does. In this study, NIRS signals were combined into EEG signals to support EEG in distinguishing left-right hand movements. The EEG-NIRS and EEG dataset were passed hybrid 1DCNN-BiLSTM to discriminate accuracy separately to compare the accuracy and the SD. As a result, EEG-NIRS can more distinguish between left- and right-hand movements than using only-EEG signals. Considering the result, the combination of EEG and NIRS signal is possible to support BMI based on EEG to distinguish the left- and right-hand movement. It may be possible to determine the non-movement and movement signals using RP that appears on EEG.

Keywords: BMI · Deep learning · EEG-NIRS

1 Introduction

In voluntary human movement, the brain activities start at the frontal area to generate the signal when planning movements. The signal sent from the frontal lobe is sent to the supplementary motor area and primary motor area to generate the signal of movements

C. Stephanidis et al. (Eds.): HCII 2023, CCIS 1957, pp. 55–61, 2024.
https://doi.org/10.1007/978-3-031-49212-9_8

before sending it to the planned moving part. Because the signal from the brain is crossed at medulla oblongata before sending to the moving part, The signal generated from the brain and the body movement side is crossed.

The readiness potential (RP) can be observed using Electroencephalogram (EEG) near the frontal lobe. The readiness potential is generated 1s to 1.5s before movement [1] in minus voltage. Similarly, the change of oxyhemoglobin, deoxyhemoglobin, etc., can be observed by Near Infrared Spectroscopy (NIRS) in the same situation [2]. The NIRS sensor have 1 cm and 3 cm length from light emission to light detection for observation at the 0.5 cm and 1.5 cm from surface of the brain [9].

The brain-machine interface (BMI) is the system that decodes and encodes the activities from the brain to control the machine or sends machine activities to the brain. The brain activities for BMI can be recorded by EEG, NIRS, fMRI, etc. [3] BMI is utilized to support handicapper to control prosthesis hand, external bone, wheelchair, etc.

1DCNN is the deep learning model that utilizes the features of the sequential input. Unlike the normal CNN that extracts features from the images [10] (the 3D data for RGB), 1DCNN is used to extract the features from the 2D data, like the time series data. 1DCNN utilize the filters on convolutional 1D layers to extract the features of the input data. This CNN type distinguishes sequential data like EEG [4] or NIRS.

LSTM is the deep learning model that utilizes the LSTM layer to learn the long-term dependencies between the time series data by remembering the information through time. Unlike the convolutional 1D layers that use the filters to extract the features, the LSTM layer utilizes the input gate, forget gate and output gate to support remembering the information. The input layer using to input the new information into the network before sending it into the next hidden state as modulation input. The forget gate is utilized to delete the remembered data that is not required. Finally, the output gate decides and sends output into the next state [5]. Bidirectional LSTM (BiLSTM) is the model that consists of two LSTMs that take the input in a forward direction and the other in a backward direction. This deep learning model is used to classify and predict sequential data like text classification [6] or financial forecasting [7].

The hybrid 1DCNN-BiLSTM is the model that connects the BiLSTM after 1DCNN to identify the information after the input data extracted the important features by 1DCNN.

The previous study [8] showed that the information from NIRS measured at the forehead area could distinguish the left-right hand movement more accurately than the information from EEG. In addition, from 1DCNN, BiLSTM, and hybrid 1DCNN-BiLSTM models, the hybrid 1DCNN-BiLSTM can distinguish the most accuracy in the lowest SD. However, NIRS may find it hard to distinguish the information invoked by hand movement and the external noise because NIRS doesn't have the shape of a signal that can show that invoked by movement or not and doesn't, like EEG, have a special shape of signals like RP from EEG that can specify the signal invoked by movement and other signal. Therefore, this study proposes to improve the cons of EEG and NIRS when distinguishing left- and right-hand movements observed in the previous study by upgrading the BMI algorithm and combining the information from EEG and NIRS to enhance the distinguished model using hybrid 1DCNN-BiLSTM.

2 Methodology

2.1 Measuring Method

This experiment was performed by nine healthy right-handed individuals between the ages of 20 and 30. The measuring instrument of EEG was used BRAIN PRODUCTS Inc. Brain Vision Recorder1.20. The recordings were based on the international 10–20 system, and the electrodes were placed on F3, F4, Fcz, C3, C4, Cz, P3, P4, A1, and A2 (Fig. 1). The electrode at Cz was utilized as system reference on this system. The EEG signals were recorded and took a reference at A1 and A2. The ground was set at the area of the cervical spine. The sampling frequency was set at 250 Hz. On the other hand, NIRS (HOT-2000, NeU) sensor placed two sensors on the left and right sides of the forehead to observe the relative change of total hemoglobin (THb) in a depth of 0.5 cm and 1.5 cm. Unlike EEG, the maximum sampling frequency that NIRS can initiate is 10 Hz. Therefore, in this study, both NIRS and EEG were measured at the same time.

In this experiment, the individuals were seated at comfortable seats, and the stimulus was presented by the stopwatch in front of the individuals. The stopwatch shows that individuals rest between digits one and five and squeeze the button once when stop-watches show digits between six and zero. During the first five seconds, individuals can choose their squeeze spots (digits 1 to 5). The experiment was done 45 times each, and the left and right hands were done Separately (Figs. 2 and 3).

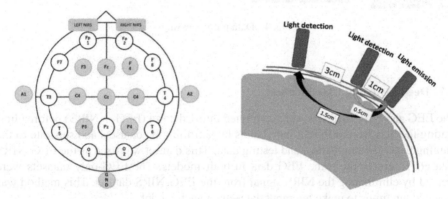

Fig. 1. EEG-NIRS measurement site   **Fig. 2.** Schematic illustration of NIRS measurement

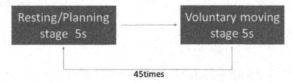

Fig. 3. Task

2.2 Data Preprocessing

On EEG, the signal from the left hemisphere was minus to A1, and the signal from the left hemisphere was minus to A2 to utilize A1 and A2 as references on each side. Hence, the signal between −1000 ms to 0 ms before the hand squeezing that use as a dataset for deep learning. On NIRS, the signal between −1500 ms before the hand squeezing to 500 ms after the hand squeezing was utilized as the dataset. However, the sampling frequency on EEG and NIRS is extremely different. This difference can decrease the accuracy of EEG-NIRS deep learning. To proof this problem, new 12 data were generated between the original data in the liner to make the data length similar to EEG (20 data to 248 data) (Fig. 4).

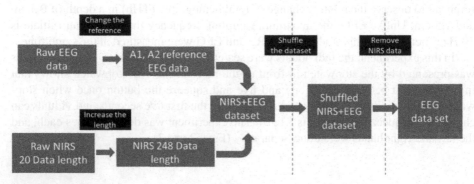

Fig. 4. Data preprocessing

2.3 Deep Learning Classification

The EEG and NIRS datasets were combined into 1 dataset (EEG + NIRS) before eliminating the bias from different individuals by shuffling the datasets and separate to the training data, validation data, and testing data. This dataset was used as the EEG-NIRS dataset. To create the same EEG data in both models, The EEG-only datasets were created by eliminating the NIRS signal from the EEG-NIRS dataset. This method was repeated ten times to make ten input datasets in each model.

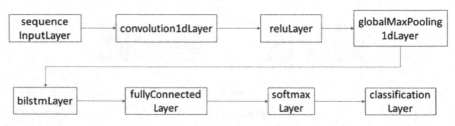

Fig. 5. Deep learning layer

The classification accuracy from the ten datasets was averaged to obtain the accuracy. In addition, the average accuracy in EEG and EEG + NIRS were compared to obtain both accuracies. Figure 5 shows the layers of the hybrid 1DCNN-BiLSTM model utilized in this research.

3 Results and Discussion

Figure 6 and Fig. 7 obtain the accuracies in EEG and EEG + NIRS datasets. Both figures show the accuracy of training data and validation data. Figure 6 shows the accuracy of EEG, and Fig. 7 shows the figure of EEG + NIRS. The x-axis represents the accuracy, and the y-axis represents the iteration numbers. The blue line represents training accuracy, and the black line represents testing accuracy. According to the results, both models' accuracies stopped increasing at 200 iterations.

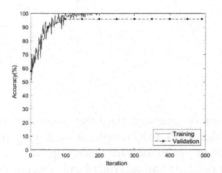

Fig. 6. Accuracy on EEG dataset   **Fig. 7.** Accuracy on EEG-NIRS dataset

Table 1 shows that the average of EEG-NIRS is higher in both validation data and testing data. In addition, the SD on the EEG-NIRS model is smaller than the EEG model. As a result, the accuracy of EEG for the validation and testing data is 96.6% and 98.5%. On the other hand, the accuracy of EEG-NIRS for the validation data was 96.9%, and the accuracy for testing data was 99%.

According to the result, the results accuracies that averaged by ten datasets in EEG and EEG-NIRS. Both models in training data can become 100% accurate. However, on validation and testing data, the EEG-NIRS model unitizing hybrid 1DCNN-BiLSTM is more accurate and does not scatter than using the signal only from the EEG.

Table 1. The accuracies on both EEG and EEG-NIRS

	EEG		EEG + NIRS	
Times	Validation (%)	Testing (%)	Validation (%)	Testing (%)
1	98	100	99	100
2	96	97	98	98
3	95	100	95	100
4	98	97	96	98
5	99	100	98	99
6	95	98	96	100
7	96	99	99	99
8	97	96	96	98
9	94	98	95	99
10	98	100	97	99
Average	96.6	98.5	96.9	99

4 Conclusion

According to the results, EEG-NIRS is the most beneficial since they present more accurately and have a low standard deviation than EEG. EEG is better at identifying the movement signal and external signal unrelated to a hand movement using appearing of RP. On the other hand, NIRS is better at distinguishing left- and right-hand movements. According to the result, NIRS can support EEG to increase the accuracy of left-right hand movements classifying by combining EEG and NIRS. Therefore, EEG-NIRS can support the disadvantage of each other on deep learning models to improve BMI classification algorithms. However, the accuracy can be improved using NIRS, which can record in the same sampling frequency as EEG. In addition, the accuracy of averaging of EEG and EEG-NIRS is not much different because the output of this research has only left- and right-hand movement. The difference in the accuracy of EEG and EEG-NIRS may increase if the classification result is more than two.

References

1. Hans, H., Kornhuber, H.H., Deecke, L.: Pflugers Archfur die gesamte Physiologie des Menschen und der Tiere (1965)
2. Denault, A.Y., Shaaban-Ali, M., Cournoyer, A., Benkreira, A., Mailhot, T.: Near-Infrared Spectroscopy. In: Neuromonitoring Techniques,Chapter 7, pp. 179–233 (2018)
3. Shedeed, H.A., Issa, M.F., El-Sayed, S.M.: Brain EEG signal processing for controlling a robotic arm. In: 2013 8th International Conference on Computer Engineering & Systems (ICCES), Cairo, Egypt, pp. 152–157 (2013). https://doi.org/10.1109/ICCES.2013.6707191

4. Giudice,M.L., et al.: 1D convolutional neural network approach to classifying voluntary eye blinks in EEG signals for BCI applications. In: 2020 International Joint Conference on Neural Networks (IJCNN), Glasgow, UK, pp. 1–7 (2020). https://doi.org/10.1109/IJCNN48605.2020.9207195
5. Hameed, Z., Garcia-Zapirain, B.: Sentiment classification using a single-layered BiLSTM model. IEEE Access **8**, 73992–74001 (2020). https://doi.org/10.1109/ACCESS.2020.2988550
6. Zhang, Y., Rao, Z.: n-BiLSTM: BiLSTM with n-gram features for text classification. In: IEEE 5th Information Technology and Mechatronics Engineering Conference (ITOEC) Chongqing, China, pp. 1056–1059(2020). https://doi.org/10.1109/ITOEC49072.2020.9141692
7. Yang, M., Wang, J.: Adaptability of financial time series prediction based on BiLSTM. Procedia Comput. Sci. **199**, 18–25 (2022). ISSN: 1877–0509
8. Leelasiri, P., et al.: A study on the relationships between readiness potential and NIRS signals evoked by voluntary hand movement, Abstract of SAS Symposium(2022). (in Japanese)
9. Chance, B., Nioka, S., Kent, J., McCully, K., Fountain, M., et al.: Time-resolved spectroscopy of hemoglobin and myoglobin in resting and ischemic muscle. Anal. Biochem. **174**(2), 698–707 (1988)
10. Sultana, F., Sufian, A., Dutta, P.: Advancements in image classification using convolutional neural network. In: 2018 Fourth International Conference on Research in Computational Intelligence and Communication Networks (ICRCICN), Kolkata, India, pp. 122–129 (2018). https://doi.org/10.1109/ICRCICN.2018.8718718

Different Ways to Deceive: Uncovering the Psychological Effects of the Three Dark Patterns Preselection, Confirmshaming and Disguised Ads

Deborah Maria Löschner[(✉)] [iD] and Sebastian Pannasch [iD]

Technische Universität Dresden, 01062 Dresden, Germany
deborah_maria.loeschner@tu-dresden.de

Abstract. Dark patterns are present in many places on the Internet in a wide variety. The multifaceted nature of deceptive designs suggests that different dark patterns may use different mechanisms to deceive, and that these may be accumulated when various dark patterns are faced at the same time. Based on this, this study examined three dark patterns that were expected to have different effects on perceptual, emotional, and motivational aspects of decision behavior. In an online experiment, the three dark patterns preselection, confirmshaming, and disguised ads were examined separately and in combination. The effects on decision behavior, negative emotions, and dwell time are collected. It is shown that disguised ads in particular increase the error rate and dwell time in decision tasks. The combination of all three dark patterns leads to both enhanced and attenuated effects for decision making and transaction costs. This highlights the need to investigate deceptive design in a more sophisticated way with respect to the mechanisms of specific dark patterns. The present work encourages to a more nuanced view on the theorizing and investigation of dark patterns.

Keywords: dark pattern · decision making · transaction costs

1 Introduction

Information, entertainment, shopping—many areas of life with low-threshold access opportunities can be found in the internet nowadays. Although most offers seem to be free of charge, users have to pay—if not with money, then with personal data, time, or attention [1]. This trend is reinforced by the increasing use of deceptive design structures, so-called "*dark patterns*" [2]. They are intended to influence behavior of users in the interest of website providers which is often contradictory to the users' intention [3]. Studies on the prevalence of dark patterns in digital design show how frequently they are used [4]. This highlights the need for technological and legal countermeasures. However, developing effective interventions requires an understanding of the underlying mechanisms of decision making in the context of dark patterns.

C. Stephanidis et al. (Eds.): HCII 2023, CCIS 1957, pp. 62–69, 2024.
https://doi.org/10.1007/978-3-031-49212-9_9

1.1 Related Work on Decision Making and Dark Patterns

Since the phenomenon was first described by Harry Brignull in 2010, a variety of design structures have been classified as "dark" [4]. What all these structures have in common is that they intervene in the process from action planning or intention building to actual behavior performance [5]. Despite the "common ground", an extensive study by the European Commission [4] revealed that different mechanisms of dark patterns can have differential effects on emerging transaction costs (i.e., cognitive load, physiological arousal, negative emotions). This implies that different dark patterns influence decision processes presumably in different ways. The identification of critical points of attack in the decision-making process in general can help to identify functional mechanisms for dark patterns.

In the first place, decision situations have to be perceived as such. Thus, dark patterns can disrupt the decision-making process by influencing perception, e.g., the visual design of stimuli. An example of this is the dark pattern preselection as the pre-selection of a choice option that suits the interests of companies or providers [4, 6].

Based on this, the current intention determines behavior. This is influenced, among others, by personal goals and thus by emotions and motivation. In the dark pattern confirmshaming, emotional influence occurs through the use of emotional language to promote a particular decision [7]. A motivational influence can be assumed for the dark pattern disguised ad. This describes advertisements embedded in website environments, which are not or not immediately recognizable as such [6]. The commercial character of the advertisements is thus intended to be hidden and users are tempted to "click" [8]. Hence, these designs may aim to motivationally reframe advertising.

We have only limited cognitive capacity to deal with these dark pattern induced "disruptions" of planned actions [9]. An even more drastic impact can be expected when multiple dark patterns appear at the same time. While the "resources" of the users remain the same, the amount of disruptive elements increases. The cumulative use of different dark patterns can thus be assumed to potentiate the influence on decision making processes.

1.2 Scope of This Study

Questions about the effects of dark patterns of varying complexity and mechanisms separately and in combination are barely investigated. This leads to the central objective of our research: How do dark patterns influence the decision making behavior and transaction costs of users? Are there differences in dark patterns deceiving mainly on a perceptual, emotional or motivational level?

This results in the research question of what impact the three dark patterns (i) pre-selection, (ii) confirmshaming, and (iii) disguised ads have, individually and in combination, on the decision-making behavior of users and the transaction costs that arise in the process. The decision behavior is understood as the error rate in the processing of an experimental task, the transaction costs are measured in the form of negative emotions, the feeling of being manipulated and the processing time. The following three hypotheses are intended to answer these questions. (H1) The use of (i) preselection, (ii) confirmshaming, and (iii) disguised ads leads to an increased error rate and (H2) increased transaction costs compared to a baseline condition. (H3) The combination of (i) preselection, (ii) confirmshaming, and (iii) disguised ads increases the error rate and transaction costs compared to the single use of dark patterns.

2 Materials and Methods

2.1 Experimental Setup

We conducted an online investigation in April and May 2023 using the online tool Labvanced. The experiment was preregistered at the Open Science Framework (osf.io/98c7w) and received a positive vote of the ethics committee of the Technische Universität Dresden. With a 5x1-factorial within-person design we tested the following five dark pattern conditions: (i) Baseline (BL, no dark pattern is presented), (ii) Preselection (PS, preselected response option on a pop-up), (iii) Confirmshaming (CS, emotionally colored language of the pop-up options), (iv) Disguised Ad (DA, advertisements designed as regular newspaper articles), (v) All Three (A3, combination of all three dark patterns). In order to avoid habituation effects, the conditions were presented on different topics (health, nature, literature, tech, mobility). The dark pattern conditions were randomized with respect to both the topic and the order of presentation. Each condition was presented as a block of six newsfeed stimuli (two test stimuli depending on the condition as a disguised ad or a regular advertisement and four distractors in the form of two news articles and two advertisements) and one pop-up stimulus, also in randomized order. Newsfeed-stimuli were displayed by website templates of a news-website with the preview of a news article or an advertisement. The pop-up stimuli appeared as pop-up windows with the question whether subjects would like to see another article related to the topic. If participants agreed to this, they were briefly shown another article to increase the credibility of the experiment. The exact design of the stimuli varied depending on the Dark pattern condition, as can be seen in Table 1.

Table 1. Design of Dark Patterns and Control Stimuli

	Design Feature	Stimulus	Control Condition
Preselection	agreeing option is already ticked	Pop-up	question whether another article on the same topic should be shown without special marking of the two possible options (agree or disagree)
Confirmshaming	agreeing option: „Yes, I'm interested" vs. disagreeing option: "No, I am missing interesting information."	Pop-up	
Disguised Ad	advertisement masked as a regular newspaper article, marked with "advertising" in the top left corner	Newsfeed-Stimulus	regular advertising, marked with „advertising" in the top left corner

2.2 Experimental Task

Based on the cover story that it was an experiment to study information processing and decision behavior online, subjects had to complete two tasks. They were instructed to determine for each newsfeed stimulus whether it was an advertisement or a newspaper article. While completing this classification task, a pop-up with a not task-related question appeared randomly. Both tasks were trained before the experiment. Repeatedly, participants were remembered to complete the tasks as efficiently as possible, i.e. accurately and quickly. It was announced in advance, that the fastest ones would have the chance to win a book voucher. This should ensure that participants had a clear task that they wanted to complete as fast as possible and without distraction in order to induce a setting that was close to website use. After each block, subjects were asked to report their emotional state. At the end of the experiment, subjects were informed that the news articles used are fictitious and does not reflect actual information.

2.3 Dependent Measures

Measures of decision behavior as well as transaction costs (negative emotionality and dwell time) were collected. Decision behavior was operationalized by the error rate in the decision tasks. For the newsfeed-test stimuli, an error was coded if the corresponding newsfeed material was misclassified as "news" and not as "advertising." The error rate for preselection and confirmshaming was measured as the consent to pop-up question, following the assumption that subjects should avoid distraction. Accordingly, the range of the error rate varied from a minimum of 0 to a maximum of 1.

Transaction costs in the form of negative emotions were assessed with two variables, each on 5-point Likert scales. The negative subscale of the short form of the Positive and Negative Affect Scale (PANAS, [10]) measured negative emotionality. The feeling of being manipulated was defined as the mean of two self-reported items, namely feeling "influenced" and "manipulated". The amount of time spent on the two relevant newsfeed stimuli (disguised ads as experimental stimuli or advertisements as control stimuli) was determined as the sum of the time spent on both stimuli. For the pop-ups, this variable resulted from the dwell time on the corresponding stimulus.

3 Results

85 people participated in the online survey. After excluding the participants whose finishing time was 75% above the average finishing time, 79 participants (62 female, 16 male, 1 diverse) remained for further analyses. The average age of the sample was 23.75 years ($SD = 7.31$), 87.34% were students and 89.87% were German native speakers. We performed Friedman rank sum tests to analyze group differences in the ordinal-scaled error rates and one-factor, Greenhouse-Geisser corrected ANOVAs with repeated measures for the emotion scales and the dwell time. All post hoc contrast results were Bonferroni-Holm adjusted for multiple testing.

3.1 Error Rates in Decision Making Behavior

As hypothesized, for newsfeed test stimuli we found an increased error rate in the DA-condition compared to the other conditions ($\chi^2[4] = 42.574, p < .001; w = 0.15$). The post-hoc Wilcox test revealed significant differences between the DA- condition and all the other conditions except PS. For the pop-up task, the error rate of the A3 condition was the highest, closely followed by the error rate of the PS condition. While these group differences were assumed in the hypotheses, very low values close to 0 were shown for CS-condition. There were slightly significant differences in the error rate of the pop-up task ($\chi^2[4] = 13.915, p = < 0.01$) between dark pattern conditions with a very weak effect size ($w = 0.05$). The Wilcox post-hoc tests revealed just slightly significant differences between the CS- and the PS- and A3-condition. The error rate frequency of all conditions for both stimuli can be seen in Fig. 1.

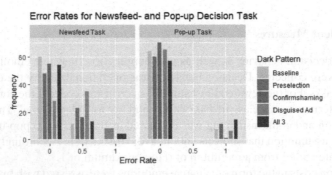

Fig. 1. Error rates for the newsfeed – and the pop-up task (error rate = 0: no errors detected)

3.2 Transaction Costs

No group differences emerged for negative emotions ($F[3.43, 239.77] = 1.50, p = 0.210$; $\eta^2_p = 0.27$) and the feeling of being manipulated ($F[3.41, 265.91, p = 0.143$; $\eta^2_p = 0.02$). For this reason, no post-hoc tests for pairwise comparisons were performed.

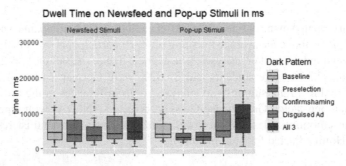

Fig. 2. Boxplots with error bars for time (ms) spent on disguised ad stimuli and pop-ups

Regarding the processing time of the newsfeed test stimuli, the dwell time was by far the highest in the condition with all three dark patterns. We found significant group differences (F[3.15, 245.8] = 9.81, $p < .001$) with a medium effect size ($\eta^2_p = 0.11$). Post-hoc testing revealed significant differences between the condition with all three dark patterns and all the other conditions except DA. Also for the dwell time in the pop-up task, significant group differences were seen (F[3.14, 245.23] = 28.38, $p < .001$) with a large effect size ($\eta^2_p = 0.27$). A post-hoc analysis revealed significant differences between almost all conditions except BL and DA as well as DA and A3. Figure 2 shows the dwell time in ms for both stimuli in each condition.

3.3 Summary of Results

Hypothesis 1 can be partially confirmed. We found increased error rates for DA and PS, while the error rate was lowest for CS. With regard to transaction costs, only DA showed a strongly increased dwell time on the dark pattern stimulus, whereas subjects remained only briefly on the pop-ups with confirmshaming and preselection. No group differences were found with regard to the emotions measured. Thus, hypothesis 2 can be confirmed just for the DA-condition and dwell time. The use of all three dark patterns at the same time was associated with increased error rates for pop-up but not for newsfeed stimuli compared to the single dark pattern conditions. Dwell time was highest for both stimuli types in the A3 condition while no differences were found in the emotional state, supporting hypothesis 3 partially.

4 Discussion

The results indicate that dark patterns influence the decision-making behavior of individuals. No altered emotional states were observed in any of the conditions. Conversely, for the stimuli dwell time especially in the pop-up task we found significant differences between almost all of the dark patterns conditions.

4.1 Error Rates

When using disguised ads, subjects were worse at deciding whether it was an advertisement or a news article. Irrelevant pop-up offers were more likely to be accepted in the PS and the A3 condition while they were most often rejected in the CS condition. Thus, confirmshaming seems to optimize the associated decision making behavior when it is used isolated. This is contrasted by the increased error rates in the A3 condition in the pop-up task. This raises the question of whether the effect of individual dark patterns is strengthened or weakened when they are combined. Besides our assumption that several dark patterns at once increase the cognitive load and that persons are therefore more susceptible to errors, another effect appears here. It seems possible that a too "obvious" manipulation increases dark pattern awareness and thus reduces vulnerability to errors. However, the low effect size in the pop-up task should be considered as a limiting factor when interpreting the results. It remains unclear whether one of these mechanisms causes the effects in our data. As dark patterns often occur together on websites [4], an understanding of these effects seems all the more important.

4.2 Emotional State

No effects were found for emotional states. The gross scaling of the measures used could be one reason for this: The five-item survey might be too insensitive to represent subtle emotional differences between conditions. The experimental manipulation, the online-setting as such, and the dark pattern induced consequences for subjects do not seem adequate to produce sufficiently drastic emotional changes. Gray and colleagues [11] identified several factors that contribute to the feeling of being manipulated in relation to dark patterns, namely distrust of providers or fear for privacy. This implies that individuals must face real and possibly noticeable consequences to report an emotional reaction. This could not be induced in our experiment.

4.3 Dwell Time

While dwell time on the newsfeed test stimuli varied between groups according to the hypotheses, an unexpected picture emerged for the pop-up task. Compared to the BL condition, dwell time was significantly decreased in the PS and CS conditions, while it was increased in the DA- and All Three conditions. The rapid processing of preselection and confirmshaming can be interpreted in the light of possible habituation effects in relation to dark patterns [4]. Perhaps, subjects are so used to dark patterns that a habituated behavior pattern is activated. This could be an explanation for the short processing time and low error rates at the same time, especially in the confirmshaming condition. Individuals hardly have to allocate cognitive capacity to deal with the pop-up and are correspondingly fast [12]. A differentiated assessment of whether fast processing can be interpreted as habituation or as avoidance of cognitive effort cannot be made on the basis of the available data. A detailed examination of the relationships between decision behavior and transaction costs could provide important insights.

4.4 Limitations and Outlook

Thus, these results condense the findings on the differentiable effects of individual dark patterns. In this context, the research method as an online experiment represents two sides of the same coin. On the one hand, it must be emphasized that even with the experiment-related low personal involvement of subjects, we see the manipulating character of dark patterns. On the other hand, it must be considered that the stimuli examined here are one representation of the respective dark patterns and not a generalizable design structure. In particular, with regard to the number of possible designs of confirmshaming it cannot be denied that other formulations might have produced different results (cf. Impact on decision making through toying with emotions [4]).

The operationalization of dark patterns and the general experimental setting limit the interpretability of the results. If we want to generate meaningful experimental evidence on deceptive design, the question of appropriate methods to manipulate behavioral manipulation should be central.

5 Conclusion

As our results show, we should not focus only on single dark patterns and single dependent variables. The combination of dark patterns provides hints on possible neutralization or potentiation effects of dark patterns. In summary, our results can be seen as an impetus for a more nuanced view of dark patterns. Assumptions about the different individual effects depending on the particular mechanism allow for a deeper understanding of the manipulation taking place. To turn dark patterns into bright patterns, we first should enlighten our understanding of the mechanisms of influence.

References

1. Garcia-Rivadulla, S.: Personalization vs. privacy. IFLA J. **42**(3), 227–238 (2016). https://doi.org/10.1177/0340035216662890
2. Gray, C.M., Chivukula, S.S.: When does manipulation turn a design 'dark'? Interactions **27**(1), 96 (2019). https://doi.org/10.1145/3375016
3. Narayanan, A., Mathur, A., Chetty, M., Kshirsagar, M.: Dark patterns: past, present, and future. Queue **18**(2), 67–92 (2020). https://doi.org/10.1145/3400899.3400901
4. European Commission. Directorate General for Justice and Consumers: Behavioural study on unfair commercial practices in the digital environment: dark patterns and manipulative personalisation: final report. Publications Office (2022)
5. Mathur, A., Kshirsagar, M., Mayer, J.: What Makes a Dark Pattern… Dark? **82**, 1–18 (2021). https://doi.org/10.1145/3411764.3445610
6. Gray, C.M., Kou, Y., Battles, B., Hoggatt, J., Toombs, A.L.: The dark (patterns) side of UX design. In: Mandryk, R. (ed) Proceedings of the 2018 CHI Conference on Human Factors in Computing Systems, CHI 2018, Montreal QC Canada, 21 April 2018–26 April 2018, ACM Conferences, pp. 1–14. ACM (2018). https://doi.org/10.1145/3173574.3174108
7. Mathur, A., et al.: Dark Patterns at Scale. Proc. ACM Hum.-Comput. Interact. **3**(CSCW), 1–32 (2019). https://doi.org/10.1145/3359183
8. Beckert, J., Koch, T., Viererbl, B., Denner, N., Peter, C.: Advertising in disguise? How disclosure and content features influence the effects of native advertising communications **45**(3), 303–324 (2020). https://doi.org/10.1515/commun-2019-0116
9. Kahneman, D.: A perspective on judgment and choice: mapping bounded rationality. A. Psychol. **58**(9), 697–720 (2003). https://doi.org/10.1037/0003-066X.58.9.697
10. Breyer, B., Bluemke, M.: Deutsche Version der Positive and Negative Affect Schedule PANAS (GESIS Panel) (2016)
11. Gray, C.M., Chen, J., Chivukula, S.S., Qu, L.: End user accounts of dark patterns as felt manipulation. Proc. ACM Hum.-Comput. Interact. **5**(CSCW2), 1–25 (2021). https://doi.org/10.1145/3479516
12. Waldman, A.E.: Cognitive biases, dark patterns, and the 'privacy paradox.' Curr. Opin. Psychol. **31**, 105–109 (2020). https://doi.org/10.1016/j.copsyc.2019.08.025

Design of Decision Tree-Based Face Emotion Interaction in Contextual Game

Patcharin Panjaburee[✉] [iD], Niwat Srisawasdi [iD], and Sasipim Poompimol [iD]

Faculty of Education, Khon Kaen University, Khon Kaen 40002, Thailand
patchapan@kku.ac.th

Abstract. With the benefits of contextual games and the applications of decision tree, well-designed games can simulate an interactive learning environment where the students can freely explore their essential knowledge and practice skills in context-based scenarios with guidance and feedback. However, on a wide development, face emotions are probably missing part of the current development of decision tree-based contextual games. Therefore, this study integrated views of facial emotions to evoke emotions in making decisions through the games. The study starts to design contextual games where the game mechanics are based on the decision tree model and interactions are based on the player's decision-making to face emotions. The games were designed as two-dimensional (2D) storytelling game prototypes with HTML5. Game designers and developers manage the user's experience and emotions along the play through visual effects, sound effects, and narration. This study conducted a pilot exploration to evaluate the effectiveness of the interactive design by collecting perceptions using a verified questionnaire about the technology acceptance model (TAM) from 30 participants. The results revealed that participants positively perceived the decision tree-based face-emotion interaction in the contextual games, and the narrative part was useful for connecting knowledge gained from the games to authentic context, and music given by emotion analysis helped adjust the decisions. They intend to play the games continually and like the design of the decision tree-based face-emotion interaction games. Further experiments are required and planned to reduce the complexity of user interfaces and increase relevant hinder in the games.

Keywords: Digital Games · Games for Learning · Interaction Design

1 Background and Motivation

Most games could be used to support enjoyment and a fun environment. In this perspective, scholars have recognized teaching and learning material using games as an effective method for fostering the students to achieve learning goals. In other words, the students can enjoyably acquire learning content to enhance their learning performance. Therefore, well-designed game-based learning element regarding user interface and flow experience is crucial for teachers and developers aiming to use the games to promote students' cognitive and affective domains. Moreover, scholars have suggested that situating the students in a particular task could help them connect the knowledge gained from the

© The Author(s), under exclusive license to Springer Nature Switzerland AG 2024
C. Stephanidis et al. (Eds.): HCII 2023, CCIS 1957, pp. 70–77, 2024.
https://doi.org/10.1007/978-3-031-49212-9_10

games to their daily life [1–3]. That is, contextual games can provide virtual context and help the students to link knowledge to authentic context. On the other hand, the decision tree is a helpful data mining approach classifying the variables into a simplified visual model and hierarchy to provide the decision for each category. The tree hierarchy also impersonates the human's cognitive process making it easy to comprehend the data [4]. The decision tree approach integrated objecting to differentiate students' movements and categorize them into right and wrong categories. The information provided by the tree model helped the students to receive appropriate recommendations to correct their learning movements and helped lessen the teacher's workload. The decision tree approach makes the games worthwhile to extract students' learning gaps and supply the most effective way to enhance individual students' learning processes [5, 6].

With the benefits of the applications of decision tree and contextual games, well-designed games can simulate an interactive learning environment where the students can freely explore their essential knowledge and practice skills in context-based scenarios with guidance and feedback. However, on a wide development, face emotions are probably missing part of the current development of decision tree-based contextual games. Therefore, this study integrated views of facial emotions to evoke emotions in making decisions through the games. The study starts to design contextual games where the game mechanics are based on the decision tree model and interactions are based on the player's decision-making to face emotions. Accordingly, this study conducted a pilot exploration to evaluate the effectiveness of the interactive design by collecting perceptions using a verified questionnaire relevant to the technology acceptance perspective.

2 Contextual Game Design

2.1 Decision Tree Method

The decision tree method is a widely used supervised machine learning algorithm that can be applied to classification and regression tasks. It adopts a flowchart-like structure to make decisions based on different conditions or features. In this method, internal nodes in the tree represent tests conducted on specific features, and each branch represents a potential outcome of the test. The tree leaves represent the final decisions or predicted outputs [4]. This method is considered common and accurate in comparison to other AI classification techniques, making it popular for various purposes, such as stock trading [7], medicine [8], and risk management [9].

Decision trees have been widely applied in educational settings for learning analytics and predicting learners' profiles and requirements [10]. They aim to understand students' learning patterns, identify variables influencing the learning process, and provide suitable teaching and learning strategies to achieve learning goals [11, 12]. For instance, Chen and Hung [13] developed a computer-assisted instructions system using a decision tree approach to differentiate students' movements and categorize them as correct or incorrect in physical education movement training. The information provided by the decision tree model helped students receive appropriate recommendations to correct their movements and reduced the teacher's workload. Furthermore, decision tree classification has been utilized in students' profiling to facilitate personalized learning [14]. Lin et al. [15]

focused on using decision trees as a data mining technique to customize learning paths for enhancing creative performance in a personalized learning system.

Accordingly, the decision tree method provided the students with the learning paths based on their good or bad actions and immediate feedback, which enabled the consistent adjustment of helpful behaviors. As a result, the students who participated in the contextual game demonstrated a decrease in bad decisions and an increase in good decisions, as shown in Fig. 1. Individual differences play a crucial part in determining learning effectiveness. The decision tree approach makes it worthwhile to extract students' learning gaps and supply the most effective way to enhance each student's learning process in the contextual game.

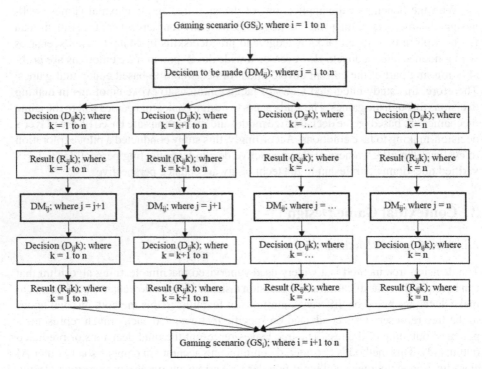

Fig. 1. A decision tree method used in designing the contextual game.

2.2 Decision Tree-Based Face Emotion Interaction Method

Based on the decision tree proposed in Fig. 1. Which presents hierarchical order of the story-telling and decision-making situations, the storyline tree can be completely used to analyze the decision in the game as follows:

(a) IF $D_{ij}k = 0$ THEN User performs Bad Decision;
(b) If $D_{ij}k = 1$ THEN User performs Good Decision.

That is to say, each decision impacts face emotional interaction of the avatar as user player:

(a) If Bad Decision THEN Avatar shows Sad facial emotion, and the gaming score is decreased;

(b) If Good Decision THEN Avatar shows Happy facial emotion, and the gaming score is increased;

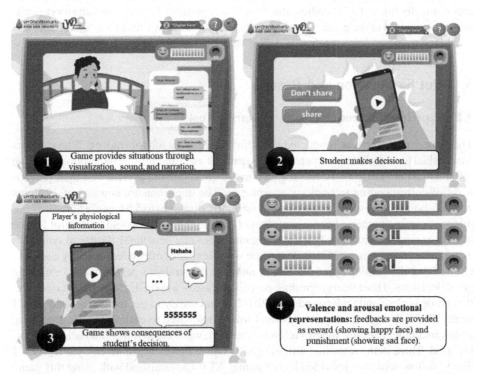

Fig. 2. A contextual game based on a decision tree-based face emotion interaction method.

The gaming scenarios will run until the user can show happy facial emotion rather than 50% of the proposed decision tree. Otherwise, the user will be diagnosed with learning understanding to trace the failure's root and restart the corresponding gaming scenario. Accordingly, the games were designed as two-dimensional (2D) storytelling game prototypes with HTML5 (see Fig. 2.). Game designers and developers manage the user's experience and emotions along the play through visual effects, sound effects, and narration. In particular, in this study, creating decision tree-based face-emotion interaction in contextual games consist of three specific aspects: visualization (text, animation effects), sound (audio effects, music), and narration (storytelling, situations). Regarding the decision tree model, the player, an avatar in the games, receives storytelling and situations to make the decisions. Making decisions of individual players was calculated for giving the rewards as showing happy facial emotion when they made a good decision;

otherwise, providing punishments as sad facial emotion was delivered when they made a bad decision. Avatar's physiological information is extracted and classified regarding happy and sad face emotions into emotional groups (i.e., valence and arousal). In this sense, the player who intends to perform more good decisions will have positive valence; otherwise, negative valence will be displayed. Moreover, arousal will be shown when the player sticks to highly bad decision-making. The valence and arousal emotional representations are directly used as an interactive input into the game interaction mechanism. In other words, the player receiving negative valence and arousal emotion will be automatically traced back to adjust the decisions regarding the decision tree storytelling. Regarding sound in the game, the game system automatically provides audio effects and music regarding positive valence, negative valence, and arousal.

3   Pilot Exploration and Results

3.1   Experimental Procedure and Measuring Tool

The pilot exploration was conducted with thirty secondary school students. The students were asked to experience and perceive the features and functions of the proposing game (60 min). Afterward, the students respond to the questionnaire to reflect on their perceptions of corresponding technology acceptance. The questionnaire consists of 12 items with a 5-point Likert scale ranging from 1 (strongly disagree) to 5 (strongly agree). Three things regarding perceived game usefulness (PGU1: This game would be helpful for me to trigger decision making; PGU2: The game would be beneficial for me to construct experience in my context; PGU3: The game would enhance effectiveness in my context.) elicited that the gaming approach would improve the student's performance in making good decisions. Three items regarding perceived ease of use (PEU1: My interaction with this game is clear and understandable; PEU2: I find it easy to get the game to do what I want; PEU3: The game is easy to use and follow.) are used to ensure that the proposing game, including features, functions, and directions, was easy to follow and achieve gaming goal. Three items regarding attitude (AT1: Game makes me more enjoyable; AT2: I like to follow scenarios provided by the game; AT3: I am satisfied with using this game as a cognitive tool.) referred to the degree to which students are comfortable or enjoyed with the gaming environment. Three items regarding gaming acceptance (GA1: I will use the game to support my decision-making in the future; GA2: I will use the situations/experiences provided by the game to practice my expertise in my context; GA3: I plan to use the game often.) could reflect the students' intention to play the proposing game in the future. The Cronbach's alpha value of the questionnaire was .84, showing acceptable reliability in the internal consistency.

3.2   Results

According to data on the student's perceptions of the features and functions of the proposing game, for the survey questions relevant to gaming usefulness, most students revealed a degree approaching or over 4 points (Agree) on the 5-Likert scale (PGU1: 100%, PGU2: 100%, PGU: 86.67%). The high degree of gaming perception can be attributed to the decision tree method's ability to present a series of learning scenarios that encourage students to make choices and receive appropriate feedback based on their decisions and actions. The game system incorporated valence and arousal emotional representations, which rewarded players for making good decisions and provided warnings to those who made poor decisions. Through facial emotion interaction, students were guided to adjust their decision-making based on their current behaviors, leading them toward more suitable learning paths. Ultimately, the decision tree contextual game facilitated students' understanding of cause-and-effect relationships, allowed them to learn from their mistakes, and enabled them to make improved decisions, aligning with the findings of Tapingkae et al. [16].

Regarding the perceived ease of use, most students responded highly positively to the contextual game and found the interaction straightforward and comprehensible (PEU1: 86.67%, PEU2: 100%, PEU3: 86.66%). These findings suggest that the game was designed and implemented with a graphical user interface that facilitated convenient navigation. Moreover, the game utilized valence and arousal emotional feedback presented through facial emotion visualization, making it easily comprehensible for students. Additionally, the game gave students hints through noticeable visual effects and sounds, effectively guiding them when they encountered uncertainties. This finding is consistent with the study by Moizer et al. [17], which highlighted the influence of game interfaces and interactive features on the functionality of the game environment.

When considering students' attitudes toward the contextual decision tree-based game (AT), most students highly expressed that the designed gaming environment enhanced their enjoyment of learning (AT1: 93.33%, AT2: 86.67%, AT3: 100%). These findings align with previous research conducted by Chan, Wan, and King [18], Cohen [19], and Yu, Gao, and Wang [20], which highlight the positive impact of game elements such as challenges, goals, interactivity, multimedia and appealing design, and immediate feedback on learners' motivation, engagement, and flow experience. These factors collectively contribute to making the game a highly enjoyable learning experience.Regarding gaming acceptance, the majority displayed a satisfying interest in using the game in the future (GA1: 73.33%, GA2: 86.67%, GA3: 60.00%). These findings align with the research conducted by Lin et al. [21], which highlights the influential factors in the acceptance of AI-enabled e-learning systems, including perceived satisfaction, interactive effects, and ease of use.

4 Conclusions

This study aimed to explore the students' perceptions of integrating facial emotions into a decision tree-based contextual game. A pilot exploration indicated that most students positively perceived the decision tree-based contextual game with face-emotion interaction. They recognized the game's usefulness in enhancing decision-making abilities and constructing contextual experiences and found the game easy to use and control, appreciating its graphical user interface and the emotional feedback provided through facial expressions. They also expressed high levels of enjoyment, satisfaction, and intent to use the game in the future, highlighting the positive impact of game elements on motivation, engagement, and learning outcomes. The findings support the effectiveness of this approach in enhancing students' decision-making skills and creating engaging learning experiences.

Accordingly, future research presents opportunities to probe into the long-term effects of this game design on learning outcomes, shedding light on its sustained impact. Additionally, exploring further avenues to incorporate facial emotion interaction can foster heightened engagement and forge deeper emotional connections with the game. Simultaneously, enhancing the introduction of pertinent obstacles will cultivate an authentic and captivating gameplay environment, closely mirroring real-life scenarios and facilitating profound immersion. These collective endeavors will contribute to a more comprehensive understanding of the game's effectiveness and provide insights for refining future educational game designs.

Acknowledgements. This work was supported by the Network Strengthening Fund of the Program Management Unit for human resources and institutional development, research, and innovation (PMU-B), Office of National Higher Education Science Research and Innovation Policy Council of Thailand [Grant number B16F640121].

References

1. Komalawardhana, N., Panjaburee, P.: Proposal of personalised mobile game from inquiry-based learning activities perspective: relationships among genders, learning styles, perceptions, and learning interest. Int. J. Mob. Learn. Organ. **12**(1), 55–76 (2018)
2. Fu, Q.K., Lin, C.J., Hwang, G.J., Zhang, L.: Impacts of a mind mapping-based contextual gaming approach on EFL students' writing performance, learning perceptions and generative uses in an English course. Comput. Educ. **137**(April), 59–77 (2019)
3. Bunyakul, N., Wiwatwattana, N., Panjaburee, P.: Effects of a mobile game on students learning achievements and motivations in a clinical chemistry course: Learning style differences. Int. J. Mob. Learn. Organ. **16**(2), 221–244 (2022)
4. Patel, H.H., Prajapati, P.: Study and analysis of decision tree based classification algorithms. Int. J. Comput. Sci. Eng. **6**(10), 74–78 (2018)
5. Fang, M., Tapalova, O., Zhiyenbayeva, N., Kozlovskaya, S.: Impact of digital game-based learning on the social competence and behavior of preschoolers. Educ. Inf. Technol. **27**(3), 3065–3078 (2022)
6. Saleme, P., Dietrich, T., Pang, B., Parkinson, J.: Design of a digital game intervention to promote socio-emotional skills and prosocial behavior in children. Multimodal Technol. Interact. **5**(10), 58 (2021)
7. Wu, M.C., Lin, S.Y., Lin, C.H.: An effective application of decision tree to stock trading. Expert Syst. Appl. **31**(2), 270–274 (2006)
8. Podgorelec, V., Kokol, P., Stiglic, B., Rozman, I.: Decision trees: an overview and their use in medicine. J. Med. Syst. **26**(5), 445–463 (2002)
9. Karnon, J.: A simple decision analysis of a mandatory lockdown response to the COVID-19 pandemic. Appl. Health Econ. Health Policy **18**(3), 329–331 (2020)
10. Rizvi, S., Rienties, B., Khoja, S.A.: The role of demographics in online learning; a decision tree based approach. Comput. Educ. **137**, 32–47 (2019)
11. Priyam, A., Abhijeeta, G.R., Rathee, A., Srivastava, S.: Comparative analysis of decision tree classification algorithms. Int. J. Curr. Eng. Technol. **3**(2), 334–337 (2013)
12. Gomes, C., Almeida, L.S.: Advocating the broad use of the decision tree method in education. Pract. Assess. Res. Eval. **22**(1), 10 (2017)

13. Chen, Y.J., Hung, Y.C.: Using real-time acceleration data for exercise movement training with a decision tree approach. Expert Syst. Appl. **37**(12), 7552–7556 (2010)
14. Kurilovas, E.: Advanced machine learning approaches to personalise learning: learning analytics and decision making. Behav. Inf. Technol. **38**(4), 410–421 (2019)
15. Lin, C.F., Yeh, Y.C., Hung, Y.H., Chang, R.I.: Data mining for providing a personalized learning path in creativity: an application of decision trees. Comput. Educ. **68**, 199–210 (2013)
16. Tapingkae, P., Panjaburee, P., Hwang, G.J., Srisawasdi, N.: Effects of a formative assessment-based contextual gaming approach on students' digital citizenship behaviours, learning motivations, and perceptions. Comput. Educ. **159**, 103998 (2020)
17. Moizer, J., et al.: An approach to evaluating the user experience of serious games. Comput. Educ. **136**, 141–151 (2019)
18. Chan, K., Wan, K., King, V.: Performance over enjoyment? Effect of game-based learning on learning outcome and flow experience. Front. Educ. **6**, 660376 (2021)
19. Cohen, E.L.: What makes good games go viral? The role of technology use, efficacy, emotion and enjoyment in players' decision to share a prosocial digital game. Comput. Hum. Behav. **33**, 321–329 (2014)
20. Yu, Z., Gao, M., Wang, L.: The effect of educational games on learning outcomes, student motivation, engagement and satisfaction. J. Educ. Comput. Res. **59**(3), 522–546 (2021)
21. Lin, H.C., Ho, C.F., Yang, H.: Understanding adoption of artificial intelligence-enabled language e-learning system: an empirical study of UTAUT model. Int. J. Mob. Learn. Organ. **16**(1), 74–94 (2022)

Complex Access Scenarios (CAS) Service Request

Rahmira Rufus[✉]

University of North Carolina, 601 S College Road, Wilmington, NC 28403, USA
rufusr@uncw.edu

Abstract. A complex access scenario (CAS) is an access event-modeling scheme that focuses on contextual and situational awareness addressing the service concerns arising for complex systems. The CAS is structured in the form of a service request establishing the following criteria: (1) satisfies classification for complexity, such as properties, characteristics, conditions, etc.; (2) concatenates the access criteria to the complexity class; otherwise, downgrades the class to complicated; and (3) confirms that the request is system generated. The significance of this work involves maturing the request analysis process within CAS to identify an effective knowledge representation scope for how to develop schemas that are applicable to the associations described in given operating environments. The scope of this work is associating CAS to human-computer interaction (HCI), where the human-in-the-loop element of this use case begins to play a factor in the complexity of the system service request. Our method surveys HCI usability factors to identify CAS service requests applicable to usage scenarios in the HCI space that address system complexity. The goal is that with increased CAS comprehension and application, networking components and their specific utilization are used effectively and securely in complex computing operating environments, which still suffer from ambiguous workload requirements. The purpose of this work and future iterations that follow are to place more emphasis on the CAS topic by demonstrating how CAS addresses access scenarios specific to complex computing environments like HCI.

Keywords: complex computing systems · autonomic computing · artificial intelligence (AI) · human-computer interaction (HCI) · autonomous agent · human-computer integration · human-centered AI (HCAI) · context awareness · situational awareness · complex access scenarios (CAS) · service request · cybersecurity · trust

1 Introduction

IBM's 2001 manifesto prescribed that to reduce the workload on the system administrator, complex computing systems should employ autonomic properties that independently take care of regular maintenance and optimization tasks [1, 2]. However, autonomic computing is still struggling to address the workload requirements for use cases tailored to address the priorities of system complexity scenarios. Some current issues are because

C. Stephanidis et al. (Eds.): HCII 2023, CCIS 1957, pp. 78–87, 2024.
https://doi.org/10.1007/978-3-031-49212-9_11

the autonomic properties promote a self-computing model, which is functioning independently of human-entity involvement. As a result, the execution will often become complicated for the human-entity end-user to detect the errors that arise. Additionally, the self-reliant autonomous agents are not influenced by human understanding, interpretation or context. Consequently, the agent's experience and learning are dependent upon previous agent information or context, which is often biased or skewed in some capacity.

1.1 HCI Concern

In 2003 the investigation conducted by [4] questioned the accountability of autonomic computing systems, where the focus was on the problem with human-computer interaction (HCI). According to [4], HCI presented a perception dilemma and the notion of accountability being a "situated matter". HCI has evolved since the 2003 investigation, however fundamentally HCI is still "premised on the principle that users act and systems react" [4]. Basically, in this interaction amongst the user and system, the user associates his/her actions executed via the user interface (UI) as input being a direct influence of system state change as output [4]. Utilizing UI input and output mechanisms solely in this fashion can mistakenly interpret or accept the system's behavior as accurate, accountable or even as criteria to establish a basis for trust [4].

Traditionally HCI focused on interaction amongst the human-entity and systems that lacked the artificial intelligence (AI) capabilities of the autonomous emergence, such as autonomic computing concepts and were considered non-AI systems. However, HCI is transitioning from the non-AI computing systems that were dependent upon human interaction represented as the "stimulus-response" effect [6]. These automation services were primarily human-entity assistants [7]. The emergence of the "autonomous/AI agent" is shifting the engagement amongst the human-entity user & the system-entity, where the system-entity or autonomous/AI agent (agent) can evolve from being an assistant service or tool to an intelligent agent collaborator with the human-entity user (end-user) [5]. The paradigm shifts in this space further compound the workload issues arising for complex computing systems and their usability factors as interaction morphs into integration of the user and the agent engagement.

1.2 Access Concern

HCI objectives focus on developing well-designed systems user-driven for usability, safety, efficiency, etc. The goal is to incorporate methodologies, techniques, tools and capabilities that grant users access to systems based on user priorities. However, what does access look like in the new age of computing as we transition into the Next-Gen era? Have we adequately assessed the scenarios that address the needs of networking and communications conduits that correlate to the current execution of data services utilized on web and other networking technologies?

One such scenario class created and analyzed by [3] introduces the notion of complex access scenarios (CAS) as a service request addressing the service concerns arising for complex systems. Specifically, CAS is an access event-modeling scheme that focuses on the contextual and situational awareness priorities for next-generation cybersecurity computing requirements within the technology emergence and convergence scope. The CAS described in [3] conducts a service request analysis case of knowledge misrepresentation where a misunderstanding of interoperability in communication was compared against interoperability of semantics. Initially the service request in Fig. 1 was communicated as a simple access request demonstrating a subject S requesting access to an object O resource as illustrated in A, while B is semantically different [3]. The visualization in A is the accepted generalization used by industry professionals.

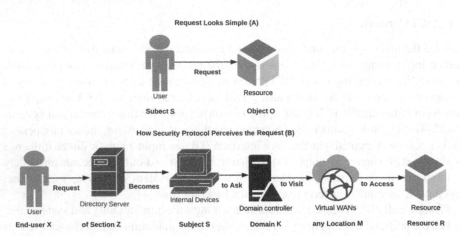

Fig. 1. CAS Service Request: Perspective (A) Simple Request & (B) Network Security Protocol [3]

This access scheme assessment impacted how resource access was perceived by a security protocol versus the traditional visualizations that were being utilized by access matrix schemes and control lists designed for centralized architectures [3]. CAS was created in response to context and situational awareness concerns [3] discovered while analyzing emerging IoT issues focusing on IoT knowledge representation, understanding their networking components requirements and usability factors. The purpose of this work and future iterations that follow are to place more emphasis on the CAS topic by demonstrating how CAS addresses access scenarios specific to complex computing environments.

The service request analysis conducted during the CAS process aids in providing required understanding a network administrative component needs to better assess acquisition of the operating environment resources. The goal is that with increased CAS comprehension and application, network components and their specific utilization are utilized appropriately. Additionally, surveying knowledge representation aspects, interconnected data and web complexity are covered. These 3 areas play a role in the difficulties associated with properly comprehending network service requests. There are numerous resource access requests for transmissions being broadcasted via future web generations and interconnected networks that can be applied to CAS scenarios, but we limit the scope of this phase of the work to the 3 mentioned.

2 Problem

As CAS was addressed in [3], the scope was streamlined to focus primarily on how the service requests continue to affect the local area network (LAN) -to wide area network (WAN) communications for decentralized distributed operating environments, specifically via the application domain [3] designed. The progression towards understanding context and situational awareness is where [3] was able to design a construct to build the awareness leveraging data analysis to service network security via an enterprise security model for the prescribed application domain. The extent of the CAS analyses also established the correlation amongst industrial control systems (ICS) networks and their prescribed application domains. The mapping in [3] demonstrates how to gather situational awareness that can be leveraged in a manner synonymous to those proven successful within the ICS domain. The context derived from the cybersecurity application domain developed by [3] also established CAS being successfully transitioned to a IoT/device technology application domain as well.

2.1 Perception Dilemma

The problem we encounter here is as contextual and situational awareness is capable of being matured, the concern addressed in the introduction is the need to address the HCI issues that are being evaluated as CAS. In the perception concern, autonomic computing and other aspects of autonomous computing are not complementary to the HCI scope. Table 2 in Appendix A provides a summary from [5] that details some issues within HCI for AI and/or non-AI systems.

Fig. 2. Human-centered AI (HCAI) Framework with Specific Design Goals [5]

Additionally, in Table 2 displayed in the last column on the right are the primary design goals of human-centered AI (HCAI). With HCAI, emerging challenges are explored with a range of approaches to address these specific issues introduced by AI technology for HCI [5]. Each HCAI design goal from Table 2 is aligned with the challenges in the middle columns and then the design goals are mapped to the HCAI framework as illustrated in Fig. 2 [5].

2.2 Interaction to Integration

As the traditional purpose for HCI makes way for a more symbiotic coupling, the way to quantify the end-user characteristics are changing [6]. Table 1 displays how a human scenario is interpreted as an example of computer interaction to what is now being modified into computer integration. The integration of AI agent technology and capabilities in the HCI space transformed system-entity engagement with the human-entity from service assistant to partner, collaborator, peer, etc. Autonomy is replacing task management in the traditional sense and in turn service requests for system resources amongst both parties more sophisticated [6].

Table 1. Human Interaction to Integration Scenarios [6]

Scenario	Interaction Example	Integration Example
Waking up	Turning the alarm off	Alarm poses a consequential choice
Driving to work	Car signals return of control	Car is semi-autonomous
Starting the workday	Reading email	Email app prioritizes messages
Prior to meeting	Reading notification	App tracks meetings, sends alert
Meeting start	Arriving connected, agenda up	Room software tracks calendar
In meeting	Watching speaker	Teleconference app magnifies speaker
Reading news	Noticing advertisements	Service selects ads based on history
Watching cartoons	Setting educational goal	Tablet negotiates with the child
Surfing social media	Scrolling news feed, seeing ads	App suggests video, selects ads

3 Method

In this work we focus on the CAS directly as being a service request to address in the HCI space. The scope here is to concentrate on the event-modeling schema that establishes the following: (1) satisfies classification for complexity, such as properties, characteristics, conditions, etc.; (2) concatenate the access criteria to the complex class; otherwise, down grade the class to complicated; (3) confirm that the request is system generated. Initially, HCI situational awareness and the system complexity of accessing resources are discussed. Following we survey access request scenarios resulting in operating environment compromise to improve and build upon the CAS service request process. Exploits of interests that were successful from the work conducted in [3] were slave device exploits, such as Mirai Botnet exposure case, host platform masquerading exploits compromise, the near-field communication (NFC) low frequency band and lateral movement exploit, etc. In this work we focus on usability factors specific to HCI and look to determine any indications of CAS criteria for HCI use cases. The next iteration of this work will focus on the interconnected data and web complexity concerns that could be identified here but not quantified. In this step we were looking for simplistic associations that can be easily misrepresented and demonstrated in a working CAS example. We demonstrate these misrepresentations as elements for building establishing CAS. Lastly, we explore knowledge reasoning techniques utilized in the respective field or being developed in R&D efforts, when executed properly can derive some explicit knowledge that is translatable.

4   Results

Two specific issues were assessed to determine if CAS criteria can be established in HCI. Initially the perspective dilemma satisfies a complexity classification by default because the difficulty to acquire situational and context awareness in HCI is high. Additionally, a system generated service request for resources and service use can be affected by the complexity of the contextual issues. Therefore, access criteria can be concatenated to the complexity and since HCI is a system assistant service for the human-in-the-loop usability function, the request would be system generated. However, the HCAI framework does propose a mechanism to reduce the complexity by correlating current HCI misrepresentations with the design goals for future improvements. Unfortunately, there is limited data to determine the effectiveness of the HCAI structure because this work is new and does not have any confirmed performance metrics to support its claims [5].

The next issue assessed involves the transition of the human-interaction focus of HCI to the human-centered modifications emerging. In Table 1, the human scenario is mapped with the interaction example and its integration successor. The leap that the interaction capability is undertaking to execute the integration presents many challenges within the HCI optimization or maturity model. Exploits leveraging vulnerabilities and weakness will increase due to promoting an assistant service to a peer-to-peer collaborator capacity without effectively testing and evaluating the impact of such a grand leap of artificial cognitive processing escalation.

Appendix A: HCI with AI Systems Issues

Table 2. Human Interaction Main Issues with AI Systems Summary [5]

Main issues	Familiar HCI concerns with non-AI systems [8]	New HCI challenges with AI systems	Main HCAI design goals
Machine behavior	• Machines behave as expected by design • HCI design focuses on usability of system output/UI, user mental model, user training, operation procedure, etc	• AI systems can be developed to exhibit unique machine behaviors with potentially biased and unexpected outcomes. The machine behavior may evolve as the machine learns [9]	• Human controlled AI
Human-machine collaboration	• Human interaction with non-AI computing system • Machine primarily works as an assistive tool • No collaboration between humans and machines	• The intelligent agents of AI systems may be developed to work as teammates with humans to form human-AI collaborative relationships but there is debate on the topic [10, 11]	• Human-driven decision-making • Human controlled AI
Machine intelligence	• By definition, non-AI systems do not have machine intelligence	• With AI technology, machines can be built to have certain levels of human-like intelligence [12] • Machines cannot completely emulate advanced human cognitive capabilities, developing machine intelligence in isolation encounters challenges [13] • How to integrate human's role into AI systems to ensure human-controlled AI [14]	• Augmenting human • Human controlled AI

(*continued*)

Table 2. (*continued*)

Main issues	Familiar HCI concerns with non-AI systems [8]	New HCI challenges with AI systems	Main HCAI design goals
Explain-ability of machine output	• Machine output is typically explainable if the user interface is usable through HCI design	• AI systems may exhibit a "black box" effect that causes the output obscure to users, users may not know how and why AI systems make decisions, when to trust AI [15]	• Explainable AI
Autonomous characteristics of machines	• Non-AI systems (e.g., automated systems) do not have autonomous characteristics • HCI design focuses on system UI, automation awareness, human-in-loop design, human intervention in emergency	• AI systems may be developed to have unique autonomous characteristics (e.g., learning, self-adaption, self-execution) [16] • AI systems may handle some operating situations not fully anticipated [10] • The output of autonomous systems may not be deterministic [16, 17] • Intelligent user interface (e.g., voice input, facial / intention recognition)	• Human controlled AI

(*continued*)

Table 2. (*continued*)

Main issues	Familiar HCI concerns with non-AI systems [8]	New HCI challenges with AI systems	Main HCAI design goals
User Interface	• Usability design of conventional user interface (graphical user interface, visible interface, etc.)	• UI may be invisible & implicit [18] • How to design intelligent UI usable and natural • AI technology adapts to human capabilities vs. humans adapt to AI [19] • The need of HCI design standards specifically developed for AI systems [20]	• Usable AI
Ethical Design	• Primary user needs include usability, functionality, security	• Ethical issues become more significant, including issues, such as privacy, ethics, fairness, skill growth, decision-making authority [21]	• Ethical & responsible

References

1. Huebscher, M.C., McCann, J.A.: A survey of autonomic computing—degrees, models, and applications. ACM Comput. Surv. (CSUR) **40**(3), 1–28 (2008). https://doi.org/10.1145/138 0584.1380585
2. Rahman, M., Ranjan, R., Buyya, R., Benatallah, B.: A Taxonomy and survey on autonomic management of applications in grid computing environments. Concurr. Comput.: Pract. Exp. **23**(16), 1990–2019 (2011). https://doi.org/10.1002/cpe.1734
3. Rufus, R.S.: Intrusion Detection via Neuroception for an Autonomic Internet of Things. PhD diss., North Carolina Agricultural and Technical State University (2021)
4. Anderson, S., et al.: Making autonomic computing systems accountable: the problem of human-computer interaction 2003, pp. 718–724 (2003).https://doi.org/10.1109/DEXA.2003. 1232106
5. Xu, W., Dainoff, M., Ge, L., Gao, Z.: Transitioning to human interaction with AI systems: new challenges and opportunities for HCI professionals to enable human-centered AI. Int. J. Hum.-Comput. Interact. **39**, 494–518 (2023). https://doi.org/10.1080/10447318.2022.204 1900
6. Farooq, U., Grudin, J.: Human-computer integration. Interactions **23**(6), 26–32 (2016). https://doi.org/10.1145/3001896
7. Wickens, C.D., Hollands, J.G., Banbury, S., Parasuraman, R.: Engineering Psychology and Human Performance. Psychology Press (2015)

8. Jacko, J.A.: Human computer interaction handbook: Fundamentals, evolving technologies, and emerging applications. CRC Press (2012)

9. Rahwan, I., et al.: Machine behaviour. Nature **568**(7753), 477–486 (2019)

10. O'Neill, T., McNeese, N., Barron, A., Schelble, B.: Human-autonomy teaming: a review and analysis of the empirical literature. Hum. Factors (2020). https://doi.org/10.1177/001872082 0960865

11. Brill, J.C., Cummings, M.L., Evans, A.W.I.I.I., Hancock, P.A., Lyons, J.B., Oden, K.: Navigating the advent of human-machine teaming. Proc. Hum. Factors Ergon. Soc. Ann. Meet. **62**(1), 455–459 (2018). https://doi.org/10.1177/1541931218621104

12. Watson, D.P., Scheidt, D.H.: Autonomous systems. J. Hopkins APL Tech. Dig. **26**(4), 368–376 (2005)

13. Zheng, N., et al.: Hybrid-augmented intelligence: collaboration and cognition. Front. Inf. Technol. Electron. Eng. **18**(2), 153–179 (2017). https://doi.org/10.1631/FITEE.1700053

14. Zanzotto, F.M.: Human-in-the-loop artificial intelligence. J. Artif. Intell. Res. **64**, 243–252 (2019). https://doi.org/10.1613/jair.1.11345

15. Mueller, S.T., Hoffman, R.R., Clancey, W., Emrey, A., Klein, G.: Explanation in human-AI systems: a literature meta-review, synopsis of key ideas and publications, and bibliography for explain- able AI (2019). arXiv 1902.01876

16. Kaber, D.B.: A conceptual framework of autonomous and auto- mated agents. Theor. Issues Ergon. Sci. **19**(4), 406–430 (2018). https://doi.org/10.1080/1463922X.2017.1363314

17. Xu, W.: From automation to autonomy and autonomous vehicles: challenges and opportunities for human-computer interaction. Interactions **28**(1), 48–53 (2021). https://doi.org/10.1145/3434580

18. Streitz, N.: From human–computer interaction to human–environment inter-action: ambient intelligence and the disappearing computer. In: Proceedings of the 9th ERCIM Workshop on User Interfaces for All, pp. 3–13. Springer, Cham (2007).https://doi.org/10.1007/978-3-540-71025-7_1

19. Cooke, N.: 5 ways to help robots work together with people. The Conversation (2018). https://theconversation.com/5-ways-to-help-robots-work-together-with-people-101419

20. Google PAIR. People þ AI Guidebook: Designing human-centered AI products (2019). https://pair.withgoogle.com

21. Ethically aligned design: a vision for prioritizing human well-being with autonomous and intelligent systems, 1st edn. The Institute of Electrical and Electronics Engineers (IEEE), Incorporated IEEE (2019)

Digital Emotion Regulation on Academic Twitter

Claudine Tinsman$^{(\boxtimes)}$ and Laura Csuka

Oxford University, Oxford OX1 3QD, UK
claudine.tinsman@cs.ox.ac.uk
https://www.cs.ox.ac.uk/research/HCC/

Abstract. Academic Twitter is increasingly seen as an essential part of career development for early career researchers (ECRs) [6]. However, engagement with the community may be associated with unwanted emotional responses to upward social comparisons. We contribute to the emerging field of digital emotion regulation (ER) by conducting fifteen semi-structured interviews with women ECRs about their use of *content curation features* to support the regulation of emotional responses to upward social comparisons when engaging with Academic Twitter. We found that (1) participants view engagement with Academic Twitter as crucial to their career progression, (2) few participants use Twitter's content curation features to support ER out of fear of missing out on critical information and (3) most participants want content curation features to afford them more control over their exposure to celebratory content on Academic Twitter.

Keywords: Academic Twitter · digital emotion regulation · social comparison theory

1 Introduction

Academic Twitter is a community where academics to exchange stories of both achievements and setbacks. It is a space where academic journeys unfold, professional identities take shape, and scholarly communities are forged [9]. Engaging with Academic Twitter can yield significant rewards such as increased research impact, beneficial collaborations, and increased readership [6]. However, it may also negatively impact individual well-being: Reading celebratory tweets about professional successes may lead users to engage in upward social comparisons with other researchers on the platform, leading to unwanted feelings such as depression and anxiety [7]. Some Academic Twitter users, such as women early career researchers (ECRs), may be more likely to engage in strong upward comparisons with others and experience negative and unwanted emotions and lower subjective well-being as a result [1,3].

Supported by King's College London.

C. Stephanidis et al. (Eds.): HCII 2023, CCIS 1957, pp. 88–95, 2024.
https://doi.org/10.1007/978-3-031-49212-9_12

Using Academic Twitter as a case study, we explore if and how users employ *content curation features*, which are platform features that users can engage with to influence, limit or promote the social media content to which they are exposed, in order to preserve their subjective well-being. To that end, we conducted fifteen exploratory semi-structured interviews with women ECRs working in the United Kingdom to explore the following research questions:

- **RQ1**: What emotion regulation (ER) strategies do women ECRs employ when engaging in upward social comparisons on Academic Twitter?
- **RQ2**: How do those users engage with content curation features to support ER processes when experiencing unwanted emotional responses to upward social comparisons on Academic Twitter?

2 Background

Social comparison theory posits that individuals have a fundamental drive to evaluate their opinions and abilities and do so by comparing themselves to others, which can lead to biased self-perceptions [4]. Individuals may compare themselves to others who they perceive as better off (upward), worse off (downward), or similar (lateral), depending on their motives [4].

Women ECRs who use Academic Twitter may be more likely to engage in higher levels of upward comparison than other academics: Research in the field of social comparison theory has linked uncertainty in professional contexts to higher levels of upward comparison [3] and decreased subjective well-being. In the United Kingdom, ECRs usually work on fixed-term contracts that provide little stability or certainty about future academic employment, with women being more likely to stay in such roles for longer periods than men [1]. In the context of social media use, upward comparison with other users based on content celebrating successes and happy events, such as work achievements and holidays, has been associated with feelings of anxiety, depression, and inadequacy [7]. When faced with such feelings, individuals engage in emotion regulation to change how they feel [5].

According to Gross's process model of emotion regulation, there are five categories of ER strategies: Situation selection, situation modification, attentional deployment, cognitive change, and response modulation. *Situation selection* refers to seeking out or avoiding certain stimuli to decrease the likelihood of experiencing unwanted emotions before they can form [5,8]. *Situation modification* involves modifying a situation to alter its emotional impact, for instance, by blocking a 'toxic' contact on Twitter so one doesn't have to see their content [8]. *Attentional deployment* involves redirecting one's attention to a different aspect of a situation to alter an emotion (e.g. focusing on a different part of the screen when seeing a gruesome photo on Instagram) [5]. *Cognitive change* involves altering the meaning of a situation, often by reappraising its personal relevance, to alter its emotional impact [5,8]. Finally, *response modulation* involves adjusting the response to a well-developed emotion, usually by suppressing its expression or venting [8]. Existing work has found suppression and avoidance to be maladaptive and associated with depression and anxiety, whereas reappraisal and problem-solving are adaptive and associated with positive mental health outcomes [8].

Academic Twitter provides an interesting context in which to explore the role of content curation features in regulating unwanted emotions resulting from upward social comparison. First, Twitter is treated by academics as the prime venue for engaging in self-promotion and dissemination of news about professional achievements [9], a setting that provides a clear dimension of upward comparison (professional success) for a well-defined set of users (women ECRs). Second, Twitter provides users with limited content curation features (see 1) that align well with situation modification and selection strategies by enabling users to block contacts, mute words or phrases, turn off notifications for certain users, create lists and topics to follow, and unfollow accounts. Third, the use of platform content curation features for ER support is a topic that has barely been explored in digital emotion regulation research [12].

3   Methods

3.1   Recruitment

We recruited women ECRs who use Academic Twitter directly on the platform. The interviews were conducted either on Zoom or in departmental offices and participants were compensated with a £10 Amazon voucher for their time.

3.2   Interview Protocol

One week before the interview, participants received an email requesting they look through their Twitter feeds for content that elicits negative responses and take screenshots of them for reference. The semi-structured interviews were conducted in three parts:

Part one pertained to general expectations for Academic Twitter as a community and feelings of upward comparison. Participants were asked about the content they expected to see when engaging with Academic Twitter, the types of content that elicited unwanted emotional responses, and the general factors that influenced how strongly they tended to respond to such tweets.

Part two investigated unwanted emotional responses to upward comparison. Participants were asked to discuss the posts they had taken screenshots of before the interview and what they thought had triggered negative responses. They were also asked what strategies they employed when experiencing such reactions.

Part three concerned user engagement with Twitter's content curation features for ER of upward comparisons. Users were shown a table (Table 1) describing the available content curation features. They were given time to review the controls and asked if they used any of them to manage unwanted feelings when confronted with stories of success from others in their field.

In *Part Four*, participants were asked about the strategies they would like to (but did not currently) use and hypothetical changes to the platform that they felt would better support ER.

Table 1. Twitter Content Curation Features [11]

Mute	Sort	Block	Unfollow
Mute notifications from specific accounts or the app in general	*Lists* You can organise accounts into lists and choose to see tweets from those lists on your account	*Block Account* Blocked accounts cannot follow you, and you won't receive notifications from them. The account holder won't know they've been blocked unless they visit your profile	*Unfollow Account* You no longer wish to see an account's Tweets in their home timeline. You can still view them by visiting their profile
Mute tweets containing specific emojis, hashtags, words, or phrase on your timeline for 24h, 7 d,30 d, or until you unmute.	*Topics* The Topics you follow are used to personalise the Tweets, events, and ads that you see and show up publicly on your profile		

3.3 Analysis

The first author conducted, recorded, and manually transcribed all interviews. Each author separately performed reflexive thematic analysis of the data, documenting all code emerging from the data and aggregating them into sub-themes and themes [2]. Both authors then compared findings and resolved discrepancies through discussion [2].

4 Themes

Between November 2022 and January 2023, interviews were conducted with fifteen ECRs who identified as women across twelve research fields and eleven UK universities. Interviews lasted on average 31.5 min. Seven major themes emerged from the interview data: 1) Academic Twitter in Context, 2) Targets of Comparison, 3) Content Highlighting Inequalities, 4) User Engagement with Emotion Regulation Strategies, 5) Lack of Engagement with Content Curation Features to support Emotion Regulation, 6) The Desire to Engage with More Strategies, and 7) The Desire for Platform Changes.

4.1 Academic Twitter in Context

Most participants only used Twitter for professional or research purposes and felt that engagement with the platform was critical to their professional advancement.

4.2 Targets of Comparison

Nearly all participants (n=13) felt stronger negative reactions to content from people with whom they had a personal connection and were at a similar, or less advanced, stage of their career.

4.3   Content Highlighting Inequalities

A significant theme emerging from the data was that success tweets highlighting unequal treatment in academia exacerbated unwanted emotional responses to upward comparisons for over one-third (n=6) of the participants:

> I struggle with how unequal academia is, especially to people from the Global South, who don't have the same privileges as Americans and North Americans and Europeans primarily. –Participant 8

4.4   User Engagement with Emotion Regulation Strategies

This theme reflects the ER strategies that participants engaged in order to regulate unwanted emotional responses to Tweets about professional successes. The five sub-themes correspond to the five categories of ER per Gross's process model of emotion regulation.

Situation Selection. The most common strategy used was avoidance (n=10): Participants cited that, to manage their emotional responses to content, they engaged primarily in being highly selective about the people followed, removing Twitter from their devices, creating physical distance with their devices in order to avoid using Twitter, or imposing time limits on the Twitter app.

Cognitive Change. Reappraisal was a common ER strategy: Nearly two-thirds (n=9) of participants engaged in reappraisal as a means to the meaning or personal relevance of a post by either engaging in self-talk about a particular concern or seeking external opinions on their feelings from people of trust, such as academic supervisors or partners.

Situation Modification. Approximately half (n = 7) of the participants engaged in strategies that modified their digital environment to reduce unwanted emotional responses to comparisons. Five of those participants actively used controls, such as blocking, muting, or unfollowing accounts for ER purposes.

Attentional Deployment. Three participants engaged in attentional deployment by switching to different types of content when they experienced unwanted emotions in order to modify their emotional responses.

Response Modulation. Three participants vented to partners or friends in order to express their frustration pertaining to posts about success in an effort to make release negative emotions.

4.5   Lack of Engagement with Content Curation Features to Support Emotion Regulation

Only one-third (n=5) of participants utilised Twitter's content curation features to support situation modification by muting keywords or phrases and blocking or unfollowing accounts.

Two-thirds (n = 10) of participants did not use any of Twitter's content curation features to manage their exposure to content that would trigger social comparisons and elicit unwanted responses. The reason most often cited by participants (n=5 respectively) was either a lack of familiarity with the features or the belief that, while using them could help reduce experiences of unwanted emotions, it might also cause them to miss out on critical information:

> If it's someone that I follow because they published papers that are interesting and relevant to my research, I don't really want to mute them. I don't really think it would be like, in my best interest to do so. –Participant 10

4.6 The Desire to Engage with More Strategies

Most (n=11) participants expressed a desire to engage with more strategies to help them regulate unwanted emotional responses to posts about professional success. Nearly half of the participants cited a desire to spend less time using academic Twitter (n=7). The others wanted to reappraise content (n=2), start using the lists feature to curate their content (n=2), or block more accounts (n=1). The remainder did not want to engage in any strategies (n=4) at all.

4.7 The Desire for Platform Changes

Most participants (n=13) expressed a desire for a range of changes to the Twitter platform to support the regulation of unwanted emotional responses to upward comparisons on Twitter. The most commonly desired platform change was the ability to curate their Twitter feed in a manner that allows easy and time-bounded content blocking and filtering (n=11):

> ...I could go into Twitter and be like, 'I just want to look at like sports things right now.' Then on days when I just know I don't have the capacity to deal with people being like, 'I'm so amazing, and my research is incredible.' I wouldn't have to look at it. –Participant 12

5 Discussion

5.1 Experiences of Social Comparison on Academic Twitter

Nearly all participants experienced unwanted feelings associated with social comparisons when engaging with Academic Twitter, suggesting that the issue may be common among women ECRs. These results indicate that further investigation into the use of ER strategies for upward social comparisons on Academic Twitter among women academics is warranted.

About one-third of participants reported stronger unwanted emotional responses to upward comparisons when content highlighted systemic inequities. The prevalence of this theme suggests that academic communities may have a role to play in supporting effective emotional regulation by engaging in interventions that address inequality in academia and research.

5.2 Engagement with Emotion Regulation Strategies and Use of Content Curation Features

Participants' unawareness of Twitter's content curation features, combined with the perception that engagement with Twitter is compulsory, indicate ECRs may benefit from receiving formal instruction on how to use Academic Twitter in a manner that allows them to advance their careers while protecting their well-being. Furthermore, participants perceived that the curation features were not useful for emotion regulation purposes.

The popularity of technologically unassisted ER strategies (both adaptive and maladaptive), such as cognitive reappraisal and avoidance, and the content curation features' perceived lack of suitability for emotion regulation suggests that users' ER needs are not being adequately met by Twitter's content curation features. Developing and designing features that support better cognitive reappraisal may be a viable direction for future research in social comparison ER on Academic Twitter. However, results for such interventions in the context of social media use have admittedly yielded mixed results in prior research [10,13].

5.3 Desired Changes to the Platform

Most participants wished for more flexibility in controlling what appears in their feed and when. Some changes are already feasible using the lists function [11]: Users can choose what lists appear on, or are hidden from, their timeline but must do so manually. A time-bounded functionality, like the one that exists for blocking and muting keywords/phrases, could provide a relatively rapid workaround for the problem. Features that enable topic labelling for particular tweets may allow users to filter by topic and may also provide a short-term solution for individuals who need to alter the content they are exposed to for short periods of time.

6 Limitations and Future Work

Our sample of participants was limited to fifteen women ECRs based in the UK and may not be representative of women researchers who use Academic Twitter. We are currently interviewing women researchers from a wider range of career stages and plan to involve them in designing content curation features that better serve their ER needs.

7 Conclusion

Participants engaged in a wide range of ER strategies both supported and unsupported by Twitter's content curation features. Our thematic analysis demonstrated that all five categories of ER were represented, though situation selection, cognitive change, and situation modification were the predominant categories. Furthermore, we found that there was low engagement with Twitter's content curation features for ER due to either unawareness of their existence or a belief that such tools would lead to negative professional outcomes. These findings suggest that future research into modifying Twitter's content curation features to better meet users' ER needs is warranted.

References

1. Precarious work in higher education: insecure contracts and how they have changed over time, Tech. rep., University College Union, London (2021). https://www.ucu.org.uk/heprecarity
2. Braun, V., Clarke, V.: Using thematic analysis in psychology. Qual. Res. Psychol. **3**(2), 77–101 (2006). https://doi.org/10.1191/1478088706qp063oa
3. Buunk, B., Ybema, J.: Social comparisons and occupational stress: the identification-contrast model. In: Buunk, B., Gibbons, F. (eds.) Health, Coping, and Well-being: Perspectives from Social Comparison Theory, pp. 359–388. Lawrence Erlbaum Associates, Mahwah, N.J. (1997), oCLC: 846494979
4. Dijkstra, P., Gibbons, F.X., Buunk, A.P.: Social comparison theory. In: Social Psychological Foundations of Clinical Psychology, pp. 195–211. The Guilford Press, New York, NY, US (2010)
5. Gross, J.J.: Emotion regulation: current status and future prospects. Psychol. Inq. **26**(1), 1–26 (2015). https://doi.org/10.1080/1047840X.2014.940781
6. Klar, S., Krupnikov, Y., Ryan, J.B., Searles, K., Shmargad, Y.: Using social media to promote academic research: identifying the benefits of twitter for sharing academic work. PLoS ONE **15**(4), e0229446 (2020). https://doi.org/10.1371/journal.pone.0229446
7. Krasnova, H., Widjaja, T., Buxmann, P., Wenninger, H., Benbasat, I.: Why following friends can hurt you: an exploratory investigation of the effects of envy on social networking sites among college-age users. Inf. Syst. Res. **26**(3), 585–605 (2015). https://doi.org/10.1287/isre.2015.0588
8. Slovak, P., Antle, A.N., Theofanopoulou, N., Roquet, C.D., Gross, J.J., Isbister, K.: Designing for emotion regulation interventions: an agenda for HCI theory and research. ACM Trans. Comput.-Hum. Interact. (2022). https://doi.org/10.1145/3569898
9. Taylor, Y., Breeze, M.: All imposters in the university? striking (out) claims on academic Twitter. Women's Stud. Int. Forum **81**, 1–8 (2020). https://doi.org/10.1016/j.wsif.2020.102367
10. Tiggemann, M., Anderberg, I.: Social media is not real: the effect of 'Instagram vs reality' images on women's social comparison and body image. New Media Soc. **22**(12), 2183–2199 (2020). https://doi.org/10.1177/1461444819888720
11. Twitter: Using Twitter (2023). https://help.twitter.com/en/using-twitter
12. Wadley, G., Smith, W., Koval, P., Gross, J.J.: Digital emotion regulation. Curr. Dir. Psychol. Sci. **29**(4), 412–418 (2020). https://doi.org/10.1177/0963721420920592
13. Weber, S., Messingschlager, T., Stein, J.P.: This is an Insta-vention! exploring cognitive countermeasures to reduce negative consequences of social comparisons on Instagram. Media Psychol. **25**(3), 411–440 (2022). https://doi.org/10.1080/15213269.2021.1968440

Characteristics of Perceived Time Depends on UI Expression of Waiting Time

Toya Yahaba[✉] ⓘ and Namgyu Kang ⓘ

Future University Hakodate, Kameda-Shi Nakano-Cho 116-2, Hokkaido, Japan
yahabatouya@gmail.com

Abstract. In recent years, there have been some displays of the order number or how long users must wait on the screen to help with waiting time in restaurants and public places.

In this study, we focus on users' waiting time on a website. We compare how the perceived time changes depending on the UI of the progress bars. Moreover, we also visualize the compared results, including participants' impressions.

Namely, this research aims to clarify what kind of UI and participants' impressions influence their perceived time.

In the experiment, 33 Participants saw the six videos with different progress bar expressions and evaluated their impressions of each expression.

We experimented with six videos divided into two groups.

Group 1 was the group that changed the speed at which they were shown, and Group 2 is the group that changed the way of display.

After evaluating the six expressions, they made a rank with six expressions and answered the reason for the rank order.

Moreover, we conducted the Factor analysis using the SD method results, and we extracted the three factors; 'Novelty,' 'Openness,' and 'Dullness.' Primarily, 'Dullness' was related to the perceived time.

From the ranking results, the perceived time can be increased or decreased by changing expression even though real-time is the same.

Keywords: Perceived Time · Progress bar · UI

1 Introduction

In recent years, to improve services in places such as restaurants and city halls, more places display the order by call number and how long to wait on a screen [1, 2].

According to a hospital satisfaction survey, outpatients' dissatisfaction is high for time-related items such as waiting time for consultation and waiting time for accounting, and it is reported that the waiting time for consultation increases significantly when it exceeds 40 min [3]. There is also a report [4] that people feel that pages displayed on the Internet are slow after two to three seconds, suggesting that acceptable waiting time varies depending on the situation. However, in situations where an unspecified number of people use the system, such as restaurants and city halls, it is difficult to increase or

C. Stephanidis et al. (Eds.): HCII 2023, CCIS 1957, pp. 96–102, 2024.
https://doi.org/10.1007/978-3-031-49212-9_13

decrease the actual waiting time because only a certain number of employees can serve customers in consideration of work efficiency and cost. Therefore, our focus in this study was to change the actual time. Therefore, we thought that service could be improved by increasing or decreasing the perceived time instead of the actual time.

2 Previous Studies

Shudo et al. [5] conducted an experiment to clarify which of three conditions (stationary, stepped, and continuous) causes the shortest waiting time. The results suggest that participants may perceive time as shorter when shown different conditions depending on the time of day. Otsubo et al. [6] experimented using a progress bar with ten different shapes. The results showed that a ring-shaped progress bar with a 90-degree central core made time seem the shortest.

Previous studies above have revealed that changing the UI may shorten the perceived time. However, the perceived time, including impressions and specific opinions focused on in this study, still needs to be clarified. There have been various studies on progress bars, such as the previous study. However, few papers still include the opinions and impressions of the experiment participants, such as why they chose the progress bar and felt it was the fastest. Since the shape and continuity of progress bars have been changed to compare the perceived time, we focused on the effect of other UIs on the perceived time without changing the basis of the progress bar.Purpose.

In this study, we focus on the situation where users are made to wait on a web page, compare how the perceived time increases or decreases depending on the UI using a progress bar as a subject, and visualize the results, including impressions. The purpose of this study is to clarify what kind of impressions influence the perceived time from the visualized results.

3 Method

3.1 Experimental Procedure

In this experiment, we have prepared six videos with different UIs. After showing one of the videos to the participants, we asked them to answer a questionnaire about their impressions. After viewing the six videos and answering the questionnaire, we divided the videos with similar UI content into two groups. Finally, we asked the participants to rank them and answer why they ranked them that way.

3.2 Video

Table 1 shows the six videos used. A total of six videos display the progress bar. All videos were 23 s long, and the progress bar was filled in the same 20 s. The progress bar was activated 1 s after the start of the video, and the progress bar was filled 21 s after the start. The rabbit jumps along with the progress bar only in video E. In the experiment, we prepared a group that changed the speed of display (Group 1) and a group that changed the way of display (Group 2). Participants watched each video and ranked.

Table 1. Group of videos used in the experiment.

Group 1 — A group that changed the speed of display		Group 2 — A group that changed the way of display	
A	100% — Constant speed from 0% to 100%	A	100% — Constant speed from 0% to 100%
B	100% — 10 seconds from 0% to 80% / 10 seconds from 80% to 100%	D	100% — Constant speed from 0% to 100% / The turtle moves with the bar
C	100% — 10 seconds from 0% to 20% / 10 seconds from 20% to 100%	E	100% — Constant speed from 0% to 100% / Rabbit moves with the bar while sleeping
		F	10000/10000 — Constant speed from 0 to 10000

3.3 Participants

A total of 33 participants (15 males and 18 females) participated in the experiment.

3.4 Questionnaire

In the questionnaire, ten adjective pairs were selected based on the literature on UI [7] to evaluate the participants' impressions using the SD method. Table 2 illustrates the selected adjective pairs. First, we instructed participants to watch one of the videos from A to F and then each participant respond with their impressions of the video. The order of the showing videos was randomly changed in the experiment to consider the effect of the order of watching the videos. After watching all of videos, the participants ranked the watched all videos from the fastest to lowest for each group. Finally, the participants answered the reason for their evaluated ranking.

4 Results

4.1 Factor Analysis by SD Method

Table 3 shows the results of the factor analysis using the results of the SD method. Factor 1 was named "Novelty" from the adjectives "Fun," "Eccentric," "Bright," and "New." Factor 2 was named "Openness" based on the adjectives "Fun," "Beautiful," "Light," and "Friendly." Finally, factor 3 was named "Dullness" based on the adjectives "Heavy" and "Slow".

Figures 1, 2, 3 illustrate the summarized three-factor scores obtained by factor analysis. Factor 1, "Novelty," showed high with the bar's illustrations of rabbits and turtles.

Table 2. Adjective pairs used

Classy —vulgar
Fun—Boring
Ugly—Beautiful
Disordered—Arranged
Heavy—Light
Plain—Eccentric
Friendly—Unfriendly
Fast—Slow
Dark—Bright
Old—New

Factor 2, "Openness," a bar with a rabbit, was the highest, but other than that, the results did not change much. Finally, factor 3, "Dullness," was the lowest in the UI with displaying up to 10,000, it enhances the sense of lightness.

Table 3. Results of Factor Analysis by SD Method

		Factor 1	Factor 2	Factor 3
Plain	Eccentric	0.956	-0.235	0.064
Old	New	0.621	0.229	-0.065
Dark	Bright	0.474	0.524	0.021
Fun	Boring	-0.48	-0.42	0.201
Friendly	Unfriendly	-0.058	-0.602	-0.014
Ugly	Beautiful	-0.026	0.554	-0.157
Heavy	Light	0.049	0.423	-0.483
Fast	Slow	-0.034	0.034	0.996
Classy	Vulgar	0.068	0.09	-0.065
Disordered	Arranged	-0.25	0.263	-0.045
Contribution		1.828	1.485	1.305
Contribution Ratio		0.183	0.148	0.13
Cumulative Contribution Ratio		0.183	0.331	0.426

4.2 Rank Evaluation

We obtained scale values from the ranked results and investigated significant differences. Figures 4 and 5 illustrate the results of ranked. That result means the perceived time

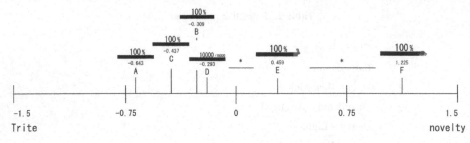

Fig. 1. Graph of factor scores for Factor 1 "Novelty".

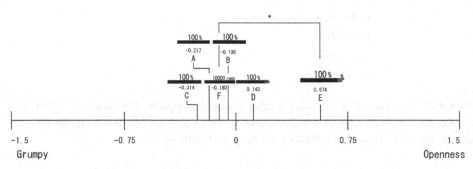

Fig. 2. Graph of factor scores for factor 2 " Openness"

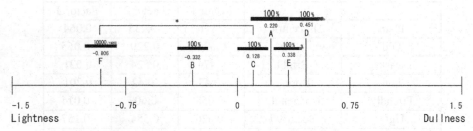

Fig. 3. Graph of factor scores for factor 3 "Dullness"

change by changing the way the figure is presented, even if the figure's appearance is the same and the speed is the same (Fig. 4). The result of Fig. 5 also suggests that bar with big moving images such as E and F are perceived as faster.

As the reasons for ranking, responses for Group 1 included comments such as, "If the speed of the last few percent is fast, it feels faster overall," and "It is stressful when the speed of the filling bar suddenly slows down in the second half. On the other hand, in response to the question about Group 2, there were opinions such as "I am not bored because the numbers move in detail" and "I feel faster than a rabbit because the progress is faster than a tortoise."

Figure 1 suggests that videos with illustrations increase the feeling of "Novelty." In addition, the opinion that "the turtle moves quickly and is not boring," which was one of the reasons for ranking the videos, it suggests that the "Novelty" of a video that is slightly different from the expected video would increase the value of "Novelty."

From Fig. 2, only video E, which has movements different from the others, had a high score. This result means the bar with moving like a jumping enhances the impression of "Openness."

Finally, in Fig. 3, "Lightness," the movie displaying F, which displays up to 10,000, is evaluated as the highest value. The reason for the videos' ranking was "The numbers move in detail, so it is not boring." The speed of the movie's first half was critical to feeling the speed of filling time, and it is to be the cause of the increase in the "Lightness" of the video, even though participants watched the same screen for 20 s.

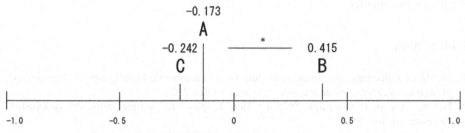

Fig. 4. Scale values for Group 1

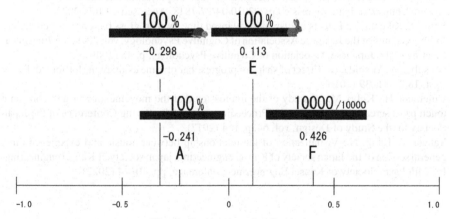

Fig. 5. Scale values for Group 2

5　Conclusion and Future Works

In this study, we conducted an experiment using the UI of a progress bar as the subject to clarify how impressions affect perceived time. The feeling of "Lightness" of UI influences the perception time since the fastest impressions, B and F (Fig. 4–5). On the other hand, the other factors, "Novelty" and "Openness," of UI showed no significant relationship with the perception time. Therefore, novel design and making people feel cheerful may not affect perceived time. However, a previous study [8] reported that the perception time becomes short when we feel joyful. Furthermore, when naming the factors, "Novelty" and "Openness" include the adjective "Fun," so a more in-depth study of these factors was also necessary. And among the responses to ranking the videos, there was an opinion that "The numbers were moving quickly, so I was not bored, and time seemed to go by faster." That means factor 3, "Lightness," might indicate that the perception time might be faster when one of the objects being viewed moves faster.

In addition, the experiment of this study was conducted in a format in which the respondents were asked to watch the video in a one-way manner and respond to their impressions. Therefore, we will also investigate the changing of the perceived time with the interactive manner.

References

1. Otorhinolaryngology Aso Hospital, Waiting Time Confirmation Display System.https://www.jibiazabu.or.jp/azabu/feature/online/. Accessed 16 Nov 2022
2. Normal Surgery Orthopedics, "Waiting Time Display" has started! https://bit.ly/3Xre1c5. Accessed 16 Nov 2022
3. Outpatient "Wait Time" Awareness. https://www.mdnt.co.jp/insight/mr/wait-time.php. Accessed 29 July 2022
4. Users begin to get frustrated after 2 seconds of page display, and one-third say "enough is enough". https://webtan.impress.co.jp/e/2010/04/27/7848. Accessed 29 July 2022
5. Shuto,J., Kikuchi, T.: Effects of displaying elapsed time by a progress bar on time perception. In: Proceedings of the Japanese Association of Cognitive Psychology, vol. 2009, the 7th Annual Meeting of the Japanese Association of Cognitive Psychology, p. 45 (2009)
6. Ohtsubo, M., Yoshida, K.: Effect of shape of progress bar on time evaluation. J. Biomed. Fuzzy Syst. 18(2), 31–39 (2016)
7. Umemura, H., Kubo, M.: A study of the impression that the movement of visual icons on a touch panel screen gives to users. In: Proceedings of the 64th Spring Conference of the Japan Society for the Study of Design, vol. 64, p. 114 (2017)
8. Yahata, T., Kang, N.: Visualization of the relationship between music and experience time, general session of the Japan society of Kansei engineering, japan society of Kansei engineering. In: 24th Japan Society of Kansei Engineering Conference, pp. 40–44 (2022)

SciTok - A Web Scraping Tool for Social Science Research

Yannick Zelle[1,2(✉)] ⓘ, Thibault Grison[2,3] ⓘ, and Marc Feger[1] ⓘ

[1] Heinrich Heine University, Duesseldorf 40225, Germany
[2] CERES, Sorbonne University, Maison de la Recherche, 75006 Paris, France
`lettres-ceres@sorbonne-universite.fr`
[3] GRIPIC, CELSA Sorbonne University, 75006 Paris, France
`https://ceres.sorbonne-universite.fr`

Abstract. This paper presents *SciTok*, a tool developed to facilitate social science and computer science researchers in the acquisition, exploration, and analysis of TikTok data. Despite TikTok's burgeoning influence in public and scientific discourse, access to its data remains an unaddressed challenge, creating a void this study aims to fill. This research achieves its objectives by first defining a theoretical model of TikTok that integrates the perspectives of both social science and computer science, followed by the design and implementation of a web scraper adapted to this model. By making the tool user-friendly and ensuring that it is adapted to a common social science research framework, we seek to foster interdisciplinary collaboration and invite more extensive analysis of social media's influence on social phenomena. Limitations and potential extensions for future research are also discussed, providing a groundwork for further explorations. (The tool can be accessed under: https://github.com/Lazel102/SciTok. For more details on this work, refer to the thesis corresponding to this paper [8]).

Keywords: TikTok · Social network analysis · Social media · Web scraping

1 Introduction

The emergence of social media has provided social science researchers with new avenues to gain a macroscopic view of social phenomena [2,6,7]. However, accessing this data can be technically challenging. Unlike some social media platforms that provide researchers with access to their data through an API, TikTok does not currently offer an official API for researchers. As a result, despite its growing importance in public and scientific discourse, TikTok remains an under-utilized resource for social science research [1].

This work addresses the issue by presenting *SciTok*, a tool that allows researchers to scrape TikTok data and bring it into a form especially suited for *social network analysis*, thereby providing a straightforward way of storing and analyzing the data. Through this approach, the work aims to facilitate interdisciplinary collaboration between social science and computer science researchers and provide social scientists with a tool to collect, explore, and analyze data from TikTok.

2   Motivation

Social media, defined as internet-based platforms for user interaction, have become a popular topic for researchers in both computer science and social sciences. Computer scientists are interested in the technical aspects of social media platforms, such as algorithms and network structures [5], while social scientists are interested in the ways in which these platforms reflect and shape social interactions and structures [2].

Despite the widespread usage of TikTok, it does not yet provide a free API like Twitter does for researchers to utilize their data. This necessitates the development of a tool that enables researchers to access and use TikTok data in a quantitative manner.

With this work we contribute the following:

1. **Theoretical Framework:** We conducted a comprehensive discussion on social media, with a focus on TikTok, to establish common ground for both social science and computer science perspectives. This process led to the development of an accessible theoretical model, reflected in the data structure (Fig. 1 and Table 1).
2. **Tool Development:** We designed and implemented the TikTok data scraper, *SciTok*, addressing technical and legal concerns. We obey the TikTok's *robots.txt*[1] by default. Additionally, we utilized existing tools, such as *Neo4j*[2], *Scrapy*[3], and *Docker*[4], for *SciTok*.
3. **Interdisciplinary Collaboration:** *SciTok* was designed to foster interdisciplinary collaboration by making it user-friendly, reducing knowledge requirements for data acquisition, and embedding it in a theoretical model that aligns with both social science methods and theories, while remaining adaptable to accommodate research questions of interest from a computer science perspective. The tool has already been employed during the development stage for a research project in information and communication sciences, with a specific focus on reality TV formats on TikTok [3]. The feedback obtained from this usage has been integrated into the development process.
4. **Evaluation and Application:** We evaluated the tool's capability and performance in collecting data from TikTok and demonstrated its potential applications through a descriptive showcase of the collected data. A visualization of a sample of the resulting graph can be seen in Fig. 2.

---

[1] The *robots.txt* is a text file placed on a website's server that instructs web robots or crawlers which pages or directories to access or avoid when indexing the site.
[2] For more information see https://neo4j.com.
[3] For more information see https://scrapy.org.
[4] For more information see https://www.docker.com.

5. **Accessible Presentation:** We ensured that technical information was presented in a comprehensible manner for both scientific domains, providing explanatory material as needed.

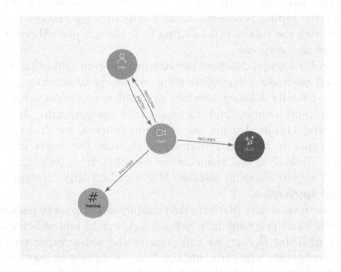

Fig. 1. Theoretical model and data structure.

Fig. 2. Example for the visualization of collected data.

3   Implementation

The main components for the implementation of this project are *Scrapy* for web crawling, *Neo4j* for storing graph-based data, and *Docker* for platform-independent deployment of *SciTok*.

Scrapy is a web scraping framework written in Python. It is specifically designed for large-scale web scraping projects. *Scrapy* offers key features such as extensibility, support for asynchronous requests, and optimized data processing, which were crucial factors in our decision to adopt it. When compared to alternative tools like *Beautiful Soup* and *Selenium*, *Scrapy* allows for more scalable and performant scraping processes. Additionally, *Scrapy* enables configuration of compliance with the robots.txt, ensuring that the scraper adheres to the legal requirements of web scraping.

Neo4j is a robust graph database management system that offers a wide range of features and seamless integration with various programming languages. It provides a user-friendly desktop interface for graph exploration using the *Cypher query language*[5] and includes built-in support for manipulating, analyzing, and visualizing stored graphs. During our scraping process, we directly connected the *Scrapy* scraper to the *Neo4j* database, allowing for direct storage of the collected data. To analyze and visualize the collected data, we primarily utilized *GraphXR*[6], a free visualization software that can be easily integrated with the *Neo4j* desktop application.

Docker is an open-source platform that enables developers to package, deploy, and run applications in containers, which are lightweight and self-contained environments. By utilizing *Docker*, we can package the web scraper and its dependencies in one container while running the *Neo4j* database in another container, allowing for easy execution of the web scraping process on any machine with *Docker* installed. This containerized version can be conveniently deployed and shared among users and developers.

The implemented scraping algorithm operates as follows: (1) When the scraper is initiated, the user provides a TikTok URL as input. The scraper (2) then visits the corresponding page. When encountering a video page, the scraper gathers all the items outlined in Table 1 and stores them using the specified data types presented in the same table. If it is not a video page, the scraper extracts the URLs of all the video pages present on the page and adds them to a queue of pages to be visited next. Additionally, on video pages, the scraper collects the associated music and hashtags, treating them as pages to be visited as well. The scraper also checks for duplicates before adding an item to the list of pages, ensuring that each page is visited only once. This recursive scraping process is summarized in the pseudocode provided in Listing 1.1 The resulting data structure can be seen in Fig. 1.

```
def collectURLs(url) -> void:
    htmlresponse = htmlrequest(url)
    responseUrls = htmlresponse.getAllSignificantURLs(htmlresponse)
    for respUrl in responseUrls:
        if isVideoUrl(respUrl):
            parse(respUrl)
        collectURLs(respUrl)
```

Listing 1.1. Pseudo code of the scraping procedure.

---

[5] For more information see https://neo4j.com/developer/cypher/.
[6] For more information see https://www.kineviz.com.

Table 1. Description of variables used and collected by SciTok.

Variable	Role	Data Type
Post	Node	String
VideoURL	Attribute and ID of Post	String
nrComments	Attribute of Post	Integer
nrLikes	Attribute of Post	Integer
nrForwarded	Attribute of Post	Integer
date	Attribute of Post	Datetime Object
created[a]	Attribute of Post	Datetime Object
INCLUDES	Edge from Post to Hashtag or Music	
MENTIONS	Edge from Post to User	
User	Node	String
UserScreenname	Attribute and ID of Username	String
username	Attribute of user	String
created	Attribute of user	String
POSTED	Edge from User to Post	
Hashtag	Node	String
created	Attribute of Hashtag	Datetime Object
Music	Node	String
created	Attribute of Music	Datetime Object

[a] created is always the timestamp that is given to the node when it is send to the database.

4 Evaluation

As our work was interest driven having both computer and social scientist participating, we decided to evaluate our tool by collecting data about the particular hashtag "LGBT", which is highly interesting for social scientist researching in the context of online moderation [4]. The process of collecting data lasted specifically from 8:00 PM on February 6, 2023, to manually terminating the scraping on February 7, 2023, at 9:00 PM, resulting in a total scraping duration of 27 h. Within this time period, a total of 4.980 items were collected. Figure 3 shows the amount of accumulated collected items over time during the collection. Moreover, Fig. 4 visually illustrates the reliable and linear progression of data collection, specifically designed for rigorous testing. This linear progression can be effectively utilized for predicting the duration required to gather a specific amount of data. By observing the steady advancement depicted in Fig. 4, one can estimate the time it would take to accumulate the desired quantity of data, thereby aiding in planning and resource allocation for future data collection endeavors.

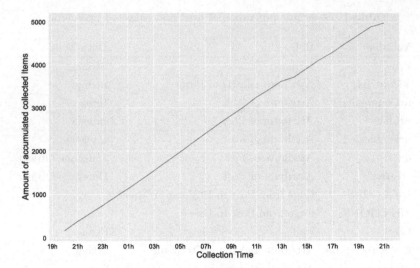

Fig. 3. Linear progression of accumulated posts over time.

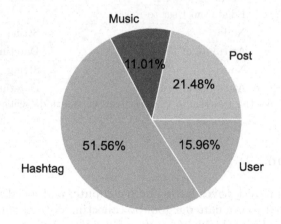

Fig. 4. Portions of collected nodes by attributes.

5   Conclusion

In this study, we present a solution to address the challenge of restricted access to TikTok data for research purposes. Our approach aims to promote interdisciplinary collaboration between the fields of social sciences and computer science. Introducing SciTok, a user-friendly platform, we cater to researchers who may not possess extensive technical expertise. By leveraging existing tools, our solution strikes a balance between guiding users towards effective data analysis methods and providing flexibility for researchers to customize their data analysis techniques based on their specific research inquiries.

By offering SciTok to the scientific community, our aim is to contribute to scientific discourse and encourage researchers to utilize TikTok data for addressing research questions. We hope that the tool can also be further developed through the valuable feedback of other researchers who utilize the framework we provide in our paper. However, we recognize a limitation in the current scraping process, which involves scraping a limited amount of data on each page. Although our scraper can handle large amounts of data, the process itself can be time-consuming. Furthermore, since only 15 items are collected on each visited page, the data may quickly become less relevant to the initial research question.

One potential approach to overcome this limitation in future research is to integrate other tools, such as *the unofficial TikTok API*[7], to address this challenge. A promising strategy would involve using the unofficial TikTok API to identify URLs of interest, and then utilizing SciTok to scrape the corresponding data. This integration would enable researchers to enrich the collected data with comments and user information. Furthermore, incorporating music features from sources like *Musicbrainz*[8] could be valuable for certain research investigations.

Overall, we are thrilled to present SciTok to the scientific community, and we anticipate that this tool will serve as a stepping stone for interdisciplinary collaboration and innovative research. We hope that the tool, along with the framework presented in our paper, can be enhanced through the feedback and contributions of other researchers.

References

1. Anderson, K.E.: Getting acquainted with social networks and apps: it is time to talk about TikTok. Library Hi Tech News (2020)
2. Boyd, D.: Social network sites as networked publics: affordances, dynamics, and implications. In: A Networked Self, pp. 47–66. Routledge (2010)
3. Grison, T., Bolz, L.: La réinvention de la télé-réalité sur TikTok: entre nouveaux formats numériques et l'émergence des «créateurs-vedettes». Télévision 14, hal-04139393 (2023)
4. Grison, T., Julliard, V., Alié, F., Ecrement, V.: La modération abusive sur twitter: Étude de cas sur l'invisibilisation des contenus lgbt et tds en ligne. Reseaux (1), 119–149 (2023). https://doi.org/10.3917/res.237.0119
5. Kwak, H., Lee, C., Park, H., Moon, S.: What is Twitter, a social network or a news media? In: Proceedings of the 19th International Conference on World Wide Web, WWW 2010, pp. 591–600. Association for Computing Machinery, New York, NY, USA, April 2010. https://doi.org/10.1145/1772690.1772751
6. Papacharissi, Z., de Fatima Oliveira, M.: Affective news and networked publics: the rhythms of news storytelling on #egypt. J. Commun. **62**(2), 266–282 (2012)
7. Varnelis, K.: Networked Publics. MIT Press (2012)
8. Zelle, L.: Bachelor thesis for a degree in computer science: let's talk about TikTok - a web scraping tool for social science research (2023). https://doi.org/10.13140/RG.2.2.10710.11843

---

[7] For more information see https://github.com/davidteather/TikTok-Api.
[8] For more information see https://musicbrainz.org.

Accessibility, Usability, and UX Design

Onírica: Device with Tangible Interface for the Development of Computational Thinking

Juliana Yuri Ando[✉][iD]

Universidade de São Paulo, São Paulo, Brazil
julianayuri@usp.br
http://ppgsi.each.usp.br

Abstract. Studies on Tangible User Interfaces (TUI) became popular from the works of Suzuki and Kata [15] and Ishii and Ullmer [7]. Among the many areas in that TUI can be explored, education stands out. Contact with interfaces beyond graphical interfaces can help and expand the way one learns. From this, this research project proposes a tangible interface focused on non-formal early childhood education to analyze whether the material used in the interface influences interaction and learning. To this end, it is intended to use the Design Science Research (DSR) methodology.

Keywords: Tangible User Interface · Computational Thinking · Materiality

1 Introduction

From different views on the construction of interactive systems, the human-computer interaction (IHC) area seeks to study how Information and Communication Technologies (ICT) relate to its users. The Computational Systems Architecture is one of the objects of study of HCI and deepens on the issue of physical means, focusing on the input and output devices [2]. Through the Tangible Interface it is possible to explore physical objects as an input or output device, providing a tangible representation for information and digital controls [12].

In the 1990s, two seminal works published served as a reference for many other later ones on Tangible Interfaces, they are: AlgoBlock [15] and Tangible Bits [7]. The first explores programming in aluminum blocks as a tangible interface, while the second presents the concept of tangible bits based on ubiquitous computing. According to Ishii and Ullmer [7], through tangible interfaces it would be possible to touch the bits in the physical world.

In relation to recent studies involving TUI and education, some common characteristics of interest are noted. Nonnis and Bryan-Kinns [8] and Al Mahmud and Soysa [1] sought to explore TUI as an educational way to develop socialization

C. Stephanidis et al. (Eds.): HCII 2023, CCIS 1957, pp. 113–117, 2024.
https://doi.org/10.1007/978-3-031-49212-9_15

in children with autism. Also on socialization, Song et al. [13] explored the TUI in educational activities in the interaction between parents and children, while Garcia, Jurdi, Jaen and Nacher [6] sought to explore collaborative learning from gamification using TUI. In relation to the teaching of specific knowledge, TUI has been applied mainly in the teaching of programming [6,11], but also in the teaching of algebra [10] and in the literacy process itself [5]. Among the research related to TUI, one can also highlight the TaPrEC [3], which is an example of tangible interface work aimed at children who seek to explore the pillars of Computational Thinking. In addition of the application by itself, TaPrEC has also been tested with other devices, such as Sphero, sometimes being an input device, sometimes being an output device [16].

2 Content

Stephanidis [14] present seven challenges faced by the area of HCI in the 21st century, among them are learning and creativity. The authors argue that digital technologies increase motivation, promote demonstrations of the topics taught, and can adapt to the pace of individual learning [14]. In addition, these technologies also contribute to the development of skills such as communication, collaboration, problem solving and critical and creative thinking.

To meet the needs of and facing the challenges of the HCI area, it is part of this research proposal the development of a device with tangible interface that uses fabric and lines as part of its materiality, as well as embroidery to compose visual communication. This device is given the name of Onírica. The idea of adding embroidery to technology in the context of learning is to stimulate creativity, seeking to provide alternatives so that other materials can also be explored in Tangible Interfaces.

The description of the materials used in Tangible Interfaces is common in the literature. Many of these are composed of plastic or wood, as illustrated in the Fig. 1. However, there are not many studies that compare the types of materials used in tangible interfaces and how these materials influence the interaction between humans and machines.

As previously described, the TaPrEC uses wooden blocks for the development of the pillars of computational thinking aimed at children. Onírica uses more malleable material, such as tissue, for teaching activities in the context of non-formal education. Being TaPrEC and Onírica applied in the same context, it would be possible to compare the influence of materiality.

Therefore, this project aims to answer the following question: in the comparison between TaPrEC and Onírica, the material used in devices with Tangible Interfaces can influence educational activities aimed at children?

3 Methodology

The proposed methodology for this research is Design Science Research (DSR). In Information Systems studies, this methodology became more frequent from

Environment	Tangible Object	Technology
AlgoBlock	Aluminum cubes	Electronic circuit
Tangible Programming Bricks	Lego blocks	Microprocessor - PIC
Eletronic Blocks	Lego blocks	Electronic circuit
Tern	Wooden cubes	Computer Vision
TanPro-Kit	Wooden cubes	SCM, wireless, infra-red, RFID, sensors

Fig. 1. Translated table by the author from Carbajal's work [3]

1990 and came up with the observation of Design processes for creating products for human purposes [9]. By systematizing the design creation process, this methodology involves a rigorous process of designing artifacts from the following steps: identifying problems, contributing to research, evaluating the project, and communicating the results with the appropriate audiences [4].

Some stages of this methodology are already underway, such as: (a) the identification of problems, through a preliminary systematic literature review, (b) contribution in research, through the development of the initial prototype as shown in the Fig. 2.

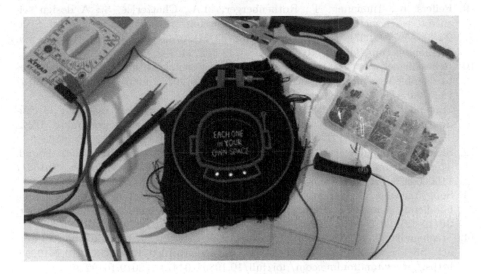

Fig. 2. Onírica: inicial prototype

To answer the research question, one of the main steps in the DSR is the evaluation. For this, it is intended to use the Self-Assessment Manikin method (SAM), which is based on a pictographic representation to evaluate emotion in three dimensions: satisfaction, motivation, and control. Finally, the communication stage of the results will be completed through the publication of scientific articles and participation in events.

References

1. Al Mahmud, A., Soysa, A.: POMA: a tangible user interface to improve social and cognitive skills of Sri Lankan children with ASD. Int. J. Hum. Comput. Stud. **144** (2020). https://doi.org/10.1016/j.ijhcs.2020.102486
2. Barbosa, S.D.J., Silva, B.S.D.: Interação Humano-Computador (2010). http://www.sciencedirect.com/science/book/9788535234183. oCLC: 870676143
3. Carbajal, M.L., Baranauskas, M.C.C.: TaPrEC: Desenvolvendo um ambiente de programação tangível de baixo custo para crianças, p. 8 (2015)
4. Dresch, A., Lacerda, D.P., Antunes, J.A.V.: Design Science Research: A Method for Science and Technology Advancement. Springer, Cham (2015). https://doi.org/10.1007/978-3-319-07374-3
5. Fan, M., Antle, A., Hoskyn, M., Neustaedter, C.: A design case study of a tangible system supporting young English language learners. Int. J. Child-Comput. Interact. **18**, 67–78 (2018). https://doi.org/10.1016/j.ijcci.2018.08.001
6. Garcia-Sanjuan, F., Jurdi, S., Jaen, J., Nacher, V.: Evaluating a tactile and a tangible multi-tablet gamified quiz system for collaborative learning in primary education. Comput. Educ. **123**, 65–84 (2018). https://doi.org/10.1016/j.compedu.2018.04.011
7. Ishii, H., Ullmer, B.: Tangible bits: towards seamless interfaces between people, bits and atoms. In: Proceedings of the ACM SIGCHI Conference on Human Factors in Computing Systems, pp. 234–241 (1997)
8. Nonnis, A., Bryan-Kinns, N.: Olly: a tangible for togetherness. Int. J. Hum. Comput. Stud. **153** (2021). https://doi.org/10.1016/j.ijhcs.2021.102647
9. Peffers, K., Tuunanen, T., Rothenberger, M.A., Chatterjee, S.: A design science research methodology for information systems research. J. Manag. Inf. Syst. **24**(3), 45–77 (2007). https://doi.org/10.2753/MIS0742-1222240302. https://www.tandfonline.com/doi/full/10.2753/MIS0742-1222240302
10. Reinschlassel, A., et al.: Multimodal algebra learning: from math manipulatives to tangible user interfaces. i-com **17**(3), 201–209 (2018). https://doi.org/10.1515/icom-2018-0027
11. Sapounidis, T., Stamovlasis, D., Demetriadis, S.: Latent class modeling of children's preference profiles on tangible and graphical robot programming. IEEE Trans. Educ. **62**(2), 127–133 (2019). https://doi.org/10.1109/TE.2018.2876363
12. Shaer, O.: Tangible user interfaces: past, present, and future directions. Found. Trends® Hum. Comput. Interact. **3**(1–2), 1–137 (2009). https://doi.org/10.1561/1100000026. http://www.nowpublishers.com/article/Details/HCI-026
13. Song, Y., Yang, C., Gai, W., Bian, Y., Liu, J.: A new storytelling genre: combining handicraft elements and storytelling via mixed reality technology. Vis. Comput. **36**(10–12), 2079–2090 (2020). https://doi.org/10.1007/s00371-020-01924-3
14. Stephanidis, C., et al.: Seven HCI grand challenges. Int. J. Hum. Comput. Interact. **35**(14), 1229–1269 (2019). https://doi.org/10.1080/10447318.2019.1619259. https://www.tandfonline.com/doi/full/10.1080/10447318.2019.1619259

15. Suzuki, H., Kata, H.: Interaction-level support for collaborative learning: Algoblock-an open programming language (1995)
16. Zanetti Panaggio, B., Luque Carbajal, M., Calani Baranauskas, M.C.: Programação Tangível no Mundo Físico: TaPrEC + Sphero. Revista Brasileira de Informática na Educação **27**(03), 32–51 (2019). https://doi.org/10.5753/rbie.2019. 27.03.32. https://br-ie.org/pub/index.php/rbie/article/view/v27n033151

Why the Wilhelm Scream, One of the Most Well-Known "Easter Egg" Sound Effects in Video Games, is Used, and How to Test Participants' Extent of Assessment by Using a Bayesian Statistical Approach

Jakub Binter[1,2]([✉]) [iD], Silvia Boschetti[1] [iD], Tomáš Hladký[1] [iD], Daniel Říha[1] [iD], and Hermann Prossinger[2,3] [iD]

[1] Faculty of Humanities, Charles University, Prague, Czech Republic
jakub.binter@fhs.cuni.cz
[2] Faculty of Social and Economic Studies,
University of Jan Evangelista Purkyně, Ústí nad Labem, Czech Republic
[3] Department of Evolutionary Anthropology, University of Vienna, Vienna, Austria

Abstract. The *Wilhelm Scream* is the sound effect that first appeared in 1951 and has been used in an almost uncountable number of movies and video games as an "Easter egg" related to pain, injury, and displeasure. The *Intensity Paradox* theory claims that vocalizations are rated valence-wise with very low accuracy. The learning hypothesis, on the other hand, suggests that repeated exposure allows for overcoming the intensity paradox. To test this, we collected a large sample of two ratings each by 902 raters and developed a novel statistical approach, based on Bayesian statistics, in which we determine the maximum-likelihood probability of Beta distributions of these responses. We asked our participants to rate the Wilhelm Scream mixed in with the other high-intensity vocalizations. The outcome showed an unexpected result—an extremely high precision of rating and consistency in repeated exposure. Furthermore, older men (but not women) rated with lower consistency. This provides, using a natural experiment, novel support for the learning effect of vocalization and the importance of using Easter eggs as a vehicle of familiarity related to gaming attractiveness and audiovisual media creation.

Keywords: Wilhelm Scream · Beta distribution · Vocalization · Game design · Intense affective states

1 Introduction

1.1 A Subsection Sample

The Wilhelm Scream (one of the "Easter eggs" of gaming sound engineers) is the sound effect that was first used in 1951 and it is often included in videogames—among these: *Battlefield 1*, *Call of Duty*, *Modern Warfare 2*, *Fallout 3*, *Grand Theft Auto V*, and *Red*

C. Stephanidis et al. (Eds.): HCII 2023, CCIS 1957, pp. 118–123, 2024.
https://doi.org/10.1007/978-3-031-49212-9_16

Dead Redemption. As the name suggests, it is a loud vocal display from a male actor and is related to a negative emotion of pain or displeasure involving fear.

The term Easter egg was originally used for the hidden function of a program that would be impossible to be called the usual way by the user. Since then, the meaning has shifted and the meaning has become broader.

In order to make audio-visual materials attractive, immersive, and enjoyable, a suite of options needs to be employed. One example of these are so-called Easter eggs, "[the] secret 'goodies'... Used in video games, movies, TV commercials, DVDs, CDs, CD-ROMs and every so often in hardware" (PC Magazine [n.d.]).

Since the early 1980s, digital Easter eggs have become a common phenomenon in the digital world. Today, they are even appearing in the automotive industry. The purpose of these Easter eggs is to enhance the experience by providing some additional excitement and surprise (within the context of familiarity so that the user can relate to the content of the Easter eggs). Academic research about Easter eggs is scarce, even though the concept is intensively used. This paper intends to fill the gap about the lack of academic research into Easter eggs, restricting our study to the Wilhelm Scream; it is one of the first scientific analyses of this legendary sound effect.

Each affective display has two main properties; the *intensity* (low-middle-high), and the *valence* (negative-neutral-positive).

To allow for comparison, we interleaved the Wilhelm Scream with other vocalizations while conducting our research project (Binter et al. 2023) in which we asked participants to rate acoustic signals (short, randomly presented vocal displays) of highly intensive affective states (pain, pleasure and fear), asking them to evaluate their valence. We found that the participants who rated these stimuli as positive, neutral, or negative affective states had extremely low accuracy in their judgment (approximately only 50% correct answers). Through further analysis, we concluded that the participants' ratings were statistically equivalent to being due to chance—the raters were guessing (Boschetti et al. 2022; Binter et al. 2023). In other words, the raters were using a trial-and-error approach unsuccessfully. All ratings were conducted twice to test for *consistency* between the first and second ratings in two randomized trials (Boschetti et al. 2022; Binter et al. 2023). The consistency was extremely low in the case of these high-intensity vocalizations (pain, pleasure, and fear).

These results are an example of the so-called *Intensity Paradox* phenomenon (CIT), which claims that the more intensive the display, the more difficult it is to assign a valid valence to it. We, therefore, investigated whether the *Intensity Paradox* also applies to the Wilhelm Scream, since it, too, is a high-intensity emotional display.

We emphasize that the Wilhelm Scream is solely employed to accompany death, injury, or some other negative experience of the portraying character on the screen. We did find a small number of media where the effect accompanied a pleasurable experience; in those cases, however, the effect was used sarcastically in order to enhance the humorous undertone.

2 Methods

2.1 The Data Set

We asked the 902 participants (526 females aged 18–50 years and 326 males aged 18–50 years) to also (in addition to the affective states mentioned above) rate the Wilhelm Scream—twice. Because, during the same session, the participants were also rating other acoustic signals, we were able to interleave the Wilhelm Scream with these others randomly.

2.2 Statistical Methods

The ratings are categorical variables, which may not be converted to computable numbers (Blalock, 1979). Instead, we use a Bayesian approach (Gelman et al., 2014, Kruschke, 2014; Lambert, 2018). In the Bayesian approach, the probability s is a random variable ($0 \leq s \leq 1$), with a distribution called the likelihood function $\otimes(s)$ (Bishop, 2006).

In the case of two categorical variables (correct versus incorrect, say), in which there are m correct responses and n incorrect responses, then the likelihood function for the probability s of being correct is (Bishop, 2006).

$$\otimes(s) = const \cdot s^m \cdot (1-s)^n.$$

This likelihood function is the *pdf* (probability density function) of the Beta distribution. The constant *const* ensures that $\int_0^1 \otimes(s)\, ds = 1$, so $const = \left(\int_0^1 s^m (1-s)^n ds \right)^{-1}$. We note that $m + n = N,$, which is the total sample size (the total number of registered ratings). The most likely probability is $\frac{m}{m+n}$ (which, for large sample sizes, approaches the Laplace limit; i.e. the traditional, elementary way of defining probability as a ratio.). In the Bayesian approach, the likelihood function includes the inference of the uncertainty (the confidence interval; see below), which the Laplace limit does not (despite the questionable approaches involving the error of the mean; for details, see Lambert, 2018).

Furthermore, the Bayesian approach allows for the determination of whether an observed outcome is due to the raters guessing. One way of quantifying this determination is to calculate depending on which side of $\frac{1}{2}$ the most likely probability s_{ML} is. If this integral is above 5% (the conventional significance level, and the one we have chosen for this publication—any other choice can be chosen, however), then the raters are guessing at the chosen significance level.

$$\int_0^{\frac{1}{2}} \mathcal{O}\otimes(s)\, ds \text{ or } \int_{\frac{1}{2}}^1 \mathcal{O}\otimes(s)\, ds.$$

Another method of determining the significance level of a result not being due to guessing is to find the boundaries s_1 and s_2, such that.

$$\int_{s_1}^{s_2} \mathcal{O}\otimes(s) \, ds = 0.95$$

for a significance level of 5%. Finding the boundaries s_1 and s_2 involves solving for $\otimes(s_1) = \otimes(s_2)$ with the above condition. The interval $\{s_1, s_2\}$ is called $\text{HDI}_{95\%}$ (highest density interval at 95% confidence; Kruschke, 2014).

We use these definitions to determine how reliably raters rated the screams—in other words, whether they were guessing.

Because the sample sizes were so large, we use Wilks' Λ (Wilks, 1938) to determine whether the two distributions (likelihood functions $\otimes(s_A)$ and $\otimes(s_B)$) for two populations A and B are significantly different.

Specifically, we calculate the log-likelihoods: $LL_A = \ln(\otimes(s_A))$, $LL_B = \ln(\otimes(s_B))$, and $LL_{AB} = \ln(\otimes(s_{AB}))$, where AB is the union of both populations. For large sample sizes

$$\Lambda = -2(LL_{AB} - (LL_A + LL_B))$$

is (therefore asymptotically) χ^2-distributed with $df = (df_A + df_B) - df_{AB}$ degrees of freedom (Wilks, 1938). We note that we can thereby calculate the significance level (as we do here) without specifying it to be 5%.

Because the number of males in our sample ($N_{\text{♂}} = 376$) is much smaller than the number of females ($N_{\text{♀}} = 526$) and the likelihood function $\otimes(s)$ is sensitive to $m + n$, we use a bootstrap method when comparing male populations with female populations. We randomly choose 376 out of the 526 females and compare their maximum likelihood with the maximum likelihood of the 376 males. We repeat this random selection one thousand times and find the computed comparison distributions.

We used ML methods to find the ML age distributions of participants in a population. We first scaled all ages (by dividing by the maximum age in the data sets—50 years) and then calculated the log-likelihood of the beta distribution, the normal distribution, the log-normal distribution, the Gamma distribution, and the Weibull distribution. (We note that many univariate continuous parametric distributions are subsets of the Gamma distribution with specific values of its parameters.) Again, we used Wilks Λ; to compute significances of comparisons.

3   Results

In contrast to other situations of highly intense affective states (Prossinger et al. 2021; Boschetti et al. 2022; Binter et al. 2021, 2023), we found some unexpected results.

For the 1st rating, 94.7% of the female raters and 91.8% of the male raters correctly rated the Wilhelm Scream. For the 2nd rating, 94.1% of the female raters and 90.2% of the male raters correctly rated the Wilhelm Scream.

In both cases we found, using the described bootstrap method, that the rating difference was not significant at $siglevel = 5\%$. . When analyzing whether the ratings were consistent (i.e. when the ratings were 'doubly correct'), we find that 91.4% of the female raters were 'doubly correct' whereas 'only' 86.2% of the male raters were. The differences between 'doubly correct' and 'not doubly correct' were not significant (females: $siglevel < 4 \times 10^{-4}$; males: $siglevel < 7 \times 10^{-3}$; Beta distribution test).

On the other hand, the distributions of ages showed a remarkable result: the ages of the 'doubly incorrect' females (*mean* = 31.7 years; *stdev* = 8.8 years) were not significantly different from the ages of the 'doubly correct' females (Wilks' Λ; test: *siglevel* = 5%), , while for the males ('doubly incorrect': *mean* = 30.9 years; *stdev* = 8.6 years) there is a highly significant difference (Wilks' Λ; test: *siglevel* $< 4 \times 10^{-6}$).

We observe several outcomes: (1) Neither do all the males, nor all the females, reliably and correctly rate the Wilhelm Scream. Yet the likelihood of correct identification is much higher than expected. All differences are, however, not significant. (2) When asked to repeat the rating, the probability of a 'doubly correct' rating decreases for both the males and the females. (3) The ages of the males rating the Wilhelm Scream incorrectly twice are significantly older (by 2.9 years on average) than those males that rate 'doubly correct'.

4 Discussion and Conclusion

For categorical variables, we could not use point estimators of the most probable q in a binomial test. Nor could we estimate the expectation (via the arithmetic mean) of a distribution. While it is commonplace to use the standard error of the mean to estimate a confidence interval (which is actually illogical, as these are point estimates), it would be useless here: only if we had in excess of 100 samples would we be able to infer that 95% of the point estimators would lie within the intervals bracketing the true mean (the expectation value). Bayesian statistics, which treats all estimators as likelihood functions, allows for a natural estimation of both the confidence interval and the ML true mean—and also the mode (Lambert, 2018).

Because the raters were very much more successful when rating the Wilhelm Scream than when rating the acoustic signals of highly intensive affective states (Boschetti et al. 2022; Binter et al. 2023), we conclude that the Wilhelm Scream is not a 'victim' of the *Intensity Paradox*. This supports the learning hypothesis of valence evaluation suggested by Corvin et al. (2022) and Boschetti et al. (2022)—both using the Bayesian methodology.

The insignificant differences, both for single ratings and combined ratings, as well as for males and females, indicate a high rating precision by the raters, ascribable to a learning effect acquired *before* participating in our study. Arguably, the 902 participants in our sample have been exposed to the Wilhelm Scream in many films and video games; consequently, an association with the negative experiences (depicted in those) will have unavoidably occurred. If so, we must infer that the deviation from 100% is most likely due to random (yet rare) concentration lapses while the participants were asked to rate not only the Wilhelm Scream but also other highly affective states in the same session.

The significant difference in ages between the 'doubly correct' and 'not doubly correct' males is quite large (2.9 years on average; 9.0%), necessitating a more detailed statistical investigation.

Both the statistical methodologies we used and the results we found have implications for game design, because of the involved evolutionary-developmental mechanisms the prospective gamer (unwittingly) underlies during game development.

The use of known sound effects and situations that have been termed "Easter eggs" can support the orientation in novel environments (such as game environments) and would then serve as building blocks so as to avoid ambiguity—consequently improving and enhancing the users' experiences.

The results show that four stages of the Easter egg experience were identified: awareness, trigger, delivery, and longevity, which are all important phases the game developer needs to incorporate into his/her design.

Acknowledgements. The study was preregistered on the OSF portal: https://osf.io/bhk6m/. We thank the reviewer for very helpful comments and suggestions.

Funding. This research was funded by the Czech Science Foundation in the project with number GACR 19-12885Y and titled "Behavioral and Psycho-Physiological Response on Ambivalent Visual and Auditory Stimuli Presentation".

This work was supported by the Cooperatio Program, research area ARTS.

Conflicts of Interest. The authors declare no conflict of interest.

References

Bishop, C.M. Pattern Recognition and Machine Learning. Springer Science + Business Media, NY (2006)

Binter. J., Boschetti, S., Hladký, T., Prossinger, H.: Ouch!" or "Aah!: Are Vocalizations of 'Laugh', 'Neutral', 'Fear', 'Pain' or 'Pleasure' Reliably Rated? Under Review (2023)

Binter, J., et al.: Quantifying the rating performance of ambiguous and unambiguous facial expression perceptions under conditions of stress by using wearable sensors. In: International Conference on Human-Computer Interaction, pp. 519–529. Springer, NY (2022)

Blalock, H.M.: Social Statistics, 2nd edn. McGraw-Hill, NY (1979)

Boschetti, S., Prossinger, H., Hladký, T., Machová, K., Binter, J.: "Eye can't see the difference": facial expressions of pain, pleasure, and fear are consistently rated due to chance. Human Ethology **37**, 46–72 (2022)

Corvin, S., Fauchon, C., Peyron, R., Reby, D., Mathevon, N.: Adults learn to identify pain in babies' cries. Curr. Biol. **32**(15), R824–R825 (2022)

Gelman, A., Carlin, J.B., Stern, H.S., Dunson, D.B., Vehtari, A., Rubin, D.B. Bayesian Data Analysis. 3rd edn. CRC Press, Boca Raton

Kruschke, J.K.: Doing Bayesian Data Analysis: A Tutorial with R, JAGS, and Stan. Academic Press, NY (2014)

Lambert, B.: A Student Guide to Bayesian Statistics. Sage Publications, London, UK (2018)

Prossinger, H., Hladky, T., Binter, J., Boschetti, S., Riha, D.: Visual analysis of emotions using ai image-processing software: possible male/female differences between the emotion pairs "neutral"–"fear" and "pleasure"–"pain". The 14th PErvasive Technologies Related to Assistive Environments Conference, pp. 342–346 (2021). https://doi.org/10.1145/3453892.3461656

Wilks, S.S.: The large-sample distribution of the likelihood ratio for testing composite hypotheses. Ann. Math. Stat. **9**(1), 60–62 (1938). https://doi.org/10.1214/aoms/1177732360

User-Centered Design of a Family-Meal Planning Tool

Vanja Blažica[1,3], Bojan Blažica[1,2]([✉]) [ID], and Antonio Solinas[3]

[1] Proventus d.o.o., Ajdovščina, Slovenia
[2] Jožef Stefan Institute, Ljubljana, Slovenia
[3] Lifely S.r.l., Sassari, Italy
bojan.blazica@ijs.si

Abstract. This paper describes the design and development of a tool for family meal planning based on data about meal planning habits from Slovenian families. The tool creates a weekly meal plan based on family preferences with corresponding shopping list and meal consumption statistics. The tool collects data on family eating habits and has potential to promote benefits associated with family meals. Future research could explore the tool's generalizability and potential improvements.

Keywords: nutrition · user research · meal planning · FNS-Cloud · food · security

1 Introduction

"The family meal has declined drastically since 1966. Families who have frequent family meals often see the following benefits with their children and youth: enhanced vocabulary, academic success, healthy food selections, demonstration of positive values, and avoidance of high-risk behaviors (substance abuse, sexual activity, depression/suicide, violence, school problems, binge eating/purging, and excessive weight loss)." [2] This sentiment echoes through literature focusing on different aspects of the benefits of family meal planning such as higher fruit and vegetable consumption [1,5], lower BMI [6], better diet quality predicted by family meal patterns during adolescence [7], reduction of high-risk behaviors [3], [8], time for conversation, feelings of togetherness, and ceremony [4].

Despite these benefits, families face several challenges in planning and executing family meals. Therefore, the purpose of this study is to investigate the challenges and opportunities to design an ICT tool that facilitates family meal planning.

2 Methodology

Following a co-creation, user-centered approach, an initial survey about meal planning habits among Slovenian families was conducted (n = 250). The questions can be grouped in three themes:

- **Household composition and dynamics:** How many adults/children are in your household, who prepares meals in your household, who does the food shopping, who decides what to eat, do other household members suggest what to cook, how much are other members involved in decision-making?
- **Menu planning and preparation:** How often do you prepare different dishes for the same meal, how do different factors affect the composition of your menu, have you ever prepared weekly menus and if so, were they useful, how far in advance do you prepare your menu, how often do you struggle with meal ideas, what do you do when you don't know what to make, how often do you buy too much food, which foods spoil the most, where do you find new recipes, are there any foods that you don't eat due to one member's preferences, do you monitor your diet?
- **Attitudes towards food and eating:** how important is it to adapt to seasonal fruits/vegetables, would you find a weekly menu planning app useful, which of features of a family meal planning app would you find most useful?

The survey gathered data that guided the next steps of preparing mock-ups for a standalone application that solves the main problems identified in the survey. After the survey, more in-depth unstructured interviews were conducted with a smaller group (n = 6) of family meal planning decision-makers from various family types, age groups, and background. The mock-ups were prepared, and the most common scenarios evaluated with this group. These included to check the weekly menu, substitute dishes that do not fit their preferences, create a list of required groceries for the week, add a recipe to their list of frequently cooked dishes, find a new recipe for chickpeas, browse recipes for new ideas in the evening, test interesting recipes and add successful ones, like Parmigiana, to their recipe bank, include a new family member in choosing recipes, check the dishes they have been cooking frequently, and look for any diet improvement recommendations in the app (what is expected from a nutritional analysis and related recommendations in such an app).

With the results of usability testing in mind, the tool was developed and used to gather feedback and initial data about family food preferences.

3   Results

The main problems identified related to family-meal planning that can be solved with an ICT tool were: 1) generation of a healthy meal plan that takes into consideration family preferences, 2) generation of a shopping list and 3) ideas for new recipes based on family taste.

3.1   Survey Analysis

Predominantly, more than 80%, survey respondents where females in charge of meal preparation in the household as well as doing grocery shopping and deciding what to eat. Participating households consists of 3 adults and 0.8 children on average.

Fig. 1. Analogue family meal planning with a paper on the fridge and its digital counterpart in a mobile phone.

Most of the respondents discuss food wants and needs with other household members and try to follow their suggestions. Some talk more often, others less, and some do not involve other members in decision-making. In some cases, other members prepare the food themselves or say what they want for the meal. One part of the respondents lives alone or has no other members in the household. Most (more than 80%) find it useful if other family members suggest what to cook.

Preparing separate dishes for the same meal is not a common practice with 66% never or seldom practicing this while only 16% claim to do this often.

The factors that most influence meal planning were ordered based on a rating from 1 (little influence) to 5 (big influence) as follows: what's currently available in the garden(4.49), fruit/vegetable seasonality (4.47), rules of a healthy diet (4.05), tastes of household members (3.83), price (2.85), special diets (2.65).

Answers to the question "Have you ever prepared weekly (or several-day) menus?" reveal that most of have not yet prepared weekly (or several-day) menus. Some have tried them in the past but abandoned them, while a few people still prepare them regularly. Of those who planned their meals, approximately half found this practice useful and half not. People have abandoned weekly meal planning for various reasons such as lack of time, loss of freshness in the ingredients, reduced interest in the planned meals, and the need to adapt to changing circumstances. Some people prefer to cook according to their current mood or preference, while others decide on their meals based on what is available from their garden or at the moment. Some find it difficult to stick to a planned meal, while others prefer to plan for only a day or two rather than for the entire week. Some have stopped planning altogether while others intend to reintroduce it in the future. The answer to the question "How far in advance do you prepare menu?" varies from person to person, but planning for the next day or at most a few days is more frequent. Work schedule or visits are also an influencing factors mentioned.

Being in the situation of not knowing what to cook at the time of a meal is not common (2.28 on a scale from 1 to 5, where 5 is very frequent). When people are unsure of what to cook, they typically search for inspiration by looking at what ingredients are available to them at home, or they may check their garden or pantry for ideas. Some may choose to make pasta with a quick sauce, utilize canned goods, prepare a simple dish like a salad, use their own preserved food, prepare a meal from leftovers, or improvise with the ingredients they have. Inquiring about what would they like to be able to do in such a situation suggested a desire for convenience and simplicity when it comes to meal preparation (having food readily available or someone else cook for them, ordering food or having pre-cooked meals that they could easily heat up, having more ideas or suggestions for what to cook with the ingredients they have, or having stocked ingredients for a pre-planned meal plan).

Similarly to the above, food spoiling is not a common problem (2.24 on a scale from 1 to 5, where 5 is very frequent). The most commonly mentioned foods that spoil in households are dairy products (yogurt, spreads, milk, cheese), bread, vegetables (due to overbuying), and fruit. Some people mentioned that they do not have any food spoilage problems because they plan and organize their food consumption carefully. A few others mentioned specific items like homemade jams without sugar, mushrooms, and deli meats that spoil quickly. Some people mentioned that they have animals that consume the food, and some mentioned that they have no such items in their household.

35% of households do not eat a specific ingredient because one member of the household does not eat it. Most commonly these ingredients are seafood and tripe.

Based on the survey question "Do you monitor your diet to ensure that you receive all the micro and macro nutrients?" the results indicate that approximately half of the respondents, 50.4%, monitor their diet to ensure that they receive all the necessary micro and macro nutrients. 26.4% of the respondents do not currently monitor their diet but would like to, while 12.4% of the respondents do not monitor their diet and do not want to do so. Others responded either no, without expressing a preference, did not understand the questions or mentioned that they follow a specific diet.

The responses to the question "How important is adapting to seasonal fruits and/or vegetables for you?" show that the majority of respondents, 62.3%, buy whatever fruits and vegetables are available at the store if they are not growing them in their garden. 36.9% of respondents only eat seasonal fruits and vegetables, indicating that eating produce that is in season is important to them. Only 0.8% of respondents indicated that it doesn't matter to them whether they eat seasonal produce or not, and they will buy whatever is available.

Respondents were asked to rate the importance of potential features for a family meal planning app on a scale from 1 to 5, where 1 indicates "not important at all" and 5 indicates "very important". The results indicate that the most highly valued feature were recommendations for improving the menu (mean rating of 4.08), followed by suggestions for new recipes according to the taste of the family (4.00), and a review of the quality the family diet against dietary guidelines (3.91). Other features that were rated highly included the option to print the menu to be hung on a fridge (3.91), automatic weekly menu suggestion based on a common set of family recipes (3.84), and a shopping list for the week (3.78). Less important features included adding snacks (3.52), family members voting on whether they liked the dishes consumed (3.5), and the option for family members to enter meals they didn't eat at home (3.49).

In a final open-ended question about any other comments quite different from each other appeared, but some wishes were repeated. Most respondents want menus that are simple, seasonal and balanced. There are also special dietary requirements and suggestions for recipes made from seasonal ingredients. Some have homegrown produce, so they don't want meals that include canned foods.

3.2   Family Meal Planning App

Insights from the survey helped us prioritize potential features and lead us to the design of a mobile application with the capability to create a weekly meal plan based on the recipes that the family usually eats. The head user is able to add their usual meals to the recipe bank - typically 30 or 40 meals the family most often consumes. The recipes can be inserted manually or found online in a recipe source connected to the app, e.g. in Slovenia the first and largest online source of recipes kulinarika.net[1] was used offering more than 18.000 recipes provided by the community. All the family members are able to vote on these recipes through the 'glance popular recipes' section (Fig. 2). Family members can glance at various recipes from the chosen public recipe source and vote on their preference on a scale from 4 to 1 ('great', 'OK', 'if needed', and 'no chance'). The recipes that are highly favored go to the family's wish list, and the other family members are asked to vote on them. After the recipe is tried out, it can be added to the regular recipes in the recipe bank or removed from the wish list. From the recipes in the recipe bank, the shopping list and weekly plan are created automatically (Fig. 1).

While the desire to have dietary recommendations present in the app emerged already from the survey, after usability testing using mock-ups, it was determined that users wanted these recommendations (preferences, nutrition analysis, and statistics) to be integrated more subtly into the app. Users can thus mark whether they consumed a meal by ticking a box, and only ticked meals are included in the statistics section where families can review their dietary habits (e.g. how many times a dish was prepared, whose tastes are better catered for)

---

[1] https://www.kulinarika.net/.

and receive basic recommendations, such as increasing their fiber intake if it's found to be lacking in their menu.

Finally, as seasonality and homegrown food are important factors for many respondents when planning meals for their household, the family meal planning app was connected to the garden planning app Tomappo[2] to help them better integrate their homegrown produce into their meal plans, e.g. users can easily see what is available in their garden within their shopping list of the family meal planning app.

Fig. 2. Features of the family meal planning tool: on the left, glancing and voting on recipes from an online source by swiping the recipe up (great), down (no chance), left (if needed) or right (OK), and the family recipe or food bank with votes from family members on the right.

4   Discussion

The development of the tool for family meal planning was based on a co-creation, user-centered approach that involved gathering data from Slovenian families. While the tool was specifically designed to meet the needs and preferences of Slovenian families, the general principles behind the design process of the tool

---

[2] Tomappo assists users in planning their garden while taking into consideration gardening best practices such as crop rotation and companion planting, and guides users through the whole gardening season. https://www.tomappo.com.

could be applied to families in other cultural and geographic contexts. The data collected from the families who participated in the survey and interviews were invaluable in identifying the main challenges and needs of families when it comes to meal planning. Additionally, the tool collects data about family eating habits, which could be of interest to researchers studying eating habits and nutrition.

One potential drawback of the tool is that it does not force a healthy diet, but rather, a diet based on family preferences. While the tool provides guidance for creating a balanced weekly meal plan, it ultimately relies on the recipes and food preferences of the family. It is important to note that the tool is not intended to be a substitute for the guidance of a registered dietitian or other qualified health professional (potentially aided by an ICT tool specific for dietary monitoring and planning). Instead, it is designed to provide a convenient and efficient way for families to plan and prepare meals together.

Another limitation of the tool is that it was developed based on data gathered in Slovenia only and from an audience pooled from users of the hobby gardening application Tomappo. While the principles behind the tool could be applied to families in other cultural and geographic contexts, there may be variations in food preferences and cultural practices that would need to be taken into account. Further research could explore the generalizability of the tool across different cultures and geographic regions and comparison with a sample more representative of the general population. For example answers related to the importance seasonality might be biased.

In terms of potential for improvement, future iterations of the tool could incorporate features such as generation of healthy meal plans, integration with popular food delivery services, and integration with wearable technology to track food intake and physical activity. Additionally, the tool could be expanded to include information beyond those usually present in single meal recipes. Some examples include general information about food preparation techniques, food storage, and food safety.

Overall, the tool for family meal planning presented in this paper provides a user-centered and convenient way for families to plan and prepare meals together. By addressing the challenges and needs of families when it comes to meal planning, the tool has the potential to promote the many benefits associated with family meals, including enhanced vocabulary, academic success, healthy food selections, demonstration of positive values, and avoidance of high-risk behaviors.

5   Conclusion

Despite their importance, family meals have been declining as families face several challenges in planning and executing family meals. This study presents a tool that facilitates the planning part of family meals by considering family preferences and generating a plausible meal plan with corresponding shopping list. The tool provides a platform for family members to vote on their preferred recipes from popular recipe sources and add new recipes to the family recipe bank. The tool has the potential to encourage families to have more frequent family meals and experience the many benefits associated with it.

Acknowledgement. This research was supported by the Slovenian Research Agency (research core grant number P2-0098) and the European Union's Horizon 2020 research and innovation programme (FNS-Cloud, Food Nutrition Security) (grant agreement 863059).

References

1. Boutelle, K.N., Birnbaum, A.S., Lytle, L.A., Murray, D.M., Story, M.: Associations between perceived family meal environment and parent intake of fruit, vegetables, and fat. J. Nutr. Educ. Behav. **35**(1), 24–29 (2003). https://doi.org/10.1016/S1499-4046(06)60323-0. http://www.sciencedirect.com/science/article/pii/S1499404606603230
2. Fruh, S.M., Fulkerson, J.A., Mulekar, M.S., Kendrick, L.A.J., Clanton, C.: The surprising benefits of the family meal. J. Nurse Pract. **7**(1), 18–22 (2011). https://doi.org/10.1016/j.nurpra.2010.04.017. http://www.sciencedirect.com/science/article/pii/S1555415510002503
3. Fulkerson, J.A., Story, M., Mellin, A., Leffert, N., Neumark-Sztainer, D., French, S.A.: Family dinner meal frequency and adolescent development: relationships with developmental assets and high-risk behaviors. J. Adolesc. Health **39**(3), 337–345 (2006). https://doi.org/10.1016/j.jadohealth.2005.12.026. http://www.sciencedirect.com/science/article/pii/S1054139X0500577X
4. Fulkerson, J.A., Story, M., Neumark-Sztainer, D., Rydell, S.: Family meals: perceptions of benefits and challenges among parents of 8- to 10-year-old children. J. Am. Dietet. Assoc. **108**(4), 706–709 (2008). https://doi.org/10.1016/j.jada.2008.01.005. http://www.sciencedirect.com/science/article/pii/S0002822308000060
5. Gross, S.M., Pollock, E.D., Braun, B.: Family influence: key to fruit and vegetable consumption among fourth- and fifth-grade students. J. Nutr. Educ. Behav. **42**(4), 235–241 (2010). https://doi.org/10.1016/j.jneb.2009.05.007. http://www.sciencedirect.com/science/article/pii/S1499404609002474
6. Hanson, A.J., et al.: Cooking and meal planning as predictors of fruit and vegetable intake and BMI in first-year college students. Int. J. Environ. Res. Public Health **16**(14), 2462 (2019)
7. Larson, N., Fulkerson, J., Story, M., Neumark-Sztainer, D.: Shared meals among young adults are associated with better diet quality and predicted by family meal patterns during adolescence. Public Health Nutr. **16**(5), 883–893 (2013). https://doi.org/10.1017/S1368980012003539
8. Warnick, J.L., Stromberg, S.E., Krietsch, K.M., Janicke, D.M.: Family functioning mediates the relationship between child behavior problems and parent feeding practices in youth with overweight or obesity. Transl. Behav. Med. **9**(3), 431–439 (2019). https://doi.org/10.1093/tbm/ibz050

Utilizing Crowdsourced Heuristic Evaluation in the Assessment of User Experience for Online Tools

Maha Faisal$^{(\boxtimes)}$ and Eng.Hadeel AlQouz

Computer Engineering Department, Kuwait University, Kuwait City, Kuwait
{dr.mahafaisal,eng.hadeel}@ku.edu.kw

Abstract. People have the power to participate in and contribute to online content not only by consuming it but through social network platforms. Crowdsourcing has huge benefits due to the increasing potential of connecting and engaging people through social network platforms. Crowdsourcing can be used with heuristic evaluation principles to appraise an online education platform by invoking people to participate in elucidating the success factors for education as well as collaborating on pertinent recommendations.

Keywords: crowdsourcing · heuristic evaluation · education · software evaluation

1 Introduction

Many academic staff use different educational tools, such as the online course system (OCS) using Moodle, along with Piazza and Microsoft Teams, which is the most famous tool. They are used for different levels of education, starting from kindergarten all the way to postgraduate studies. In addition, many companies use it for meetings.

Such tools were shown to be vital during the Covid-19 pandemic. The importance of these tools was recognized previously, but after the years of the pandemic, acknowledgment of their prominence grew. We noticed many difficulties faced by users with different backgrounds, ages, and education degrees. Therefore, we aimed to measure the difficulties that the users of such tools face.

The heuristic evaluation technique is a method for testing usability. It is recommended that heuristic evaluation principles are used by 5 to 8 experts to address user interface problems. These principles can be used with any system or application to shake the design and find out the issues that could face users at any phase of a system.

We applied the heuristic evaluation principles on the OCS, Piazza, and Microsoft Teams, by testing these tools with 144 different users of different ages and with different experiences of computers; approximately 56.3% of them were trained HCI students, who can be considered experts.

© The Author(s), under exclusive license to Springer Nature Switzerland AG 2024
C. Stephanidis et al. (Eds.): HCII 2023, CCIS 1957, pp. 132–137, 2024.
https://doi.org/10.1007/978-3-031-49212-9_18

2 Crowdsourcing

Crowdsourcing—a conjunction of "crowd" and "outsourcing" that was coined by Jeff Howe in a June 2006 *Wired* magazine article—is defined as "the process by which the power of many can be leveraged to accomplish feats that were once the province of a specialized few" (Howe, 2008). Howe (2010) further defined crowdsourcing as "the act of taking a job traditionally performed by a designated agent (usually as an employee) and outsourcing it to a unified, generally large group of people in the form of an open call" [5].

3 Education

Education is a targeted activity destined to allocate knowledge or strengthen essentials and characteristics. Online educational software has certain requirements for students that include the following criteria:

1. The software should provide relevant feedback.
2. Students should be able to create and post material easily.
3. Students should be able to incorporate their choices for assignments and assessment.
4. Discussion protocols should be available so that all students can contribute.
5. The system should provide students with tech support options, such as virtual examples, so that students do not get lost.
6. The system should be designed with the assumption that not all students have the same level of technological ability.
7. Online courses need to be supportive of students' success.
8. The system should have clear content and presentation.
9. In addition, online educators should participate with good presentations.

Educators can be the conduits of knowledge, skills, and values, but they do not have the conceptual tools and skills to design an online learning environment.

Students' experiences with online learning environments are influenced by the design of the environments. To measure good design, usability evaluation metrics can be used. With fast and continually changing online learning environments, optimal usability should be reached. This will optimize the efficiency of the user's task and performance, helping them to complete specific tasks and have the best learning outcomes.

4 Heuristic Evaluation

Difficulties and trouble areas for end users can be understood by establishing and evaluating usability evaluation criteria. These criteria address the user interface and are cost-effective, efficient, and simple to apply. To identify potential usability problems with a user interface, we used a usability checklist in the form of a survey.

The heuristic evaluation principles addressed essential factors that affect students' success during the undergraduate education experience. We tried to make sure that the principles had been used in multiple ways over the years to integrate technology into the classroom or outside the classroom.

Our research analyzed existing online applications to get an excellent perception of applications that reframe problems, resolve conflict requirements, and address the challenge of guaranteeing impact and efficiency through actionable knowledge.

In our survey, we used a usability inspection technique, namely the heuristic evaluation of Jakob Nielsen. It is easy to learn, efficient, and widely used in software development. In addition, it is time- and cost-efficient.

There are 10 usability heuristics for user interface design:

1. Visibility of system status

    The design should always keep users informed about what is going on through appropriate feedback within a reasonable amount of time.

2. Match between system and the real world

    The design should speak the users' language. It should use words, phrases, and concepts familiar to the user, rather than internal jargon, and follow real-world conventions, making information appear in a natural and logical order.

3. User control and freedom.

    Users often perform actions by mistake. They need a clearly marked "emergency exit" to leave the unwanted action without having to go through an extended process.

4. Consistency and standards

    Users should not have to wonder whether different words, situations, or actions mean the same thing. The design should follow platform and industry conventions.

5. Error prevention

    Good error messages are important, but the best designs carefully prevent problems from occurring in the first place. The design should either eliminate error-prone conditions or check for them and present users with a confirmation option before they commit to the action.

6. Recognition rather than recall

    The design should minimize the user's memory load by making elements, actions, and options visible. The user should not have to remember information from one part of the interface to another. The information required to use the design (e.g., field labels or menu items) should be visible or easily retrievable when needed.

7. Flexibility and efficiency of use

    Shortcuts — hidden from novice users — may speed up the interaction for the expert user such that the design can cater to both inexperienced and experienced users. Allow users to tailor frequent actions.

8. Aesthetic and minimalist design

    Interfaces should not contain information which is irrelevant or rarely needed. Every extra unit of information in an interface competes with the relevant units of information and diminishes their relative visibility.

9. Help users recognize, diagnose, and recover from errors

    Error messages should be expressed in plain language (no error codes), precisely indicate the problem, and constructively suggest a solution.

10. Help and documentation

    It's best if the system doesn't need any additional explanation. However, it may be necessary to provide documentation to help users understand how to complete their tasks.

5   Findings

To address the findings, the best strategy to remedy those problems is to violate multiple heuristics at a time.

Usability issues could affect the experience across the web instead of doing a single task. We conducted a survey on 144 students and experts.

Example of heuristic violation presented as follows:

1. Visibility of system status

   The violation of heuristic "Visibility of system status "specifies that the design should always keep users informed about what is going on, through appropriate feedback within a reasonable amount of time. 70.7% didn't agree. That means the users were lost while they were using the application. To remedy this issue, feedback should be present immediately.

2. Match

   The violation of heuristic "Match between the system and the real word" indicates that terms, phrases, and language do not match the terms used by the users daily or arranged in unnatural order.

   The issue that signified on the website that the web site used unfamiliar terms. 43.7% of the users were confused.

   The potential solution for this issue is to work with a group of end users to find familiar and appropriate terms to represent these types of content.

3. User control and freedom

   The user needs a clear way to undo, redo or exit a process to feel the control of his action.

   72.9% face difficulty in getting back out or undoing a task.

   The application should support the undo and redo. In addition to clear labeling of exit.

4. Consistency and standards

   A violation of the heuristic "Consistency and adherence to standards" signifies that the same word, symbol, action, or concept do not refer to the same thing. 90.3% of the users disagree on this point.

   There could be two links within the same text box that are labeled the same, but when the user clicks it, it will lead to different locations within the site.

5. Error prevention

   88.1% of the users found that the application didn't prevent errors from occurring. It needs more effort to prevent the high-cost errors.

6. Recognition rather than recall

   77.8% of the users faced difficulty in retrieving information to complete their task. Since the human has limited short-term memory, the information should be reduced and offer help in context.

7. Flexibility and efficiency of use

   46.5% (experienced users) to 77.1%(normal) of the users didn't find shortcuts to speedup their work.

8. Aesthetics

A violation of the heuristic "aesthetic and minimalism in design" occurs when site dialogue has irrelevant information that is distracting to users, when the page is not minimized, or when display is overly complex.

When a task required an excessive number of pages for the user to search through in order to access information.

94.4% of the users didn't find that the application was focused on the essentials. To solve this issue, remove the unnecessary elements to minimize distractions. Also consolidate all links for the same task in one page.

It could use nested tasks.

9. Help users recognize, diagnose, and recover from errors

90.3% of the users needed help to recover from their errors.

10. Help and documentation

9.2% of the users need additional explanation.

6 Conclusion

In our study, the heuristic evaluation factors were used to evaluate the online learning environment as a methodology.

The potential issues were highlighted through the heuristic evaluation and could be modified to match the user design principles. They could be used as guidelines and frameworks to satisfy the online learning design principle.

In our survey, we found that the feedback should be present immediately so the user will not be lost while using the application.

Work with a group of end users to find familiar and appropriate terms to minimize confusion. The user needs a clear way to undo, redo or exit a process to feel the control of his action.

The application should focus on the essentials by removing the unnecessary elements to minimize distractions. Also, the users need shortcuts to speed up their work.

The information should be reduced and offer help in context to make it more convenient and easily accessible.

In addition, some applications need more effort to prevent high-cost errors. And the users needed help to recover from their errors.

References

1. Molich, R., Nielsen, J.: Improving a human-computer dialogue. Commun. ACM **33**(3), 338–348 (1990)
2. Nielsen, J., Molich, R.: Heuristic evaluation of user interfaces. In: Proceedings of ACM CHI'90 Conference (Seattle, WA, 1–5 April), pp. 249–256 (1990)
3. Nielsen, J.: Enhancing the explanatory power of usability heuristics. In: Proceedings of ACM CHI'94 Conference (Boston, MA, April 24–28), pp. 152–158 (1994a)
4. Nielsen, J.: Heuristic evaluation. In: Nielsen, J., and Mack, R.L. (eds.), Usability Inspection Methods, Wiley, New York (1994b)
5. Dunlap, J., Lowenthal, P.: Online educators' recommendations for teaching online: crowd-sourcing in action. Open Praxis 10(1), 79–89 (2018). ISSN 2304–070X

6. Han, K., Zhang, C., Luo, J.: Taming the uncertainty: budget limited robust crowdsensing through online learning. IEEE/ACM Trans. Networking **24**(3), 1462 (2016)
7. Hildebrand, E.A., Bekki, J.M., Bernstein, B.L., Harrison, C.J.: Online learning environment design: a heuristic evaluation. Am. Soc. Eng. Educ. (2013)
8. Garreta-Domingo, M., Hernández-Leo, D., Sloep, P.B.: Evaluation to support learning design: lessons learned in a teacher training MOOC. Australasian J. Educ. Technol. **34**(2) (2018)
9. Nantongo, P.S.: Framing heuristics in inclusive education: the case of Uganda's preservice teacher education programme. Afr. J. Disabil. **8**(1), 1–10 (2019). ISSN: (Online) 2226–7220, (Print) 2223–9170.
10. Granića, A., Ćukušić, M.: Usability testing and expert inspections complemented by educational evaluation: a case study of an e-learning platform. Educ. Technol. Soc. **14**(2), 107–123 (2011)

Quantifying User Experience Through Self-reporting Questionnaires: A Systematic Analysis of the Sentence Similarity Between the Items of the Measurement Approaches

Stefan Graser$^{(\boxtimes)}$ ⓘ and Stephan Böhm ⓘ

Center for Advanced E-Business Studies (CAEBUS), RheinMain University of Applied Sciences, 65195 Wiesbaden, Hesse, Germany
{stefan.graser,stephan.boehm}@hs-rm.de

Abstract. Standardized questionnaires are a common way to collect self-reported data about users. User experience (UX) questionnaires are metrics with multi-dimensional factors. These factors represent specific UX qualities based on items measuring the user's subjective perception. However, UX questionnaires vary in factor sets, factors names, or measurement items. This study examined 705 items of such factors from 27 popular UX questionnaires. This study aimed to identify the underlying semantic similarity of UX factors on the measurement item level. Augmented SBERT was applied to measure the sentence similarity between the items. Highly similar items were then grouped based on their cosine similarity to identify similarity clusters by the Fast Clustering approach. As a result, 14 similarity clusters could be identified.

Keywords: User Experience (UX) · Usability · UX Factors · UX Questionnaires · UX Measurement · SBERT · cosine similarity · Fast Clustering · t-SNE

1 Introduction

A satisfying user experience (UX) is a critical success factor for all IT-related offerings [1]. UX refers to different aspects of a person's perception of a product, system, or service [2]. Measuring UX is essential to improve IT systems and solutions designs. UX goes beyond the usability defined as "the extent to which a product can be used by specified users to achieve specified goals with effectiveness, efficiency, and satisfaction in a specified context of use" [2]. Usability is a fundamental concept in Human-Computer-Interaction (HCI) and can be seen as an integral component of the UX [3]. So UX and Usability complement each other [3–5]. UX is a multi-dimensional construct evaluating the overall impression of a user interacting with a system covering pragmatic and hedonic qualities [6].

Various empirical methods can be found in scientific literature to measure UX, including objective and subjective methods. Every measurement approach aims to gain high

C. Stephanidis et al. (Eds.): HCII 2023, CCIS 1957, pp. 138–145, 2024.
https://doi.org/10.1007/978-3-031-49212-9_19

qualitative insights based on empirical data. Objective methods gather analytical data, e.g., log files or other system reports. Subjective methods, e.g., questionnaires, focus on evaluating the user's experience through self-reported data, which means that the study subjects give feedback on the survey questions independently. Self-reported data is one of the most important sources of information about users' perceptions. Questionnaires can gather this data quickly, simply, and cost-effectively. Hence, self-reported metrics are popular in Human-Computer Interaction [7, 8].

Self-reported metrics include the usage of standardized questionnaires as summative techniques. Standardized questionnaires are a consistent evaluation method established to cover user-related issues comparably. Typically, these questionnaires break down the construct of UX into different influencing factors intended to reflect different sub-dimensions, perspectives, or qualities of UX. The factors are, in turn, measured by items and scales. The measurement items characterize the user's subjective impression concerning a specific factor.

Existing UX questionnaires differ in the UX factors, items, and scales. Moreover, UX factors with different names can measure the same thing, but factors with the same name can also measure different aspects [4, 5, 9]. However, if questionnaires are based on a shared understanding of UX, the questionnaire approaches of different origins and authors should measure the same. The guiding principle of our study is that common ground among the UX factors can be identified despite different interpretations in detail. If no shared understanding could be identified, the construct of UX would become arbitrary and without substance. Therefore, we move away from the author-specific cat-egorization of UX factors and try to find similar approaches at the level of measurement models. In this regard, the study focuses on the semantic structure of the textual items concerning the most well-established UX questionnaires. Semantic textual similarity analysis can be conducted using Sentence Transformers. By applying the innovative data-augmentation method Augmented SBERT [10] from that field, we computed and visualized the sentence similarity between the items to identify whether different items measure the same or not. Based on the similarity, we applied Fast Clustering to group similar items and visualized the similarity clusters using t-SNE [11–14]. Against this background, we address the following research question:

RQ1: Can a Sentence Similarity approach like Augmented SBERT be used for semantically similar Measurement Items of different UX surveys?

RQ2: How many Similarity Clusters can be identified among the measurement items of popular UX questionnaires, and how can they be interpreted?

This article is structured as follows. Section 2 describes the NLP approach applying the Augmented SBERT method as a data science technique for measuring sentence similarity. The resulting outcomes of the study and derived UX factors are presented in Sect. 3. Finally, the article concludes with a discussion of findings and an outlook on future research in Sect. 4.

2 Approach

For this study, we conducted a machine learning approach by implementing a sentence similarity model to determine how similar the different items of the UX questionnaires are. In general, so-called cross-encoders or bi-encoders can be used to measure sentence similarity. For further details, we refer to the respective literature [10]. Sentence BERT (SBERT) is the most common model for measuring sentence similarity concerning this study's research objective. SBERT, developed by Reimers and Gurevych [15], modifies the original cross-encoder BERT. The model comprises a network architecture that encodes textual input into a vector representation. Each vector is called a sentence embedding. Due to the spatial distance between the embeddings in the vector space, the similarity between the individual vectors can be computed using cosine similarity. The detailed approach of SBERT is discussed in [15].

However, applying Sentence Transformers such as SBERT requires a lot of data. As often in practice and in this study, the data set is rather small. Takhur et al. developed the extended model Augmented SBERT combining cross-encoder and bi-encoder to cope with this situation. In their approach, the researchers used "the cross-encoder to label a larger set of input pairs to augment the training data for the bi-encoder" [10]. Figure 1 shows the simplified approach of Augmented SBERT. In this short paper, we refer to the literature for further details [10].

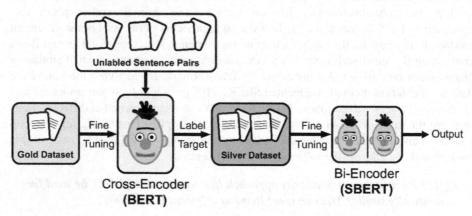

Fig. 1. Augmented SBERT architecture [10].

The study's methodological approach is structured into five steps. In step (1), we analyzed the most established UX questionnaires. UX questionnaires with various focuses have been proposed in the scientific literature over the last decades. In a recent literature survey from 2020, Schrepp identified 40 questionnaires for Usability and UX evaluation [5]. Since our study aims at sentence similarities in the questions of the items, we excluded all questionnaires with a semantic differential scale. After this adjustment, 27 UX questionnaires remained in the scope of our study. All items from these 27 questionnaires were extracted in step (2). In step (3), the Augmented SBERT was applied to a total of 705 extracted items. In particular, we first implemented the source code[1] from the developers [16] and trained the bi-encoder model. We used the model 'all-mpnet-base-v2' for the bi-encoder, providing the best quality among all other models [17]. After training, we applied the trained Augmented SBERT bi-encoder model to the items encoding vector embeddings in a vector space. Lastly, cosine similarity between all vectors was computed, and a similarity matrix was performed [11].

Fast Clustering was applied in step (4) to identify the similarity clusters, i.e., to group similar vectors based on their cosine similarity. This clustering approach is referred by the developers of the Augmented SBERT [11]. Therefore, a scikit-learn and Sentence Transformer libraries were used [18]. The algorithm uses a start vector as a cluster center item. Afterward, the encoded embeddings are analyzed and merged into clusters using a similarity threshold. As the cosine similarity was calculated in step (3), all similarity values of the embeddings range between -1 and 1 whereas 1 refers to the highest similarity. Based on this, the threshold defines the limit above which the different embeddings are classified into a similarity cluster based on their cosine similarity values. The threshold needs to be determined by the researchers. Concerning literature, no benchmark threshold could be found. The threshold depends on the respective dataset. For this study, we adjusted a threshold of 0.60.

In the last step (5), we visualized the identified similarity clusters using t-SNE which is a widespread method in the field of machine learning for exploring and visualizing high-dimensional data in a vector space [13, 14]. The detailed approach is illustrated in Fig. 2.

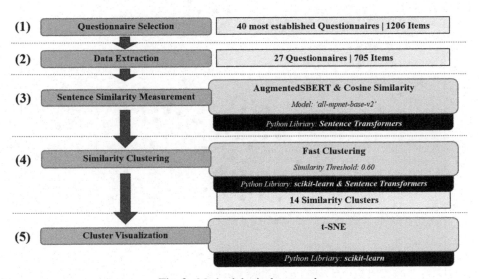

Fig. 2. Methodological approach.

---

3 Results

Data analysis revealed a total of 14 similarity clusters based on a setup with a similarity threshold of 0.60. Figure 3 shows the t-SNE visualization in a 2D vector space. The main purpose of t-SNE is to transform high dimensional into a low-dimensional space. The visualization shows the relative positions of the embeddings to each other in the vector space. The axis values are automatically scaled to achieve the best possible visualization. It can be stated that the clusters are partly overlapping, and no clear distinction is provided. Especially in the center, the concentration of the vectors can be seen. More precious, five similarity clusters can be seen. Moreover, in the upper space, two clusters partially merge into each other. This indicates, that the similarity clusters can not be entirely separated and, thus, the measurement items are partly similar. However, t-SNE only provides a data visualization of the vector space. For further insights, the clusters must be examined more detailed and interpreted.

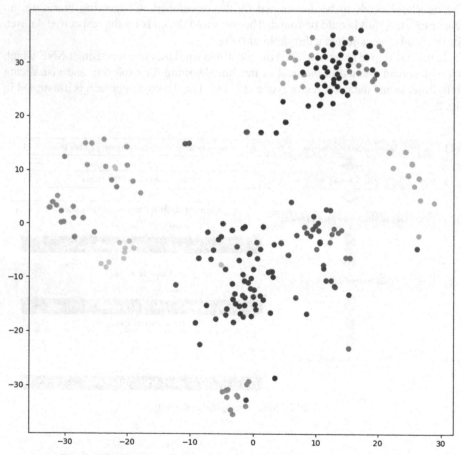

Fig. 3. Visualized similarity clusters using t-SNE in a 2D vector space.

Lastly, the different questionnaire items of the similarity clusters can be investigated to get insights into what the items are measuring. By applying the Fast Clustering approach with a similarity threshold of 0.6, 240 of the 705 items were grouped. The number of items within a cluster ranges between 10 and 52 items. Each cluster consists of a cluster center, represented by a specific item and its corresponding sentence from the UX questionnaire. Table 1 shows the respective center items of the similarity clusters.

Table 1. Similarity clusters.

Cluster	Cluster Center Items	Item Numbers
1	I could quickly get to know the structure of the website by skimming its home page	52
2	From time to time, I use the software to do tasks for which it is not actually intended	40
3	The software makes it easy for me to move between the different menu levels	18
4	Does the system provide the precise information you need?	17
5	The product is creatively designed	16
6	I thought the amount of information displayed on screen was appropriate	12
7	If I had interest in the content of the website in the future, I would consider visiting the website	11
8	The organization of the website was clear	11
9	The software makes my task processing difficult due to inconsistent design	11
10	Is the system user friendly	11
11	This application X was attractive	11
12	Occasionally I use the software in unusual ways to achieve my goal	10
13	The system was not complicated to use	10
14	Are the results of control entry compatible with user expectations?	10

Considering the allocated items, the similarity clusters can be interpreted to identify shared UX factors among the underlying UX questionnaires. The text sentences of the items in a cluster can indicate what the items and their respective factors are measuring. Each resulting cluster needs to be examined to determine if the combined items address a shared UX factor and are suitably represented by the center item. The applied cluster analysis methods are thus only an assisting tool. Further processing requires an interpretation of the authors. For example, cluster 13 contains ten items. These include, for example, *"It is easy to use"*, *"it is simple to use"*, and *"I easily remember how to use it"*. Hence, the items refer to the **Ease of Use** of a system. It might be possible to investigate in further work whether AI-based text processing methods could also be used to summarize further a cluster's items or even to refine the center item question to represent the cluster content better. Due to paper restrictions, this cluster interpretation cannot be completed in this short paper. Further interpretations are the subject of future research.

4 Conclusion

This paper presents a machine learning approach measuring the sentence similarity of 705 items of 27 popular UX questionnaires. The AugmentedSBERT model combining cross-encoders and bi-encoders was applied, and cosine similarity was measured. Based on the similarity, clusters were grouped using Fast Clustering. In the end, the similarity clusters were visualized by applying t-SNE. As a result, 14 similarity clusters could be identified.

The major limitation of this study is the unspecified similarity threshold for Fast Clustering—any adjustment of the threshold results in a change in the number of similarity clusters. Concerning this threshold, evaluation metrics must be considered to provide insights into the quality of the similarity clusters. Based on these metrics, the best-fitting threshold could be determined [19–22].

However, this pre-study provides insights into the textual similarity of the items concerning the UX factors in questionnaires. More research using other Sentence Transformer models and other clustering techniques could be applied to gain insights into UX item similarity clusters. For example, Agglomerative Clustering as a bottom-up approach or BERTopic as a specified Topic Modeling approach concerning sentence similarity [23] could reveal further insights within this research topic.

The clusters and contained items must also be interpreted to derive shared UX factors. Furthermore, the items within a cluster could be traced back to the original UX factors of the respective questionnaire. These UX factors can be matched and consolidated to identify a common ground within the factors of different UX questionnaires. Moreover, based on the shared factors and the corresponding clustered items, a generalized UX questionnaire could be derived as a standardized tool to measure the UX in different application scenarios. This research indicates that further research is required to establish a basis for a common understanding of the UX factors.

References

1. Rauschenberger, M., Schrepp, M., Cota Pérez, M., Olschner, S., Thomaschewski, J.: Efficient measurement of the user experience of interactive products. How to use the user experience questionnaire (UEQ) (2013)
2. DIN EN ISO 9241–210.: Ergonomics of human-system interaction – part 210: human-centred design for interactive systems (2010)
3. Hassan, H.M., Galal-Edeen, G.H.: From usability to user experience. In: International Conference on Intelligent Informatics and Biomedical Sciences (ICIIBMS), pp. 216–222. IEEE (2017)
4. Hinderks, A., Winter, D., Schrepp, M., Thomaschewski, J.: Applicability of user experience and usability questionnaires. J. Univ. Comput. Sci. 25(13), 1717–1735 (2019)
5. Schrepp, M.: A comparison of UX questionnaires – what is their underlying concept of user experience?. In: Mensch und Computer 2020 Workshopband (2020)

6. Santoso, H.B., Schrepp, M.: The impact of culture and product on the subjective importance of user experience aspects. Helion **5**, 1–12 (2019)
7. Assila, A., Oliveira, K., Ezzedine, H.: Standardized usability questionnaires: features and quality focus. Comput. Sci. Inf. Technol. **6**(1), 15–31 (2016)
8. Albert, B., Tullis, T.: Measuring the user experience: Collecting, analyzing, and presenting UX metrics. Morgan Kaufmann, Burlington (2022)
9. Schrepp, M., et al.: On the importance of UX quality aspects for different product categories. Int. J. Interact. Multimedia Artif. Intell. (2023)
10. Thakur, N., Reimers, N., Daxenberger, J., Gurevych, I.: Augmented SBERT: Data Augmentation Method for Improving Bi-Encoders for Pairwise Sentence Scoring Tasks. ArXiv, abs/2010.08240. (2020)
11. Manning, C.D., Raghavan, P., Schütze, H.: Introduction to Information Retrieval. Cambridge University Press, Cambridge (2008)
12. Reimers, N.: Clustering (2022). https://www.sbert.net/examples/applications/clustering/REA DME.html#fast-clustering. Accessed 05 2023
13. Maaten, L.V.D., Hinton, G.: Visualizing data using t-SNE. J. Mach. Learn. Res. **9**, 2579–2605 (2008)
14. Wattenberg, M., Viégas, F., Johnson, I.: How to use t-SNE Effectivley, Distill (2016)
15. Reimers, N., Gurevych, I.: Sentence-BERT: sentence embeddings using Siamese BERT-networks. In: Conference on Empirical Methods in Natural Language Processing (2019)
16. Reimers, N.: Augmented SBERT (2022). https://www.sbert.net/examples/training/data_a ugmentation/README.html. Accessed 05 2023
17. Reimers, N.: Pretrained models (2022). https://www.sbert.net/docs/pretrained_models.html# sentence-embedding-models. Accessed 05 2023
18. Pedregosa, F., et al.: Scikit-learn: machine learning in python. J. Mach. Learn. Res. **12**(85), 2825–2830 (2011)
19. Allwrigth, S.: Which are the best clustering metrics? (explained simply) (2022). https://ste phenallwright.com/good-clustering-metrics/. Accessed June 2023
20. Rousseeuw, P.J.: Silhouettes: a graphical aid to the interpretation and validation of cluster analysis. Comput. Appl. Math. **20**, 53–65 (1987)
21. Calinski, T., Harabasz, J.: A dendrite method for cluster analysis. Commun. Stat. (1974)
22. Davies, D.L., Bouldin, D.W.: A cluster separation measure. IEEE Trans. Pattern Anal. Mach. Intell. **PAMI-1**(2), 224–227 (1979)
23. Grootendorst, M.R.: BERTopic: Neural topic modeling with a class-based TF-IDF procedure. ArXiv, abs/2203.05794. (2022)

Design and Development of a Deep Learning-Based Sign Language Learning Aid for Deaf Teenagers

Wenchen Guo(✉), Jingwen Bai(✉), Hongbo Li, Kuo Hsiang Chang, and Jie Xu

Peking University, Beijing, China
beihuanfanchen@sina.com, baijingwen@pku.edu.cn

Abstract. In this paper, we developed HearUsNow, a deep learning-based system designed to assist deaf teenagers in correcting speech order and learning sign language, thereby improving their communication skills. This interactive system incorporates a deep learning-based back-end with a user-friendly front-end interface, aiming to bridge the gap between these individuals and their real-world communication needs. In this system, deaf teenagers receive corrections on sentence structure and accompanying sign language instructional images after entering sentences, and sign language practice is facilitated through a camera interface that provides real-time feedback. The results of a pilot study (n = 6) showed high usability, interaction fluency, and accuracy of correction and recognition of the interactive system. Over a seven-day period, the participants mastered more than 30 gesture combinations for everyday communication, and parents noted improved self-confidence and parent-child relationships.

Keywords: Accessibility · Deaf Teenagers · Sign Language Learning · HCI

1 Introduction

Communication is fundamental to human interaction, shaping our connections and experiences in the world. However, for around 300 million people globally who are deaf and one million who are mute, as reported by the World Health Organization, communication becomes a significant challenge. Unlike many other physical disabilities, the vulnerability of these individuals is reflected in the loss of function of their expressive organs, compelling them to rely on body language and facial expressions to connect with the external world [1]. Sign language has emerged as the primary communication method for deaf individuals, fostering a more seamless dialogue and enabling participation in social activities beyond their immediate circles.

It increases the ease of communication for deaf people and allows them to participate in social life beyond their internal group. Research has shown that teenager is a crucial period for learning sign language, but due to regional differences in the level of educational development (concepts, methods, technology, teachers, etc.) and other factors,

---

W. Guo and J. Bai—Co-first authors of this poster.

C. Stephanidis et al. (Eds.): HCII 2023, CCIS 1957, pp. 146–150, 2024.
https://doi.org/10.1007/978-3-031-49212-9_20

teenagers in many developing countries are faced with an unpromising environment for learning sign language [2].

Unfortunately, numerous obstacles impede the acquisition of sign language, especially during the teenage years, a critical period for language learning. In many developing countries, variations in educational development levels, encompassing pedagogical concepts, methods, technology, and the quality of teachers, create an unfavorable environment for learning sign language. Moreover, a considerable number of learners fail to develop complete linguistic logic due to their impaired listening and speech perception abilities, thus struggling to express ideas accurately and precisely [3]. Many deaf teenagers feel the pain of not being able to express their emotions and inner thoughts, which often come to a screeching halt along with their voices, especially when they are at a crucial time in their mental and psychological development [4].

Key innovation points in the system are as follows: 1) a text correction feature tailored for the deaf population that visualizes corrected text in sign language, 2) a camera interface for users to assess their sign language skills, and 3) plans for scenario-based learning content to increase engagement. Ultimately, the system aims to contribute to the well-being of deaf people, particularly in less developed areas.

2 Methods and Implementation

Recognizing the potential of recent developments in artificial intelligence and human-computer interaction technologies to address these challenges, our team developed HearUsNow, a system that uses natural language processing and computer vision to facilitate sign language learning for deaf teenagers. Because the sign language of deaf people is different from the spoken language of normal people. With the dual mission of correcting speech order and improving sign language skills, HearUsNow aims to bridge the communication gap between these young people and the world around them.

HearUsNow is a comprehensive system based on state-of-the-art technology. At its core, it consists of two components: a deep learning back-end and a front-end user interface.

The back-end is the heart of the system. It uses MacBERT a BERT-based model to interpret and correct speech order, providing a vital support tool for deaf young people who struggle with this aspect of communication. BERT is an NLP pre-training method proposed by Google in 2018, known as "the strongest NLP model". BERT, which stands for Bidirectional Encoder Representations from Transformers, pre-trains a bidirectional encoder by using the context in all layers. In terms of model architecture, BERT provides a unified structure for solving different downstream tasks. When fine-tuning specific tasks, it is only necessary to add some additional output layers on top of the original structure [6]. MacBERT is a chinese pre-trained language model which improves upon RoBERTa in several ways, especially the masking strategy that adopts MLM as correction (Mac) and could achieve state-of-the-art performances on many NLP tasks [7].

The algorithms work by parsing the input text, identifying potential errors in structure and order, and then offering corrections. This process is enhanced by the use of natural language processing. By incorporating semantic understanding capabilities, HearUsNow not only corrects grammar and syntax, but can also understand the intended meaning behind sentences, ensuring that corrections still convey the same overall message.

To further enhance its capabilities, HearUsNow's back-end also uses computer vision. It uses this technology to visualize text in sign language, allowing users to see and learn how corrected sentences are expressed in sign language [8].

Complementing the technological prowess of the back-end, HearUsNow's front-end provides a seamless and user-friendly interface. The design is minimalist, in keeping with the aesthetic sensibilities of teenagers and ensuring ease of use. The main colour scheme features shades of plant green, a deliberate choice to create a visually pleasing and calming effect. This soothing palette, combined with an intuitive layout, helps to reduce potential learning stress and promotes a more enjoyable learning experience.

Understanding the importance of accessibility in today's fast-paced world, HearUs-Now has been optimized for mobile use. Users can access the system via their smartphone, allowing them to learn and practice anytime, anywhere. This feature greatly expands the potential reach and impact of HearUsNow, as users are not tied to location or access to a desktop computer (Fig. 1).

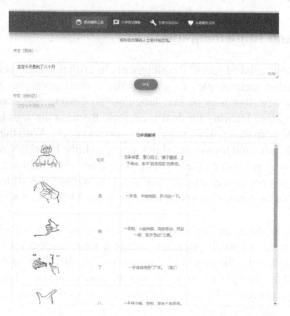

Fig. 1. User interface and a running example

A sample scenario demonstrating the functionality of the system involves Alice, a deaf teenager who faces challenges with word order and sign language learning. Alice enters her intended sentence into HearUsNow's user-friendly interface. The deep learning back-end then springs into action, providing a corrected version of the sentence and corresponding instructional images in sign language. Alice can then turn on the camera on her mobile phone or computer to practise the sign language expressions. HearUsNow, equipped with real-time feedback technology, assists her in this process, providing prompts and comments to help her refine her skills. The system's ability to provide immediate, personalized feedback underscores its practical utility and potential to revolutionize sign language education (Fig. 2).

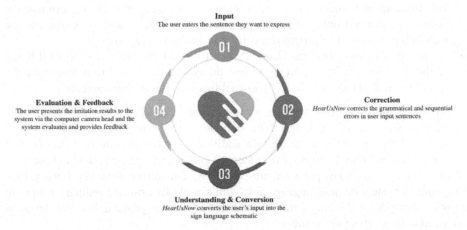

Fig. 2. User workflow of the system

3 Pilot Study

A pilot study conducted with six deaf teenagers demonstrated HearUsNow's ease of use, smooth interaction and accurate correction and recognition capabilities. During a seven-day trial period, the participants mastered over 30 combinations of everyday communication gestures. More importantly, the system significantly increased their confidence and enthusiasm for learning, as evidenced by interviews with their parents. HearUsNow also served to improve parent-child communication, fostering a stronger bond during the learning process.

4 Conclusion

HearUsNow's innovations include a customized text correction feature for the deaf population, a camera interface for real-time learning feedback, and future enhancements to include scenario-based learning content. These features overcome the limitations of existing API services, increase learning efficiency and motivation, and provide a more engaging learning experience.

In summary, the Innovation and Main Contributions of our work are as follows:

- The system breaks the limitations of existing API services for the correction of utterances of special groups by building a text correction function specifically for the deaf population and visualizing the corrected text in sign language.

- The system uses a camera to allow users to view their learning results and make accurate judgments and assessments of their sign language input, thereby increasing the efficiency and motivation of their learning.
- In the future, we will continue to improve the system by adding scenario-based learning content to make it more interesting and engaging. We also believe that the system, as an open online platform, will also contribute to and work towards the well-being of more deaf groups (especially in less developed areas).
- As an open online platform, HearUsNow strives to contribute to the well-being of the deaf community, especially in less developed areas, and to demonstrate the transformative power of technology in enabling accessible communication.

However, after practical operation, we found that the image display of sign language translation is far less effective than dynamic video. From this perspective, there is still room for improvement in our project. In addition, how to integrate gamification and scenario elements into the interactive system to enhance the participation and pleasure of deaf youth is also a key point for subsequent system enhancement [9]. Finally, how to connect or integrate deaf language aids with social platforms for ordinary people to provide strength for the long-term development of deaf language aids is the direction we need to think about in the future.

References

1. Aran, O., et al.: Signtutor: an interactive system for sign language tutoring. IEEE Multimedia **16**, 81–93 (2009)
2. Hein, Z., Htoo, T.P., Aye, B., Htet, S.M., Ye, K.Z.: Leap motion based myanmar sign language recognition using machine learning. In: 2021 IEEE Conference of Russian Young Researchers in Electrical and Electronic Engineering (ElConRus), pp. 2304–2310. IEEE (2021)
3. Rastogi, R., Mittal, S., Agarwal, S.: A novel approach for communication among blind, deaf and dumb people. In: 2015 2nd International Conference on Computing for Sustainable Global Development (INDIACom), pp. 605–610. IEEE (2015)
4. Marschark, M., Spencer, P.E.: The Oxford Handbook of Deaf Studies, Language, and Education, vol. 2. Oxford University Press, Oxford (2010)
5. Sultan, A., Makram, W., Kayed, M., Ali, A.A.: Sign language identification and recognition: a comparative study. Open Comput. Sci. **12**, 191–210 (2022)
6. Devlin, J., Chang, M.-W., Lee, K., Toutanova, K.: Bert: pre-training of deep bidirectional transformers for language understanding. arXiv preprint arXiv:1810.04805. (2018)
7. Cui, Y., Che, W., Liu, T., Qin, B., Wang, S., Hu, G.: Revisiting pre-trained models for Chinese natural language processing. arXiv preprint arXiv:2004.13922. (2020)
8. Rastgoo, R., Kiani, K., Escalera, S.: Sign language recognition: a deep survey. Expert Syst. Appl. **164**, 113794 (2021)
9. Guo, W., Li, S., Zhang, Z., Chen, Z., Chang, K.H., Wang, S.: A "magic world" for children: design and development of a serious game to improve spatial ability. Comput. Anim. Virtual Worlds **34**(3), e2181 (2023)

FUNgi: An Interactive Toy Designed for Young Children Based on e-Textile Material

Xinyi Guo and Qiong Wu(⊠)

Tsinghua University, Beijing, People's Republic of China
guo-xy22@mails.tsinghua.edu.cn, qiong-wu@tsinghua.edu.cn

Abstract. Electronic toys are almost necessary in young child's childhood as a companion. However, more and more electronic toys in the market can provide a richer sensory experience for children but still not soft and skin-friendly enough, and allow limited ways for children to interact with them. Eletronic textile, as a new type of intelligent material, has both characteristics of traditional fabric and the ability of communication. In this research, we want to create a soft toy with eletronic textiles. We focus on the textile characteristic of e-textiles, and utilize different colors and textures of them to guide children play naturally with their full body and obtain organic and synesthetic feedback. The research provides an alternative solution to improve the common hard shell electronic toys for young children, and extend the interactive modes of e-textiles.

Keywords: Interface for Children · Electronic Textiles · Tangible Interaction · Soft User Interface · Multisensory Design

1 Introduction

Early childhood education toys have become a necessity for the majority of parenting families. Good toys can cultivate young children's sensory, cognitive and motor systems. Various types of electronic toys have emerged in recent years, providing children with richer experiences to some extent, but also have problems such as homogeneous interaction patterns, excessive stimulation, and using hard shells. As a new type of smart material, electronic textiles have the potential to develop electronic toys which provide a multi-sensory experience. It is not only soft and skin-friendly, but can also be used as an information carrier for more functional extensions, creating rich synesthesia experiences for children to support their sensory development.

Most interactions with electronic toys on the market are triggered by pushing buttons or other controllers. Children's interactions are limited, and seldom do electronic toys allow interaction with children's whole bodies [1]. This paper explores ways in which young children interact with e-textile toys in multiple postures, and how they get emotional multi-sensory experiences during the process, which is of innovative significance and value.

C. Stephanidis et al. (Eds.): HCII 2023, CCIS 1957, pp. 151–158, 2024.
https://doi.org/10.1007/978-3-031-49212-9_21

2 Tactile Interaction Based on e-Textile

2.1 The Development and Application of e-Textile

Electronic textiles (or e-textiles), also referred to as intelligent fabrics, emerged in the 1990s that integrate actuators, and digital components seamlessly into traditional textile substrates, thus creating a novel computational platform. E-Textiles possess wearable and aesthetically flexible properties while also enabling environmental monitoring, computing tasks, and wireless communication capabilities [2].They find extensive applications in healthcare, personal protection, flexible sensing, and intelligent clothing [3–5].

The basic materials of e-textiles include conductive fibers, intelligent fibers, and conductive polymers. In contrast to previous intelligent garments, which affixed miniature sensors onto inner fabric layers or concealed cables within the fabric, current e-textiles integrate sensors and wires into fabrics by incorporating conductive yarns during the weaving process to achieve diverse sensing functions [6].

2.2 Tactile Interaction Interface Based on e-Textile

The tactile experience of fabric is the user's perception of its tactile properties, shaping their overall emotional response toward fabrics. Before touching the fabric, users predict the tactile feedback based on their previous life experiences, forming an expectation of the fabric, which is known as the expectancy effect [7]. Visual information precedes tactile sensation, generating psychological expectations that subsequently impact interactive experience. Consistency between visual and tactile stimuli evokes a comfort, security, and synesthetic experience, which foster users' repeated touch interactions.

The tactile interaction of e-textiles represents a form of tangible interaction. Many tangible interactions are built upon the act of pressing, while e-textiles possess a soft texture and excellent deformability because of their textile characteristics, supporting various interaction modes such as stretching, folding, squeezing, flipping, twisting, and penetrating.

3 Design of an Interactive Toy for Young Children Based on e-Textile

3.1 Design Target and User Research

The aim of this study is to create an interactive toy device for young children, based on e-textile materials, which enables full-body interaction and provides diverse sound feedback. All feedback is triggered by the electronic fabric, without buttons or sensors. The form, texture, and color of the fabric encourage children to explore naturally based on their instinct and experience. Simultaneously, children's tactile and auditory senses are stimulated, providing them with a synesthetic experience.

The target users for this toy are defined as children aged 1 to 2 years. By the age of 1, children already demonstrate the ability to sit upright independently, and also to stand and walk with the assistance of their parents. Their physical development allows for diverse interactive postures, while their visual development enables a recognition of various colors, accompanied by a strong desire for exploration.

Color Recognition and Preference of Young Children. Visual perception is the primary way for children to acquire external information. Children aged 0–3 years are in the period of color enlightenment, lacking distinct color preferences but being attracted to vibrant and stimulating primary colors like red and yellow. It is beneficial to expose children to bright, warm colors. However, the color variety should be limited, with clear segmentations between color blocks, creating a stronger visual impact to capture their attention and interest.

Characteristics of Tactile Perception of Young Children. Tactile sense is the earliest and most widespread sensory system in the human body [8]. Children are driven by curiosity to interact with unfamiliar objects using their hands to explore the temperature, texture, and quality of surrounding objects. Children aged 0–3 years have highly sensitive skin receptors. Children at seven months can actively explore and touch their surroundings, displaying excitement when encountering preferred objects. By the ages of 2–3, children demonstrate improved control and coordination in lifting, gripping, and manipulating objects, engaging in repetitive behaviors such as observing, touching, and shaking.

Characteristics of Auditory Perception of Young Children. Young children aged 0–3 years already possess the ability to distinguish sound volume, source, timing, direction, and frequency. Different sounds elicit various emotional responses from children. Children show preferences for beloved melodies, while becoming annoyed by loud and noisy sounds. By the age of 9 months, children demonstrate an interest in various external sounds and try to locate their sources. They become delighted upon hearing rhythmic sounds or music, prompting them to move their bodies and limbs. It is benefitial to expose them to various kinds of sounds.

3.2 Appearance Design

The design of the toy's form takes into account the ergonomic dimensions, interactivity, aesthetics, and stability. During early childhood, children can already differentiate simple geometric shapes and begin to develop abstract thinking. Therefore, the toy's form is appropriately shaped with and biomimetic elements, taking on an open structure that closely resembles a tree stump. The soft, stretchable characteristics of the e-textile material can effectively shape organic forms. The interactive components resemble moss and fungi in the jungle, clinging to the surface of the toy with vibrant, lively, and warm colors (see Fig. 1).

The toy employs both knitting and weaving techniques which offer versatility in creating diverse textures and tactile sensations. Yarns of similar colors are combined into different thicknesses to create multi-ply yarns for weaving. From a distance, the woven pieces exhibit harmonized colors, while up close, the colors appear delicate, rich, and varied.

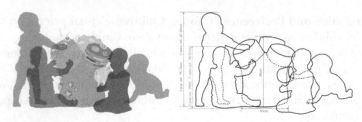

Fig. 1. Sketches of the toy's form design.

3.3 Interaction Design

The Toy's Modeling Semantic Guides Children's Natural Interactive Behavior. By providing accurate form information, a toy guides children in its proper usage, conveying its intended functionality. Therefore, the shape of interactive components on the toy should align with children's cognition in their daily lives to reduce the learning effort. For instance, young children are inclined to insert their fingers into hollow openings, press on raised hemispheres, and stroke plush fabric surfaces.

The Toy Incorporates Seven Interactive Zones with Varying Heights and Shapes. The interactive zones are designed according to their respective semantic meanings. They offer young children multiple possibilities for interactive engagement, and appropriate sound mappings are selected to provide synesthetic feedback based on the tactile sensation and interaction mode of each zone. The following Table 1 gives a summary of all interactive zones.

4   Implementation

4.1   Experiments and Implementation of e-Textile

Selection of Conductive Yarn. The performance of e-textiles largely depends on the material composition and textile structure of conductive yarns. In this study, several common types of conductive yarns were compared by reviewing relevant literature, focusing on their resistance variations concerning stretching length.

Conductive yarns used in textiles can be classified into metallic conductive yarns, carbon-based conductive yarns, and composite conductive yarns. Metallic conductive yarns offer good conductivity but have low tensile strength, leading to potential breakage and deformation. Carbon-based conductive yarns provide high stability but lack flexibility. Composite conductive yarns, such as silver-plated yarns, are soft, durable, and exhibit significant changes in resistance with stretching, making them suitable for sewing threads in smart textiles. Therefore, our toy incorporates a blend of silver-plated yarn and baby yarn (see Fig. 2).

Blending Experiments and Technical Implement. This toy employs two types of interaction sensing: capacitive sensing (touch-based interaction) and resistive sensing (stretch-based interaction). Several tests were conducted, focusing on the relatively typical stirring units and stretching units.

Table 1. Seven Interactive Zones

Zone	Shape and Texture	Interaction and Feedback	Picture
Tapping Area	Plump round bulges with a diameter of around 5cm, deisgned to fit in the hands of target children. The surface of each bulge is adorned with crochet floral motifs.	Units are distributed on the top surfaces of the toy. Children tap and press them with their hands in a standing position, eliciting bongo hitting sounds from the toy.	
Kicking Area	Plump round bulges with lace trim, around 6cm in diameter, designed to fit in the feet of target children. The surface is smooth and adorned with small bulges.	When in a seated position, children can kick and strike the bulges with their feet. The toy will produce resonant sounds like bass drums.	
Stirring Area	Composed of green bowl-shaped units. The opening of the units guide children to explore out of curiosity by inserting their fingers into it.	Units are scattered at the lower part of the toy. When seated, children insert their fingers into these units, and the toy produces rustling sounds.	
Squeezing Area	The raised pieces resemble mushroom caps growing on tree trunks. The units have a soft and delicate texture, filled with a small amount of cotton.	Children can squeeze them in a standing postion. The toy will produce sounds akin to squeezing toys.	
Stretching Area	The elongated droplet-shaped small balls are suspended for graspping. The small balls have a firm touch. The elongated part is softer with strong elasticity.	Children use fingers to pull the small balls downward. The toy will produce string instrument sounds depending on the extent of stretching.	
Stroking Area	Woven with yarn of varying thickness, having a plush texture and curved surface. Children can embrace it with both hands in a seated position.	When children stroke the area, the toy emits a vague, gentle, and soothing white noise.	
Sliding Area	Strips with different color and lengthwise are like strings on an instrument. The raised strips with the smooth base fabric provide a strong contrast in texture and a tactile experience.	Children slide or flick their fingers along the strips. Different strips will produce distinct chord-like string sounds.	

Fig. 2. Silver-plated yarn and fabric pieces woven with both conductive yarn and baby yarn.

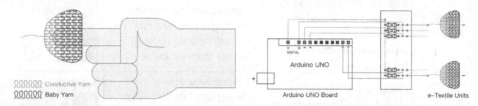

Fig. 3. Silver-plated yarn and fabric pieces woven with both conductive yarn and baby yarn.

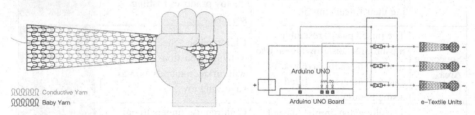

Fig. 4. Silver-plated yarn and fabric pieces woven with both conductive yarn and baby yarn.

Touch-Based Interaction (Capacitive Sensing). In this experiment, conductive yarn is woven with baby yarn to create a unit where the inner part is conductive while the rest remains insulated (see Fig. 3). By measuring changes in capacitance between digital pin 12 and other digital pins on an Arduino UNO board, the feedback is only triggered when a finger touches the conductive part. This principle applies to other touch-based areas such as kicking, tapping, stroking, and sliding areas.

Stretch-Based Interaction (Resistive Sensing). In this experiment, the unit is woven using a long stitching technique to provide more elasticity (see Fig. 4). When the unit is stretched, increased contact points between the conductive yarn result in reduced resistance [9]. By measuring voltage division using an analog pin on an Arduino UNO board, children can control input and obtain corresponding feedback.

4.2 Final Product

The texture of e-textiles largely depends on the knitting technique and the thickness of the yarn. To achieve a soft curved shape and fill adequate cotton inside, the fabric is made thick, and the stitches dense. Additionally, to enhance the tactile experience for children, a variety of yarns with different thicknesses, ranging from a maximum of 9 strands to a minimum of 3 strands, are blended. Different knitting techniques are employed to create fabric with varying roughness and elasticity. We integrate the circuit, filled the toy with PP cotton, and sew them together. The final product is shown in Fig. 5.

Fig. 5. Display effect of toy "FUNgi".

5   Conclusion

The objective of this research is to explore the cognitive, sensory, and behavioral aspects of young children, as well as the application of e-textiles to create multi-sensory toys for this age group. This paper proposes an alternative solution to the commonly used hard-shell electronic toys, offering gentler and more organic feedback, and supporting the sensory and motor development of young children. Additionally, this paper emphasizes the fabric and emotional characteristics of e-textiles. Based on functionality, designers can control the texture, shape, and pattern of e-textiles to facilitate natural interaction and emotional experiences for young children. This represents a novel exploration of expanding the application domain of electronic textiles.

Acknowledgement. This research is supported by "Dual High" Project of Tsinghua Humanity Development (No. 2021TSG08203).

References

1. Berzowska, J., Mommersteeg, A., Rosero Grueso, L.I., Ducray, E., Rabo, M.P., Moisan, G.: Baby Tango: electronic textile toys for full-body interaction. In: Proceedings of the Thirteenth International Conference on Tangible, Embedded, and Embodied Interaction, pp. 437–442 (2019)
2. Zheng, N., Wu, Z., Lin, M., Yang, T., Cheng, W.: A survey on electronic textiles. Chin. J. Comput. **34**(07), 1172–1187 (2011)
3. Luo, Y., Wu, K., Palacios, T., Matusik, W.: KnitUI: fabricating interactive and sensing textiles with machine knitting. In: Proceedings of the 2021 CHI Conference on Human Factors in Computing Systems, pp. 1–12 (2021)
4. Honauer, M., Moorthy, P., Hornecker, E.: Interactive soft toys for infants and toddlers-design recommendations for age-appropriate play. In: Proceedings of the Annual Symposium on Computer-Human Interaction in Play, pp. 265–276 (2019)
5. Li, L., Au, W., Li, Y., Wan, K., Wan, S., Wong, K.: A novel design method for an intelligent clothing based on garment design and knitting technology. Text. Res. J. **79**(3), 1670–1679 (2009)
6. Chen, D.: Smart fabrics and clothing: the second skin of human beings. Design **255**(24), 72–75 (2016)
7. Zeng, D., Zhou, Z., Cheng, H., Li, K., Qiu, S.: Tactile experience in product design. Packag. Eng. **42**(02), 134–141 (2020)
8. Zhang, B., Li, J.: Design of the infants' toy based on the development of tactile. Packag. Eng. **33**(10), 65–69 (2012)
9. Ou, J., Oran, D., Haddad, D., Paradiso, J., Ishii, H.: SensorKnit: architecting textile sensors with machine knitting. 3S Printing Addit. Manuf. **6**(1), 1–11 (2019)

Proposal of a Home Aquarium Using Change Viewpoints

Youngjun Lee(✉) ⓘ and Namgyu Kang ⓘ

Future University Hakodate, 116-2 Kamedanakanocho, Hakodate, Hokkaido 041-8655, Japan
g2122010@fun.ac.jp

Abstract. The aquarium market is growing and becoming popular. Many aquariums and zoos attempt to satisfy the visitors' new experiences based on considering the characteristics of each animal and fish. For example, the Asahiyama Zoo has designed a water tank to allow visitors to see seals moving up and down and penguins swimming like flying in the sky. We focused on a home aquarium in this research. Because there are only a few studies aimed at enjoying a home aquarium. When we enjoy a home aquarium, the existing one-sided viewpoint method of seeing the inside of the aquarium from the outside of it has a blind spot and cannot be seen. That means the one-sided viewpoint method from outside limits the various information inside the aquarium. Therefore, we experimented with the effect of changing viewpoints when we see a home aquarium. In the experiment, participants saw the movie recorded inside a home aquarium with four different viewpoints. One existing viewing point and three new viewpoints. Next, they evaluated these four movies using the SD method. After that, we conducted Factor Analysis using the evaluated results of the SD method. As a result, we extracted the following three factors: 1) Novelty factor, 2) Dynamism factor, and 3) Unity factor. However, the factor scores differed depending on the home aquarium's viewpoints. That means we feel these three impressions when we see the home aquarium. Based on the results, we created a new device for a home aquarium with the keyword 'changing viewpoints.'

Keywords: Home aquarium · Kansei evaluation · Viewpoints

1 Introduction

The ornamental fish market is growing at 7–8% annually, and aquariums are becoming popular for viewing aquatic life in aquariums and zoos and at home [1]. Large-scale aquariums are diversifying the shapes of tanks and exhibition techniques, considering the aquarium's characteristics and the audience's flow lines. Many attempts are to provide new experiences for the audience [2]. For example, Asahiyama Zoo has devised a cylindrical tank so that visitors can see the habits of seals that move up and down (see Fig. 1) and a "behavioral exhibition" [3, 4] that allows visitors to view the ecology of penguins that swim as if flying underwater from various visitor viewpoints, which is contributed significantly to the rapid increase in visitors.

© The Author(s), under exclusive license to Springer Nature Switzerland AG 2024
C. Stephanidis et al. (Eds.): HCII 2023, CCIS 1957, pp. 159–166, 2024.
https://doi.org/10.1007/978-3-031-49212-9_22

Fig. 1. Cylinder tank at Asahiyama Zoo

As shown in the above examples, aquariums and zoos have attempted various methods to satisfy viewers by focusing on the visual experience through aquariums. On the other hand, most of the previous studies on home aquariums focused on ornamental fish, rather than on the aquarium itself.

In the case of a study [5], in which the status of fish was informed by a speech bubble on a display at the back of the aquarium, the fish were intuitively shown and the fish-keepers were guided to observe them. In the case of the study on interaction with fish using bubbles [6], users became interested in fish by subjectively interpreting their reactions. The reality is that there is no research on interaction that focuses on the visual experience of home aquarium viewers in this way.

Against this background, the authors conducted a previous study and proposed "change of viewpoint" as a new way to appreciate home aquariums. Unlike pictures or moving images, aquariums are three-dimensional objects, and changes in the angle and position of the viewpoint from which the aquarium is observed will change the image of the aquarium that is projected to the viewer. Therefore, it is thought that the viewer can obtain more diverse visual experiences through the new viewing method.

To clarify the effect of the new viewing method, an evaluation experiment was conducted. The aquarium was photographed from four viewpoints, including three new viewpoints such as inside the tank and a conventional viewpoint, and the impression of the aquarium was evaluated using the SD method. Then, "novelty factor," "dynamism factor," and "Unity factor" were extracted by factor analysis, and created a graph based on the mean and significant difference of the factor scores for each viewpoint (Figs. 2, 3, 4 and 5).

Fig. 2. Examples from each of the perspectives taken.

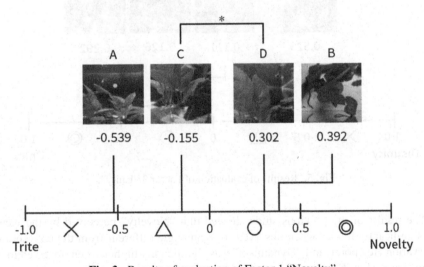

Fig. 3. Results of evaluation of Factor 1 "Novelty".

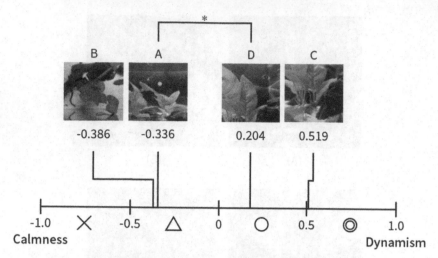

Fig. 4. Results of evaluation of Factor 2 "dynamism".

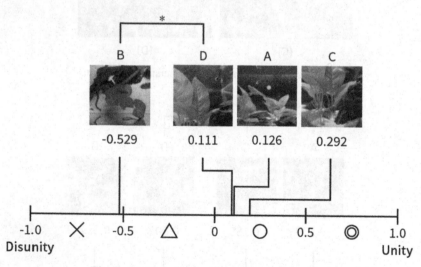

Fig. 5. Results of evaluation of Factor 3 "Unity".

The results of the previous study showed that "Novelty" perceived by the viewer was significantly higher when observed from an angle different from the conventional observation viewpoint, and "Dynamism" was significantly higher when observed inside the aquarium (Fig. 6).

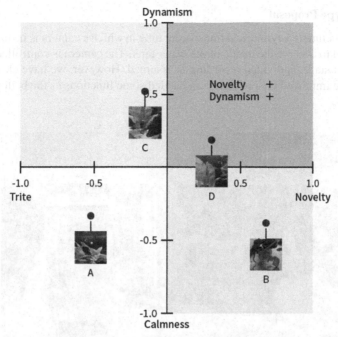

Fig. 6. Factor Rating Distribution Chart

2   Purpose of the Study

Through previous studies, we have visualized the effects of new viewing methods on viewers' impressions. However, installing a camera inside the aquarium to change the viewpoint of observation is complicated. In other words, it is not easy for a home aquarium viewer to experience a new viewing method under general circumstances. Therefore, this study aims to devise an interaction and create a device for the new viewing method, which has been proven effective through previous studies. Therefore, it can be easily applied to aquariums in general situations.

3   Device Proposal

3.1   Concept of the Device

We established the device concept based on the evaluation experiments conducted in the previous study. The two main concepts of the device were "changing the observation viewpoint inside the tank" and "changing the angle of the observation viewpoint. The device should not be shaped to harm the fish to minimize the impact on the organisms, nor should it significantly change the water flow.

3.2 Prototype Proposal

The basic structure is a cylindrical transparent tube in which a camera is installed, which can be moved to observe the inside of the water tank. The camera is controlled manually at the present stage, and video recording is assumed. However, we have checked some problems and improved the problems, and added some functions as the better prototype (Fig. 7).

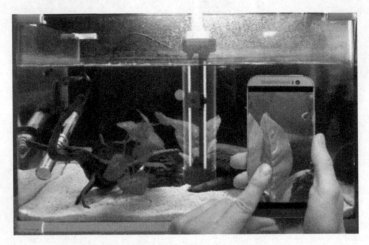

Fig. 7. Conceptual image of prototype

3.3 Prototype Creation

The prototype was made of transparent acrylic and aluminum pipes, and other necessary parts were printed by a 3D printer and the acrylic was cut by a laser cutting machine. The diameter of the acrylic pipe, which determines the size of the device, is 70 mm.

4   Evaluation of Prototypes

4.1 Prototype 1

The camera can be moved up and down by turning the handle on the upper section to adjust its position. However, since the camera had only one fixed axis, there was a problem that the screen was not stable because it swayed from side to side in the process of moving up and down.

4.2 Prototype 2

The camera was fixed on two axes, and the process of moving up and down made it possible to take a stable picture of the screen without shaking. In addition, a function to fix the vertical movement of the camera was applied to make it easier for the user to view the image, but it was not smooth and needed to be improved (Fig. 8).

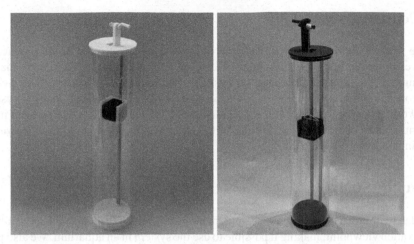

Fig. 8. Prototype 1, 2

4.3 Prototype 3

During the creation of the prototype, adding a function to feed the fish would induce the fish's behavior and draw the user's interest. Therefore, we added a baiting function to the upper section. Since the structure of the upper section became more complex with the addition of the function, we used gears to change the direction of the handles so that the user could easily control them (Fig. 9).

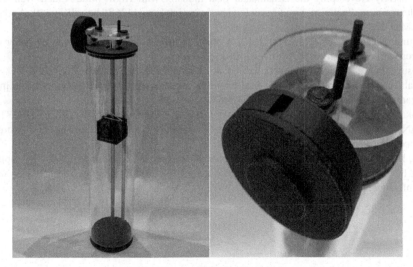

Fig. 9. Prototype 3, Feeding device.

5 Consideration

While working on the prototype, we 5 were able to implement some of the interaction features proposed in the previous study. However, at this stage, the function to change the angle of the observation viewpoint has yet to be implemented. Also, since we are still concentrating on implementing functions, we have yet to assume that the system will work underwater. Therefore, waterproofing the device so that it can be used in an aquarium and positioning it stably inside the aquarium in consideration of buoyancy remain issues to be addressed.

6 Future Study

We plan to improve the prototype by implementing a function to change the angle of the observation viewpoint, making it possible to use the system in an aquarium. We also plan to implement appropriate functions when deemed necessary, as in the case of the feeding function in Prototype 3. Furthermore, although it is currently intended to be operated manually, remote control using an Arduino or similar device is also being considered. Finally, once the prototype is completed, we plan to conduct evaluation experiments to clarify the effect of the new interaction on the viewer's impression.

References

1. Aquaculture Industry Division, Department of Marine and Fisheries: Department of Seawater, Intensively Developing the Ornamental Fish Industry with High Value-Added Well-Being Industry. https://www.mof.go.kr/article/view.do?articleKey=11268&boardKey=10. Accessed 10 May 2021
2. Chung, J.-H., Jung, S.-Y., Yoon, S.-K.: A study on the exhibition space plan by water tank types in the aquarium. KICA J. 67–74 (2011)
3. Kosuge, M.: Activities of Asahiyama Zoo. J. Jpn. Vet. Med. Assoc. 364–367 (2006)
4. Asahikawa City Asahiyama Zoo: Seal Pavilion. https://www.city.asahikawa.hokkaido.jp/asa hiyamazoo/facilityinformation/d055081.html. Accessed 14 July 2022
5. Isokawa, N., Nakazawa, J., Nishiyama, Y., Takashio, K., Okoshi, T., Tokuda, H.: TalkingNemo: aquarium fish talks its mind for breeding support. In: ACM International Conference Proceeding Series, pp. 15–17 (2016)
6. Ko, D., Kwon, D., Kim, E., Lee, W.: BubbleTalk: enriching experience with fish by supporting human behavior. In: DIS 2018: Proceedings of the 2018 Designing Interactive Systems Conference, pp. 919–930 (2018)

Competition or Collaboration? Exploring Interactive Relationships in Live-Streaming Audience Participation Game

Yifan Luo[1], Ke Fang[1], Xiaojun Wu[1], Jiahao Li[1], Zeyan Dao[1], Yunhan Wang[1], and Wai Kin (Victor) Chan[2]([✉])

[1] Interactive Media Design and Technology Center, Shenzhen International Graduate School, Tsinghua University, Beijing, China
{luoyf21,wuxj22,lijiahao21,daozy22, wangyunh22}@mails.tsinghua.edu.cn, fang.ke@sz.tsinghua.edu.cn
[2] Tsinghua-Berkeley Shenzhen Institute, Shenzhen International Graduate School, Tsinghua University, Beijing, China
chanw@sz.tsinghua.edu.cn

Abstract. Interactivity is the key to enhancing audience engagement and immersion during the live-streaming process. Viewer-streamer interaction is a research field worth exploring in live streaming. The live-streaming audience participation games break down the boundaries between viewers and streamers, allowing viewers to participate in live streaming using their virtual avatars, which effectively expands the existing ways of interaction in live streaming. To explore the interactive relationships in live streaming, we designed a quiz game that viewers can play by sending comments as answers to questions during live streaming. The game has two different modes. In competitive mode, viewers who answer any question incorrectly will lose the game, and only the last viewer left will win. In collaborative mode, viewers who answer any question correctly will get points, and all viewers will win when their total points reach the target set by streamers in advance. We also incorporated some entertaining elements into the game. We conducted a comparative experiment to investigate how the different modes affected viewers' experiences. We utilized a mixed-methods approach including semi-structured interviews (N = 7) and questionnaires (N = 30). The results indicated that in the competitive mode, viewers were more focused on answering questions. They also had a stronger sense of participation and were more easily influenced by other viewers and the streamer. In the collaborative mode, viewers were more relaxed and less influenced by other viewers, and the streamer played a smaller role. The findings provide guidelines for the design and further research of games in which viewers participate.

Keywords: Live streaming · Audience Participation Game · Audience experience

1   Introduction

Live streaming has gained tremendous popularity with the rise of live-streaming platforms, attracting a large number of viewers. Interactivity plays a crucial role in enhancing audience engagement and immersion during the live-streaming process. Among various forms of viewer-streamer interaction, the most common is sending comments that are visible to both viewers and streamers. Additionally, many live-streaming platforms offer interactive features such as likes and donations to streamers [1]. However, these existing forms of interaction have limited impacts on enhancing audience engagement.

Live-streaming Audience Participation Games (APGs) allow viewers to directly participate in the streamer's gameplay, blurring the boundaries between viewers and players. APGs introduce a fresh form of interaction within the live-streaming context [2]. For example, "Twitch Plays Pokémon" allows viewers to control the game character in real-time by sending comments [3], while "HedgewarsSGC" is an APG version of "Hedgewars" that explores sharing game control in a live-streaming context [4]. Another example is "CowardChess", which enables viewers to play chess against an AI and investigates the impact of live-streaming APGs on viewers' experiences [5]. These APGs have expanded the existing ways of interaction in live streaming. However, there is limited research on how different relationships among viewers, such as competitive and collaborative relationships, influence the audience experience. Therefore, we have designed a game system that incorporates a different way of interaction, aiming to investigate the impact of competition and collaboration among viewers on their engagement and experience within the live-streaming context.

In this research, we have developed a live-streaming quiz game where viewers can engage by sending likes and comments. The game offers two modes: competitive mode and collaborative mode. By setting different game objectives, we aim to investigate how these modes affect viewers' engagement and experience in live streams.

2   Quiz Game Design

In this research, we have developed a multiplayer quiz game that runs on a live-streaming platform. Viewers participate by sending comments as their answers during the live stream, aiming to correctly answer as many questions as possible. Upon joining the game, viewers' virtual avatars are displayed on the screen, standing on a platform, and are visible to both viewers and the streamer.

During the game, the streamer announces questions that are displayed on the screen. The streamer determines the content of these questions. To select their answers, viewers simply send comments containing options A, B, C, or D. Once an answer is chosen, the platform on which the viewer's virtual avatar stands changes color, indicating that the selected answer is visible to all viewers in the live stream. The streamer sets a time limit for each question and can choose to reveal the correct answer once the time is up. Viewers who answer correctly will have their corresponding virtual avatars remain on the platform. However, viewers who answer incorrectly will fall off the platform. The streamer has the discretion to decide whether viewers who answer incorrectly can rejoin the game. In addition to answering questions, the game also incorporates entertaining elements where viewers can send comments to change the appearance and actions of their virtual avatars.

In this research, the quiz game offers two modes to investigate the different impacts of competition and collaboration on audience engagement in live-streaming APGs (Fig. 1). In the competitive mode, viewers who answer questions incorrectly are eliminated from the game and cannot rejoin. Only the last remaining viewer will emerge as the winner. In the collaborative mode, viewers who answer questions incorrectly and fall off the platform have the opportunity to rejoin the game. Viewers accumulate points for each correct answer, and the total points are displayed as a progress bar visible to both viewers and the streamer. The game concludes when the total points reach the target, and all viewers achieve victory together.

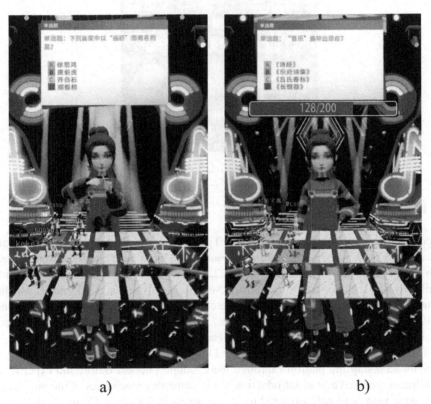

a)   b)

Fig. 1. a) Competitive mode of the quiz game, b) Collaborative mode of the quiz game

The quiz game is played on Douyin, a popular live-streaming platform in China. The streamer initiates the live stream on Douyin and serves as the game host. Viewers who access the live channel can see the streamer's avatar and the game interface. They can participate in the game by sending likes and real-time comments (Fig. 2).

Fig. 2. The game interface on Douyin

3 Experimental Details

To conduct the experiment, we recruited 30 participants through online platforms and social media channels. Among the participants, 53% were male and 47% were female, with ages ranging from 20 to 26 (M = 22.50, SD = 1.74). To ensure participants' familiarity with the live-streaming platform, we specifically selected individuals who had a minimum of one month's experience in watching live streams. Among the participants, 71.4% had three or more years of experience, 10.7% had one to two years of experience, and 17.9% had less than one year of experience.

The experiment was conducted on the Douyin live-streaming platform, with participants accessing the platform through their mobile phones. Before the experiment, participants received a brief introduction to the gameplay mechanics of the quiz game. They were then randomly assigned to two experimental groups: Group A and Group B. Each group experienced both the competitive mode and the collaborative mode, but in different orders. Both modes of the game consisted of 15 questions. During the experiment, participants had to select answers within a limited time frame and submit them by sending comments. The streamer was responsible for announcing the questions, monitoring the answers, and providing timely feedback to facilitate the progress of the game. Participants were free to use the entertainment elements of the game at any time, including sending commands to change their virtual avatars' appearance and actions.

Each game session lasted approximately one hour. After the completion of each game session, participants were given 20 min to complete a questionnaire. The questionnaire included the Audience Experience Questionnaire (AEQ) [6] and the Social Presence Gaming Questionnaire (SPGQ) [7] to assess participants' game experience. Additionally, qualitative questions were included in the questionnaire to investigate the impact of the entertainment elements in the game on the participants. Within one week after the experiment, seven participants were randomly selected for semi-structured interviews, which were recorded and transcribed for further analysis.

4   Results and Analysis

4.1   Questionnaire Results and Analysis

Figure 3 presents the statistical results of the questionnaire, demonstrating that scores across various dimensions were generally similar in both modes. The collaborative mode exhibited slightly higher median scores in the dimensions of Enjoyment, Mood, Empathy, and Change Dance. This suggests that participants experienced more delight, were more attentive to others, and were more engaged with entertaining elements. On the other hand, the competitive mode had a slightly higher median score in the Participation dimension, indicating that participants experienced higher levels of tension and primarily focused on answering questions.

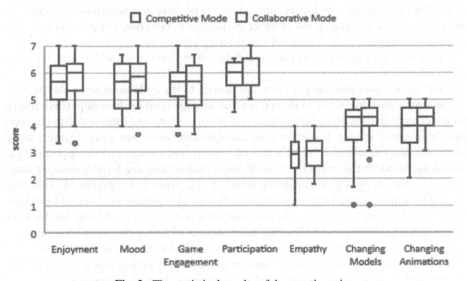

Fig. 3. The statistical results of the questionnaire

To examine the differences in game experience between the two modes, the Mann-Whitney test was conducted, and the results are presented in Table 1. The results show no significant differences across the seven dimensions. This absence of significant differences may be attributed to the relatively small sample size and limitations of the experimental conditions, such as potential network latency.

Table 1. The results of the Mann-Whitney test

Dimensions	Game Mode – Median (P$_{25}$, P$_{75}$)		U	Z	p
	Competitive	Collaborative			
Enjoyment	5.667 (5.0, 6.2)	6.000 (5.3, 6.3)	265.500	−.469	.639
Mood	5.667 (4.7, 6.3)	5.833 (5.3, 6.3)	262.000	−.542	.588
Game Engagement	5.667 (5.1, 6.0)	5.667 (4.8, 6.2)	286.000	−.042	.967
Participation	6.000 (5.5, 6.4)	5.500 (5.5, 6.5)	279.000	−.190	.849
Empathy	2.900 (2.4, 3.4)	3.000 (2.5, 3.4)	250.500	−.778	.437
Changing Models	4.333 (3.4, 4.6)	4.333 (4.0, 4.7)	241.000	−.985	.325
Changing Animations	4.000 (3.3, 4.7)	4.333 (4.0, 4.7)	240.500	−.992	.321

4.2 Interview Results and Analysis

The semi-structured interviews focused primarily on the differences in participants' experiences between the competitive mode and the collaborative mode. The interview questions explored various aspects, including (1) positive and negative experiences in different modes, (2) perception of other participants' behavior, (3) perception of the streamer's behavior, and (4) usage of entertaining elements.

We randomly selected seven participants for online interviews, which were recorded in audio format.

R1) In terms of game experience, compared to the collaborative mode, participants had a stronger sense of objectives and engagement in the competitive mode. In the competitive mode, the experience was more exciting and intense due to the presence of a single winner. In contrast, the collaborative mode was more relaxing, as all participants accumulated points together and eliminated viewers had the opportunity to rejoin the game. In the competitive mode, most participants displayed a stronger motivation to win, along with a heightened sense of objectives and engagement. They also tended to be more cautious in answering questions and were more influenced by others' responses. Some interviewees mentioned that in the competitive mode, they wanted to be the only one answering correctly while others answered incorrectly, in order to maintain their position in the game and sustain high levels of focus throughout. Another interviewee mentioned being more afraid of answering incorrectly in the competitive mode and would modify their answers based on others' responses. In the collaborative mode, most participants were more relaxed and had less motivation to achieve the goal, and their answers were less influenced by others. Some interviewees mentioned that since they could rejoin the game after being eliminated and others were also accumulating points, they didn't worry about choosing the wrong answer and didn't mind if their answers matched others. Some interviewees also mentioned that in the collaborative mode, they were less concerned about completing objectives and were more curious about what kind of questions would come next.

R2) Regarding the usage of entertaining elements, participants in the collaborative mode were more likely to explore these elements. In both modes, most participants frequently used these elements during the preparation phase but rarely during the game process. However, participants in the collaborative mode utilized the entertaining elements more frequently. Some interviewees mentioned using the entertaining elements more in the collaborative mode due to the more relaxing atmosphere. One interviewee mentioned paying more attention to other participants' virtual avatars on the platform in the collaborative mode, so she was influenced and had a greater incentive to change her appearance and actions.

R3) In terms of the relationship between participants and the streamer, participants in the competitive mode were more likely to be influenced by the streamer. Participants in the competitive mode exhibited a stronger susceptibility to the streamer's influence. Timely feedback from the streamer was deemed crucial to the game experience. In the competitive mode, the streamer seemed to have more control and participants were more likely to pay attention to the streamer's behavior. Some interviewees mentioned that in the competitive mode, they wanted to stay in the game to gain recognition from the streamer and receive more feedback. Conversely, one interviewee mentioned that, in the collaborative mode, her contributions were less likely to attract the streamer's attention, resulting in a sense of disappointment.

5   Discussion and Conclusion

In this research, we developed a live-streaming quiz game with two modes to enhance viewers' engagement within the live-streaming context. Through a comparative experiment, we investigated the impact of the competitive mode and the collaborative mode on viewers' engagement and experience. The results showed that the competitive mode fostered focused participation, susceptibility to viewer influence, and strong responsiveness to the streamer's feedback. On the other hand, the collaborative mode created a relaxed environment with less influence from other viewers and reduced emphasis on the streamer's role. Strengthening streamer-viewer interaction and highlighting the streamer's presence is more suitable for competitive modes, while the collaborative mode promotes independent thinking and knowledge learning in educational scenarios.

This research has some limitations. The distinction between the competitive and collaborative modes in game design may not have been clear enough, potentially resulting in minimal differences between the modes. Additionally, the sample size and collected questionnaire data were limited. Future work should focus on refining game mechanisms to better differentiate the two modes and conducting larger-scale experiments to further explore viewers' engagement and experience in live-streaming APGs.

References

1. Striner, A., Webb, A., Hammer, J., Cook, A.: Mapping design spaces for audience participation in game live streaming. In: Proceedings of the 2021 CHI Conference on Human Factors in Computing Systems, pp. 1–15. Association for Computing Machinery, Yokohama (2021). https://doi.org/10.1145/3411764.3445511
2. Glickman, S., McKenzie, N., Seering, J., Moeller, R., Hammer, J.: Design challenges for livestreamed audience participation games. In: Proceedings of the 2018 Annual Symposium on Computer-Human Interaction in Play, pp. 187–199. Association for Computing Machinery, Melbourne (2018). https://doi.org/10.1145/3242671.3242708
3. Lessel, P., Mauderer, M., Wolff, C., Krüger, A.: Let's play my way: investigating audience influence in user-generated gaming live-streams. In: Proceedings of the 2017 ACM International Conference on Interactive Experiences for TV and Online Video, pp. 51–63. Association for Computing Machinery, Hilversum (2017). https://doi.org/10.1145/3077548.3077556
4. Lessel, P., Altmeyer, M., Hennemann, M., Krüger, A.: HedgewarsSGC: a competitive shared game control setting. In: Extended Abstracts of the 2019 CHI Conference on Human Factors in Computing Systems, pp. 1–6. Association for Computing Machinery, Glasgow (2019). https://doi.org/10.1145/3290607.3313024
5. Lessel, P., Vielhauer, A., Krüger, A.: CrowdChess: a system to investigate shared game control in live-streams. In: Proceedings of the Annual Symposium on Computer-Human Interaction in Play, pp. 389–400. Association for Computing Machinery, Amsterdam (2017). https://doi.org/10.1145/3116595.3116597
6. Downs, J., Vetere, F., Howard, S., Loughnan, S.: Measuring audience experience in social videogaming. In: Proceedings of the 25th Australian Computer-Human Interaction Conference: Augmentation, Application, Innovation, Collaboration, pp. 217–220. Association for Computing Machinery, Adelaide (2013). https://doi.org/10.1145/2541016.2541054
7. Poels, K., de Kort, Y.A.W., IJsselsteijn, W.A.: D3.3: game experience questionnaire: development of a self-report measure to assess the psychological impact of digital games, p. 46. Technische Universiteit Eindhoven, Eindhoven (2007)

Using ProAut Process to Prototype a Social Story Repository for Autistic People

Eduardo Feitosa Nunes[1,2], Marcela Pessoa[1,2], Jr. Jucimar Maia[1,2], and Áurea Melo[1,2(✉)]

[1] Universidade do Estado do Amazonas (UEA), Manaus, Brazil
{efn,eng21,mpessoa,jmj,asmelo}@uea.edu.br
[2] Escola Superior de Tecnologia (EST), Manaus, Brazil
https://est.uea.edu.br/

Abstract. Social stories represent a rich resource to support the treatment of autistic people, aiming to minimize their stereotyped behaviors and also improve social interaction. However, most of these stories are based on common everyday situations, such as washing hands, taking a shower, among others, that is, they are composed of predefined stories always with the same figures. In this context, this work presents the prototyping of a repository to support the creation of social stories not only statically (predefined stories), but mainly dynamically (customized stories). The user will be able to consult the existing pictures and stories in the repository, as well as include new pictures, including photos of the autistic person and the environments with which he interacts. For this, ProAut was used as a prototyping process, and for which we made an evaluation of its use.

Keywords: Autism · Social Story · ProAut

1 Introduction

Delay in communication, difficulty in social interaction and repetitive behavior are the main characteristics of an autistic individual [12] The individual is called low-functioning autistic if he has many of these characteristics, otherwise he is called high-functioning. Because it exists in various intensities, autism is defined using the term Autistic Spectrum Disorder (ASD).

There are several tools to support autistic people therapies. Among them are social stories, used for education in specific situations, especially in the social skills development [4]. Social stories are excellent for help improve the behavior

---

This article is result of Academy STEM Project developed by Universidade do Estado do Amazonas and is funded by Samsung Electronica da Amazônia Ltda, under terms of Brazilian Federal Law n° 8,387/1991, and its disclosure is in accordance with the provisions of Article 39 of Decree No. 10,521/2020.

C. Stephanidis et al. (Eds.): HCII 2023, CCIS 1957, pp. 175–182, 2024.
https://doi.org/10.1007/978-3-031-49212-9_24

and social interaction of autistic people. Generally, social stories are predefined
to teach you how to deal with everyday situations, such as washing your hands,
bathing, brushing your teeth, getting ready to sleep, among others. In addition,
most stories is presented to the autistic person in print.

Currently, the use of computer technologies in autistic treatments is common,
especially in applications form [13,16]. However, few of them address social stories dynamically. Thus, the development of a repository to support the creation
of social stories, either for everyday situations or for unexpected, seems a very
promising idea. ProAut [8], is a process focused on low-functioning autistic. The
objective of ProAut is to support development teams in interface design activity,
whether these lay teams are in the process of software construction or the theme
of autism. In this context, this work presents the use of ProAut by a lay team
both in software development processes and autism themes. The scope of the
work is the prototyping of a repository to support the creation of dynamic social
stories.

2   Context and Related Works

2.1   Autism and Social Stories

American Psychiatric Association [12] characterizes ASD from two aspects: (a)
deficits in communication and social interaction; and (b) behaviors or interests stereotyped or repetitive. The deficit in social interaction implies difficulty
in interacting with other people, resulting in restrictions in understanding the
social rules properly. Thus, teaching programs for autistic people must focus on
improving and adapting their social skills.

Social skills are developed and learned throughout life through interaction
between individuals, but some people do not develop these skills spontaneously.
For these cases, it is necessary to perform systematic teaching and structure,
using specific mechanisms and according to individual particularities. Social
story [3] is a mechanism that consists of the use of images and written words to
describe social situations in which an individual may have difficulty identifying
relevant social signs or expected behaviors. Additionally, Social Story addresses
understanding the consequences of behaving appropriately or inappropriately.

Authors such as [5,6] used social stories describing behavioral contingencies
to support adjustment to everyday changes, provide insight into what others feel
or think, and teach specific social skills that are alternative or incompatible with
inappropriate behavior. Thus, social stories are used because they are easy to
produce without wasting time on apply [5]. They constitute a social learning tool
that supports the safe and meaningful exchange of information between parents
and/or professionals and people with ASD of all ages and. In addition, social
stories are very useful in teaching process and in the therapies of autistic people.

2.2   ProAut

The use of software for therapeutic purposes became a frequent reality. In the
context of autism, there are several applications developed [2,11]. However, many

of these applications have been developed following traditional or own methods without considering the particularity of autistic people concerning the software construction process and its interfaces. Considering this, there is the ProAut, which is a process based on Design Thinking [1] with a focus on the prototyping of interfaces but is also an inclusive process that counts on stages capable of immersing those involved in the context of individuals with ASD. The ProAut address at developers/designers who are laypeople both in Software Engineering processes and in Autism topic.

ProAut has four stages: (i) Immersion - composed of activities that allow obtaining relevant information for the understanding and knowledge of the characteristics, limitations, and potential of people with ASD, the context of the application to be developed as well as requirements gathering; (ii) Analysis - includes activities of triangulation of the data obtained in the Immersion phase, focusing on the generation of empathy between developers/designers and autistic people; (iii) Ideation - consists in the specification of requirements and the filling out of an artifact called Table of Requirements/Restrictions (TRR) [15], The TRR allows each requirement to be detailed, drawing its representation in the interface. (iv) prototyping - represents the construction of the prototype in itself.

The most of the low-functioning autistic people present limited verbal communication. For this reason, each step of ProAut generates a set of artifacts that are filled in with data extracted from family members, caregivers, as well as professionals who interact with them. Among these artifacts, the following stand out: (i) Interview Script [7] - containing a set of questions to interview the parents/caregivers/guardians, therapists, and the client (person or group of people who have an interest in the software). The data obtained from the answers to these interviews are consolidated in another artifact called CANVAS; (ii) EmpthyAut [9] and PersonAut [10], representing Empathy Map and Personas respectively, and are tools to support the generation of empathy between developers/designers and the autistic person; (iii) Autistic Characterization Form (ACF) [14], a form containing characteristics about Social Interaction, communication, behavior and cognition of autistic people.

3   Methodology

The work was done by a team of five students of the Computer Engineering Course, and scholarships of the STEM academy at the Escola Superior de Tecnologiada Universidde do Estado do Amazonas. These students neither had experience in developing systems aimed at the autistic public nor in software development, and so they decided to adopt ProAut. The work was based on the action research methodology, following the phases: *(i) Interviews* - consist of to interview professionals specialized in therapies for autistic people, as well as parents and anyone else who lives with them. These interviews aim to understand the needs of low-functioning autistic people and gather requirements for application; *(ii) Scope Defining* - we identified the need to create a repository to provide ready-made stories as well as elements to create new stories. The repository will aim to help therapists, teachers, parents, caregivers, and anyone who has interaction and needs to develop social skills of autistic people. In this way, the user will be able to create personalized, being able to adapt to any situation where there is a need; *(iii) Development* - the prototyping of the application was carried out using the ProAut process because of its applicability in the context of low-functioning autistic people, moreover the support of ProAut in directing inexperienced teams; and *(iv) Evaluation* - consists of analysis performance of ProAut during the repository development.

4   Results

4.1   Interviews

In the Interviews stage, we interviewed two professional experts in autism, a psychologist and a speech therapist. The experts reported the difficulties of finding social stories in the regional context. In addition, stories are usually already predefined in Apps and books, not allowing changes or customization for specific situations of certain patients.

4.2   Scope Definition

From the analysis of the interviews with the psychologist and the speech therapist, it was possible to identify the need for a repository to store both elements that will compose a specific social story (for example, an explanation about sexuality), as well as predefined such as washing hands, bathing, brushing teeth, among others. This way, the application will have functionalities to allow the user to customize social stories, according to his/her needs, from the elements contained in the repository, or insert real photos of environments and even of the autistic individual himself.

4.3   Development

The results obtained from conducting the PROAUT are presented following: *(i) Immersion Phase* - in this stage, we conducted research to gain knowledge about social stories and their application in the treatment of autistic people. Two people were interviewed: *(a)* a father of a 23 years old low-functioning autistic girl, presenting echolalic language (repeats what she hears, out of context), and with resistance in breaking routine; *(b)* a speech therapist who assists autistic children in a specialized institute and who highlighted the importance of creating personalized social stories. The speech therapist assumed the role of client, passing on some application requirements. This ProAut step produces three Canvases, but in this paper, we only present the customer's canvas (1). After completing the ACF, the Autistic Overview Graph (AOG) was generated and used in the PersonAut (2); *(iii) Analysis Phase* - we performed an analysis through the triangulation of the data contained in the canvas, identified the main requirements of the application, and we also created the PersonAut (2) and the EmpathyAut (which we do not show due to lack of space). In addition, we generated the initial TRR, in which the requirements and restrictions of the application. During the elaboration we identified of the TRR, twenty functional requirements, four business rules, and two restriction; *(iii) Ideation Phase* The result of this phase was the elaboration of the final TRR, in which we detailed the application requirements. Each requirement (column 3) is associated with its respective specification (column 5) and a low-fidelity prototype (column 6). For that, we consider the characteristics contained in PersonAut and EmpathyAut. Figure 3 presents the TRR resulting from this phase, which for lack of space, has only one requirement; *(iii) Prototyping Phase* - from the TRR specifications, at last, the prototype is created (Figs. 1 and 2).

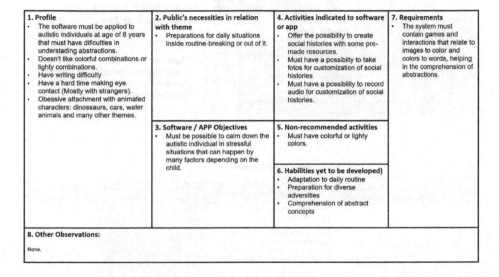

Fig. 1. Client canvas resulting from the immersion phase.

4.4   Evaluation

The team of five students evaluated ProAut through a focal group. Everyone agreed that ProAut serves lay teams both in software development and autism theme, directing the activities step by step. Thus, all team members evaluated ProAut positively. However, the team suggested that the documentation of the ProAut be done through self explanatory video to ensure that other lay teams better understand how, when, and why to use each of the artifacts, making filling them easier.

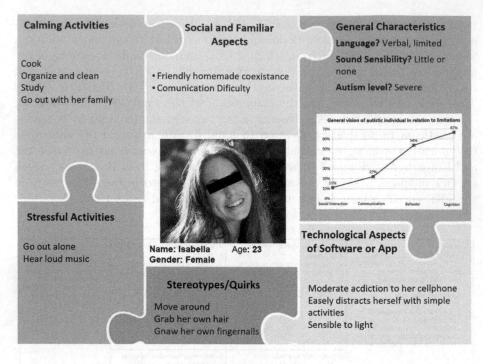

Fig. 2. PersonAut.

Requirement / Restriction Table

App Objective: the system must be applied to create and present social history

1.ID	2.Type	3. Requirement / Restriction	4. Requirement / Restriction Items	5. Item requirement specification	6. Requirement / Item requirement interface sugestions	7. Recommendation / Observations
RQ12	RQ	The system must permit the images to maintain themselves saved	Edit image	1. User selects an option "Edit image" after selecting an image 2.System must give edition tools to permit user's modification of selected image according to his necessity. 3. After modifying an image, user must click in the option "Save Image" or "Save as copy". 4. The system must save a new image at device folder if it has been chosen to "save image" edited image must replace original image and if "saved as copy" is chosen, a new image must be saved and placed at image table		

Fig. 3. Final TRR.

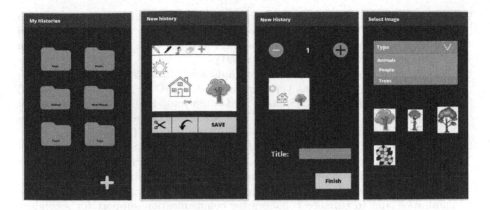

Fig. 4. Some screenshots of the prototype.

5 Conclusion

In this work, we concluded that ProAut achieved its objective of supporting inexperienced teams in the interface design activity for applications addressed for autistic people. After using ProAut became easy to conduct each project phase and generate the artifacts correctly. The interview script was fundamental in requirements gathering, considering lay developers do not feel secure about what to ask. At each stage, as the project progressed, the team learned about relevant aspects of an interface project, such as empathy with the end user and the association of each requirement with its respective design. Therefore, process ProAut is easy-to-apply, and supports the construction of interfaces through its various phases, from requirements gathering to prototyping. Future work includes development and its respective validation with the client (Fig. 4).

References

1. Brown, T., et al.: Design thinking. Harv. Bus. Rev. **86**(6), 84 (2008)
2. Cena, F., et al.: A personalised interactive mobile app for people with autism spectrum disorder. In: Ardito, C., et al. (eds.) INTERACT 2021. LNCS, vol. 12936, pp. 313–317. Springer, Cham (2021). https://doi.org/10.1007/978-3-030-85607-6_28
3. Gray, C.A., Garand, J.D.: Social stories: improving responses of students with autism with accurate social information. Focus Autistic Behav. **8**(1), 1–10 (1993)
4. Ivey, M.L., Juane Heflin, L., Alberto, P.: The use of social stories to promote independent behaviors in novel events for children with PDD-NOS. Focus Autism Dev. Disabil. **19**(3), 164–176 (2004)
5. Kuoch, H., Mirenda, P.: Social story interventions for young children with autism spectrum disorders. Focus Autism Dev. Disabil. **18**(4), 219–227 (2003)
6. Lorimer, P.A., Simpson, R.L., Smith Myles, B., Ganz, J.B.: The use of social stories as a preventative behavioral intervention in a home setting with a child with autism. J. Posit. Behav. Interv. **4**(1), 53–60 (2002)

7. Melo, A., Oran, A., Santos, J., Rivero, L., Barreto, R.: Requirements elicitation in the context of software for low-functioning autistic people: an initial proposal of specific supporting artifacts. In: Proceedings of the XXXV Brazilian Symposium on Software Engineering, pp. 291–296 (2021)

8. Melo, A., et al.: Desenvolvimento de uma aplicação educativa para o ensino derotinas diárias e quebra de rotinas a crianças autistas. RENOTE **19**(1), 166–175 (2021)

9. Melo, Á.H.D.S., Rivero, L., Santos, J.S.D., Barreto, R.D.S.: EmpathyAut: an empathy map for people with autism. In: Proceedings of the 19th Brazilian Symposium on Human Factors in Computing Systems, pp. 1–6 (2020)

10. Melo, Á.H.D.S., Rivero, L., Santos, J.S.D., Barreto, R.D.S.: PersonAut: a personas model for people with autism spectrum disorder. In: Proceedings of the 19th Brazilian Symposium on Human Factors in Computing Systems, pp. 1–6 (2020)

11. O'Rourke, J., Kueh, C., Holly, C., Brook, L., Erickson, C.: Co-designing a communication app to enhance collaborative communication support for secondary students with autism. Educ. Technol. Res. Dev., 1–26 (2022)

12. de Psiquiatria, A.A.: Manual de diagnóstico e estatística das perturbações mentais. Climepsi Editores, Lisboa (2014)

13. Sharma, P., Upadhaya, M.D., Twanabasu, A., Barroso, J., Khanal, S.R., Paredes, H.: "Express your feelings": an interactive application for autistic patients. In: Antona, M., Stephanidis, C. (eds.) HCII 2019. LNCS, vol. 11573, pp. 160–171. Springer, Cham (2019). https://doi.org/10.1007/978-3-030-23563-5_14

14. Hiléia da Silva Melo, Á., Oran, A.C., Silva dos Santos, J., Rivero, L., da Silva Barreto, R.: ACF: an autistic personas' characteristics source to develop empathy in software development teams. In: Stephanidis, C., et al. (eds.) HCII 2021. LNCS, vol. 13096, pp. 223–236. Springer, Cham (2021). https://doi.org/10.1007/978-3-030-90328-2_14

15. da Silva Melo, Á.H., et al.: From requirements to prototyping: proposal and evaluation of an artifact to support interface design in the context of autism. In: HCI International 2022-Late Breaking Papers: HCI for Health, Well-Being, Universal Access and Healthy Aging: 24th International Conference on Human-Computer Interaction, HCII 2022, Virtual Event, 26 June– 1 July 2022, Proceedings, pp. 307–321. Springer, CHam (2022). https://doi.org/10.1007/978-3-031-17902-0_22

16. de Urturi, Z.S., Zorrilla, A.M., Zapirain, B.G.: A serious game for android devices to help educate individuals with autism on basic first aid. In: Omatu, S., De Paz Santana, J.F., González, S.R., Molina, J.M., Bernardos, A.M., Rodríguez, J.M.C. (eds.) Distributed Computing and Artificial Intelligence. AISC, vol. 151, pp. 609–616. Springer, Heidelberg (2012). https://doi.org/10.1007/978-3-642-28765-7_74

Voice vs Mouse: The Input Preference of People with Upper-Limb Impairments in a Multi-modal Block-Based Programming Environment

Obianuju Okafor(✉) ⓘ

University of North Texas, Denton, TX 76203, USA
obianujuokafor@my.unt.edu

Abstract. Voice-Enabled Blockly is a multi-modal block-based programming environment that allows people with upper limb motor impairments to create block-based programs using voice as an input modality, while also retaining the mouse and keyboard as a form of input. In this paper, a study was conducted to compare the performance of participants with upper limb motor impairments when creating a program in Voice-Enabled Blockly using voice and when creating the same program using a mouse. The results showed that although participants performed tasks faster with a mouse and they rated it higher, they recommend voice as the input modality for people with upper limb motor impairments.

Keywords: Block-based Programming · Accessibility · Speech Recognition

1 Introduction

Block-based programming environments (BBPE) such as Scratch[1], Blockly[2], and Pencil Code[3] are visual programming interfaces where programs are constructed by dragging blocks to a workspace and joining them [1,2]. Due to their simplicity, BBPEs are often used to introduce programming concepts and computational thinking to novices [3]. As advantageous as they are, they have some limitations [1,4,5]. One drawback they have is their dependence on the use of a pointing device to drag and drop elements on the screen. This has made them inaccessible to people with upper limb motor impairments (ULMI) such as cerebral palsy, multiple sclerosis, muscular dystrophy, etc. [5–8] (Fig. 1).

To address the challenges people with ULMI face in the BBPE Blockly, a voice-enabled version of Blockly was created, that allows people with dexterity impairments to perform actions using voice as a form of input. The goal was not to replace the mouse or keyboard as a form of input, but to provide an

---

[1] https://scratch.mit.edu/.
[2] https://developers.google.com/blockly/.
[3] https://pencilcode.net/.

C. Stephanidis et al. (Eds.): HCII 2023, CCIS 1957, pp. 183–191, 2024.
https://doi.org/10.1007/978-3-031-49212-9_25

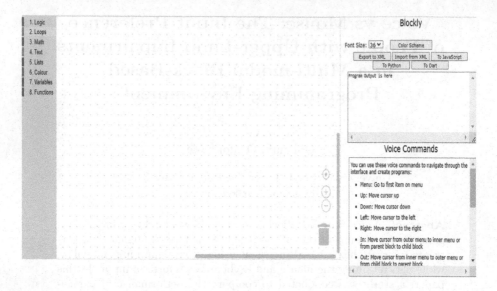

Fig. 1. User interface of Voice-enabled Blockly

alternative option for those who cannot use the mouse or keyboard. Hence, in Voice-enabled Blockly, users can perform actions in Blockly using speech, as well as with a mouse or keyboard.

Similar work exists where they attempted to make the BBPE Scratch, accessible to people with ULMI, by creating a tool called Myna. Myna is an application that runs parallel to Scratch to allow people with ULMI to create programs in Scratch using their voice [6–8]. In contrast to Myna, speech was added as an alternative input modality in Voice-enabled Blockly, and not as a separate entity. The rationale behind doing this is to make the user experience seamless and to allow collaboration among people with and without dexterity skills. Furthermore, Myna was only evaluated by 2 people with a ULMI. In the two studies conducted with Voice-enabled Blockly so far [9], there has been a total of 14 participants with ULMI.

Before implementing Voice-enabled Blockly, a preliminary study was conducted [10,11]. The study aimed to confirm the feasibility of using voice as an input modality, particularly for people with cerebral palsy who were the target audience at the time, as they are known to sometimes have speech impediments [12,13]. The study also helped us test the appropriateness of the voice commands. In the study, 5 people with cerebral palsy voiced 10 commands to a speech recognition engine. The results of the preliminary study revealed the need to expand the target population from people with cerebral palsy to anyone with ULMI. Furthermore, the study showed the need to modify some voice commands. After creating Voice-enabled Blockly, a usability study was performed. In the study, 9 people with ULMI used Voice-enabled and gave feedback at the end [9]. The results revealed that the system can be used by people with motor impairments. However, it also exposed some shortcomings of the tool and gave some suggestions on how to fix them.

This paper presents the results of an experiment conducted on Voice-enabled Blockly with 7 participants with ULMI. The study aimed to compare the performance of participants when using two different input modalities in Voice-enabled Blockly, mouse and voice. It also sought to understand the input preference of people with ULMI, and what they recommend to other users with ULMI. The results of the study showed that users recommend voice as an input modality for people who cannot use their hands, despite the fact that they rated the mouse higher than they rated voice, and took less time to perform the study task using a mouse.

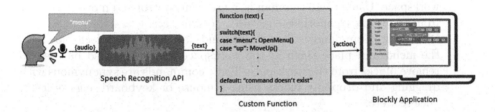

Fig. 2. System Overview

2   Voice-Enabled Blockly

The system is a voice-enabled version of the Blockly application, hence the name. Blockly's primary input method is a mouse or keyboard. In Voice-enabled Blockly, speech was added as an alternative input modality for people with ULMI while keeping the mouse as a form of input. This section presents the components of Voice-enabled Blockly. Figure 2 gives an overview of Voice-enabled Blockly's components and how they work together.

Voice-enabled Blockly consists of four main components:

1. Blockly Application: Blockly is a browser-based block-based programming environment. Originally, in Blockly, actions are performed using a mouse or keyboard. Modifications were made to Blockly's source code so that the same actions can also be performed using speech. Blockly's source code was made available online via GitHub[4], and therefore the code used in this research project was downloaded from Blockly's GitHub repository.
2. Speech Recognition API: Speech recognition API is a robust pre-built library that records speech in real-time, converts it to text, and returns the text. As with every API, it can be added to your website or application by adding

---

[4] https://github.com/google/blockly

a few lines of code. The speech recognition API chosen was the Web speech API[5]. This API was used in several research studies [14,15].

3. Voice Commands: The voice commands are the words uttered by users when performing actions in the system. They are limited and predefined. This helps prevent any ambiguity associated with more verbose speech recognition systems. A voice command consists of one or two words, e.g., "delete", "edit field", etc. Each voice command has an action that they perform, e.g., selecting, deleting, etc. For example, to delete a block from the workspace, the user will say "delete".

   Voice commands can be broken down into 5 categories:

   - Navigation Commands: These are the commands used to navigate through menus, dropdown menus, and between a stack of blocks in the workspace. Using these commands, a user can control and move the cursor from one point to another. e.g. "up", "down", etc.
   - Placement Commands: These commands are used to select blocks in the menu and place them in the workspace. They can also be used to remove blocks from the workspace. These commands are synonymous with dragging and dropping blocks using a mouse or keyboard. e.g. "select", "delete", etc.
   - Control Commands: These set of commands are responsible for controlling elements in the interface, such as opening and closing menus, e.g. "menu", "close", etc.
   - Edit Commands: These commands are used to edit a block's text value or to add a comment to a block. It can also be used to change the option selected from the dropdown menu, e.g. "edit field", "save", etc.
   - Mode Commands: These commands are used to switch between the 3 modes in the system. The modes are navigation mode, connect mode, and edit mode. e.g. "edit", "connect", etc.

4. Custom function: To perform actions in Blockly using speech, a function was created that translates voice commands to actions. This function entails a switch statement [16]. In the switch statement, each case is a voice command. Each voice command is paired with a corresponding action function to be executed. For instance, the voice command "delete" is paired with the delete function.

3   Experiment

This experiment compares two modalities in the Voice-enabled Blockly environment, voice and mouse. The objective of this study was to find out the following: (i) the preferred input modality for people with ULMI and (ii) the relative performance of the participant when using voice versus when using the mouse.

---

[5] https://developer.mozilla.org/en\discretionary-US/docs/Web/API/Web_Speech_API.

Table 1. Participant Information

Participant ID	Age	Gender	Condition
P1	49	Male	Cerebral Palsy
P2	52	Male	Multiple Sclerosis
P3	51	Male	Charcot Marie Tooth Disease
P4	25	Female	Cerebral Palsy
P5	41	Male	Cerebral Palsy
P6	26	Male	Limb Pelvic Hypoplasia
P7	25	Male	Muscular Dystrophy

3.1   Participants

There were a total of 7 participants. Table 1 shows information about each participant, such as age, gender, and condition. There were 5 males and 2 females. The mean age was 38.28 years (SD = 12.9). More than 40% of the participants had Cerebral Palsy, 14% had Muscular Dystrophy, 14% had Amyotrophic Lateral Sclerosis, 14% had Charcot Marie Tooth Disease, and 14% had Limb Pelvic Hypoplasia. Although the participants selected could use the mouse to some extent, they all had difficulty using the mouse, some more than others.

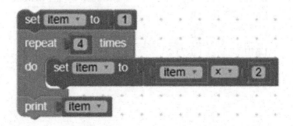

Fig. 3. Block-based program to be created using mouse and voice

3.2   Procedure

This study was conducted remotely. Participants were individually met on Zoom. They used a prototype of Voice-enabled Blockly that was deployed online. They shared their screen as they performed tasks and they were observed. Before starting the tasks, each participant was told that they could stop or pause at any time if the tasks became too cumbersome for them. They were also told that they could ask questions during the study if they felt stuck.

At the start of each session, they were given a demo of Voice-enabled Blockly and 3 tasks were assigned. The first was a training task to familiarize themselves with the system. If they performed well in the training task, then they moved on to the two main tasks; otherwise, more explanations were given. The two main tasks were to create a program using voice and to create the same program

using a mouse. Figure 3 shows the block-based program to be created. The order
in which the participant performed the tasks was changed for each participant.
Some started with a mouse, and others started with voice.

Participants answered survey questions as they went through the study tasks.
Before starting the training tasks, they answered 5 general questions asking them
their gender, age, condition, etc. After completing each of the main tasks, they
answered more survey questions relating to the input modality they used to
perform the task. At the end of the session, more questions were asked, such as
"Which modality do you prefer?" and *"Which modality are you more likely to
recommend to a friend with upper-limb motor impairments?"*.

Table 2. Results from the A/B test

Participant ID	Voice Rating (1–5)	Mouse Rating (1–5)	Preferred Input method	Recommended Input Method
P1	3	5	Mouse	Voice
P2	2	5	Mouse	Voice
P3	5	5	Voice	Voice
P4	3	4	Mouse	Voice
P5	4	4	Mouse	Mouse
P6	4	5	Mouse	Voice
P7	4	5	Mouse	Voice
Average	3.571	4.714	-	-

3.3   Results

The results of the experiment are presented in this section. The result is divided
into two categories, preferred and recommended input modality, and relative
performance. Table 2 shows a summary of the results.

Preferred and Recommended Input Modality. When asked *"Which
modality do you prefer?"*, approximately 86% of the participants stated that
they would prefer to use a mouse to perform actions in Voice-enabled Blockly.
One in seven participants stated that they preferred to use voice. A reason mentioned as to why the mouse was preferred to the voice was time. According to P4
*'I liked the voice system, but I found it to be more time consuming so, I prefer
the mouse'.*

On the other hand, when asked *"Which modality are you more likely to
recommend to a friend with upper-limb motor impairments?"*, all participants
except one said that they recommend voice. However, verbally, they all agreed

that for someone who is not able to use their hands at all, the voice will be a better alternative. According to P7 *"I personally like using the mouse because that's what I'm used to, and I have enough control to just use the mouse but I think if you weren't able to use your hands at all the voice thing would be very easy"*.

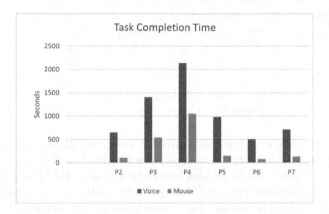

Fig. 4. Task completion time when using a mouse versus when using voice

Relative Performance. The performance of the participants were compared when creating a program using both mouse and voice, based on the following metrics: task completion time and overall experience rating. Figure 4 is a bar chart showing the time each participant took to complete the task using a mouse and voice.

Looking at Fig. 4, you can see that all participants took longer to perform the task using a mouse compared to when using voice. The maximum time spent performing the task using a mouse was 1052.56 s, while that for voice was 2137.79 s. The minimum time spent on the task by any participant using the mouse was 74.4 s, while that for voice was 505.74 s. On average it took the participants 344.4 s when using a mouse and 1066.2 s when using voice. This means that on average, participants spent about three times as much time completing the study task when using voice than they did when using a mouse. It is important to note that some participants took longer using the mouse than others did when using voice; e.g., P4's voice task completion time was more than P5's mouse task completion time.

Regarding the overall experience rating of the mouse versus that of voice. Table 2 shows how each participant rated their experience using the mouse and voice. Most of the participants rated their experience when using a mouse higher than their experience when using voice. However, P3 and P5 rated them the same. On average, the user rated their experience with a mouse as 4.714 while voice had an average rating of 3.571. The minimum voice experience rating was given as 2, while the mouse had a minimum rating of 4. Both the voice and the mouse had a maximum rating of 5.

4   Discussion

The results of the experiment are promising. Although most participants said that they preferred mouse, and they rated their experience using a mouse higher than their experience using voice, they all concurred that the use of voice could benefit people who are not able to use their hands at all. 6 out of 7 stated that for someone who cannot use their hands at all, they will recommend the use of voice over a mouse. This supports the main objective of this project. The use of voice was not created to replace the mouse or keyboard, but rather to provide an alternative for a user who has a severe motor impairment and cannot use the mouse at all.

Some of the reasons participants gave for preferring the mouse were because they are accustomed to a mouse and because it takes less time to perform tasks using a mouse. Voice's lengthier task completion time could be attributed to the faulty speech recognition system. The speech recognition system did not always accurately recognize the commands uttered, hence the participant sometimes had to repeat a command several times. According to P1 *'Voice recognition needs work '*. Therefore, with more experience using voice and if the speech recognition system is improved, then potentially more users may prefer the use of voice.

5   Conclusion

In this paper, Voice-enabled Blockly was presented, a speech-driven BBPE for people with ULMI. Additionally the result of an experiment comparing two input modalities in Voice-enabled Blockly, mouse and voice, was given. The study results showed that although most participants preferred the mouse and rated their experience using a mouse higher than their experience using voice, they all agreed that voice will be a better option for people with dexterity impairments. The results also showed that on average the participants performed the task 3 times faster using the mouse than using voice; this time difference contributed to why some of the participants preferred to use a mouse.

In future work, the speech recognition system will be replaced with a more efficient one. Furthermore, another study will be conducted to compare the use of voice to other modalities such as eye tracking.

References

1. Biyani, A.: What is block coding for kids and how does it work? (2022). Accessed 16 Apr 2023. https://insights.gostudent.org/en/block-coding-for-kids
2. Computer Hope: Block-based programming (2019). Accessed 16 Apr 2023. https://www.computerhope.com/jargon/b/block-based-programming.htm

3. Humble, N.: Developing computational thinking skills in K-12 education through block programming tools. In: ICERI2019 Proceedings, Series 12th Annual International Conference of Education, Research and Innovation. IATED, 11–13 November 2019, pp. 4865–4873 (2019). https://doi.org/10.21125/iceri.2019.1190

4. Weintrop, D., Wilensky, U.: To block or not to block, that is the question: students' perceptions of blocks-based programming. In: Proceedings of the 14th International Conference on Interaction Design and Children, Series IDC 2015, pp. 199–208. Association for Computing Machinery, New York, NY, USA (2015). https://doi.org/10.1145/2771839.2771860

5. Computer Science Educators: Advantages and disadvantages of teaching block-coding languages such as MIT's app inventor? (2017). Accessed 16 Apr 2023. https://cseducators.stackexchange.com/questions/4099/advantages-and-disadvantages-of-teaching-block-coding-languages-such-as-mits-ap

6. Wagner, A., Rudraraju, R., Datla, S., Banerjee, A., Sudame, M., Gray, J.: Programming by voice: a hands-free approach for motorically challenged children (2012)

7. Wagner, A., Gray, J.: An empirical evaluation of a vocal user interface for programming by voice **8**, 47–63 (2015)

8. Wagner, A., Gray, J.: An empirical evaluation of a vocal user interface for programming by voice (2017)

9. Okafor, O., Ludi, S.: Voice-enabled blockly: usability impressions of a speech-driven block-based programming system. In: Proceedings of the 24th International ACM SIGACCESS Conference on Computers and Accessibility, Series ASSETS 2022. Association for Computing Machinery, New York, NY, USA (2022). https://doi.org/10.1145/3517428.3550382

10. Okafor, O.: Helping students with cerebral palsy program via voice-enabled block-based programming. SIGACCESS Access. Comput. (132) (2022). https://doi.org/10.1145/3523265.3523267

11. Okafor, O., Stephanie, L.: Helping students with upper-body motor disabilities program via voice-enabled block-based programming. In: Antona, M., Stephanidis, C. (eds.) Universal Access in Human-Computer Interaction. User and Context Diversity. LNCS, vol. 13309, pp. 62–77. Springer, New York (2022). https://doi.org/10.1007/978-3-031-05039-8_5

12. Centers for Disease Control and Prevention: What is cerebral palsy? November 2021. https://www.cdc.gov/ncbddd/cp/facts.html

13. National Institute of Neurological Disorders and Stroke: Cerebral palsy: hope through research, July 2013. https://www.ninds.nih.gov/Disorders/Patient-Caregiver-Education/Hope-Through-Research/Cerebral-Palsy-Hope-Through-Research

14. Rosenblatt, L., Carrington, P., Hara, K., Bigham, J.: Vocal programming for people with upper-body motor impairments, pp. 1–10 (2018)

15. Lin, P., Van Brummelen, J., Lukin, G., Williams, R., Breazeal, C.: Zhorai: designing a conversational agent for children to explore machine learning concepts. In: Proceedings of the AAAI Conference on Artificial Intelligence, vol. 34, pp. 13 381–13 388 (2020)

16. W3Schools: JavaScript Switch Statement (2022). Accessed 14 Apr 2022. https://www.w3schools.com/js/js_switch.asp

Usability of Reservation Systems of Japanese Airlines

Emiri Otsuka(✉) [ID] and Namgyu Kang [ID]

Future University Hakodate of Japan, Hakodate, Japan
g2122014@fun.ac.jp

Abstract. In recent years, the style of travel in Japan has changed with the epidemic COVID19. As a result, the chances of making individual reservations for hotels and planes have increased. Based on the background, online reservations using reservation systems are the mainstream when purchasing airline tickets. Therefore, the website's usability for making reservations is one of the critical factors for users. However, there needs to be more research on Japanese airlines' websites and reservation systems. In our study, therefore, we conduct an evaluation experiment using three reservation systems (= applications) of domestic Japan. This research aims to visualize design and usability issues and points for system improvement. The evaluation objects are JAL, ANA, and Peach, significant airlines in Japan. For the experiment, we created a system based on the existing ones. At that time, we made the system with black and white color to avoid the influence of the brand color and erased all the brand information like a logo. Then, participants conducted the task of reserving the determined domestic flight ticket. After that, we analyzed the obtained responses using the Normalized Rank Method. As a result, JAL's application scored the highest in 5 evaluation items, followed by ANA and PEACH. In addition, when participants selected flight fares and times, he/she felt that the reservation system with various functions was easy to access. In addition, the size and placement of letters and the use of icons on the system are strongly connected with reservation behavior.

Keywords: Airlines Application · Reservation · Usability

1 Introduction

In recent years, the style of travel in Japan has changed with the epidemic COVID19. In the past, the most popular tour style was a group tour. However, now many people want to avoid contact with an unspecified number of people [1]. In addition, in 2021, From a questionnaire regarding airlines' use, about 50% of individual users answered that they used the "official website of the airline" when reserving airline tickets. The result means many people buy airline tickets online [2]. This way, small-group travel will likely become established even after the COVID-19 epidemic subsides, and opportunities to arrange air tickets and accommodations on each own will increase. The reservation system's usability significantly influences the willingness to purchase when booking air tickets and accommodation online [3].

© The Author(s), under exclusive license to Springer Nature Switzerland AG 2024
C. Stephanidis et al. (Eds.): HCII 2023, CCIS 1957, pp. 192–199, 2024.
https://doi.org/10.1007/978-3-031-49212-9_26

Therefore, the degree of satisfaction with airline ticket reservation sites also affects the choice of airlines [4]. As a result, reservation systems such as websites and applications play an essential role in airline ticket reservations. In recent years, many airlines have significantly improved their websites and newly introduced mobile applications as a marketing strategy to make it easier for customers to book and manage their airline tickets.

There are studies on web accessibility and Usability. For example, a study on the web accessibility of Indian government websites using Google Lighthouse for analysis found issues such as the difficulty of use for people with disabilities and broken links [5]. Based on this background, we conducted a study on Japanese airline websites using Google Lighthouse [6]. As a result, all Japanese airlines passed the criteria set by Google Lighthouse in all categories. However, some airlines had issues such as insufficient color contrast and long loading times.

According to a study on personal use of flight reservation applications, demand for booking flights has been increasing yearly [7]. Thus, airlines need to provide users with more interactive and attractive features. Furthermore, by conducting objective and subjective evaluations of websites, it is possible to identify new issues and improvement points. However, more research about Japanese airlines' websites and reservation systems needs to research more.

Therefore, in this study, we conduct experiments targeting the reservation system of domestic airline applications as a subjective evaluation. Furthermore, this study aims to visualize the issues and improvement points regarding the reservation system's design and usability based on the experiments' results.

2   Method

2.1   Prototype of the Application

For this experiment, we created a prototype of an application that performs the same functions as the reservation systems of three Japanese airlines. In our experiment using Google Lighthouse, we targeted four airline companies, but one did not offer an application. Therefore, for this experiment, we selected the applications of JAL, ANA, and

Fig. 1. Prototype of the application

PEACH, which are airlines that the experiment participants frequently use. To minimize the influence of brand image and colors used by each airline, we created the prototype using only black and white. We removed any text or logos that could reveal the identity of each airline. The following is the prototype we created (Fig. 1).

2.2 List of Questions

This experiment targeted 27 participants aged 10 to 20 between November 20th and November 22nd. First, we instructed the participants to book a round-trip ticket from Sapporo to Tokyo for December 12th to December 15th. After that, we prompted them to select the earliest flight from the available choices with the cheapest fare on the specified dates. The participants completed the experiment by pressing the "finish" on the application's prototype when they accurately selected the date, location, and price, among other options. Finally, we experimented with the same process with each of the three application prototypes.

2.3 Experimental Method

After the experiment, the participants ranked and described the reasons for their rankings of the three applications. The following are the five question items.

1. Ease of use
2. Easy operation until reservation
3. Easy selection of departure and arrival places
4. Easy selection of date
5. Easy selection of price/fare

3 Results and Discussion

Among the 27 participants, about 80% answered that they fly on planes about 1–3 times a year. Regarding the essential point when reserving plane tickets, around 75% of the participants indicated that price/fare is the most significant factor. Using the responses obtained, we analyzed the normalized ranking method for each of the five question items presented in 2.3 [8].

3.1 Ease of Use

In the first question, the participants used the applications and sorted them in the order they felt they were easy to use. The results showed that the order was JAL, ANA, and PEACH. We then conducted a t-test to examine the significance of the differences between the rankings. The results showed that there were significant differences between JAL and ANA (t0(JAL, ANA) = 3.118 < t (52, 0.01)) and between ANA and PEACH (t0(ANA, PEACH) = 6.102 < t (52, 0.01)) (Fig. 2).

In the participants' open-ended responses, many described that JAL's application, which received the highest evaluation, was intuitively easy to understand what to do next. On the other hand, for PEACH, which received a low evaluation, some answers

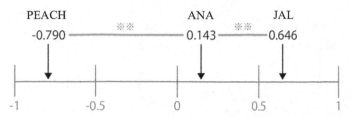

Fig. 2. "Ease of Use" Score

indicated difficulty in comprehending the information and finding which button to press, resulting in mistakes.

Regarding the difference between JAL and ANA's application, some responses mentioned the font size and the icons displayed on the top page. For example, comparing the top page of JAL and ANA, JAL's page included icons suitable for each item, such as departure point, arrival point, departure date, arrival date, and the number of people (Fig. 3).

Therefore, usability is essential in achieving intuitive operations by using icons. Moreover, users will realize it is difficult to use the application if they need help determining which parts are tappable.

Fig. 3. Top screens of JAL and ANA application.

3.2 Easy Operation Until Reservation

In the second question, the participants used the application and sorted in the order in which they felt that the operation up to the reservation was easy. Again, the result was in the order of JAL, ANA, and PEACH. Furthermore, we conducted a t-test to examine the significance of the differences. As a result, t0(JAL, ANA) = 3.373 < t (52, 0.01) and t0(ANA, PEACH) = 9.379 < t (52, 0.01), and each pair had a significant difference (Fig. 4).

Regarding usability, some participants mentioned that the buttons on JAL's application were easy to understand, and the perceived time for completing the operations

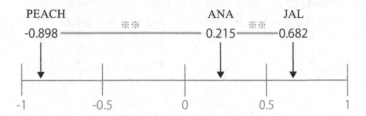

Fig. 4. "Easy Operation until Reservation" score

was shorter than others. On the other hand, some answers regarding PEACH stated that it took more work to know where to tap and longer to proceed to the next operation. When comparing the number of screens up to the fare and time selection between the prototypes, JAL could proceed to the search with a minimum of 7 screens, while PEACH had a minimum of 5 screens. However, the participants felt that JAL took less time than Peach because there was less gap between the next operation they wanted to perform and the actual screen. From this, the design of the screen is related to the ease of use that users feel when they perform the next operation.

3.3 Easy Selection of Departure and Arrival Places

In the third question, participants used the application and sorted the order in which they felt it was easy to select the departure and arrival locations using the application.

The result was in the order of JAL, ANA, and PEACH. Furthermore, we conducted a t-test to examine the significance of the differences. The results showed that t0(JAL, ANA) = 9.352 < t (52, 0.01) and t0(ANA, PEACH) = 4.800 < t (52, 0.01), and each pair had a significant difference (Fig. 5).

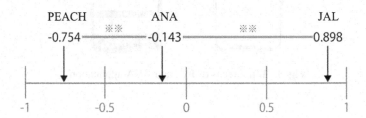

Fig. 5. "Easy Selection of Departure and Arrival Places" score

Participants indicated that JAL's application was easy to understand as it had drop-down menus for each region (Fig. 6). In contrast, some participants found locating their targets on ANA's application difficult due to the need for lines and color coding. PEACH's application with the lowest rating answered that it is easy to make mistakes because the list includes overseas airports. In addition, there was an answer for functionality that the application could be more apparent because it is a single screen for selecting the departure and arrival points.

JAL   ANA   PEACH

Fig. 6. Location selection screen for each application

3.4 Easy Selection of Data

In the fourth question, subjects used the application to sort the dates in the order they felt was easier to select. The result was in the order of JAL, ANA, and PEACH. Furthermore, we conducted a t-test to examine the significance of the differences. The results showed that $t0(JAL, ANA) = 3.765 < t(52, 0.01)$ and $t0(ANA, PEACH) = 3.605 < t(52, 0.01)$, and each pair had a significant difference (Fig. 7).

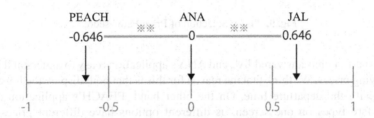

Fig. 7. "Easy Selection of Data" score

All applications included a feature to select dates using a calendar. However, participants needed help finding Peach's application for selecting dates. The reason was that the calendar would slide up once a departure date was selected (Fig. 8). Thus, the large amount of eye movement required by this approach may increase cognitive load.

3.5 Easy Selection of Price/Fare

In the fifth question, participants used the application and sorted the prices in the order in which they felt that it was easier to select the price. The result was in the order of JAL, ANA, and PEACH. We conducted a t-test to examine the significant differences between the applications. The results showed that there was no significant difference between JAL and ANA's applications, with $t0(JAL, ANA) = 2.009 < t(52, 0.05)$. On the other hand, there was a significant difference between ANA and PEACH's applications, with $t0(ANA, PEACH) = 2.678 < t(52, 0.01)$ (Fig. 9).

Departure data   Arrival data

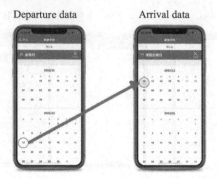

Fig. 8. Date selection screen of PEACH application

PEACH   ANA   JAL
-0.826 ※※   0.359 0.467

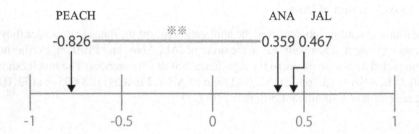

Fig. 9. "Easy Selection of Price/Fare" score

Many participants answered JAL and ANA's applications easy to understand in terms of displaying prices. We think that the reason for this is that both display the lowest price together with the departure time. On the other hand, PEACH's application displays multiple fare types on one screen, as different options have different prices, which resulted in participants making more mistakes.

Therefore, we suggest that reducing the likelihood of user error in fare selection can be achieved by adjusting the text size and displaying the lowest price near the fare type. When there are multiple fare types, it would be easier for users if they are able to select them on the first screen.

4 Conclusion

We studied the usability of reservation systems using the applications of three Japanese airlines. Participants performed the same task using the three applications and answered questions related to the task. As a result, JAL's application received the highest evaluation, followed by ANA and then PEACH. In this regard, we summarize our analysis and observations.

1. Users feel that an application that can be operated intuitively, even if the number of operations is high, results in a shorter perceived time.
2. By minimizing the user's eye movement, cognitive load can be reduced.

3. When users must choose one option from multiple ones, it's necessary to apply Gestalt's principles to font size and lines.

In addition, the amount of information included on one screen was also an important factor. Specifically, many participants valued price when choosing a flight, displaying the cheapest option was effective. In the future, we plan to investigate the error rate and task completion time when using the application.

References

1. Sonoda, S., Aoyama, Y.: New life and society suggested by the corona disaster. Keishin J. Life Health **4**(2), 1–13 (2020)
2. PR TIMES: We asked 1,200 people! How do I purchase a ticket? https://prtimes.jp/main/html/rd/p/000000636.000044800.html. Accessed 3 Sept 2022
3. Ani, N., Noprisson, H., Ali, N.M.: Measuring usability and purchase intention for online travel booking – a case study. Int. Rev. Appl. Sci. Eng. **10**(2), 165–171 (2019)
4. Yazid, M.A., Jantan, A.H.: User experience design (UXD) of mobile application - an implementation of a case study. J. Telecommun. Electron. Comput. Eng. **9**, 197–200 (2017)
5. Agrawal, G., Kumar, D., Singh, M., Dani, D.: Evaluating accessibility and usability of airline websites. In: Mayank Singh, P.K., Gupta, V.T., Flusser, J., Ören, T., Kashyap, R. (eds.) ICACDS 2019. CCIS, vol. 1045, pp. 392–402. Springer, Singapore (2019). https://doi.org/10.1007/978-981-13-9939-8_35
6. Otsuka, E., Kang, N.: Study on the measurement of the web performance of Japanese airlines using Google lighthouse. In: COWEKO 2022 International Conference, pp. 111–116 (2022)
7. Suki, N.M., Suki, N.M.: Flight ticket booking app on mobile devices-examining the determinants of individual intention to use. J. Air Transp. Manag. **62**, 146–154 (2017)
8. Tadahiko, F., Ryoko, F.: Ergonomics guide-how to do the science of kansei, pp. 41–71. Scientist Company

A Design Space for Digital Augmentation of Reading

Pedro Ribeiro[1]([✉]) [iD], Wolfgang Müller[2] [iD], Ido Iurgel[1] [iD], Christian Ressel[1] [iD], and Carrie Ching[1] [iD]

[1] Rhine-Waal University of Applied Sciences, Kamp-Lintfort, Germany
`{pr,ii,cr}@hsrw.eu`, `kar-wai-carrie.ching@hsrw.org`
[2] University of Education Weingarten, Weingarten, Germany
`mueller@md-phw.de`

Abstract. To comprehend a text readers can benefit from their capacity to bodily interact with the environment to construct the meaning of a text. Specifically, they use their perception, action, and emotion systems to gain a deeper understanding of the text. Readers' mental simulations of perceptions, actions, and emotions associated with a text can therefore facilitate reading comprehension, motivation and learning. The digital augmentation of reading aims at the artificial enrichment of reading through digital media. This concept has the potential to digitally synchronise the text with the surrounding environment and to promote an embodied reading experience, effectively fostering comprehension and learning. To harness the potential, recent relevant work about digital augmentation of reading was reviewed and analysed in our ongoing research to construct a design space. The resulting design space aims to support researchers, designers or educators to systematically explore design parameters that enable the effective creation of embodied reading experiences. The under-explored configurations of the design space, as well as the most frequently used configuration patterns, are also identified to reveal trends and opportunities for future applications. The paper also exemplifies how the design space can be utilised.

Keywords: Augmented Reading · Digital media · Education

1 Introduction

When preparing to delve into a captivating romantic novel, we adapt the light settings, brew a comforting cup of tea, perhaps play some serene piano music, and then we sit down in our preferred armchair, legs up, take our book, and start reading. The interplay between our body and environment is always present, influencing our reading experience. However, imagine if the lights and the music would automatically adapt to the atmosphere of each chapter in our novel. Such enhancement could certainly intensify the reading experience. Moreover, what if our beverage somehow could adaptively support the reading experience? Is it conceivable that our TV set would display illustrations, in synchrony to our reading? How can the environment support the reading experience?

C. Stephanidis et al. (Eds.): HCII 2023, CCIS 1957, pp. 200–208, 2024.
https://doi.org/10.1007/978-3-031-49212-9_27

The embodied cognition perspective [1] emphasises that our comprehension of the world and learning is deeply tied to our embodied experiences. When we read, we mentally simulate realities and draw upon experiences and knowledge. Despite technological advancements in reading, most innovation focused on the text itself, neglecting the potential for designing technologies that consider the holistic interactions between the reader, text and environment. This oversight limits the exploration of the environmental support of reading. With a systematic overview of all the possibilities to augment reading via changes in the environment, we will be able to discover and study further innovative opportunities. This is the leading question of the current research: considering the emphasis of environmental factors what is the design space of Augmented Reading?

This paper focuses on options to modulate the reading environment to enhance the reading experience. It involves adjusting various parameters to influence the reader's interaction with the text and the environment, including synchronising the text with the surrounding environment. To effectively implement this approach, an understanding of Augmented Reading is crucial. Augmented Reading entails enhancing the reading experience through the integration of digital elements and technologies. However, the current body of research does not fully covers all Augmented Reading dimensions. Existing work [2–4] explored specific contexts and dimensions but does not address the environmental support of reading holistically. There is a need for a systematic approach to create meaningful and engaging reading experiences that promote effective learning.

As an endeavour to fulfil the need, this paper aims to complement prior work by defining a design space that explores and analyses the underlying factors associated with interactions in the reading environment. It provides a framework for designers and researchers to understand and shape these interactions and create meaningful and engaging learning experiences. The contributions of this paper include proposing a three-dimensional design space and demonstrating its application.

2   Methodology

A literature review analysed 79 artefacts, including research papers, prototypes, and projects, dated between 2000 and 2021 to examine the underlying concept of Augmented Reading. While not exhaustive, the review identified trends and opportunities. The process involved tagging the artefacts, identifying the dimensions involved, constructing the design space, evaluating contributions, and conducting multi-dimensional analysis to identify trends and uncover potential opportunities.

3   Design Space Dimensions

Within the design space, this paper primarily focuses on exploring the dimensions of the surrounding environment to enhance Augmented Reading experiences. However, it is important to acknowledge the dimensions associated with the text itself. The text, as a conveyor of a message, has an extensive list of relevant characteristics such as medium (e.g., paper, electronic visual displays, and projection surfaces) or dynamism (static or dynamic).

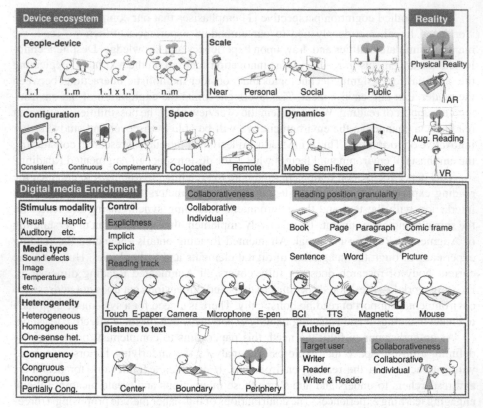

Fig. 1. The proposed three-dimensional design space for Augmented Reading.

3.1 Reality

The reader's perceived environment, known as reality, can exist along a continuum [5] ranging from *physical reality* (composed of atoms) to *virtual reality* (composed of digitally synthesized artefacts). Additionally, there is a *mixed reality* configuration that combines both physical and virtual elements. *Augmented Reading Reality*, a specific sub-configuration of mixed reality focuses on tracking and enhancing the reading activity rather than simply augmenting physical objects like books.

3.2 Digital Media Enrichment (DME)

It can be described as reading digital media artefacts which manifest in the reading environment with the purpose to support the reading activity. The following present sub-dimensions that characterise the DMEs.

The *stimulus modality* distinguishes between the five human senses: visual, auditory, haptic, olfactory and gustatory.

Media type refers to the concrete type of media that stimulates one or more human senses. Different media types are organised based on their respective stimulus modality, such as visual (text, pictures, motion pictures, light effects, shadow, fog), auditory (sound effects, speech, music, soundscape), haptic (wind, temperature, vibration), olfactory (scent), gustatory (taste), and hybrid (combining multiple stimulus modalities).

The *relative distance to text* dimension describes the position of a DME in relation to the location of the text. It can be classified as *center* (existing in the same medium and area as the text, such as illustrations on a digital tablet, that also serves to read the text), *boundary* (sharing borders with the text, such as an illustration on a tablet that extends an illustration on a paper book [6]) or *periphery* (not sharing borders with the text, such as triggering a light effect in a physical location that is not near the text).

Heterogeneity entails the notion of diversity of media types employed in an Augmented Reading experience. The three possible categories are: *homogeneous* (only one media type is used), *single-sense heterogeneous* (more than one media type from a single stimulus modality is employed) and *heterogeneous* (if the media types used belong to multiple stimulus modalities).

Congruency is the degree to which the DME is contextualised with the text's meaning. There are three possible categories: (1) *congruous* - DME has a strong and literal connection, (2) *incongruous* - DME has no direct connection with the text being enriched, or (3) might combine the usage of *congruous and incongruous* DMEs.

Control pertains to the reader's ability to operate Digital Media Enrichments (DMEs). This dimension can be characterised by four sub-dimensions: *reading position tracking, reading position granularity, explicitness, and collaborativeness. Reading position tracking* involves determining the real-time reading position using various methods such as touchscreens, cameras, or text-to-speech. *Reading position granularity* refers to the precision of measuring the reading position, ranging from the entire book to specific levels like paragraphs or words. *Explicitness* relates to whether control over the enrichment is consciously expressed or implicit. *Collaborativeness* signifies the capacity for multiple readers to collaboratively control the DMEs.

Authoring can be understood as the process of creating a DME and synchronising it with a specific part of the text. An important subdimension of authoring is *collaborativeness* which refers to the possibility to author DMEs individually or collaboratively.

3.3 Device Ecosystem

The incorporation and adaptation of the Cross-Device taxonomy [7] into the design space allow for the exploration of various configurations within the device ecosystem, such as device coordination. In the following, we describe the related dimensions:

People-to-device relationship refers to the number of readers that is in a direct relationship with a specific amount of devices. Accordingly, there are four categories represented in Fig. 1: (1) *single reader of a single device* - one reader interacting with one device, (2) *single reader of multiple devices* - one reader interacts with more than one device, (3) *multiple single readers of a single device* - more than one reader can interact with their own device and (4) *multiple readers of multiple devices* - more than one device can be controlled by more than one reader in a collaborative setting.

Scale of a device ecosystem depends on the dimensions of the devices and how close they are to the user. Accordingly, there are four categories represented in Fig. 1: (1) *near* devices are in contact with the reader's body, (2) *personal* limited by the reader's reach,

(3) *social* comprises devices which are being collaboratively manipulated by a group of readers, and (4) *public* represents the larger possible area in which the devices and readers can occupy.

Space makes the distinction between ecosystems in which devices are *co-located* and ecosystems of interconnected *remote* devices (see Fig. 1).

Dynamics is concerned with the mobility capacity of the devices that compose the ecosystem. Accordingly, there are three categories represented in Fig. 1: (1) *mobile*, where devices can easily change their location, (2) *semi-fixed*, where devices have limited portability and (3) *fixed*, where the devices cannot be moved.

Configuration addresses the spatial and logical distribution of the interfaces across devices. Three design approaches for designing multi-device experiences are considered [8]: *consistent* (same content replicated on each device), *continuous* (spatial distribution of content across multiple devices) and *complementary* (supplemental content on each device). See Fig. 1 for reference.

4 Outcomes

The design space presented in the previous section serves as a tool for exploring Augmented Reading. Through a preliminary exploration of the design space and a comprehensive analysis of existing literature, it becomes possible to provide an overview of emerging trends and opportunities for further exploration. Our analysis also offers insights into the prevailing directions of research and development. In this section, we showcase applications that not only embody these trends and opportunities but also provide tangible examples within the Augmented Reading design space.

4.1 Trends and Opportunities

Regarding the reality configuration dimension, around 30.4% focused on physical reality (e.g. the interactive pop-up book Popables [9]), while 59.5% explored mixed reality applications (e.g. SequenceBook [10]). Among these, 27.8% specifically investigated Augmented Reading Reality (e.g. the Augmented HE-Book [11] or the LIT ROOM [12]). A small portion (7.6%) delved into virtual reality, and 5.1% employed multiple reality configurations. These findings underscore the underexplored nature of virtual reality in the context of Augmented Reading and its innovation potential.

Regarding the digital media enrichment dimension and concretely the stimulus modality, 48.10% of the studies explored multimodal stimulation, while 16.45% did not focus on any specific modality. Visual stimulation was prominent in 73.41% of the studies, with 26.58% exclusively exploring visual stimuli. Auditory stimulation was examined in 53.16% of the studies, followed by haptic stimulation (11.39%) and olfactory stimulation (2.53%). However, gustatory and other less emphasised senses were neglected. Nevertheless, there is a growing trend towards exploring multimodal stimulation, including visual, auditory, haptic, and olfactory combinations (e.g. the augmented HE-Book [11] or the Multisensory book [13]). Popular multimodal approaches included audio-visual (40.50%), visual-auditory-haptic (3.79%), visual-auditory-haptic-olfactory (2.53%), and auditory-haptic (1.26%) combinations.

Among the visual media types, still pictures were the most frequent (53.16%), primarily consisting of 2D computer-generated images (34.17%, e.g. Flippin [14]) and 3D computer-generated images (6.33%). Motion pictures (44.30%) included 3D animation-based (e.g. MagicBook [2]), 2D animation-based (e.g. Bridging Book [6]), photographic, and motion graphic formats (e.g. Lost Cosmonaut [15]). Text (21.52%) constituted the third most frequent visual media type. Light (15.18%, e.g. LIT ROOM [12]), shadow (1.26%, in LIT ROOM [12]), and robots (8.86%, e.g. the Robot tutor for children [16]) were utilized as visual media types in other studies. Regarding auditory media types, four main types were extensively explored. Sound effects (30.37%, e.g. the Embodied reading project [17]) were the most used type. The speech was also recurrently employed (16.45%), either through text-to-speech or pre-recorded methods. Music was the third most used auditory media type (12.65%, e.g. the Listen Reader [18]), while soundscape was the least explored (6.32% e.g. the Listen Reader [18]).

Haptic media types were rarely used. The vibration was employed in five studies (6.32%, e.g. Embodied Reading system [17]). Other haptic types were used once: friction was used to emphasise scene features [19], the wind was used to direct scent and intensify embodiment [13], force conveyed emotions and physical events [11], and temperature influenced identification and para-social relationship [20]. Finally, no study utilised gustatory media types, while only one study incorporated limited olfactory effects [13]. The exploration of underutilised stimulus modalities (e.g. haptic, olfactory), and media types (e.g. data visualisation), as well as its multimodal usage in Augmented Reading, presents an opportunity for enhancing and enriching the reading experience.

Concerning the control sub-dimension, it is noteworthy that 46.83% of the analysed papers lack a reading track mechanism. Among those that do have a mechanism, 22.78% utilise a camera-based reading track. The remaining mechanisms, such as touchscreen, electronically augmented paper, and brain sensor, each represents less than 8.86% of the total. These underutilised mechanisms hold the potential to spur innovative advancements when the appropriate conditions are met. The reading position granularity also presents innovative potential, with only 3.79% of the papers offering word-level granularity. The most commonly offered granularity is page granularity (31.64%), followed by paragraph granularity (16.45%). Regarding the control explicitness, 29.11% used an implicit approach (e.g. the SequenceBook [10]) and 12.66% a combination of implicit and explicit approaches (e.g. the Listen reader [18]). 11.39% employed an explicit control mechanism (e.g. e.g. the Robot tutor for children [16]). Implicit control is advantageous as it requires less effort and attention but readers may lose control and become frustrated. Finally, regarding the control sub-dimensions, only 7.59% of the studies incorporated collaborative functionalities for controlling digital media enrichments (DMEs). This aspect holds significant potential, particularly in application areas like education and entertainment.

Concerning authoring, only 15.19% of the analysed material included authoring functionalities, with a mere 5.06% offering collaborative ways. Surprisingly, this dimension remains vastly underexplored in the design space, despite the immense potential it holds for promoting active engagement and embodied cognition, particularly in educational settings. Authoring, can empower individuals to create and personalise content fostering comprehension and knowledge retention.

Regarding the remaining digital media enrichment sub-dimensions, 48.10% offer heterogeneity, using diverse media types from multiple stimulus modalities. 26.58% employed a homogeneous configuration (only one media type was used) and 10.12% explored a single-sense heterogeneous configuration. Congruent DMEs were used in most studies (74.68%). Only 6.32% used incongruous DMEs for specific purposes, such as refocusing readers [21]. Regarding the relative distance to text, the most frequent position for DMEs was the center (35.44%), followed by the peripheral position (31.64%). Locating the enrichments exclusively in the boundary position was the least common option (7.59%). Some studies combined different positions: center and periphery (3.79%), center and boundary (1.26%), boundary and periphery (1.26%), and center, boundary, and periphery (1.26%). Opportunities also arise when exploring these sub-dimensions. For instance, considering the exploration of incongruous DMEs such as utilising the environment as a source of pleasure [22] rather than solely using it to reinforce text interpretation, which is the more common approach.

Preliminary analysis of device ecosystem dimensions indicates a focus on personal use, with limited exploration of the near and public scale configuration. Immersive reading in virtual environments or Augmented Reading in public settings remain largely untapped with great innovation potential. In terms of dynamics, there is a need to explore Augmented Reading approaches that encourage mobile reading and effectively use the reader position and associated surroundings as a way to improve the reading experience such as synchronising the text with the environment.

4.2 Exemplary Applications

The design space facilitates the exploration of the Augmented Reading design dimensions, enabling the identification of trends and opportunities to design innovative Augmented Reading applications. Here, we present two applications that exemplify how the design space serves as a valuable tool to understand design patterns and unlock new possibilities. For instance, the design space has been instrumental in the development of a location-based story generator, showcased in Pranay Bhatia's thesis [23]. This approach enables the creation of interactive and engaging narratives tailored to tourists.

The design space analysis can also play a vital role in identifying the innovativeness of systems and in driving their improvement. One such example is STREEN [24], an augmented reading environment developed for primary school students to foster collaboration and active engagement during reading activities. STREEN offers a range of innovative features, including collaborative authoring and control of DMEs, and the use of not-so-conventional digital media types, such as data visualisation graphs. It seamlessly operates across diverse device ecosystem scales from personal to public scales (e.g. reader's theatre public performance). Furthermore, we can identify the potential to extend STREEN to provide the usage of other media types e.g. haptic or to explore the potential of STREEN in remote configurations. These applications demonstrate the practical outcomes that emerge from utilising the design space as a framework to explore innovative approaches and capitalise on emerging trends.

5 Conclusion

The analysis and exploration of the Augmented Reading design space have revealed promising insights and opportunities for enhancing the reading experience. Underexplored areas and potential avenues for innovation were identified, highlighting the potential of environmental support of reading. This approach promotes embodied cognition, active engagement, and learning. Furthermore, exemplary applications showcased the practical use of design trends and the translation of opportunities into meaningful reading experiences. By leveraging the design space as a tool to analyse and shape the future of Augmented Reading it is possible to pave the way for transformative advancements not only in learning to read but also in the broad area of reading to learn.

References

1. Glenberg, A.M.: Embodiment as a unifying perspective for psychology. WIREs Cogn. Sci. **1**, 586–596 (2010). https://doi.org/10.1002/wcs.55
2. Grasset, R., Dunser, A., Billinghurst, M.: The design of a mixed-reality book: is it still a real book? In: 2008 7th IEEE/ACM International Symposium on Mixed and Augmented Reality, pp. 99–102 (2008). https://doi.org/10.1109/ISMAR.2008.4637333
3. Campos, C., Ducasse, J., Čopič Pucihar, K., Geroimenko, V., Kljun, M.: Augmented imagination: creating immersive and playful reading experiences. In: Geroimenko, V. (ed.) Augmented Reality Games II, pp. 57–81. Springer, Cham (2019). https://doi.org/10.1007/978-3-030-156 20-6_3
4. Cardoso, J.C.S., Ribeiro, J.M.: Tangible VR book: exploring the design space of marker-based tangible interfaces for virtual reality. Appl. Sci. **11**, 1367 (2021). https://doi.org/10.3390/app 11041367
5. Milgram, P., Kishino, F.: A taxonomy of mixed reality visual displays. IEICE Trans. Inf. Syst. **77**, 1321–1329 (1994)
6. Figueiredo, A.C., Pinto, A.L., Branco, P., Zagalo, N., Coquet, E.: Bridging book: a not-so-electronic children's picturebook. In: Proceedings of the 12th International Conference on Interaction Design and Children, pp. 569–572. ACM, New York (2013). https://doi.org/10.1145/2485760.2485867
7. Brudy, F., et al.: Cross-device taxonomy: survey, opportunities and challenges of interactions spanning across multiple devices. In: Proceedings of the 2019 CHI Conference on Human Factors in Computing Systems, pp. 1–28 (2019)
8. Levin, M.: Designing Multi-Device Experiences: An Ecosystem Approach to User Experiences Across Devices. O'Reilly Media, Inc. (2014)
9. Qi, J., Buechley, L.: Electronic popables: exploring paper-based computing through an interactive pop-up book. In: Proceedings of the Fourth International Conference on Tangible, Embedded, and Embodied Interaction, pp. 121–128. ACM, New York (2010). https://doi.org/10.1145/1709886.1709909
10. Yamada, H.: SequenceBook: interactive paper book capable of changing the storylines by shuffling pages. In: CHI 2010 Extended Abstracts on Human Factors in Computing Systems, pp. 4375–4380. ACM, New York (2010). https://doi.org/10.1145/1753846.1754156
11. Rahman, A.S.M.M., Alam, K.M., El Saddik, A.: Augmented HE-Book: a multimedia based extension to support immersive reading experience. In: Kamel, M., Karray, F., Gueaieb, W., Khamis, A. (eds.) AIS 2011. LNCS (LNAI), vol. 6752, pp. 321–330. Springer, Heidelberg (2011). https://doi.org/10.1007/978-3-642-21538-4_32

12. Schafer, G.J., Fullerton, S.K., Walker, I., Vijaykumar, A., Green, K.E.: Words become worlds: the LIT ROOM, a literacy support tool at room-scale. In: Proceedings of the 2018 Designing Interactive Systems Conference, pp. 511–522. Association for Computing Machinery, New York (2018). https://doi.org/10.1145/3196709.3196728

13. Silva, E.P., et al.: Using multisensory content to impact the quality of experience of reading digital books. ACM Trans, Multimedia Comput. Commun. Appl. (TOMM) **17**, 1–18 (2021)

14. Yoshino, K., Obata, K., Tokuhisa, S.: FLIPPIN': exploring a paper-based book UI design in a public space. In: Proceedings of the 2017 CHI Conference on Human Factors in Computing Systems, pp. 1508–1517. Association for Computing Machinery, New York (2017)

15. Vogelsang, A., Signer, B.: The lost cosmonaut: an interactive narrative environment on the basis of digitally enhanced paper. In: Subsol, G. (ed.) ICVS 2005. LNCS, vol. 3805, pp. 270–279. Springer, Heidelberg (2005). https://doi.org/10.1007/11590361_31

16. Gordon, G., Breazeal, C.: Bayesian active learning-based robot tutor for children's word-reading skills. In: Proceedings of the Twenty-Ninth AAAI Conference on Artificial Intelligence, pp. 1343–1349. AAAI Press, Austin (2015)

17. Sanchez, S., Dingler, T., Gu, H., Kunze, K.: Embodied reading: a multisensory experience. In: Proceedings of the 2016 CHI Conference Extended Abstracts on Human Factors in Computing Systems, pp. 1459–1466 (2016)

18. Back, M., Cohen, J., Gold, R., Harrison, S., Minneman, S.: Listen reader: an electronically augmented paper-based book. In: Proceedings of the SIGCHI Conference on Human Factors in Computing Systems, pp. 23–29. ACM, New York (2001). https://doi.org/10.1145/365024.365031

19. Cingel, D., Blackwell, C., Connell, S., Piper, A.M.: Augmenting children's tablet-based reading experiences with variable friction haptic feedback. In: Proceedings of the 14th International Conference on Interaction Design and Children, pp. 295–298. ACM, New York (2015). https://doi.org/10.1145/2771839.2771900

20. Tal-Or, N., Razpurker-Apfeld, I.: When the physical coldness in the viewer's environment leads to identification with a suffering protagonist. Int. J. Psychol. **56**, 394–406 (2021)

21. Eid, M., Fernandez, A.: ReadGoGo!: towards real-time notification on readers' state of attention. In: 2013 XXIV International Conference on Information, Communication and Automation Technologies (ICAT), pp. 1–6 (2013). https://doi.org/10.1109/ICAT.2013.6684047

22. Kuzmičová, A.: Does it matter where you read? Situating narrative in physical environment. Commun. Theory **26**, 290–308 (2016). https://doi.org/10.1111/comt.12084

23. Bhatia, P.: Location-based story generation. Bachelor thesis, Rhine-Waal University of Applied Sciences (2022)

24. Ribeiro, P., et al.: The Impact of a Digitally-Augmented Reading Instruction on Reading Motivation and Comprehension of Third Graders. In: Brooks, E.I., Brooks, A., Sylla, C., Møller, A.K. (eds.) DLI 2020. LNICSSITE, vol. 366, pp. 3–25. Springer, Cham (2021). https://doi.org/10.1007/978-3-030-78448-5_1

Research on Inclusive Design Elements of Urban Innovative Migrants Based on KANO Model

Yuwei Wu[✉] [iD], Chengwei Wang[iD], and Shuran Li

Tongji University, Zhangwu Road 281, Yangpu District, Shanghai, China
2131935@tongji.edu.cn

Abstract. Purpose to explore the demand preferences of innovative immigrants towards cities, obtain demand priorities, and propose a framework for inclusive design elements of innovative immigrants. Research methods from the perspective of inclusive design, interviews were conducted on urban innovative immigrants, and a detailed classification of their demand preferences was conducted. Eight evaluation dimensions and 19 evaluation indicators were established. Quantitative analysis of effectively recovered samples was conducted using the KANO model and correlation analysis. Research results based on preliminary research, KANO model, and correlation analysis, a framework for innovative immigrant inclusive design elements is proposed. Conclusion Urban innovative immigrants attach great importance to seeking innovative and diverse life experiences, as well as the convenience of urban areas and the importance of community interaction activities. At the same time, research has found that differences in marriage and culture among urban innovative immigrants can also affect their demand for the city. Limitations the limitation of this study is that the sample size is limited, resulting in only a certain degree of local representativeness in the research results. Value the value of this study lies in exploring the living needs of innovative urban immigrants and providing effective references for designing and optimizing urban inclusivity.

Keywords: KANO Model · Urban Innovative Immigrants · Inclusive Design · indicator Framework

1 Introduction

1.1 Research Background and Significance

With the acceleration of urbanization, immigration has become a new issue of concern. As an important component of the urban population, the diverse cultural backgrounds and lifestyles of immigrant groups have brought rich cultural and social resources to the city, but they also face various difficulties and challenges, especially in terms of social, cultural, and economic isolation and exclusion. Although there are many studies on urban migration, most of them are quantitative studies based on the results of the "population census", mainly focusing on low-income migrant workers or social surveys on marginalized life [1]. However, there is little research and analysis on the living needs

C. Stephanidis et al. (Eds.): HCII 2023, CCIS 1957, pp. 209–223, 2024.
https://doi.org/10.1007/978-3-031-49212-9_28

of innovative immigrants. Urban innovative immigrants refer to immigrants who possess innovative spirit, strong abilities, and play an important role in urban areas. Their characteristics include: (1) possessing rich experience and skills, bringing innovation and creativity to the city; (2) Familiarity with different cultures and languages facilitates cross-cultural communication and cooperation; (3) Good at creating and seizing opportunities, with strong inclusiveness and openness; (4) Have a profound understanding and understanding of the social, cultural, economic, and political development of cities. Faced with innovative immigration, cities need to be more inclusive to stimulate their creativity [2]. In this context, inclusive design, as an important design concept and practice, provides us with a more comprehensive approach to solving the problems faced by urban innovative immigrants. By breaking the framework of people's bottom thinking and comfort zones, inclusive design can provide a more open and adaptable urban environment, creating a more friendly and diverse life for innovative immigrants.

This study takes inclusive design as the starting point and combines the KANO model to analyze the social phenomenon and cultural background of urban innovative immigrants. It deeply understands and analyzes the factors that affect the survival and living conditions of today's urban innovative immigrant groups, thereby providing more comprehensive and effective strategic support for urban planning, social management, and design practices.

1.2 Immigrants Needs List Evaluation

Currently, many studies have explored the research directions and methods of inclusive design and urban innovative immigration.

Some studies focus on the meaning of urban infrastructure and public services, as well as their positioning and construction in immigrant settlements. These studies explore how to establish cultural diversity and inclusivity, strengthen inclusive and sustainable human settlements planning [3] and management by exploring and evaluating urban site selection strategies, and make cities more inclusive, safe, resilient, and sustainable [4].

Other research focuses on the role of inclusive design in integrating innovative immigrants into urban life as one of the stakeholders [5]. The focus of these studies is on the spatial functional layout of cities [6], the attractiveness of social networks, transportation, and tourism facilities to immigrants, and the impact of these facilities on promoting social communication among immigrants [7].

In addition, there are some studies based on community participation aimed at exploring how direct community participation can better adapt to the design of immigrants [8] and provide them with better living conditions and opportunities for interpersonal interaction [9].

In summary, there are various attempts to study innovative immigrants, but due to the different backgrounds and cultures involved in innovative immigrant groups, their needs and interests are also more distant. Therefore, current research lacks more detailed and in-depth research on the needs of innovative groups.

2 Research Design and Implementation

2.1 Research Framework

In the research process, we first established evaluation dimensions and evaluation characteristics based on literature research, in order to further analyze the needs and preferences of the research objects. Then, we used the bidirectional KANO quality satisfaction survey to understand consumers' satisfaction with products and services and the factors that influence them, so as to provide a basis for improving their daily needs. Next, we used the SII-DDI matrix analysis to classify the evaluation dimensions, understand the relationship between the evaluation dimensions, and the importance of the evaluation characteristics. Finally, we used correlation analysis to explore the correlation between the evaluation characteristics, in order to gain a deeper understanding of consumers' needs and preferences, and provide more powerful data support for product and service optimization. The results of this research process will provide powerful data support for the improvement and continuous optimization of products and services (Fig. 1).

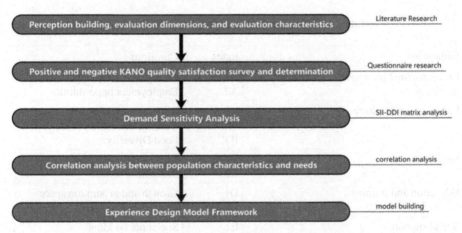

Fig. 1. Research framework. Source: Author's self drawing

2.2 Development of the Immigrants Needs List

The initial version of the innovative immigrants needs list was developed by literature review and in-person interview with innovative immigrants.

The process of literature review. Firstly, a literature review was conducted to establish the evaluation dimensions and features based on perception. This involves extracting the main dimensions and features that influence users' perceived evaluation of products or services from relevant theoretical and empirical research, forming a preliminary evaluation index system.

Collecting data from online social media. We used the social media platform Weibo to collect geotagged information posted by users. We screened cities with a population greater than 1 million to ensure that the data we collected is sufficiently representative. Then, we use natural language processing technology (such as keyword extraction and part of speech tagging) to process the text to extract the crowd attribute and city attribute we need. For crowd attributes, we extract and classify keywords such as personal information, behavior, and interests involved in the text. For urban attributes, we extract and classify vocabulary and expressions related to cities in the text.

Last, We conduct five one-on-one semi-structured interview with innovative immigrants. During the interview, every participants was invited to talk about the key reasons brought them to living and working in the new city. Each interview last about 15 min.

Based on the result from literature review, online data analysis and in-person interview. We created an initial version of the immigrants needs list. All co-authors run a discuss session to refine the list. During the discussion, similar items was eliminate. A final list include 8 categories and 19 needs was created (see Table 1).

Subsequently, multiple innovative immigrants were invited to rate each element based on their own preferences, and Likert's five-point scale was used to measure these elements (see Table 2).

Table 1. Evaluation indicators established in this study.

Dimension	Index	Questions
Entrepreneurship support resources and networks	A1 A2	Entrepreneurship opportunities Employment opportunities
Language and Culture	B1 B2 B3	Dialect penetration rate Cultural Inclusion Food Diversity
Settle	C1 C2	Settlement conditions Settlement benefits
Education and training	D1 D2	Growth and promotion space Children's education
Social support	E1 E2 E3 E4	Social net building Peer Counseling Looking for partners Social activity
Cost of living	F1 F2	Housing price Consumption level
Natural environment	G1 G2	Climate Natural scenery
Basic equipment	H1 H2 H3 H4	Transportation Large supermarket School Medical treatment

Table 2. Comparison table of classification of evaluation results.

Function/Service		Negative question					Function/Service	
		Very important	Generally important	in-different	not too important	not important		
Positive question	**Very important**	Q	A	A	A	O	**Positive question**	**Very important**
	Generally Important	R	I	I	I	M		**Generally Important**
	Indifferent	R	I	I	I	M		**Indifferent**
	not too important	R	I	I	I	M		**not too important**

A: Attractive Quality **O:** One-dimensional Quality M: Must-be Quality I: Indifferent Quality R: Reverse Quality

2.3 Immigrants Needs List Evaluation

In order to further investigate the needs of innovative immigrants, we conduct designed a questionnaire to learn the opinion from the target audience in a boardly way.

Data Collection and Validation. This study has the following requirements for the tested participants: they are innovative workers who have come to live in a new city, such as designers, design students, etc. Throughout the entire questionnaire process, the identity of the respondents is kept confidential, and only demographic data such as gender, age, and marital status are required. All respondents need to click on the survey link to view the research survey instructions. They voluntarily answer research questions and can withdraw from the survey at any time. Therefore, all participants agreed to fill out the questionnaire on the principle of full knowledge and voluntary participation. The questionnaire consists of 19 evaluation characteristics, from the perspective of innovative immigrants, to evaluate the multi-faceted attributes of innovative immigrant lifestyles based on demand attributes and overall satisfaction (see Table 3). The questionnaire contains a series of paired items to investigate the opinions of the respondents.

In this study, a total of 331 questionnaires were collected, and the answering time of each questionnaire was not less than 120 s. To ensure the validity of the data, we conducted multiple screening during the data cleaning stage. Firstly, we excluded all questionnaires with answering time less than 120 s to ensure that the research objects had enough time to answer the questions seriously. Secondly, we checked all the answers to the questions and screened out all the questionnaires with the same selected options. After the above screening, we finally obtained 201 valid questionnaires. In order to verify the accuracy of the data analysis results, we also randomly selected 55 research objects for questionnaire survey to observe the consistency of the results. Through the above data cleaning process, we obtained a reliable data foundation, which provided strong support for subsequent data analysis. The specific demographic data are shown in Table 3.

Table 3. Sample basic data statistics.

Category	Option	Frequency	Percentage%
Gender	Male	93	46.27%
	Female	108	53.73%
Age group	18–25	53	26.37%
	26–30	68	33.83%
	31–40	44	21.89%
	41–50	36	17.91%
The highest education	Undergraduate	133	66.17%
	Master	43	21.39%
	Doctor	25	12.44%
	Other	0	0%
Duration of settlement	Less than 1 year	30	14.93%
	1–3 years	42	20.9%
	4–6 years	39	19.4%
	7–10 years	37	18.41%
	Over 10 years	23	11.44%
	There are plans to work in cities other than home, but have not been implemented yet	30	14.93%
Annual income	Currently unemployed	27	13.43%
	below 100000	90	44.78%
	100000 to 300000,	48	23.88%
	300000–500000	18	8.96%
	Over 500000	18	8.96%
Marital status	Single (no potential spouse)	24	11.94%
	In Love	32	15.92%
	Married	52	25.87%
	Married and childbearing	86	42.79%
	Single (but with potential partners)	7	3.48%

Development of the immigrants needs list. A Bi-directional KANO quality satisfaction determination was implemented to the study. The KANO model was proposed by Noriaki Kano [10]. This method was mainly inspired by Frederick Herzberg's two-factor theory. Compared to the traditional method of determining satisfaction through one-dimensional quality, it has wider applicability and is a tool for classifying and prioritizing consumer preference factors [11]. Based on the analysis of the impact of needs on satisfaction, the KANO model reflects the non-linear relationship between product service function, quality and user satisfaction. The KANO model is shown in Fig. 2, with the abscissa representing the degree of quality attributes and the ordinate representing the degree of satisfaction. These five attributes are determined based on the relationship between the degree of quality possession and satisfaction [12]. Using the KANO model to define quality categories helps designers determine the real needs of the research object, enabling them to more accurately control quality and satisfaction in the pattern design and development process.

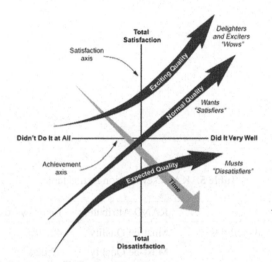

Fig. 2. KANO model. Source: Gorelova et al. 2021

Based on the KANO model, when collecting questionnaire data, the respondent's opinions or views need to be divided into five dimensions: "important", "generally important", "indifferent", "not very important", and "unimportant" [13]. The KANO evaluation result classification reference table is used to determine the final classification of each demand feature (see Table 4).

For the bi-directional KANO model analysis, respondents are required to perceive their satisfaction with 19 evaluation characteristics in two hypothetical scenarios (positive or negative) [14]. The satisfaction indicator uses the Likert 5-point scale, and the higher the score, the higher the perceived satisfaction.

3   Results

3.1   Attribute of the Indicators

The results of the questionnaire analysis are used to attribute the KANO evaluation dimensions and features to attribute categories [15]. Among the 19 design evaluation characteristics, 9 are classified as attractive attributes (A), 0 as One-dimensional attributes (O), 6 as must- be attributes (M), 4 as indifferent attributes (I), and 0 as reverse attributes (Q) (see Table 5).

Table 4. Sample questionnaire for this study.

Questions	Very important	Generally important	indifferent	not too important	not important
If the city can provide more entrepreneurial opportunities, your evaluation is:					
If there are few or no cities that can provide entrepreneurial opportunities, your assessment is:					

Table 5. KANO evaluation results table.

Function	KANO Attributes	Better-words	Worse-words
Number of educational facilities	Must-be Quality	42.19%	−45.83%
Urban Climate	Must-be Quality	42.02%	−45.21%
Conditions for urban settlement	Must-be Quality	41.49%	−45.21%
Urban consumption level	Must-be Quality	40.64%	−40.64%
Cities to provide personal growth and promotion space	Must-be Quality	39.89%	−45.21%
Urban transportation facilities	Attractive Quality	49.21%	−36.65%
The city provides peer support	Attractive Quality	49.21%	−39.78%
Urban housing price level	Attractive Quality	48.92%	−41.88%
Urban cultural tolerance	Attractive Quality	48.69%	−40.11%
Urban hospitals	Attractive Quality	47.06%	−41.67%
Cities provide entrepreneurial opportunities	Attractive Quality	46.35%	−43.37%
Diversity and urban cuisine	Attractive Quality	44.79%	−43.75%
Urban large-scale commercial supermarkets	Attractive Quality	43.98%	−43.46%

(continued)

Table 5. (*continued*)

Function	KANO Attributes	Better-words	Worse-words
Cities help establish local social networks	Attractive Quality	42.47%	−41.4%
Urban settlement benefits	Indifferent Quality	41.54%	−40%
Employment opportunities provided by cities	Indifferent Quality	41.36%	−40.31%
Prevalence of urban dialects	Indifferent Quality	39.06%	−40.63%
Providing children's education in cities	Indifferent Quality	38.17%	−38.71%

3.2 SII-DDI Matrix Analysis

According to KANO's two-dimensional quality concept, changing attribute performance has different benefits for increasing customer satisfaction and decreasing customer dissatisfaction [16]. To improve customer satisfaction, both the increase in satisfaction and the decrease in dissatisfaction need to be considered simultaneously. Berger et al. proposed the Satisfaction Increment Index (SII) and the Dissatisfaction Decrement Index (DDI) to measure the improvement performance of satisfaction and dissatisfaction, respectively [17], which have been cited or modified in most subsequent studies. The absolute values of SII and DDI range from 0 to 1, and the larger the value, the greater the improvement benefit; conversely, the smaller the value, the smaller the improvement benefit (see **Error! Reference source not found.**).

The formulas for calculating these two coefficients are as follows:

$$SII = (A + O)/(A + O + M + I) \tag{1}$$

$$DDI = (O + M)/(A + O + M + I)(-1) \tag{2}$$

Furthermore, a two-dimensional quadrant can be established using SII and DDI, with the X-axis at the average SII value and the Y-axis at the average DDI value, to determine the priority of attributes that can be improved. These four quadrants are as follows [18]:

Quadrant 1: High SII and high DDI, which represent quality expectations attributes that can eliminate user dissatisfaction and increase consumer/user satisfaction. The functions/services in this quadrant should be prioritized.

Quadrant 2: High SII but low DDI, which represent quality attractive attributes that cannot eliminate user dissatisfaction but can increase consumer/user satisfaction. These are attributes that consumers/users do not have excessive expectations for.

Quadrant 3: Low SII and low DDI, which represent quality indifferent attributes that neither eliminate user dissatisfaction nor increase consumer/user satisfaction. These are attributes that users do not care about.

Quadrant 4: Low SII but high DDI, which represent necessary attributes that can eliminate user dissatisfaction but do not increase consumer/user satisfaction. These are demands that users feel obligated to be met, and the functions/services in this quadrant must be satisfied.

According to the sensitivity ranking of the attractive attributes of urban innovation immigrants, urban transportation, urban peer support, and urban housing prices are the three important factors affecting the selection of cities by innovation immigrants. Among them, urban transportation ranks first, which means that innovation immigrants value the convenience of urban transportation more. Urban peer support ranks second, indicating that innovation immigrants also value the support of their peers in the same industry. The ranking of urban housing prices is third, which shows that innovation immigrants also consider the level of housing prices when selecting a city (Fig. 3).

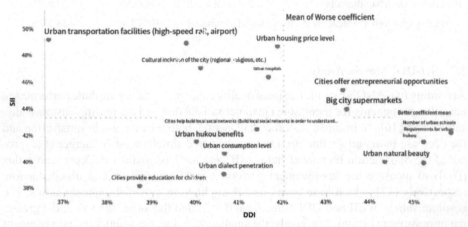

Fig. 3. SII-DDI two dimensional quadrant results. Source: Author's self drawing

3.3   Correlation Analysis

Based on the analysis above, we studied the correlation between six demographic attributes and 19 city attributes. We found that although all the factors showed weak or negative correlation with each other, the differences in their correlations still reflected certain patterns. Firstly, marital status was somewhat related to the popularity of local dialects and peer support in the city; time of settlement was correlated with the city's entrepreneurial opportunities, cultural inclusiveness, and housing prices, indicating that innovative immigrants need to strengthen language integration and career links while considering the cost of living for long-term stability. Education background was strongly associated with the city's employment opportunities, the popularity of local dialects, and the welfare benefits of the city's household registration, indicating that people with higher education tend to value the advantages of employment and settlement. Gender was related to the diversity of food, the conditions for settling down, and the city's provision of personal growth and promotion opportunities, indicating that there are still differences between men and women in these aspects. Annual income and age group were related to the welfare benefits of settling down and the provision of educational facilities in the city, indicating that innovative immigrants increasingly value long-term welfare of the city with age and income growth (Fig. 4).

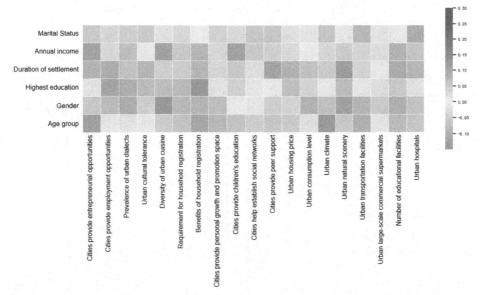

Fig. 4. Heat map of the correlation between the attributes and needs of innovative immigrants. Source: Author's self drawing

The KDE distribution graphs of the factors show that the grouping of demographic attributes often corresponds to the differentiation of their preference options. Taking the two groups of factors with the highest correlation, gender-city food diversity and education background-city household welfare, for example, the KDE graph of the former shows that males (group 1) tend to choose cities with high food diversity over females (group 2), and the KDE graph of the latter shows that innovative immigrants with a bachelor's degree are insensitive to household welfare benefits, those with a master's degree are divided on this issue, while those with a doctoral degree tend to value household welfare benefits. Overall, different groups of demographic attributes will choose suitable cities to settle in according to their specific needs and preferences when facing various city attributes (Fig. 5).

3.4 Framework for Innovative Immigration Inclusive Design Elements

The Framework for Innovative Immigration Inclusive Design Elements is a framework aimed at helping designers and planners create a more inclusive and friendly urban environment for new immigrants. The framework mainly includes the following contents(see Fig. 6):

1. Community integration: Provide opportunities and support for new immigrants to join the community.
2. Employment opportunities: Provide employment opportunities for new immigrants while ensuring fair wages and benefits.
3. Public services: Provide appropriate public services, including education, healthcare, and social services.

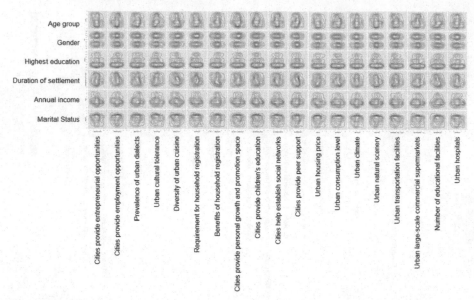

Fig. 5. The KDE diagram of the attributes and needs of innovative immigrant. Source: Author's self drawing

4. Cultural adaptation: Respect and support the cultural background and values of new immigrants.
5. Participation and governance: Ensure that new immigrants have the opportunity and right to participate in urban governance.
6. Urban environment: It should be open and inclusive, so that immigrants can find a sense of belonging and social support within it.

These elements aim to provide support and encouragement for new immigrants to integrate into the urban environment, and provide a guiding framework for designers to develop more inclusive and friendly urban design solutions.

First level design attributes	KANO Attributes	Second level design attributes	KANO Attributes	Third level design attributes	KANO Attributes
Urban transportation facilities	Attractive Quality	Urban Climate	Attractive Quality	Diversity and urban cuisine	Attractive Quality
The city provides peer support	Attractive Quality	Conditions for urban settlement	Attractive Quality	Urban large-scale commercial supermarkets	Attractive Quality
Urban housing price level	Attractive Quality	Urban consumption level	Attractive Quality	Cities help establish local social networks	Attractive Quality
Number of educational facilities	Must-be Quality	Urban cultural tolerance	Attractive Quality		
Cities to provide personal growth and promotion space	Must-be Quality	Urban hospitals	Attractive Quality		
Urban Natural Scenery	Must-be Quality	Cities provide entrepreneurial opportunities	Attractive Quality		

Community integration   Growth opportunities   Public services   Cultural adaptation

Participation and governance   Urban environment

Fig. 6. The KDE diagram of the attributes and needs of innovative immigrant. Source: Author's self drawing

4 Discussion

In this study, the authors aimed to explore the demand preferences of innovative immigrants towards cities, identify their demand priorities, and propose a framework for inclusive design elements to meet their needs. The research employed interviews with urban innovative immigrants and conducted a detailed classification of their demand preferences. Through the use of the KANO model and correlation analysis, the study established eight evaluation dimensions and 19 evaluation indicators.The results of the research, based on the analysis using the KANO model and correlation analysis, led to the proposal of a framework for inclusive design elements targeting innovative immigrants. This framework takes into account the importance placed by urban innovative immigrants on seeking innovative and diverse life experiences, the convenience of urban areas, and the significance of community interaction activities. The study also identified that differences in marriage and culture among urban innovative immigrants can influence their demand for the city.

However, it is important to acknowledge the limitations of this study. One notable limitation is the relatively small sample size, which may limit the generalizability of the research findings to a broader population. The study primarily represents the preferences and perspectives of the local context in which the research was conducted. Despite the limitations, this study holds significant value in its exploration of the living needs of innovative urban immigrants. The proposed framework for inclusive design elements can serve as a valuable reference for urban planning and design professionals seeking to create more inclusive and accommodating cities. By understanding the demand preferences and priorities of innovative immigrants, urban environments can be optimized to provide the necessary resources, opportunities, and experiences that contribute to their successful integration and overall satisfaction.

References

1. Odame, H.S., Okeyo-Owuor, J.B., Changeh, J.G., Otieno, J.O.: The role of technology in inclusive innovation of urban agriculture. Curr. Opin. Environ. Sustain. 43, 106–111 (2020)
2. Bartzokas-Tsiompras, A., Photis, Y.N.: Measuring rapid transit accessibility and equity in migrant communities across 17 European cities. International Journal of Transport Development and (2019)
3. Lowe, N., Vinodrai, T.: The maker-manufacturing nexus as a place-connecting strategy: implications for regions left behind. Econ. Geogr. **96**, 315–335 (2020)
4. Duconseille, F., Saner, R.: Creative placemaking for inclusive urban landscapes. J. Arts Manage. Law Soc. **50**, 137–154 (2020)
5. Rinaldi, A., Angelini, L., Abou Khaled, O., Mugellini, E., Caon, M.: Codesign of public spaces for intercultural communication, diversity and inclusion. In: Di Bucchianico, G. (ed.) AHFE 2019. AISC, vol. 954, pp. 186–195. Springer, Cham (2020). https://doi.org/10.1007/978-3-030-20444-0_18
6. Benson, M.C.: The context and trajectory of lifestyle migration: the case of the British residents of southwest France. Eur. Soc. **12**(1), 45–64 (2010). https://doi.org/10.1080/146166 90802592605
7. Benson, M., Osbaldiston, N.: New horizons in lifestyle migration research: theorising movement, settlement and the search for a better way of life. In: Benson, M., Osbaldiston, N. (eds.) Understanding Lifestyle Migration, pp. 1–23. London: Palgrave Macmillan UK (2014)
8. Fleury, S., Vanukuru, R., Mille, C., Poinsot, K., Agnès, A., Richir, S.: CRUX: a creativity and user experience model. Digit. Creativity **32**(2), 116–123 (2021). https://doi.org/10.1080/146 26268.2021.1915339
9. Ermacora, G., Lupetti, M.L., Pei, L.: Design for ALL.L making and learning for and with people with disabilities In: 2020 12th International Conference on Education Technology (2020)
10. Kim, T., Hong, H., Magerko, B.: Design requirements for ambient display that supports sustainable lifestyle. In: Proceedings of the 8th ACM Conference on Designing Interactive Systems, pp. 103–112. Aarhus Denmark: ACM (2010)
11. Kaufman, J.C., Beghetto, R.A.: Beyond big and little: The four C model of creativity. Rev. Gen. Psychol. **13**(1), 1–12 (2009). https://doi.org/10.1037/a0013688
12. Lo, C.-H.: Application of refined Kano's model to shoe production and consumer satisfaction assessment. Sustainability **13**(5), 2484 (2021). https://doi.org/10.3390/su13052484
13. Becerra, L., Carenzo, S., Juarez, P.: When circular economy meets inclusive development. Insights from urban recycling and rural water access in Argentina. Sustainability **12**, 9809 (2020)
14. Gorelova, I., Dmitrieva, D., Dedova, M., Savastano, M.: Antecedents and consequences of digital entrepreneurial ecosystems in the interaction process with smart city development. Adm. Sci. **11**(3), 94 (2021). https://doi.org/10.3390/admsci11030094
15. Ginting, R., Hidayati, J., Siregar, I.: Integrating Kano's model into quality function deployment for product design: a comprehensive review. IOP Conf. Ser. Mater. Sci. Eng. **319**, 012043 (2018). https://doi.org/10.1088/1757-899X/319/1/012043
16. Mishra, A., Dash, S.B., Cyr, D.: Linking user experience and consumer-based brand equity: the moderating role of consumer expertise and lifestyle. J. Prod. Brand Manage. **23**(4/5), 333–348 (2014). https://doi.org/10.1108/JPBM-12-2013-0459

17. Naylor, T.D., Florida, R.: The rise of the creative class: and how it's transforming work, leisure, community and everyday life. Can. Public Policy/Anal. de Politiques **29**(3), 378 (2003). https://doi.org/10.2307/3552294
18. Saleh, M.A.E.: Reviving traditional design in modern Saudi Arabia for social cohesion and crime prevention purposes. Landscape Urban Plan. **44**(1), 43–62 (1999). https://doi.org/10.1016/S0169-2046(98)00107-8

User Experience of the Portrait Mode of Smartphone: A Comparative Case Study

Xu Zhang and Mickey Mengting Zhang[(✉)]

Faculty of Humanities and Arts, Macau University of Science and Technology, Macau 999078, China
mtzhang@must.edu.mo

Abstract.

Purpose - Portrait mode refers to a particular setting in smartphone cameras, which mimics the effect of professional cameras with specialized lenses, larger sensors, and high focal lengths. The mode is popular as it can remove the distractions in the background while making the main figure - usually a person more outstanding. The function is so powerful if correctly used, as users can enjoy the professional effect of photos as well as the portability of smartphones. However, as the mode relies on the smartphone's processor, camera hardware, and computational algorithm, different smartphones have different specific functional features and results.

Research Methodology and Approach - This study intends to compare the portrait mode of six smartphones based on iOS and Android systems. Twelve user interviews were conducted first to investigate users' evaluation, needs, and expectations of smartphone portrait mode. Based on this, we develop a survey with current problems, expected functional features of portrait mode, and suggestions for smartphone companies.

Finding - After data analysis, we found that users are not satisfied with the current offering of portrait mode on the market. Smartphone companies have great potential for innovation in this area. Portrait modes from different brands have similar problems: poor interaction logic, hard-to-access shooting assistants, lack of notice information in the shooting process, and hard to customize according to users' needs. We also found that users expected four functions related to the automatic justification of photo composition (75%), better lighting angle (69.44%), parameter setting (63.89%), and figure angle (52.78%). All four functions require the algorithm to recognize the 'aesthetics' of a human being from a personal perspective. Design implications of portrait mode were provided based on the results.

Contribution - The study analyzed the current problems and expected functional features of portrait mode with a comparative case study method. The research can be valuable for the design and development team to discover innovative opportunities, create meaningful functions, and provide a better user experience for a smartphone camera.

Keywords: Portrait mode · user interface · user experience · smartphone

C. Stephanidis et al. (Eds.): HCII 2023, CCIS 1957, pp. 224–238, 2024.
https://doi.org/10.1007/978-3-031-49212-9_29

1 Introduction

Since 2016, Apple has introduced a new camera mode called Portrait Mode, which has gained significant popularity due to its ability to create a depth-of-field effect that allows users to capture photos with a sharp focus on the subject and a blurred background (Apple, 2021). By leveraging advanced algorithms and camera lenses, Portrait Mode enables users to capture photos with a sharp focus on the subject and a blurred background, creating a depth-of-field effect. This feature has become increasingly significant in today's digital age, as more people take and share photos online. By mastering Portrait Mode, even users without a background in photography can consistently capture high-quality images. However, despite its powerful visual performance, Portrait Mode can be challenging for novice users to understand and operate. Typically, mobile phone cameras default to standard photo mode, and users must select Portrait Mode manually. Additionally, different smartphone models have varying Portrait Mode settings, requiring users to have a basic knowledge of photography to adjust relevant parameters. As a result, beginners face a learning and technical barrier when attempting to learn and use Portrait Mode. In conclusion, while Portrait Mode is a valuable feature for capturing stunning photographs, its complexity can hinder user adoption and may require some level of prior knowledge and practice to master.

The purpose of this study is to compare the portrait mode features of six mobile phone models available in the market, with a focus on exploring users' experiences. The study aims to propose an interface design for portrait mode that aligns with users' habits and preferences and provides a wireframe and user interface for mobile phones' portrait mode. The research analyzes the portrait mode on six mobile phone models that operate on Android, IOS, and HarmonyOS systems. The paper begins with an analysis of the six cases, followed by conducting a user interview and a questionnaire to better understand users' needs. The study is centered on the users to develop an interface for portrait mode that accommodates their preferences and habits.

The concept of User Interface Design (UID) has been discussed by Marcus (2002) who suggested that UID plays a significant role in enabling effective communication between human beings or between humans and an artifact. UID is concerned with both the physical and communicative aspects of input and output, which are essential components of interactive activity. Therefore, an efficient user interface design should aim to enhance the communication and usability of an artifact by considering the user's needs and preferences. This can be achieved through a comprehensive understanding of the user's cognitive, emotional, and behavioral characteristics, which should be considered during the design process to create a user interface that is intuitive and user-friendly.

Shneiderman (1998) proposed The Eight Golden Rules of Interface Design including strive for consistency; seek universal usability; offer informative feedback; design dialogs to yield closure; prevent errors. Permit easy reversal of actions; keep users in control; reduce short-term memory load.

Based on Shneiderman's research, Gong and Tarasewich (2004) proposed fifteen principles for mobile device interface design, including to enable frequent users to use shortcuts; offer informative feedback; design dialogs to yield closure; support internal locus of control; consistency; reversal of actions; error prevention and simple error handling; reduce short-term memory load; design for multiple and dynamic contexts; design for small devices; design for limited and split attention; design for speed and recovery; design for "top-down" interaction; allow for personalization; design for enjoyment.

Nielsen's Ten Heuristics are also used to evaluate user interfaces to find their usability problems (Nielsen, 2005). Ten principles were discussed, including visibility of system status; match between system and the real world; user control and freedom; consistency and standards; error prevention; recognition rather than recall; flexibility and efficiency of use; aesthetic and minimalist design; help users recognize, diagnose, and recover from errors; help and documentation. In Don Norman's book "The Design of Everyday Things", seven basic design principles are presented including discovery, feedback, conceptual models, affordance, signifiers, mapping, constraints (Norman, 2013) (Table 1).

Table 1. Comparison of design principles

	Shneiderman (1998)	Gong and Tarasewich (2004)	Nielsen (2005)	Norman (2013)
1.Consistency	√	√	√	
2.Shortcuts	√	√		
3.Feedback	√	√	√	√
4.Dialog	√	√	√	√
5.Error Prevention	√	√	√	
6.Reversal	√	√	√	
7.Control and freedom	√	√		√
8.Reduce memory load	√	√	√	√
9.Personalization		√		
10."Top-Down" Interaction		√		
11.Enjoyment		√	√	
12.Constraints				√
13.Flexibility and Efficiency		√	√	
14.Help			√	

After comparison, we summarized the fourteen principles that could guide the interface design, including consistency, shortcuts, feedback, dialog, error prevention, reversal, control and freedom, reducing memory load, personalization, "Top-Down" Interaction, enjoyment, constraints, flexibility and efficiency, and help. The aforementioned principles hold considerable significance in the realm of mobile device interface design. The present study focuses on the design of the portrait mode interface and seeks to incorporate and analyze the aforementioned principles.

2   Research Methodology and Approach

The present study employed a mixed-methods approach to collect and analyze data, which incorporated a case study, questionnaire, and user interview.

2.1   Case Study

We select portrait mode on six mobile phones based on Android, IOS, and HarmonyOS Six popular and representative mobile phones, namely iPhone 13 Pro, Huawei P50 Pro, Vivo X70 Pro+, Xiaomi 11 Ultra, OnePlus 9, and OPPO Reno7 Pro (Table 2), were selected for the study. These mobile phones are widely used and have a significant user base. The portrait mode of these devices was analyzed and compared in terms of their information structure, function, and user experience.

Table 2. Systems and Models of mobile phones selected.

Native System	Mobile Phone System	Mobile Phone Model
iOS	IOS 15	iPhone13 pro
HarmonyOS	HarmonyOS 2.0	Huawei P50 pro
Android	OriginOS 1.0	Vivo X70 pro+
	MIUI 12	Xiaomi 11 Ultra
	Color OS 11.2	OnePlus 9
	Color OS 12	OPPO Reno7 pro

2.2   Questionnaire

We conducted an onlinequestionnaire with 100 valid questionnaires that were collected and analyzed (Table 2). From the demographic analysis, we found that 48% of the respondents are male, while 52% are female. 9% are under twenty years old. 91% are between twenty to thirty-one years old. 11% of respondents are with professional experience in photography. 44% are without professional experience in photography. The Demographic Analysis shows that most respondents are between twenty to thirty-one years old, the main group that uses the phone camera portrait mode.

2.3   User Interview

We interviewed twelve users, including eight iPhone users, two Huawei users, and two Android system phone users (Table 3). The 12 interviewees were: X2, L7, C3, S4, C5, C6, Y9, Y12, W1, T11, Z10, Z8. Respondents were between twenty-three and twenty-five years old, seven females and five males. The interview time ranged from between twenty and forty-five minutes and was conducted offline face-to-face and online via video chat. Interview questions included their habits, experiences of using portrait mode, and preference (Table 4).

Table 3. Demographic Analysis by the authors.

Demographic characteristic	Category	N	%
Gender	Male	48	48
	Female	52	52
Age	Under 20	9	9
	20–30 Years	91	91
Experience	With professional experience in photography	11	11
	Without professional experience in photography	89	89

Table 4. Information of interviewees.

Demographic characteristic	Category	N	%
Gender	Male	5	41.67
	Female	7	58.33
Age	21–25	12	100
Phone System	IOS	8	66.67
	HarmonyOS	2	16.67
	Android	2	16.67
Frequency of use	Frequent	7	58.33
	General	5	41.67
Time of use	0–2 years	3	25
	3–4 years	9	75

3 Result

3.1 Functional Features of Portrait Mode

In the ensuing section, we scrutinize and juxtapose the functional characteristics of the portrait mode across six mobile phone models, highlighting their differences, similarities, strengths, and weaknesses. Upon transitioning from the standard photo mode to portrait mode, all six devices exhibit a comparable interface featuring a circular shutter icon centered at the bottom, an album icon situated at the left side at the bottom, and a Flip Lens icon positioned at the right side at the bottom (as illustrated in Fig. 1). These three functions are frequently utilized and are presented for user convenience, facilitating one-handed operation.

After a thorough analysis and comparison of the first level of the portrait mode interface, we proceeded to evaluate the second level, which includes seven functional features such as buttons, zoom functions, composition assistance, beautification, lighting,

Fig. 1. First level of portrait mode interface.

depth, and other functions (Fig. 2, Table 5). It is worth noting that the number of function buttons plays a crucial role in determining the user's experience in the interface, as it can significantly affect the simplicity, flexibility, and efficiency of use. Based on our research, most of the portrait modes have four to five functional features (e.g., iPhone 13 Pro, Xiaomi 11 Ultra, Huawei P50 Pro, OnePlus 9, and OPPO), whereas the Vivo X70 Pro + offers eight functional features.

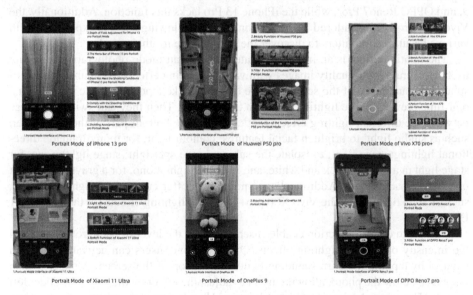

Fig. 2. Second Level of portrait mode interface comparison.

The zoom function enables users to adjust the captured image's magnification level and varies in its presentation across different mobile phones. By selecting a focal length, users can adjust the level of out-of-focus blurring at the tele end to emphasize the main subject and create separation from the foreground or background. As the zoom is increased towards the tele end, the out-of-focus area's blurriness becomes more pronounced. In contrast, the wide-angle end is suitable for pan-focus shots and offers a distinct representation. When framing the image with a focus on a middle or long-distance view, the tele end delivers sharp results across the entire range, much like the wide-angle. The zoom function allows for more personalized representations. After comparing the zoom function of six models, we found that the iPhone 13 Pro, Huawei P50 Pro, Vivo X70 Pro+, and OnePlus 9 offer zoom functions ranging from $1\times$ to $5\times$, whereas the Xiaomi 11 Ultra and OPPO Reno7 Pro lack this feature.

The present portrait mode incorporates various fundamental composition assistance functions, which enable users to discern if they are too close or too far from the subject. Certain portrait modes also offer composition tips, a nine-pane grid, and horizontal lines that facilitate better composition. The Huawei P50 Pro's rear-facing camera can detect a person's face to capture a portrait mode photo. Among all of the six mobile phones, the Vivo X70 pro+ provides a "pose" function, which provides users with posing inspiration.

Beautification is a recent and widespread functional feature that appeals to young users. The primary objective of this function is to improve the appearance of the photograph and create a more impressive and dazzling image by enlarging the eyes, enhancing the lips, and smoothing the skin to create a more radiant look. One-click beautification is provided by four of the models (namely, Huawei P50 Pro, Xiaomi 11 Ultra, OnePlus 9, and OPPO Reno7 Pro), while the iPhone 13 Pro lacks this function. Additionally, the Vivo X70 Pro+ offers tailored beautification features, allowing users to experiment with various beautification filters to discover the optimal one for their needs.

The lighting effect is an important feature in portrait mode photography, allowing users to capture high-quality images with various lighting effects to enhance the atmosphere and ambiance of the scene. IPhone users can take a portrait mode photo with a real-time preview of the lighting effect on their screen. Then they can swipe to choose between the different lighting effects that appear in the bottom part of the viewfinder, such as studio light, to brighten facial features; contour light, for more dramatic directional lighting; stage light, to isolate the subject in the spotlight; stage light mono, for stage light in a classic black and white, and high-key light mono, for a grayscale subject on a white background. Additionally, some models offer customized lighting effects, such as style lighting for the Vivo X70 pro+ and neon lighting effects for the Xiaomi 11 Ultra.

The depth control function enables users to adjust the level of background blur and the intensity of portrait lighting effects. On the iPhone, users can activate the Depth Control by tapping the corresponding button on the top of the screen. A slider is then displayed below the photo, allowing users to adjust the effect by dragging the slider left or right. The original value of the photo is marked by a gray dot above the slider. Notably, three of the six mobile phones in the study offer depth control functions, including the iPhone 13 Pro, Vivo X70 Pro+, and Xiaomi 11 Ultra.

In addition to the functional features mentioned above, there are four features provided by various models, such as foreground effect, AI depth control filter, shooting prompts, and portrait introduction. Two of the mobile phones have foreground effects (Huawei P50 Pro and Vivo X70 pro+). Visual elements are positioned between the camera and the subject. The AI-assisted depth control of Xiaomi 11 Ultra allows users to apply different types of depth filters, such as for humans, animals, and food, etc. The shooting condition prompts remind users to stay near or far to trigger the portrait mode. iPhone displays terms like "Stay away", or "Place the subject within a distance of 2.5 m", which sounds like orders. While OnePlus 9 does not use words for alert, a green box is a signal for a successful trigger of portrait mode, which is clearer and more user-friendly. Only the Huawei P50 Pro has an introduction function for beginners on the upper right side of the interface. It explains the difference between portrait mode and standard mode with cases.

Table 5. Comparison of portrait mode interface of six mobile phones.

	iPhone 13pro	Huawei P50 pro	Vivo X70 pro+	Xiaomi 11 Ultra	OnePlus 9	OPPO Reno7 pro
Number of buttons	5	4	8	5	4	4
Zoom	"1×" "3×"	"1×" "2×" "3×"	"1×" "2×" "5×"	None	"1×" "2×"	None
Composition Assistance	Basic assistance	Basic assistance	Basic assistance, Pose composition assistance	Basic assistance	Basic assistance	Basic assistance
Beautification	No beauty	One-click beauty	Custom Beauty	One-click beauty	One-click beauty	One-click beauty
Lighting	Studio Light, Contour Light, Stage Light, Stage Light Mono, High-Key Light Mono	None	Style Lighting	Neon Lighting	None	None
Depth	Have	None	Have	Have	None	None
Other Functions	Shooting prompts	Foreground Effect, Introduction	Foreground Effect	AI assistance	shooting prompts	None

3.2 Analysis of Portrait Mode with Design Principles

In the following section, the portrait modes of six mobile phones are examined according to the interface design principles examined in a literature review. After analysis, the first level of portrait mode functions is designed and developed reasonably and user-friendly considering user interaction, behaviors, and habits. While the second level of functional features has its strength and weakness (Table 6).

Table 6. Matching portrait mode with design principles

	iPhone 13pro	Huawei P50 pro	Vivo X70 pro+	Xiaomi 11 Ultra	OnePlus 9	OPPO Reno7 pro
1.Consistency	✓	✓	✓	✓	✓	✓
2.Shortcuts						
3.Feedback	✓				✓	✓
4.Dialog						
5.Error Prevention	✓	✓	✓	✓	✓	✓
6.Reversal						
7.Control and freedom	✓	✓	✓	✓	✓	✓
8.Reduce memory load						
9.Personalization						
10."Top-Down" Interaction	✓	✓	✓	✓	✓	✓
11.Enjoyment						
12.Constraints	✓				✓	
13.Flexibility and Efficiency				✓		
14.Help		✓		✓		

Consistency of Portrait Mode. Consistent sequences of actions should be required in similar situations; identical terminology should be used in prompts, menus, and help screens; and consistent color, layout, capitalization, fonts, and so on, should be employed throughout (Shneiderman, 1998). Consistency takes on an additional dimension with mobile applications: the consistency across multiple platforms and devices for the same application (Gong and Tarasewich, 2004). Users should not have to wonder whether different words, situations, or actions mean the same thing. Follow platform conventions (Nielsen, 2005).

According to the questionnaire responses, 47.2% of users have perceived the interface design of the portrait mode across various models as similar and consistent. Moreover, from level one to level two, the interface is consistent. Based on the interview results, some users have found it relatively easy to comprehend and familiarize themselves with the fundamental portrait mode functions among different models. Nevertheless, users may encounter difficulties in learning and understanding new, model-specific features when switching between different mobile phone models.

Within the portrait mode category, inconsistency in page jumping can impede user operations and cause confusion. For instance, in the iPhone series, the depth of field setting button located in the upper right corner of the interface can jump to the depth of field setting page. However, clicking on the depth of field setting button situated in the lower left corner of the interface can result in jumping to a different page. Such inconsistency in page jumping can lead to a logical conundrum for some unfamiliar users.

Dialog and Feedback of Portrait Mode. For every user action, there should be interface feedback. Sequences of actions should be organized into groups with a beginning, middle, and end (Shneiderman, 1998). For every operator action, there should be some system feedback, such as a beep when pressing a key or an error message for an invalid input value. Sequences of actions should be organized into groups with a beginning, middle, and end (Gong & Tarasewich, 2004). The system should always keep users informed about what is going on, through appropriate feedback within reasonable time (Nielsen, 2005). The term signifier refers to any mark or sound, any perceivable indicator that communicates appropriate behavior to a person. Some way of letting you know that the system is working on your request (Norman, 2013).

Approximately 66.67% of the survey respondents acknowledged the usefulness of the feedback provided by portrait mode. Nonetheless, some of the interviewees expressed divergent views. Specifically, some interviewees reported that the shooting prompt feature can be a hindrance when users need to capture a photo quickly. They felt that portrait mode requires users to invest more time and effort to adjust the settings, and in an emergency situation where the camera fails to recognize the user, the user has to quickly swipe back to standard mode. To enhance the user experience, the interface should be refined to enable automatic swiping to standard mode if portrait mode cannot be triggered. Some interviewees opined that the interactive prompts do not aid users, but instead create confusion and even engender resentment towards the function.

Regarding the intelligent assistant function, the survey results indicate that 63.89% of respondents are interested in adjusting parameter settings. In addition, 52.78% of respondents believed that camera angle tips are necessary, while 75% considered photo composition tips to be useful. A majority of 75% of respondents also acknowledged the importance of photo lighting tips (Fig. 3).

Error Prevention of Portrait Mode. As much as possible, design the interface so that users cannot make serious errors (Shneiderman, 1998). Preventing and handling errors on mobile interfaces are similar to those for desktop interfaces, although the need becomes more critical due to the more rapid pace of events in the mobile environment (Gong & Tarasewich, 2004). Even better than good error messages is a careful design that prevents a problem from occurring in the first place either eliminating error-prone

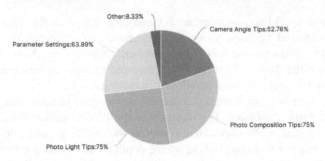

Fig. 3. Portrait mode photo assistance function.

conditions or checking for them and presenting users with a confirmation option before they commit to the action (Nielsen, 2005).

The shooting condition prompts serve as an aid to assist users in achieving their desired bokeh effects, while also providing consistent feedback without a mandatory format. To best suit user preferences, shooting conditions should not impose strict orders but rather adapt to their desired photographic outcomes. Instead of the current phrase "Stay away", suggested language such as "To meet the bokeh conditions" and "0.5–2.0 m to achieve better bokeh" could be used.

It is important to clearly display reminder information regarding whether or not the portrait mode shooting conditions are met. Some users may use portrait mode despite not meeting the necessary conditions, resulting in photos without the desired portrait mode effects. This can cause confusion and a negative experience for the user. To address this issue, shooting condition prompts can be used to inform users of the current situation through a dialog box that indicates whether the bokeh effect is enabled or not. This approach, similar to the shooting condition prompt used in the portrait mode interface of OnePlus series phones, should avoid any misleading prompts and be tailored to the user's needs.

Control of Portrait Mode. Experienced users strongly desire the sense that they are in charge of the interface and that the interface responds to their actions (Shneiderman, 1998). Users want to be in charge of the system and have the system respond to their actions, rather than feeling that the system is controlling them (Gong & Tarasewich, 2004). The system should speak the users' language, with words, phrases, and concepts familiar to the user, rather than system-oriented terms. Follow real-world conventions, making information appear in a natural and logical order. Users often choose system functions by mistake and will need a clearly marked "emergency exit" to leave the unwanted state without having to go through an extended dialogue. Support undo and redo (Nielsen, 2005). It is possible to determine what actions are possible and the current state of the device. The design projects all the information needed to create a good conceptual model of the system, leading to an understanding and a feeling of control (Norman, 2013).

Based on the results of the questionnaire, a majority of 57.3% of users found the information presented on the interface to be easy to comprehend. However, certain interviewees held the view that a considerable number of functional features were conveyed through mere icons, lacking sufficient accompanying prompts to enhance their understandability. In particular, some distinctive functions of specific mobile phone models were difficult to grasp without prior experience, thus adding to the learning curve and leaving an unfavorable impression on users.

Moreover, based on the interview findings, certain camera features can pose challenges to users. For instance, users may struggle to differentiate among the five available lighting effects on the iPhone. X2 interviewee expect that "the lighting function seems advanced, but I do not know how to use it. It is better that the phone can adjust lighting effect automatically for me". This suggests that some users may require further guidance or assistance in utilizing certain camera features effectively.

Personalization of Portrait Mode. Allow users to configure the output to their needs and preferences (e.g., text size, brightness). Allow for single or no-handed operation. Have the application adapt itself automatically to the user's current environment. Provide users the ability to change settings to their needs or liking (Gong and Tarasewich, 2004).

According to the survey results, 30.56% of participants expressed a desire to customize the interface using the options button. However, the portrait mode interfaces are currently fixed and do not allow for personalization. Some users have reported that the fixed frame provided by the current portrait mode is too restrictive and inconvenient. In response to this, the Xiaomi 11 Ultra has implemented various presets for different shooting themes to cater to the needs of subgroups of users. W1 suggested, "providing more intelligent, one-touch settings and environmental self-adaptation".

The design of function keys aims to maintain simplicity and minimalism by avoiding an excessive number of buttons. In addition, customizable settings may be provided to empower users to select which function keys to display and their location, thereby tailoring the interface to individual preferences.

To optimize shooting settings, it is recommended to provide a diverse range of presets in addition to custom settings. To prevent overly complicated parameter settings that may impede some users, the Xiaomi 11 Ultra presets for people, pets, still life, and other categories can be used as a reference to offer a one-click mode selection to most users. This approach enables users to select functions and interface subdivisions based on their preferences and needs, thus providing a more personalized and convenient experience.

"Top-Down" Interaction of Portrait Mode. Present high levels of information and let users decide whether or not to retrieve details (Gong & Tarasewich, 2004).

In the design of the portrait mode interface, the function keys' logic should aim for maximum convenience without an excessive number of jumping pathways. The number of interface levels should be minimized, with the second-level interface capable of meeting most needs, except for a few that require the third-level interface. For instance, the depth-of-field adjustment function key located in the upper right corner of the iPhone 13 Pro interface can be used without reappearing in the secondary interface of the idle part of the top setting function button. The interface for depth-of-field setting does not need to jump to the interface of the setting function to prevent users from making jumping logic errors, mistakenly regarding the setting function interface as the third-level interface.

Enjoyment of Portrait Mode. Applications should be visually pleasing and fun as well as usable (Gong and Tarasewich, 2004). Dialogues should not contain information that is irrelevant or rarely needed. Every extra unit of information in a dialogue competes with the relevant units of information and diminishes their relative visibility (Nielsen, 2005).

From the questionnaire result, 58.33% of the respondents prefer a simple and elegant interface style. 59.9% of users are satisfied with the aesthetics of the interface design of portrait mode. However, from the interviewee, we found that some problems that need to be addressed. The portrait mode interface is not designed with delicate details. Take iPhone as an example, its visual aesthetics are not well managed. For instance, the Chinese version of "a little farther away" has a period of "." in the middle, which is not inconsistent with the Chinese writing style and is not necessary. And the rectangle for the prompt is not delicately de-signed and inconsistent with the overall style of interface design.

Flexibility and Efficiency of Portrait Mode. Accelerators – unseen by the novice user – may often speed up the interaction for the expert user such that the system can cater to both inexperienced and experienced users. Allow users to tailor frequent actions (Nielsen, 2005).

Some interviewee reflects that the overall functional features are too complicated for general users and not professional enough for professional users. For general users, the portrait mode provides more intelligent assistance and automatic parameter settings. For professional users, the portrait mode should allow maximum manual parameter settings and control like a professional camera. Therefore, it can provide different interfaces for different types of users. C6 said "I have always felt that the iPhone portrait mode settings are not easy to use. Some beauty cameras do a better job and they also disclose the parameters for taking better photos. iPhone can learn from beauty cameras to set the presetting parameters for users to take a beautiful photo." The interface should be designed and developed as convenient as possible.

Help. Error messages should be expressed in plain language (no codes), precisely indicate the problem, and constructively suggest a solution. Even though it is better if the system can be used without documentation, it may be necessary to provide help and documentation. Any such information should be easy to search, focused on the user's task, list concrete steps to be carried out, and not be too large (Norman, 2013).

The majority of prior studies have focused on user assistance, without addressing intelligent assistance, which is likely to become an essential principle as technological advancements continue to evolve. The technology of shooting posture assistance (Amir, 2022) enables the device to offer users more efficient and sensible aid. It can recognize the images uploaded by the user to provide shooting assistance through analysis. Moreover, it offers interactive forms of assistance, such as voice prompts and indicator lights, instead of imposing restrictive constraints on the user.

Providing clear information cues is crucial, particularly for primary or infrequent functions that require explanation and instruction. In the case of iPhone 13 Pro's portrait mode, the lighting effects feature could be included in a help button that, when clicked, displays a comparison chart and concise textual guidance to aid the user in understanding the feature's purpose and usage. A similar approach is seen in Huawei P50 Pro's portrait mode interface, which includes an introduction to the portrait mode feature in the help button.

3.3 Proposed Wireframe and Prototype of Portrait Mode

Based on the principles of interaction interface design that have been researched, and studying the existing portrait model of cell phones, the following interface wireframe and prototype diagram (Fig. 4) are proposed to improve on this basis. The interface framework comprises two major components.

(1) Main interface: Zoom, Beautification, Depth, Flash, Shooting Assistance, Other Settings, Intelligent Assistance, Information Description.

(2) Bottom interface: Shutter, Album, and Lens Conversion, which are basically the same as those of the six phones.

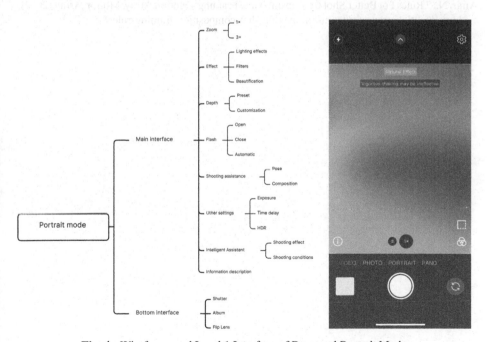

Fig. 4. Wireframe and Level 1 Interface of Proposed Portrait Mode.

References

Apple. Using Portrait Mode on iPhone. Support (2021). https://support.apple.com/en-us/HT2 08118

Marcus, A.: Dare we define user-interface design? Interactions **9**(5), 19–24 (2002)

Shneiderman, B.: Designing the user interface: strategies for effective human-computer. Interaction **3** (1998)

Gong, J., Tarasewich, P.: Guidelines for handheld mobile device interface design. In: Proceedings of DSI 2004 Annual Meeting, pp. 3751–3756 (2004)

Norman, D.: The Design of Everyday Things: Revised and Expanded Edition. Basic Books (2013)

Nielsen, J.: Enhancing the explanatory power of usability heuristics. In: Proceedings of the SIGCHI Conference on Human Factors in Computing Systems, pp. 152–158 (1994)

Nielsen, J.: Ten usability heuristics (2005)

Apple. iPhone 13 pro (2022). https://www.apple.com/iphone-13/

Vivo. Vivo X70 (2022). https://www.vivoglobal.ph/phone/vivo-X70/

HUAWEI. HUAWEI P50 Pro (2022). https://consumer.huawei.com/en/phones/p50-pro/

Xiaomi. Xiaomi 11 Ultra (2022). https://www.mi.com/in/mi-11-ultra/

OnePlus. OnePlus 9 (2022). https://www.oneplus.com/global/9

OPPO. OPPO Reno7 Pro (2022). https://www.oppo.com/en/smartphones/series-reno/reno7-pro-5g/

Amir, N.: 7 Rules For Better Shot Composition and Framing - Motion Array. Motion Array (2022). https://motionarray.com/learn/filmmaking/shot-composition-framing-rules/

User Experience Centred Design for Chinese Seniors' Community Employment

Tianrui Zhu[✉]

School of Design, South China University of Technology, Guangzhou 510006,
People's Republic of China
2531174527@qq.com

Abstract. Against an accelerating aging population, China bears a heavy burden of old age. Many older people face a poverty crisis due to a lack of social security. Therefore, focusing on the resources of older people and using the old clothes recycling project as a breakthrough point, this paper designs an online and offline process to help older people find employment in the community. This paper first uses literature research to propose that clothing recycling projects can re-employ older people in the community. Then User Requirements Analysis was conducted using the interview method based on Maslow's Hierarchy of Needs to improve the user experience. Afterward, a specific design framework was proposed for the innovative transformation of clothing for commercializing community clothing recycling and disposal. At the same time, the online process APP was developed with a gamified interaction design to motivate users to participate. This research aims to drive community employment for the low-aged elderly, to allow older people to train in relevant activity participation skills, improve their living conditions, build new interpersonal networks with community activities, and enhance older people's sense of community integration. Based on previous research, this paper proposes a community-led recycling process for clothes to help older people find employment. Also, it provides a reference for subsequent community employment designs for the lower-aged elderly.

Keywords: Older people · Employment · Community clothing recycling process · UX

1 Introduction

1.1 Aging in China

Population aging has become a universal social issue worldwide. China is entering an aging society at a catch-up stage, facing enormous pension pressures and insufficient financial resources to provide more social benefits for older people [1]. China's elderly are at risk of poverty without adequate pension protection, and there are many obstacles to re-employment.

At the same time, we cannot ignore the massive potential of elderly resources. As of November 2020, the number of lower-aged older people (aged 60–74) in China will exceed 147 million, accounting for 55.83%, the highest number of older people [2]. Suppose that we include this low-age elderly population in human resource development. In that case, it will play an essential role in promoting the construction and development of the social economy and effectively alleviate the burden and pressure of the aging population.

1.2 Current Status of Clothing Recycling in China

As the ecological environment deteriorates, a global awareness of environmental protection is beginning to emerge. Sustainable development is now the theme of national and even global development. People are concerned that improper methods of disposing of used clothes, such as landfill or incineration, cause serious environmental pollution and waste the earth's resources. The recycling of old clothes has become a hot topic of social concern, as the project is developed with the issues of environmental protection, energy conservation and social welfare in mind.

However, clothing recycling in China is in the exploratory stage. The overall recycling rate of old clothes cannot meet the expected standards. The recycling system has not yet reached scale, and no effective operating mechanism is truly government-led, market-driven and public-led [3].

2   Related Work

Through literature research, this paper reviews keywords related to employment for the low-age elderly and clothing recycling, summarizing cases and methods in the literature.

Galkin, KA [4] mentioned that employment strategies in developed economies are characterized by tax incentives for employers and retraining for older people. Cho et al. [5] referred to improvements to promote the employment of older people. For example, making the best use of short-time work, expanding the range of social service jobs in social enterprises, and then there are more employment opportunities for older people.

Richard J. Wirth et al. [6] organized participatory design community events with public interactive displays. Their design promoted social interaction and community engagement, facilitate co-production among older people in the community.

Guo Yan et al. [7] studied GRACER Ltd, the largest used clothing sorting enterprise and second-hand clothing exporter in China, and analyzed its recycling model of integrated used clothing treatment. GRACER regularly organizes used clothing recycling activities in the community, and the integrated back-end processing of used clothing also provides many jobs for the community. Sun Rui [8] proposed organically combining used clothing recycling services with urban community management to build a comprehensive community-used clothing recycling system.

Based on these studies, the paper changes the direction of thinking. For the first time, the paper proposes to provide jobs for older people in the less complex processes of used goods recycling. The community committee can act as an intermediary between the company and older people. Using clothing recycling as an example to develop a community employment user experience design. User Requirements Analysis is conducted on the potential elderly employed in the community.

3 User Requirements Analysis

A user interview form based on Maslow's Hierarchy of Needs (see Table 1) was developed to gain insight into the needs of older people regarding the employment process and workshop activities.

A small sample size was chosen for this interview, and interviews were conducted one-on-one with older people. The interviews took 6 days to interview 10 older people in different situations. The interviews were conducted in Suishi Village, Zengcheng Xiangjiang Gifted Community, Guangzhou Book Buying Centre and Dongshankou. The transcripts were collated from the interviews to obtain a record sheet of relevant views and keywords.

Table 1. User Interview Form.

Physiological need	1. Please introduce your basic information? For example, age, education, income (pension), etc
Safety need	2. What is your present occupation?
	3. Would you like to be re-employed in the community?
	If you are re-employed, how long can you physically support your current work schedule?(Half an hour as a work unit)
	Have you previously developed skills and experience in the workplace?
Belongingness and love need	Are you a native of the community or did you come to the city with your children?
	Do you know your neighbors well?
	Would you like to participate in a community clothes workshop to meet new friends?
Esteem need	Do you need care for grandchildren?
	Would you want time for yourself if you had to take care of your grandchildren?
	Do you want to try to express your will and show yourself?
Self-actualization need	Would you like to learn about new ideas such as clothing recycling?
	Would you like to learn new skills about clothing recycling?

Based on the ten older people recorded, three types of User Persona were drawn up (see Fig. 1. User persona.): illiterate migrant people (brought to the city by their children and living away from their native villages), indigenous people with a skills base, and indigenous people with low income or no pension. They will provide a user reference for the subsequent design of the solution.

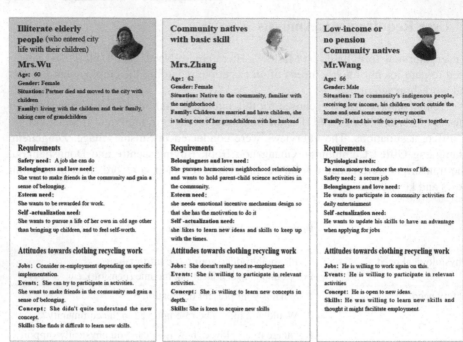

Fig. 1. User persona

4 Solution

4.1 A Design Framework for the Innovative Transformation of Used Clothing for Community Employment

This paper conceptualizes a design framework for the innovative transformation of used clothing for community employment (see Fig. 2) to guide the development of the design practice. The design framework clarifies the functional roles of the various departments.

The framework is community-led, with government departments and social enterprises working together to recover and recycle clothing. The community is the initiator, and community managers are matched with public benefit enterprises and low-income seniors. Public benefit enterprises provide jobs and technical training to obtain low-cost employees provided by the community. Seniors apply to obtain jobs and achieve employment within the community. Government departments are indirectly involved through regulation or legislative and planning guidance to protect personnel's labor rights, encourage enterprises' active participation, and ensure an orderly process [9].

4.2 Process Design of Clothing Recycling for Seniors' Community Employment

The public recycling business separates two low-technology processes from the assembly line: sorting and packing. They offer these positions to match the community. Community managers post job openings on the app. The managers assign suitable jobs based on the health status and interests of the applicants.

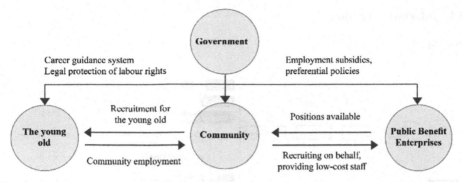

Fig. 2. A design framework for the innovative transformation of used clothing for community employment.

The clothes are sorted according to the 70% newness standard. Unusable scraps less than 70% new are recycled into fiber material at a partner recycling company's fabrication facility. A small portion of the scrap can be used to hold community clothing transformation workshops. The community clothing transformation workshop invites professionals from companies to popularize the knowledge of recycling, environmental protection concepts and provide professional tutorials on transformation so that seniors can learn to transform old clothes at low cost. Most available shredded materials are shipped to Cooperating companies, which clean and disinfect the materials and then process materials into products or clean clothes. If there are relevant demands from public welfare organizations, company and workshop products will be donated to needy people. Remaining products are sold at low prices in the community's idle space. This puts the clothing into the recycling process. Older people can redeem work credits for new clothing at a low price, as well as for needed coupons, as shown in Fig. 3

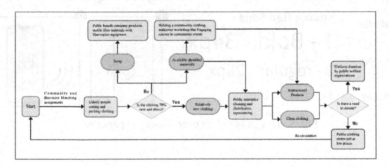

Fig. 3. Process design of clothing recycling for seniors' community employment.

5 Prototype Interface Design

An app is designed to assist in the flow of this UX design online process.

5.1   Interface Structure

See Fig. 4.

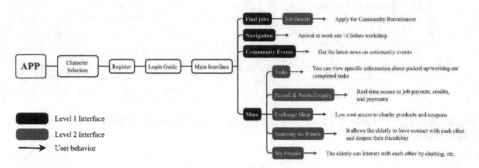

Fig. 4. Interface structure.

5.2   Gamified Interaction Design

User Sensory Experience. In the visual aspect, the design is based on the visual habits of older people in order to allow them to receive messages better. The font size is larger than 18dp/pt, and the line spacing is 1.5 times and above. At the same time, warm and bright colors improve the contrast between the text and the interface. Haptic interaction during use gives the user a more engaged sense of reality, and the slight vibration when completing tasks creates an immediate feedback experience, as shown in Fig. 5.

Fig. 5. Design based on user sensory experience.

Login Process and Guidelines. Illiterate older people who do not know most of the words will retreat if they do not understand the interface after logging in, so this design provides detailed guidelines after logging in, using visual expressions, mostly in everyday language, and adding a slow voice reading to assist older people in understanding. Considering the poor memory of older people, the guidelines exist as a hover button for a long time in case of emergency.

Wayfinding Design. The app automatically locates the current location and displays the situation of nearby community work sites, providing navigation services for older people unfamiliar with the location of work sites. At the same time, to avoid the problem that older people do not trust the product enough and older people get lost, the app will synchronize the elderly location information to their children's cell phones in real time (see Fig. 6).

Fig. 6. Login interface and wayfinding design.

User Emotional Incentives. The app helps record the hours older people work and their remuneration. The seniors can check the amount of payment at any time. The points earned from older people's work can be exchanged for products from the community's unmanned clothing store, as well as for older people's favorite vouchers for supermarket consumption, household goods, phone bill recharge and laundry consumption (see Fig. 7).

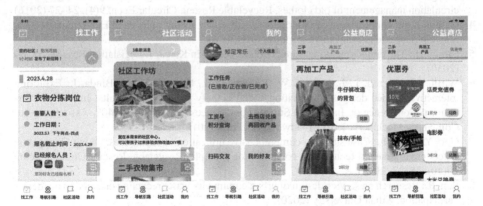

Fig. 7. Emotionally motivating interface design

6   Conclusion

Based on the background of China's severe aging and the fact that clothing recycling is at an exploratory stage, this paper explores how lower-aged older people engage in the clothing recycling process for employment in the community. This paper summarizes previous views through literature research, conceives the innovation point of this paper for design, finds the user pain points through the interview method of Maslow's Hierarchy of Needs, conceives the design framework of waste clothing transformation for community employment, constitutes the economic industry chain of old things recycling, designs the community clothing recycling processing experience process with the breakthrough point of low-aged elderly users, and designs the app to assist the process Conduct.

The design innovatively proposes a community-led design framework for the innovative transformation of old stuff recycling, allowing older people to participate in the community-used clothing recycling for re-employment. Which on the one hand, can meet the needs of the elderly of low age, allowing them to recognize their self-worth and gain a sense of belonging in the community by participating in community employment and clothing transformation workshops, and reducing the social pressure brought by aging. On the other hand, it can provide a reference for the subsequent design of a comprehensive user experience for older people and attract more attention to the direction of community employment for older people.

References

1. Zou, B.: Status quo of China's population aging and positive response on it. Soc. Policy Res. 3–9 (2017)
2. National Health Commission of the People's Republic of China. http://www.nhc.gov.cn/
3. Wang, Y., Zhang, S., Wang, Z.: New idea to develop the vintage industry and regulate the circulation management of old clothes. Recyclable Resour. Circular Econ. 9(4), 24–27 (2016)
4. Galkin, K.A.: Employment of older people and active ageing policies in Europe and Russia. Sotsiologicheskie issledovaniya (11), 99–110 (2016)
5. Cho, S.H.: The employment measure for older people in Korea. J. Legislation Res. 38, 35–80 (2010)
6. Wirth, R.J., Carroll, J.M., Yuan, C.W., Rosson, M.B., Hanrahan, B.V., Binda, J.: Exploring interactive surface designs for eliciting social activity from elderly adults. In: ACM International Conference on Interactive Surfaces and Spaces (ISS), pp. 403–408. Association for Computing Machinery, 1515 Broadway, New York (2016)
7. Guo, Y., Chen, L.: Case study on comprehensive utilization of old clothes: taking Guangzhou gracer environmental technology company for example. Recyclable Resour. Circular Econ. 10(10), 25–27 (2017)
8. Sun, R.: Research on service design of urban community waste recycling oriented to residents' participation, Xihua University (2020)
9. Zhang, Y.: the research on innovation and transformation design of used clothing oriented to social innovation, Guangdong University of Technology (2018)

HCI in Education and Collaborative Learning

AR-Classroom: Investigating User-App-Interactions to Enhance Usability of AR Technology for Learning Two and Three Dimensional Rotations

Samantha D. Aguilar, Heather Burte(✉), Philip Yasskin, Jeffrey Liew,
Shu-Hao Yeh, Chengyuan Qian, Dezhen Song, Uttamasha Monjoree,
Coby Scrudder, and Wei Yan

Texas A&M University, College Station, TX 77845, USA
{heather.burte,yasskin,jeffrey.liew,cyqian,uxm190002,
cobyscrudder,samdyanne,wyan}@tamu.edu, dzsong@cse.tamu.edu

Abstract. AR-enabled applications have the potential to contextualize math concepts within a concrete situation, like rotating an aircraft, where students can physically manipulate objects and develop their spatial skills. The AR-Classroom application utilizes AR to make 2D and 3D rotations underlying matrix algebra visible and interactive, enabling embodied learning. Previous usability tests on the AR-Classroom assessed user-app interactions, the functionality of app features, and overall ease of use. The findings from the previous studies led to several modifications and improvements to the app. The present study uses a mixed-method approach to assess the usability of the latest version of the AR-Classroom. Results indicate that the latest version is associated with improved user experience, increased ease of use, and an overall increase in users' understanding of the app's functionality. Findings are discussed in the context of previous user studies with earlier AR-Classroom versions. Implications for conducting iterative usability studies and recommendations for developing educational technologies are provided.

Keywords: Augmented Reality · Educational Technology · User Interaction · Spatial Rotations · Matrices

1 Introduction

The importance of spatial skills as an essential element of mathematical thinking is well documented in the literature [1, 2]. Research has demonstrated that spatial skills, specifically performing spatial rotations, can be improved with targeted interventions [3] and that certain types of technology may aid in strengthening these skills. Spatial visualization is the skill of imagining an object in one's mind and manipulating or moving the object; whereas spatial rotation is a skill that only involves rotations. Interactive technology such as augmented reality (AR) can enhance learning experiences for math

C. Stephanidis et al. (Eds.): HCII 2023, CCIS 1957, pp. 249–256, 2024.
https://doi.org/10.1007/978-3-031-49212-9_31

by visualizing the theoretical and abstract concepts underlying rotations in a real-world environment [4, 5]. Utilizing AR-enabled applications can contextualize math concepts in a concrete situation, like rotating an aircraft, where students can manipulate physical objects and build spatial skills. The present study uses a mixed-method approach to assess the usability of two of the latest workshops in the AR-Classroom application.

1.1 BRICKxAR/T

The present usability study of the AR-Classroom app was informed by the authors' previous research on the AR-enabled educational app, BRICKxAR/T [6]. BRICKxAR/T uses AR to display the mathematical concepts behind geometric transformations by visualizing the entries within transformation matrices (for more about BRICKxAR/T development see [7]). A benchmark usability study was conducted to investigate the usability of the BRICKxAR/T app's AR and non-AR workshops in its standard condition. Then an updated usability study was done to investigate the impact of changes made based on the benchmark study's findings. Guided by the BRICKxAR/T usability studies, the present study used a usability test format to evaluate the usability and efficacy of the AR-Classroom.

1.2 AR-Classroom

The AR-Classroom assists in learning two-dimensional (2D) and three-dimensional (3D) geometric rotations and their mathematics through a virtual and physical interactive environment. The AR-Classroom application utilizes AR to make 2D and 3D rotations underlying matrix algebra visible and manipulative, enabling embodied learning (for more about AR-Classroom development, see [8]). Previous usability tests on the AR-Classroom assessed user-app interactions, the functionality of app features, and overall ease of use (for review, see [9]). The findings from the previous studies led to several implemented modifications and improvements to the app.

The current version of the AR-Classroom consists of a model registration tutorial and virtual and physical workshops. Users can perform rotations using a physical LEGO model (i.e., physical workshop) or by manipulating the application's x, y, and z axes sliders to rotate a virtual model (i.e., virtual workshop). Both workshops share similar features, such as a green wireframe model superimposed onto the LEGO model to represent rotation transformations, color-coded x, y, and z axes lines, degree or radian units, z-axis direction (up versus down), multiple types of model views, and 2D or 3D matrices (Fig. 1 and Fig. 2). Building on previous usability studies [6, 9] the present study focused on assessing the usability of the AR-Classroom in its most recent version, and reflecting on changes in discoverability, usability, and quantitative measures compared to the last two versions of the app.

2 Method

Participants were fifteen undergraduate psychology students recruited via a large public university's Department of Psychological and Brain Sciences' research sign-up system. The experiment took 1 h, and participants received research credits for participation.

Fig. 1. AR-Classroom Virtual Workshop: 3D y-axis rotation with z-axis down

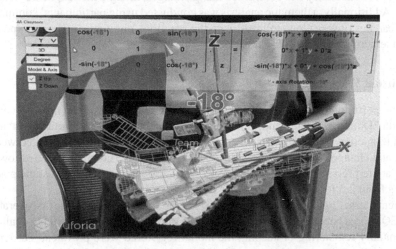

Fig. 2. AR-Classroom Physical Workshop: 3D y-axis rotation with z-axis up

Participants were randomly assigned to interact with the app's virtual (N = 7) or physical (N = 8) workshop. All participants completed a pre-test consisting of demographic information, previous experience with matrix algebra, and a sixteen-question multiple-choice matrix algebra test developed by the research team, including a mathematics professor. After each question, participants rated their confidence in their answer (1 = "not at all confident" to 5 = "very confident"). After the pre-test, participants watched a brief introductory video on matrix algebra, then a second video showing how to set up and register the space shuttle LEGO model. Then participants interacted with the AR-Classroom using a computer with a webcam.

While interacting with one of the workshops, participants completed tasks related to the app's functionality. Tasks consisted of discoverability (i.e., five minutes of free play), registering the LEGO model, utilizing in-app features such as rotations around the x-, y-, or z-axis (either using the model or rotation sliders), reporting the degree or radian of rotation, changing model views, and changing the z-axis direction. While interacting with the app, participants thought out loud by explaining what they were trying to do and any thoughts about interacting with the app. After each task, participants rated how easy or difficult the task was to complete on a 7-point scale using the Single Ease Question rating scale (SEQ). Higher SEQ scores indicate that a task was easy to complete, with lower scores indicating the inverse. Finally, participants completed a post-test with the same matrix algebra test with confidence ratings and the System Usability Scale (SUS) to assess the overall usability.

3   Results

Due to the small sample size, we used descriptive statistics to review the pre- to post-test matrix algebra accuracy and confidence rating changes, along with SEQ scores and SUS ratings. Additionally, a thematic analysis was conducted using participants' commentary and researcher observations to investigate the reactions, thoughts, and user experience while interacting with the AR-Classroom.

3.1   Virtual Workshop

The eight participants were majority freshmen males with all but one reporting experience with 2D matrix algebra and varied experience with 3D. Virtual participants' matrix algebra test score accuracy appeared consistent as pre-test accuracy ranged between 25 to 75% and changed to 50 to 75% at post-test. However, participants reported low confidence at the pre-test (ranging from 1.75 to 2.75), moderately increased at the post-test (ranging from 2.5 to 3.75).

When interacting with the app, virtual participants reported moderate discoverability, with SEQ scores between four and five. Themes of participants experiencing challenges when initially registering or keeping the model registered were prevalent. Participants needed an adjustment period to correctly line up the physical model with the wireframe once they realized the camera was inverted. Moreover, participants reported struggling with aligning the physical model within the wireframe initially (n = 3), and some participants also had difficulty maintaining registration (n = 4), participants further stated that "seems a little harder to register this time" and "I'm having more trouble this time." However, participants were ultimately able to effectively utilize the app's functions after the initial learning curve. Observations highlighted participants' ability to find and switch between the 2D/3D and degrees/radians buttons. They exhibited curiosity about how the 2D, and 3D visuals differed by clicking the button to see what would change; one participant even stated, "Visually, there seems to be nothing different between 2D and 3D besides the equations". Though it was unclear if the participants' understood the theoretical differences between 2D and 3D matrix algebra, their 5 min of free play introduced them to differences in the size of the matrix and length of the equation.

After discoverability, participants rated registering the LEGO model favorably, with most participants (n = 4) rating it a seven. Additionally, participants found rotating the virtual model about the 3 axes particularly easy, rating these three separate tasks a seven, with the minimum reported rating being a five. Salient themes further emphasized the ease of performing rotations using the virtual workshop. Themes such as an immediate understanding of the dropdown axis selection function and the ability to accurately rotate the virtual model using the in-app sliders highlight the virtual workshop's intuitiveness and accessibility. In addition to the favorable SEQ scores, the thematic analysis of participant feedback and researcher observations provided insight into participants' intuitive knowledge of the app. Participants recognized how to bring up the desired axis using the dropdown and correctly reported the model rotation in degrees or radians. Moreover, participants could quickly change the z-axis direction, with six participants rating it a seven and one rating it a six. Finally, regarding changing the model view, SEQ scores ranged between scores of five (n = 2), six (n = 2), and seven (n = 3) as they could find and use the function to change the view of the model without guidance or hints. Preference of the model view varied; some participants preferred the axis-only type, citing the "clutter" brought forth by the green wireframe model, while others preferred the model and axis together, claiming the type "gave better visuals" for understanding the underlying matrix algebra.

3.2 Physical Workshop

The seven participants were freshmen with equal distribution across participants who identify as male (n = 4) and female (n = 4). All but one physical workshop participant had experience with 2D matrix algebra with reported mixed experience with 3D. At the pre-test, confidence level (ranging from 0.5 to 3.25) and accuracy in math answers were relatively low (ranging from 25 to 75%), with confidence level (ranging from 1.75 to 3.5) and accuracy increased slightly at the post-test (ranging from 50 to 75%).

During the five minutes of discoverability, participants reported a range of SEQ scores from two to seven. Participants reported that the app's features were inviting and could easily be used once found; However, registration could have been easier for some participants. When participants tried moving the model (i.e., not necessarily performing rotations), they lost registration, which was frustrating (n = 4). These issues diminished as participants became more familiar with the app and were given more direct tasks to complete (e.g., "Rotate the LEGO model on the x-axis").

After discoverability, the physical workshop participants also quickly registered the model, with five participants rating registration a seven. Participants appeared to have trouble performing an x-axis rotation as they would attempt to rotate on x without clicking the dropdown menu; some required a hint to click the dropdown menu (n = 4). However, SEQ scores for these tasks were relatively high, as five participants rated it a six. The difficulties performing an x-axis rotation may have been an initial period of orienting oneself to using the app, as the later tasks of rotating the model about the y- and z-axis were performed with greater ease. Participants showed intuitive knowledge of the app as they could use the dropdown functionality to rotate the LEGO model properly and complete the tasks. The y-axis task SEQ scores ranged from five to seven, with over half of the participants reporting a six or higher, and the z-axis task scores of most participants (n = 7) reporting a six or higher.

For the features of changing the z-axis direction and the model view, participants appeared capable of finding these features, effectively using them, and describing their preferences. Participants knew the function of the z-axis direction change button when given the task with half of the participants (n = 4) rating the task a six. Participants also reported a preference for the z-axis direction being up; one participant stated that "… [the up direction] makes it easier to picture in my head for rotating", while some participants did not provide or know their reason for this preference. Next, changing the model view seemed particularly easy for participants as all rated the task a five or higher. Additionally, like the virtual workshop, participants preferred the axis visualization (n = 6), citing the "cleaner" view with "lack of clutter." Finally, participants could change between 2D/3D and degree/radians while discerning the differences in the app when switching between dimensions.

4   Discussion and Conclusion

Prior to the present study, two usability tests of the AR-Classroom were performed to assess the app's usability and functionality under various versions (see Aguilar et al., 2023b). In its starting version (i.e., benchmark usability test), participants found the AR-Classroom challenging to use, and its features needed to be more intuitive. Results indicated that users needed additional guidance on model set-up and registration, could utilize most of the app's functions effectively, and could quickly complete most tasks using the app with instructions. Based on these findings, recommendations were formulated to address issues and enhance users' experience. Changes to AR-Classroom app included enhancing AR tracking, reformatting the in-app instructions, creating a video to guide setting up and registering the LEGO model, restructuring app functions to increase accessibility and enhance utilization, and adding additional functionality (e.g., false rotation error message). After implementing these changes, another usability test (i.e., an updated usability test) was conducted to investigate how changes to the app impacted its discoverability and usability. The updated usability study revealed that users could effectively use the app's features, perform correct rotations about the x, y, or z axis, and found interacting with the app relatively easy. The changes made to the virtual and physical workshops of AR-Classroom improved usability and enhanced user-app interactions. However, based on the results of the updated usability test, there were still salient issues in user-app interactions. Thus, additional recommendations were formulated to address concerns and enhance users' experience with AR-Classroom further.

In its current version (i.e., the present usability study), the AR-Classroom includes a reformatted video for setting up and registering the app's companion LEGO model to give more precise step-by-step instructions, a button to switch between 2D/3D matrices, a button to present degrees/radians, a toggle to change z-axis direction, and an updated model view button with additional model views. This usability study examined the impact of these incremental changes. Participants in both workshops reported higher confidence in their answers, increased math test accuracy, and rated the app's usability moderately high. Additionally, qualitative findings from the thematic analysis showed that the instructional video for model set-up and registration greatly improved users' ability to start using the app and that users could navigate the app's functions effectively. These findings were further supported by users' reported SEQ scores for each task. For example, after completing the first task of registering the model, most participants rated all sequential tasks more favorably.

These results highlight the impact of data-informed insights based on iterative usability testing and the changes made to the AR-Classroom based on those insights. After three usability tests and respective updates to the app, the latest version of the AR-Classroom is associated with improved user experience, increased ease of use, and an overall increase in users' understanding of the app's functionality.

5 Limitations and Future Work

A significant strength of the present work is its use of thematic analysis of observations with quantitative measures (i.e., SEQ and SUS, and math test accuracy and confidence). By using this mixed-method approach, we holistically investigated undergraduate students' experience interacting with and usability of previous versions (i.e., benchmark and updated), and the current version of the AR-Classroom. Another strength is using a five-minute discoverability period (i.e., free play) for users to become familiar with the AR-Classroom before executing specific functions. By allowing users to explore the app's features, they became familiar with how to interact with the app and, during later tasks, effectively used those features.

Though these noted strengths add to the study's efficacy, several limitations must be addressed to contextualize the present findings' impact. First, the study's sample size of fifteen participants limits the ability to determine any statistical significance of the quantitative measures. The smaller sample size allowed for a deeper analysis of users' experiences through qualitative and observation data analysis; however, if statistical significance or measure validity is important to researchers, then a quantitative usability test with a large sample size should be run (n < 30). Next, the AR-Classroom was created to be implemented in STEM education settings where students typically have higher spatial and math skills. However, the current study's participants were recruited through convenience sampling. Though our participants varied in strength of these skills, participants with lower math or spatial abilities may have felt more significant frustration, impacting user-app interaction.

In conclusion, this paper reviewed the most recent usability test run on the AR-Classroom and reflected on changes in discoverability, usability, and quantitative measures compared to two previous usability tests. In the development of the AR-Classroom and its predecessor, BRICKxAR/T [6], our research team, and tech development team have been very collaborative. The tech team will develop new versions of the app, the research team will test those versions in a usability test and provide recommendations based on user insights, then the tech team will implement these recommendations along with adding new features and upgrades as they see fit. Then the cycle continues with more research, recommendations, and app changes. This research process has produced observable improvements across all usability test measures. These improvements demonstrate the effectiveness of taking a data-informed and iterative approach to developing educational technologies.

Acknowledgements. This material is based upon work supported by the National Science Foundation under Grant No. 2119549.

References

1. Uttal, D.H., Cohen, C.A.: Spatial thinking and STEM education: when, why, and how? In: Psychology of Learning and Motivation, vol. 57, pp. 147–181. Academic Press (2012)
2. Hawes, Z.C., Gilligan-Lee, K.A., Mix, K.S.: Effects of spatial training on mathematics performance: a meta-analysis. Dev. Psychol. **58**(1), 112 (2022)
3. Uttal, D.H., et al.: The malleability of spatial skills: a meta-analysis of training studies. Psychol. Bull. **139**(2), 352 (2013)
4. Estapa, A., Nadolny, L.: The effect of an augmented reality enhanced mathematics lesson on student achievement and motivation. J. STEM Educ. **16**(3) (2015)
5. Chen, Y.C.: Effect of mobile augmented reality on learning performance, motivation, and math anxiety in a math course. J. Educ. Comput. Res. **57**(7), 1695–1722 (2019)
6. Aguilar, S.D., Burte, H., Shaghaghian, Z., Yasskin, P., Liew, J., Yan, W.: Enhancing usability in AR and non-AR educational technology: an embodied approach to geometric transformations. In: Zaphiris, P., Ioannou, A. (eds.) Learning and Collaboration Technologies. HCII 2023. Lecture Notes in Computer Science, vol. 14041, pp. 3–21. Springer, Cham (2023). https://doi.org/10.1007/978-3-031-34550-0_1
7. Shaghaghian, Z., Burte, H., Song, D., Yan, W.: Learning spatial transformations and their math representations through embodied learning in augmented reality. In: Zaphiris, P., Ioannou, A. (eds.) Learning and Collaboration Technologies. Novel Technological Environments. HCII 2022. Lecture Notes in Computer Science, vol. 13329, pp. 112–128. Springer, Cham (2022). https://doi.org/10.1007/978-3-031-05675-8_10
8. Yeh, S., et al.: AR-classroom: augmented reality technology for learning 3D spatial transformations and their matrix representation. In: The IEEE ASEE Frontier in Education Conference Proceedings (2023)
9. Aguilar, S.D., et al.: AR-classroom: usability of AR educational technology for learning rotations using three-dimensional matrix algebra. In: The IEEE ASEE Frontier in Education Conference Proceedings (2023b)

Personalized Cybersecurity Education: A Mobile App Proof of Concept

Yusuf Albayram[⊠], David Suess, Yassir Yaghzar Elidrissi, Daniel P. Rollins, and Maciej Beclawski

Department of Computer Science, Central Connecticut State University, New Britain, CT, USA
yusuf.albayram@ccsu.edu,
{davidsuess,yassiry,dprollins,m.beclawski}@my.ccsu.edu

Abstract. Online users are confronted with many privacy and security decisions every day. However, users often fail to understand online privacy, security risks and the importance of security solutions. Instead of using a *"one-size-fits-all"* approach in educating people about the security and privacy implications of their technology use to stay safe online as they often vary widely in their level of IT knowledge, personality traits etc., we developed an Android application that provides personalized cybersecurity training using a machine learning algorithm. The app recommends a variety of cybersecurity materials (e.g., videos, articles, tips) for each individual based on their personality traits and IT expertise. The project is a proof of concept, but has the potential to be extended for use by schools, government organizations, and businesses to personalize their cybersecurity training programs.

Keywords: Personalized cybersecurity education · Security · Privacy

1 Introduction

The rapid shift to digitization and remote operations has led to an increase in internet and device usage, exposing users to privacy and security risks. Educating users about cybersecurity is becoming increasingly important to keep them safe online. Existing cybersecurity training materials are based on a *"one-size-fits-all"* assumption and their effectiveness is limited due to the diversity of users' characteristics such as demographics, mental model, personality traits and IT knowledge etc. We believe that effectiveness of cybersecurity education can be amplified by providing users materials that are tailored to their demographics, personality traits and decision making styles. While recent studies have shown promising results about the effectiveness of personalizing nudges in the context of security (e.g., improve password strength) [7,11,12], to the best of our knowledge, there is no study investigating the effectiveness of a personalized cybersecurity education for users to improve their security and privacy awareness. Towards that, we developed an Android application that provides personalized

C. Stephanidis et al. (Eds.): HCII 2023, CCIS 1957, pp. 257–263, 2024.
https://doi.org/10.1007/978-3-031-49212-9_32

cybersecurity training using a machine learning algorithm. The app recommends a variety of cybersecurity materials (e.g. videos, articles, tips) for each individual based on their personality traits and IT expertise. The project is a proof of concept, but can be expanded to be used by schools, government, and business employees to personalize their cybersecurity training.

2 High Level Overview

We developed an Android application that provides personalized cybersecurity training using a machine learning algorithm that takes into account a set of attributes, features, and information obtained from users to personally recommend various cybersecurity materials (e.g., videos, articles). Figure 1 shows several screenshots from the app.

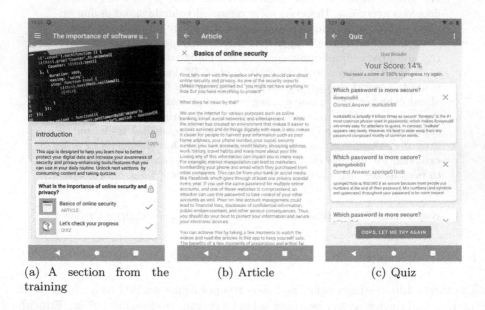

(a) A section from the training   (b) Article   (c) Quiz

Fig. 1. Screenshots showing a sample of course content.

The app uses Firebase (i.e., a cloud based database) to persist any data necessary, such as user profile and personalized cybersecurity training materials. After account creation, the app directs the user to take a survey to determine their personality traits and their level of IT knowledge. The data collected in the survey will then be consumed by a recommender algorithm for presenting a personalized training curriculum and content (e.g., articles and videos) for the user to improve their security and privacy awareness. Figure 2 depicts the system architecture and main components. We describe each of these components in details in the following sections.

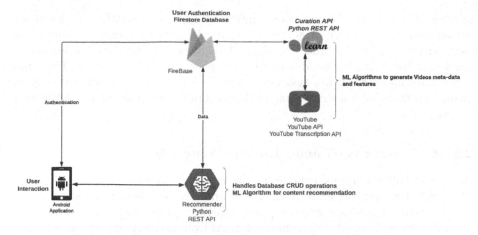

Fig. 2. System architecture and components.

2.1 Survey/Data Collected by Users

The survey serves as a starting point of the application, and the survey data collected from the user is used to capture their personality traits (i.e., personality profile), and classify them based on their levels of knowledge of digital security topics (i.e., knowledge profile). For personality traits, we used BFI-10 scale [13] measuring the Big Five personality traits: Extraversion, Agreeableness, Conscientiousness, Neuroticism, and Openness. For knowledge profile, users are asked about their level of computer proficiency, IT experience, quiz questions measuring their digital knowledge on security and privacy topics (adopted from PEW Research's Digital Knowledge Quiz [8]). This is used to classify the user into three levels: Beginner/Novice, Intermediate/Competent and Advanced/Proficient.

To create a personalized training for each user, the app requires the user to complete the survey after the signup process. The survey questions are asked to users only once when they start using the app for the first time. Once the survey is completed by the user, the collected information is sent to the backend server for processing by the Recommender Algorithm. To render the survey questions, we used SurveyKit[1] library, which allows us to generate a user interface dynamically.

2.2 User Learning Progression

Upon the user's initial login and completion of the survey, they can begin their personalized cybersecurity training course in our app. The course is structured into sections and subsections, each containing various content options such as videos or articles for a user to watch or read. To maintain a linear learning experience, users can only progress through the course sequentially. They are unable

---

[1] https://github.com/QuickBirdEng/SurveyKit.

to view contents from later sections until they have successfully completed the earlier ones. Each section or subsection typically includes a quiz, serving as an assessment of the user's understanding. To advance to the next section, users must pass the quiz associated with the current section or subsection. This app-roach provides users with a systematic and comprehensive learning experience, ensuring a thorough understanding of the material before moving on to the next section.

2.3   Cybersecurity Training Content/Materials

As cybersecurity training content in the app, we determined five key topics: 1) multifactor authentication, 2) software updates, 3) passwords and password management, 4) phishing awareness, and 5) privacy protection. These topics were carefully selected based on recommendations from security experts as enabling multifactor authentication, using strong and unique passwords with the assis-tance of password managers, promptly updating software, and adopting privacy-enhancing technologies are essential security and privacy behaviors that users should incorporate into their online practices [5,6,9,10,14,15].

We identified awareness materials in the form of articles, videos and quizzes from multiple non-profit web sites such as government, non-profit organization promoting security behaviors (e.g., National Cyber Security Alliance (NCSA) [2], National Cyber Security Centre (NCSC) [4], Surveillance Self-Defense [3], Cyber.org [1], YouTube channels (e.g., All Things Secured[2], Techlore[3] and CyberNews[4]) owned by security professionals/experts.

2.4   Algorithm for Personalizing Content

We used Content-Based Filtering for narrowing down a group of videos and articles to a select few to recommend to the user. As part of the recommendation algorithm, the app uses the Cosine Similarity formula for comparing a content's feature (e.g., duration of the video) scores with the user's feature scores. When recommending contents for the user, the app compares these feature scores with the user feature scores to predict which contents the user would like to view or should be shown. More specifically, the cosine can be calculated as the dot product of the two vectors divided by the product of their magnitudes. Contents that strongly exhibit a feature the user likes but also exhibit more features the user does not like will almost never be recommended. We chose the Cosine Similarity because it is simple to implement, and only dependent on how large or small the feature scores are relative to each other within the same vector and not on how they compare with corresponding scores from other vectors. In other words, only the direction the vectors point in matters while how long or short

---

[2] https://www.youtube.com/@AllThingsSecured.
[3] https://www.youtube.com/@techlore.
[4] https://www.youtube.com/@cybernews.

they are does not. A mathematical formula for calculating the Cosine similarity between two vectors A and B is shown below:

$$\cos(\theta) = \frac{\mathbf{A} \cdot \mathbf{B}}{\|\mathbf{A}\|\|\mathbf{B}\|} = \frac{\sum_{i=1}^{n} A_i B_i}{\sqrt{\sum_{i=1}^{n} A_i^2}\sqrt{\sum_{i=1}^{n} B_i^2}}$$

2.5 Automatic Content Curation and Feature Collection

In order to provide personalized cybersecurity education, a key factor is the proper curation of a wide range of content. This includes selecting various videos that cover different aspects such as personality traits and IT experience. Ideally, the process of identifying materials/content (e.g. videos, articles) to be made available to users should be automated. As a proof of concept in our system, we manually identified several videos and articles for each proficiency level (i.e., beginner, intermediate, and advance), as described in Sect. 2.3. To reduce and potentially eliminate manual curation in the future, we developed an auto curation and feature collection application that automatically classifies videos based on their content's proficiency level and extracts features from the video's metadata.

To recommend personalized videos to users, our system utilizes a video training list to build and train a classifier model. We leverage the Natural Language Toolkit (NLTK) to preprocess the transcript of each video, applying techniques like stemming and removing stopwords to optimize the transcript's size for faster and more efficient machine learning (ML) processing. Using Scikit-Learn ML, the system then trains the classifier model based on the preprocessed transcripts and their corresponding labels. This enables the model to classify content into categories such as Beginner, Intermediate, or Advanced.

3 Implications and Future Work

The application we have developed holds significant implications for the future of cybersecurity training. It addresses the growing need for effective and engaging training methods to enhance users' awareness of security and privacy in today's digital landscape where cyber threats increase and users increasingly rely on the internet for work and personal activities.

Traditional cybersecurity training materials are often based on a *"one-size-fits-all"* assumption, which can be perceived as complex, tedious, and lacking engagement. However, by leveraging the concept of personalized cybersecurity training such as the one we proposed, we can reduce complexity and make the training process more engaging by tailoring it to individual users' needs. By considering factors such as their knowledge level, skillset, and learning preferences, we can customize the training content and delivery to better resonate with each user. This not only makes the material more accessible and relevant but also encourages active participation and deeper understanding, which, in turn, can result in higher adoption rates of essential security and privacy behaviors such as enabling 2FA, using password manager, and privacy-enhancing tools etc. Our personalized training application, has the potential to revolutionize cybersecurity awareness. It can be employed in various settings, such as classrooms, to educate students from an early age. Additionally, businesses and government organizations can utilize apps like ours to keep their employees well-trained and engaged in cybersecurity practices.

Moving forward, there are several areas for improvement and expansion of the proposed application. One potential avenue is to incorporate user feedback mechanisms to enhance the fitness of the training material for each individual. Allowing users to provide feedback on the personalized content can enable the application to continuously improve and refine its training recommendations, resulting in an increasingly tailored and effective learning experience. Additionally, the Curation application could curate and process videos, websites, and articles automatically to generate more content automatically. Finally, continued development and research in such personalized cybersecurity training applications can pave the way for more effective cybersecurity training experiences, ultimately bolstering the overall security posture of individuals, organizations, and society as a whole.

Acknowledgments. This work was supported by the Central Connecticut State University AAUP University Research Grant.

References

1. CYBER.ORG: Cybersafety. https://cyber.org/cybersafety. Accessed 23 June 2023
2. Stay Safe Online: Online Safety Basics. https://staysafeonline.org/resources/online-safety-basics/. Accessed 23 June 2023
3. SURVEILLANCE SELF-DEFENSE: Tips, tools and how-tos for safer online communications. https://ssd.eff.org/. Accessed 23 June 2023
4. The National Cyber Security Centre. https://www.ncsc.gov.uk/. Accessed 23 June 2023
5. Albayram, Y., Khan, M.M.H., Fagan, M.: A study on designing video tutorials for promoting security features: a case study in the context of two-factor authentication (2fa). Int. J. Human-Comput. Interact. **33**(11), 927–942 (2017)
6. Albayram, Y., Liu, J., Cangonj, S.: Comparing the effectiveness of text-based and video-based delivery in motivating users to adopt a password manager. In: Proceedings of the 2021 European Symposium on Usable Security, pp. 89–104 (2021)
7. Albayram, Y., Suess, D., Elidrissi, Y.Y.: Investigating the effectiveness of personalized content in the form of videos when promoting a tor browser. In: Proceedings of the 2022 European Symposium on Usable Security, pp. 216–232 (2022)
8. CENTER, P.R.: Digital knowledge quiz (2019). https://www.pewresearch.org/internet/quiz/digital-knowledge-quiz/
9. Centre, N.C.S.: Password managers: How they help you secure passwords (2021). https://www.ncsc.gov.uk/collection/top-tips-for-staying-secure-online/password-managers
10. Ion, I., Reeder, R., Consolvo, S.: "... no one can hack my mind" comparing expert and non-expert security practices. In: Proceedings of the Eleventh USENIX Conference on Usable Privacy and Security, pp. 327–346 (2015)

11. Peer, E., Egelman, S., Harbach, M., Malkin, N., Mathur, A., Frik, A.: Nudge me right: personalizing online security nudges to people's decision-making styles. Comput. Hum. Behav. **109**, 106347 (2020)
12. Qu, L., Xiao, R., Wang, C., Shi, W.: Design and evaluation of cfc-targeted security nudges. In: Extended Abstracts of the 2021 CHI Conference on Human Factors in Computing Systems, pp. 1–6 (2021)
13. Rammstedt, B., John, O.P.: Measuring personality in one minute or less: a 10-item short version of the big five inventory in English and German. J. Res. Pers. **41**(1), 203–212 (2007)
14. Redmiles, E.M., et al.: A comprehensive quality evaluation of security and privacy advice on the web. In: 29th USENIX Security Symposium, pp. 89–100. USENIX (2020)
15. Story, P., et al.: Awareness, adoption, and misconceptions of web privacy tools. Proc. Priv. Enhan. Technol. **2021**(3), 308–333 (2021)

Enhancing Prototyping Skills of K-12 Students Through Lemon: A Bio-Inspired Robotics Kit

İremsu Baş, Demir Alp, Ceren Dolu, Melis Alsan, Andy Emre Koçak, Irmak Atılgan, and Sedat Yalçın[✉]

Hisar School Computer Science ideaLab, Istanbul, Turkey
{iremsu.bas,demir.alp,ceren.dolu,melis.alsan,emre.kocak,
sedat.yalcin}@hisarschool.k12.tr,
irmak.atilgan@hisarschool.k12.t

Abstract. While the popularity of 3D printers and open-sourced materials and the subsequent demand for makers have increased at numerous educational facilities and fabrication laboratories in recent years, there are still many who have yet to utilize 3D printers, laser cutters, and other similar resources within the context of prototyping. This lack of skill and knowledge prevents the resources in such maker spaces from being used effectively. Our proposed project, "Lemon," aims to fix this issue by providing an educational kit to standardize introductory education for modeling, mechanics, electronics, and programming. Thus, users can engage with all these concepts while enhancing their computational and design thinking skills, providing a solid introduction to prototyping and similar design processes. With the kit, the users can build three robots that each represent a level of learning and a stage of complexity by introducing consecutive bio-inspired robots that incorporate newer and more complex mechanical, electronic, and programming systems as opposed to their predecessors. This way, the user's abilities naturally improve as they interact with the kit, reflecting a sense of evolution. The most straightforward stage is the Lime (a fish robot), the next is Satsuma (a turtle robot), and the third is Lemon (a dog robot). The kit includes inexpensive materials such as Raspberry Pi Zeros, MG90S servo motors, and PCA9685 servo boards to increase accessibility. Lemon has a gamification element that encourages students to design their ideal pets. This feature aims to flourish the creativity of children by encouraging them to use the skills that they acquired through Lemon and adopt these skills to the pet robots that they design and build from scratch. Additionally, the kit has a platform where individuals can find documentation about the equipment, step-by-step instructions on the building process, a custom library, and related built-in features while interacting with the platform and the robot they build, amending its attributes in creative manners urged by the guidance of our platform. Lemon stands out as a kit not only for prototyping but also for STEAM education in general, with various applications within schools and maker spaces.

Keywords: STEAM · Gamification · HCI · Prototyping · Robot · Design · Creativity

C. Stephanidis et al. (Eds.): HCII 2023, CCIS 1957, pp. 264–270, 2024.
https://doi.org/10.1007/978-3-031-49212-9_33

1 Introduction

1.1 Learning and Creativity

Creativity is one of the most vital skills of contemporary society [1] and proves its applicability and importance in a diverse range of areas, from the arts to STEAM. It garners increasing importance when paired with digital technologies. Therefore, emphasizing creativity within educational systems is increasingly essential, especially with technological education [2]. However, such modes of instruction that integrate creativity into curricula are still in development [2]. Additionally, recent years suggest an increase in the development of educational resources in both technology and creativity, such as Lego Mindstorms, which only strengthened the idea that efforts in this area need to be furthered [3]. Moreover, it is also evident that educational styles that focus on developing intrinsic motivation as one of the primary motivators behind creativity [3]. Our project, Lemon, emphasizing this aspect of teaching, focuses on a more open learning environment with minimum extrinsic control to the point that our users could complete, customize, and fabricate with the Lemon Kit without teacher assistance as such an open environment is more suitable to nurturing a sense of creativity [3].

An attribute of child education gamification is defined as a process of enhancing a service with affordances for gameful experiences in order to support users' overall value creation [4]. Children like coming up with play-like storified games where they assign roles to themselves and game companions [5]. These games thrive on children's creativity and imagination. Game companions are suitable for supporting these "pretend" games of children. On this note, Lemon stands out as after the fabrication process of robots, they get to create their own ideal companions or pets as Lemon encourages children to customize the robots (Lime, Satsuma, and Lemon) that they assemble guided by our kit resources. As a result, the process of fabrication with Lemon begins to assume aspects of gamification. In the context of the body of research that connects creativity and gamification to learning or education, Lemon can assert its strengths in prototyping education when compared to the large body of works already present in prototyping or technological education.

2 Related Works

There are different tangible and interactive educational systems developed to enhance the programming and computational thinking skills of children. Code Notes is an affordable, accessible, tangible tool for supporting the programming education of children. It uses basic code function cardboards that children can form simple sequences with. These sequences are executed through an Android application utilizing the device's camera [6]. Another programming and logical reasoning education proposal is Roboquedo, which is a turtle robot that can be navigated by using arrows and buttons on either a mobile or a tangible device to complete logical tasks on a map [7]. Pomelo is a friendly robot dog that focuses on teaching children basic algorithmic skills and enhances classroom collaboration through games. Pomelo is programmed utilizing the patterns on tangible code blocks. It also has a question-answering system using natural language processing which helps the students to understand the simpler parts of the lecture they did not comprehend without waiting for the teacher in the classroom to answer [8]. Lemon's proposal is unique in the sense that it pushes students to the more active role of creators as opposed to passive users. They program the robots that they build however they like with the guidance of our videos and booklets within our open-sourced website. Plus, they can implement these skills in another project that they created and observe new implementations there.

An open-source robotic dog similar to Lemon is the Stanford Pupper. It is a quadruped robot to get K-12 and undergraduate students more involved in robotics research. It uses Raspberry Pi 4 for the robot's brain. Building Pupper takes around 8 h to build, and it costs 900$, electronic and mechanical parts included [9]. We were inspired by Stanford Pupper while designing the Lemon kit. We wanted Lemon to go step by step for learning assembly, electronics, and programming rather than trying to teach it in one go so that every essential topic is fully embraced by the children. We tried to achieve this by adopting three different robots in our kit that each focus on these main areas. In addition, we wanted the Lemon kit to be accessible to everyone everywhere. Thus, both the electronics and mechanical components that we utilize cost cheaper than Pupper, which makes Lemon more accessible. Also, if the student has access to 3D printers or laser cutters, they can provide their own parts using our open-sourced models featured on our website (Fig. 1).

Fig. 1. Satsuma the robot turtle (left), Lime the robot fish (center), Lemon the robot dog (right)

3 The Lemon Kit and Discussion

Lemon is a prototyping educational kit that is comprised of three levels of increasing difficulty inspired by biological complexity. The first level, Lime, teaches the basics of assembly, electronics, and coding. In Lime, the users learn how to integrate servo motors into a design, to connect servos to and move them through Raspberry Pi pico microcontrollers by integrating adafruit circuit python libraries (as it is both simple and compatible with parts used in our kit) in the coding process to teach a coding foundation for prototyping in a mechanical fabrication process. Afterward, however, the kit starting with Lime pushes its users to express themselves creatively. For example, with Lime, after the user creates a fish that can move through the educational instructions, then they can modify, color, or customize the fish to reflect their own identity and culture. Building on this foundation, Satsuma further develops these skills by adding to the curriculum by integrating electronic breadboards, voltage regulators, and servo boards into its fabrication process to allow more complicated movements, as well as improving the model thematically by adding ultrasonic sensors. Finally, Lemon, the final model, adds inverse kinematics principles to the coding process to significantly further the foundational skills of users in prototyping in mathematics, electronics, design, and coding. Paired with the utilization of ultrasonic sensors and speaker systems, the final model stands out as a prototype that can replicate specific actions of a dog, such as following individuals and barking. These features notably develop the thematic component and engage the users further.

Lemon stands out in education due to its direct focus on gamification and its tangibility to further engage users. It is important to note that robotics is a significantly helpful tool in education as it facilitates stimulation and engagement as an instructive aid due to the tangible quality of robotics [10]. In the case of using a simple and guided mechanism for education in prototyping methods, Fortunati et al. compared arts and crafts robots and Lego Mindstorms robots. They found that building robots from scratch using recycled materials increased students' skills and knowledge. On the other hand, making a LEGO Mindstorms robot using structured materials increased their awareness of the robotization of machines [11]. The kit, Lemon, while structured in a fashion similar to LEGO Mindstorms robots, also invites users to customize the end products and develop original models to be shared on our website. This practice creates an environment that promotes not only the growth of cerebral skills and an understanding of robotization but also of creativity, which is essential to individuals' skills and knowledge, as mentioned above. This feature also functions as a mode of gamification for our users, as they get to create their ideal pet, whether it be an incredibly unique fish, a dog that follows the user, or another fabrication of their imagination (Fig. 2).

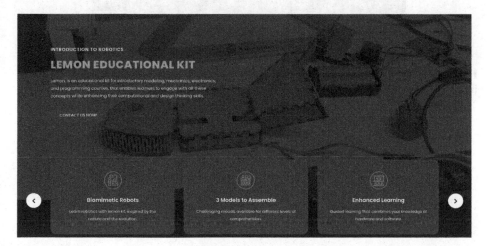

Fig. 2. The main menu of our online platform

Lemon, however, is also unique in its mode of Human-Computer interaction. Firstly, with our online platform, users continuously engage with the kit itself may it be through informative content such as tutorials or the opportunity to customize and request changes to a model. Moreover, our kit also functions as an intermediary between the computer and the individual, as it encourages a direct dialogue through changes to models and codes regarding optimizations or customizations in the context of our gamification system. And the user also interacts directly with the end product, the robot that they have built. Being directly involved in its manufacturing and assembly process also functions in a way, as a manner of interaction between the user and their creation.

We introduced the Lemon kit to the newcomer middle and high school students in our lab. As they built the robots with no prior experience, they provided extensive feedback on what was difficult to implement and what should be improved (Figs. 3 and 4). After completing the Lemon kit successfully, we challenged the students to design their own pet robots. One of the students, combining the creativity they gained through the Lemon kit, is now working on building a snake robot (Fig. 5).

Fig. 3. Lime models built by newcomers to our lab. The one on the bottom is designed with the inspiration of shiny fishes.

Fig. 4. Lime creative design inspired by a fish on a Victorian wall tile

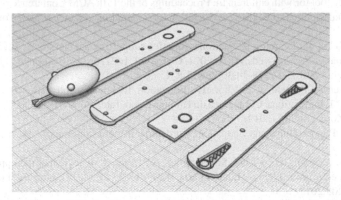

Fig. 5. The 3D model of the snake robot a middle school student from our lab designed

4   Conclusion

Education is heavily influenced by creativity and gamification, as both dramatically increase the benefits of educational resources. When applied to education in technology, creativity, and gamification can be increasingly important as creative thinking is an integral part of contemporary skills in technology. Thus, by integrating such principles into prototyping education, Lemon stands out as an effective kit that can introduce its users to the fabrication process while developing them creatively. Lemon works as an interacting mode of human-computer interaction as Lemon, through optimization and customization of robots made using the kit, simulate direct communication between users and computer systems. Moreover, the utilization of Lemon in an educational context have shows great promise as it not only allowed users to significantly improve their skills in fabrication, but also it has pushed its users to create further, utilizing their creativity and knowledge strengthened by Lemon to design and build new robot companions, showing the potential of the Lemon Kit's gamified education for K-12.

References

1. Craft, A.: Creativity and Education Futures: Learning in a Digital Age. Trentham Books, Staffordshire (2010)
2. Henriksen, D., Henderson, M., Creely, E., et al.: Creativity and technology in education: an international perspective. Tech. Know. Learn. **23**, 409–424 (2018)
3. Apiola, M., Lattu, M., Pasanen, T.: Creativity-supporting learning environment—CSLE. ACM Trans. Comput. Educ. **12**(3), Article 11. New York, USA (2012)
4. Huotari, K., Hamari, J.: Defining gamification. In: Proceeding of the 16th International Academic MindTrek Conference, pp. 17–22. Finland (2012)
5. Verenikina, I., Herrington, J.: Computer game design and the imaginative play of young children. In: Proceedings of the 8th International Conference on Interaction Design and Children (IDC 2009). Association for Computing Machinery, pp. 254–257. New York, NY, USA (2009)
6. Sabuncuoglu, A., Buruk, O., Erkaya, M., Goksun, T.: Code notes: designing a low-cost tangible coding tool for/with children. In: Proceedings of the 17th ACM Conference on Interaction Design and Children (IDC 2018). Association for Computing Machinery, New York, NY, USA (2018)
7. Barros, G., et al.: Learning interactions: robotics supporting the classroom. In: Stephanidis, C., Antona, M., Ntoa, S. (eds.) HCII 2021. CCIS, vol. 1421, pp. 3–10. Springer, Cham (2021). https://doi.org/10.1007/978-3-030-78645-8_1
8. Nasi, L. et al.: Pomelo, a Collaborative Education Technology Interaction Robot. In: 14th ACM/IEEE International Conference on Human-Robot Interaction (HRI), 2019, pp. 757–758. Daegu, Korea (South) (2019)
9. Stanford Pupper Homepage. https://stanfordstudentrobotics.org/pupper. Accessed 17 Mar 2023
10. Mubin, O., Stevens, C., Shahid, S., Mahmud, A., Dong, J.: A review of the applicability of robots in education. Technol. Educ. Learn. **1**(209-0015), 13 (2013). https://doi.org/10.2316/Journal.209.2013
11. Fortunati, L., Manganelli, A.M., Ferrin, G.: Arts and crafts robots or LEGO® MINDSTORMS robots? A comparative study in educational robotics. Int. J. Technol. Des. Educ. **32**, 287–310 (2022)

It Takes Sperm and Egg: Improving Social Interdependence by Integrating Asymmetrical Game Design into Collaborative Learning

Jiajia He, Ke Fang, Yunxuan Li, Zeyan Dao, and Wai Kin (Victor) Chan[✉]

Tsinghua Shenzhen International Graduate School, Shenzhen 518055, China
hejj21@mails.tsinghua.edu.cn, chanw@sz.tsinghua.edu.cn

Abstract. Computer-supported collaborative learning (CSCL) is a growing trend in education, emphasizing the importance of social interdependence for effective collaboration. Conversely, the absence of social interdependence can result in negative group dynamics. To address this, we propose an approach called asymmetrical game design, which aims to provide players with distinct abilities, information, and tasks, fostering interdependencies that require close cooperation to achieve game objectives. To examine the impact of asymmetrical game design on social interdependence in collaborative learning, we developed "It Takes Sperm and Egg," an augmented reality game for two players, designed to educate players about human sexuality. The game utilizes physical Lego blocks and foam models to construct interactive scenes. The "sperm player" engages in a first-person perspective augmented reality (AR) game, controlling a Lego block car through the physical scene using a controller. The car's camera captures live footage relayed to a monitor, enabling the "sperm player" to view both the physical scene and augmented reality content. In contrast, the "egg player" observes the physical scene from a top-down perspective and has the sole responsibility of guiding the sperm and manipulating the AR world through actions such as removing Lego bricks, pressing buttons, and solving puzzles. The game presents unique clues to each player, necessitating effective communication and understanding to acquire knowledge and complete the game. Based on preliminary experiments and interviews, it can be concluded that this game has a positive impact on enhancing social interdependence. In summary, this study introduces the integration of asymmetrical game design into collaborative learning, providing comprehensive design guidance for cooperative educational games that can inspire further innovation and exploration in this field.

Keywords: CSCL · Asymmetrical game design · Augmented Reality

1 Introduction

Collaborative Learning (CL) [1] is an important educational approach aimed at encouraging students to learn together with shared task goals. However, the current development of collaborative learning theory faces a major issue – inequality [5]. As collaborative learning considers group goals as individual goals, students inevitably encounter issues of unequal resource allocation and task distribution during group cooperation. This inequality is primarily reflected in the uneven abilities of group members and the uneven assignment of group tasks. Such unequal distribution puts students in an "asymmetric" situation, making it easy for problems like free-riding and unwillingness to cooperate to arise [3].

Asymmetric game design holds promise for addressing the issue of inequality in collaborative learning. In the context of rapid technological advancement, Computer-supported Collaborative Learning (CSCL) [4] has emerged as a new trend in collaborative learning. Among the various approaches, game-based learning has proven to be highly effective [6]. Recently, the concept of asymmetric games [2] has been introduced, cleverly utilizing differences in abilities and actions among individuals in team games to create "asymmetric" scenarios and gameplay that foster mutual cooperation among players.

Building upon existing research, we have designed a non-symmetric Augmented Reality (AR) game titled "It Takes Sperm and Egg", with a focus on sexual education. The game incorporates the design framework of asymmetric games, including settings of information asymmetry and ability asymmetry, to foster interdependence and close cooperation between players. By utilizing AR image recognition technology, the game creates a combination of virtual and real-world asymmetric scenarios. Players collaborate and communicate to solve puzzles at each level, achieving common goals and learning relevant sexual education knowledge. Additionally, a pre-experiment was conducted to test the game, and the preliminary effectiveness was verified through interviews. This represents a new attempt and exploration in the field of collaborative learning.

2 Method

2.1 Design Guide

Based on the MDA framework, Harris [2] innovatively proposed the theory of asymmetric game design. Including the following aspects.

Mechanics of Asymmetry: In game mechanics design, the following actions in Table 1 can be employed to create an asymmetric gaming experience for players.

Interdependence and the Dynamics of Asymmetry: During the dynamic process of the game, players' actions will influence the game's development. Especially in cooperative game environments, the interplay between players and the correlation between players' actions and timing will both impact the progress of the game. The main design points are outlined in Table 2.

Table 1. Types of asymmetry in mechanics.

Mechanics of Asymmetry	Description
Asymmetry of Ability	Players with different abilities
Asymmetry of Challenge	Players face different challenges
Asymmetry of Interface	Players engage in the game using different forms
Asymmetry of Information	Players receive different information
Asymmetry of Investment	Players invest different amounts of time in the game
Asymmetry of Goal	Players have different objectives in the game

Table 2. Types of asymmetry in interdependence and the dynamics.

Interdependence and the Dynamics of Asymmetry	Type
Directional Dependence	Mirrored Dependence
	Unidirectional Dependence
	Bidirectional Dependence (AKA Symbiosis)
Synchronicity and Timing	Asynchronous Timing
	Sequential (Disjoint) Timing
	Expectant Timing
	Concurrent Timing
	Coincident Timing

2.2 Game Design

We have designed an asymmetric collaborative AR game with a sexual education theme called "It Takes Sperm and Egg". The game requires two players, with one player assuming the role of a sperm and the other player assuming the role of an egg. As shown in Fig. 1(d), the game scene is constructed using physical LEGO blocks and foam models, simulating the first part of the sperm's adventurous journey—from the vaginal opening to the cervical opening.

The "sperm player" experiences a first-person augmented reality (AR) game, controlling a Lego-block car through the physical environment using a controller (Fig. 1(a), (b)). The car is equipped with a WiFi camera that captures real-time footage and streams it to a monitor. The scene includes various recognizable stickers, and if the sperm player's camera detects the relevant images, the monitor displays text information, puzzles, and more (Fig. 1(c)). However, the sperm player has a limited field of view and cannot see the entire map.

In contrast, the "egg player" has a broader perspective and can overlook the entire physical scene (Fig. 1(d)). The "egg player" assist in guiding the sperm player's actions and solving puzzles through activities such as assembling LEGO blocks and pressing buttons, fostering cooperation between the two players.

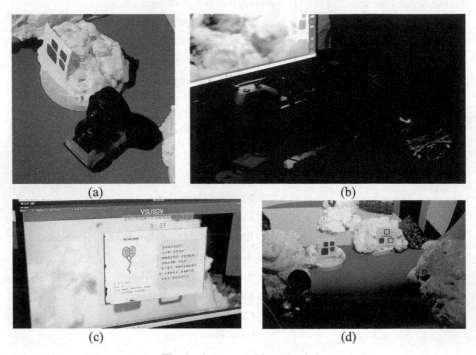

(a)   (b)

(c)   (d)

Fig. 1. Game scene introduction

The entire game consists of two main stages. In the first stage, the sperm player constantly faces the corrosive effects of the acidic environment and must find a protective shield within the scene before the 5-min countdown ends. The egg player is provided with information about several potential locations where the shield might be present. They need to guide the sperm player to the relevant spots, allowing the sperm player to use their AR scanning capabilities to identify and obtain relevant clues. Through cooperation and puzzle-solving, they ultimately secure the shield and deactivate the countdown.

In the second stage, the egg player encounters a crisis and must solve a puzzle to progress towards the fallopian tube. Failure to do so will lead to a negative outcome for both players. The puzzle is related to the hormonal regulation of the female menstrual cycle. The sperm player can utilize the AR recognition feature to search for clues and assist the egg player in solving the puzzle. Ultimately, the egg player obtains crucial information and completes the related task through LEGO assembly, signifying the successful completion of the game—where the sperm reaches the cervical opening and the egg reaches the fallopian tube.

Throughout the entire game process, the two players must collaborate closely and work together to solve puzzles in order to complete the game. In the entire game design process, we adhered to the key principles of asymmetric game design and incorporated the following asymmetric elements.

Mechanics of Asymmetry

- *Asymmetry of Ability.* The sperm and egg players possess different abilities. The sperm player can control the movement of the "sperm car" and engage in AR image recognition. The egg player, on the other hand, has a broader observation perspective, more background knowledge clues, and the ability to modify the physical environment.
- *Asymmetry of Challenge.* The sperm player needs to maneuver the car to identify and obtain the correct clues, while also assisting the egg player. The egg player relies on the terrain map to guide the sperm player's movements and cooperates with them to solve puzzles.
- *Asymmetry of Interface.* The sperm player can only view the virtual scene's visuals, while the egg player can only observe the visuals of the real-world scene.
- *Asymmetry of Information.* The sperm player's information is derived from AR scanning and recognition, while the egg player's information is provided through textual descriptions specific to their role. The information available to the sperm player primarily relates to sperm biological characteristics, while the information accessible to the egg player predominantly pertains to the vaginal environment and menstrual cycle of the female reproductive system.

Interdependence and the Dynamics of Asymmetry

- *Directional Dependence.* Based on the level and puzzle design, the relationship between players in this game can be described as bidirectional dependence. In the first stage of the game, the egg player has a better understanding of the overall terrain, and the sperm player relies on the guidance of the egg player to navigate the environment. In the second stage, the sperm player utilizes their AR recognition abilities to gather more information, which the egg player depends on to solve puzzles and achieve success in the game. This interdependence between the players provides them with more cooperative opportunities, encourages mutual collaboration, and enhances positive social interdependence among them.
- *Expectant Timing.* When player B completes their preparation action, player A can trigger a specific discrete action. This creates a one-way dependency between the players, leading to a closer cooperative relationship. In the game, the egg player guides the sperm player to reach specific locations, allowing the sperm player to perform AR recognition on relevant images. Similarly, when the egg player needs to solve a puzzle, the sperm player must answer questions to obtain relevant clues and inform the egg player, enabling them to solve the puzzle together.
- *Concurrent Timing.* Both players perform continuous actions simultaneously. The egg player and the sperm player need to jointly control the movement of the sperm car,

with the egg player responsible for giving directions and the sperm player responsible for maneuvering the car.

3 Pilot Study

To examine the cooperative and knowledge learning effects of the game players, we conducted a pilot study. Firstly, we recruited 8 participants through a friend community, aged between 22 and 35 years (mean $= 25.6$, SD $= 3.99$), with an equal gender distribution (50% male, 50% female). Among them, 1 person reported having no knowledge of sexual education, 2 people considered themselves highly knowledgeable, and the rest had some level of knowledge but not extensive.

Prior to the start of the experiment, we divided the participants into groups of two, resulting in a total of 4 groups, with three groups consisting of members who were already acquainted with each other. Once the players selected their respective roles, the experiment began. The duration of the experiment ranged from 10 to 25 min, depending on the completion time of each group. After all the group members completed the game, we randomly selected 5 individuals for semi-structured interviews. With their consent, the interviews were recorded, with each interview lasting approximately 25 min.

4 Result and Analysis

After the completion of all the experiments, we transcribed the 5 interviewers' content into written form. The interviews mainly focused on two aspects: game experience and knowledge acquisition. After conducting qualitative analysis on the interview transcripts, we categorized the players' gameplay process into the following aspects:

- *Role Identification.* This is the preparation phase of the game, where players familiarize themselves with the background introductions of their respective characters. During this phase, P4 said, *"I found the role-playing aspect quite interesting."*
- *Ability Limitations.* During the early stages of the game, many sperm players expressed a sense of limitation in their abilities. As P2 pointed, *"It's challenging to control, and from my perspective, I can't judge the distance between the left and right doors accurately, so I often collide with the edges of those doors."* On the other hand, egg players rarely experienced such feelings in the initial stages. These feelings often appeared when they also needed assistance in the second phase. *"Now it's like we've switched roles, and I have to rely on the other person"* (P4).
- *Clear Objectives.* After realizing the limitations in their abilities, players became aware that they could only complete the game by helping each other. *"I think the goal is quite clear"* (P2).
- *Collaborative Gameplay.* During the collaborative gameplay, two main behavior patterns emerged--information sharing and puzzle solving. In the information sharing phase, players could directly access their own information or acquire the other player's information through communication. For example, a player mentioned, *"I don't know the pH value here, so I have to ask him"* (P2). Additionally, during the puzzle-solving phase, both players could operate the car simultaneously or wait for one player to explore and provide assistance to the other player in solving the puzzle.

- *Knowledge Acquisition.* Through the interviews, three main ways of acquiring knowledge were identified: passive acquisition, active acquisition, and active dissemination. Passive acquisition refers to information obtained from the environment itself, including AR-recognized images and highlighted information in the text. For example, a player mentioned, *"I remember the appearance of those sperm very clearly. Maybe because the visual impact is stronger than text, the impression is more profound"* (P2). Active acquisition refers to knowledge obtained through communication with the partner when encountering challenges during the game. For instance, *"I remember the answer to that pH value"* (P3). Active dissemination indicates voluntarily providing assistance to the partner when they encounter difficulties and reviewing related knowledge. As mentioned by P3, *"He needed the answer to that hormone, so I carefully examined the image and memorized it"* (P3).

Based on the above analysis, we have come to two conclusions:

R1) Among all the design elements, the Asymmetry of Ability and Expectant Timing stand out as the most effective in promoting mutual dependence and enhancing player experience.

These two design aspects are primarily manifested during the information sharing and puzzle solving stages of collaborative gameplay. Through the interviews, we discovered that the design of Asymmetry of Ability necessitates players to rely on information communication, thereby strengthening their interdependence. Many sperm players found that jointly operating the car compensated for their own limitations. One player expressed, *"I'm not very accurate in fine adjustments. So, I have to completely rely on Miss Egg's instructions, yes. But when the two are combined, I feel that my operation becomes more precise and accurate"* (P3). Similarly, during the puzzle-solving stage, we found that it was the most enjoyable phase for players. The design of Expectant Timing, as a form of asymmetrical gameplay, was mentioned multiple times by players. For example, *"There was a 30-s countdown question, and there were three or four consecutive questions that created a sense of tension. I was reading the problem on my side while waiting for Miss Egg to help me with the answer. It felt both tense and enjoyable"* (P3). It is evident that the Asymmetry of Ability and Expectant Timing, as two key asymmetrical design elements, effectively promote player interdependence and enhance the overall gaming experience.

R2) Players acquired sexual education-related knowledge during the game, and among the three ways of obtaining knowledge, interacting with interdependent peers resulted in the most profound impressions of the learned knowledge.

Through analysis, it was found that all players reported gaining new knowledge after completing the game. Regarding the "most memorable knowledge," 56% of the responses were related to actively acquired knowledge, 35% were related to actively disseminated knowledge, and only 9% were related to passively obtained knowledge. This indicates that the probability of acquiring knowledge is higher when there is interactive interdependence between the players throughout the game. As P5 mentioned, *"The knowledge wasn't given to me directly, but rather encountered during puzzle-solving moments where the other player told me or I had to remember to tell the other player"*

(P5). Because of the collaborative relationship based on mutual interdependence, players faced and solved difficulties together. In this interactive process, the incorporated knowledge was more easily learned and understood.

5 Conclusion

In this study, we developed a dual-player asymmetric AR game with a theme of sexual education, aiming to explore new approaches in collaborative learning. We designed seven forms of asymmetric gameplay and incorporated sexual education-related knowledge points. Through experiments, we examined the cooperative effects and learning outcomes of players. The results showed that the design elements of Asymmetry of Ability and Expectant Timing had the greatest impact on fostering mutual dependence among players and enhancing their game experience. Moreover, in terms of knowledge acquisition, interactions with interdependent partners had a more profound impact on knowledge retention.

However, our study also had certain limitations. Firstly, in the puzzle-solving aspect of game design, many players pointed out that the hints were not clear, leading to situations where they were unsure of what to do. In future iterations, we will refine the coherence of clues and game prompts in this part. In terms of experimentation, this study only conducted a preliminary experiment with a relatively small sample size. In future research, we plan to expand the scale of experiments to further explore the role of asymmetric games in cooperative learning.

References

1. Ashman, A., Gillies, R.: Cooperative Learning: The Social and Intellectual Outcomes of Learning in Groups. Routledge, Abingdon (2003)
2. Harris, J.: Leveraging asymmetries in multiplayer games: investigating design elements of interdependent play. In Proceedings of the 2016 Annual Symposium on Computer-Human Interaction in Play, Austin Texas, pp. 350–361. ACM, USA (2016). https://doi.org/10.1145/2967934.2968113
3. Isaac, M.L.: "I Hate Group Work!" social loafers, indignant peers, and the drama of the classroom. Engl. J. 101(4), 83–89 (2012)
4. Jeong, H., Hmelo-Silver, C.E.: Ten years of computer-supported collaborative learning: a meta-analysis of CSCL in STEM education during 2005–2014. Educ. Res. Rev. 28, 100284 (2019). https://doi.org/10.1016/j.edurev.2019.100284
5. Sharan, Y.: Cooperative learning for academic and social gains: valued pedagogy, problematic practice, Par I. Eur. J. Educ. 45(2), 300–313 (2010). https://doi.org/10.1111/j.1465-3435.2010.01430.x
6. Wendel, V.: Designing collaborative multiplayer serious games: escape from Wilson Island—a multiplayer 3D serious game for collaborative learning in teams. Educ. Inf. Technol. 18, 287–308 (2013). https://doi.org/10.1007/s10639-012-9244-6

Digital Administration in the Improvement of Information Quality Processes in Teachers. Case, Local Educational Management Unit in Peru

Edgar Mitchel Lau-Hoyos[1]([✉]) [iD], Yessica Erazo-Ordoñez[2] [iD],
Juan Máximo Santa Cruz Carhuamaca[2] [iD], Magaly Natalie Uceda-Bazán[3] [iD],
Armando José Moreno-Heredia[4] [iD], María Alejandra Castro-Navarro[1] [iD],
Blanca Elisa Ramírez-Medina[1] [iD], Flor Elizabeth Obregón-Vara[1] [iD],
Claudia Emperatriz Rodríguez-Ortiz[1] [iD], and Jhoselit Lisset Facho-Cornejo[5] [iD]

[1] Cesar Vallejo University, Pimentel, Peru
mlauh@ucvvirtual.edu.pe
[2] Cesar Vallejo University, Lima, Peru
[3] Technological University of Peru, Chiclayo, Peru
[4] Pedro Ruiz Gallo National University, Lambayeque, Peru
[5] San Matin de Porres University, Pimentel, Peru

Abstract. This research presents the objective of proposing digital administration in the improvement of information quality processes in teachers. Case, Unit of Local Educational Management Peru. The research presents a quantitative, non-experimental and purposeful approach, supported by validated instruments. The information collected by the collaborators who work in the local educational management unit in Peru was analyzed. This research is based on the theories of information quality and digital government. Likewise, the instrument that measured the Digital Administration and Information Quality variables obtained a reliable value with Cronbach's Alpha. The most relevant results show that the intrinsic dimension obtained a low level of 38.2% and a medium level of 41.2%, both indicating that there is no digitized information, nor organized in databases. Likewise, the contextual dimension obtained a medium level of 45.6% and a high level of 35.3%, both indicating that a large percentage of the information is received in digital files of different formats, incomplete, outdated to generate real, reliable and timely reports in the event of any eventuality. -dad. The proposed proposal is based on law 1412 digital government law and the proper use of digital technologies, decentralization, modernization and improvement of public management at the service of the citizen. Finally, the proposal was validated by professional experts in the field.

Keywords: Digital administration · information quality · administrative processes

C. Stephanidis et al. (Eds.): HCII 2023, CCIS 1957, pp. 279–286, 2024.
https://doi.org/10.1007/978-3-031-49212-9_35

1 Introduction

1.1 Problematic Reality

Information is the most precious treasure we have, through it we can solve problems and make the right decisions for personal or collective benefit. It is necessary to digitize information in all public entities, to optimize and speed up information processes. For this reason, digital administration (AD) is the strategy that helps all users who participate in the processes of said processes.

The Ministry of Education (MINEDU) requires that each Regional Directorate of Education (DRE) and each Local Educational Management Unit (UGEL) comply with the current requirements given in the regulations and at the times indicated, in order to make decisions that improve, correct on time and guarantee the quality of teaching in educational institutions (IIEE) in the country.

In the different administrative activities of a UGEL in Peru, critical problems were identified in the execution of their processes, which affected their work carried out by various officials and collaborators, as well as the pedagogical work of teachers and students. Among the common problems that follow the information processes (PI) in some areas we have that:

Procedures for receiving massive information were found through physical paper documents and digital files sent by IIEE professors, this information must be processed, studied and informed in due time to the officials of UGEL, DRE and MINEDU. The information received is enormous, in different formats, without structures and without automation, making it very difficult to prepare timely, truthful and quality reports for those who require it; In addition, they present difficulties to supervise the attendance of the teachers in 730 IIEE, how to know, if in an educational institution (IE) their teachers attend and fulfill their responsibilities? How to know immediately, when teachers do not attend due to health problems or resignations and replace their places on time and not affect students? Another difficulty is the existing delay in updating the rank information of teachers who move up the ranks, unfortunately it can take months and the information is never updated. Finally, another common problem is the requirements for educational materials that are requested from the supply area, which, due to lack of knowledge of the regulations and inaccuracies in the information, delay the delivery of educational materials for months, affecting students.

For these reasons, it was essential to examine the information quality processes (PCI) in teachers of a UGEL in Peru, and according to the problems expressed, an attempt is made to answer the question: How to improve the PCI in teachers? of a UGEL from Peru?

The intention was to examine the PCI in the teachers of a UGEL in Peru, following the route of the PI in all areas of this UGEL and how the satisfaction of teachers and UGEL workers is affected. as well as understand the requirement of proposing the implementation of digital administration.

1.2 Literature Review

Theory of Digital Goverment. The United Nations Educational Scientific and Cultural Organization (UNESCO 2018) in its agenda for 2030 projects that the diffusion and implementation of information and communication technologies (TIC) and global communication are factors that accelerate the development of the humanity and closing digital gaps. Many governments around the world have implemented digital administration policies and recognize the great influence of TIC and e-government (GE) in transforming improvements in public management (GP).

The United Nations (2020), points out that the GE improves the links between the state and the citizen, reflecting on the services provided by the public administration. Likewise, the International Telecommunications Union (2022), strengthens social inclusion through the electronic services provided by the government, considering that by 2030 citizens will improve their quality of life by applying TIC towards a digital state (ITU 2020).

The Economic Commission for Latin America and the Caribbean (CEPAL 2021) points out that the digital transformation (TD), in addition to including TIC in the GP, should also be considered in its context the 4.0 revolution, which considers democratization, the study of public policies, techniques and government tools to better understand the challenges of GP.

To implement digital administration, one must consider the fast pace of technology and communications. Digital administration implements TIC in governments to bring benefits to citizens, access them, improve the services they receive and be more socially connected (World Bank 2018).

Toro-García et al. (2020), Digital administration is based on the use of digital technologies applied to the GP, this allows very quickly to attend to the efforts made by citizens, helping them to make the right decisions and improve their quality of life. It is also an environment made up of people who want to improve public management and who participate by building digital services (SD) to guarantee the best service to the citizen in the use of technology in public management (Carlos, 2021).

Theory of Quality of the Information. Sauvageot (2017), in his article before UNESCO, states that quality has types of patterns to refer to the productions made by people with the capacity, intelligence and power to build them.

According to Richard (2017), details that the information is linked to procedures such as accepting the lack of information, accessing, building and receiving the information, as well as developing digital systems, using and publishing the information. These open systems processes demarcate the idea indicating that organizations work converting information into knowledge, processes and structures to generate other results and services (Choo 1996).

Ohly (2011), indicates that the information is of quality as long as it helps in decision making and solves questioned problems. On the contrary, if there is a process that leads to the quality of information failing, this will affect decision-making and therefore the problem in question will not be resolved. Furthermore, Van Birge-len et al. (2001), consider quality information if, during the process and at the end of an investigation, users express their satisfaction.

Lee et al. (2002), indicate that CI presents the following dimensions: intrinsic, contextual, representation and accessibility (see Fig. 1). Strong et al. (1997) coincides in the same, pointing out that these categories provide higher quality information. These researchers point out that information is intrinsically inherent to quality. They also point out that the contextual dimension requires that the information be prominent, accurate, complete and adequate to determine its quality. Lastly, the representation and accessibility dimensions highlight the importance of information systems and their access to them.

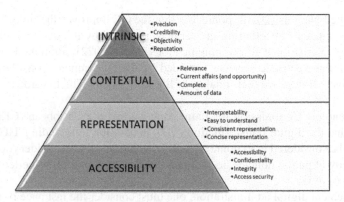

Fig. 1. Information Quality Dimensions

Lee et al. (2002) consider that CI is based on four dimensions. Likewise, it studies the environment where the information circulates, for example: database, information systems, social networks or website, considering the people who generate and use information (Strong et al. 1997). This also implies that the information is punctual and concise, allowing correct decisions to be made, combined with other information, in accordance and remarkable to the requirements of the users. In addition, CI means that the information must be specific and allow you to decide correctly.

Objectives. Propose the digital government in the improvement of information quality processes in teachers. Case, local educational management unit Peru. In addition, it includes specific objectives: i) Diagnose the current situation of PCI in teachers. Case, local educational management unit Peru. ii) Design the digital administration proposal to improve PCI in teachers. Case, local educational management unit Peru. iii) Validate the digital administration proposal to improve PCI in teachers. Case, local educational management unit Peru.

2   Method

This research approached the quantitative approach (Sánchez 2015), using numerical data, systematically analyzed, organized and structured. It is a non-experimental investigation, because only the variables are measured and not manipulated, cross-sectional with data collected at a single moment and descriptive depth, revealing the characteristics of the study population using an instrument validated and reliable (Hernández 2018).

Sierra (2001), determines that the sample is a correctly selected part of the population group; presenting common characteristics to optimize the total study of the population group, in order to collect true and reliable data. On the contrary, when the population is small, like that of this UGEL in Peru, which has 78 workers, it was decided to work with 68 for the census population and 10 for the pilot test. Thus, clarifying that sampling was not applied.

3 Results

3.1 Results by Dimensions and Variable

(See Tables 1, 2 and 3).

Table 1. Intrinsic dimension of PCI

		Frequency	Valid Percentage
Valid	1 None	6	8.8
	2 Little	26	38.2
	3 Median	28	41.2
	4 High	6	8.8
	5 Very High	2	2.9
	Total	68	100.0

Table 2. Context dimension of PCI

		Frequency	Valid Percentage
Valid	1 None	1	1.5
	2 Little	9	13.2
	3 Median	31	45.6
	4 High	24	35.3
	5 Very High	3	4.4
	Total	68	100.0

Observing the results of Table 3, we identified that the PCI variable presents unfavorable results, because if we add the percentages of the Medium, High and Very High levels they reach 83.83% (57). Therefore, we understand that the dimensions: intrinsic, context, representation and accessibility are at a high-risk level and in a state of alert, continuously generating problems in PCIs.

Table 3. Variable information quality processes

		Frequency	Valid Percentage
Valid	1 None	5	7.4
	2 Little	6	8.8
	3 Median	29	42.6
	4 High	16	23.5
	5 Very High	12	17.6
	Total	68	100.0

3.2 Digital Administration Model for a UGEL Peru

(See Fig. 2).

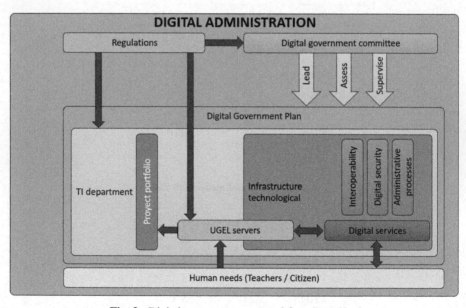

Fig. 2. Digital government proposal for a Peru Ugel

3.3 Digital Administration Proposal for a UGEL Peru

The digital administration proposal is based on Law 1412, called the digital government law, determines the format to apply the digital government strategy in the state, making the correct use of digital technologies in public administration; also, in Law 29158, in charge of the decentralization process and modernizing public management by coordinating the country's multisectoral policies; and Law 27658, focused on building a state with democracy and decentralized to serve the citizen.

The purpose of the proposal is to optimize the PCI in the teachers of a UGEL in Peru, this also leads to improving the services provided in the public administration. Its activity begins with a socio-technological reality, which is why the state, with its different government entities and digital transformation, create public management policies to include them in the implementation of digital administration, to improve services using technologies and digital systems designed with clear and simple methodologies so that all public servants can access, integrate and process the required quality information.

Digital governance integrates the processes of directing, evaluating and supervising; necessary for the construction of the digital government plan, requiring any public entity to implement digital administration with clear strategies, with activities, techniques and tools focused on improving and consolidating public management through digital systems at the service of the citizen in any possible situation; facilitating and promoting TD.

The benefit of this digital administration proposal contributes to improve the PCI in teachers. In recent years, teachers have been neglected, due to poorly recorded and outdated information, the information they present is not yet digitized or automated, therefore, there are no databases that help to organize the information for when reporting is required. And make accurate decisions. Added to this the time and money lost, there are also complaints from them. For these reasons, it is necessary to propose proposals that help improve results.

The digital administration proposal is developed considering the results of the study, the requirements of the teachers and the difficulties of the PCI that both teachers and workers of a UGEL in Peru have; and most importantly, the need to strengthen the digital skills of the staff working in a UGEL in Peru.

4   Conclusions

The current situation of the dimensions of the PCI of a UGEL in Peru was diagnosed, we found very adverse results, considering that the Medium level presents 42.65% (29), then the High level with 23.53% (16) and Very High with 17.65% (12). Percentages that when added reach 83.83% (57) of 100% (68); Which means that it presents a very high percentage of difficulties and continuous deficiencies that do not allow reaching the level of quality information.

The digital administration proposal was built to improve the PCI in teachers of a UGEL in Peru, based on the most outstanding elements that affect the PCI, such as: abundant information without digitizing or automated, information with errors, unorganized and unstructured, lack of databases that do not allow timely and reliable reports to be generated. This proposal is made up of a set of tasks, strategies and appropriate methods.

The validation of the proposal was carried out by expert specialists in digital administration, CI and GP. The average reached by the experts was 98%, who considered the proposal with a high level of relevance to be applied in a UGEL in Peru.

References

Carlos Sáenz, A.E.:. Gobierno Digital. Política de Gobierno Digital; Publicación de las Naciones Unidas (2021). https://cdn.www.gob.pe/uploads/document/file/3114412/RS_PCD_0412022. pdf.pdf

CEPAL. Tecnologías digitales para un nuevo futuro (LC/TS.2021/43), Santiago. Comisión Económica Para América Latina y El Caribe, 98 (2021). https://www.google.com/search?q= CEPAL%2C+En+los+procesos+de+transformación+digital+no+solo+se+debe+incorporar+ las+TIC+en+la+gestión+pública%2C&rlz=1C1SQJL_esPE939PE939&oq=CEPAL%2C+ En+los+procesos+de+transformación+digital+no+solo+se+debe+incorporar+las+TI

Choo, C.W.: The knowing organization: how organizations use information to construct meaning, create knowledge and make decisions. Int. J. Inf. Manag. **16**, 329–340 (1996)

Hernández, R., Mendoza, C.: Investigation methodology. Quantitative, qualitative and mixed routes. Mexico: Editorial Mc Graw Hill Education (2018)

International Telecommunications Union. Digital Government. In: Digital Government (2011). https://doi.org/10.4018/978-1-59140-122-3

ITU. Conectar 2030 – Una Agenda para la conexión de todos a un mundo mejor (2020). https:// www.itu.int/es/mediacentre/backgrounders/Pages/connect-2030-agenda.aspx

Lee, Y.W., Strong, D.M., Kahn, B.K., Wang, R.Y.: AIMQ: A methodology for information quality assessment. Inf. Manag. **40**(2), 133–146 (2002). https://doi.org/10.1016/S0378-7206(02)000 43-5

Ohly, H.P.: Information: a question of quality? Scire **17**, 17–21 (2011). https://www.ibersid.eu/ 9f7d1ff9-ca1e-4ff9-adf1-4df44c37f8b1

Rubin, R.E.: Foundations of Library and Information Science (Fourth Edi) (2017). https://books. google.es/books?hl=es&lr=&id=muk_DwAAQBAJ&oi=fnd&pg=PT8&dq=information+ is+related+to+six+processes:+recognition+of+information+needs,+obtaining+information,+ construction+and+collection+of+information,+creation+of+digital+products+and+service

Sánchez Gómez, M.C.: The qualitative-quantitative dichotomy: integration possibilities and mixed designs. Open Field **1**(1), 11–30 (2015)

Sauvageot, C.: Quality and learning indicators I Unesco IIEP Learning Portal (2017). https://lea rningportal.iiep.unesco.org/en/issue-briefs/monitor-learning/quality-and-learning-indicators

Bravo, R.S.: Técnicas de investigación social: Teoría y Ejercicios, 14 edn. (2001)

Strong, D.M., Lee, Y.W., Wang, R.Y.: Data quality in context. Commun. ACM **40**(5), 103–110 (1997). https://doi.org/10.1145/253769.253804

The United Nations. Peace, justice and strong institutions. Naciones Unidas (2020). https://www. un.org/sustainabledevelopment/es/peace-justice/

Toro-García, A.F., Gutiérrez-Vargas, C.C., Correa-Ortiz, L.C.: Estrategia de gobierno digital para la construcción de Estados más transparentes y proactivos. Trilogía Ciencia Tecnología Sociedad **12**(22), 71–102 (2020). https://doi.org/10.22430/21457778.1235

UNESCO. United Nations Educational, Scientific and Cultural Organization. Water **571**, 2 (2018). https://www.un.org/es/desa

Van Birgelen, M., De Ruyter, K., Wetzels, M.: What factors determine use of quality-related marketing research information? an empirical investigation. Total Qual. Manag. **12**(4), 521–534 (2001). https://doi.org/10.1080/09544120123611

World Bank. E-Government (2018). https://www.mineducacion.gov.co/portal/micrositios-instit ucionales/GobiernoDigital/371905:E-Government

Don't Let Your Remotes Flop! Potential Ways to Incentivize and Increase Study Participants' Use of Edtech

Grace C. Lin[1]([⊠]) ![iD], Ilana Schoenfeld[1] ![iD], Brandon Hanks[1] ![iD], and Kathryn Leech[2] ![iD]

[1] Massachusetts Institute of Technology, Cambridge, MA 02139, USA
{gcl,ilanasch,bhanks}@mit.edu
[2] University of North Carolina at Chapel Hill, Chapel Hill, NC 27599, USA
leechk@unc.edu

Abstract. Studies that require participants to use educational apps or other technologies have often struggled with fidelity of implementation and even user uptake [e.g., 1]. That is, it is often unclear how much the participants have used the designated technologies at home or in the classroom when only self-reports are used to assess participants' usage. In the event that the information can be objectively obtained using process data, the participants' actual usage tends to be lower than what has been reported or observed via synchronous sessions [2]. Because remote studies on the impacts of technological innovations or interventions can often depend upon how much study participants actually use them independently, it is important to have strategies on-hand to increase the at-home use of these technologies. Our poster presents two years of data from a study focused on an educational app meant to improve children's early literacy through modeling dialogic reading practices with an AI-powered conversational agent. The app features a virtual rabbit-agent who asks questions to prompt caregiver-child interactions as the caregiver reads a physical book aloud with their child. In the first year, focused on usability, we discovered there was sparse usage of the app, with 6 of the 20 participants procrastinating until the day before their post-test session to use it. We implemented four key changes–device, reading diary, text reminders, and compensation structure–to increase and incentivize participant usage of the app during the study's second-year efficacy phase. Although we are unable to distinguish the unique contribution of the four changes implemented to increase user engagement with the app, clustering of the process data patterns suggests a clear increase in the app's usage during the second year of the study. Our findings can be useful to researchers and practitioners facing similar implementation challenges.

Keywords: Implementation · Conversational Agent · Early Literacy

1 Introduction

Teacher Alex has just completed a professional development workshop where they learned of a mobile game app that has the potential to improve their students' arithmetic skills. They assigned the game to a struggling student, Brandon, asking him to play the game daily for 30 min over a two-week period. Being a free spirit, Brandon, unbeknownst to Teacher Alex, played the game only every now and then when he felt like it.

Lo and behold, two weeks later, Alex observed that Brandon's arithmetic skills had not improved. To the omniscient reader, this result was not surprising, given that Brandon did not carry out the plan to fidelity. However, not knowing how much Brandon had actually played the game, Alex thought that perhaps the intervention just did not work.

This simple scenario illustrates challenges faced often by educators, researchers, and developers of new educational technologies. When investigating how well or if a new intervention or technology works, it is difficult to reach a valid conclusion if the intervention or technology is not implemented or used as intended.

2   Fidelity of Implementation

The importance of fidelity of implementation–how well an intervention is implemented in comparison to the way it is designed to be implemented–is well established in educational research [e.g., 1, 3, 4]. Poor implementation can often result in ineffective learning outcomes; thus, implementation scientists have worked on refining the definitions and types of fidelity as well as developing multiple measures to capture fidelity of implementation [1, 5, 6]. For example, Dane and Schneider [5] emphasized adherence to the intervention components, exposure (or dosage) to the intervention, quality of implementation (e.g., attitudes of the implementer), responsiveness of the participants, and differentiation between treatment and control group of participants. Traditionally, fidelity measurements are based on self-reports or observations [1], both of which may be subject to biases or other observational effects (e.g., an implementer adhering to the program more closely when being observed). More recently, web-based applications that log participants' activities opened up another measurement for implementation fidelity. In fact, researchers found that the objectively and remotely obtained process data indicated a lower level of fidelity than what was captured in synchronous observations [2].

Considering the threat to educational technology intervention studies posed by low fidelity of implementation, this poster aims to showcase 1) the use of metadata from an educational app to track the exposure/dosage component of implementation fidelity, and 2) the changes we enacted to improve fidelity.

3   Method

3.1   Research Context

Studies in early childhood settings have identified dialogic reading–where a more experienced reader asks the new reader questions about the story as they read–to be an effective method of promoting early literacy [7–12]. To promote dialogic reading practices, particularly among socioeconomically disadvantaged populations, we developed an app meant to train caregivers on dialogic reading practices.

3.2 The Floppy App

There are two components to the Floppy App. The first component consists of several short videos explaining and modeling the use of five simple dialogic reading strategies (Recall the past, Explain new words or ideas, Ask questions, Discuss the future, and You can make a difference).The second component features a cartoon rabbit named Floppy. Floppy is a semi-intelligent conversational agent who "listens in" as a caregiver and their child read a physical book out loud together. When it hears a target word indicating which page the dyad is reading, it asks a relevant question. By doing so, Floppy models dialogic reading practices for the caregiver. In order for Floppy to "listen in," the app records the conversation between the dyads when they begin their reading session.

Participants begin reading with Floppy by selecting a book to read aloud. Floppy then gives instructions on how to use the app. When the dyads are ready, they press the "start" button and Floppy starts listening (i.e., the device starts recording). The recording ends when participants press the "end" button. (As a precaution, in case participants forget to end the session, the recording terminates automatically after 30 min of inactivity). An audio file is generated in this process, and when the participant presses "resume" or "start" again, a new audio file is created.

3.3 Year 1 and Year 2

We conducted a usability study in the summer of 2021 with 20 parent-child dyads (18 mothers, 2 fathers) from across the United States. The following summer, we conducted an efficacy study with 40 parent-child dyads (38 mothers, 2 fathers), with 20 of the dyads in the intervention group (who used the app) and the other 20 in the waitlist control group (who did not use the app). All of the children were between the ages of 3 and 6, and all of the families had annual income levels below US $75,000.

Study Procedure
In the 2021 usability phase, the study team mailed participating families children's books as well as an Android phone with the app already installed. (They also received a prepaid envelope for returning the Android phone.) The families participated in two Zoom sessions with the researchers and conducted at-home readings with the Floppy app during the 2–4 weeks between the first and last Zoom sessions. When the dyads first met with the researchers, they did a baseline reading without using the app. After the researchers introduced the families to the app (both the video and Floppy portions), the dyads read another book with Floppy. The session ended with the researchers interviewing the parent for their initial thoughts about the app, providing them with a link to a survey, and asking the parent to read three books with the app before the second Zoom session. The families returned to a second Zoom meeting 2–4 weeks later, and the procedure was largely the same except that they no longer needed to be introduced to the app.

The study procedure of having two Zoom sessions bookending the at-home, remote reading sessions remained largely unchanged in the 2022 efficacy phase with a few exceptions: 1) as an efficacy study, early literacy measures were included in both Zoom sessions, 2) the waitlist control group did not receive the Floppy app or engage in tasks related to Floppy until the second Zoom session, 3) the at-home reading time was increased from the usability phase's 2–4 weeks to 4–6 weeks in the efficacy phase.

Implementation Changes in Efficacy Study Phase

Beyond increasing the length of the at-home reading period, we implemented additional changes to help increase participants' usage of the app at home. First, we recruited families who already use Android devices. Instead of mailing the families the phones, we provided them with the Floppy app's APK file to download and install on their own devices. Second, we asked all families in the 2022 efficacy phase to record their reading sessions. We provided each family a bookmark with a QR code. The code linked them to an individualized Google form that allowed the caregiver to report any books they had read during the study period. Third, the study team sent the families weekly text reminders to read with their children. Finally, we changed the compensation structure. In the 2021 usability phase, participants received a lump sum payment at the end of the study. In the 2022 efficacy phase, smaller payments were disbursed at three points over the course of the study such that the total was equal in value to the lump payment from the previous year. The participants received the payments after the first Zoom session, in the middle of the at-home reading period, and after the second Zoom session.

3.4 Data Source and Wrangling

For this study, we focus on the metadata generated by the dyads' use of the Floppy app as the primary data source. As such, only data from the participants from the 2021 usability phase (n = 20) and the intervention group from the 2022 efficacy phase (n = 20) were included. We used the reading diary data as a secondary data source to double check the efficacy phase participants' self-reports and use of the app. Participants read additional books without Floppy (we only provided five books), and their self-report/recollection of reading with Floppy was remarkably accurate. The metadata include the date and time the dyads accessed the app, which books they were reading, and the length of the generated audio files (i.e., the duration of the reading session). To ensure participant anonymity, each login was assigned a random string of characters as their session ID. Each generated audio file was also assigned a random string of characters as its filename. We matched and merged the participant data with their random strings of session IDs and audio files. Because separate mp3 files were generated every time the dyads hit "pause," we also identified which particular audio files were supposed to go together, thereby obtaining the number of reading sessions that were conducted with Floppy. Because participants started the study on different days, we recoded all the dates to reflect how long participants had been introduced to the app such that day0 indicates the day of their first Zoom session. To prepare for the analysis, we aggregated the information (number of reading sessions and total reading time in minutes) by the participants and by the time (in days) since the start of the study.

4   Analysis and Findings

Participants from the usability phase generated 118 reading sessions, and those in the intervention group of the efficacy phase generated 395 reading sessions with Floppy. (As a reminder, participants in the waitlist control group did not have access to the

Floppy app until their second Zoom session, so they were excluded from the analysis.) Sheer comparison of the total volume of reading using Mann-Whitney tests indicated that participants in the intervention group from the efficacy phase read longer (total minutes), $z = -4.17, p < .001$ (see Fig. 1), and read more times (total reading sessions), $z = -2.72, p = .0067$. However, there was no difference in the average time per reading session between the participants in the usability phase and those in the intervention group of the efficacy phase, $t(511) = 1.20, p = .23$.

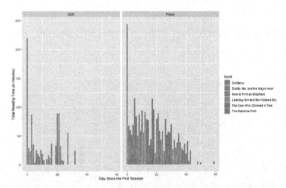

Fig. 1. Participants in the 2022 efficacy phase who read with Floppy spent more time using the app than the participants from the 2021 usability phase did.

Considering that participants in the efficacy phase had double the amount of time between the Zoom sessions, it is not surprising that their total reading volume was significantly different. Thus, we also investigated the pattern of app usage by the families and applied clustering methods (e.g., K-medians, Ward method) as the first pass to categorize the patterns. Two human coders then sorted through the machine clusters, settled any discrepancies, derived meaning, and created labels for the clusters. Before applying the clustering methods, we adjusted for the differential time span each family experienced between their two Zoom sessions by further aggregating the reading time data by four time segments: the first day of the study (i.e., day0), the last couple of days, the first half of their reading period after day0, and the second half of the reading period before the last couple of days.

When we conducted the clustering analysis by only the 2021 usability participants, we discovered that two participants exhibited the "get it over with" (GIOW) pattern where they read the three books the day after their first session and never used the app again until the second Zoom session. In contrast, six dyads showed "procrastinating" behavior where they only read the day before or the day of their second Zoom session. (See Fig. 2 for sample graphs exhibiting these patterns.) The rest of the participants paced their readings or were considered "fans" based on how much they read with the app. However, when we included the 2022 participants, the groupings from the original analysis with only the 2021 data disappeared. Most of them became lumped together in the "sparse user" group. Even the most avid users from the usability phase paled in comparison with the average users from the efficacy phase (see Fig. 3).

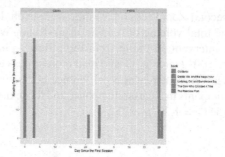

Fig. 2. Sample graphs of the "Get it Over With" pattern (left) and the "procrastinating" pattern (right).

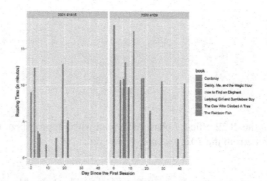

Fig. 3. Participant #1815 was one of the most avid users from the usability phase in 2021. Participant #109 was a typical, average user from the efficacy phase in 2022.

5 Discussion and Conclusion

After the initial Year 1 usability study phase of an educational app meant to improve children's early literacy through the modeling of dialogic reading practices for parents/caregivers by an AI-powered conversational agent, our data showed sparse, independent use of the app during the remote portion of the study (See Figs. 2 and 3). Understanding that exposure or dosage is a crucial component of fidelity of implementation that can substantially affect efficacy research validity and findings [4], we set out to increase and incentivize at-home, remote usage of the app during the study's Year 2 efficacy phase. Specifically, we implemented four key changes—use of participants' own device, a reading diary, text reminders, and a new participant compensation structure. The analyses of the metadata indicated that our efforts were largely successful in ensuring an increased use of the educational app during the second year of the study.

Our findings can be useful to researchers and practitioners facing similar remote implementation challenges. These findings may also prove useful from a design perspective. Design-based research of innovative educational tools and interventions is an iterative process informed by both data and qualitative user feedback [13]. Early-on incorporation of strategies that encourage remote engagement and testing by users of educational tools under development can increase access to helpful user feedback at every step of the design process–from early prototype to final production and implementation. Additionally, metadata and process data generated by web-based applications or other digital tools can function as additional feedback and measure of implementation fidelity [2]. This ongoing feedback from users enables designers to create tools that are better suited to user needs, which in turn increases the potential for user engagement. The resulting increase in usage frequency or user responsiveness, which are components of implementation fidelity [4], enhances the validity of intervention efficacy studies.

5.1 Limitations

While we managed to enhance the app's dosage/usage in Year 2, it remains challenging to differentiate the specific impact of each of the four implemented changes. Future studies can investigate the individual effects of various compensation structures, text reminders to participants, reading diaries, and participants using their own devices.

Acknowledgments. This work was funded by the Chan Zuckerberg Foundation as part of the Reach Every Reader project. We would like to thank all the participating families as well as all past and present members of the design and research teams.

References

1. McKenna, J.W., Flower, A., Ciullo, S.: Measuring fidelity to improve intervention effectiveness. Interv. Sch. Clin. **50**(1), 15–21 (2014). https://doi.org/10.1177/105345121453 2348
2. Helsabeck, N.P., Justice, L.M., Logan, J.A.R.: Assessing fidelity of implementation to a technology-mediated early intervention using process data. Comput. Assist. Learn. **38**(2), 409–421 (2022). https://doi.org/10.1111/jcal.12621
3. Berman, P., McLaughlin, M.W.: Implementation of educational innovation. Educ. Forum **40**(3), 345–370 (1976). https://doi.org/10.1080/00131727609336469
4. Gage, N., Macsuga-Gage, A., Detrich, R.: Fidelity of implementation in educational research and practice. The Wing Institute (2020). https://www.winginstitute.org/systems-program-fid elity
5. Dane, A.V., Schneider, B.H.: Program integrity in primary and early secondary prevention: are implementation effects out of control? Clin. Psychol. Rev. **18**(1), 23–45 (1998). https://doi.org/10.1016/S0272-7358(97)00043-3
6. O'Donnell, C.L.: Defining, conceptualizing, and measuring fidelity of implementation and its relationship to outcomes in K-12 curriculum intervention research. Rev. Educ. Res. **78**(1), 33–84 (2008)
7. Arnold, D.S., Whitehurst, G.J.: Accelerating language development through picture book reading: a summary of dialogic reading and its effect. In: Dickinson, D.K. (ed.) Bridges to Literacy: Children, Families, and Schools, pp. 103–128. Blackwell Publishing, Malden (1994)
8. Doyle, B.G., Bramwell, W.: Promoting emergent literacy and social–emotional learning through dialogic reading. Read. Teach. **59**(6), 554–564 (2006). https://doi.org/10.1598/RT. 59.6.5
9. Hargrave, A.C., Sénéchal, M.: A book reading intervention with preschool children who have limited vocabularies: the benefits of regular reading and dialogic reading. Early Childhood Res. Q. **15**(1), 75–90 (2000). https://doi.org/10.1016/S0885-2006(99)00038-1

10. Lever, R., Sénéchal, M.: Discussing stories: on how a dialogic reading intervention improves kindergartners' oral narrative construction. J. Exp. Child Psychol. **108**(1), 1–24 (2011). https://doi.org/10.1016/j.jecp.2010.07.002

11. Towson, J.A., Fettig, A., Fleury, V.P., Abarca, D.L.: Dialogic reading in early childhood settings: a summary of the evidence base. Top. Early Childhood Spec. Educ. **37**(3), 132–146 (2017). https://doi.org/10.1177/0271121417724875

12. van der Wilt, F., Bouwer, R., van der Veen, C.: Dialogic classroom talk in early childhood education: the effect on language skills and social competence. Learn. Inst. **77**, 101522 (2022). https://doi.org/10.1016/j.learninstruc.2021.101522

13. Barab, S., Squire, K.: Design-based research: putting a stake in the ground. J. Learn. Sci. **13**(1), 1–14 (2004)

Identification of the Types of Strategies for the Development of Social Competencies in Virtual Environments of Management Students in Colombian Universities

Evaristo Navarro[1](✉), Esperanza Díaz[1], Enrique Otalora[1], Alberto Mena[1], Delia Robles[2], and Silena Paba[1]

[1] Universidad de la Costa, 58 Street #55 66, Barranquilla, Colombia
{enavarro3,Spaba1}@cuc.edu.co
[2] I.E Técnico del Santuario, 47B Street #8d-60, Barranquilla, Colombia

Abstract. The present study is directed towards the identification of the types of strategies for the development of social competences in virtual environments of administration students at Colombian universities. The sample is taken from a group of 25 teachers, who teach in the business administration program of a private university located in the city of Barranquilla, Colombia. A questionnaire consisting of a total of 15 items applied to this sample, which was validated by experts and its reliability was determined by means of the Cronbach's Alpha coefficient, yielding a value of 0.84. Thus, the results show the indicators of the dimension Types of strategies for the development of social competence, which in turn are organized into indicators as follows: Pre-instructional Strategies, Co-instructional Strategies and Post-instructional Strategies. Each of these indicators obtained a respective weighting of 2.89, 3.35 and 2.40. In relation to the teaching strategies for the development of social competence, which constitute the object of study of the research presented, low frequencies were obtained for this variable in its two dimensions, which reveals that the teachers in the sample exhibit low levels of application of these strategies in the classroom. This situation highlights the need to train students in this type of competencies, given their impact on the achievement of school success.

Keywords: Pedagogical strategies · social competences · virtual training · synchronous and asynchronous education

1 Introduction

The development of competences as the purpose of the educational system is highly recognized for its importance towards the integral formation of people; Agreed then the so-called education by competences in one of the most relevant models of today and being the standard of various countries in the world [1]. The case of Colombia as a developing nation is highlighted, which adopts competency-based training in order to standardize the process of measuring the impact of education in order to allow the

C. Stephanidis et al. (Eds.): HCII 2023, CCIS 1957, pp. 295–302, 2024.
https://doi.org/10.1007/978-3-031-49212-9_37

implementation of effective strategies and programs in the improvement of education [2, 3].

In this sense, social competences are mentioned, referring to the capacities for the development of social processes that happen within their environment. Currently, within the educational field, strategies focused on strengthening this type of skills in schools, universities and other educational institutions are presented [4]. However, it is important to mention that social changes since the entry of information and communication technologies (ICT) have been increasingly accelerated, where the interaction between two people no longer requires a face-to-face from which new codes, standards and ways of perceiving Coexistence within these new communication environments had been created. [5]. Certainly, today's society is experiencing a process of increasingly accelerated change in which globalization, technologies 4.0 and new welfare paradigms, Equality and diversity completely change the traditional standards of interaction between individuals whether in the workplace, academic or personal environments [6, 7]. On the academic it is necessary to mention how the educational system and more specifically the University has adapted more and more to these new trends, not only acquiring installed capacity for the Development of its mixed missionary activities (between virtual and face-to-face) or in a total virtuality, but for the training of skills of professionals considering that they can develop effectively in areas mediated by new technologies such as ICT [8].

This awakens the need to develop scientific knowledge that allows recognizing the implementation of these strategies within universities, taking as a reference social competences as a support factor for assertive communication processes within ICT. That said, the present study is directed towards the identification of the types of strategies for the development of social competences in virtual environments of administration students at Colombian universities.

2   Theorical Approach

2.1   Social Competences

The new education models impose roles on education professionals for the performance of their duties. Today, a teacher combines the standards of an educator and an individual in their behavior, not as in traditional pedagogy, but with both characteristics. In the new school he searches, investigates and responds to the need and responsibility to find answers to the questions that arise from his personal experience and professional practice in his cultural and social context. The above will undoubtedly stand out from the new technologies that are applied in the field of education [9].

In this way, the educator is the reference base for the formative practice and contrast for the evaluation, on what, how, when, where, why and what to teach; What are the important dimensions of acquired personal and social knowledge? In addition to this, teachers are also responsible for promoting, expanding and reinforcing various knowledge about students [10].

From this point of view, it is necessary to generate feedback with the teacher, instead of simply highlighting the weaknesses of the students, which otherwise affects their performance and progress. The dialogues should highlight the strengths and weaknesses of the students to encourage support and make them part of their performance so that they are recognized, nurtured and rewarded.

It is important that the teacher, from his pedagogical conduct, manages to communicate orientation to the social environment, which positively complements his work, to cooperate effectively in the direction of the student's attention, in order to achieve the goals set and strengthen the academicity of the students. Themselves [10].

Therefore, the social competence development strategy is a continuous and systematic process that, with the participation of all members of the educational community, helps the individual to reach their maximum development through better self-awareness and optimization of environmental conditions - Individual development in each discipline [9].

The strategy for the development of social competences, developed by educators from the classroom, has as its main objective cooperation to create an inclusive educational environment that allows the ecological adaptation of people and their environment, as well as a truly quality education, com -mutual promise and constant communication.

In this sense, according to Álvarez, when referring to the process of effectiveness of the strategies for the development of social competences, he indicates: "It is a social praxis aimed at facilitating the processes of human development in the dimensions of Being, Living Together, Serving, Knowing and Doing in the personal, social and community context throughout the continuum of life with the purpose of empowering talents and generating processes of self-determination, freedom, and emancipation in the permanent construction of development and well-being of people and communities" [11].

In this sense, the human development of the person will be strengthened, and in this study it is of great importance, since the task of the teacher is to wonder about strategies that can strengthen the self-concept through emotional intelligence, and for this, teacher. It is sought as part of self-development and potential protagonist, which allows in the classroom to promote an effective rapprochement between the actors and thus respond positively to problems in the school and social space that can negatively affect performance, achievement and progress. For students.

2.2 Social Competences on Virtual Environments

Social competences in virtual environments refer to the skills necessary to interact effectively with others through online platforms and social networks. With the increasing importance of technology in our lives, the ability to communicate and network online has become increasingly important [12].

It is important to emphasize that social competence in virtual environments is not only about using technology, but also about knowing how to interact effectively with others online. As technology continues to evolve, social skills in virtual environments become increasingly important to navigating and succeeding in the online world [12].

2.3 Types of Strategies

As described by Moreno, one of the stages that determine human behavior occurs in the field of education; Based on the interactions created in these spaces, it is possible to define which strategies teachers will use to develop the social skills that will later define them as active subjects in society. However, determining the first strategies to develop social competences is the responsibility of the family, in fact, the educational system simply improves behavior and places students in the body of knowledge learned in a formal way [13].

These relational skills are not only defined in relation to the child, but also play an important role for the other members and form a support function in the various life transitions of the individual: education, adolescence, beginning of working life, new social life. Relationships, retirement and more.

In this way, the following figure shows the types of pedagogical strategies according to the moment of their development (Fig. 1):

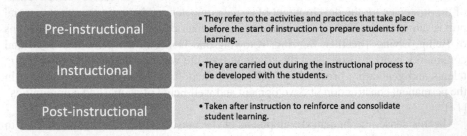

Fig. 1. Types of strategies for the development of social competence in virtual environments

3   Material and Method

This study is developed from the quantitative approach, with a descriptive level and a field and non-experimental design framed in the identification of the types of strategies for the development of social competences in virtual environments of administration students at Colombian universities. In this way, it is mentioned that the sample is taken from a group of 25 teachers, who teach in the business administration program of a private university located in the city of Barranquilla, Colombia.

A questionnaire consisting of a total of 15 items applied to this sample, which was validated by experts and its reliability was determined by means of the Cronbach's Alpha coefficient, yielding a value of 0.84. The analysis process is carried out with a Likert scale, where the following interpretation establishes the scales (Table 1):

Table 1. Scale of analysis of the findings

Score	Interpretation
1	Very inappropriate implementation of strategies for the development of social competencies in the virtual environment from the pre-instructional, co-instructional and post-instructional
2	Inappropriate implementation of strategies for the development of social competencies in the virtual environment from the pre-instructional, co-instructional and post-instructional
3	Neither appropriate nor inappropriate the implementation of the strategies for the development of social competences in the virtual field from the pre-instructional, co-instructional and post-instructional
4	Appropriate implementation of strategies for the development of social competencies in the virtual environment from the pre-instructional, co-instructional and post-instructional
5	Very appropriate implementation of strategies for the development of social competencies in the virtual field from the pre-instructional, co-instructional and post-instructional

4 Results

In the analysis of the results, they are grouped from three types of indicators which describe the type of strategies implemented by the 25 teachers surveyed for the identification of the types of strategies for the development of social competences in virtual environments of administration students at Colombian universities. In this way, the results are as follows (Table 2):

Table 2. Types of strategies for the development of social competence in virtual environments

Indicador	Media
Pre-instructional strategies	2.89
Co-instructional Strategies	3.35
Post-Instructional Strategies	2.40

Having reviewed the previous table referring to the types of strategies for the development of social competence in virtual environments, It is possible to observe that for strategies of a pre-instructional nature with an average of 2.89 and those of a post-instructional nature with an average of 2.40 are within the range of analysis considered inappropriate, which implies that there is little implementation of this type of strategies by the teachers surveyed.

In turn, the co-instructional strategies demonstrate a better performance with an average of 3.35 referred to an intermediate level where there is no appropriation or misappropriation of these within the training processes developed. In this way, for a clearer analysis of the dimensions referred to above, the findings obtained by each reagent of the three student dimensions in the present research are shown (Table 3):

Table 3. Pre-instructional strategies

Item	Mean
1	3.32
2	2.61
3	2.89
4	2.80
5	2.85
Total	**2.89**

When reviewing the results of the statistical averages related to pre-instructional strategies, there is little appropriation on the part of teachers in relation to the generation of knowledge based on student experiences, the implementation of diagnostic processes and the use of introductory materials for the development of social competences within the communication platforms of the Universities (Table 4).

Table 4. Co-instructional strategies

Item	Mean
1	2.97
2	3.44
3	3.75
4	3.43
5	3.18
Total	**3.35**

Within the approach of co-instructional strategies, it is observed how these are neither appropriate nor inappropriate, most referring to the application of strategies that allow the understanding of the student and the use of discussion as a means of developing competencies in virtual environments, while evidencing higher levels of appropriation in the use of graphic tools for the training process (Table 5).

With the findings shown in the previous table, it is possible to observe how there are low levels of appropriation of post-instructional strategies within the processes of virtual formation of social competences, such as conducting debates for the consolidation of knowledge or the use of digital tools and resources for the content synthesis process. Conclusions and discussions.

Table 5. Post-instructional strategies

Item	Mean
1	2.44
2	2.00
3	2.23
4	2.33
5	3.01
Total	**2.4**

From the processing of the findings of the study it is possible to conclude in the first instance that education, like other sectors of society, has undergone extremely significant changes thanks to the support and use of new technologies, especially information and communication technologies which intervene directly in communication as it is known today [14]. In this way, the survey shows unfavorable results in the use of both pre-instructional and co-instructional or post-co-instructional strategies for the strengthening of social competencies in university students; This could be due to the complexity for the faculty to effectively adapt the dynamics and contents of face-to-face subjects towards virtuality.

It is certainly not enough to have technological equipment and modern platforms for the adequate development of students' skills in virtuality, It requires a strong involvement of the teaching staff in this process and that they are trained and sensitized on how to achieve the goals of training from the tools provided by new technologies today [15].

However, it must be clear that social competence does not develop naturally in people, so teaching interventions must be aligned with their development to mediate their training and improvement. In this sense, this is the beginning of its development. The decisive factor of development. It develops from youth, through adolescence, and even into adulthood, as it can easily change when it comes to phenomena such as perception, understanding, and proper behavior.

It can be concluded that the greatest contribution of the research on strategies for the development of social competence in the school environment is that its most important role is to promote healthy coexistence and the creation of an environment conducive to the promotion of interpersonal relationships. Efficiency and quality, since through them individuals are capable of displaying appropriate social behavior in response to the environmental or situational demands they face.

Within the framework of the previous observations, social competence development strategies as a continuous and systematic process help individuals to demonstrate their personal potential, since it gives them greater self-confidence and preparation to face environmental conditions. in which they are found. It is recommended that the institution involved in the data collection process implement an intervention strategy aimed at accompanying the faculty in the training exercise within the virtual environments, taking advantage of the virtues and opportunities that this represents for the generation of value in the work of higher education institutions, especially in the missionary teaching function.

References

1. Lay, N., Ramírez, J., Parra, M.: Desarrollo de conductas ciudadanas en estudiantes del octavo grado de una institución educativa de Barranquilla. In: Memorias del I congreso internacional en educación e innovación en educación superior. Caracas, Venezuela (2019)
2. Niebles, W., Martínez-Bustos, P., Niebles-Núñez, L.: Competencias matemáticas como factor de éxito en la prueba pro en universidades de Barranquilla, Colombia. Educación y Humanismo **22**(38) (2020)
3. Díaz, E., Reyes, R.: Flipped Classroom para el desarrollo de competencias digitales en educación media. Edutec. Revista Electrónica De Tecnología Educativa **79**, 182–198 (2022)
4. Romera, E.M., Luque-González, R., García-Fernández, C., Ortega-Ruiz, R.: Competencia social y bullying: el papel de la edad y el sexo. Educación XX1 **25**(1), 309–333 (2022)
5. Olivar, A.J., Daza, A.: Las tecnologías de la información y comunicación (TIC) y su impacto en la educación del siglo XXI. Revista negotium **7**, 21–46 (2022)
6. Mendoza-Ocasal, D., Navarro, E., Ramírez, J., García-Tirado, J.: Subjective well-being and its correlation with happiness at work and quality of work life: an organizational vision. Polish J. Manag. Stud. **26**(1), 202–216 (2022)
7. Orellana-Daube, D.F.: El efecto global de la actual revolución tecnológica 4ª revolución industrial y la industria 4.0 en acción. Revista GEON (Gestión, Organizaciones y Negocios) **7**(2), 1–24 (2020)
8. Hernández-Sánchez, I., Romero-Caballero, S., Acuña-Rodríguez, M., Rocha-Herrera, G., Acuña-Rodríguez, J., Ramírez, J.: Traditional face-to-face educational modality vs. remote face-to-face: its impact on academic performance in the context of the Covid 19 pandemic. In: Meiselwitz, G., et al. (eds.) HCI International 2022 - Late Breaking Papers. Interaction in New Media, Learning and Games. HCII 2022. Lecture Notes in Computer Science, vol. 13517, pp. 266–275. Springer, Cham (2022). https://doi.org/10.1007/978-3-031-22131-6_20
9. Marín, F., Meroño, M., Peña-Acuña, B.: Experiencias de trabajo cooperativo en la educación superior: Percepciones sobre su contribución al desarrollo de la competencia social. Vivat Academia **1**(147), 87–108 (2019)
10. Torres, M.P. Ponce, F.C.: Análisis del rol del docente universitario a partir de una crisis sanitaria: el proceso de una resignificación de lo presencial a lo virtual. Revista electrónica interuniversitaria de formación del profesorado **24**(2) (2021)
11. Álvarez, G.: Orientación Profesional. CEDECs, Barcelona (1995)
12. Garay-Núñez, J.R.: Representaciones sociales de las competencias docentes en entornos virtuales de aprendizaje en tiempos de pandemia. Dilemas contemporáneos: educación, política y valores **8**(2) (2021)
13. Moreno, N.: Estrategias Didácticas Preinstruccionales para Promover Aprendizajes Significativos. SINOPSIS EDUCATIVA. Revista venezolana de investigación **12**(1), 44–49 (2017)
14. González-Pérez, L., Ramírez-Montoya, M.: Components of Education 4.0 in 21st century skills frameworks: systematic review. Sustainability **14**(3), 1493 (2022)
15. Herrera, H., Barrera, A., Ramírez, J., Ballestas, M., Ballestas, I., Duran, S.E.: Educational quality in virtuality during the Covid 19 pandemic in Colombia. In: Meiselwitz, G., et al. (eds.) International Conference on Human-Computer Interactio, pp. 276–285. Springer, Cham (2022). https://doi.org/10.1007/978-3-031-22131-6_21

A Study on the Development of Digital Characters for Learning Contents

Heehyeon Park[(✉)]

Hanseo University, Seosan-si Chungcheongnam-do, 31962 Seosan, South Korea
hpark@hanseo.ac.kr

Abstract. Since the COVID-19 pandemic, educational content using digital-based media has received significant public attention, and various methods to enhance educational effects, such as educational content using digital illustration characters, are emerging. Characters have long been an essential element of media content based on OSMU (One Source Multi Use), and their utilization is outstanding. In this paper, we propose a study on the production process of digital characters, especially the production of educational content through the characteristics of characters. For a case study, a character considering the elements of 20 chemical elements was created and applied to an elementary school student's after-school class. Digital illustrated characters can be used in various online and offline learning content. As a result, students' interest has increased, and they focused on the more.

Keywords: Digital Character · Character Design · Character · Learning Content · Online Education · Digital Learning Content

1 Introduction

1.1 A Subsection Sample

Digital content in various fields is continuously appearing; among them, education has progressed towards significant development in conjunction with digital content. Since the COVID-19 pandemic, educational content with the assistance of digital-based media has attracted considerable public attention. Various methods to increase the effectiveness of education are emerging, such as educational content using digitally illustrated characters. Characters have been an essential element of media content for a long time based on One Source Multi Use (OSMU), and their utilization is prominent in today's society. Characters are used frequently on various platforms, from traditional to new media. Characters have been widely used in traditional media such as print media, newspapers, and magazines. Their interest is increasing with the recent development of immersive media and metaverse technology. A Digital Character is a digitally created character that looks and acts like a real or imaginary creature in a computer-generated environment [1]. The roles of digital characters have emerged, serving as a medium for delivering information to users and making information communication more effective through the

C. Stephanidis et al. (Eds.): HCII 2023, CCIS 1957, pp. 303–310, 2024.
https://doi.org/10.1007/978-3-031-49212-9_38

traits of digitally illustrated characters. In this paper, the process of digital characters is proposed—particularly a study on the production of educational content through the traits of characters.

2 Digital Characters for Learning Contents

2.1 Character

There are numerous encounters with characters in real life as content or products of various media. The dictionary definition of a character is a person who appears in a novel, play, movie, or entity endowed with a unique personality and image by the content of the work. Or in the context of product design, incorporating the appearance of a unique person or animal appearing in a novel, cartoon, or movie into the design (Toys, stationery, children's clothing, etc.) [2]. However, a character has a comprehensive meaning that includes objects that appear in works and mascots and caricatures expressed for symbolism, as well as products that commercialize real people [3]. Traditionally, characters played the role of mascots with religious or shamanistic characteristics before mankind began to use letters. Through the development of digital media in modern society, characters' roles as resources for commercial purposes or image delivery have become more diverse. In addition, the character itself holds the value of the product, playing a role in further accelerating repeated purchases, liking and trust, purchase impulse, and differentiation from other products [4]. Recently, with the development and expansion of smart devices, it is easy to share information through various mobile applications. Thus, the utilization and importance of characters are increasing. Many companies collaborate with famous characters or develop their characters, as shown in [Fig. 1], and using them for marketing. Characters have many strengths from a branding point of view: They are easy to apply to media, give intimacy and attention to the public, and have the advantage of being expandable to various contents [5].

Fig. 1. Corporate character brand

Characters have the ability to communicate visually, surpassing barriers such as gender, age, and cultural differences. They are now being utilized in the creative industry to create cultural products in collaboration with various industries [6].

2.2 Learning Content Using Digital Characters

A digital character is a digitally created character that looks and behaves like a real or imaginary creature in a computer-generated environment [1]. Computer-generated digital characters are easy to apply to digital content; they can add liveliness by adding movement or animation; they can give intimacy and interest to the public; and can be expanded to various contents. These characteristics of characters play a role in bringing about positive effects by becoming tools that can empathize with children in educational content. In previous research, 58% of users chose a character as the criterion for selecting an early childhood educational application for learning. Additionally, there is a research finding that learning using an application featuring a character significantly affects the sense of achievement in oneself [7]. Already, education companies are collaborating with existing popular characters and developing their character commercialization in textbooks and toys. Representatively, characters such as 'Yoonieiyoon' and Friends (see Fig. 2) by Mr. Yoon, an English education company, 'Pinkfong' from Smart Study, and 'Dash' and 'Dot' from PBS (see Fig. 3) are the fun of young children using educational content. It leads to active learning activities and enhances the learning effect.

Fig. 2. 'Yoonieyoon' and Friends

Fig. 3. 'Pinkfong' and 'Dash' and 'Dot'

2.3 Learning from Character

The roles of characters in learning content are very diverse. Still, in many cases, most are introducing learning content or acting as learning mediators. However, if a character is created with their traits becoming the main education factor, users can approach learning and memorization with increased ease and effectiveness. Characters created with information present in their characteristics can become powerful educational tool. Throughout this research, its effectiveness, along with production examples, will be evaluated.

3 Case Study

3.1 Character Creation Based on Learning Content

This study uses examples of character creation and utilization, assuming that characters with principal meanings necessary for learning will effectively learn beyond simple character creation. The following process is required to create a character that contains learning elements. First, before character creation, it is necessary to define the learning content to be delivered clearly. Second, select keywords for character creation. Third, determine the shape, color, props, etc., based on keywords. In case several characters have to be introduced together, the unity of the characters will also be an important factor.

Fig. 4. The process of creating a digital character.

Take "Chemistry Friends" developed with support from the Korea Foundation for the Advancement of Science and Creativity. This is a character set based on the fundamental properties of elements to educate elementary school students about 20 basic chemical elements. In the first step, the traits of the first 20 chemical elements were investigated, and select 2–3 keywords among them. The next step is the visualization of each character. The character creation process for each element is as follows (see Table 1).

3.2 Application and Survey

The 20 characters were used online and offline for elementary school students' after-school classes (see Fig. 5). Many students showed great interest in the chemistry class through characters, and 82% of the students who participated in the class answered that they were interested in studying chemistry using characters.

Table 1. Character design for the first 20 chemical elements

The first 20 chemical elements and their trait		Keywords	Character Visualization
1. H (Hydrogen)	• The lightest element • Easily burns • Makes up 81.5% of the mass of the sun	• burning • lightness • sun	
2. He (Helium)	• Stable • Used to float balloons	• balloon • party • lightness	
3. Li (Lithium)	• The lightest metal • Widely used in electronic devices	• battery • electricity	
4. Be (Beryllium)	• An emerald or aquamarine gemstone • For special springs or tools	• Emerald • Spanner	
5. B (Boron)	• Black solid • Very hard • Resistant to heat	• Black • Strong	
6. C (Carbon)	• Has a hexagonal structure • Diamond raw material • Very hard	• Hexagon • Diamond • Hardness	
7. N (Nitrogen)	• 80% of the air • The construction of an animal's • Laugh when used as an anesthetic	• Air • Laughing • Happiness	
8. O (Oxygen)	• Very stable • colorless • Unscented • Use for life support	• stability • symbol O	

(continued)

Table 1. (*continued*)

The first 20 chemical elements and their trait		Keywords	Character Visualization
9. F **(Fluorine)**	• Fluoride • Use in toothpaste • Kitchen Appliances Coating	• Toothpaste • Coating	
10. Ne (Neon)	• Colorless, odorless gas with trace amounts in the air • When other elements are mixed, they create a neon light in a rainbow	• Neon light • Night	
11. Na **(Sodium)**	• Components of salt and soda • Explosive • Used for sodium lamp streetlights	• Lamp • Explosive	
12. Mg (Magnesium)	• It is often used as an alloy material such as cameras and airplanes • Can be used as a coagulant when making tofu	• Tofu • alloy	
13. Al **(Aluminum)**	• Silver and white • Light and firm • Airplane, spacecraft fuselage	• Silver and white • Firmness	
14. Si **(Silicon)**	• The richest mineral on Earth • Components of sand, mica, quartz, and glass • Materials for semiconductors	• Semiconductors • Sand, mica, quartz, and glass	

(continued)

Table 1. (*continued*)

The first 20 chemical elements and their trait		Keywords	Character Visualization
15. P (**Phosphorus**)	• White, Red, Black • The identity of the goblin fire • The raw materials of fertilizer and matches	• Red • Matches • Fire	
16. S (**Sulfur**)	• Strong smell • Exists in the human body (nail toenail hair • A deep yellow • A fiery temper	• Strong smell • Human body • Deep Yellow	
17. Cl (**Chlorine**)	• Toxic green and yellow • Used for disinfection of tap water • Used in bleach, disinfectant	• Disinfectants • Toxic green and yellow	
18. Ar (**Argon**)	• Low responsiveness • Stable • Used in fire extinguishers	• Fire extinguisher • Stable shape	
19. K (**Potassium**)	• Raw materials such as soap, glass, and gunpowder • Metallic potassium gets excited easily and reacts violently to water • Easy to oxidize	• Easy excitement (expressed in triangles) • Used as fertilizer	
20. Ca (**Calcium**)	• Maintain the shape of a person or building • The elements that make up bones, teeth, cement, or marble • Shells, milk	• Teeth • Bone, Shell, Millk	

Fig. 5. "Chemistry Friends" Learning Products

4 Conclusion

Characters have long been an essential element of media content, and their utilization is outstanding in the digital era. In this study, we looked at the "Chemistry Friends" case study for the production process of digital characters, mainly producing educational content through character characteristics. "Chemistry Friends" was created considering the factors of 20 chemical elements and applied to elementary school students' after-school classes. Digital illustration characters can be used in various online and offline learning content. As a result, it was found that students' interest increased, and they became more focused. In this study, we focused on the manufacturing process. More in-depth research on the educational effect will be conducted in the future.

Acknowledgment. This work was supported by 2023 Hanseo University Research Fund.

References

1. ICI Global Homepage. https://www.igi-global.com/chapter/the-use-of-digital-characters-in-interactive-applications-for-cultural-heritage/248600 Accessed 15 Jun 2023
2. Author, K.: A study on the design strategy according to the generation of a character product. KDK. J. **15**, 125–134 (2010)
3. Wikipedia, https://ko.wikipedia.org/wiki/%EB%93%B1%EC%9E%A5%EC%9D%B8%EB%AC%BC
4. Author, L.: A study on the character design as the image of Korea. Korea Entertain. Indust. **2**(1), 31–33 (2008)
5. http://www.openads.co.kr/nTrend/article/3246
6. Author, K.: A study on the purchase intention of character product and the attribute factors of character design. J. Korean Soc. Design Cult. **16**(3), 11–23 (2010)
7. Author, Y., Author, K., Author, S.: Analysis of character preference according to ex-pression motive in the educational applications for children. Korea Dig. Design Council **12**(3), 95–104 (2012)
8. The financial news Homepage, http://www.fnnews.com/news/201608021706230921 Accessed 15 Jun 2023

Phone-Based Speech Recognition for Phonetic E-Learning System

Chang Ren, Jueting Liu, Dongji Feng, and Cheryl D. Seals[✉]

Auburn University, Auburn, AL 36849, USA
{czr0049,jzl0122,dzf0023,sealscd}@auburn.edu

Abstract. The APTgt system is a web-based phonetics educational training tool that aims to improve teachers' linguistics pedagogical experience and provide phonetic transcription training for students. Based on this system, we proposed an Automatic Speech Recognition (ASR) system to convert speech to a stream of phones, automatically generating the phonetic transcription of both standard speech and disordered speech. With the help of the phone recognizer, the instructors can generate a large number of phonetic transcription exams without manual transcription.

This phone-level ASR system applied Mel-frequency cepstral coefficients (MFCCs) as features and bidirectional Long-Short Term Memory (LSTM) as an encoder. The Speech Exemplar and Evaluation Database (SEED) data set, including disordered and non-disordered speech, was used for training and further testing. The proposed recognizer will make our phonetic E-learning system more intelligent and better serve students with their performance on phonetic transcription.

Keywords: E-learning · Phonetic Transcription · Automatic Speech Recognition · Recurrent Neural Network

1 Introduction

As technology has been widely adopted by younger generations and becomes a primary necessity in the classroom over the past decade, the demand for e-learning has increased significantly in recent years [1,2]. In the field of communication disorders, the clinical phonetic transcription skill is a critical part of students' clinical preparation to become speech-language pathologists. However, students often report feeling unprepared to apply the skill in clinical practice as the practice opportunities can be impeded by the limited resources to manage the grading of additional assignments through traditional learning approaches [3].

The Automated Phonetic Transcription Grading Tool (APTgt) was developed to facilitate online course content delivery and automate the grading of phonetic transcription assignments, thereby improving the efficiency and effectiveness of grading and providing timely feedback to students. It provides interactive phonetic exams through the use of an embedded International Phonetic

C. Stephanidis et al. (Eds.): HCII 2023, CCIS 1957, pp. 311–317, 2024.
https://doi.org/10.1007/978-3-031-49212-9_39

Alphabet (IPA) keyboard (see Fig. 1) and adopts a word bank (see Fig. 2) as the exam resource for the instructors to generate the linguistic exams effortlessly [4].

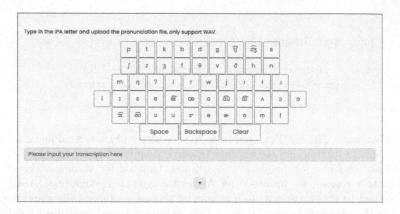

Fig. 1. The Embedded IPA keyboard in APTgt system

However, generating a large-scale word bank to support diverse exam resources is often challenging due to the high cost and time-consuming nature of manual transcription. To overcome this, we propose deploying an ASR module that can convert speech to a stream of phones, automatically generating phonetic transcriptions for both standard and disordered speech.

Word Bank

Word File	File Pronunciation	Difficulty Score	Difficulty Level	Listen	Edit
1597114369971_file_example_WAV_1MG.wav θvrəfˌuwr	θvrəfˌuwr	40.0	adv 1	Listen	Edit x
1598327296330_file_example_WAV_1MG.wav ǔ	ǔ	18.5	medium 1	Listen	Edit x
1598327856027_file_example_WAV_1MG.wav eĩeeɪ	eĩeeɪ	17.0	medium 1	Listen	Edit x
1598327869819_file_example_WAV_1MG.wav bʃpv̌	bʃpv̌	9.5	easy 2	Listen	Edit x
1598327883683_file_example_WAV_1MG.wav mkǐ	mkǐ	20.5	medium 1	Listen	Edit x
1598327929896_file_example_WAV_1MG.wav anɾhoˌ	anɾhoˌ	38.5	adv 1	Listen	Edit x
1598327940111_file_example_WAV_1MG.wav ʌæꬲeɾe	ʌæꬲeɾe	19.5	medium 1	Listen	Edit x
1598327956548_file_example_WAV_1MG.wav hvƷɔaǔɛn	hvƷɔaǔɛn	14.5	medium 1	Listen	Edit x
1598327971578_file_example_WAV_1MG.wav rθʔæʌmˌʊ	rθʔæʌmˌʊ	26.5	medium 2	Listen	Edit x
1598327981255_file_example_WAV_1MG.wav ðbz	ðbz	3.0	easy 1	Listen	Edit x

Fig. 2. The Word bank of APTgt system

2   System Design

APTgt enables the automatic generation of interactive phonetic exams for instructors by allowing them to upload audio files and store correct answers in a word bank. Students can then listen to the selected audio and use an IPA keyboard to spell out pronunciations. The system utilizes the Levenshtein distance algorithm to automatically grade student responses by comparing them to the stored solutions [4].

To further enhance the efficiency of generating a large-scale word bank without concerns about typos or misspellings, we propose the integration of a Speech-To-IPA system. This phone-based ASR system directly converts the audio speech signal into IPA symbols, bypassing text mediation. It employs a neural network architecture with an encoder and a decoder component (see Fig. 3). During the encoding stage, the system extracts feature vectors from the input speech signal. The acoustic model in the encoder utilizes these feature vectors as input and generates a sequence of phoneme probabilities. The decoder then produces a sequence of IPA symbols based on the sequence of phoneme probabilities.

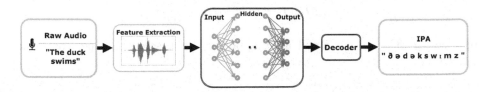

Fig. 3. Overview of the phone-based ASR system

3 Method

3.1 Data Preparation

Our dataset for training and evaluation is SEED, which was specifically created for clinical training in articulatory phonetics and speech science. It comprises of over 16,000 high-quality speech samples recorded from 33 adults and 69 children, along with corresponding English text [5]. The dataset is organized based on age (child vs. adult) and speech health status (with or without speech disorder), providing a comprehensive and diverse set of speech data for training and testing our model.

The data preparation process includes converting the English text of audio to its IPA phonetic forms and in some cases changing the sampling rate of the speech sample. We used our previously proposed grapheme-to-phoneme (G2P) converter to do translation [6], and manually inspected the result to ensure all samples and phonetic transcriptions matched up properly.

3.2 Mel-Frequency Cepstral Coefficients (MFCCs)

MFCCs are the most widely used parametric representations for acoustic signals in ASR systems [7]. The MFCCs feature extraction algorithm involves the following implementation steps:

1) Pre-emphasis increases the magnitude of energy at higher frequencies.
2) Split the signal into short frames.

3) For each frame, apply the Fast Fourier Transform (FFT) to convert the signal from the time domain to the frequency domain.
4) Calculate the power spectrum of each frame using the following equation:

$$P = \frac{|FFT(x_i)|^2}{512} \qquad (1)$$

5) Apply Mel-scale filter banks to the power spectrum of the signal and take the logarithm of all filter bank energies. The Mel scale maps the actual frequency to the frequency that human beings perceive. The formula for the mapping is:

$$Mel(f) = 2595 \log(1 + \frac{f}{700}) \qquad (2)$$

6) The MFCCs are extracted after applying the Discrete Cosine Transform (DCT).

3.3 Bidirectional Recurrent Neural Network

A recurrent neural network (RNN) is a type of neural network commonly used in speech recognition. The network consists of an input layer, a hidden layer, and an output layer, where each output layer unit has a feedback connection to itself. The feedback loops remember historical inputs which allows them to make decisions by considering current inputs while learning from previous inputs [8]. In this way, RNNs can gain a deeper understanding of the sequence and its context than other types of deep learning algorithms, enabling more precise prediction results.

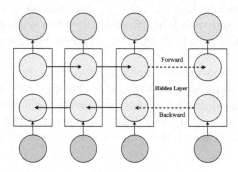

Fig. 4. Bidirectional LSTM network architecture

LSTM is an RNN architecture used in ASR systems. It contains special units called memory blocks in the recurrent hidden layer and is better for maintaining long-range connections, recognizing the relationship between values at the beginning and end of a sequence [9]. Bidirectional LSTM adds one more LSTM layer, which reverses the direction of the information flow. The architecture of a one-layer bidirectional LSTM network is illustrated in Fig. 4. Unlike standard LSTM, the input flows in both directions and is capable of utilizing information from both sides.

4   Implementation and Analysis

This work utilized the NVIDIA GeForce RTX 3080 graphics cards to train the model. The encoder was built using PyTorch and consisted of a 5-layer bidirectional LSTM, with each layer having a hidden size of 1024. The model was trained on 40-dimensional MFCCs, using the SGD optimizer with an initial learning rate of 0.01. Table 1 demonstrates the performance of the model evaluated on 10131 speech samples in SEED, of which 30% are words and 70% are sentences. 95% of the dataset is used as the training set, and the remaining data are used for testing/validation.

Table 1. Accuracy in % on the SEED dataset

Dataset	Accuracy	
	Training	Testing
Word SEED	87.1	73.9
Sentence SEED	96.9	83.8
Full SEED	91.4	**81.5**

We assess the performance of the system using the Phone Error Rate (PER), which is used to identify speech errors at the phone level, instead of the classic Word Error Rate (WER). The PER metric evaluates all mismatches between the recognizer hypothesis and the manual phone-level annotated reference (see Eq. 3), with C, I, S, and D respectively, referring to the number of correct detections, insertions, substitutions, and deletions [10].

$$PER = \frac{I + S + D}{C + S + D} \tag{3}$$

The resultant model provides a PER of 26.1% on the word task and 16.2% on the sentence task (see Fig. 5). The PER for the entire dataset is 18.5%, which means the overall accuracy is 81.5%.

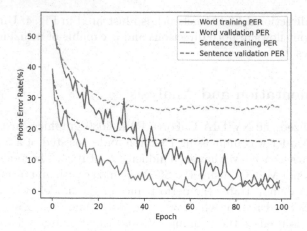

Fig. 5. Phone error rate for dataset SEED

5   Conclusion and Future Work

This phone recognizer will be initially incorporated into APTgt and serve as an auxiliary tool for automatically generating training and examination resources in the field of phonetic transcription, but it has great potential for various applications beyond just E-learning. It can bypass text mediation and directly converts the audio speech signal into IPA symbols, which is helpful in the research of communication disorders where understanding the exact errors of speech is critical. In this preliminary work, we focus on the LSTM-based model with only the MFCCs feature as the first step in identifying phones in speech samples from the SEED dataset. Future work will explore other deep architectures and combine additional features with MFCCs to improve accuracy. In addition, we will finetune the model on multiple datasets to enhance its robustness.

References

1. Seals, C.D.: Applied webservices platform supported through modified edit distance algorithm: automated phonetic transcription grading tool (APTgt). In: Zaphiris, P., Ioannou, A. (eds.) HCII 2020. LNCS, vol. 12205, pp. 380–398. Springer, Cham (2020). https://doi.org/10.1007/978-3-030-50513-4_29
2. Kim, K., et al.: The impact of CMS quality on the outcomes of e-learning systems in higher education: an empirical study. Decis. Sci. J. Innov. Educ. **10**(4), 575–587 (2012)
3. Atkins, M.S., Bailey, D.J., Seals, C.D.: Implementation of an automated grading tool for phonetic transcription training. Clin. Linguist. Phonetics **37**(3), 242–257 (2023)
4. Liu, J., et al.: Optimization to automated phonetic transcription grading tool (APTgt) – automatic exam generator. In: Zaphiris, P., Ioannou, A. (eds.) HCII 2021. LNCS, vol. 12784, pp. 80–91. Springer, Cham (2021). https://doi.org/10.1007/978-3-030-77889-7_6

5. Atkins, M.S., Bailey, D.J., Boyce, S.E.: Speech exemplar and evaluation database (SEED) for clinical training in articulatory phonetics and speech science. Clin. Linguist. Phonetics **34**(9), 878–886 (2020)
6. Liu, J., et al.: Transformer-based multilingual G2P converter for e-learning system. In: Artificial Intelligence in HCI: 3rd International Conference. AI-HCI 2022, Held as Part of the 24th HCI International Conference, HCII 2022, Virtual Event, 26 June–1 July , 2022, Proceedings, pp. 546–556. Springer-Verlag, Heidelberg (2022). https://doi.org/10.1007/978-3-031-05643-7_35
7. Han, W., et al.: An efficient MFCC extraction method in speech recognition. In: 2006 IEEE International Symposium on Circuits and Systems (ISCAS), p. 4 (2006). https://doi.org/10.1109/ISCAS.2006.1692543
8. Amberkar, A., et al.: Speech recognition using recurrent neural networks. In: 2018 International Conference on Current Trends towards Converging Technologies (ICCTCT), pp. 1–4 (2018). https://doi.org/10.1109/ICCTCT.2018.8551185
9. Sak, H., et al.: Long short-term memory recurrent neural network architectures for large scale acoustic modeling. In: Proceedings of the Annual Conference of the International Speech Communication Association, pp. 338–342. INTERSPEECH (2014)
10. Gelin, L., et al.: End-to-end acoustic modeling for phone recognition of young readers. Speech Commun. **134**, 71–84 (2021)

Tell Me What I See: Universal Design and Educational Video for Inclusive Digital Education

Andreas Schille and Robin Støckert[✉] (iD)

Norwegian University of Science and Technology, Trondheim, Norway
{andreas.h.schille,robin.stockert}@ntnu.no

Abstract. This paper is based on the film *Tell Me What I See*, a documentary about Simen, a student at NTNU with hearing and visual impairment. We present process elements from the idea to the finished product and elaborate on various interacting themes ranging from accessibility and constraints (defined by standards) to artistic expression in telling a good story. By presenting the film in various contexts across campus and beyond, different aspects and functions evolve and show the film's many facets. First, it can act as a digital learning resource accessible in all learning spaces supporting various pedagogies like student-active learning with, for instance, group discussions and flipped classrooms. Secondly, it can act as a medium for raising awareness about the situation of students with disabilities (SWD) and be a starting point for discussion and reflection amongst all stakeholders within Higher Education (HE).

Keywords: Educational Video · Universal Design · Accessibility · Documentary

1 Introduction

Seen from the perspective [1] of disabled students, many factors still harm the learning experience and access to HE. For example, the additional time and stress involved in being a disabled student and organizing their own required support for access to rooms, information, exams, or in general, "making the system work".

In the film, *Tell Me What I See*, these issues absorb much of the main character's energy, Simen, a student at NTNU with hearing and visual impairment. For him, carrying out ordinary activities requires both assistance and careful planning.

These vexing issues are not new but are perceived and handled differently depending on the stakeholder's role or perspective. The stakeholders range from the individual level as a student, teacher, or administrative staff to the organizational level at the university and governmental and international institutions concerning strategies, standards, resources, and policies [2–5]. When examining studies and papers from various countries, Several studies describe that students with disabilities experience a gap between their rights as expressed in policy and how their rights and issues are addressed in practice [6]. Hence, there is a need for awareness of student population diversity and practical knowledge on inclusive teaching with student variability in mind, leaving the "one size fits all" approach behind [7].

© The Author(s), under exclusive license to Springer Nature Switzerland AG 2024
C. Stephanidis et al. (Eds.): HCII 2023, CCIS 1957, pp. 318–324, 2024.
https://doi.org/10.1007/978-3-031-49212-9_40

2   Digital Educational Video

Digital educational video has become an integral part of university teaching, supporting student active and multimodal learning. In online learning especially, digital video is often the central learning object and often "represents an essential point of contact between teacher and student as they replace the traditional lecture in the course." [8, 9].

The HE-video landscape has a previous history filled with talking heads and presentation slide videos [10]. However, there are examples of different formats, also involving genres known from the industry, such as animation, documentary films, featurettes, and dramatizations spreading into HE [11, 12]. The competencies to produce these different formats are becoming increasingly present at universities. Typically, producing this type of content requires a cross-disciplinary approach, where academics work with video producers to create engaging video content to convey the learning content in alternative ways than recording a traditional lecture. The benefits of videos in higher education include (Adapted from Dinmore, 2019):

- increased flexibility – time, place, speed, hearing ability
- sense of personalization and social presence for the learner – especially in online courses
- video allows for unlimited repetition and revision
- perceived higher levels of student engagement
- promotion of active learning pedagogies
- additional language acquisition

Professionals working with video for online teaching must be aware of students' limited attention span and how the digital video *affordances* mentioned above connect engagement to different video formats. Furthermore, elaborate on how video is distributed and made accessible as an asynchronous or synchronous resource in the physical, hybrid, and online learning space [13]. There are also indications that well-produced marketing videos for online courses raise expectations for course content and that this causes dropout when the learning content does not meet expectations [14]. Looking at digital video as a personal, flexible, and engaging way of communicating with students opens up the unique affordances of video compared to text.

3   Accessibility and Video

Various standards and frameworks illustrate the many sides of accessibility. For instance, the Disability Inclusion Institutional Framework (DIIF) [5] focuses on the overall needs of SWD. The framework builds on three overarching constructs glued together by a "culture of shared understandings".

- Shared ownership: Disability inclusion as the responsibility of all.
- Empowerment: Focused on enabling access and addressing the physical and emotional labor involved in advocating for basic needs.
- Independence: Enabling disabled students and staff to have equal access to manage their HE context for themselves.

More specific standards and regulations are available for videos since videos must be accessible to provide added value for all learners [15]. Different approaches are available when producing educational video content, and sacrifices may have to be made, based on the requirements for accessibility, as pointed out in WCAG [16]. Alternatively, the Universal Design for Learning (UDL) framework [2] gives an overview of what inclusive education can entail. Concerning video, UDL is relevant when looking at the educational activities that video support. The UDL framework is a set of different strategies, and implementation in Norway focuses more on some parts of the framework than the whole. The framework has met criticism but stands out as a guide for inclusive education, looking past technical requirements. Good teaching practice can be observed through many different lenses, and UDL is one of them [17].

Access to education is crucial in a democratic society providing access to attractive careers and representation in influential societal positions. The right to education is both a part of the UN's sustainability goals and a part of Norwegian legislation. Through EUs Web Accessibility Directive [18], requirements for the Universal Design of video content are prevalent in European HE institutions. Comparing these requirements with theories on good practice for educational video design reveals discrepancies and overlapping.

There are three critical requirements of universal design in learning videos [16]:

- Same-language subtitles (SLS)
- Audio description (AD)
- Inclusive use of graphics (Visual accessibility)

There are also other factors affecting the level of accessibility to mention, such as:

- Technical audio and video quality
- The tone of voice and language use
- Speed, pace, and other editing techniques

We can find evidence for these additional factors affecting accessibility, such as Mayer's Multimedia principles [19]. There are arguments that online learning using digital video, when executed correctly, can be more inclusive and appeal more broadly to learners than traditional lectures.

It is possible to see creative limits that the requirements may put on media designers, but at the same time, those limitations can foster creativity [20]. Coming to terms with the fact that educational media represents something other than ordinary media production, as accessible media is a prerequisite for having access to higher education, may give a different context for media production. The variability in the target group shows that everyone benefits from universally accessible solutions [21].

Fig. 1. Poster for the short documentary *Tell Me What I See* (2023)

4   Tell Me What I See – a Documentary

At NTNU, some of the work of staff training and strengthening the motivations of academic staff took the form of film production. A film team followed a student needing accommodation on campus and in everyday situations. By having Simen, a student in sociology, tell the story of how limited vision and hearing affect his everyday life and studies and listening to his reflections, educators at the university should be better prepared to meet a diverse crowd of students in their classroom. Both know what practical adjustments are needed and see the person behind the needs.

The background for creating the documentary film was to emphasize the necessary accommodations for students with visual disabilities. New requirements for Audio Description of pre-recorded audiovisual material occurred in Norway in 2023, seemingly putting the extra workload on academics. The film aims to motivate educators to have students who benefit from universally designed content in mind when confronted with requirements of accessibility.

Testimonials like the one in the film *Tell Me What I See* can push the development of solutions to help students with the need for accommodations or Universal Design. Increased knowledge about universal design can also help promote more positive attitudes toward people with disabilities [22]. Furthermore, after watching the film, the effort of educators should be more targeted in investigating what resources are necessary to achieve the appropriate level of accessibility. Screening the film as an educational video can trigger discussions and support the target group with the mental context necessary to learn [23]. Hence, the pedagogical aims of the documentary film focus on the experiences of and identification with the main character, affecting the audience emotionally and possibly changing attitudes and creating a reflection. After screening the film, the discussion is essential to the pedagogical activity. Here students and teachers are encouraged to share their thoughts and have a discussion afterward.

The film itself takes accessibility into account by having an alternative version with Audio Descriptions and captioning in both English and Norwegian. Also, parts of the film have integrated descriptions, as an interpreter who follows Simen gives him visual descriptions of his surroundings.

5 Artistic and Practice-Based Methodologies

The strategies behind the film *Tell Me What I See* are similar to the advice for designing digital video for online learning. Giving access, using storytelling, and showing rather than telling are affordances used to present the situation of a student with disabilities [11]. These actions give context to the issue and interest in exploring the topic further.

By working practice-based with interviews and other observations with the camera, a goal is to reflect on the process as a filmmaker. Furthermore, to reflect on the creative process to find tools, models, theories, and concepts that can provide an analytical perspective to the creative process behind the fact-based film, providing a self-reflexive component in communicating the scientific content with cinematic devices and being able to work practice-based with one's reflections and ideas. (As we take our cameras out into the world to explore and record, we also travel with notions and concepts that speak powerfully to us) [24].

The practice-based approach here explores the potential of shorter documentary films and contributes to creating new knowledge by developing "a space of constellations and connections where practices, methods, and understandings meet and shape new methodologies."

6 Conclusion

This paper addresses a pragmatic approach toward education using well-known and established pedagogical methods with videos produced according to UDL standards. Aligning inclusive design of educational videos that are easy to use and used in UDL-informed teaching practice can be a powerful tool in providing opportunities for education to more students.

Using a film like *Tell Me What I See* to promote openness, awareness, and inclusion across campus will hopefully create a strong commitment in students, teachers, and other stakeholders to put accessibility as a high priority. The DIIF builds precisely on the same values promoted by the film, and hence the film can act as a glue for shared understanding amongst all stakeholders within HE. In addition, we hope that the film can motivate students with impairments to put in the necessary effort to make the best out of their situation as students. And not to be afraid of telling the professor or other students about his or her situation and to be conscious of their rights.

Acknowledgment. NTNU and the Norwegian Directorate for Higher Education and Skills for supporting the making of this documentary.

Production and presentation of this paper/poster are co-funded with support from the European Commission through the project Learning Through Innovative Collaboration Enhanced by Educational Technology (iLikeIT2) (Nr. 2020–1-NO01-KA203–076434).

References

1. Holloway, S.: The experience of higher education from the perspective of disabled students. Disability Soc. **16**(4), 597–615 (2001). https://doi.org/10.1080/09687590120059568
2. "About Universal Design for Learning," *CAST*. https://www.cast.org/impact/universal-design-for-learning-udl Accessed Jun 06 2023
3. W. W. A. Initiative (WAI), "Introduction to Web Accessibility," *Web Accessibility Initiative (WAI)*. https://www.w3.org/WAI/fundamentals/accessibility-intro/ Accessed Jun 06 2023
4. "Education Policy," *European Disability Forum* 2020. https://www.edf-feph.org/education-policy/ Accessed Jun 06 2023
5. "Disability Inclusion Institutional Framework (DIIF) - Eleanor Glanville Centre." https://eleanorglanvilleinstitute.lincoln.ac.uk/di-hub/inclusion-resources/diif Accessed Jun 05 2023
6. Järkestig Berggren, U., Rowan, D., Bergbäck, E., Blomberg, B.: Disabled students' experiences of higher education in Sweden, the Czech Republic, and the United States – a comparative institutional analysis. Disability Society, vol. 31, pp. 1–18 (2016). https://doi.org/10.1080/09687599.2016.1174103
7. Kennette, L.N., Wilson, N.A.: Universal design for learning (udl): student and faculty perceptions. J. Effect. Teach. High. Educ. **2**(1), 1–26 (2019)
8. Dinmore, S.: Beyond lecture capture: Creating digital video content for online learning - a case study. J. Univ. Teach. Learn. Pract. **16**(1), 98–108 (2019). https://doi.org/10.53761/1.16.1.7
9. Reutemann, J.: Differences and Commonalities – A comparative report of video styles and course descriptions on edX, Coursera, Futurelearn and Iversity (2016)
10. Reutemann, J.: Framing the Talking Head Challenges of Academic Broadcast Studios. (2018). https://doi.org/10.17605/OSF.IO/M5U4V
11. Hustad, J.L., Schille, A., Wattengård, E.: Escaping the talking head: experiences with three different styles of MOOC video. In: Proceedings of the 6th European Conference on Massive Open Online Courses, pp. 151–156 (2019)
12. Hansch, A., Hillers, L., McConachie, K., Newman, C., Schildhauer, T., Schmidt, P.: Video and online learning: critical reflections and findings from the field. SSRN Electron. J. (2015). https://doi.org/10.2139/ssrn.2577882
13. Støckert, R., Van der Zanden, P., De Caro-Barek, V.: An education spaces framework to define interactive and collaborative practices over the physical-hybrid-virtual continuum. In: Proceedings of the 16th International Scientific Conference "eLearning and Software for Education," Bucharest: Editura Universitara, pp. 486–496 (2020). https://doi.org/10.12753/2066-026X-21-061
14. Reutemann, J.: To tease somebody – advertised educational intro vs. Lecture Videos. (2018). https://doi.org/10.17605/OSF.IO/SKZ5F
15. Authentic and Effective: Rescuing Video from Its Role as the Villain of Online Learning. https://er.educause.edu/articles/2021/12/authentic-and-effective-rescuing-video-from-its-role-as-the-villain-of-online-learning Accessed Jun 20 2023
16. W. W. A. Initiative (WAI), "WCAG 2 Overview," *Web Accessibility Initiative (WAI)*. https://www.w3.org/WAI/standards-guidelines/wcag/ Accessed Jun 20 2023

17. "UDL Now! A Teacher's Guide to Applying Universal Design for Learning in Today's Classrooms," CAST Professional Publishing. https://publishing.cast.org/catalog/books-products/udl-now-novak Accessed Jun 20 2023
18. "Web Accessibility | Shaping Europe's digital future," Apr. 18, 2023. https://digital-strategy.ec.europa.eu/en/policies/web-accessibility Accessed Jun 20 2023
19. Mayer, R.E. (ed.): The Cambridge Handbook of Multimedia Learning. Cambridge University Press (2014). https://doi.org/10.1017/CBO9781139547369
20. Kerrigan, S., McIntyre, P.: The 'creative treatment of actuality': rationalizing and reconceptualizing the notion of creativity for documentary practice. J. Media Pract. **11**(2), 111 (2010)
21. Sapp, W.: Universal design: online educational media for students with disabilities. J. Visual Impairm. Blind. **103**(8), 495–500 (2009)
22. Hitch, D., Dell, K., Larkin, H.: Does universal design education impact on the attitudes of architecture students towards people with disability? J. Access. Design **6**, 26–48 (2016). https://doi.org/10.17411/jacces.v6i1.103
23. Schwartz, D., Hartman, K.: "It is not television anymore: Designing digital video for learning and assessment," Video research in the Learning sciences (2007)
24. Rogers, C., Gough-Brady, C., Berry, M.: Breathing places: three filmmaking investigations. Cult. Geograph. **29**(1), 99–113 (2021). https://doi.org/10.1177/14744740211003628

A Multi-modal Interactive Picture Book for Chinese Left-Behind Children: A Case Study Based on Dear Ducklings

Zhengming Si[1], Wantong Du[1], Wenchen Guo[2]([envelope]) [iD], Menghan Shi[3]([envelope]), and Xiacheng Song[4]

[1] Harbin Institute of Technology, Harbin, China
sunnyzmsi@126.com, djingjing21@gmail.com
[2] Peking University, Beijing, China
beihuanfanchen@sina.com
[3] Hong Kong Polytechnic University, Hong Kong, China
m2shi@polyu.edu.hk
[4] Guangzhou Academy of Fine Arts, Guangzhou, China

Abstract. In this poster, we designed and developed *Dear Ducklings*, a multi-modal interactive picture book for Chinese left-behind children, set in the animal world, where the children take on the role of a visitor accompanied by a virtual tutor to follow the adventures of a group of ducklings. In the picture book, children can interact with characters, watch science videos, and share learning output with their parents. The picture book provides multi-modal interaction, enabling children to gain diverse knowledge and communicate with their parents. We conducted a pilot study (n = 12), and the results showed that the book had a positive impact on reducing loneliness and expanding children's learning perspectives. In the future, we will develop more series of books for children left behind to empower the childhood lives of left-behind children.

Keywords: Digital Picture Books · Left-behind Children · Multi-modal Experience · Emotional Companionship · Human-computer Interaction

1 Introduction

The wave of modernization in China has intensified the siphoning effect of cities on less developed areas, triggering a massive movement of the labor force. Parent-child separation is extremely common in less developed areas of China, especially in rural areas. Approximately 61.03 million children in China experience parent-child separation [1]. Children who experience parent-child separation at an early age are more likely to grow up with low academic performance, psychological deformities, and even criminality [2]. However, at present, the issue of how to enhance the well-being of left-behind children and compensate for the lack of parental companionship is still a hot topic, and there are still few companionship-based products designed for left-behind children.

C. Stephanidis et al. (Eds.): HCII 2023, CCIS 1957, pp. 325–332, 2024.
https://doi.org/10.1007/978-3-031-49212-9_41

The rapid advancement of new media technology has opened up possibilities for designing products tailored to the needs of left-behind children. Digital picture books, for instance, offer enriched emotional interaction and reading experiences through multi-media elements such as audio and interactive games. Studies have indicated that children exhibit higher levels of interest, focus, and engagement when reading digital picture books [3]. Furthermore, these books facilitate vocabulary acquisition, story retelling, and comprehension [4].

Based on extensive research, we designed and developed *Dear Ducklings* (see Fig. 1), a multi-modal picture book targeting left-behind children aged 4–7. The story unfolds in an animal world, following the adventures of Grandmother Duck and her ducklings in the wilderness. Our picture book allows children to interact with the characters, watch educational videos, engage in mathematical exercises, and share their learning outputs with their parents. Consequently, children gain a multi-modal interactive experience while acquiring knowledge in various domains, including science, literature, and more. The book employs a cartoon art style that appeals to children's visual preferences. From a technical standpoint, the picture book utilizes the Unity platform and integrates voice interaction, audio-visual elements, augmented reality, and other immersive methods, utilizing mobile phones as the primary interactive tool.

In summary, the main contributions of our work are as follows: (1) Identification of the unique product requirements for left-behind children in China through comprehensive literature reviews and user interviews. (2) Design and development of a multi-modal interactive picture book tailored to the needs of left-behind children in China. This book combines storytelling and functionality to address their specific learning needs (literacy, mathematics, natural knowledge, and cultural understanding), emotional needs (companionship and communication), and value guidance requirements (behavioral guidelines and social norms).

Fig. 1. Prototype display image of *Dear Ducklings*

2   Related Work

2.1   Digital Products for Left-Behind Children

As society pays more attention to the issue of left-behind children, some scholars have developed digital products for left-behind children, bringing inspiration to the design of products for left-behind children.

To meet the emotional needs of left-behind children, several scholars have explored the development of smart interactive products that aim to alleviate psychological issues. Haoran Zeng developed Toubot, a pair of wearable haptic robots that strengthened the emotional bond between left-behind children and their parents. Through interactive behaviors, such as touch, this study revealed that left-behind children can develop a sense of companionship, thus mitigating emotional problems such as depression, loneliness, and alexithymia [5]. Pinghong Wang designed an online parent-child communication platform based on smart TVs for left-behind children, which made communication between left-behind children and their parents more convenient [6]. Another critical aspect is the lack of access to quality educational resources and guidance for left-behind children [7]. The Magic House App is a mobile platform that allows left-behind children to connect with children and teachers in large cities. The App aims to provide a channel for left-behind children to access good educational resources [8].

These digital products provide insights into the design for left-behind children. The findings highlight the significance of developing products that adequately address the specific learning and emotional requirements of left-behind children, thereby recognizing the importance of tailoring interventions to their unique circumstances.

2.2 Digital Products for Left-Behind Children

New media technologies have been combined with children's publications to add digital multimedia information, making the messages conveyed in the publications more vivid and easier to understand. *What is What* are a series of German AR science books developed for children aged 5–8 years old, which enable children to learn about various aspects of knowledge, such as architecture, astronomy, and archaeology. Distributed in tens of millions of copies worldwide, the picture books are widely popular with children. Additionally, the Tokyo Shimbun, a Japanese newspaper, has developed an augmented-reality newspaper specifically designed for children. When the mobile phone camera scans a specific article in the newspaper, an animated online version of the corresponding article appears on the phone screen. With fewer out-of-the-ordinary words and short articles, the online version makes the newspaper accessible to children through a cartoonish, flat, easy-to-understand graphic design style and cute, lively voice explanations.

Through our analysis of existing picture books, we have recognized their ability to captivate children through engaging storytelling and a visually appealing cartoonish, flat design style. Furthermore, we acknowledge that new media technologies, such as augmented reality (AR), can enhance children's learning experiences.

3 Design Study

Our design research was conducted through literature reviews and user interviews with over 10 left-behind children, their teachers and guardians.

China's rapid economic development has triggered a massive movement of people from less developed areas (mostly rural) to developed areas (mostly large cities). The migrant workers are often unable to bring their children to live with them in cities, and the children instead stay at home to be cared for by non-parent guardians [9]. This group of children is known as "left-behind children". Most of the guardians of left-behind children are less educated grandparents who are almost not concerned about whether their children obtain quality companionship and knowledgeable education [10]. The absence of parents can lead to a series of cascading reactions, such as higher levels of psychological, behavioral and school adjustment problems among left-behind children [11]. Additionally, a recent meta-analysis found that, compared with non-left-behind children, left-behind children had more safety problems and emotional distress problems [12].

Through the literature review, we clarified the main causes of the social problem of left-behind children and gained a conceptual understanding of the current life situation. On this basis, we conducted real-name online interviews with more than 10 left-behind children aged 5–7, their teachers and guardians.

For the left-behind children, we first learned about their basic family situation, then interviewed them about communication activities with their parents, the state of getting along with their peers, daily behavioral activities and family education in four areas. For their teachers and guardians, we mainly asked about their educational background and the way they educated the left-behind children.

Through the interviews, we found that the communication frequency of the left-behind and their parents maintain 3–4 times a week, but the calls are basically in the form of voice calls. The content of parent-child communication is rather homogeneous, and the few parent-child exchanges are limited to parents' unilateral inquiries about their children's basic living conditions, resulting in inefficient communication. While getting along with their peers, left-behind children are easily bullied by their peers due to insufficient behavior and poor personal hygiene. This in turn leads to the left-behind children becoming more introverted and withdrawn. Additionally, many left-behind children are required to perform household chores such as washing vegetables and feeding livestock in their daily lives. Due to the low level of education of their guardians, many left-behind children lack early education, basic behavioral manners and social etiquette. Through interviews with the teachers and guardians of the left-behind children, we learned that teachers and guardians are mostly concerned with the basic survival needs of the children such as food and clothing, but show little concern for the children's inner feelings.

By reading literature reviews and conducting user interviews, we plan to adopt a gamified, scenario-based concept [13], and summarized three core needs of left-behind children: learning needs (literacy, algebra, knowledge of nature and culture), emotional needs (companionship, communication) and values guidance (rules of behavior, social rules).

4 Implementation

Based on the above research, we have developed *Dear Ducklings, a* multi-modal interactive picture book for children aged 5–7 years old, based on the Unity platform (see Fig. 2).

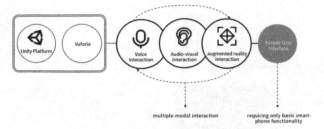

Fig. 2. Technical framework diagram

4.1 Storyline Design

The story introduces the children to the duckling family. The ducklings' mum and dad are working in the big city and Grandma Duck is living in the countryside with the ducklings. One day, Grandma Duck takes the three ducklings to the pond to catch fish. On their way to catch food, they first pass by a meadow full of flowers. The ducklings want to pick some flowers, but Grandma tells them that flowers have life, and not to pick the beautiful flowers. Then they need to cross a road full of cars. The ducklings have to remember the rules of the road so that they will not get into a traffic accident. When they reach the pond, the dangerous white spotted dogfish tempts the ducklings with lies and tries to trick them to go to the center of the pond. Luckily, Grandma Duck arrives just in time to chase away the white spotted dogfish and take the ducklings back home.

The storyline is designed to combine educational functions with narrative storytelling, and to fit in with the life situations of left-behind children, aiming to enhance their sense of immersion and interest in reading, so that they can understand and accept the knowledge and values conveyed in the picture book.

4.2 Picture Design

The book is designed in a flat and cartoonish style, which is more approachable and in line with children's reading and information-receiving habits. The pictures are made up of blue, green and yellow colors with a high degree of purity and contrast, and are bright and lively, aiming to attract children's attention and enhance their interest in reading. In terms of text design and layout, the picture book chooses a large font size and applies a highlighted white color as the text color and a black and green background color for the text to highlight the text. In addition, all the text in the picture book is marked with Chinese phonetic alphabets to meet children's needs for Chinese character recognition (see Fig. 3).

Fig. 3. Picture design for *Dear Ducklings*

4.3 Interaction Function Design

In the picture book, we have designed a variety of interactive activities to meet the unique needs of left-behind children, such as watching science videos, reading and singing along with the voice, calculating mathematics, writing Chinese characters, and sharing screenshots of their learning with their parents (see Fig. 4).

Fig. 4. Partial interactive effect display

Research has found that children have a more enjoyable reading experience when interacting with the characters in dynamic electronic picture books [14]. To address the psychological needs, a virtual tutor, 'Tinkerbell', is set up to help children read the story and understand the problem challenges designed in the picture book. In addition, children can scan the picture of the book by their mobile phones to see the 3D characters and click on the character to change its movement. They can also scan the book to play the children's songs on their mobile phones. When the villainous white spotted dogfish appears, children can scan the picture book to watch the white spotted dogfish science video on their mobile phones. When reading the book, children are given maths problems and step-by-step solutions to assist them with their maths calculations. In addition, all interactive parts of the picture book include light background music and interactive touch points with simulated sound effects to integrate children's perceptions into the virtual environment. In addition, the picture book is designed with a screenshot-sharing function so that children can share their learning with their parents and friends after completing interactive tasks.

5   Pilot Study

5.1   Participants and Procedure

12 left-behind children aged 5–7 years participated in our user pilot study. We gave the picture books to the left-behind children, downloaded the apk file used for picture book interaction to the guardians' mobile phones, and informed the children how to read the book. 15 days later, we interviewed the children and their guardians. The interview process and the disclosure of the results were agreed upon by the subjects.

5.2   Results and Discussion

Through the interview, we found that the children could quickly pick up on the picture books and become immersed in the picture book stories. This reflects the ease of handling and comprehension of the picture books. The children were attracted by the colorful pictures, vivid stories and rich interactive features of the picture books, and they wanted to be able to interact more with their favorite picture book characters. Some children said they had more topics to talk about with their parents and friends after sharing what they had learned from the book. This demonstrates the important role that picture books play in reducing children's feelings of isolation and low self-esteem. The children found the augmented reality interactions in the picture books very interesting and were thrilled each time the 3D characters appeared in their scans. When asked if they would like to continue reading the picture books, the children all answered in the affirmative. Three of the 7-year-olds said that the story was somewhat brief. This reflects the fact that the current picture book stories are still not abundant enough and more storylines need to be designed to meet the children's long-term reading learning needs. In addition, some of the children showed behaviors that were guided by the values in the picture books, such as taking the initiative to greet their elders and taking care of flowers and plants.

The feedback proves that *Dear Ducklings* has a measurable positive impact on reducing children's isolation and broadening their learning horizons by providing some companionship, knowledge education and values guidance.

6   Limitations and Future Work

At present, *Dear Ducklings* is limited by the fact that there is only one story at present. Furthermore, it caters specifically to the age group of 5–7-year-old left-behind children, thus failing to address the needs of other age groups. In the future, we will enrich the story content and interaction of Dear Ducklings and improve the functionality of the picture book through more user testing. In addition, we will conduct more detailed research to comprehensively understand the unique requirements of children across different age groups. Guided by these findings, we aim to elevate the narrative and interactive aspects, ultimately culminating in the design of a comprehensive series of picture books expressly tailored to accompany and support left-behind children.

References

1. National Bureau of Statistics Homepage. http://www.stats.gov.cn. Accessed Nov 2020
2. Xue, L.F., Zhang, Y.S.: The impact of family separation on the mental health of rural-urban migrant children in China. Int. J. Mental Health **7**(4), 287–295 (2021)
3. Daisy, J.H., Smeets, F., MSc, S., Marianne, J.T.: Using electronic storybooks to support word learning in children with severe language impairments. J. Learn. Disabilities **47**(5), 435–449 (2014)
4. Zsofia, K., Takacs, F., Elise K Swart, S., Adriana G Bus, T.: Benefits and pitfalls of multimedia and interactive features in technology-enhanced storybooks: a meta-analysis. Rev. Educ. Res. **85**(4), 698–739 (2015)
5. Haoran Zeng, F., Yuyang Qi, S., Yao Lu, T.: Toubot: a pair of wearable haptic robots that strengthen the emotional bond between left-behind children and their parents by enhancing instant interactions. In: 2023 18th ACM/IEEE International Conference on Human-Robot Interaction(HRI). IEEE, pp.816–819 (2023)
6. Hongping Wang, F.: Research on Family Communication Product. Design **261**(6), 122–124 (2019)
7. Wei, Y.F., Gong, Y.S.: Understanding Chinese rural-to-urban migrant children's education predicament: a dual system perspective. Int. J. Educ. Develop. **69**, 48–57 (2019)
8. Shengfeng Duan, F., Yongsheng Pi, S.: Design intervention in education poverty alleviation. Packag. Eng. **39**(10), 1–7 (2018)
9. Fellmeth, G.F., Rose-Clarke, K.S., Zhao, C.T.: Health impacts of parental migration on left-behind children and adolescents: a systematic review and meta-analysis. The Lancet **392**, 2567–2582 (2018)
10. Li Z, F., Zou X, S., Zhu P, T.: The empirical research on the competency of rural skip-generation guardians for left-behind children. China Journal of Health Psychology 21(3), 422–425 (2013)
11. Wang, L.F., Mesman, J.S.: Child development in the face of rural-to-urban migration in China: a meta-analytic review. Perspect. Psychol. Sci. **10**, 813–831 (2015)
12. Chen, M.F., Sun, X.S., Chen, Q.T., Chan, K.L.: Parental migration, children's safety and psychological adjustment in rural China: a meta-analysis. Trauma, Violence, Abuse **21**(1), 113–122 (2020)
13. Guo, W., Li, S., Zhang, Z., Chen, Z., Chang, K.H., Wang, S.: A "magic world" for children: design and development of a serious game to improve spatial ability. Comput Anim Virtual Worlds **34**(3), e2181 (2023)
14. Barnyak, N.C.F., MeNelly, T.A.S.: The literacy skills and motivation to read of children enrolled in titlel: a comparison of electronic and print nonfiction books. Early Childhood Educ. J. **44**(5), 527–536 (2016)

Exploring Mixed Reality Group Activity Visualisations for Teaching Assistants to Support Collaborative Learning

Ryota Takahashi[1], Shizuka Shirai[1]([✉]), Hiroyuki Nagataki[1], Tatsuya Amano[1], Mehrasa Alizadeh[2], Mayumi Ueda[3], Noriko Takemura[4], Mutlu Cukurova[5], Hajime Nagahara[1], and Haruo Takemura[1]

[1] Osaka University, Osaka, Japan
takahashi.ryota@lab.ime.cmc.osaka-u.ac.jp,
shizuka.shirai.cmc@osaka-u.ac.jp
[2] International Professional University of Technology, Osaka, Japan
[3] University of Marketing and Distribution Sciences, Hyogo, Japan
[4] Kyushu Institute of Technology, Fukuoka, Japan
[5] University College London, London, UK

Abstract. This paper presents the intermediate results of our Mixed Reality (MR)-based visualisation prototype for teaching assistants (TAs) to support collaborative learning. Many universities have introduced TA programs; however, it is not easy for TAs to understand students' engagement states in collaborative learning activities due to their lack of teaching experience. The proposed MR-based visualisation overlays student activity states above each group location to facilitate decision-making for TAs as to whether support is needed or not. To examine the proposed solution's impact, we conducted an exploratory experiment using a prototype with a Wizard of Oz method. The results indicated that the prototype has the potential to support TAs in noticing groups that need support and increases their efficiency.

Keywords: mixed reality · collaborative learning · teaching support

1 Introduction

Teaching assistant (TA) programs have been widely introduced in higher education. TAs play a significant role in providing instruction tailored to individual students' progress. However, most TAs do not have enough preparation to teach [5], so it is not easy to make appropriate decisions to support students. In previous studies for supporting instruction, Egi et al. [2] proposed a tablet-based TA support system for programming exercises. Holstein et al. [3] presented a Mixed Reality (MR)-based real-time teacher awareness tool. However, these

---

This work was supported by MEXT "Innovation Platform for Society 5.0" Program Grant Number JPMXP0518071489.

studies focused on individual learning, and the rich analytics for supporting students were generated by learning management or intelligent tutoring systems. In collaborative learning involving group work, where multiple students work together and multiple groups proceed with their tasks simultaneously, it is more difficult to grasp each student's and the group situation. Previous studies show the effectiveness of analysing students' activity for understanding the quality of student group collaboration [1], and it is expected to be helpful if teachers and TAs know the learner's state in teaching activities. However, few studies have examined the effectiveness of visualisation methods and evaluated them in actual classes. This research aims to develop a collaborative learning support system for TAs based on student activity states. As an initial step, the study examined whether visualising activity states in group work using MR is effective for TAs.

2   Group Activity Visualisation Framework Using MR

The proposed visualisation framework overlays students' and group activity states above each group location as shown in Fig. 1. The advantage of using the MR technique is that TAs can see students' activity state while looking around the classroom in real-time, so it is intuitive to understand which groups or students need support. The activity states are shown as binary to represent an active or a passive state, which is calculated using an engagement coding scheme explained later. The active state means engaged in tasks and taking an initiative, and the passive state means engaged in tasks but passively. The passive state includes the situation of stalled tasks so that the visualisation system can inform TAs of groups with passive students.

To calculate the activity state, we defined three types of engagement levels during group learning, as shown in Table 1. However, providing excessive support to students decreases their motivation to solve problems and reduces effective learning [6]. Therefore, we did not use these activity states directly but changed the activity state gradually. Specifically, Active is coded as 2, Passive as 1, and Not Engaged as 0, and the moving average of these values over the last 60 s is

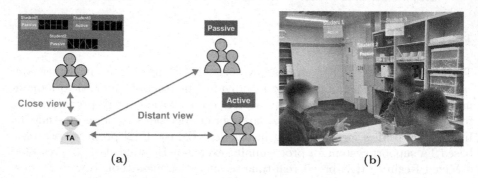

Fig. 1. (a) The system displays the activity level of the entire group at a distance and the activity level of an individual at a short distance. (b) Example of close view.

Table 1. Engagement coding scheme.

Level	Coding scheme
Active (2)	Engaged in tasks and takes initiative
	e.g., Talks about tasks, works on tasks proactively
Passive (1)	Engaged in tasks but passively
	e.g., Reads documents, listens to other members speak
Not Engaged (0)	Not engaged in tasks
	e.g., Talks about things unrelated to tasks

the activity level. Let us define the state of a student S_i at a time t as $A_{S_{i,t}}$, then the activity state at the time is defined as:

$$A_{S_i,t} = \frac{1}{60} \sum_{k=t-59}^{t} S_{i,k} \tag{1}$$

The group activity state used the 60-s moving average of the product of students' activity states belonging to that group. Specifically, the group activity $A_{group,t}$ belonging to students S_1, S_2, S_3 at time t is defined as:

$$A_{group,t} = \frac{1}{60} \sum_{k=t-59}^{t} S_{1,k} S_{2,k} S_{3,k} \tag{2}$$

Since a group with a Not Engaged student needs assistance, we used this definition where the group value is set to 0 if there is even one Not Engaged student.

With regard to the implementation, we used MR to visualise the activity states. Although MR has the advantage of intuitive visualisation, the cognitive load increases when excessive information is presented in MR systems [4]. Therefore, the proposed system suppressed the cognitive load by dynamically changing the information presented. Specifically, the proposed framework turns the displays according to the distance between each group and TAs as shown in Fig. 1(a). When the distance between each group and a TA is far, only the activity level of the entire group is displayed. At a near distance, detailed information on each student using a line graph is displayed, which displays the progress of the activity state. This method ensures that the amount of information for TAs is not too much when looking at the entire classroom. We used Magic Leap One (https://www.magicleap.com) and Unity (https://unity.com/) to implement the proposed MR-based visualisation framework.

3 Evaluation

3.1 Methodology

We conducted a trial lesson to examine the effectiveness of the proposed visualisation framework. The learning activity was physical programming using micro:

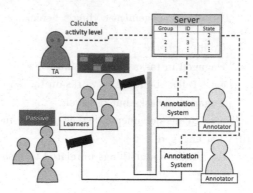

Fig. 2. Annotator inputs activity level in real time based on the group's video and sends it to the server. The system calculates the activity level using these data.

bit (https://makecode.microbit.org/). We designed the lesson based on group work with three students in each group. The 46 undergraduate and graduate students (29 females and 17 males, mean age:22.5 (SD:3.1)) participated in the experiment, all of whom had little programming skill. We conducted the experiment over two days; 24 students joined on the first day and 22 on the second. The lesson consisted of six sessions of 20-minute long exercises. Students were divided into six groups (two groups consisted of two students on the second day due to member absence) and they were assigned programming tasks to complete by themselves, referring to supplementary materials. We designed a within-subjects experiment involving two conditions: the condition of no MR-based system (noMR conditions) and the condition of using the proposed system (MR condition). Six graduate students with programming skills joined the experiment as TAs, and each TA participated in two sessions with each condition. For the MR condition, we used the Wizard of Oz (WOZ) methodology, a research method of interaction with a mock system controlled by a human, for collecting student engagement levels to avoid the effects of estimation accuracy. We assigned eight annotators to groups and they observed the group activity in real-time and input the engagement level of each student. As shown in Fig. 2, every student engagement level input by annotators is sent to the server in real-time. The visualisation module refers to these labels in the server to calculate the student and group activity state. Note that annotators input activity levels in both conditions.

For the analysis, we measured the number of times that TAs supported groups marked by annotators and the TAs' movement distance using LiDAR (Light Detection and Ranging), a remote sensing method, for objective evaluation. As a measure of subjective evaluation, we asked TAs to answer questionnaires about the system usability and mental workload after each condition. For usability, we used the System Usability Scale (SUS), and the mental workload is a 10 Likert-scale original questionnaire based on the items of NASA-TLX. In addition, we collected responses to five original questions as shown in Table 2.

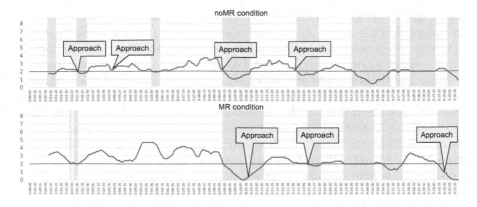

Fig. 3. The graph shows the group activity states of group 5 at sessions 3 and 4 on the first day, with the timing of TA assistance.

Table 2. The results of TA's questionnaire ((Strongly Disagree 0–Strongly Agree 5)).

Item	Questionnaire Items	Mean (SD)	
		noMR	MR
1	I could notice the group needed observation or assistance	3.33 (1.03)	3.67 (1.03)
2	I could approach the group needing assistance with appropriate timing.	3.33 (0.82)	3.33 (1.03)
3	The overall system displayed data clearly.	–	4.00 (1.10)
4	In student assistance, I utilised the feature that changes the visualisation with the distance.	–	2.00 (1.10)
5	The graph in the details view helped to understand each student's state.	–	2.22 (0.82)

3.2 Results and Discussion

Our sample size is small for statistical analysis; therefore, we report the descriptive statistics values and qualitative assessment of the data from TAs. Regarding the objective evaluation, the number of support provided, which means TAs approaching the groups to support them, was 9.83 (SD: 4.91) in the noMR condition, and 10.83 (SD: 6.88) in the MR condition. The assistance number slightly increased by using the proposed system. The mean movement distance with the noMR condition was 298.9 m (SD: 74.8), and the MR condition was 252.3 m (SD: 49.5). Although the number of assistance is almost the same across conditions, the movement distance in the MR condition was shorter than in the noMR condition. Figure 3 shows the group activity states of group 5 at sessions 3 and 4 on the first day, with the timing of TA assistance. The red lines in each graph represent the threshold value for changing the panel between Active and Passive. Also, the tags represents the TA assistance timing. In the MR condition (lower graph), the TA could assist the group after the group activity state went under the threshold, while in the noMR condition (upper graph), the same TA helped before the group activity level fell below the threshold. These results indicate that the visualisation prototype helps TAs to notice groups that need support.

Regarding the subjective evaluation, the mental workload of the noMR condition was 5.75 (*SD*: 1.96), and the MR condition was 5.39 (*SD*: 1.61). The results are not much different between the two conditions. However, the result of the SUS was 53.8 (*SD*: 17.3), and it varied with each individual. Regarding the original questionnaire about whether they could notice the groups that needed support, TAs scored higher at the MR condition than at the noMR condition. In contrast, the questionnaire about whether they could support the group with appropriate timing showed no difference. One TA reported, *"It was a great help to understand the timing when assistance was needed"* in the comments. On the other hand, another TA reported that *"even if the system displayed 'Passive,' some groups did not need support because they tackled the tasks that lie ahead compared to the other groups."* This indicates that TAs still had to make final decisions of whether an intervention was needed or not. The decision of whether students need support or not is influenced by multiple factors such as the class goal, task, and progress which are not considered in the visualisation prototype provided. Regardless, initial results and participant comments indicate that the proposed framework has the potential to support TAs in terms of initial alerting and potentially prioritising of support for their intervention decisions. Finally, regarding the feature of detailed view, most TAs did not find it helpful. One TA reported that he had his hands full with checking group activities and approaching them, so he had no room to check each student's activity level in a one-to-many situation with limited time. We need to confirm the efficiency of the close view feature with a long-term experiment.

4   Conclusion

In this study, we proposed an MR-based visualisation framework that displays students' activity state to assist TAs. The proposed framework overlays student activity states directly above the group location and turns the display content based on distance. The experiment results indicated that the proposed framework has the potential to help TAs, particularly for detecting which groups need immediate attention and prioritise them to improve the efficiency of their practice. In the future, we will incorporate a student activity state estimation model to the proposed framework and evaluate the system with a larger number of students.

References

1. Cukurova, M., Luckin, R., Millán, E., Mavrikis, M.: The NISPI framework: analysing collaborative problem-solving from students' physical interactions. Comput. Educ. **116**, 93–109 (2018)
2. Egi, H., Yokoyama, Y., Imamura, R.: Development and practice of a TA support system for programming exercise based on learning support strategies. IPSJ Trans. Comput. Educ. **8**(2), 1–11 (2022)
3. Holstein, K., McLaren, B.M., Aleven, V.: Student Learning Benefits of a Mixed-Reality Teacher Awareness Tool in AI-Enhanced Classrooms. In: Penstein Rosé, C., Martínez-Maldonado, R., Hoppe, H.U., Luckin, R., Mavrikis, M., Porayska-Pomsta, K., McLaren, B., du Boulay, B. (eds.) AIED 2018. LNCS (LNAI), vol. 10947, pp. 154–168. Springer, Cham (2018). https://doi.org/10.1007/978-3-319-93843-1_12
4. Lindlbauer, D., Feit, A.M., Hilliges, O.: Context-aware online adaptation of mixed reality interfaces. In: Proceedings of the 32nd Annual ACM Symposium on User Interface Software and Technology, UIST 2019, pp. 147–160 (2019)
5. Luo, J., Bellows, L., Grady, M.: Classroom management issues for teaching assistants. Res. High. Educ. **41**(3), 353–383 (2000)
6. Miwa, K., Terai, H., Nakaike, R.: Tradeoff between problem-solving and learning goals: two experiments for demonstrating assistance dilemma. In: Proceedings of the Annual Meeting of the Cognitive Science Society, vol. 34 (2012)

The Role of Media and Advance Organizers in Learning for 5-Year-Old Children

Yijia Wang(✉) , Lihanjing Wu , and Ting Zhang

Central China Normal University, 152 Luoyu Road, Wuhan 430079, Hubei, China
1430739910@qq.com

Abstract. Children are increasingly exposed to educational videos in their daily life. Video learning is popular for children to acquire information and knowledge. However, there is a lack of research to compare video and face-to-face learning directly. Moreover, the advance organizer is a kind of guiding material often used in teaching, but there are also few researches aimed at children. Whether an interaction between the learning media and the advance organizer is a good question to explore. The present study examines the effects of two types of learning media (video and face-to-face) and advance organizer on 5-year-old children's learning of biological knowledge. Eighty 5-year-old children were taught biology knowledge in four experimental conditions: video learning with advance organizer, video learning without advance organizer, face-to-face learning with advance organizer, and face-to-face learning without advance organizer. The results indicated that only the learning media showed a significant main effect, while the advance organizer and the interaction between the two were not significant. We could infer that compared with watching videos, children learn biological knowledge better in face-to-face condition. The advance organizer in different learning media conditions does not have a significant impact on children's learning. The research results are explained by children's mental representations and other related theories, and some suggestions are put forward to improve children's video learning.

Keywords: Learning Media · Video · Advance Organizer · Learning Effects

1 Introduction

Nowadays, the media is booming and it has become an important channel for children to acquire knowledge. Studies have shown that television and video are the most commonly used media for American children aged 0–8, with children aged 2–4 watching more than an hour a day on average [1]. Through media, children can get access to information, images, emotions, rules and values in life [2]. They actively choose media and actively absorb the information it provides into their value system [3].

Compared with traditional face-to-face teaching, what is the impact of teaching video on children's learning effect? In a 2010 review, Barr focused on the *"video deficit effect"*, the phenomenon that "young children tend to learn less well after watching a video presentation than after watching a face-to-face presentation [4]." In 2021, Strouse and Samson [5] further found through meta-analysis and empirical research that children would show the peak of this *"video deficit effect"* at the age of 3, and it was mainly reflected in the aspects of imitation, language learning and object retrieval tasks. Previously, reviewing the American Academy of Pediatrics study on television and young children, Anderson and Pempek found that when assessing learning via video versus a live presentation of equivalent content, children typically learn much less from video. In addition, Anderson et al. [6] believe that children's TV programs have negative effects on children's language, cognition and attention development.

Therefore, compared with face-to-face learning, video learning will have more adverse effects on children. However, previous studies on the"video deficit effect" did not involve learning tasks such as recall and understanding. Therefore, we plan to explore whether the video will also negatively affect learning tasks such as recall or understanding.

When AuSubel proposed the "advance organizer" concept, he pointed out that it could help learners learn new knowledge. Since then, scholars have carried out research on the influence of advance organizers successively. Barnes and Clawson [7] argue that advance organizers do not promote learning. At the very least, according to Corkill [8], advance organizers help learners perform recall tasks. Mayer and Stone's [9, 10] study found that advance organizers only work if properly designed and applied. Corkill [8] went further and found that the best conditions for the advance organizer include the following: learners will not make proper connections between prior knowledge and the material to be studied without outside help, learners must participate in the advance organizer, learners have enough time to learn the advance organizer and the material, recall tests were given at least after a brief delay. In addition, Neuman et al. [11] found that the advance organizer was an effective mediator in improving children's understanding and memory of important information in television storylines.

Previous studies on the influence of advance organizers on learning results have drawn quite different conclusions. However, based on that, we have reason to speculate that advance organizers can play a positive role under appropriate conditions. In addition, few studies have compared the use of advance organizers in different learning media. Based on this, we will explore the influence of advance organizers across different media (mainly video and face-to-face).

We choose biological knowledge as the main learning content. Experience shows that preschoolers can understand a range of biological knowledge and are curious about the unknown animal world. In addition, some scholars have found that early science skills are essential for children's later academic success, suggesting that educational media could be used to close the gap in children's scientific achievement [12].

Based on our literature review, it makes sense to further explore the influence of advance organizers across different learning media. This study includes two experimental conditions, video and face-to-face, and advance organizers are designed according to the learning materials of biological knowledge. Among them, the learning effect is mainly measured by children's "recall" of key content. Based on previous research, we would expect children to learn less effectively under video conditions. We also expect the adding advance organizers will improve learning effect for children. In addition, we also expect the learning effect to be better in the video condition with advance organizers.

2   Method

2.1   Participants

Eighty 5-year-olds children (M = 67.9 months, SD = 2.7; 38 boys) participated in the experiment. These children are from a public kindergarten in Binzhou City, Shandong Province. Most of them come from middle-class families, and the parents of these children are doctors. All of the participants were native Chinese speakers. The children are known to have no speech or other developmental disabilities. After screening the questions before the experiment, no children were excluded, and they all said they did not know the informant. This experiment used a 2 (Media: video vs. face-to-face) × 2 (Condition: with advance organizer vs. without advance organizer) between-subjects design. Children were randomly assigned to one of four conditions: video learning with advance organizer (n = 20, M = 68.2 months, SD = 2.3; 12 boys), video learning without advance organizer (n = 20, M = 67.4 months, SD = 2.7; 11 boys), face-to-face learning with advance organizer (n = 20, M = 67.7 months, SD = 2.8; 7 boys), face-to-face learning without advance organizer (n = 20, M = 68.5 months, SD = 2.8; 8 boys).

2.2   Materials

Learning content. We choose the "secret of hummingbird flight" with pictures and gestures. The script used in learning materials (see Appendix A for details) was formed based on previous research by Chinese scholars, and it took about 75 s.

Advance organizer. We refer to the research of Chinese scholars [13]. Before learning, a language description is presented, then the learning script includes an opening question, general introduction, content summary and guiding questions. The length of time the advance organizer clips is about 30 s, and the interval between the advance organizer and the learning content is 3 s, in case children's exhaustion may influence subsequent learning.

Learning material. The differences in materials among the four conditions are as follows: in Condition A, an advance organizer was added before the learning content, and children learned through prerecorded videos; In Condition B, the learning content was presented to the children without any advance organizer, and the children learned through the prerecorded video. In Condition C, the advance organizer was added before the learning content, and the children learned through face-to-face teaching by the informant. In Condition D, the children were presented with the learning content without any advance organizer, and the children learned through face-to-face teaching. The subject and the informant were the same adult female under the four conditions, and the pictures and gestures of the informant were consistent, to ensure that the learning materials presented to the children were as identical as possible.

Pre-test questions. The six questions in the pre-test were relative to the learning content, which was to explore whether they mastered the knowledge of "hummingbird flapping its wings and flying". We scored children's answer as 1 for "correct", 0 for "I don't know", and as -1 for "wrong".

Learning effect test. In order to control the practice effect, the same six questions were used as in the pre-test. In order to reflect the influence of experimental treatment, a total of 4 multiple-choice questions and two essay questions were designed to assess the children's recall and retention of key content. The learning effect score was equal to the post-test score minus the pre-test score.

Subjective assessment. The subjective assessment questions were respectively adapted from the "Pressure", "Effort" and "Enjoyment" parts of the Intrinsic Motivation Inventory [14]. There are five questions in total: (1) "Did you find yourself relaxed while learning the secrets of hummingbird flight?", (2) "Did you find yourself nervous while learning the secrets of hummingbird flight?", (3) "Did you feel like using up a lot of energy when learned the secrets of hummingbird flight?", (4) "Would you like to learn the secrets of hummingbird flight by watching the video/face-to-face as you just did?", (5) "Would you like to learn the secrets of hummingbird flight by face-to-face/watching the video?". The first three questions were used to test the efforts children devoted to the learning process. The last two questions are used to judge whether children have any preference for learning media. A three-point Likert scale was used for all questions, with children selecting "No" (scored as 0), "A little bit" (scored as 1), and "A lot" (scored as 2). Among them, question (1) adopts reverse scoring (Fig. 1).

See Appendix B for details about all the questions in the experiment.

(a)   **(b)**

Fig. 1. Materials under video conditions. (A) with advance organizer; (B) without advance organizer

2.3 Procedure

Before the experiment began, we conducted an preliminary online experiment on a 5-year-old child, aiming to test the child's understanding of learning content and questions, to further modify and improve the problems to ensure the experiment's feasibility.

The experiment was conducted in an empty classroom in the kindergarten. Children individually came into the classroom to meet the experimenter. The four conditions were carried out in sequence. In all conditions, the subjects were first asked whether they knew the informant. All children responded "No". Before the experiment began, children were taken the pre-test. Next, the children were taught the "secret of hummingbird flight" according to their conditions. After learning, children were taken the post-test. Finally, children in the four conditions were asked to finish the subjective assessment.

3 Results

This study used a two-factor, two-level, between-subjects design to measure whether media and advance organizers affect 5-year-old children's learning of biological knowledge. Descriptive data are shown in Table 1.

Table 1. Means of learning effect (SDs in parentheses) according to media and with or without advance organizer.

	advance organizer	Learning effect			The cognitive load	Learning media preference	
		Pre-test	Post-test	Final score		Video	Face-to-face
video	with advance organizer	-0.70 (1.76)	2.50 (2.01)	3.20 (2.40)	2.15 (1.65)	1.80 (0.40)	1.80 (0.40)
	without advance organizer	-0.60 (2.13)	2.10 (2.70)	2.70 (3.32)	2.00 (1.55)	1.85 (0.36)	1.75 (0.43)
Face-to-face	with advance organizer	-0.65 (1.35)	3.25 (2.09)	3.90 (2.74)	2.30 (1.38)	1.30 (0.84)	1.45 (0.80)
	without advance organizer	-0.75 (1.58)	4.20 (1.69)	4.95 (2.31)	2.35 (1.49)	1.55 (0.67)	1.55 (0.74)

Note. 1.By paired-samples T test, the test scores before and after the experiment were significantly different ($p < 0.001$). 2. Keep two decimal places in the data

3.1 Learning Effect

In order to test whether there is an interaction between media and advance organizer on children's learning of biological knowledge, we used two-way ANOVA, with learning media (video versus face-to-face) and advance organizer (with versus without advance organizer) as the between-subjects variables. The results showed that there are significant differences in the mean scores of children's learning among different experimental conditions (see Fig. 2), but there is no interaction between media and advance organizers (see Table 2), $F(1, 75) = 1.037, p = 0.312, \eta_p^2 = 0.014$. In addition, the results of main effect analysis showed that the influence of media on the learning effect was statistically significant, $F(1,75) = 4.659, p < 0.05, \eta_p^2 = 0.058$, while there is no significant main effect of the advance organizer, $F(1, 75) = 0.479, p = 0.491, \eta_p^2 = 0.006$.

In order to further test the main effect of learning media, pairwise-comparative analysis was conducted. The results showed (see Table 3) that the means of learning effect under face-to-face condition was 1.325 points higher than that under video condition (95% confidence interval: 0.102–2.548), $p < 0.05$.

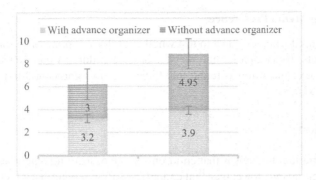

Fig. 2. Means of learning effect under different conditions.

Table 2. Analysis of interaction between media and advance organizers.

Variable	Two-way ANOVA				
	Tape III SS	df	F	p	η_p^2
Media	34.656*	1	4.659	0.034	0.058
Advance organizer	3.566	1	0.479	0.491	0.006
Media × Advance organizer	7.711	1	1.037	0.312	0.014

Note. 1.*, $p < 0.05$. 2. Keep three decimal places in the data

Table 3. Main effect analysis of media (SDs in parentheses).

Media	Learning effect M	pairwise-comparative analysis	
		MD	p
Video	3.100(0.437)	-1.325*	0.058
Face-to-face	4.425(0.431)	1.325*	0.006

Note. 1.*, $p < 0.05$. 2.Keep three decimal places in the data. 3.The significant was Bonferroni's adjusted

3.2   The Cognitive Load

In order to test whether the cognitive load is one of the reasons for the differences in children's learning effects, one-way ANOVA was conducted with the cognitive load as the dependent variable, the media and advance organizer as independent variables. The results showed no significant difference in children's cognitive load caused by different media or advance organizers ($p = 0.480$; $p = 0.897$), which could not be used as a scientific basis for the discussion of subsequent results.

3.3   Learning Media Preference

We adopted paired-samples T-test to test whether children's preference for media influences the results. By comparing the mean scores of children's preference for learning media in the experiment, it was found that there was no significant difference between them ($p = 0.883$).

4   Discussion

One of our important findings is that children's score of learning outcomes under video condition is significantly lower than that under face-to-face condition, which is consistent with the research results of "video defect" mentioned above [4, 5], confirming hypothesis 1. It indicates face-to-face learning is more effective than video learning for 5-year-old children.

According to the theory of mental representation, preschool children's cognitive and social immaturity make it difficult to transfer information obtained from two-dimensional videos to three-dimensional real life [4]. For example, in the video condition, some answers to "Can hummingbirds fly upside down?" "Can hummingbirds stop in the air?" in the post-test are "No" instead of "I don't know", which reflects that children can receive the information about hummingbird flight provided by the video, but they have wrong cognition between the video and real information, resulting in poor learning effect. From a practical point of view, we observed that the children in the video condition frequently appeared inattention, eye wandering and other phenomena in the second half of the video. Moreover, compared to video learning, in face-to-face conditions, the informant inevitably interacted with children in expression, paid attention to their eyes and showed more natural and fluent voice and intonation. However, the informant in videos was stereotypical in expression, voice and intonation, and interaction. Further research should explore whether these objective factors lead to the gap in learning effects between video and face-to-face.

Another important finding was that the advance organizer has no significant main effect on children's learning, which is inconsistent with previous studies [8, 15–19], and also contradicts the second hypothesis of this study. According to the theory of mental representation, an effective advance organizer should act as a giant with higher mental representation and play the role of "scaffolding" in children's learning.

There are two possible reasons to explain the contradiction. First, Mayer and Stone [9, 10] pointed out that the effectiveness of advance organizers is subject to certain conditions. One concerns the subjective factor, that is, the rationality of the advance organizer. The advance organizer in this study was designed according to the concept defined by scholars, and its scientificity, effectiveness and compatibility with the correct concept need to be further evaluated by experts. Therefore, advance organizer did not play a significant role in this study is understandable. In addition, objective factors depend Corkill [8] proposed that it is necessary for the advance organizer to perform recall test to evaluate the learning effect of learners after a short delay. However, this factor was not considered in this study, and there was no time interval between the learning and recall test, which may be one of the reasons why the advance organizer did not show certain advantages.

Second, though a three-second interval before learning was added, we found that advance organizer would make children tired, leading to poor learning effect on the subsequent learning, which is the deficiency of this study. Of course, we do not rule out that the extra 30 s gives children a greater opportunity to learn. Neuman [20] has responded to this in a study on joining advance organizers before reading, two comparative teaching methods are used to control experimental bias caused by treatment effects, and similar methods can be used in subsequent experiments to exclude experimental errors in this part.

In addition, the advance organizer accounted for about 28% (30s/108s) of the total learning time in this study. Whereas in a related study by Neuman et al., [11] the advance organizer accounted for 6.25% (1.5 min/24 min). Unfortunately, previous studies have not clearly stated that the time ratio of advance organizers is the reason for the difference in learning outcomes, so further studies are needed to examine this.

Finally, there was no interaction between the media and the advance organizer on the learning effect. However, they did show some differences: the learning effect with the advance organizer was relatively better in the video condition, while the learning effect without the advance organizer was relatively better in the face-to-face condition. Calvert et al. [21] found that the advance organizer combined with relevant visual effects may be more effective, which provides an explanation for this result and is also the basis for hypothesis 3 above. However, this view has not been fully verified by the facts. On the one hand, the sample size is insufficient and the representative is not high. On the other hand, the design of the advance organizer and its use under different media conditions are not scientific enough, so the experimental results are inconsistent with the previous research conclusions. Based on the different but insignificant results of media and advance organizers on learning effect in this study, future research should expand the sample size, continue to conduct repeated experiments and determine more universal conclusions.

According to the above results, in the future children's teaching, we should appropriately reduce the time of video teaching in addition to the necessary time and space restrictions. Use face-to-face teaching as much as possible, pay attention to emotional communication and facial interaction with children, and give children words and actions feedback at all times. Of course, video can also be combined with face-to-face teaching, to learn from each other, enrich the role of educational forms, and maximize the learning efficiency of children. At the same time, following the new trend of media development, we can try to use advance organizers to improve the quality of teaching video. However, further research is needed to determine what form the advance organizer should present to achieve the best optimization effect, how to design the content to be more scientific and practical, and whether there is an upper limit on the duration.

Appendix A

Advance Organizers

Have you ever seen a hummingbird? Do you know how hummingbirds fly in the air? Hummingbirds are among the most beautiful birds in the world. Their light body and fast movements in flight have impressed people. Now you will hear the story of the hummingbird's flying secret, Listen carefully to the introduction of hummingbirds, and see what is the unique flying ability of them? Pause three seconds.

Secret of Hummingbird Flight

Hummingbirds come from the rainforests of South America, they are the smallest birds on the earth, because they look like bees, so people call them hummingbirds. They also make a "humming" sound when flying, so they are also called humming birds. Although hummingbirds are so small, don't underestimate them just because they're small. Hummingbirds have a special ability to flap their wings. Our hands can only flap twice a second, but their wings can flap 90 times a second. So not only can they fly through the sky like other birds, but they have no problem staying in the sky and flying backwards! They are also the only birds in the world that can fly and stop in the air. This flying ability of hummingbirds is the same as that of helicopters we see in our life.

Appendix B

Question	Question type	Answer score
1.1 Is the hummingbird the smallest bird in the world? Please tell me "Yes", "No" or "I don't know"	Pre-test	Yes (scored as 1) / No (scored as 0) / I don't know (scored as -1)
1.2 Do you know what a hummingbird is also called?	Pre-test	Humming birds (scored as 1) / No (scored as 0) / Other answers (scored as -1)
1.3 Do you know how many times a hummingbird's wings can flap in a second?	Pre-test	90 (scored as 1) / No (scored as 0) / Other answers (scored as -1)
1.4 Can hummingbirds stay in the sky? Please tell me "Yes", "No" or "I don't know"	Pre-test	Yes (scored as 1) / No (scored as 0) / I don't know (scored as -1)
1.5 Can hummingbirds fly backwards? Please tell me "Yes", "No" or "I don't know"	Pre-test	Yes (scored as 1) / No (scored as 0) / I don't know (scored as -1)

(continued)

(*continued*)

Question	Question type	Answer score
1.6 Is this flying ability of hummingbirds same as helicopters we see in our life? Please tell me "Yes", "No" or "I don't know"	Pre-test	Yes (scored as 1) / No (scored as 0) / I don't know (scored as -1)
2.1 Is the hummingbird the smallest bird in the world? Please tell me "Yes", "No" or "I don't know"	Post-test	Yes (scored as 1) / No (scored as 0) / I don't know (scored as -1)
2.2 Do you know what a hummingbird is also called?	Post-test	Humming birds (scored as 1) / No (scored as 0) / Other answers (scored as -1)
2.3 Do you know how many times a hummingbird's wings can flap in a second?	Post-test	90 (scored as 1) / No (scored as 0) / Other answers (scored as -1)
2.4 Can hummingbirds stay in the sky? Please tell me "Yes", "No" or "I don't know"	Post-test	Yes (scored as 1) / No (scored as 0) / I don't know (scored as -1)
2.5 Can hummingbirds fly backwards? Please tell me "Yes", "No" or "I don't know"	Post-test	Yes (scored as 1) / No (scored as 0) / I don't know (scored as -1)
2.6 Is this flying ability of hummingbirds same as helicopters we see in our life? Please tell me "Yes", "No" or "I don't know"	Post-test	Yes (scored as 1) / No (scored as 0) / I don't know (scored as -1)

(*continued*)

(*continued*)

Question	Question type	Answer score
3.1 Did you find yourself relaxed while learning the secrets of hummingbird flight? Please tell me "No", "A little bit" or "A lot" (Scored as 2, 1 and 0)	Pressure	 ■ No ■ A little bit ■ A lot
3.2 Did you find yourself nervous while learning the secrets of hummingbird flight? Please tell me "No", "A little bit" or "A lot" (Scored as 2, 1 and 0)	Pressure	 ■ No ■ A little bit ■ A lot
3.3 Did you feel like using up a lot of energy when learned the secrets of hummingbird flight? Please tell me "No", "A little bit" or "A lot" (Scored as 2, 1 and 0)	Effort	 ■ No ■ A little bit ■ A lot
4.1 Would you like to learn the secrets of hummingbird flight by watching the video/face-to-face as you just did? Please tell me "No", "A little bit" or "A lot" (Scored as 2, 1 and 0)	Enjoyment	 ■ No ■ A little bit ■ A lot

(*continued*)

(*continued*)

Question	Question type	Answer score
4.2 Would you like to learn the secrets of hummingbird flight by face-to-face/watching the video? Please tell me "No", "A little bit" or "A lot" (Scored as 2, 1 and 0)	Enjoyment	 ■ No ■ A little bit ■ A lot

References

1. Rideout, V.: The common sense census: Media use by kids age zero to eight. R/OL, America: Common Sense Media. https://www.commonsensemedia.org/research/the-common-sense-census-media-use-by-kids-age-zero-to-eight-2017
2. Gerbner, G., Gross, L., Morgan, M., et al.: Growing up with television: The cultivation perspective. M. In Bryant J, Zillmann D eds., Media effects: Advances in theory and research. Lawrence Erlbaum Associates, 17–41(1994)
3. Brown, J.D.: Cantor J. An agenda for research on youth and the media. J. J. Adolescent Health **27**(2), 2–7(2000)
4. Barr, R.: Transfer of learning between 2D and 3D sources during infancy: informing theory and practice. J. Develop. Rev. **30**(2), 128–154 (2010). https://doi.org/10.1016/j.dr.2010.03.001
5. Strouse, G.A., Samson, J.E.: Learning from video: a meta-analysis of the video deficit in children ages 0 to 6 years. J. Child development **92**(1), e20–e38 (2021)
6. Anderson, D.R.: Television and very young children. J. American Behav. Sci. **48**(5), 505–522 (2005). https://doi.org/10.1177/0002764204271506
7. Barnes, B.R., Clawson, E.U.: Do advance organizers facilitate learning? recommendations for further research based on an analysis of 32 studies. J. Rev. Educ. Res. **45**(4), 637–659 (1975)
8. Corkill, A.J.: Advance organizers: facilitators of recall. J. Educ. Psychol. Rev. **4**(1), 33–67 (1992). https://doi.org/10.1007/bf01322394
9. Mayer, R.E.: Can advance organizers influence meaningful learning? J. Rev. Educ. Res. **49**(2), 371–383 (1979)
10. Stone, C.L.: A meta-analysis of advance organizer studies. J. J. Experiment. Educ. **51**(4), 194–199 (1983). https://doi.org/10.1080/00220973.1983.11011862
11. Neuman, S.B., Burden, D., Holden, E.: Enhancing children's comprehension of a televised story through previewing. J. Educ. Res. **83**(5), 258–265 (1990). https://doi.org/10.1080/002 20671.1990.10885967
12. Schroeder, E.L., Kirkorian, H.L.: When seeing is better than doing: preschoolers' transfer of STEM skills using touchscreen games. J. Front. Psychol. 7, 1377 (2016). https://doi.org/10. 3389/fpsyg.2016.01377
13. Jing, M., Kirkorian, H.L.: Teaching with televised stories: a story-focused narrative preview supports learning in young children. J. Child develop. **91**(5), e1101–e1118 (2020). https://doi.org/10.1111/cdev.13385

14. Choi, J., Mogami, T., Medalia, A.: Intrinsic motivation inventory: an adapted measure for schizophrenia research. J. Schizophrenia Bull. **36**(5), 966–976 (2010)
15. Mendelsohn, D.: Applying learning strategies in the second/foreign language listening comprehension lesson. J. A guide for the teaching of second language listening, 132–150(1995)
16. Marvin Willerman, Richard A. Mac Harg,: The concept map as an advance organizer. J. Res. Sci. Teach. **28**(8), 705–711 (1991). https://doi.org/10.1002/tea.3660280807
17. Hudson Shihusa, Fred N. Keraro,: Using advance organizers to enhance students' motivation in learning biology. EURASIA J. Math. Sci. Technol. Educ. **5**(4),(2009). https://doi.org/10.12973/ejmste/75290
18. Ausubel, D.P., Novak, J.D., Hanesian, H.: Educational psychology: A cognitive view. M. New York: holt, rinehart and Winston(1968)
19. Fisch, S.M.: A capacity model of children's comprehension of educational content on television. J. Media Psychol. **2**(1), 63–91 (2000). https://doi.org/10.1207/S1532785XMEP0201_4
20. Neuman, S.B.: Enhancing children's comprehension through previewing. J. National Read. Conf. Yearbook **37**, 219–224 (1988)
21. Sandra L. Calvert, Tracey L. Gersh,: The selective use of sound effects and visual inserts for children's television story comprehension. J. Appl. Develop. Psychol. **8**(4), 363–375 (1987). https://doi.org/10.1016/0193-3973(87)90027-X

Chemist-Computer Interaction: Representation Learning for Chemical Design via Refinement of SELFIES VAE

Tom Xu, Nick Velzeboer, and Yoshihiro Maruyama$^{(\boxtimes)}$

School of Computing, The Australian National University, Canberra, Australia
{tom.xu,yoshihiro.maruyama}@anu.edu.au

Abstract. Representation learning for molecular structure is essential in helping chemists with novel drug discovery and other scientific tasks. Here we refine neural networks for chemical representation learning, especially for SELFIES VAE, and thereby improve upon generative models for chemical design and discovery. For model evaluation we propose five metrics (syntactic/semantic validities; degeneracy; emptiness proportion; and diversity of generation) and experimentally demonstrate that our refined model outperforms the standard models that exist in the scientific literature today, which is achieved by integrating the symbolic grammatical structure of compounds with statistical representation learning.

Keywords: Variational Autoencoder · SMILES Representation · SELFIES Representation · Chemical Compound Design · Drug Discovery

1 Introduction

The advent of computational chemistry has presented researchers with multiple methods for molecular structure learning, each offering distinct advantages and challenges. Graphical methods, for example, are often used for their intuitive visual representation, enabling easy perception of molecule structure and chemical bonding [4,13]. However, graphs-based methods are currently more limited than string-based ones (see, for example, [1]); the methods become complex for larger molecules, and they may pose challenges in terms of computational processing. On the other hand, there are string-based representation methods with the most common representation being SMILES [11]. String-based representation methods offer benefits such as lower computational complexity, ease of integration into existing neural network architectures, and suitability for sequence generation tasks. Given these advantages, our focus in this study lies with string-based representation.

Grammatical structure can be incorporated into string-based methods either explicitly as a set of rules [2,6] or implicitly in the string representation [5,8]. Introducing grammar decreases the number of invalid outputs, allowing for more reliable molecular design. Additionally, it allows for more control over the model's interpretability, as one can manage the amount of grammar information introduced. This could potentially mitigate overfitting. In terms of the neural architecture, in this study, we use a Variational Autoencoder (VAE). VAEs have shown promise in their ability to learn the complex distribution of molecular structures and generate new, unseen molecules. The specifics of the VAE architecture will be elaborated upon in a later section.

Several existing grammar-based approaches, such as the Grammar Variational Autoencoder (GVAE) [6] and the Syntax-Directed Variational Autoencoder (SD-VAE) [2], have made significant strides in this field. They have been instrumental in producing syntactically valid string representations. However, despite these advancements, these models struggle to guarantee complete syntactic and semantic validity, such as ring closure. This does not invalidate the potential of grammar-based approaches. Rather, it elucidates the need for a more sophisticated grammar that can tackle these complexities. To address this, we turn to the Self-referencing Embedded Strings (SELFIES) representation. SELFIES provides a robust string-based representation, where every string corresponds to a semantically valid molecule. This means it passes RDKIT's [7] grammatical and semantic validity tests, and follows valency rules. One possible perspective on a SELFIES string is that it is a set of instructions to create semantically valid SMILES strings. In the original paper, [5] show how to convert a SELFIES string into a SMILES string. In this process, each SELFIES symbol represents a rule vector, which is replaced with a part of a SMILES string or another derivation state. This sequence of rule-driven transformations takes into account chemical and syntactical constraints, such as the maximum number of valence bonds, resulting in a valid SMILES string.

Nevertheless, SELFIES is not without its limitations. Certain challenges, such as the degeneracy problem where different SELFIES strings can represent the same molecule, must be addressed. In addition, while the SELFIES representation guarantees semantic validity, it does not imply chemical stability issues [1]. In this study, we endeavour to improve upon the original SELFIES VAE architecture. We aim to address its limitations and build a more effective generative model, demonstrating this through a robust proof of concept. Additionally, we explore the fascinating possibilities of algebraic operations within this model. Our research seeks to enhance the performance and potential of SELFIES, propelling the capabilities of molecular structure learning forward.

2   Neural Architecture

VAE-based generative models have been demonstrated to be well suited for string generation tasks, and have several advantages:

1. **Versatility in architecture design**: Encoder and decoder architectures as well as objective functions can be independently designed and varied to suit different tasks. Combinations of encoder and decoder design can take advantages of different neural networks. In our implementation, we chose an

asymmetrical design that leverages the pattern detection power of a CNN encoder as well as the memory capability of a GRU decoder.

2. **Efficiency in training**: VAEs are relatively easy to train compared to other generative models like Generative Adversarial Networks (GANs) or transformer-based Large Language Models (LLMs). VAEs use a straightforward optimisation objective that combines a reconstruction loss and a regularisation term, which can be optimised using standard backpropagation and stochastic gradient descent. The efficiency in training boosts iterative improvement in model design and fine-tuning.

3. **Ease of access to latent representation**: The latent space is usually clearly defined in a VAE and the embedding of training data can be accessed and analysed on demand. Tracing the encoding and decoding process end-to-end from training data to reconstruction is relatively easy, enabling easy interpretability of the model. Furthermore, a clearly defined latent space allows sampling methods to be easily implemented and interpreted for the associated generative model (the trained decoder).

Apart from these inherent advantages of a VAE, the techniques from the previous DisCoPyro research [10] give a theoretical foundation for exploring methods to incorporate grammatical structure into VAEs. In particular, the variational inferencing technique from DisCoPyro [10] allows us to explore the model parameters more efficiently. Furthermore, we employ Neural String Diagrams [12] to reason and design models. They allow us to describe different neural network components in a mathematically rigorous manner while maintaining a good level of readability. This study was conducted based on these theoretical foundations.

The overall VAE architecture in this study can be summarised into the following components: (1) SMILES-SELFIES Pre-processing; (2) CNN encoder; (3) latent space; (4) GRU decoder, as illustrated below. Note that the input and output of our VAE model are both in SELFIES format. After the VAE model is trained, the GRU decoder is used as a generative model together with post-processing to convert SELFIES to SMILES (Fig. 1).

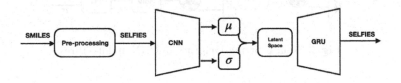

Fig. 1. Overview of SELFIES VAE

2.1 Architecture Specification

Dataset. The raw dataset used in this study is the QM9 dataset, which can be found in this reference [9]. It comprises 132,000 SMILES representations of small organic molecules. The SMILES strings in this dataset have a maximum length of 22 characters and an average length of about 15.11 characters.

Pre-processing. The SMILES strings from the dataset are first translated into SELFIES strings for training. As part of the translation, a SELFIES alphabet is automatically generated based on the SMILES characters present in the original dataset. The resulting SELFIES strings are then pre-processed into one-hot matrices according to the generated SELFIES alphabet for model training. Following the translation, each SELFIES string is one-hot-encoded as a matrix. In such a matrix, each row is a one-hot vector that identifies a particular element in the SELFIES alphabet. The position of a row in the matrix corresponds to the position of the element in the SELFIES string. Furthermore, the number of rows in the one-hot encoded matrix is fixed according to the length of the longest SELFIES string in the training dataset. In addition, a no-operation symbol [NOP] is introduced to the SELFIES alphabet to pad the matrix to the correct dimension.

CNN Encoder. The encoder consists of two 1-dimensional convolutional layers followed by a fully connected layer. The decision of using 1-dimensional convolution is based on the sequential nature of the input data. As a simple architecture it allows efficient training while maintaining good explainability of the model.

GRU Decoder. The decoder is a single stack Gated Recurrent Unit (GRU) and consists of 100 neurons. It is well established that GRUs are particularly effective for sequential data. We purposely limited the decoder's complexity as compared to the encoder to mitigate the common posterior collapse problems with VAE models. Furthermore, as the dataset is not particularly complex, we expect a simple architecture is sufficient for the task and will give indicative results to validate our approach (Figs. 2 and 3).

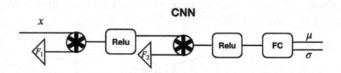

Fig. 2. Neural String Diagram of CNN architecture

Loss Function. At the current stage we decided to use the classic reconstruction loss together with a small KL-divergence weight to account for posterior collapse problem.

Latent Space. Based on the size and complexity of the dataset we decided on a range of low dimensions (5 to 20 dimension vector spaces) to experiment. The processed training data (18×21 one-hot matrices) seem to warrant a high

GRU

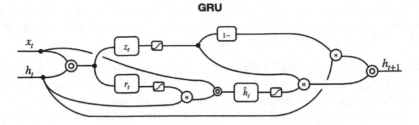

Fig. 3. Neural String Diagram of GRU architecture

dimensional latent space, but they are obviously sparse matrices. Therefore, we chose latent dimensions that are comparable to the actual SELFIES length. This is to avoid model overfitting problems.

Generative Model. The trained decoder can be used as a generative model by first sampling from the prior distribution (multidimensional standard Gaussian distribution) over the latent space. The sampled latent vectors are then decoded into SELFIES. Finally, the decoded SELFIES are translated into SMILES.

3   Experiments and Results

Based on experiments with GVAE we established several metrics to evaluate the output of the generative model. These are:

- **Syntactical validity**: Whether the generated strings follow the specified grammar exactly. This evaluates whether the grammatical information is properly introduced to the model. It is also the basic prerequisite towards a useful generative model.
- **Semantic validity**: Whether the generated strings can pass the semantic checks provided by the RDKit package, setting the sanitize argument in the MolFromSmiles method to True (rdkit.Chem.MolFromSmiles(smiles, sanitize=True)) [7]. This is one of the most important metrics because if a model doesn't generate a high proportion of semantically valid strings, it would jeopardise downstream tasks.
- **Degeneracy**: The average length of the generated SMILES string compared to the average length of the dataset. Due to the way SELFIES representation is formulated, it introduces the complication of degeneracy problem where seemingly long and complex strings actually represent very simple SMILES. Therefore, we calculated this metric specifically for SELFIES based models.
- **Empty SMILES**: The proportion of null results in a batch of generated (translated in case of SELFIES) SMILES strings. High proportion of null results directly indicate that the model is overfitted.
- **Diversity**: Number of unique strings in a batch over the batch size. While ensuring robustness in both syntactic and semantic validity, diversity is the

key metrics we set out to improve. High generative diversity indicates that the latent space is well regularised; the model is not overfitted; and the grammatical information is well integrated.

First, we evaluated SMILES-based GVAE generative model published on their GitHub page. Then we recreated the example VAE experiment from SELFIES's GitHub repository and used the result as a baseline. Based on their model we experimented with several improved architecture designs and hyperparameter specifications. The current best result was achieved through a CNN encoder and GRU decoder with a 12-dimensional latent space as introduced in the last section.

Below is a model comparison table. We also included the results from our experiment with GVAE and reported results from SD-VAE to demonstrate the differences between the SMILES-based approach and SELFIES based approach.

Table 1. Comparing SMILES-based models and SELFIES based models.

	GVAE [6]	SD-VAE [2]	SELFIES VAE [5]	**Our Model**
Dataset	250k ZINC [3]	250k ZINC	QM9 [9]	QM9
Syntactical Validity	99.6%	Not Reported	100%	100%
Semantic Validity	6.8%	43.5%	100%	100%
Degeneracy	NA	NA	8.31 / 15.11	**13.67/15.11**
Empty SMILES	20%	Not Reported	11.25%	**2.95%**
Diversity	–	–	14.8%	**65.4%**

4   Discussion

As mentioned above, being able to generate valid results is essential to the utility of a generative model. There are two levels of validity involved in string representations: syntactic validity and semantic validity where the prior underlies the latter. As shown in Table 1 above, the GVAE demonstrated near-perfect syntactic validity with respect to an explicit context-free SMILES grammar. It introduced many helpful techniques of integrating grammatical information into neural network models. However, the semantic validity of the SMILES strings generated by the GVAE was poor. Unfortunately, downstream tasks such as de novo molecule design rely heavily on chemistry semantic information. The semantic validity deficiency of GVAE is expected, after all, context free grammar by its nature is not meant to capture semantic information. Despite the drawbacks, the GVAE's approach is still well-suited for systems and tasks that can be well described by context-free grammars. With these findings, we investigated several other SMILES-based models, including SD-VAE which attaches semantic constraints to syntax trees generated during the decoding process. As shown in Table 1, the

SD-VAE reported a significant increase in semantic validity compared to the GVAE. However, we considered the result still appears insufficient to facilitate downstream tasks. On the other hand, SELFIES was designed from the ground up to address the validity problem by incorporating valence-bond rules, ring closure and branch location handling. Based on our results, all SELFIES strings were semantically valid, which aligns to the claim of 100% robustness from its authors. That is, any combination of the SELFIES alphabet rule vectors results in a SELFIES string that can be deterministically translated into a semantically valid SMILES string via SELFIES derivation algorithm. This is a strong advantage compared to SMILES-based approaches in terms of utility for downstream tasks. In this sense, we can consider SELFIES as a completely compatible set of instructions to create SMILES strings. However, as we discovered through extensive experimentation, the 100% robustness is achieved not without compromise. The main complication SELFIES introduces is degeneracy: seemingly sophisticated and diverse SELFIES strings can quickly degenerate into very simple molecules. For example, the following two seemingly complex SELFIES strings that appear different

- [F][F][=O][N][#C][C][Ring][Branch1][O][#N][O]
- [F][F][=C][#N][#C][=C][O][Branch1][O][Branch1][C][=C][#N][#C][=C]

can degenerate into the same SMILES string **FF** which is the molecule fluorine gas. This is because the first two SELFIES characters [**F**][**F**] already saturate the valence-bond and the characters following them are discarded during translation as the result. Therefore, directly calculating the diversity of generated SELFIES strings is an inaccurate assessment of the generative model's performance. Considering this, we translated the generated SELFIES string into SMILES strings. As shown in Table 1 our model significantly improved the diversity score which fulfilled our main objective. Moreover, with our model, we observed less degeneracy problem and improved structural complexity. Below is a further comparison between the generative model based on the original SELFIES VAE and our model. We sample 10,000 latent points according to the standard Gaussian prior distributions, decoded and post-processed them into SMILES. We recorded the top 3 most common strings from both models and respective proportions (Table 2).

Table 2. Comparison of top 3 most common generated SMILES.

	SELFIES VAE			Our Model		
Latent Dimension	50			12		
Top 3 Common	FF	F	NF	O = O	FF	N#N
Proportion	51.30%	7.64%	2.57%	7.46%	2.26%	2.18%

Although the SELFIES VAE generative model produced only semantically valid strings, the low diversity, high rate of empty strings, as well as low structural complexity signify that the model is significantly overfitted and did not learn to navigate the degeneracy problem of SELFIES. Our model, on the other hand, significantly improved the generative quality in all these aspects. Nevertheless, there is considerable space for improvement for our model. We would like to further increase the generative diversity and eliminate the empty generative results. However, as mentioned previously, QM9 dataset only contains small molecules with low structural diversity. Hence, to obtain better performance in those regards, our future models would be trained on the larger and more diverse ZINC dataset.

5   Concluding Remarks

Given the improvement we saw from our proof-of-concept model, we intend to explore more sophisticated upgrades to the current version. Furthermore, the model enabled us to experiment with encoding chemical reaction information as algebraic operations in the latent space. Some of the immediately actionable upgrades are: (1) fine-tune the CNN encoder architecture by introducing different types of convolutional kernels; (2) deepen the neural network; (3) train the model with the larger ZINC dataset; (4) tweak the objective function to include structural information beyond simple reconstruction rate, such as reconstruction length, number and length of rings, location and length of branches; (5) debug the generative model to drive down null string to 0%. On top of that we have started some preliminary exploration of possible algebraic operations on the latent space that can reasonably encode simple chemical reactions.

Acknowledgements. The authors would like to thank Eli Sennesh and Ichiro Takeuchi for informative discussions. This work was supported by JST (JPMJMS2033; JPMJFR206P).

References

1. Bilodeau, C., et al.: Generative models for molecular discovery: recent advances and challenges. Comput. Molec. Sci. **12**(5), e1608 (2022)
2. Dai, H., et al.: Syntax-directed variational autoencoder for structured data. In: Proceedings of ICLR (2018)
3. Irwin, J.J., et al.: Zinc-a free database of commercially available compounds for virtual screening. J. Chem. Inf. Model. **45**, 177–182 (2005)
4. Jin, W., et al.: Hierarchical generation of molecular graphs using structural motifs. In: Proceedings of ICML (2020)
5. Krenn, M., et al.: Self-referencing embedded strings (selfies): a 100% robust molecular string representation. Mach. Learn. Sci. Technol. 1 (2020)
6. Kusner, M.J., et al.: Grammar variational autoencoder. In: Proceedings of ICML (2017)
7. Landrum, G.: Rdkit: open-source cheminformatics software (2016). https://github.com/rdkit/rdkit/releases/tag/Release_2016_09_4
8. Lo, A., et al.: Recent advances in the self-referencing embedding strings (selfies) library. arXiv:2302.03620 (2023)

9. Ramakrishnan, R., et al.: Quantum chemistry structures and properties of 134 kilo molecules. Sci. Data **1**, 1–7 (2014)
10. Sennesh, E., Xu, T., Maruyama, Y.: Computing with categories in machine learning. In: Hammer, P., Alirezaie, M., Strannegard, C. (eds.) AGI 2023. LNCS, vol. 13921, pp. 244–254. Springer, Heidelberg (2023). https://doi.org/10.1007/978-3-031-33469-6_25
11. Weininger, D.: Smiles, a chemical language and information system. 1. introduction to methodology and encoding rules. J. Chem. Inf. Comput. Sci. **28**(1), 31–36 (1988)
12. Xu, T., Maruyama, Y.: Neural String Diagrams: A Universal Modelling Language for Categorical Deep Learning. In: Goertzel, B., Iklé, M., Potapov, A. (eds.) AGI 2021. LNCS (LNAI), vol. 13154, pp. 306–315. Springer, Cham (2022). https://doi.org/10.1007/978-3-030-93758-4_32
13. You, J., Liu, B., Ying, R., Pande, V., Leskovec, J.: Graph convolutional policy network for goal-directed molecular graph generation (2019)

9. Rangarajan, V. et al., Quantum chemistry from ... at finite temperature, Int. J. Chem. ... 57 (2023).

10. Scargle, J. D. ... State-space ... Contributing to astronomical time series. Astrophys. J. 263 (1982).

11. Thompson, K. ... Shannon ... C., Lalley ... ACL (2018), ... 52 (2019), ...

12. Wang, L. ... Spillmann, H. ... Physics ... Review D ... 100 (2019).

13. Sutskever, I. ... Neural information ... quantum ... prediction ... to probabilities and describing Rule 30 ... Int. J. Comput. Sci. 28 (2).

14. Smith, A. ... Neural Shannon ... Comput. ... Learning ...

15. ... Chaos and Mechanical ... old view ... J. Phys. M. ... W. Lalley ... N. ...

16. Lalley, S. ... K. D., Lalley ... S. Springer, Chem. 2022. https ... doi:10.1007/... System 123456 ...

17. Young, J. ... Liu, P.-X. ... Wu, R.-Z., Thompson ... Bayes ... A ... composite network for ... nonlinear and non-stationary ...

HCI for Health and Well-Being

Fighting the Increasing Shortage of Qualified Personnel in the Formal and Informal Care Sector with the HEROES App: Co-creation and Design with Older Adults

Simone Eicher(✉) 🆔 and Cornelia Ursprung 🆔

Institute for Ageing Research, University of Applied Sciences of Eastern Switzerland, Rosenbergstrasse 59, 9001 St. Gallen, Switzerland
{simone.eicher,cornelia.ursprung}@ost.ch

Abstract. Europe is projected to face a shortage of 1.5 million informal care-givers by 2060, while the formal care sector will also experience shortages of qualified personnel [1]. The share of older people (65 +) is expected to raise to 22% worldwide by 2050 [2]. Almost 90% felt health and social care systems should help older people stay in their homes longer [3]. However, family support is declining, while the formal sector cannot fill this gap. In the care industry, trust is essential. Recruiting trustworthy caregivers is time-consuming and costly, while many private people lack experience [4]. Recruitment support could be provided by experienced nurses and retired people looking for flexible work or financial stability [5, 6].

The *HEROES* project aims to solve these challenges by facilitating remote recruitment with an app, allowing experienced nurses and retirees to review candidates online. This ensures quality matching between candidates and job offers, helping recruiters to find trustworthy caregivers. Using candidates' video applications could make the recruitment process almost 25% faster and 90% cheaper [7].

To assure an inclusive and user-friendly solution, the *HEROES* app was developed with a user-centered approach [8], involving seniors, nurses, and families early on through co-creation iterations. This has proven especially valuable for vulnerable user groups, and in the health sector (e.g., 9–12). After each testing iteration, participants shared their findings in group discussions. Additionally, aspects of privacy and data protection, an important current challenge [13], as well as liability were considered by consulting experts from different fields.

Keywords: Ageing · Care · Co-creation · Data Protection · Older Adults · Recruitment · Smartphone App · User-centered design

1 Introduction

Europe is projected to face a shortage of 1.5 million informal caregivers by 2060, while the formal care sector will also experience shortages of qualified personnel [1]. The share of older people (65 +) is expected to raise to 22% worldwide by 2050 [2]. Alber, Köhler

[3] found that almost 90% felt health and social care systems should help older people stay in their homes longer. To achieve this, older adults will require assistance – infrequent at first – with daily tasks, e.g., groceries, or seeing a doctor. Families – especially adult women in their 40s and 50s – were traditionally helping with these activities, without pay, thus increasing the income inequality for older women. However, family support is rapidly declining due to the breakdown of families into smaller units, children living further away from their homes due to professional commitments, and rising female labor participation. [1].

In the care sector, not only numbers are important but also other factors like trust. Trust is the essence in the care industry and recruiting trustworthy caregivers is a time-consuming and costly process at best. Additionally, many private people not only lack time to find a suitable caregiver, but they also have limited or no experience in caregiving themselves [4]. The recruitment process needs to be simplified and made more time- and cost-efficient. Support in recruitment could be provided by experienced nurses and by retired people who are looking for flexible activities to do from home, to feel included and connected [5]. Some retirees long for their experience and accumulated knowledge across their lifetime, to be recognized and appreciated [5]. Others need an occupation to make use of their additional free time. Some might look for activities they can do from home, at any time to feel included and connected. A lack of such purposeful activities can impact older adults' mental health and reduce their perceived quality of life [14, 15]. Finally, increasing financial stability with additional flexible income might be another motivation. This could also be an interesting opportunity for nurses that are working parttime or are unemployed. In lower-income countries such as Romania this might be an especially fitting option [6].

One key challenge with solutions for older adults is that they are oftentimes excluded from the development process of technologies and their design [16]. A participatory design approach can be a solution to counteract the amplification of digital exclusion of older adult technology users. It is an attempt to democratically involve marginalized groups, such as people aged 65 +, in innovation processes of digital technologies, and thus increase their chances of digital inclusion [17]. To assure an inclusive and user-friendly solution, the *HEROES* (HomE woRk fOr retireES) app was developed with a user-centered approach [8], involving seniors, nurses, and families early in the process of designing, developing and testing the app. This has proven especially valuable for vulnerable user groups, and in the health sector (e.g., 9–12).

2 The HEROES App

HEROES is a research project embedded within the European Assisted Active Living (AAL) funding program which aims to create better quality of life for older adults, fostering cooperation between research and industry. Its mission is to support ageing communities by connecting them with caregivers and nurses. To achieve this, a platform was built making hiring trustworthy caregivers for older and vulnerable people fast and cost-effective. The platform intends to connect the following user group ecosystems:

- Recruiters: families, care organizations and people in need of care, looking for trustworthy caregivers;

- Candidates: individuals with formal or informal experience as caregivers or nurses who are looking for work; either people who are already working in the care sector, e.g., as (certified) nurses, or nursing assistants, and are looking for a new and / or more flexible job, or people who are not yet working in this field but are interested in supporting elderly people in situations of need, e.g., in daily life, shopping, cooking, cleaning;
- Reviewers: a community people that screen and rate candidates online; on one hand, people who are retired and would like to use their life experience for a meaningful activity working a few hours a week reviewing candidates during their retirement; on the other hand, people with a professional care or nursing background, e.g., (certified) nurses, or nursing assistants, who would like to use their knowledge and skills for the evaluation of candidates.

For each of the three user groups, a separate app was developed with specific relevant use cases. To easily distinguish the three apps, they have a unique color scheme: the recruiter app is kept in blue, while the candidate app is green in color, and finally the reviewer app is colored red. The core use case for the recruiter app is that recruiters create their own profile, as well as a job for caregivers or nurses. They can select predefined questions or write their own questions relevant to their job posting. These questions will then be presented to interested candidates (see Fig. 1).

Fig. 1. Three screenshots of the recruiter flow "creating a job" in the recruiter app (1: the recruiter's active jobs; 2: predefined questions for recruiters; 3: app screen after publishing a job).

Candidates create their own profile to see jobs that fit with their own interests and expertise. Once they choose to apply for a job, candidates answer the questions of the recruiters with a video reply (see Fig. 2).

Fig. 2. Three screenshots of the candidate flow "applying for a job" in the candidate app (1: details of a selected job; 2: predefined questions to answer with video or audio; 3 app screen after a video response has been recorded).

Finally, the reviewers support the recruiters by screening the job description, the candidate's profile, as well as the candidate's video-answer. Reviewers provide the recruiters with suggestions. Once a recruiter has chosen a candidate for a job, they can get in contact with them. The *HEROES* app is a matchmaking solution, this means it does not provide the parties with an employment contract at the end of the process. However, frequently asked questions on the project website provide additional, country specific information regarding legal aspects for employment in the field of homecare to meet an important user need.

3 Research Design and Methods

3.1 Interdisciplinary Approach with End-User Involvement

The duration of the entire project spans 30 months, starting in April 2021 and ending in September 2023. The project consortium consists of six project partners from Switzerland[1], Romania[2], and Austria[3]. While some of the project partners are mainly involved in data collection based on co-creation workshops, end-user testing, and evaluation, as well as validation, others focused on processing the generated results, planning, implementation, and design of the platform, as well as development of the business plan. Consequently, team discussions and the gathering of different perspectives are an important

---

[1] University of Applied Sciences of Eastern Switzerland (Institute for Ageing Research, IAF) and terzStiftung.

[2] The Care Hub SRL, Tricubiq Solutions SRL.

[3] Rapid user feedback GmbH (RUF), FH Kärnten - gemeinnützige Gesellschaft mbH (Austria),

part within the development process of the platform. By following a very user-centered approach throughout the entire project, the new *HEROES* project was developed in close exchange with the potential customers and end-users to avoid missing the market and customers' needs. Therefore, end-users were recruited from all three target groups of the future *HEROES* project.

3.2 Development and Testing Plan

The first half of the project focused on understanding the needs of the stakeholders involved, planning, and conducting three rounds of co-creation workshops together with end-users. Feedback gathered from the workshops was used to compile technical requirements with the objective of developing an app prototype according to the end-users' needs. The second half of the project focused on testing the usability and user friendliness of the app. A one-year long field trial with three iteration cycles was conducted to continuously improve the usability and functioning of the app.

Co-creation Workshop 1. To gather early feedback from the target user-groups, co-creation workshop 1 was planned while the *HEROES* app was still only a concept. The purpose of the workshop was to collect impressions, topics of concerns, attitudes about the entire concept, as well as ideas and suggestions from possible future end-users which the technical partners considered during the development process. The NUF test [18], a decision-making technique, was used for team members to rate the suggestions on three criteria (novel, useful, and feasible; NUF) to indicate which app aspects developers should focus on in the next stages.

Co-creation Workshop 2. The focus of the second workshop was to gain a deeper understanding of how participants respond to certain aspects of the application, such as the interface and layout tested on a mock-up. Comments and suggestions were transcribed and categorized using the NUF score and rated by the team members.

Co-creation Workshop 3. Finally, in the third workshop a prototype of the app was tested with the users. The focus was to test the accessibility and usability of the prototype. Unlike in previous workshops, a beta version of the application was tested with the participants who acted as recruiters, candidates, or reviewers. Another focus was to investigate how participants interact with the app and its interface, including its' layout and navigation. While participants completed each task, moderators observed the participants' behavior and recorded their feedback. The observations were noted in a data collection form with the following categories: usability, navigation, and content.

Field Trial. The one-year field trial phase was conducted to evaluate the platform itself, as well as single features and new ideas, while collecting real and authentic user feedback. Therefore the app was tested with potential end-users in their real-life contexts in their homes, but with artificial content. A mixed-methods approach, combining qualitative and quantitative measures was used for this "living lab" approach. The field trial started in April 2022 and ended in April 2023. Overall, it was divided into three different cycles (see Fig. 3), wherein participants tested the three apps in a real life setting and discussed their findings at the end in a group discussion. This was followed by a "passive" phase (no tasks for the participants), which was used for further development of the apps based on the user feedback. However, based on feedback from the very first test cycle resulting in fundamental changes, the consortium decided to rework the flows in the app. Before implementing these changes, the second cycle was replaced with a friendly user test to make sure, that the new features and flows are well received by potential users.

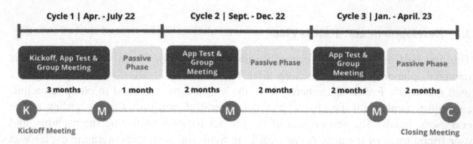

Fig. 3. Overview of the three initially planned cycles and group meetings with participants during the field trials.

4   Results of the Field Trials

A total of 91 participants started the field trials in three countries, of which 89 participated to the end. The main reasons for dropouts were lack of time, and problems with downloading the app. Participants' age distribution varied strongly in each group: candidates' median age was $M = 43$ years, recruiters' median age was $M = 51$ years, and reviewers' median age was $M = 68.5$ years. Overall, more women participated in the field trials (90% of the candidates, 60% of the recruiters, and 70% of the reviewers were female). Value propositions for the *HEROES* project (i.e., user needs, gains, and pains) as well as qualitative feedback on participants' observations and experiences were collected in the group discussions.

4.1   Qualitative Feedback from Recruiters

The recruiter app was tested by $N = 30$ participants during the field trials. Overall, the app was appreciated for its clarity, simplicity, and design, which made it easy to use for participants. The concept of the app was highly appreciated, and participants perceived it as an effective way to recruit caregivers. The video answers were seen as helpful to get a better impression of suitable candidates. However, several participants criticized spelling mistakes and unclear expressions. Additionally, data privacy concerns were raised,. Participants missed guidelines and explanations addressing the legal aspect of recruiting, especially in the homecare sector.

4.2   Qualitative Feedback from Candidates

In total, $N = 29$ participants tested the candidate app during the field trials. Most reported it to be very user-friendly and intuitive, mainly due to its simplicity and clarity, as well as its layout and structure. Navigation was described to be easy with straightforward instructions. However, some participants found the registration process repetitive. Many participants found the candidate app to be a helpful tool to find a job easily and quickly. While many participants did not report any issues with the app, several others reported issues when trying to find a fitting job (e.g., due to a lack of location filters, or desired qualifications) or reported technical issues with the app (e.g., with audio and video upload). Additionally, the color choice of the candidate app (green) was criticized by a few participants. An imbalance between the information provided by the recruiters regarding the person needing care compared to the information provided by candidates, as well as a lack of information regarding the app security was mentioned as well.

4.3 Qualitative Feedback from Reviewers

A total of $N = 30$ participants tested the reviewer app during the field trials. The app was perceived as self-explanatory and easy to use. The participants appreciated the innovative idea of the platform and see a demand for such an app. The structure of the app was found to be logical and consistent. However, some participants reported technical issues (e.g., uploading photos), while others criticized that candidates can only apply with video or audio answers, as not all candidates might feel comfortable presenting themselves in this format, and that in particular older candidates might not want to apply for jobs using these formats.

5 Conclusion and Outlook

To some extent, all participants have already dealt with the topic of care either in a private or professional context (e.g., as private caregivers, or former professional nurses). Most of them sees a lot of potential in the *HEROES* project to find support for themselves or loved ones in need of care. Therefore, this project could provide much needed relief for the formal and informal care sector, which are facing more and more pressures due to lack of caregivers in the coming years [1]. Provided that the app works well, most participants reported that they would use it privately and even recommend it to friends. The participants recognized that the app can create new opportunities in a professional and social context, and that local networks may help to reduce the consequences of a shortage of care professionals. This in turn can help older and vulnerable people to stay in their homes longer as recommended by Alber, Köhler [3].

In line with some studies [5, 14, 15], feedback from participants was able to demonstrate that the flexible work opportunity as a recruiter was appreciated by participants.

Overall, most of the participants enjoyed participating in the field trials and appreciated the opportunity to contribute with their opinions and experience. The *HEROES* project was able to address end-user needs (e.g., regarding user-friendliness), resolve issues and continuously improve the solution with the participatory, user-centered design approach by including the diverse group of end-users very early in the project [8–12]. A challenge that many solutions ignore, especially when designing for older adults [16].

Even though participants did mention a risk that older candidates might not feel comfortable recording their own video or audio to apply for a job, the process of designing the solution in a user-centered process improves user-friendliness and might help increase digital inclusion nevertheless [17].

Regarding the user-friendliness and usability of the *HEROES* app, participants appreciated the simple and clear layout and structure, its intuitive and straightforward navigation, and that it is easy to use. However, the lack of guidelines, information about app security as well as some technical issues were criticized. These concerns will need to be addressed before entering the market. A live trial is planned to gather further insights on the feasibility under real world conditions. Finally, analysis of the quantitative data will be part of the next phase.

References

1. Geerts, J., Sowa, A., Schultz, E., et al.: Projections of use and supply of long-term care in Europe: Policy implications (2012)
2. World Health Organization Ageing and health (2022). https://www.who.int/news-room/fact-sheets/detail/ageing-and-health
3. Alber, J., Köhler, U.: Health and care in an enlarged Europe. Ofice for the Official Publications of the European Communities, Luxembourg (2004)
4. Birtha, M., Holm, K.: Who Cares? Study on the challenges and needs of family carers in Europe. COFACE Families Europe, Brussels (2017)
5. Sewdas, R., de Wind, A., van der Zwaan, L.G.L., et al.: Why older workers work beyond the retirement age: a qualitative study. BMC Public Health 17, 672 (2017). https://doi.org/10.1186/s12889-017-4675-z
6. Rodrigues, R., Ozdemir, E,, Ward, T., et al.: Employment of Older Workers. European Commission Research Note no. 5/2015. Unpublished (2015)
7. Cober, R.T., Brown, D.J., Blumental, A.J., et al.: The quest for the qualified job surfer: it's time the public sector catches the wave. Public Personnel Manag. 29, 479–496 (2000). https://doi.org/10.1177/009102600002900406
8. Tullis, T., Albert, B.: Measuring the user experience: Collecting, analyzing, and presenting usability metrics, Second edition. Elsevier/Morgan Kaufmann, Amsterdam, Boston (2013)
9. Mansson, L., Wiklund, M., Öhberg, F., et al.: Co-Creation with older adults to improve user-experience of a smartphone self-test application to assess balance function. Int. J. Environ. Res. Public Health 17,(2020). https://doi.org/10.3390/ijerph17113768
10. Zuniga, M., Buffel, T., Arrieta, F.: Analysing Co-creation and co-production initiatives for the development of age-friendly strategies: learning from the three capital cities in the basque autonomous region. Soc. Policy Soc. 22, 53–68 (2023). https://doi.org/10.1017/S1474746421000282
11. Frow, P., McColl-Kennedy, J.R., Payne, A.: Co-creation practices: their role in shaping a health care ecosystem. Ind. Mark. Manage. 56, 24–39 (2016). https://doi.org/10.1016/j.indmarman.2016.03.007
12. Palumbo, R.: Contextualizing co-production of health care: a systematic literature review. Int. J. Public Sect. Manag. 29, 72–90 (2016). https://doi.org/10.1108/IJPSM-07-2015-0125
13. Stephanidis, C., Salvendy, G., Antona, M., et al.: Seven HCI grand challenges. Inter. J. Hum.-Comput. Interact. 35, 1229–1269 (2019). https://doi.org/10.1080/10447318.2019.1619259
14. Gesundheitsförderung Schweiz Psychische Gesundheit über die Lebensspanne: Grundlagenbericht. Bericht 6, Bern und Lausanne (2016)

15. Patel, R.P.: A study of impact of post-retirement work on psychological well-being of elderly. IJMH **5**, 63 (2018). https://doi.org/10.30877/IJMH.5.1.2018.63-67
16. Mannheim, I., Schwartz, E., Xi, W., et al.: Inclusion of older adults in the research and design of digital technology. Int. J. Environ. Res. Public Health **16** (2019). https://doi.org/10.3390/ijerph16193718
17. Björgvinsson, E., Ehn, P., Hillgren, P.-A.: Participatory design and democratizing innovation. In: Robertson, T., Bødker, K., Bratteteig, T. et al. (eds.) Proceedings of the 11th Biennial Participatory Design Conference, pp 41–50. ACM, New York (2010)
18. Gray, D., Brown, S., Macanufo, J.: Gamestorming: a playbook for innovators, rulebreakers, and changemakers. O'Reilly, Sebastopol, CA (2010)

Study on Sharing Health Guidance Contents Using Health Guidance Visualization System

Kaori Fujimura[✉], Taiga Sano, Tae Sato, and Yasuo Ishigure

NTT Social Informatics Laboratories, 1-1 Hikarinooka, , Yokosuka-Shi 239-0847, Japan
kaori.fujimura@ntt.com

Abstract. In Japan, "Specific Health Checkups" and "Specific Health Guidance" are implemented to prevent lifestyle-related diseases [1]. In the specific health guidance, health professionals (e.g., public health nurses and dietitians) interview patients and guide them toward a healthy lifestyle. We have analyzed the interview dialogues and found that experienced health professionals learn the characteristics of patients (biological, psychological, and social aspects [2], and lifestyle habits) and select intervention methods (motivational methods, action plans, etc.) in accordance with these characteristics, leading to behavioral change and improved health examination results.

However, although health professionals have learned from experience and know ways to effectively interview patients in accordance with their characteristics, they have few opportunities to share their knowledge and experience and learn from each other. In this study, we developed a system to visualize intervention methods in accordance with patient's characteristics, which are the findings of health professionals, with the aim of contributing to improving health guidance skills by sharing knowledge among health professionals. To verify the usefulness of the system, an experiment using health guidance interviews was conducted in February 2023. Post-experiment interviews suggested that the system would be effective in sharing health guidance knowledge.

Keywords: Behavior Change · Knowledge Sharing · Health Guidance

1 Introduction

1.1 Specific Health Guidance

In Japan, specific health checkups and specific health guidance focusing on metabolic syndrome have been implemented since 2008 to prevent lifestyle-related diseases [1]. On the basis of the results of the specific health checkup, specific health guidance provides support for lifestyle improvement to those who are at high risk of developing lifestyle-related diseases and for whom lifestyle improvement can be expected to be effective in preventing lifestyle-related diseases. In specific health guidance, health professionals give advice on which lifestyle habits to change and how to change them, on the basis of the patient's health checkup results, lifestyle habits at that time, and the patient's personality, interests, and hobbies. The health professionals who interview patients are public

C. Stephanidis et al. (Eds.): HCII 2023, CCIS 1957, pp. 374–379, 2024.
https://doi.org/10.1007/978-3-031-49212-9_46

health nurses, dietitians, physicians, etc. We analyzed the interview dialogues and found that experienced health professionals learn patients' characteristics (biological, psychological, and social aspects [2] (hereinafter referred to as BPS), and lifestyle habits) and choose interventions (motivational methods, action plans, etc.) in accordance with these characteristics, while leading to behavioral change and improved health examination results.

Health professionals have learned from experience and know ways to effectively interview patients on the basis of their characteristics, but they have few opportunities to share their knowledge and experience and learn from each other.

1.2 Motivation

We believed that storing and sharing the health professionals' knowledges through human computer interaction would improve the quality of health guidance and support effective health guidance. Therefore, the purpose of this study is to develop a system to visualize intervention methods in accordance with patients' characteristics, which are known by health professionals, and to contribute to improving health guidance skills by sharing knowledge among health professionals.

2 Health Guidance Visualization System

2.1 System Configuration

To visualize and share health guidance knowledge, we developed a health guidance visualization system. The system consists of an interview management system, a visualization system, and client PCs.

The interview management system manages the interviewers and patients for each interview, displays data input interface, and saves input data. The visualization system draws a picture of the patient's lifestyle, intervention details, intentions, and action plan when the health guidance content stored in the interview management system is input (Fig. 1).

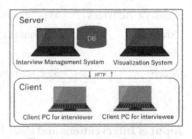

Fig. 1. System Configuration

2.2 System Functions

The health guidance visualization system allows the input of a patient's BPS information (Table 1), as well as the patient's lifestyle (Table 2), as information on the patient to be ascertained through health guidance. The system then allows the input of the content and intention of interventions for the patient, the patient information used to select the intervention content, and the action plan made with the patient.

Characteristics of the Patient, Items Related to Lifestyle. The items related to the characteristics of the patients to be captured in the health guidance (Table 1) and the items related to lifestyle (Table 2) were extracted on the basis of the dialogues in the 14 previously conducted health guidance sessions and were determined on the basis of the opinions of the experts (Fig. 2).

Table 1. Examples of items related to BPS

Aspects	Data item
Biological	Results of physical examination (height, weight, blood pressure, blood sugar, etc.), chief complaint, body shape, etc.
Psychological	Personality tendencies, health consciousness, preferences, etc.
Social	Family and relationships, work relationships, community, etc.

Table 2. Examples of items related to lifestyle

Lifestyle item	Data item
Diet	Content, amount, and time of breakfast, lunch, dinner, and snacks
Physical Activity	Type, exercise, amount, duration, frequency, past experience
Lifestyle Activities	Type, amount, duration, frequency
Alcohol	Amount per dose, frequency
Smoking	Number of cigarettes per day, smoking history
Sleep	Sleep duration, chief complaint

Input of Interventions and their Intentions. The interviewer can freely describe what he/she recommended (intervention details). Examples include explaining the meaning of the health checkup results, explaining the risks of the patient continuing their current lifestyle, etc.

The interviewer can enter a free description of his/her intention for selecting the intervention. For example, "I explained the meaning of the results of the medical checkup because the patient was very anxious about them."

On this screen, a health professional can record the patient information used when he/she selects interventions.

Visualization of Health Guidance Content. After a health professional (interviewer) inputs the health guidance data, health guidance content is visualized as a diagram. The format of the visualized diagram is shown in Fig. 3. The patient's BPS is displayed on the left; lifestyle habits, intervention details for lifestyle habits, and intentions of the interviewer are displayed in the center; and an action plan is displayed on the right. At the bottom, options of the patient's BPS that were not selected are displayed and can be

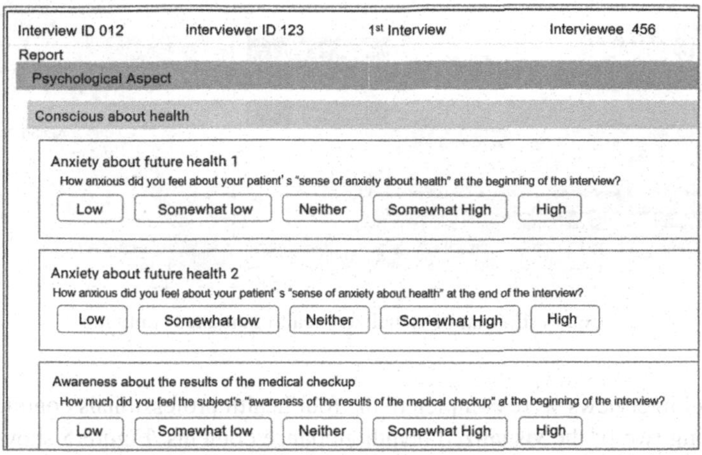

Fig. 2. Input screen image of BPS and lifestyle (originally Japanese)

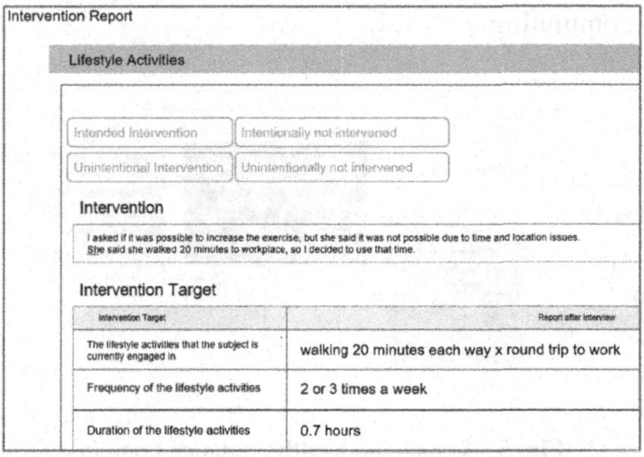

Fig. 3. Input screen image of intervention report

moved freely using the drawing application to show their relationship to lifestyle habits and interventions with arrows (Fig. 4).

3 Experiment

To test the feasibility and usefulness of the system, a health guidance interview experiment was conducted in February 2023, involving 4 experienced health professionals (3 public health nurses and 1 dietitian) and 26 participants (22 men and 4 women, average age 45). Before the interviews, the participants (interviewees) submitted the results of their most recent and previous health examinations and answers to a medical questionnaire. Among 26 interviews, 14 interviews were conducted in person and 12 online. After the interview, the interviewer entered the patient characteristics and intervention details from the system.

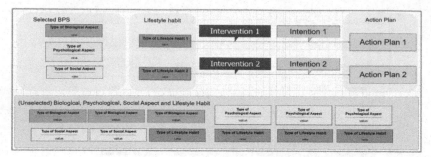

Fig. 4. Format of visualized health guidance content

After all interviews were completed, the four health professionals conducted a conference using two of the visualized health guidance contents. Figure 5 shows a part of the figure used for the conference. As this patient expressed a desire to lower her body fat percentage, but she did not have time to exercise, the interviewer decided to recommend that she use her commute time. Finally, she made an action plan involving fast walking at intervals during commuting.

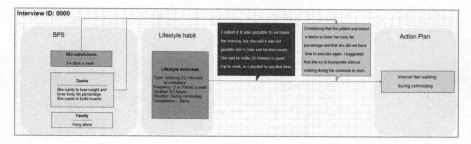

Fig. 5. Visualized health guidance content

4   Results

A group interview was conducted with four health professionals after the conference regarding their use of the visualization system.

- Self-reflection: Some participants commented that the visualization diagram and input process helped them to reflect on their own interviews. Some said it would be nice to be able to depict the relationship between lifestyle habits as well.
- Handover: It was commented that visualizations were easier to understand than text-only materials, and that the written intent was easier to understand.
- Sharing of interviews of other health professionals: Since conferences are held only once a month, some participants said it would be helpful to visualize and immediately see the interviews of others and to compare cases.

- Training: The possibility of utilization was raised, such as inexperienced people being easily consulted on the basis of diagrams or being able to provide guidance on the basis of diagrams of inexperienced people.

5 Consideration

The results of the post-experimental interviews suggest that visualization of health guidance content has the potential to support knowledge sharing. It also has the potential to be used as an educational tool for inexperienced health professionals and as an information sharing tool in multidisciplinary collaboration.

6 Conclusion

A visualization system was developed to share the knowledge accumulated by individual experts in health guidance. An experiment was conducted using the developed system. The results of post-experimental interviews suggested that visualization of the content of health guidance has the potential to support knowledge sharing. The system may also be used as an educational tool for inexperienced health professionals and as an information sharing tool in multidisciplinary cooperation.

In the future, we will accumulate health guidance knowledge using this system and study effective IT support through human computer interaction for health professionals using the accumulated data.

Acknowledgements. We are grateful to Ms. Tamae Ogata, a health professional, and her colleagues for helpful discussion. We also thank the members of NTT-TX and JSP for developing the system and supporting for the experiment.

References

1. https://www.mhlw.go.jp/stf/seisakunitsuite/bunya/kenkou_iryou/kenkou/seikatsu/index.html (Japanese)
2. Engel, G.L.: The need for a new medical model: a challenge for biomedicine. Science **196**(4286), 129–136 (1977)

Early Stage Design of a mHealth Intervention for Managing Gestational Diabetes Mellitus in Bangladeshi Women

Ashraful Islam[1,2]([✉]) [ID], Eshtiak Ahmed[3] [ID], and Md Rakibul Islam[4] [ID]

[1] EMPATHY Lab, Center for Computational and Data Sciences, Independent University, Bangladesh, Dhaka, Bangladesh
[2] Department of Computer Science and Engineering, Independent University, Bangladesh, Dhaka, Bangladesh
ashraful@iub.edu.bd
[3] Faculty of Information Technology and Communication Sciences, Tampere University, Tampere, Finland
eshtiak.ahmed@tuni.fi
[4] Computer Science Department, University of Wisconsin - Eau Claire, Eau Claire, WI, USA
islamm@uwec.edu

Abstract. Gestational Diabetes Mellitus (GDM) is a rising concern worldwide, particularly in low-resource countries such as Bangladesh, where access to healthcare facilities is limited and awareness of GDM management is inadequate. This work proposes an early-stage design of user interfaces (UIs) for a mobile health (mHealth) intervention using the Bengali language that allows users to input daily measures of blood glucose, weight, and other GDM-related health data. The intervention is designed to provide users with personalized feedback based on their input and the necessary coaching for managing GDM. It also reminds users to take medication if prescribed by their doctors. The app has six key features: blood glucose tracking, food logging, medication reminders, activity tracking, educational resources, and personalized recommendations. Overall, this work provides a valuable contribution to the field of mHealth-based maternal and child health in Bangladesh. However, further research is necessary to evaluate the effectiveness and feasibility of the intervention in real-world scenarios. Such evaluations will provide valuable insights into its potential impact and help refine the design to better serve the needs of GDM patients in Bangladesh.

Keywords: Gestational diabetes · mHealth · Bangladesh

1 Introduction

Gestational Diabetes Mellitus (GDM), a type of diabetes occurring during pregnancy, presents notable challenges and concerns for women in Bangladesh [4, 6]. The prevalence of this condition has been on the rise, emphasizing the immediate need for effective management and attention [6]. The escalating prevalence of GDM among pregnant women in Bangladesh has become a growing cause for alarm. Managing GDM poses numerous challenges in Bangladesh [3,7]. Limited access to healthcare services, particularly in rural areas, impedes timely diagnosis and effective management of the condition. Moreover, the dearth of healthcare professionals specializing in GDM exacerbates the situation. Cultural norms surrounding pregnancy and dietary practices further hinder women from adopting healthier lifestyles and adhering to recommended treatment plans [3]. Prior research demonstrates that mobile health (mHealth) interventions can significantly improve the health services available to women with GDM [1,5,8–10].

For this work, we surveyed the relevant literature and related works and found that there was not a single mHealth app in the Bengali language that had all features required for helping GDM patients in Bangladesh. All of these aspects are included in our proposed mHealth app which is in Bengali, allowing users who are not fluent in English to use it effectively during GDM. This work proposes an early-stage design of a mHealth intervention which is a prototypical smartphone app and it allows users to input daily measures of blood glucose, weight, and other GDM-related health data. The intervention is designed through an understanding of the socio-cultural context of Bangladesh and the barriers faced by pregnant women in accessing healthcare services during their GDM [2–4,7]. The app is designed to provide users with personalized feedback based on their input and the necessary coaching for managing GDM. The intervention is designed to be user-friendly, culturally appropriate, and accessible to women living in rural areas. The proposed mHealth app has six key features: (i) Blood glucose tracking; (ii) Daily food diary; (iii) Medication reminders; (iv) Daily activity tracking; (v) Educational resources for GDM; and (vi) Personalized recommendations.

Overall, this work provides a valuable contribution to the field of maternal and child health in low-resource settings, particularly in Bangladesh. The proposed mHealth intervention has the potential to address the current gap in GDM management and improve health outcomes for pregnant women and their babies. These evaluations will offer valuable insights into the potential impact of the intervention and facilitate the refinement of its design to better cater to the specific needs of GDM patients in Bangladesh.

2 Design Methodology

2.1 Requirements Analysis

For gathering the initial design requirements, we started with reviewing the existing literature on GDM in Bangladesh to see what factors are wanted by the women having GDM. We have also explored the available mHealth tools for managing GDM in different countries and languages. This strategy assisted us in coming up with features for the proposed intervention. A few of the articles that we reviewed are summarized as follows-

Varnfield et al. [10] presents the development and evaluation of a mHealth platform for the management of GDM in women of Australia that includes a smartphone app for data entry of BGL and other health data, delivery of multimedia content, and secure cloud data storage. Also, a clinician portal is there for the review of patient data and communication with patients.

Al Hashmi et al. [1] developed and experimented with a self-efficacy-enhancing mHealth app for women in Oman with GDM. This app is featured to promote behavioral modifications among patients with the components of goal setting, tracking healthy behaviors (e.g., body weight, diet, physical activity), and self-monitoring of BGL. Their findings found that the app was a feasible and acceptable intervention for behavioral modifications among women with GDM.

Mackillop et al. [5] compared the efficacy of a mHealth-based BGL management system with standard clinic care in women with GDM in the United Kingdom. This mHealth system allowed users to record, tag, and review their BGL readings in real-time and provided personalized feedback and support to the users based on their BGLs. They found that the mHealth-based system was as effective as standard care in controlling BGLs.

Scar et al. [8] explored the experiences of women with GDM with controlling their BGLs by recording BGLs and receiving health and nutrition information accordingly using a mHealth app in Norway. Their findings suggested that a mHealth app may have the potential for supporting women with GDM, particularly in their blood glucose management.

Surendran et al. [9] investigated the usage behavior and perceived usefulness of a mHealth application for managing GDM in Singapore. The app consists of three main elements: engaging educational lessons, monitoring tools for self-tracking of BGLs, physical activity, diet, and weight, and personalized coaching.

2.2   Prototype Design

Referencing the findings from the requirement analysis, we brainstormed various design ideas and settled on a few by establishing scenarios. After several iterations of screen sketches for these designs, sketches were transformed into a prototypical app using a web-based wireframing tool called MockPlus[1].

3   Prototypical mHealth Intervention

The proposed mHealth application encompasses a range of valuable features to support individuals with GDM. The language used in the user interface (UI) is Bengali. The proposed prototypical app has six key components (Fig. 1) and sample UIs for each component are illustrated in Fig. 2a, 2b, 3a, 3b, 4a, and 4b:

---

[1] https://app.mockplus.com/.

3.1   Blood Glucose Tracking

The app facilitates users in recording their blood glucose readings conveniently. Whether manually inputted or automatically synced with a glucose meter, this functionality enables easy monitoring of blood sugar levels over time.

3.2   Daily Food Diary

Users can effortlessly log their food intake within the app, aiding in the management of carbohydrate consumption. This aspect holds particular significance for individuals with diabetes as it empowers them to make informed decisions about their diet and adjust accordingly to maintain stable BGLs.

3.3   Medication Reminders

Incorporating timely medication intake reminders, the app assists users in adhering to their prescribed insulin or other medications. This feature ensures users are prompted to take their medications as per their designated schedules, thereby enhancing medication compliance and overall disease management.

3.4   Daily Activity Tracking

The app enables users to track their physical activity and exercise routines effectively. Regular exercise has been proven beneficial for individuals with diabetes, positively impacting blood sugar control. Monitoring physical activity levels through the app keeps users motivated and aware of their exercise habits, facilitating better condition management.

3.5   Educational Resources for GDM

To foster an understanding of GDM and its management, the app offers a diverse range of educational resources. These resources may comprise articles, videos, or interactive tools that furnish information on various aspects of the condition. Users can access these resources to acquire knowledge about healthy lifestyle choices, dietary recommendations, monitoring techniques, and other pertinent information for making informed decisions about their health.

3.6   Personalized Recommendations

Leveraging the user's BGLs, diet, and exercise habits, the app generates personalized recommendations. These tailored suggestions encompass dietary adjustments, exercise routines, and reminders for specific actions, all designed to meet the individual's unique needs. Such personalized guidance aids users in achieving optimal blood sugar control and effectively managing their GDM.

By integrating these six fundamental features, the mHealth app empowers individuals with GDM, equipping them with indispensable tools for self-management, education, and support. The app enhances their ability to monitor BGLs, make informed dietary choices, adhere to medication schedules, engage in regular physical activity, access educational materials, and receive personalized recommendations, all contributing to improved management of their condition.

4   Current Limitations and Future Works

One limitation of the proposed design is that it may not sufficiently consider the cultural and contextual factors involved in managing gestational diabetes in Bangladesh. Since there were no user studies conducted with the target population before designing, it becomes difficult to fully grasp their specific needs, beliefs, and healthcare practices. Additionally, without user studies, the early-stage design may overlook important insights into user preferences, cognitive abilities, and interaction patterns. Consequently, the user interface and overall usability might not meet the expectations and capabilities of the intended users.

At present, the features for the proposed intervention have been generated through brainstorming sessions, incorporating design requirements identified in existing related works. However, the next immediate step is to conduct user studies involving the target population in Bangladesh. This user-centered approach aims to gather valuable insights into the perceptions and thoughts of the users regarding the tool's functionality and usability specifically for GDM management. Furthermore, it is crucial to validate the designs with domain experts,

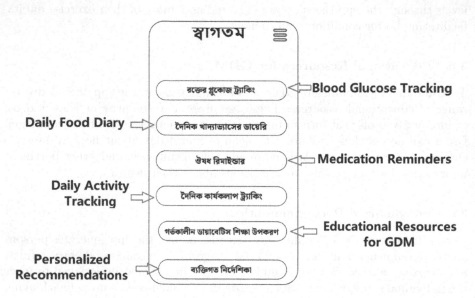

Fig. 1. Home page of the proposed prototypical mHealth app. The language of the app UI is Bengali. The corresponding English translation is given for understanding.

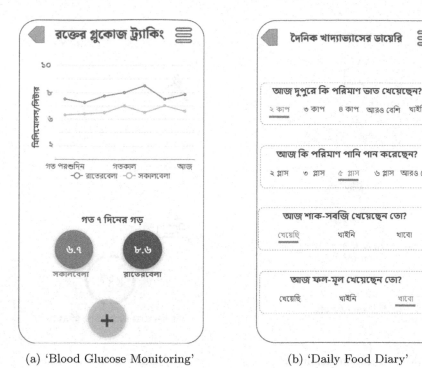

(a) 'Blood Glucose Monitoring'   (b) 'Daily Food Diary'

Fig. 2. Sample UIs of 'Blood Glucose Monitoring' and 'Daily Food Diary' features.

specifically, healthcare professionals (HCPs) who have experience in treating patients with GDM in Bangladesh. Their expertise and input will ensure that the tool aligns with the requirements and expectations of HCPs, facilitating seamless integration into existing healthcare practices. The findings from the user studies with the target population and the input from HCPs will inform the redesign process of the prototypical app. The aim is to incorporate the identified user preferences, needs, and expectations, as well as the professional expertise of HCPs. This iterative design process will help refine the tool to better suit the requirements and context of managing GDM in Bangladesh.

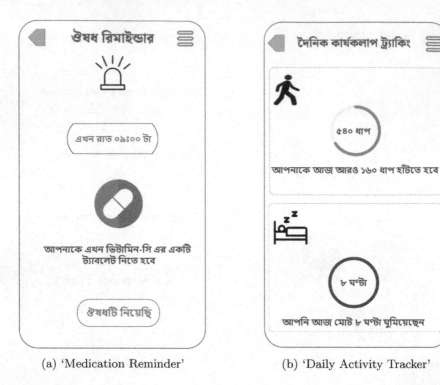

(a) 'Medication Reminder'   (b) 'Daily Activity Tracker'

Fig. 3. Sample UIs of 'Medication Reminder' and 'Daily Activity Tracker' features.

Following the redesign, another round of user studies will be conducted, utilizing well-established usability measurements scales such as the System Usability Scale (SUS) and the Mobile Application Rating Scale (MARS). These standardized scales will provide quantitative and qualitative feedback on the usability and user experience of the tool. By leveraging these measurement scales, researchers can gain insights into user satisfaction, effectiveness, efficiency, and learnability of the redesigned tool. Through this iterative process of user studies, expert validation, and usability evaluation, the mHealth tool for managing GDM can be continually refined, ensuring its effectiveness, acceptance, and suitability for the target users in Bangladesh.

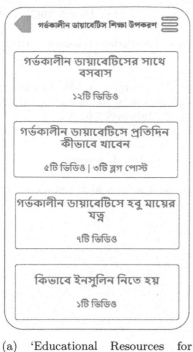

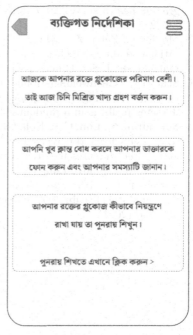

(a) 'Educational Resources for GDM'

(b) 'Personalized Recommendations'

Fig. 4. Sample UIs of 'Educational Resources for GDM' and 'Personalized Recommendations' features.

References

1. Al Hashmi, I., Alsabti, H., Al Omari, O., Al Nasseri, Y., Khalaf, A.: Development, feasibility and acceptability of a self-efficacy-enhancing smartphone application among pregnant women with gestational diabetes mellitus: single-arm pilot clinical trial. BMC Preg. Childbirth **22**(1), 1–15 (2022)
2. Bhowmik, B.: Evaluation of knowledge regarding gestational diabetes mellitus: a Bangladeshi study. Public Health **161**, 67–74 (2018)
3. Biswas, A., Dalal, K., Abdullah, A.S.M., Rahman, A.F., Halim, A.: Gestational diabetes: exploring the perceptions, practices and barriers of the community and healthcare providers in rural bangladesh: a qualitative study. Diab. Metabolic Synd. Obesity Targets Therapy **13**, 1339 (2020)
4. Jesmin, S., et al.: Screening for gestational diabetes mellitus and its prevalence in Bangladesh. Diab. Res. Clin. Pract. **103**(1), 57–62 (2014)
5. Mackillop, L., et al.: Comparing the efficacy of a mobile phone-based blood glucose management system with standard clinic care in women with gestational diabetes: randomized controlled trial. JMIR Mhealth Uhealth **6**(3), e9512 (2018)
6. Mazumder, T., Akter, E., Rahman, S.M., Islam, M.T., Talukder, M.R.: Prevalence and risk factors of gestational diabetes mellitus in Bangladesh: findings from demo-

graphic health survey 2017–2018. Int. J. Environ. Res. Public Health **19**(5), 2583 (2022)

7. Monir, N., Zeba, Z., Rahman, A.: Comparison of knowledge of women with gestational diabetes mellitus and healthy pregnant women attending at hospital in bangladesh. J. Sci. Found. **16**(1), 20–26 (2018)

8. Skar, J.B., Garnweidner-Holme, L.M., Lukasse, M., Terragni, L.: Women's experiences with using a smartphone app (the pregnant+ app) to manage gestational diabetes mellitus in a randomised controlled trial. Midwifery **58**, 102–108 (2018)

9. Surendran, S., Lim, C.S., Koh, G.C.H., Yew, T.W., Tai, E.S., Foong, P.S.: Women's usage behavior and perceived usefulness with using a mobile health application for gestational diabetes mellitus: Mixed-methods study. Int. J. Environ. Res. Public Health **18**(12), 6670 (2021)

10. Varnfield, M.: Mther, an mhealth system to support women with gestational diabetes mellitus: feasibility and acceptability study. Diab. Technol. Therapeut. **23**(5), 358–366 (2021)

The Testing of EEG and HRV Parameters to Quantitatively Differentiate between the IGD and Healthy Group

Jung-Yong Kim[1]($\boxtimes$) (iD), Sungkyun Im[2] (iD), Dong Joon Kim[2] (iD), Mincheol Whang[3] (iD), and Mi Sook Kim[4] (iD)

[1] Department of HCI, Hanyang University, Ansan 15588, Republic of Korea
jungkim@hanyang.ac.kr
[2] Department of Industrial and Management Engineering, Hanyang University, Ansan 15588, Republic of Korea
[3] Department of Human-Centered Artificial Intelligence, Sangmyung University, Seoul 03016, Republic of Korea
[4] Department of Clothing and Textiles, Kyung Hee University, Seoul 02447, Republic of Korea

Abstract. Studies have been conducted to determine the status of the internet gaming disorder (IGD) using various bio-signals, including quantitative studies using electroencephalography (EEG) and heart rate variability (HRV) that have suggested discriminant models to identify IGD subjects. This study aimed to test the accuracy of the suggested models especially when the EEG and HRV parameters were used together to build up a discriminant equation. An experiment was designed based on previous studies. The subjects consisted of 25 college students with an average age of 22.7 ($\pm$2.5) and were classified into the IGD group (n = 13) and the healthy group (n = 12) by using Young's Internet Addiction Test (IAT) and Compulsive Internet Use Scale (CIUS). The subjects played the League of Legends game for 30–40 min and collected EEG (16 channel) and ECG data throughout the game. The 240 EEG parameters (16ch. * 15) and 14 HRV parameters were used to extract the most effective sets of parameters. The t-test was conducted to sort out the parameters differentiating between the IGD group and the healthy group. Factor analysis was used to select parameters with the eigen value greater than 0.8. To remove multicollinearity, Pearson correlation was employed in this analysis. Finally, six sets of parameters were selected for logistic regression to differentiate two groups. As a result, the highest accuracy of the model was found to be Model 4. The HRV parameter has been dropped during the process of parameter elimination. The observed accuracy ranged from 63.3 to 71.4% whereas the existing accuracy ranged from 63.5 to 73.1%. In this study no synergy was observed when using both EEG and HRV parameters. In future study, a refined model can be further investigated focusing on EEG signals. Otherwise, bio-signals at particular events during game play can be explored to find a statistical model with a high and robust accuracy value.

Keywords: Classification of IGD · Electroencephalography · Heart rate variability · Logistic regression model

C. Stephanidis et al. (Eds.): HCII 2023, CCIS 1957, pp. 389–396, 2024.
https://doi.org/10.1007/978-3-031-49212-9_48

1   Introduction

Since the American Psychiatric Association (APA) highlighted the need for additional research on addictive gaming behavior in *Diagnostic and Statistical Manual of Mental Disorders* (5th Ed., DSM-5) [1]. In 2018, the World Health Organization (WHO) added "gaming disorder" to the 11th revision of International Classification of Diseases (*ICD-11*) with the code 6C51 [2].

Many subjective questionnaires for diagnosing gaming disorder have been studied over the years. However, there were limitations that have been reported by many authors. Kuss et al. [3] stated that subjective questionnaires could result in bias due to subjectivity, and King and Delfabbro [4] mentioned that subjective questionnaires could result in multiple interpretations due to the lack of standardization. In addition, Stevens et al. [5] noted that there might be limitations due to cultural differences. According to Andreetta et al. [6], there might be restrictions due to cultural distinctions.

In order to overcome the limitation of subjective questionnaire, quantitative studies have been conducted. Kim et al. [7] studied the differences between the IGD group and the control group by using HRV parameters when specific events occurred during gameplay. They reported the maximum classification accuracy of 70.3%. Furthermore, Kim et al. [8] investigated the relative power of EEGs measured during the entire gameplay, and they classified the IGD group with the accuracy of 73.1%. The results from these studies motivated authors to further investigate both EEG and HRV parameters for enhancement of classification.

Therefore, the purpose of this study is to develop a statistical model for the differentiation between the IGD group and control group by using both EEG and HRV parameters.

2   Method

2.1   Subject

The IGD and healthy groups were determined by using both the IAT [9] and the CIUS test by Meerkerk et al. [10]. The subjects who scored 50 on the IAT and 2.5 on the CIUS were classified to the IGD group, and the subjects who scored 30 on the IAT and 1.5 on the CIUS were classified as belonging to the healthy group. 364 volunteers were recruited from the Hanyang University community, and finally 13 IGD subjects and 12 healthy subjects were selected based on the IAT and CIUS scores. The ages of the healthy group and IGD group were 24.7 ($\pm$2.77) and 22.9 ($\pm$1.91) respectively. Each of the subjects had a minimum of two years of gaming experience. Subjects had no history of mental disorders, including depression and ADHD. To have the proper level of intensity, subjects played the 'Ranked game' that could affect their levels, and they were compensated at the end of the study to maintain the motivation. The experiment was conducted in accordance with the Declaration of Helsinki and regulations under consideration of the Institutional Review Board of Hanyang University in the Republic of Korea (IRB number: HYU-2019–08-004–1).

2.2 Apparatus

League of Legends (LOL) from Riot Games Inc. (Los Angeles, CA, USA) was used for the experiment. In 2022, the average monthly player count for League of Legends was 180 million, with a daily peak of 32 million players worldwide [11]. In 2022 Hangzhou Asian Games, 'e-sports' was an official event, and League of Legends was one of the official nine games.

For the experiment, the 'QEEG-64FX' from LAXTHA Inc. Was used for measuring EEG and ECG. The data collection software was 'Telescan' by LAXTHA Inc. A testing room was isolated to minimize the external stimuli that could influence the subjects. Figure 1 shows the experimental setting. For data collection, EEG cap was worn according to the 10–20 system electrode attachment method with 16 channels: Fp1, Fp2, F3, F4, F7, F8, C3, C4, P3, P4, P7, P8, T7, T8, O1, O2. And the surface electrodes for ECG were also attached according to Standard limb lead II method, with the active electrode (+) at the right chest, the reference electrode (-) above the left chest, and the ground electrode behind the neck. The stability of signals was verified before running the experiment.

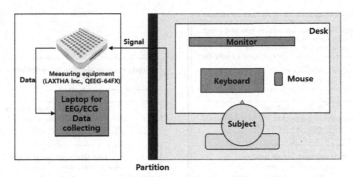

Fig. 1. Experimental setting

2.3 Procedure

The experimental procedure was shown in Fig. 2.

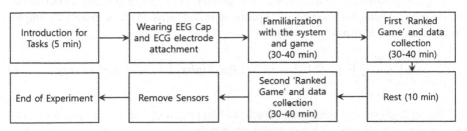

Fig. 2. Experimental procedure

2.4 Experimental Design and Data Analysis

A between subject design was used in this study. The independent variable was the type of group with two levels: IGD group and healthy group. The dependent variables were EEG and HRV/ECG parameters: 15 EEG parameters * 16 channels and 14 HRV/ECG parameters. A total of 254 parameters were used for dependent measures.

The sampling rate was 500 Hz. The window size for data collection was 30 to 40 min, and the analysis was performed with 20 min high quality data. Fast Fourier Transform (FFT) was used to compute the relative power of parameters: theta 4–8 Hz, alpha 8–12 Hz, SMR 12–15 Hz, mid-beta 15–20 Hz, high-beta 20–30 Hz, beta 12–30 Hz.

The Christov ECG R-peak division algorithm was used to extract HRV parameters: mean NN-interval, SDNN, RMSSD, pNNI50, pNNI20, SDSD, and average of HR. FFT was also used to extract the ECG frequency parameters: LF, HF, normLF, normHF, LF/HF ratio, Total Power. The statistical process for parameter elimination is summarized in Fig. 3. SPSS 26 was used for statistical computation in this study.

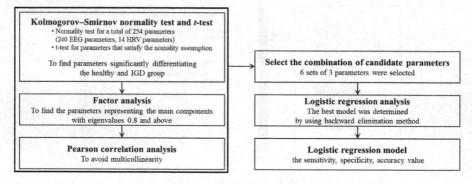

Fig. 3. Statistical process for parameter elimination

3 Results

Among 254 parameter candidates, the 13 parameters (12 EEG parameters, 1 HRV parameter) were selected after t-test out of 23 parameters that satisfied the normality assumption by Kolmogorov-Smirnov test (Table 1)

$$\ln\left(\frac{P}{1-P}\right) = -0.131 - 19.372\,Rel.Alpha_{F4} + 5.409\,Rel.Theta_{F3} \qquad (1)$$

Factor analysis was conducted in order to find principal components among 12 EEG parameters. Parameters with eigenvalue greater than or equal to 0.8 were selected and presented (Table 2). For HRV, only one parameter demonstrated a significant difference between groups. To avoid multicollinearity, Pearson correlation analysis was used

(Table 3), and parameter pairs with greater than 0.60 correlation coefficient value were discarded for the logistic regression models. The model was constructed with principal parameters in factor 1, factor 2, and HRV parameter (Table 4). Finally, the six final logistic regression models were presented along with accuracy values (Table 5). The classification accuracy ranged from 63.3% to 71.4%. The most sensitive parameters were Rel.Alpha (F3), Rel.Alpha (F4), Rel.Theta (F3), and Rel.Theta (F7). On the other hand, SDSD, the only HRV parameter, was not selected due to lack of discriminant power in this statistical process. The final logistic regression model is presented in Eq. 1.

Table 1. Twelve EEG parameters and one HRV parameter that significantly differentiate two groups (Rel. = relative power)

Parameter (ch.)	Group	Mean	t	sig
Rel.Theta (F3)	IGD	0.485(±0.255)	2.061	0.045
	Healthy	0.344(±0.223)		
Rel.Alpha (F3)	IGD	0.251(±0.175)	−2.087	0.042
	Healthy	0.378(±0.248)		
Alpha/Theta (F3)	IGD	0.369(±0.218)	−3.022	0.004
	Healthy	0.571(±0.249)		
(SMR + Midbeta)/Theta (F3)	IGD	0.235(±0.157)	−1.755	0.086
	Healthy	0.328(±0.21)		
Rel.Alpha (F4)	IGD	0.324(±0.162)	−2.475	0.017
	Healthy	0.463(±0.227)		
Alpha/Midbeta (F4)	IGD	0.282(±0.217)	−1.758	0.085
	Healthy	0.398(±0.243)		
Alpha/Theta (F4)	IGD	0.333(±0.175)	−1.999	0.051
	Healthy	0.457(±0.255)		
Rel.Theta (F7)	IGD	0.715(±0.142)	3.069	0.004
	Healthy	0.541(±0.243)		
Alpha/Midbeta (F7)	IGD	0.351(±0.233)	1.683	0.099
	Healthy	0.254(±0.158)		
Rel.Alpha (O1)	IGD	0.344(±0.123)	-2.776	0.008
	Healthy	0.477(±0.204)		
Midbeta/Alpha (O1)	IGD	0.48(±0.193)	1.924	0.060
	Healthy	0.379(±0.175)		

(continued)

Table 1. (*continued*)

Parameter (ch.)	Group	Mean	t	sig
Midbeta/Alpha (O2)	IGD	0.622(±0.218)	2.110	0.040
	Healthy	0.499(±0.188)		
SDSD	IGD	0.351(±0.207)	-1.691	0.098
	Healthy	0.45(±0.202)		

Table 2. Factor analysis results for 12 EEG parameters (excluding HRV parameters) that showed significant differences in the t-test

	Component	
	Factor 1	Factor 2
Rel.Alpha (F3)	0.890	
Rel.Alpha_(F4)	0.866	
Rel.Theta_(F3)		−0.926
(SMR + Midbeta)/Theta (F3)		0.864
Rel.Theta_(F7)		−0.827

Table 3. Results of Pearson correlation analysis among five parameters with high eigenvalues

Correlations		Component 1		Component 2		
		Rel.Alpha (F3)	Rel.Alpha (F4)	Rel.Theta (F3)	(SMR + MidBet)/Theta (F3)	Rel.Theta (F7)
Rel.Alpha (F3)	Coef.	1.000	0.888	-0.121	0.058	−0.291
	p-value	0.000	0.000	0.408	0.692	0.042
Rel.Alpha (F4)	Coef.	−	1.000	-0.108	0.098	−0.342
	p-value	−	0.000	0.460	0.502	0.016
Rel.Theta (F3)	Coef.	−	−	1.000	−0.865	0.651
	p-value	−	−	0.000	0.000	0.000
(SMR + MidBeta) /Theta (F3)	Coef.	−	-	−	1.000	−0.616
	p-value	−	−	−	0.000	0.000
Rel.Theta (F7)	Coef.	−	−	−	−	1.000
	p-value	−	−	−	−	0.000

Table 4. Six sets of parameters selected from factor analysis

Model Candidates No	Final Candidate Parameters
1	Rel.Alpha (F3), Rel.Theta (F3), SDSD
2	Rel.Alpha (F3), (SMR + MidBeta)/Theta (F3), SDSD
3	Rel.Alpha (F3), Rel.Theta (F7), SDSD
4	Rel.Alpha (F4), Rel.Theta (F3), SDSD
5	Rel.Alpha (F4), (SMR + MidBeta)/Theta (F3), SDSD
6	Rel.Alpha (F4), Rel.Theta (F7), SDSD

Table 5. The performance of six logistic regression models based on the final six sets of parameters

Model No	Model Variable	B	p	Sensitivity	Specificity	Accuracy
1	Rel.Alpha (F3)	−19.018	0.073	0.640	0.708	67.3%
	Rel.Theta (F3)	5.576	0.075			
	Constant	−0.277	0.906			
2	Rel.Alpha (F3)	−20.294	0.054	0.720	0.542	63.3%
	Constant	3.031	0.053			
3, 6	Rel.Theta (F7)	8.052	0.011	0.680	0.583	63.3%
	Constant	−4.942	0.014			
4	Rel.Alpha (F4)	−19.372	0.037	0.720	0.708	71.4%
	Rel.Theta (F3)	5.409	0.084			
	Constant	−0.131	0.954			
5	Rel.Alpha (F4)	−21.238	0.027	0.640	0.667	65.3%
	Constant	3.197	0.028			

4 Conclusion

In this study, the authors have attempted to develop a classification model by combining the parameters of EEG and ECG bio-signals. The statistical process demonstrated that five EEG parameters and one HRV parameter could best discriminate between IGD and healthy group. However, the final logistic regression models were constructed only by EEG parameters. This indicated that the EEG signals have prevailed in differentiating bio-signals of two groups. Conclusively, the final model presented in Eq. 1 showed the accuracy of 71.4%. This level of accuracy was not sufficient for diagnostic purpose. Thus, it needs to be further refined. The further study can be conducted by focusing on EEG parameters that were proven to be effective in this study. Moreover, the study can be extended by using event related data that could be the outcome of strong stimuli for game players.

Acknowledgement. This research was funded by an Institute of Information & communications Technology Planning & Evaluation (IITP) grant funded by the Korean government (MSIT) (No. RS-2022–00155885, Artificial Intelligence Convergence Innovation Human Resources Development (Hanyang University ERICA)).

References

1. American Psychiatric Association.: Diagnostic and statistical manual of mental disorders: DSM-5, vol. 5(5). American psychiatric association, Washington (2013)
2. World Health Organization.: The ICD-11 Classification of Mental and Behavioral Disorders: Diagnostic Criteria for Research; World Health Organization: Geneva, Switzerland (2018)
3. Kuss, D.J., Griffiths, M.D., Pontes, H.M.: Chaos and confusion in DSM-5 diagnosis of internet gaming disorder: Issues, concerns, and recommendations for clarity in the field. J. Behav. Addiction **6**, 103–109 (2017)
4. King, D.L., Delfabbro, P.H.: Internet gaming disorder treatment: a review of definitions of diagnosis and treatment outcome. J. Clin. Psychol. **70**(10), 942–955 (2014)
5. Stevens, M.W., Dorstyn, D., Delfabbro, P.H., King, D.L.: Global prevalence of gaming disorder: A systematic review and meta-analysis. Aust. N. Z. J. Psychiatry **55**(6), 553–568 (2021)
6. Andreetta, J., Teh MSc, J., Burleigh, T.L., Gomez, R., Stavropoulos, V.: Associations between comorbid stress and Internet Gaming Disorder symptoms: are there cultural and gender variations? Asia-Pacific Psychiatry **12**(2) (2020)
7. Kim, J.Y., Kim, H.-S., Kim, D.J., Im, S.K., Kim, M.S.: Identification of video game addiction using heart-rate variability parameters. Sensors **21**(14) (2021)
8. Kim, J.-Y., Kim, D.-J., Im, S.-K., Kim, H.-S., Park, J.-S.: EEG parameter selection reflecting the characteristics of internet gaming disorder while playing league of legends. Sensors **23**(3) (2023)
9. Young, K.S.: Internet addiction: the emergence of a new clinical disorder. Cyberpsychol. Behav. **1**, 237–244 (1998)
10. Meerkerk, G.J., Van Den Eijnden, R.J., Vermulst, A.A., Garretsen, H.F.: The compulsive internet use scale (CIUS): some psychometric properties. Cyberpsychol. Behav. **12**, 1–6 (2009)
11. RiftFeed. League of Legends Player Count: Here Are The Stats. https://riftfeed.gg/more/player-count, (Accessed 18 June 2023)

Dreadphobia: Evaluating the Usability of a Virtual Reality Application in Support of Mental Health

Shaimeira Meekins, Elijah Ballou, and Naja A. Mack(⊠)

Morgan State University, Baltimore, MD 21251, USA
{shmee1,elba1,naja.mack}@morgan.edu

Abstract. Mental health disparities within African American communities are a significant concern, as research shows that they often receive poor quality care and lack access to culturally competent mental health services due to various barriers. Culturally responsive care can be facilitated through the integration of virtual reality (VR) technology, which has become more accessible and affordable in recent years. This research aims to design, develop, and evaluate the usability of Dreadphobia, a VR application built in Unity cross-platform engine, that provides evidence-based information and resources about mental and behavioral issues in African American communities in an engaging way. The Meta Quest 2 headset was used to create a VR escape room environment that allows individuals to explore and find hidden facts about different mental health illnesses surrounding Black communities. The application has gamification features such as music, sound effects, teleportation, and scoring. The goal is to bring awareness to mental health disparities within African American communities and help individuals with mental illnesses seek treatment. This study aimed to test the functionality of Dreadphobia and identify areas of confusion in the user experience, as well as uncover opportunities for improvement. Out of a total of nine participants who evaluated the system, two of them rated it poorly, indicating that there were issues with its performance. However, despite this negative feedback, the average SUS score given by all participants was 74.44, which is above average and falls between a good and excellent rating. Although there are areas for improvement, the pilot study had promising results, and this research is a positive step toward creating a more equitable and comprehensive mental health learning tool accessible to everyone.

Keywords: Mental Health · Disparities · African-American Communities · Virtual Reality · Usability Testing

1 Introduction

According to the Centers for Disease Control and Prevention (CDC), mental health refers to a person's psychological and emotional well-being, which affects their thoughts, feelings, and behaviors [3]. Good mental health enables individuals to manage daily life stressors, work efficiently, and contribute meaningfully to

C. Stephanidis et al. (Eds.): HCII 2023, CCIS 1957, pp. 397–402, 2024.
https://doi.org/10.1007/978-3-031-49212-9_49

their communities [8]. Conversely, poor mental health can lead to various mental illnesses such as depression, anxiety, bipolar disorder, and schizophrenia [6]. There are inequalities in mental health outcomes among African Americans in the US. Due to a range of social and environmental factors, African Americans are more likely to experience mental health problems and less likely to receive culturally responsive appropriate care and treatment compared to other racial counterparts [2].

A significant factor contributing to mental health disparities in African American communities is discrimination and racism [9]. Discrimination can cause chronic stress and lead to feelings of anxiety and depression. Additionally, African Americans are more likely to face systemic racism and experience trauma from police brutality and other forms of violence, which can have long-term effects on mental health. Additionally, African Americans are more likely to face socioeconomic challenges, such as poverty, unemployment, and inadequate access to health care services. These issues can lead to higher levels of stress and affect mental health. African Americans are also more likely to lack health insurance coverage, which can limit their access to mental health services.

Furthermore, cultural factors may influence mental health disparities in African American communities. The stigma and shame associated with mental health problems can discourage people from seeking help. African Americans are also more likely to rely on religious and spiritual beliefs to help deal with mental health issues, which can be a barrier to seeking professional care. Finally, the shortage of culturally competent mental health professionals may also contribute to mental health disparities in African American communities. Many mental health professionals may not understand the cultural experiences and perspectives of African Americans, which can make it difficult to provide effective treatment. To address mental health disparities in African-American communities, it is essential to provide appropriate and culturally responsive care, increase access to mental health services, and reduce the stigma surrounding mental health. Additionally, efforts need to be made to address systemic racism and socioeconomic factors that contribute to mental health disparities. By recognizing and addressing these issues, we can work to improve mental health outcomes in African-American communities.

Virtual Reality (VR) has been the focus of several research studies examining its effectiveness in treating different mental health conditions such as phobias, eating disorders, PTSD, and psychosis [5]. Lucia Valmaggia has recently reviewed the growing interest and popularity of VR [7]. VR is an immersive technology where a person wears a head-mounted display, and the computer generates images/sounds that are synchronized with their movements, aiming to simulate real-life experiences. Researchers and certified clinicians can use VR to bring real-life experiences to a laboratory setting, making it an effective therapeutic, educational, and exciting tool to support various mental health conditions [4]. This paper aims to evaluate the use of VR and its potential for supporting mental health in African American communities.

2   System Overview

Dreadphobia is a VR application built in Unity cross-platform engine that provides evidence-based information and resources about mental and behavioral issues in African American communities. It is designed to raise awareness about mental health disparities within African American communities and help individuals with mental illnesses seek treatment. The application takes the form of a VR escape room environment where users can explore and find hidden facts about different mental health illnesses surrounding Black communities. It includes gamification features such as music, sound effects, teleportation, and scoring to engage users and make learning about mental health issues more fun and interactive. The goal of Dreadphobia is to address the persistent and complex issues of mental health within African American communities by providing culturally responsive care through the use of VR technology.

3   Study Design

The purpose of this study was to test the functionality of Dreadphobia by observing real users as they attempted to complete the designated tasks. The goal was to identify any areas of confusion and discover opportunities to improve the overall user experience.

3.1   Participants

The study was completed by 9 participants in its entirety. All participants (100%) identified as African-American or Black. Among the participants, 7 (77.8%) were male and 2 (22.2%) were female. In terms of age, 5 (55.6%) were between 18–20 years old, and 4 (44.4%) were between 21–25 years old. Additionally, 6 (66.7%) of the participants had used VR before the study, while 3 (33.3%) had never used VR before.

3.2   Procedure

At the beginning of the study, the informed consent was explained to the participants by the researchers. After obtaining consent, a pre-survey was administered to collect demographic information. Participants were then instructed to complete five tasks using a headset that had Dreadphobia preloaded onto the screen. These tasks included reading instructions, exploring the entire virtual environment, teleporting to a claw machine, resetting their position in the environment, and finding five hidden facts. The System Usability Scale (SUS) was used to ask participants 10 questions to evaluate the app's usability. Lastly, a post interview was conducted where participants were asked to share their likes, dislikes, and suggested changes for the system.

4   Results

4.1   Usability

Out of a total of nine participants who evaluated the system, two of them rated it poorly, indicating that there were issues with its performance. However, despite this negative feedback, the average SUS score given by all participants was 74.44, which is above average and falls between a good and excellent rating according to Bangdor's [1] scale. While the overall score suggests that the system performed well, the fact that some of the participants had negative experiences highlights the importance of considering individual user feedback when evaluating a system's effectiveness. It is also worth noting that the context and specific tasks involved in the evaluation may have played a role in shaping the overall score, so further investigation and refinement may be necessary to fully optimize the system's performance.

4.2   Task Completion

All participants completed Tasks 1 through 3. Task 4 (Reset Yourself) and Task 5 (Find 5 hidden facts) had the highest rates of incompleteness among the five tasks, and the usability scores were negatively impacted by unanticipated technical and design issues. One participant encountered a design flaw that caused them to be outside of the virtual environment's boundaries, while two others experienced headset malfunctions while performing the task. Additionally, some participants may not have adequately read instructions for resetting themselves due to eagerness to explore the virtual environment. The resulting frustration from these unaccounted issues likely contributed to the lower usability scores.

4.3   Post-interviews

During the post-interview, participants provided feedback on what they liked, disliked, and would change about the system. They generally liked the overall idea of Dreadphobia, the look of the map, and the fact that it uses virtual reality. However, participants also expressed several dislikes, including the controls for moving around, the fact that the system only displayed information in one eye of the Oculus lens at times, the inability to use any of the arcade machines, and the music selection. In terms of changes, participants suggested that Dreadphobia should have continuous movement instead of teleportation, allow users to play games on some of the machines for entertainment, display the facts in both lenses of the Oculus simultaneously, make the lighting dimmer to create a feeling of dread, allow users to pause music, and add a tutorial or training session to teach users how to toggle the controller. Overall, these suggestions could improve the user experience and make Dreadphobia more engaging and effective for its intended purpose.

5   Future Work

Based on post-interview feedback from participants, the team has decided to make some modifications to the Dreadphobia system. One major suggestion was to add more features and playing levels to enhance the overall experience and increase engagement. Additionally, the system will be made cross-platform by optimizing it for use on mobile devices, allowing users to access the system on-the-go. Another area of focus is investigating the ease of use and satisfaction of the modified user interface. User testing will be conducted, and feedback will be gathered to ensure that the interface is intuitive and user-friendly.

An investigation will also be conducted into the effectiveness of the system, including its impact on knowledge acquisition, attitude change, and behavioral intentions related to mental health. This will involve collecting data from users before and after interacting with the system and analyzing the results to determine its effectiveness. Finally, a comparison will be made between Dreadphobia and traditional methods for teaching about mental health, such as textbooks, lectures, and workshops. This will allow for an assessment of the unique strengths and weaknesses of the system and identify areas for improvement. Overall, these modifications and investigations will help to further enhance the effectiveness and impact of Dreadphobia.

6   Conclusion

The hypothesis that Dreadphobia would have below-average usability was disproven since the system was found to be usable and well-received by undergraduate students, as demonstrated by the high SUS score and positive feedback. However, it's crucial to recognize that the conclusion is based on limited data, and further research may be required to fully evaluate the system's usability and likability. A significant proportion of participants also learned at least one piece of information inadvertently, highlighting the potential of Dreadphobia as a mental health learning tool. Although there are areas for improvement, the pilot study had promising results, and this research is a positive step toward creating a more equitable and comprehensive mental health learning tool accessible to everyone.

Acknowledgments. This research was supported by the NIGMS RISE 5R25GM-058904 grant and the RISE-ReACHES program.

References

1. Bangor, A., Kortum, P., Miller, J.: Determining what individual SUS scores mean: adding an adjective rating scale. J. Usability Stud. 4(3), 114–123 (2009)
2. Bailey, R.K.: Racial and ethnic disparities in depression: current perspectives. Psychol. Res. Behav. Manag. 12, 343–352 (2019)
3. Centers for Disease Control and Prevention: Mental health (2021). https://www.cdc.gov/mentalhealth/

4. Freeman, D., et al.: Virtual reality in the assessment, understanding, and treatment of mental health disorders. Psychol. Med. **47**, 2393–2400 (2017)
5. Valmaggia, L.R., Latif, L., Kempton, M.J., Rus-Calafell, M.: Virtual reality in the psychological treatment for mental health problems: an systematic review of recent evidence. Psychiat. Res. **236**, 189–195 (2016)
6. National Alliance on Mental Illness: Mental health conditions (2022). https://www.nami.org/About-Mental-Illness/Mental-Health-Conditions
7. Valmaggia, L.R.: The use of virtual reality in psychosis research and treatment. World Psychiat. **16**, 246–247 (2017)
8. World Health Organization: Mental health: Strengthening our response (2021). https://www.who.int/news-room/fact-sheets/detail/mental-health-strengthening-our-response
9. Zapolski, T.C., Beutlich, M.R., Fisher, S., Barnes-Najor, J.: Collective ethnic-racial identity and health outcomes among African American youth: Examination of promotive and protective effects. Cult. Div. Ethnic Minority Psychol. **25**(3), 388 (2019)

Assessing ChatGPT's Performance in Health Fact-Checking: Performance, Biases, and Risks

Zhenni Ni[1]([✉]) [iD], Yuxing Qian[1] [iD], Pascal Vaillant[2] [iD], Marie-Christine Jaulent[2] [iD], and Cédric Bousquet[2] [iD]

[1] School of Information Management, Wuhan University, Wuhan, China
`jennie_n@whu.edu.cn`
[2] Laboratoire d'Informatique Médicale et d'Ingénierie des Connaissances en eSanté (LIMICS), Sorbonne Université, Inserm, Paris, France

Abstract. The increasing use of ChatGPT by the general public has prompted us to assess ChatGPT's performance in health fact-checking and uncover potential biases and risks arising from its utilization. In this study, we employed two publicly accessible datasets to evaluate ChatGPT's performance. We utilized BERTopic for clustering health claims into topics and subsequently employed the gpt-3.5-turbo API for fact-checking these claims. ChatGPT's performance was appraised on multi-class (False, Mixture, Mostly-False, Mostly-True, True) and binary (True, False) levels, with a thorough analysis of its performance across various topics. ChatGPT achieved a F1-score of 0.54 and 0.64 in the multi-class task and 0.88 and 0.85 in the binary task on the two datasets, respectively. In most health topics (e.g., vaccines, Covid-19), ChatGPT's F1-score exceeded 0.8, except for specific topics, such as novel or contentious cancer treatments, which yielded a F1-score below 0.6. We scrutinized the erroneous fact-checking labels and explanations provided by ChatGPT, revealing that it may produce inaccurate results for claims with misleading intent, inaccurate information, emerging research findings, or contentious health knowledge.

Keywords: Misinformation · Large language model · Health information retrieval

1 Introduction

Large language models (LLMs) have demonstrated extraordinary capabilities in the comprehension and generation of the natural language across various domains including health and medicine, promising richer cooperation and integration between humans and AI [1–3]. With growing user adoption and public interest, LLMs like ChatGPT are being used by a wide range of people. LLMs have the potential to revolutionize how people access health knowledge in their daily lives by serving as efficient tools for fact-checking and retrieving health information [4]. Thus, a critical evaluation of its performance, biased, and risk in health fact-checking is warranted to ensure its effective and ethical utilization in this sensitive domain.

C. Stephanidis et al. (Eds.): HCII 2023, CCIS 1957, pp. 403–408, 2024.
https://doi.org/10.1007/978-3-031-49212-9_50

In this study, we employed two publicly accessible datasets comprising a broad range of health-related claims accompanied by expert-annotated fact-checking labels, to evaluate ChatGPT's performance. We utilized BERTopic for clustering health claims into topics and subsequently employed the gpt-3.5-turbo API for fact-checking these claims. ChatGPT's performance was appraised on multi-class (False, Mixture, Mostly-False, Mostly-True, True) and binary (True, False) levels, with a thorough analysis of its performance across various topics.

2 Methods

2.1 Datasets

We utilized two misinformation datasets, namely Monant [5] and PUBHEALTH [6]. Details of the two datasets are shown in Table 1.

Monant [5] contains both medical news articles/blogs and fact-checked claims. For the scope of this research, the focus is intentionally directed toward the claims, primarily due to their succinctness and the inclusion of veracity ratings. Monant comprises 3,424 claims, each labeled as false, mostly false, true, mostly true, true, mixture, or unknown.

PUBHEALTH [6] pertains to a wide spectrum of health topics including biomedical subjects, government healthcare policy, and other public health-related stories, along with explanations offered by journalists to support the veracity labeling of these claims. It comprises 11,832 claims, each labeled as true, false, mixture, or unproven.

Table 1. Public misinformation datasets on health and medical topics.

Name	Timespan	Topic	Labels	Number of claims
Monant	2019/12–2022/01	Medical information	False, Mostly False, Mixture, Mostly true, True, Unknown	3,424
PUBHEALTH	1995/10–2020/05	Health information	True, False, Mixture, Unproven	11,832

2.2 Experiment Procedure

Our experiment procedure consists of three parts: topic modeling, performance evaluation, and content analysis.

BERTopic [7] were applied to group health claims into topics. We manually reviewed each topic and removed non-health-related topics such as guns and political elections. In addition, we removed claims with fact-checking labels of unproven and unknown. Given the timespan of ChatGPT's training data, claims created before September 2021 were removed. Finally, there are 1,308 claims with 29 topics in the Monant dataset and 11,003 claims with 171 topics in the PUBHEALTH dataset.

We then call the gpt-3.5-turbo API to evaluate the veracity of the health claims. For the Monant dataset, ChatGPT's performance was evaluated on a multi-class scale, categorized into five distinct labels: False, Mostly False, Mixture, Mostly True, or True. For the PUBHEALTH dataset, the performance was assessed on a slightly different multi-class scale, categorized as True, False, or Mixture. Alongside these multi-class evaluations, we also evaluated the performance at a binary level, considering only the categories of True or False. We added the additional category "Not enough information" due to the short length of the claims text and the lack of context. Claims that are classified as "Not enough information" are not included in the performance evaluation. The API call looks as follows:

```
response = completions_with_backoff(
    model="gpt-3.5-turbo",
    max_tokens=400,
    messages=[
{"role": "system", "content": "You are a medical ex-
pert. Please judge the veracity of health infor-
mation and give an explanation. Output format: Verac-
ity: True/False/Mixture/Mostly-false/Mostly-true/Not
enough information; Explanation"},
    {"role": "user", "content": claim}
    ]
)
```

Word clouds were used to visualize the topics with F1 higher than 0.9 and the topics with F1 lower than 0.6. Finally, we manually reviewed the misclassified claims and compared the differences between ChatGPT's explanations and experts' explanations.

3 Results and Discussion

Figure 1 depicts the multi-class scale evaluation results for Monant and PUBHEALTH datasets. The lower-than-expected weighted average F1-scores in both Monant (0.54) and PUBHEALTH (0.64) might be attributed to the divergent perceptions of 'True' and 'False' degrees between ChatGPT and human experts, as well as the inherent blurred boundaries among the datasets' multi-class categories. For instance, claims deemed unambiguously True or False by experts were often classified by ChatGPT as a Mixture. Despite this ambiguity, ChatGPT excelled in identifying false claims with high precision, scoring 0.87 in Monant and 0.79 in PUBHEALTH. This suggests a lower risk of the AI incorrectly labeling true health claims as false, highlighting ChatGPT's potential value in health fact-checking scenarios.

Table 2 illustrates the binary classification evaluation results of the Monant and PUB-HEALTH datasets. In terms of the weighted average F1-scores, both datasets yielded satisfactory results, with 0.88 for Monant and 0.85 for PUBHEALTH, indicating an over-all effective performance by ChatGPT. However, careful analysis uncovers potential risks

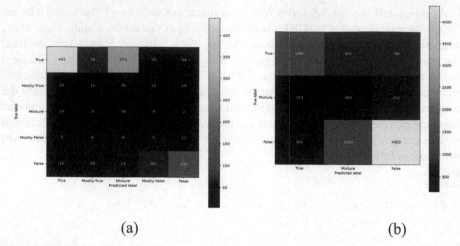

(a)   (b)

Fig. 1. Evaluation of performance on multi-class scales: (a) Monant Dataset and (b) PUB-HEALTH Dataset

and biases. In both datasets, the 'False' category had a lower recall than precision; the 'True' category presents lower precision than recall. This pattern implies that ChatGPT is more likely to misidentify false claims as true, potentially leading to false affirmations and the propagation of incorrect health information.

Table 2. Evaluation of performance on a binary scale

Monant		Precision	Recall	F1-score	Support
	FALSE	0.95	**0.88**	0.92	854
	TRUE	**0.68**	0.86	0.76	250
	Accuracy			0.88	1104
	Macro Avg.	0.82	0.87	0.84	1104
	Weighted Avg.	0.89	0.88	**0.88**	1104
PUBHEALTH		Precision	Recall	F1-score	Support
	FALSE	0.89	**0.64**	0.74	2185
	TRUE	**0.85**	0.96	0.90	4528
	Accuracy			0.86	6713
	Macro Avg.	0.87	0.80	0.82	6713
	Weighted Avg.	0.86	0.86	**0.85**	6713

In the Monant dataset, 89.66% of topics (26 out of 29) achieved a F1-score exceeding 0.80. In the PUBHEALTH dataset, 59.65% of topics (102 out of 171) achieved an F1 score above this threshold. For a more visual perspective, we have illustrated the topic terms with a F1-score higher than 0.9 in Fig. 2, and those with a F1-score lower than 0.6 in Fig. 3, providing a clear representation of ChatGPT's performance across various topics. As seen in Fig. 2, ChatGPT performed well on the verification of health claims related to topics such as vaccines and Covid-19. However, when it comes to new or controversial cancer treatments or drug use (see Fig. 3), the F1-score of ChatGPT is below 0.6.

Fig. 2. Word cloud for topics with F1 higher than 0.9

Fig. 3. Word cloud for topics with F1 lower than 0.6

We found that ChatGPT tends to misclassify false claims as true when these involve misleading intent, emerging research findings, or contentious health knowledge. The divergence appears to stem from differing focuses. Medical experts emphasize the intent behind claims, such as marketing, and they scrutinize potential side effects and costs. Conversely, ChatGPT prioritizes the verification of new treatments' existence and their descriptions.

For instance, consider the claim, 'New study finds that proton therapy has fewer side effects in esophageal cancer patients.' Experts rate this as false because the claim does not address crucial questions like the extent of the side effects reduction, whether it actually decreases patients' health risks, or if proton therapy effectively treats cancer.

However, ChatGPT considers it true, recognizing the existence of such a study. This highlights the unique challenges and biases in AI-driven health fact-checking.

4 Conclusion

The results of this study shed light on ChatGPT's performance, potential risks, and inherent biases in the realm of Health Fact-Checking. In conclusion, ChatGPT demonstrates commendable competence in binary health fact-checking tasks. However, upon closely examining ChatGPT's incorrect fact-checking labels and explanations, we found that it may produce inaccurate results when handling claims characterized by misleading intent, emerging research findings, contentious health knowledge, or health-related anecdotes. In future work, we plan to delve deeper into understanding the limitations and strengths of ChatGPT in complex health fact-checking scenarios.

References

1. Nori, H., King, N., McKinney, S.M., et al.: Capabilities of gpt-4 on medical challenge problems. arXiv preprint arXiv: 230313375 (2023)
2. Singhal, K., Azizi, S,, Tu, T,, et al.: Large Language Models Encode Clinical Knowledge. arXiv preprint arXiv: 221213138 (2022)
3. Singhal, K., Tu, T., Gottweis, J., et al.: Towards Expert-Level Medical Question Answering with Large Language Models. arXiv preprint arXiv: 230509617 (2023)
4. Zuccon, G., Koopman, B.: Dr ChatGPT, tell me what I want to hear: How prompt knowledge impacts health answer correctness. arXiv preprint arXiv: 230213793 (2023)
5. Srba, I., Pecher, B., Tomlein, M., et al.: Monant medical misinformation dataset: mapping articles to fact-checked claims. In: Proceedings of the 45th International ACM SIGIR Conference on Research and Development in Information Retrieval, pp 2949–2959. ACM, Madrid Spain (2022)
6. Kotonya, N., Toni, F.: Explainable automated fact-checking for public health claims. In: Proceedings of the 2020 Conference on Empirical Methods in Natural Language Processing (EMNLP), pp 7740–7754. Association for Computational Linguistics, Online (2020)
7. Grootendorst, M.: BERTopic: Neural topic modeling with a class-based TF-IDF procedure (2022)

Digital Animation, Health Education in Post COVID-19 Scenario

Jose A. Oleas-Orozco[✉], Carlos Aguayza-Mendieta, Franklin Castillo, and Diego Sanchez

Universidad Indoamérica, Ambato, Ecuador
joleas@indoamerica.edu.ec

Abstract. In post pandemics scenario, viral respiratory diseases are show up very often in changeable and usually cold weather locations. Ecuadorian cities in Andean region have altitude and unpredictable climate characteristics where respiratory diseases are frequent. COVID-19, influenza, flu and other infections are still present in the environment This research shows a development and application of digital animation, showing the audiovisual production processes developed through digital tools, products in educational contexts, adapted to the global health situation post pandemics.

The study shows a mixed-type research divided into two phases. The first stage, for information collection, determined the needs for learning topics that collaborates in COVID-19 prevention in elementary education population through digital cartoons as a tool using social media as broadcast medium. The second stage, the animated product evaluation, inside an application scenario, in elementary schools in Riobamba city, that was exhibited through social networks. Through qualitative and quantitative research approaches, it has been possible to demonstrate the animation (digital cartoons) relevance in educational areas. Likewise, the study shows teachers and parents positive predisposition of digital animation use, as a learning tool and its use for educational content transmission, which is something new in the Ecuadorian school scene.

Keywords: Digital Animation · Health education · Covid-19 · educational content · Cartoons

1 Introduction

The World Health Organization WHO, declared a global public health emergency on January 30, 2020, recommended supporting world organizations to promote global solidarity due to COVID-19 [1]. On April 27, 2020, assistance to educational centers at all levels was suspended, affecting 115 million students. In Ecuador, more than five million students were affected by the suspension, 952,993 was at the basic level. Twenty-one Latin American countries, continued their studies remotely [2]. Isolation in educational field, activities in these conditions have generated tensions and difficulties for students, teachers and parents by assuming an active role as co-educators. For teachers, it has caused more work by having to teach content from their curriculum, review tasks and implement learning strategies in a different scenario [3, 4]. It is necessary to take emerging measures to satisfy the consequences generated by the change in teaching procedure from the face-to-face to virtual process, which is framed in economic and social problems, such as the learning interruption, little or no parents preparation for distance learning, the students conditioned access (economic, technological, regional factors) to digital resources [5–7].

Teaching Tools. Didactic tools have been very helpful since they allow the knowledge acquisition and provide impetus towards individual learning [8], audiovisuals have potential and aptitude as teaching resources [9]. Before social networks, audiovisual and animated consumption, there were studies of educational cartoons potential were presented on television. As well, television can be merged with educational dynamics, they combine emotion and curiosity to learn through audiovisual content [10]. Cartoon series can be class part, adding ICT in classrooms, along with digital whiteboards and computers [11]. Within didactic tools, there are games applied in classroom for children, however due to COVID-19 situation, these tools cannot be used physically, but through digital animation the message can reach the infants, becoming a learning effective channel, audiovisual resources are in children's daily lives, approach their interests outside and inside school, which benefits teachers because they have great potential to transmit curricular content [12].

Cartoons and Education. UNESCO [13], points out: "inequality in education is the main cause of the global learning crisis". In Ecuadorian territory, the interest in improving educational processes is framed in state laws, which cite the Radio and Television Broadcasting Law and the Organic Communication Law. "Art.- 8.- Prevalence in content dissemination. - The media, in general, will disseminate an informative, educational and cultural nature content, in a predominant way" [14]. Although it has not always been that way, nevertheless, antecedents can be found that relate animation (cartoons) to education. It can be mentioned that in the mid-1990s, UNICEF and *Ministerio de Salud Pública* worked on communication campaigns on child care and disease prevention with the character *Yo soy Máximo,* with Disney production company advisory [15].

In Latin America, animation and education have been reflected in *The Cantinflas Show* (1972), a partnership between Hanna-Barbera and Televisa [16]. In the Panamanian scenario, Mornhinweg and Herrera [17], point out cartoons in academic production should articulate projects to explain scientific concepts, history, culture, values, traditions, national symbols, social problems, among others. In Ecuador since 2012, *Educa*, a project with government support, of animated content, multiplatform [18]. Ecuadorian universities, the digital animation projects like Llígallo [19], in ancestral knowledge diffusion, Beltrán [20], animation and urbanity, Bermúdez [21], journalism and digital animation, Zumba [22], animation in diseases prevention, Méndez [23], with animation on interpersonal relationships and Oleas et al. [24], in teaching special education with animated avatars APP.

Animation works as educational resource, through entertainment, understand and conveyed educational content, acts as psychological filters were the viewer connects with reality, captures attention and arouses curiosity [25]. Also, use characters and role design, to generate positive impact and learning in children [26]. Audiovisual language contributes to infant personal identity who observes the story [17, 27]. This has evolved from experimental and artisanal to industrial [28, 29], technological advances allowed their processes evolution. García [30], points out "it could be affirmed that the evolution of society emerges in an accelerated manner, showing multiple communication and information products". The digital revolution has made animation faster and more accessible production, has made it ICT part [31]. The animation software used allowed new production forms and several application areas [32]. As well, Digital animation production technique known as Motion Graphics [33], stands out, which is made up of graphic design, infographics and animation, elements that move in a 2D and 3D environment, its essential characteristic provides dynamism and better capture attention [34].

Methodology. The research was qualitative and quantitative type, developed in two moments at the end of the year 2020 and the beginning of 2021. In the qualitative aspect, a sample of experts was used, applied interviews to basic education teachers, on teaching methods and tools. The quantitative section, surveys to 31 parents, by means clusters probabilistic criterion [35] in Unidad Educativa España from Ambato city for diagnosis, and Unidad Educativa Jose María Roman, in Riobamba city for evaluation phase to 35 parents, using focus groups [35]. The ICT usefulness for data collection, in diagnosis and verification, Zoom was used for interviews, surveys in both phases was applied through google forms.

Results Diagnostic Stage. The structured interviews conducted online with four teachers of basic education 2nd to 4th year, to Lic. Mg. Olga Astudillo and Lic. Mg. Gabriela Romo in Ambato and Lic. Patricia Asqui and Lic. Mercy Bravo in Riobamba. Information on didactic topics was obtained, summarized in the following Table 1:

Interviewees responses general synthesis.

Quantitative Section, Results of Parent Surveys. Surveys were carried out through questions about parent's perception about the ICT use for virtual teaching and cartoons use as teaching tool. The answers have been synthesized in the following items:

- Children, in pandemic and isolation scenario, spend their time on ICT in mobile device, from 3 to 4 h a day in 54%, from 2 to 3 h in 37% and 9% less than 2 h.
- Parents consider that ICTs collaborate in the students' learning process, in a 97% positive way.
- There is a considerable parent's ignorance about animation potential in 40%, they are unfamiliar about discipline.
- 87% consider cartoons as an ideal medium for transmitting information on education and health care.
- Knowledge reinforcement in their children learning, consider educational cartoons, would be a proper way in 93%.
- 96% consider cartoons are adequate resources, for education in health issues such Covid-19 virus.

After completing the first stage field research (diagnosis stage), qualitative, quantitative information interpretation and interpretation analysis it could be determined:

- The animated short production for health information about COVID-19 to basic education students is viable.
- Audiovisual media, become a transmitting information opportune way due to social networks and mobile devices.

Table 1.

Questions for teachers	Interviewees answers
Teaching methods during pandemic	Affectation in physical and leisure activities, due to confinement and little control in virtual classes. Also, family integration has increased, Parents integrated in their children educational process. Connectivity problems, internet and technological devices (cell phones, tablets, computers) access have arisen. Teaching creativity has been present in resources such as videos, images, interactive content and social networks (WhatsApp) use
Digital tools use	Increased use of own and third-party audiovisuals for classes and social networks use to teach classes, disseminate resources, send and receive tasks
Animation, education, health and COVID-19	Prior to confinement, audiovisuals use was sporadic, but they agree that cartoons, due to their playful and versatile nature, capture attention and generate greater retention. By other hand, teaching hygiene habits, was carried out with tools requested from parents, but in virtual class, emphasis was placed on health care through audiovisuals. Videos were used to prevent COVID-19 for cleaning, disinfection, mask wearing and distancing. Likewise, animation is considered to be an optimal medium, as it makes children pay more attention and learn better. Children learn by watching animated characters actions

Animation and cartoons, are playful, fun and clear tool within children teaching and learning process.

Proposal and Validation Stage. The animation proposal follows White [36] and Mínguez [37] process, as a creative base, audiovisual production procedures [38] were used. In this way, the following methodology is applied (Table 2):

Table 2.

1. Subject 2. Idea	
3. Preproduction	• Script • Sketch • Character/Scenario • Storyboard
4. Production	• Digitalization • Animation
5. Postproduction 6. Exhibition/distribution	

Audiovisual production process adapted to digital animation project

Storyboard

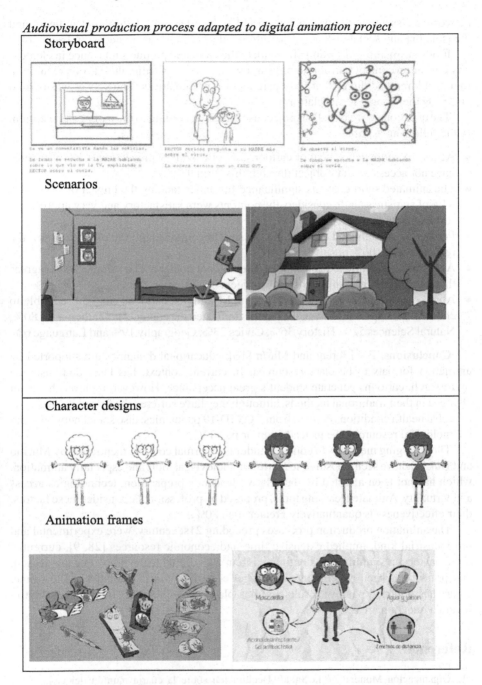

Scenarios

Character designs

Animation frames

Exhibition and Distribution. Before Internet ICT and irruption, audiovisual exhibition and distribution was very complicated, traditional media implied costs and schedules that limited the scope of products [39]. Independent productions have found in social networks a dissemination space at low cost [40]. In order to reach the target audience and the isolation and social distancing conditions, the cartoon was broadcast in Facebook.

Evaluation and Validation. To validate the animated products relevance in elementary education content transmission, a survey was carried out after the cartoon exhibition to the children and directed at forty parents or representatives. The survey was carried out using the Google forms platform.

The questions were based on project usefulness according to the parent's perception. In the following aspects:

- Access to animated content or cartoons about Covid-19 prevention, 42% of parents have not access on that subject through this format.
- The animated short contents significance for understanding the impact of Covid-19, 84% of statistic sample considers the contents were satisfactory and very appropriate for understanding by children.
- Perception of animated cartoon and possible recommendation to other families, the response was 100% positive.
- Acceptance of animated cartoon for educational content. The sample 100% agrees that its children receive educational subjects in animation format.
- About educational subject's types in which animated cartoons can be used, able to choose more than one answer, the parents indicated the contents in Mathematics 80%, Natural Sciences 52%, History 36%, Civics 23%, Geography 19% and Language 6%.

Conclusions. For Llorent and Marín [10], educational dynamics are supported by animation formats to be class resources. In current context, has been demonstrated by research, cartoons generate student's great acceptance. However, relations have not changed in their traditional methods, although they have suffered the forced increase due to global health conditions derived from COVID-19 pandemics, also social networks and technological resources use instead open or pay TV.

The emerging measures to educate students in virtual context, mentioned by Murillo and Duk [5], have seen a positive scenario for audiovisual tools and especially animation, which has not been affected by the relative teacher's preparation, technologies access and virtuality. Animated learning tools, prepared by professionals, consider these factors, their effectiveness is quantitatively greater than 80%.

The animation production processes preceding 21st century, were experimental and pre-industrial kind, implied extensive time and economic resources [28, 9], currently, these have been simplified and optimized thanks to digital technology. For this reason, this project has been experimented to target consideration, in a relatively short time, where has obtained positive results and has placed new prospects for collaboration in several education areas.

References

1. Organización Mundial de la Salud: Declaración sobre la cuarta reunión del Comité del Reglamento Sanitario Internacional, 1 Agosto 2020. [En línea]. https://www.who.int/es/news-room/detail/01-08-2020-statement-on-the-fourth-meeting-of-the-international-health-regulations-(2005)-emergency-committee-regarding-the-outbreak-of-coronavirus-disease-(covid-19)

2. CEPAL: CEPAL (2020). [En línea]. https://www.cepal.org/es/publicaciones/45527-desafio-social-tiempos-covid-19?utm_source=CiviCRM&utm_medium=email&utm_campaign=20200513_tercer_informe_covid19

3. Hernández Mondragón, A.R.: COVID-19: el efecto en la gestión educativa, Revista Latinoamericana de Investigación Social, 37–41 (2020)

4. CEPAL: Informe COVID-19 CEPAL-UNESCO (2020). [En línea]. https://www.cepal.org/sites/default/files/publication/files/45904/S2000510_es.pdf

5. Murillo, F.J., Duk, C.: El Covid-19 y las Brechas Educativas. Revista Latinoamericana de Educación Inclusiva, 11–13 (2020)

6. Vélez Calvo, X., Rodas Espinoza, C.: COVID-19: contexto educativo de niños ecuatorianos y establecimiento de normas para el cuidado de su salud. Coloquio. Reflexiones desde la Academia, 38–45 (2020)

7. Vásquez-Ponce, G.O.A., Indacochea-Figueroa, J.F., Forty-Moreira, R.J., Chara-Plúa, E.J.: Educación virtual en tiempos del covid-19 desde la perspectiva socioeconómica de los estudiantes de la Universidad Estatal del Sur de Manabí del cantón Jipijapa. Polo del Conocimiento, 798–823 (2020)

8. Ovando Almaguer, F.R.: Recursos didácticos y herramientas tecnológicas para la motivación, Editorial Digital UNID (2018)

9. Larrosa, J.: Niños atravesando el Paisaje. Notas sobre cine e infancia. de Educar la mirada. Políticas y pedagogías de la imagen, Buenos Aires, Ediciones Manantial SRL, pp. 113–134 (2006)

10. Llorent, V.J., Marín, V.: La integración de los dibujos animados en el currículo de Educación Infantil. Una propuesta teórica. REICE. Revista Iberoamericana sobre Calidad, Eficacia y Cambio en Educación, 73–82 (2013)

11. Malosetti Costa, L.: Algunas reflexiones sobre el lugar de las imágenes en el ámbito escolar. de Educar la mirada. Políticas y pedagogías de la imagen, Buenos Aires, Ediciones Manantial SRL, pp. 155–163 (2006)

12. Sonsoles Ramos, A., Botella Nicolás, A.M., Gómez Jiménez, M.: El audiovisual como recurso didáctico en el aula: Creación de dibujos animados con Muvizu, El Artista (2016)

13. UNESCO: Informe de seguimiento de la Educación en el mundo, Servicio de Prensa, Quito (2018)

14. ARCOTEL: ARCOTEL [En línea]. https://www.arcotel.gob.ec/wp-content/uploads/downloads/2013/07/ley_organica_comunicacion.pdf. Último acceso: 2021

15. Oleas-Orozco, J.: Animación Ecuatoriana: Orígenes y Futuro, de Narrativa de la Imagen. 1er Congreso Internacional de la Imagen y su Narrativa, Escuela Superior Politécnica de Chimborazo ESPOCH. Facultad de Informática y Electrónica. Escuela de Diseño Gráfico (2018)

16. Silva Escobar, J.P.: Cantinflas: mito, gestualidad y retórica despolitizada de lo popular, Atenea, pp. 107–120 (2017)

17. Mornhinweg, G., Herrera Montenegro, L.C.: Los Dibujos Animados: herramienta para la educación, Investigación y Pensamiento Crítico, pp. 21–37 (2017)

18. Alvarez Cedeño, E.N., Rodas Soto, B.I.: Análisis de la propuesta "Educa Radio" como recurso didáctico para los docentes de la educación básica elemental. INNOVA Res. J., 127–141 (2018)

19. Llígalo, T.: La animación digital en la difusión de saberes ancentrasles de la comunidad Chibuleo de la proviencia de Tungurahua. Universidad Tecnológica Indoamérica, Ambato (2019)

20. Beltrán, M.: Aplicación de las Técnicas de Animación Digital basado en un vídeo animado, que muestra la convivencia vecindaria (2013). [En línea]. http://dspace.udla.edu.ec/bitstream/33000/3728/1/UDLA-EC-TTADT-2013-08(S).pdf

21. Bermúdez, D.: La animación gráfica digital como recurso enriquecedor de los contenidos periodísticos-audiovisuales del sitio web www.elcolombiano.com (2015). [En línea]. http://repository.lasallista.edu.co/dspace/bitstream/10567/1785/1/Animacion_gra fica_digital_sitio_web_elcolombiano.pdf
22. Zumba, K.: Elaboración de historieta digital mediante animación 2D multimedia para dar a conocer los riesgos de contagio de transmisión sexual en los estudiantes de la Unidad Académica de Ciencias de la Ingeniería y Aplicadas de la Universidad Técnica de Cotopaxi (2016). [En línea]. http://repositorio.utc.edu.ec/handle/27000/2296
23. Méndez, Z.G.: Producción de un Cortometraje animado utilizando la técnica del stopmotion y la animación digital, Septiembre 2013. [En línea]. http://biblioteca2.ucab.edu.ve/anexos/biblioteca/marc/texto/AAS5752.pdf
24. Oleas-Orozco, J.A., Mena, A., Ripalda, D.: Hearing loss, mobile applications and inclusive social environments: approach to learning sign language for children without disabilities. de Intelligent Human Systems Integration (IHSI 2022) Integrating People and Intelligent Systems, Venecia (2022)
25. Grade-Lopez, V., Pérez García, Á.: Personajes de Animación con discapacidad a través de una perspectiva educativa, Creatividad y sociedad: revista de la Asociación para la Creatividad, pp. 259–283 (2016)
26. Navas, E., Armendariz, S.: Interactive application with motion comics in the school bullying awareness process. In: Mesquita, A., Abreu, A., Carvalho, J.V., de Mello, C.H.P. (eds.) Perspectives and Trends in Education and Technology. Smart Innovation, Systems and Technologies, pp. 219–230. Springer, Singapore (2023). https://doi.org/10.1007/978-981-19-6585-2_20
27. Saneleuterio, E., López-García-Torres, R.: Las películas de animación Infantil en la Actualidad: El hombre como contraejemplo. Edetania: Estudios y propuestas socio-educativas, pp. 203–221 (2019)
28. Maltin, L.: Of Mice and Magic. A history of american animated cartoons, Plume (1987)
29. Castro, K., Sánchez, J.R.: Dibujos animados y animación, Quito: Ciespal (1999)
30. García-Umaña, A., Ulloa, M.C., Córdoba, É.F.: La era digital y la deshumanización a efectos de las TIC. ReiDoCrea: Revista electrónica de investigación Docencia Creativa, pp. 11–20 (2020)
31. Cortés, A.: Experiencias en innovación educative. Ediciones de la U, Bogotá (2018)
32. Dueñas, B.: El potencial de la animación como recurso pedagógico y publicitario (2015). [En línea]. http://dspace.uhemisferios.edu.ec:8080/xmlui/bitstream/handle/123456789/235/CAROLINA%20DUENAS.pdf?sequence=1&isAllowed=y
33. Alonso Valdivieso, C.: Qué es Motion Gráphics, Con A de animación, pp. 104–116 (2016)
34. Alonso Valdivieso, C.: Enseñar con Motion Graphics. Revista Latinoamericana de Tecnología Educativa, pp. 75–84 (2015)
35. Hernandez Sampieri, R., Fernandez Collado, C., Baptista Lucio, P.: Metodología de la Investigación. McGraw Hill, México (2010)
36. White, T.: Animation from Pencil to Pixels. Elsevier, Burlington (2006)
37. Mínguez, N.: Itinerarios y formas del ensayo audiovisual. Editorial Gedisa, Barcelona (2019)
38. Worthington, C.: Bases del cine: Producción, Parramon (2009)
39. Sequera Díaz, R.: Televisión y Redes Sociales: nuevo paradigma en la promoción de contenidos televisivos. Ámbitos. Revista Internacional de Comunicación (2013)
40. Ortiz, C., Suing, A., González, V.: Gestión de redes sociales del proyecto audiovisual EnchufeTV. de La pantalla insomne, Tenerife, Congreso Internacional Latina de Comunicación Social (2016)

A Study on Improving the Medical Treatment System for Rural Elderly by Using Service Design Thinking – A Case Study of Huangbu Village

Bingxuan Shi[✉], Limin Tong, and Haimei Luo

Beijing Institute of Technology, Zhuhai, People's Republic of China
13004935@qq.com

Abstract. This paper presents a design case that discusses how to solve the problem of difficult access to medical care for the elderly in a more remote rural area of China. Using service design thinking, this paper fully understands the actual situation of Huangbu Village and the local elderly through fieldwork and other methods, integrates the actual needs of multiple stakeholders, and uses tools such as stakeholder maps and service blueprints and organizational framework diagrams to construct a service system and form a set of service processes, thereby improving the current rural elderly access system and attempting to form a universally applicable model that can be extended to other rural areas. Finally, we analyze the rationality and sustainability of the system through the evaluation criteria of service design innovation.

Keywords: Rural elderly · Service design · Medical treatment system

1 Introduction

1.1 Current Situation of Rural Medical Treatment

Since entering an aging society in 2000, China's aging population has continued to deepen. By 2022, 14% of China's population will be over the age of 65. In some remote rural areas, the health care system is incomplete, lacking medical facilities and medical personnel, and access to medical care for the elderly is a problem for those in power at all levels. The elderly in these areas are generally not well educated and have few ways to seek medical help, thus missing many opportunities to seek medical care and causing hardship in their old age. Rural health care is a priority for China's health sector, and it is directly related to the interests of the majority of farmers. However, the actual situation is not optimistic, as the medical system in rural areas of China has been suffering from poor organization and coordination, a general lack of medical knowledge, a shortage of medical personnel, loopholes and gaps in the medical management system platform, and unbalanced allocation of medical resources, which makes the medical system in rural areas face great challenges and complexity. According to relevant data, the number of rural doctors in China is being gradually reduced by 50,000 per year, and most of them are over 45 years old. It is evident that the loss of young village doctors is very serious. The issues of treatment, management system, and business capacity enhancement of rural doctors need further attention so that rural medical care can be taken to another level [1].

1.2 Service Design Intervention in Public Affairs

The search for solutions to complex social problems is the domain of sociology, management and economics, but with the multidimensional development of design, the design community has also responded to the search for solutions to complex problems. The discipline of design, because of its openness, systematization of the design process, and practicality, can be associated with the power of multiple disciplines for innovation. There are also examples of practice in many social issues, such as coping with aging, rural poverty alleviation, and social innovation [2]. As one of the most interdisciplinary design disciplines, service design has been making its mark in the field of public affairs systems in recent years, playing an increasingly important role in decision-making to solve complex social problems. The goal of service design is to bring better experience and higher user satisfaction. Human-centeredness is the basic concept of service design, and in the process of designing services, people, objects, environment and behavior are organically integrated to form a more rational system. As a college teacher, I have made various attempts in the course of Service Design, such as using the thinking and methods of service design to realize rural revitalization, solve the problem of campus waste classification, and solve the problem of stray cats in the community, and have achieved good results. The example of Huangbu Village studied in this thesis is one of the topics in my Service Design course.

2 Literature Review

Wu Jian and You Donggui pointed out in their "Research on the Design of Medical Services for Rural Elderly" that the existing problems of medical services for rural elderly mainly lie in three aspects: difficulty in obtaining medical services in a timely manner, vulnerability to errors in the transmission of disease information, and relatively outdated diagnostic and treatment equipment. They divided the medical service process for rural elderly people into four parts: "seeking assistance", "on-site diagnosis and treatment", "emergency transfer", and "completing treatment", and formed three corresponding processes. At the same time, they proposed strategies for designing medical services in rural environments: establishing an internal family medical security system, establishing a neighborhood mutual assistance security system, establishing an online family doctor system, conducting regular health examination activities (obtaining health data for the elderly), establishing medical information networking and sharing, and establishing fast emergency stations. Finally, according to the severity of the patient's condition, a rural medical service model was established. This model divides patients into mild and critically ill patients, and divides them into two situations: assisted and unattended, forming four different targeted service processes [3].

Wu Yue (2020), "Research and Design of Rural Emergency Medical Service System under the Background of" Beautiful Rural Construction" Starting from the thinking mode of service design, using service design tools and methods, we conducted research on rural emergency medical service systems. After analyzing the regional characteristics of rural areas, the current situation of rural emergency medical care models, and investigating and analyzing the pain points and needs of stakeholders, we deeply explored the gaps and opportunities of rural emergency medical services, and determined the core value propositions of service-oriented and technology-oriented rural emergency medical service systems, Combining the technological advantages of modern 5G development, a rural emergency medical service system centered on the 120 emergency data management platform will be ultimately constructed. The main innovation of this study is to construct a complete implementation path for service systems in different modes from a new perspective of service design research, combining four aspects: the need for contact points in rural emergency services - the feasibility of technology - the cohesion and integrity of service experience - and the specificity of rural regional environment, and ultimately improve the application contact design under the main rural emergency service modes [4].

The scope of this study, excluding emergency medical aspects, focuses on medical solutions for non-acute patients as a complement to existing studies.

3 Methods

3.1 Field Investigation and In-depth Interviews

This article uses the method of field research to understand the detailed local situation of Huangbu Village, including the medical organization structure of Huangbu Village, the organizational structure of the public sector, the basic situation of the elderly and their medical habits.

In the in-depth interview, the interviewees mainly include Huangbu villagers (mainly the elderly), Huangbu village committee staff, rural medical workers, and urban medical workers. Among them, 8 villagers were interviewed, 5 village committee staff members, 2 rural medical workers, and 5 urban medical workers. The purpose of the interview is to understand their feelings and thoughts about the current medical service system. Their opinions mainly focus on two aspects: one is that the access to medical care for elderly villagers is not smooth, and the other is that the number and level of rural doctors are insufficient.

3.2 Quantitative Survey - Questionnaire Survey Method

The questionnaire was mainly used to survey the villagers in Huangbu Village, and was conducted in an online format. Based on the field research, we prepared a questionnaire on the "Health Care Situation of the Elderly in Huangbu Village", which included socio-demographic variables, as well as the basic conditions and health care habits of the elderly. Since the elderly are generally not well educated and not familiar with the use of smart terminals, the questionnaire was mainly targeted at the middle-aged and young

420   B. Shi et al.

people around the elderly, in order to understand the medical condition of the elderly from the side. A total of 38 questionnaires were sent out, and 35 valid questionnaires were returned. From the questionnaires, we can see that the rural elderly is generally afraid of spending money and unwilling to go to the hospital for fear of trouble. The root of the problem lies in the distrust of the elderly to the village doctors and the poor access of the elderly to medical treatment.

Based on the above survey, we identify user pain points, paint user portraits, and use tools such as stakeholder maps and service blueprints and organizational framework maps to build a new healthcare service system.

4 Conclusions

4.1 Demand Analysis and User Portrait

Old Villagers. From the in-depth interviews and questionnaires, we can conclude that the current situation of rural elderly people's medical treatment mainly includes the following aspects: 1. fear of spending money, thinking that small diseases can be cured without treatment, but it costs too much to cure big diseases; 2. distrust of existing doctors' technology; 3. most of the elderly people have inconvenient legs and legs, so it is troublesome to go out for medical treatment; 4. there are no hospitals in rural areas, only small clinics, so some diseases cannot be detected and treated in time. In this paper, through the analysis and summary of the survey results, the following rural elderly characters are fictitiously created to build a representative user portrait of the elderly residents of Huangbu Village (see Fig. 1).

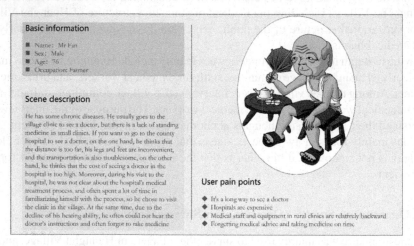

Fig. 1. The user portal Huangbu Village elderly patient.

Doctors. China's existing medical system, according to the size of the hospital, research direction, talent and technical strength, medical hardware and equipment on the hospital qualification assessment is divided into primary, secondary and tertiary.

Health stations in rural areas are level one, equipped with village doctors. Doctors from higher-level hospitals also occasionally go down to villages to practice medicine. There are two main types of such rural medical practice: one is mission-based, where the hospital will make tasks and plans to assign some doctors to the village on a regular basis, and also occasionally assign professors and deans to the village; the other is public service, where the second-level hospital will assign volunteers to the village to provide assistance and help. Since the villagers' distrust of village doctors was fully felt during the research process, this study tries to seek help from higher level hospitals in the hope that it can really solve the villagers' needs for medical treatment. Therefore, village doctors were basically avoided in the survey process when selecting survey respondents, and doctors from higher-level hospitals were found directly, hoping that through certain effective ways, more urban doctors would be encouraged to open clinics in villages to improve the level of medical services in villages and truly solve the rural medical problems. Through comprehensive survey and result analysis, the role of a first-level hospital doctor was virtualized, and a user portrait with a representative group of urban hospital doctors was constructed (see Fig. 2).

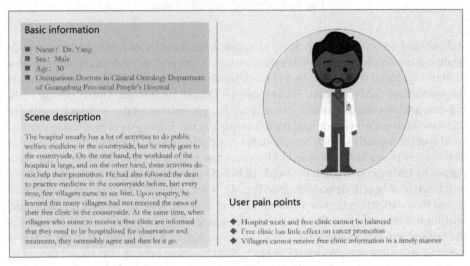

Fig. 2. The user portrait of the doctor who provide medical assistance in rural areas.

4.2 Stakeholder Map

Currently, stakeholders in the rural medical system mainly include interest providers, interest participants, and interest demanders. In the traditional stakeholder Map (see Fig. 3), the relationship between them is basically one-way, with no other connections.

By synthesizing the results of the survey and summarizing the user pain points, we can learn that the core conflict between supply and demand in rural healthcare services is that the needs of stakeholders are not sufficiently valued, and the needs of some

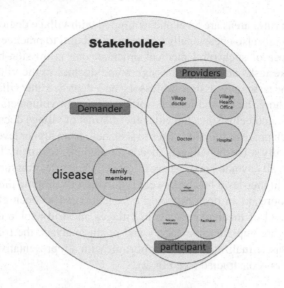

Fig. 3. Traditional stakeholder map.

stakeholders are even ignored. How to balance the interests of multiple parties in the healthcare system is the key to solve the problem. At present, more demand identification methods are based on various types of model analysis under quantitative samples, such as the mainstream KANO model, FBS model, QFD model and so on. This is similar to the big data analysis method, which can achieve the generalized analysis of user needs, but these methods are a bit superficial for the multiparty needs analysis of medical systems in rural specific scenarios. Therefore, with the basic principle of "human-centered" service design, this paper builds a stakeholder map that can satisfy the interests of multiple parties by taking into account the needs of benefit providers and participants in addition to the needs of benefit demanders (see Fig. 4). What distinguishes this stakeholder map is that the relationship between stakeholders is multi-directional, and each stakeholder will form a mutually beneficial relationship with each other. It takes full advantage of the holistic and systematic thinking of service design to bring attention to the needs of a certain party that was previously neglected. At the same time, it also allows the public sector to play a greater role, so that the interests of all parties are balanced.

4.3   Service Process

Touchpoint Design. Since a multi-party evaluation mechanism was added to the stakeholder map, electronic touchpoints were added to the process touchpoint design, and a smart terminal application was created to facilitate users to do evaluation and record. Increase the touchpoint between doctors and village doctors, and gradually improve the level of village doctors, so as to better solve the problems of rural medical care in the future. Increasing the contact point between the village committee and the elderly patients, so that the village committee can play the role of informing and assisting the

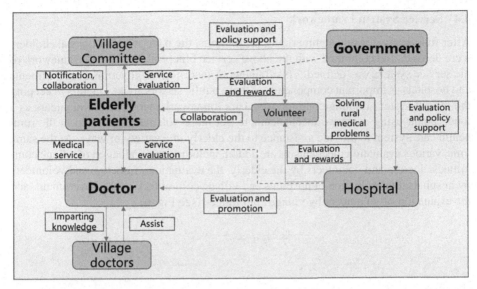

Fig. 4. New stakeholder map.

elderly to travel, can enable the elderly to better receive high-level treatment. The addition of volunteers as a contact point will enable the elderly with limited legs and reduced sensory functions to be better served.

Service Blueprint. Based on the stakeholder map, we redefined the service process by combining the design of touchpoints in the service system to depict a service blueprint for geriatric patients. The service blueprint is divided into online and offline parts, making full use of modern information technology to make the whole service process more detailed and in-depth, and more in line with the "people-oriented" design principle (see Fig. 5).

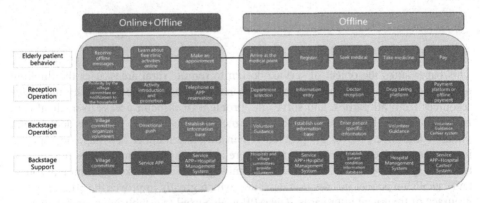

Fig. 5. Service Blueprint.

4.4 Service System Framework

After fully analyzing and summarizing the findings, the pain points of the stakeholders were derived, and combined with the above service blueprint, the overall framework of the service system was defined. This framework incorporates government departments and hospitals as important components, as these public sectors are key factors in keeping the overall system running continuously. This framework incorporates volunteers as a touch point, using incentive mechanisms to get more volunteers involved in the rural health care system to provide assistance to the elderly in a variety of ways. At the same time, various evaluation mechanisms are added, including the evaluation of village committees, doctors and volunteers by the elderly, the evaluation of doctors and volunteers by hospitals, the evaluation of hospitals and village committees by the government, and the evaluation of volunteers by village committees (see Fig. 6).

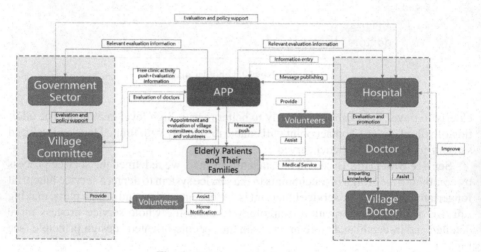

Fig. 6. Service system framework.

4.5 Service System Evaluation

This paper sinks the object of service design to remote rural areas, uses the thinking of service design to establish an organizational operation framework, fully mobilizes resources from all parties, and solves the problem of difficult access to medical care for rural elderly. This paper uses incentive mechanisms to fully mobilize doctors and village committees, solves the problems of insufficient number of village doctors and incomplete service system, constitutes a more rational system, and ensures the sustainability of system operation. Information technology is used to make appointments, push, and establish a patient information database, which greatly improves the efficiency and accuracy of treatment afterwards. The APP is also used to establish a sound evaluation mechanism and to improve the motivation of various stakeholders through merit evaluation and promotion, which are key factors for the service system to be able to maintain its operation.

The system has universal applicability and is a high reference for other rural areas and can be used to good effect as long as it is used in conjunction with local realities. Although the prototype of this service system has not yet been built out, after the initial return visits, all parties in the system have a high opinion of the rationality and feasibility of the system.

Acknowledgements. The completion of this paper is the result of joint collaboration. The preliminary research and user study were mainly done by my students, Yonghao Fan, Xuanqi Zhong, Rongsheng Lin, Shengyuan Chen, and Junjie Wang. The charts in the later stage are the result of our joint efforts. I would like to thank them for their hard work.

References

1. Rural Medical Research Report_ Report on in-depth analysis and investment analysis and prediction of China's rural medical industry from 2023 to 2028_ China Industry Research Network. https://www.chinairn.com/report/20230112/143554221.html?id=1861502&name=wuy anan. Accessed January 2023
2. Liu, T.: Research on the supply of rural public cultural services from the perspective of service design. Design (22), 121–123 (2022)
3. Wu, J., You, D.: Research on medical service design for rural elderly. Ind. Des. (10), 100–102 (2022)
4. Wu, Y.: Research and design of rural emergency medical service system under the background of "beautiful rural construction". Master's thesis, Nanjing Academy of Arts (2020)

Evaluation of Websites of City and Medical Association Emergency Medical Institutions in Hokkaido

Yuki Uenoya[✉] [ID] and Namgyu Kang[ID]

Future University Hakodate of Japan, Hakodate, Japan
p4122001@fun.ac.jp

Abstract. With the spread of the Internet, many medical institutions have established and are operating Web sites. According to the results of the "Survey on Medical Examining Behavior" conducted by the Ministry of Health, Labor and Welfare in 2020, "Information on the Internet provided by medical institutions" was the second most common source of information when visiting a medical institution. Therefore, it is necessary to design a website and UX design that is easy for patients to understand and operate. However, according to a previous survey, about 80% of all hospitals in Hokkaido have a website. However, only about 45% of them are updated within a month. In addition, prior research on websites of emergency duty medical institutions is still scarce in Japan. Therefore, the purpose of this study is to visualize improvements and issues in the websites of emergency duty medical institutions. Therefore, we selected the following four cities in Hokkaido: Sapporo, Asaikawa, Hakodate and Obihiro. And we objectively evaluate the websites of emergency medical institutions in the four cities and a medical association using Google Lighthouse with the four categories: Performance, Accessibility, Best Practices, and Search Engine Optimization (SEO). As a result, among the city emergency duty sites, Obihiro City and Hakodate City had a score of 90 or higher for two out of four items. No site operated by a medical association has calculated values of 90 or higher for more than two of the four items.

The site operated by the Asahikawa Medical Association also revealed no values above 90. As a point for improvement, visualization of the minimum and maximum values revealed that there are large differences in values by region. In addition, the Obihiro and Sapporo websites were below the 50 criteria set by Google Lighthouse in Performance, indicating the need for immediate improvement.

Keywords: Web Performance · Google Lighthouse · Medical Website

1 Introduction

With the spread of the Internet, many medical institutions have established and are operating websites. According to the results of a survey on medical treatment behavior conducted by the Ministry of Health, Labour and Welfare of Japan in 2020, "information on the Internet provided by medical institutions" was the second most common source of information when visiting a medical institution, following "An opinion from family, acquaintances and friends" [1]. That means it is necessary to design websites and UX designs that are easy for patients to understand and operate. As a previous study on medical institution websites, a survey of medical institution websites targeting hospitals and clinics in Hokkaido, Japan, was conducted to determine the degree to which medical information is available on their websites. In that study, 79.9% of all hospitals in Hokkaido had publicly available websites. In contrast to that result, only 44.7% of the websites were updated within one month [2]. In addition, three websites of Hokkaido hospitals with specific functions were evaluated using a web accessibility validation tool [3]. The results indicated that the three websites had not only web accessibility problems but also accessibility problems to medical information. In addition, a survey of 413 parents of children who visited pediatric emergency rooms in two cities in prefecture A was conducted to examine the actual and perceived use of the Internet by parents who visited pediatric emergency rooms and their decisions on whether to visit a pediatric emergency room or not. The results showed that the most common means for parents to obtain medical information sources were the city newsletter (52.8%), followed by INET (Internet) (46.9%). Furthermore, about half of the mothers reported that even a fever of less than 38 °C was a source of fear [4]. Therefore, using emergency medical services via the Internet is not uncommon. On the other hand, using an on-duty emergency medical service is unusual, urgent, and likely to cause anxiety and fear in families with children and the elderly. However, only some studies exist on websites of on-duty emergency medical services in Japan. In this study, we objectively evaluate the websites of emergency medical institutions in four cities and a medical association in Hokkaido using Google Lighthouse. The purpose of this study is to visualize the essential points, points for improvement, and issues in the websites of emergency medical service organizations based on the evaluation results.

2 Method

2.1 About Google Lighthouse

In this study, we conduct an objective evaluation using Google Lighthouse. The purpose of this study is to visualize the essential points, points for improvement, and issues in the websites of emergency medical service organizations based on the results.

As a previous study, a marketplace performance analysis using Google Light-house was conducted on Tokopedia and Shopee. Although, as a result of the research and testing, Tokopedia is superior to Shopee in various aspects of the tested metrics. In particular, Tokopedia and Shopee are reported to be 85 and 13, respectively, in terms of performance; Shopee needs to be improved as soon as possible [5]. That means this evaluation using Google Lighthouse can visualize some problems and improvement points of websites.

The 1st item is "Performance. This item measures loading speed, image display speed, and speed of response to user operations. In a previous study, this item showed that even when there were no changes to the website, the results varied depending on the time of day and the environment in which it was conducted. Measuring a single website five times reduced the variation and produced valid results [6]. The 2nd item is "Accessibility. This item evaluates whether the text and contrast are easy to read and equally usable by all website users and whether buttons have names. The 3rd item is "Best Practices. This item measures whether the site is trustworthy and safe by checking whether the code on the page is written correctly. The 4th item is Search Engine Optimization (SEO). This item evaluates whether the web page is optimized for search engine ranking results. The results of these evaluations are displayed as a score of − 0–49, □50–89, ○90–100 for each item, with details for improvement indicated for each (Fig. 1).

Fig. 1. Evaluation picture using google lighthouse

2.2 Study Method

This study used Google Lighthouse, a tool provided by Google for analyzing and diagnosing websites. The websites of emergency duty medical institutions operated by the four cities of Sapporo, Asahikawa, Obihiro, and Hakodate, and the websites of emergency duty medical institutions operated by the respective medical associations of the four cities were included in the study (Fig. 2, 3, 4, 5, 6, 7, 8 and 9). As mentioned in Sect. 2.1, the "Performance" item may vary depending on the environment, such as the time when the evaluation is conducted. Therefore, we conducted five trials for one website during the same time period and calculated the average value for comparison.

Fig. 2. Sapporo City Website

Fig. 3. Asahikawa City Website

Fig. 4. Obihiro City Website

Fig. 5. Hakodate City Website

Fig. 6. Website of Sapporo Medical Association

Fig. 7. Website of Asahikawa Medical Association

Fig. 8. Website of Obihiro Medical Association

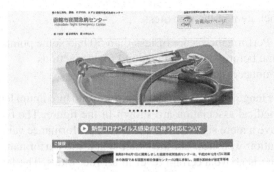

Fig. 9. Website of Hakodate Medical Association

3 Results and Discussion

Using Google Lighthouse, we evaluated the websites of emergency duty medical institutions in four cities and medical associations in Hokkaido and discussed the results.
Table 1 shows the measurement results of the websites of the four cities in Hokkaido, and
Table 2 shows the measurement results of the medical associations' websites (Table 1)
(Table 2). As described in Sects. 2.1 and 2.2, the Performance item was calculated as
an average value of five times after five attempts. Therefore, the numbers above 90 in
the table indicate little or no improvement based on the criteria established by Google
Lighthouse.

Table 1. City Website

	Sapporo	Asahikawa	Obihiro	Hakodate	Average
Performance	47.2	78	39	94.8	64.75
Accessibility	97	81	100	79	89.25
Best Practices	67	75	83	67	73
SEO	83	97	90	92	90.5

Table 2. Medical Association Website

	Sapporo	Asahikawa	Obihiro	Hakodate	Average
Performance	50.6	87.2	73.6	58.8	67.5
Accessibility	91	54	94	84	80.75
Best Practices	83	83	75	67	77
SEO	89	58	67	90	76

We analyzed each item of the websites:

1. Websites with a Performance score of less than 50 had some points in common.
2. It took a long time before they could respond to user actions.
3. The presence of unnecessary code.

One factor is the length of the Web. The minimum and maximum lengths of the city's websites and the medical association are shown in the figure. The results suggest that the city websites have a more significant variation of performance values by region than the medical association websites. On the other hand, the performance of the medical association's website is above a certain level in all four cities. The fact that the performance of the websites differs significantly from region to region is a point that needs to be improved.

In the second category, "Accessibility," all websites except for the Asahikawa Medical Association's website scored 75 or higher. In particular, the websites of the cities of Sapporo and Obihiro recorded very high values of 95 or higher. On the other hand, Asahikawa Medical Association's Accessibility score is low compared to other websites. The Asahikawa Medical Association's website could be improved using more appropriate tag names. In addition, the contrast ratio between the background and foreground colors needs to be increased. On the other hand, the websites of the cities of Sapporo and Obihiro, which have high values, are highly rated for their easy-to-read text color and contrast. That is because they are equally usable by all users who access them, including those with visual impairments.

In the fourth category, "SEO," all of the four city websites had a score of 75 or higher. In addition, Asahikawa, Obihiro, and Hakodate recorded high scores of 90 or higher. The factors evaluated include links, tags, and codes easily understood as content by search engines and an appropriate web page summary. For example, the websites of medical institutions on emergency duty are often used in emergencies. Therefore, the websites are created with texts and codes easily understood by search engines so that users can reach the necessary information as quickly as possible. On the other hand, the Asahikawa and Obihiro websites of medical associations had a score of less than 75. The reasons for this are the use of unreadable font sizes in documents and the wrong size of tap targets.

As in Fig. 10, the evaluation results for the medical association and the city are expressed in minimum and maximum values. As a result, the minimum value for the medical association's website is 58, and the maximum value is 90, indicating a difference in the SEO values by region. On the other hand, the city websites have a minimum value of 83 and a maximum value of 97. Compared with the SEO values of the medical associations, all city websites have a value of 80 or higher, and there is little difference in the SEO values among the regions. This result indicates that the differences in SEO values that affect search rankings on the websites of emergency duty medical institutions with urgent care should be improved, as well as the decrease in importance due to the use of unreadable font sizes and inappropriate tap target sizes (11, 12 and 13).

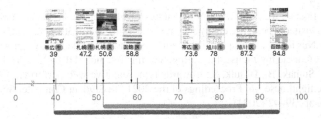

Fig. 10. Performance Evaluation

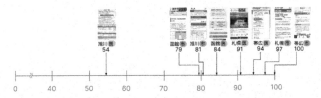

Fig. 11. Accessibility Evaluation

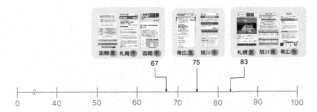

Fig. 12. Best Practices Evaluation

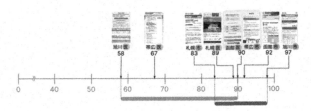

Fig. 13. SEO Evaluation

References

1. Ministry of Health, Labour and Welfare, Survey of Patient Behavior (2020). https://www.mhlw. go.jp/toukei/saikin/hw/jyuryo/20/dl/kekka-gaiyo.pdf. Viewed 20 June 2022
2. Suzuki, T., Sasaki, A., Hayashi, K., Tanigahara, A.: Katsuhiko Ogasawara: the degree of enrichment of medical information on medical institution websites. Med. Inf. **35**(3), 133–140 (2015)
3. Ohba, H.: Information accessibility evaluation of public hospital websites: a case study of a specified functional hospital in Hokkaido. J. Japan. Soc. Healthcare Manage. **15**(4), 261–266 (2015)

4. Kusano, J., Takano, M., Fujita, Y.: Actual status of Internet use and consultation decision of parents who visited a pediatric emergency room. J. Nurs. Sci. **13**(35–42), p35-42 (2015)
5. Muna, S.S., Nurdin, N., Taufiq, T.: Tokopedia and Shopee marketplace performance analysis using Metrix Google lighthouse. Int. J. Eng. Sci. Inf. Technol. (IJESTY) **2**(3), 106–110 (2022)
6. Heričko, T., Šumak, B., Brdnik, S.: Towards representative web performance measurements with Google lighthouse. In: Proceedings of the 2021 7th Student Computer Science Research Conference, pp. 39–42 (2021)

Designing a Strain Textile Sensing System for Shoulder Compensation Monitoring of Stroke Patients

Qi Wang$^{(\boxtimes)}$, Shiwen Fang, Yuxuan He, and Yucong He

College of Design and Innovation, Tongji University, Shanghai, China
{qiwangdesign,2241626,195344}@tongji.edu.cn

Abstract. Stroke is a leading cause of death and physical disability worldwide. Early rehabilitation plays a crucial role in helping stroke survivors regain their basic daily living abilities. However, the effectiveness of training can be influenced by compensatory movements during upper extremity rehabilitation. To address this issue, wearable motion monitoring technology with spatial flexibility features has been an increasing research focus to support rehabilitation training. Recently, the emerging textile strain sensors offer advantageous features such as comfortable wearability and conforming to the human form. In this study, we propose a wearable system including a smart garment equipped with a network of strain textile sensors, along with a screen-based visual feedback platform. Subsequently, we reported the results of preliminary usability testing.

Keywords: Strain textile sensor · stroke patients · shoulder compensation monitoring · wearable system

1 Introduction

Stroke is the second leading cause of death globally and ranks third as the leading cause of disability in adults, and 80 million people worldwide suffer from the effect of a stroke [1]. After a stroke, upper limb movement disorders are common, affecting approximately 80% of stroke survivors [2]. This dysfunction significantly impacts patients' quality of life. During the patient's long-term rehabilitation process, compensatory movements often occur due to the reduced control of the affected limb, using the alternative muscle groups to complete the training task [3], which seriously affects the effectiveness of the rehabilitation training. Currently, therapists rely on verbal and auditory guidance based on experience to supervise and help patients control compensatory movements, which is time-consuming [4].

In recent years, wearable motion monitoring technology with spatial flexibility features has also been an increasing research focus to support rehabilitation training. While inertial sensing units (IMUs) are widely used, they may suffer from alignment errors and have difficulty fitting the shoulder peak angle, making it difficult to achieve effective monitoring of compensatory movements of the shoulder joint complex. The emerging textile

C. Stephanidis et al. (Eds.): HCII 2023, CCIS 1957, pp. 435–441, 2024.
https://doi.org/10.1007/978-3-031-49212-9_54

strain sensor [5], which utilizes the electronic textile itself as the sensing component, can comfortably fit the human form and is expected to monitor human motion.

In this study, we proposed a wearable system that consists of a smart garment equipped with strain textile sensor networks to monitor the shoulder complex and a screen-based visual feedback platform that demonstrates the training task and compensation status in real time. We designed the wearable system with considerations for sensor performance and focused on the design of the interfaces.

2 Related Works

2.1 Interactive Wearable System for Upper Limb Rehabilitation

Various interactive wearable systems with feedback in multi-modality have been proposed. For example, Markopoulos et al. [6] developed Us'em, a wearable device specifically designed to record real-time upper limb activity in stroke patients during their daily lives. It captures data from both the affected and healthy sides of the patient, allowing for a comparison between the functioning of the upper limbs on each side. This comparative analysis provides valuable insights into the progress of rehabilitation. Wang et al. [7] introduced the smart rehabilitation garment (SRG), which addresses symptoms like low back pain and shoulder pain, the system monitors both trunk and shoulder posture, and they adopted the metaphor of a pointer and dashboard to visualize the real-time compensation movement. Guillén-Climent et al. [8] reported the MERLIN robotic system based on serious games for upper limb rehabilitation in the home setting. This study not only demonstrates the feasibility of using this low-cost, easy to learn, easy to use and easily transportable rehabilitation system but also represents a substantial advancement in the implementation of intensive rehabilitation at home.

2.2 Smart Fabric-Based Motion Monitoring

Among the wearable motion monitoring systems, lots of researchers are paying attention to smart textile sensors. For instance, Sang-Ho Han [9] introduced a method for identifying upper limb movement postures using an e-textile sensor consisting of a bilayer structure with complementary resistive properties, and the functional feasibility of the method was verified using data from 10 participants performing six interactive gestures. Jorge et al. [10] proposed a wearable monitoring method involving a sensor array that tracks three geodesic distances between specific points on the shoulder surface and the lower back. This sensor array can be integrated into custom garments or used with a mobile application. Esfahani et al. [11] designed and developed a lightweight and portable trunk motion system (TMS) utilizing printed body-worn sensors (BWS). This non-invasive system combines 12 BWS printed on stretchable garments to measure the three-dimensional motion of the torso; the VUL team [12] used 10 fabric strain sensors placed on the torso to assess complex lumbar motion.

3 Design Process

3.1 Hardware Design

In this study, we used a new fabric strain sensor (Fig. 1.a) to precisely monitor shoulder joint angles by detecting resistance changes when the fabric stretches. To ensure efficient sensing performance, a resistance test was conducted using a tensile test platform (Fig. 1.b), and the test confirmed the stability and linearity of the sensor's data. Machine learning techniques were employed to establish a mapping model between the sensor data and angles calculated from an optical motion capture system, enabling accurate monitoring.

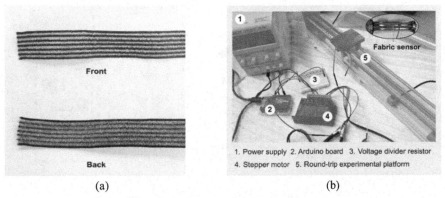

(a)   (b)

Fig. 1. An experiment was conducted to investigate the resistance characteristics of the novel fabric strain sensor. a) Tensile strain fabric sensing materials, b) Experimental set-up

Taking the left shoulder as an example, we deployed a total of five fabric strain sensors. This layout scheme (see Fig. 2) effectively monitored the movements of the scapula and humerus while minimizing the number of sensors. To ensure that wearing the prototype garment during rehabilitation training does not hinder force exertion or impose excessive motion burden, we used a "z" stitching along the direction of stretch

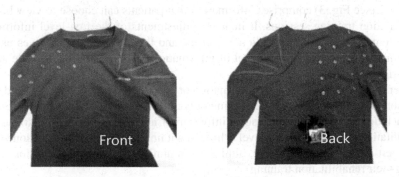

Fig. 2. Smart garment prototype with fabric strain sensors

variation. Additionally, the development board was sewn onto the back of the garment, enabling sensor data collection through the Arduino hardware circuit.

3.2   Feedback Design

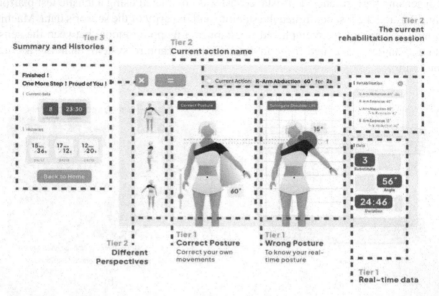

Fig. 3. Functional hierarchy diagram of the user interface

The interface is organized into three levels to present information. Taking the core interface as an example (see Fig. 3), Tier 1 comprises real-time information that requires the patient's attention during the rehabilitation process, including the target movement and the patient's current action status. The avatar is positioned at the center of the interface. Details such as angle, compensation level, and training time are located in the bottom right corner of the interface, represented by large numbers for better visibility and comprehension.

Tier 2 (see Fig. 3) comprises information that patients can choose to view between rehabilitation training sessions. It includes adjustments of the first-level information, the current session of rehabilitation exercises, and the different perspectives used for rehabilitation comparison. This level of information is located on the left side and the upper right corner of the interface.

Tier 3 (see Fig. 3) consists of information or functionalities that patients need to pay attention to when interrupting the training or completing the rehabilitation session. This part includes a history record, personal information, and the choice to return to the initial rehabilitation movements. This level is hidden within a thumbnail icon positioned at the upper left corner of the interface, aiming to minimize visual distractions for patients during their rehabilitation training.

Furthermore, in order to create a more immersive interactive experience, we have conceptualized a rehabilitation system for stroke patients based on motion-sensing games (see Fig. 4). The patients wear smart garments and as they perform shoulder rehabilitation movements, they can control a game character jumps between the mushrooms in the game, ultimately reaching the endpoint to complete a rehabilitation session. If a compensatory behavior occurs during rehabilitation, the game character may slide off the mushroom, prompting the patient to repeat the movement until acceptable compensatory behaviors occur.

Fig. 4. Scene design of the motion-sensing game.

4 Usability Evaluation

4.1 Protocol

To assess the usability and feasibility of the system, this study invited five participants for a functional test. The test procedure was as follows: the five participants completed the test independently in a lab-setting environment, following the interface prompts. The participants wore the smart garment and performed five specified movements, including two normal movements and three compensatory movements. After the test, the five participants evaluated the interface comprehensively using the SUS questionnaire [13].

4.2 Result

In this study, the average score of SUS is 83.3, demonstrating good system usability. All five participants were able to comprehend the information conveyed by the interface effectively. They can make corrections to compensatory movements based on the interface feedback. Participants expressed that the interface colors were soothing, and they experienced no pressure or sense of urgency. Participants also mentioned the overall experience to be smooth, including wearing the smart garment, conducting the rehabilitation training with real-time monitoring, and reviewing the results at the end of the rehabilitation process.

5 Discussion and Limitations

The smart garment and its visual feedback platform were developed to support the rehabilitation training. Ultimately, we demonstrated that the system has the capability to monitor real-time shoulder motions, detect compensatory movement during rehabilitation tasks, and provide immediate visual feedback to enhance patients' rehabilitation efficiency. Additionally, the system generates quantifiable patient data, enabling clinicians to better evaluate the patient's rehabilitation progress in the future.

During the design practice, the following points require further optimization:

- Integration method: the integration between the fabric substrate and the fabric strain sensors requires manual stitching, which is time-consuming and costly. Further research can explore integrated methods for more efficient integration.
- Power supply and data transmission: future optimizations could involve transitioning to a wireless smart garment, offering convenience, comfort, and unrestricted space limitation. This would enable monitoring of movement posture anytime and anywhere.
- Testing and follow-up: in the future, it is anticipated to recruit a larger sample of general participants and patients at various stages of recovery for testing. Changes in recovery progress and attitude will be recorded monthly to enhance the overall robustness of the system design.

6 Conclusion

This study focuses on upper limb rehabilitation for stroke patients. A wearable system is proposed that consists of a smart garment equipped with a strain fabric sensor network and a screen-based visual feedback platform. During the system design process, various considerations were included for the feedback contents design. The system was validated through preliminary usability tests, which demonstrated the system's potential for shoulder joint rehabilitation.

References

1. Campbell, B.C.V., Khatri, P.: Stroke. Lancet **396**, 129–142 (2020)
2. Masiero, S., Armani, M., Ferlini, G., Rosati, G., Rossi, A.: Randomized trial of a robotic assistive device for the upper extremity during early inpatient stroke rehabilitation. Neurorehabil. Neural Repair **28**, 377–386 (2014)
3. Cirstea, M.C., Levin, M.F.: Compensatory strategies for reaching in stroke. Brain **123**, 940–953 (2000)
4. Wang, Q., et al.: Stroke patients' acceptance of a smart garment for supporting upper extremity rehabilitation. IEEE J. Transl. Eng. Health Med. **6**, 1–9 (2018)

5. Shi, J., et al.: Smart textile-integrated microelectronic systems for wearable applications. Adv. Mater. **32**, 1901958 (2020)
6. Markopoulos, P., Timmermans, A.A.A., Beursgens, L., van Donselaar, R., Seelen, H.A.M.: Us'em: the user-centered design of a device for motivating stroke patients to use their impaired arm-hand in daily life activities. In: 2011 Annual International Conference of the IEEE Engineering in Medicine and Biology Society, pp. 5182–5187 (2011). https://doi.org/10.1109/IEMBS.2011.6091283
7. Wang, Q.: Designing posture monitoring garments to support rehabilitation. In: Proceedings TEI 16 Tenth International Conference on Tangible, Embedded, and Embodied Interaction, pp. 709–712. Association for Computing Machinery (2016). https://doi.org/10.1145/2839462.2854106
8. Guillén-Climent, S., et al.: A usability study in patients with stroke using MERLIN, a robotic system based on serious games for upper limb rehabilitation in the home setting. J. NeuroEngineering Rehabil. **18**, 41 (2021)
9. Han, S.-H., Ahn, E.-J., Ryu, M.-H., Kim, J.-N.: Natural hand gesture recognition with an electronic textile goniometer. Sens. Mater. **31**, 1387 (2019)
10. Caviedes, J.E., Li, B., Jammula, V.C.: Wearable sensor array design for spine posture monitoring during exercise incorporating biofeedback. IEEE Trans. Biomed. Eng. **67**, 2828–2838 (2020)
11. Mokhlespour Esfahani, M.I., et al.: Trunk Motion System (TMS) using printed Body Worn Sensor (BWS) via data fusion approach. Sensors **17**, 112 (2017)
12. Vu, L.Q., Kim, K.H., Schulze, L.J.H., Rajulu, S.L.: Lumbar posture assessment with fabric strain sensors. Comput. Biol. Med. **118**, 103624 (2020)
13. System Usability Scale (SUS). https://www.usability.gov/how-to-and-tools/methods/system-usability-scale.html

Exploring the Usage, Interpretation, and Implications of Disease Metaphors in Cancer Reports: A Case Analysis of the People's Daily

Yuhan Wang[✉] and Yuanbing Deng

School of Journalism and Communication, Zhengzhou University, Zhengzhou 450001, China
wangyuhan0520@126.com

Abstract. Cancer's invasive characteristics have been metaphorically represented for over seven decades in China. This study examines the utilization of metaphors in digital news of cancer. Its objective is to identify prevalent metaphors used in cancer reporting, the factors that influence their usage, and the social interactions that follow as a result of the depiction of cancer and cancer patients in digital news. The study utilizes a metaphorical criticism analysis method, which involves selecting language samples, identifying and categorizing metaphors, and analyzing their use and effects. The findings reveal that the cancer report of People's Daily (1949–2022) utilized seven metaphors, namely war, demon, killer, opportunistic, plague, star, and hell metaphors. Among them, the war and killer metaphors were the most frequently used. The study suggests that the prevalence of war metaphors in Chinese mainstream media can be attributed to China's historical and ideological background. Furthermore, the results indicate that the use of metaphors in cancer reporting follows a distinct pattern influenced by political and social factors across different periods.

Keywords: Cancer · Metaphor · Digital News · Critical Metaphor Analysis

1 Introduction

1.1 Background

Cancer poses a significant global public health challenge. As reported by the World Health Organization (WHO) in 2019, cancer is currently the leading or second leading cause of death in 112 countries, and the third or fourth leading cause of death in 23 countries [1]. According to the latest national cancer statistics released by the National Cancer Center in 2022, the incidence and mortality rates of numerous cancers in China have continued to rise from 2000 to 2016 [2]. According to the 2020 cancer burden data published in the CA Journal by the World Health Organization, there will be an estimated 19.29 million new cancer cases worldwide in 2020, with China alone accounting for 4.57 million of these cases, representing 23.7% of the global total. Additionally, there will be approximately 9.96 million cancer-related deaths worldwide in 2020, with China accounting for 3 million of these deaths, making up 30% of the total number of cancer deaths [3].

In China, cancer has been metaphorically represented to capture its invasive nature for over seven decades. Effective health communication in China heavily relies on mainstream media and mass communication channels. Metaphor can be understood as a means of comprehending and relating to present experiences by drawing upon something else. It serves as a direct way to name a life experience or a novel concept, involving the mapping of one conceptual domain onto another. Metaphor is not merely a linguistic phenomenon; it is a fundamental cognitive tool that humans employ to make sense of the world and develop concepts. In the context of news reporting, metaphors have also become a significant element in framing news stories [4–8]. Through emphasizing or obscuring particular categories within a structural concept, metaphorical concepts reinforce certain aspects of the concept, creating a "metaphorical frame" in cognitive thinking, which is referred to as the "news frame" in news reporting.

1.2 Related Work

There has been limited research on metaphors in digital news reporting, and previous studies primarily focused on the implicit ideologies conveyed by these metaphors [9]. One study examined the usage of metaphors in public health crisis reporting and discovered that while these metaphors enhanced the expressiveness of the news, they also instilled fear and led to potential agenda drift [10]. Scholars have analyzed metaphors in media reports related to occupational diseases, such as pneumoconiosis, to investigate their origins and impacts. Additionally, researchers have conducted metaphorical analyses of news reports on new coronaviruses using corpus-based methods. Furthermore, the metaphor of the doctor-patient relationship has been analyzed by some scholars [11].

During the 18th century, as medicine underwent a transformation, the discourse surrounding medical taxonomy shifted the focus from the patient's subjective experience of discomfort to the objective concept of "disease" as an entity residing within a segmented body space. This shift was based on certain predetermined "configurations" of disease. Within the discourse of clinical medicine, a system was established to categorize and distribute diseases, thereby making the patient's body the subject of medical intervention and granting healthcare professionals a form of control or "power" over the patient's body [12, 13]. In the realm of digital media, coverage of diseases and patients often tends to construct a specific representation of the human body. The formation of this representation is closely intertwined with the discursive rhetoric employed by the media.

1.3 Research Questions

RQ1: What are the most frequently used disease metaphors in People's Daily's digital coverage of cancer?
RQ2: What are the probability factors for the use of metaphors in the People's Daily digital report on cancer?
RQ3: What are the consequences of the use of disease metaphors in People's Daily's digital coverage of cancer?

2   Method

2.1   Procedure

The study utilizes a metaphorical criticism analysis method, which involves selecting language samples, identifying and categorizing metaphors, and analyzing their use and effects. The study is conducted in four steps: Firstly, the corpus is selected, and the rhetorical context is presented. Secondly, metaphorical texts are extracted and thoroughly read to identify all the metaphors relating to cancer and cancer patients in relevant news reports. Thirdly, the relevant metaphors are coded and categorized, and the frequency of different metaphor types used at different times is counted. Finally, the analysis examines how and why cancer metaphors are used in mainstream media reports at different times and explores whether and how cancer patients are characterized.

2.2   Data Collection

People's Daily, the oldest daily newspaper in China, holds significant influence and appeal among the general population, serving as a platform for representing China's policy. Thus, studying the construction of cancer metaphors in health communication within People's Daily carries practical importance. For this study, the People's Daily Graphic Database (1949–2022) was selected. Using the keyword "cancer" and applying the search condition "title & text," the search period spanned from January 1, 1949, to January 1, 2023. A total of 397 relevant reports were retrieved initially. After thoroughly reviewing all the reports, non-cancer-related articles, advertisements for cancer drugs, and newsletters from academic conferences were filtered out, resulting in a final selection of 321 cancer reports that met the screening criteria.

3   Results and Discussion

3.1   Metaphorical Description

This part focuses on the analysis of metaphors in cancer report discourse, which are categorized into three subject types: metaphors related to the cancer disease, metaphors concerning cancer patients, and metaphors describing the situations faced by cancer patients (Table 1). A notable trend observed in People's Daily is the increasing preference for employing metaphors in their cancer reports (Fig. 1). The findings demonstrate that the cancer reports of People's Daily (1949–2022) utilized seven metaphors, namely war, demon, killer, opportunistic, plague, star, and hell metaphors. Among these, the war and killer metaphors were the most frequently used (Fig. 2). The study suggests that the prevalence of war metaphors in Chinese mainstream media can be attributed to China's historical and ideological background. Furthermore, the results indicate that the utilization of metaphors in cancer reporting follows a distinct pattern influenced by political and social factors across different time periods.

Table 1. Table captions should be placed above the tables.

Subject	Metaphor type	Word frequencies	Text examples
Cancer Diseases	War (a)	victory(18); overcome(16); fight(12); conquer(9); eliminate(9); anti-cancer(7); attack(8); invade(8); resist(5); enemy(5); defend(3); imperialism; reactionary faction; Paper Tiger; fortress; bio-missile; iron army; blocking; defender; culprit; surrender; revolution; combat;	Cancer, like imperialism and all reactionary factions, is a paper tiger. We should treat cancer the same way as we treat our enemies. (1969–1-2-a)
	Demon (b)	disease demon(7); death(4); cancer demon(2);	To conquer this vicious disease demon.(1990–1-2-b)
	Killer (c)	kill(23); killer(13);	The No. 1 killer is lung cancer. (1989–2-1-c)
	Opportunistic (e)	escape(3); sly(3); interference(2); play tricks(2); cunning; disguise;	Cancer cells are very cunning and play tricks to disguise themselves in order to avoid detection by the immune system. (1988–1-7-e)
	Plague (f)	plague(2);	There are still four major "plagues" threatening humanity. (1994–2-1-f)
Cancer Patients	Star (g)	star(4); hero;	Many cancer-fighting stars have emerged. (1999–1-2-g)
Situation of Cancer Patients	Hell (d)	hell;	Falling to the gates of hell.(1990–1-4-d)

During the 1970s, war metaphors were exclusively used to describe cancer. In the following decades of the 1980s and 1990s, both killer metaphors and war metaphors became increasingly common, with the latter comprising the majority of their usage, accounting for 15% (Fig. 3a). The utilization of war metaphors declined after China's reform and opening up, indicating a shift away from the emphasis on struggle consciousness in Chinese ideology (Fig. 3).

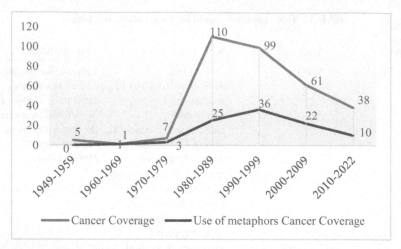

Fig. 1. Amount of cancer coverage and use of metaphors in *People's Daily (1949–2022)*

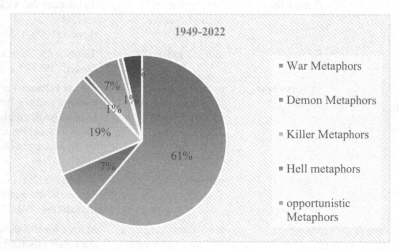

Fig. 2. Use of metaphor types for cancer coverage in *People's Daily (1949–2022)*

3.2 Metaphorical Interpretation

Political Factors. The war metaphor serves as both a political discourse and a rhetorical tool within news media. Following the establishment of the People's Republic of China, there existed a pervasive sense of ideological struggle, which was reflected in news coverage and led to the widespread use and acceptance of war metaphors. During this period, the notion of struggle permeated society and contributed to the prominence of these metaphors. However, with the implementation of China's reform and opening-up policies, the usage of war metaphors has generally declined. This can be attributed to China's adoption of a more open policy and the subsequent weakening of the ideological struggle.

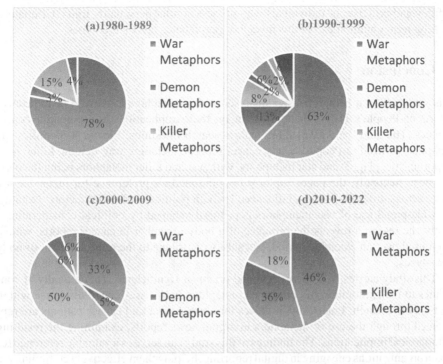

Fig. 3. Use of metaphorical types for each time period in *People's Daily(1949–2022)*

Social Factors. Raising awareness about a disease that is not fully understood necessitates effective packaging and guidance to resonate with mainstream society and effectively establish a social consensus and norm. In the Chinese social context, the mainstream media, with its significant credibility and influence, plays a crucial role in shaping social ideology, constructing new interpretations, capturing the public's attention, and arguably, it possesses the ability to define a disease through the use of metaphors.

3.3 Consequences of the Cancer Metaphor

In various cancer reports from 1980, 1999, 2005, and 2013, the People's Daily made references to the concept of a "cancer personality" and emphasized its significance and scientific nature. For instance, in 2005, the People's Daily reported that individuals with a "cancerous personality" are more susceptible to developing cancer. While the intention behind the People's Daily's use of this metaphor may be to encourage people to maintain a positive and optimistic mental state, it is important to consider the potential unintended consequences of employing such a metaphor. Over time, the persistent use of this metaphor can unintentionally contribute to implicit and rigid stereotypes concerning the body. This study argues that human personality is a deeply personal trait that is not suitable for media judgment in the public sphere. Labeling individuals with a "cancer personality" can result in the transfer of that label to a larger group, leading to public scrutiny and criticism of individuals who possess similar personality traits. Ultimately, the long-term common use of this metaphor perpetuates body stereotypes.

4 Conclusion

This study offers a comprehensive analysis of the metaphors employed in the cancer reports of People's Daily, shedding light on their implications and potential consequences. The study addresses three main research questions. Firstly, it identifies the metaphors utilized in People's Daily cancer reports, including war, demon, killer, hell, Opportunistic, plague, and star metaphors, with war and killer metaphors being the most prevalent. Secondly, the paper explores how the media's preference for metaphor use varies across different periods, influenced by both political and social factors. Notably, the widespread use of war metaphors is primarily shaped by political considerations. Lastly, the research reveals the presence of a body metaphor in cancer reports, which, when used over an extended period, can subtly contribute to the reinforcement of body stereotypes.

This study carries both theoretical and practical significance. Theoretically, it contributes to the exploration of conceptual metaphors in disease-related discourse within the field of research. Practically, it delves into how cancer and cancer patients are represented through the use of metaphors in digital news reports, examining the resulting metaphorical implications. The findings of this study can serve as a valuable reference for media organizations engaging in digital reporting, helping them effectively communicate health knowledge and information.

One limitation of this study is that it relies on speculation and hypothesis regarding the potential consequences of stereotypical representations of the body. These hypotheses have not been empirically tested. Future research can build upon this aspect and further investigate the actual outcomes of such stereotypical representations.

References

1. WHO. Global Health Estimates: Deaths by Cause, Age, Sex, by Country and by Region, 2000–2019. Global health estimates: Leading causes of death (who.int) (2020)
2. Zheng, R., Zhang, S., Zeng, H., et al.: Cancer incidence and mortality in China, 2016. J. Natl. Cancer Center 2(1), 1–9 (2022)
3. Sung, H., Ferlay, J., Siegel, R.L., et al.: Global cancer statistics 2020: GLOBOCAN estimates of incidence and mortality worldwide for 36 cancers in 185 countries. CA Cancer J. Clin. 71(3), 209–249 (2021)
4. Koteyko, N., Brown, B., Crawford, P.: The dead parrot and the dying swan: the role of metaphor scenarios in UK press coverage of avian flu in the UK in 2005–2006. Metaphor. Symb. 23(4), 242–261 (2008)
5. Casarett, D., Pickard, A., Fishman, J.M., et al.: Can metaphors and analogies improve communication with seriously ill patients? J. Palliat. Med. 13(3), 255–260 (2010)
6. Hendricks, R.K., Demjén, Z., Semino, E., et al.: Emotional implications of metaphor: consequences of metaphor framing for mindset about cancer. Metaphor. Symb. 33(4), 267–279 (2018)

7. Hanne, M., Hawken, S.J.: Metaphors for illness in contemporary media. Med. Humanit. **33**(2), 93–99 (2007)
8. Rodehau-Noack, J.: War as disease: biomedical metaphors in prevention discourse. Eur. J. Int. Rel. **27**(4), 1020–1041 (2021)
9. Chen, Y., Zhou, S.: War metaphor, state-as-a-body and the family-country imagination: a corpus approach to the metaphor analysis on COVID-19 media coverage. Chin. J. Journal. Commun. **44**(02), 37–57 (2022). 陈阳, 周思宇.战争隐喻、国家身体与家国想象——基于语料库的新冠肺炎疫情报道隐喻研究. 国际新闻界 **44**(02), 37–57 (2022). https://doi.org/10.13495/j.cnki.cjjc.2022.02.003
10. Zhou, M., Lin, D.: Use and introspection of metaphor in the reports for public health crisis issues: a case study on media reports for influenza A/H1N1. Chin. J. Health Educ. **26**(01), 39–42+54 (2010). 周敏,林丹燕.公共卫生危机报道中隐喻的使用与反思——以甲型H1N1流感的媒体阐释现象为例. 中国健康教育 **26**(01), 39–42+54 (2010). https://doi.org/10.16168/j.cnki.issn.1002-9982.2010.01.024
11. Xu, K., Wan, P.: Highlighting and ignoring: a metaphorical analysis of the doctor-patient conflict in Chinese mainstream newspapers. Chin. J. Journal. Commun. **40**(11), 63–81 (2018). 徐开彬,万萍.凸显与遮蔽:国内主流报纸新闻评论中医患矛盾的隐喻分析. 国际新闻界 **40**(11), 63–81 (2018). https://doi.org/10.13495/j.cnki.cjjc.2018.11.004
12. Annas, G.J.: Reframing the debate on health care reform by replacing our metaphors. N. Engl. J. Med. **332**(11), 745–748 (1995)
13. Montgomery, S.L.: Codes and combat in biomedical discourse. Sci. Cult. **2**(3), 341–390 (1991)

Product Appearance Design of In Vitro Diagnostic Card Using Colloidal Gold Method Based on Kansei Engineering

Yuan Xu [iD] and Meiyu Zhou[(✉)]

School of Art Design and Media, East China University of Science and Technology, Shanghai, China
zhoutc_2003@163.com

Abstract. In vitro diagnostic (IVD) tests using immune colloidal gold technique are widely used in home disease prevention and disease diagnosis and have great potential for development. However, as a medical product, the existing design of the test card tends to focus on the satisfaction of the product's function rather than the user's emotions, so it is necessary to design the appearance of products from an emotional perspective and bring care to users. This study takes IVD cards using colloidal gold method as the design object, combines with Kansei Engineering (KE) as the theoretical guidance, quantifies the product characteristics by using Quantification Theory Type 1 (QT1), and constructs the correlation model with high confidence between Kansei words and design elements through multiple linear regression analysis. Finally, the test card design strategy is proposed according to the data, which can help relevant enterprises determine the direction of product form development.

Keywords: Kansei Engineering · Product design · In vitro diagnostic card · Quantification Theory Type 1

1 Introduction

In Vitro Diagnosis (IVD) is a technique for biomedical testing of tissue, body fluids, blood and other samples extracted from the human body to obtain diagnostic information, and is one of the important pillars of modern medical technology [1]. Among them, IVD tests using immune colloidal gold technique can be used for self-testing in a home environment with ease of operation, low cost, rapid detection and high accuracy [2]. At present, there have been detection products for Corona Virus Disease 2019 (COVID-19), Influenza A/B virus (FLUA/B), and human immunodeficiency virus (HIV) and so on. With the continuous development of economic level, the maturity of immune colloidal gold technique and the improvement of public health awareness, IVD tests (colloidal gold method) may have huge development space and demand [3].

However, as a medical product, the existing design focuses more on the product function and ignores the emotional reactions during the using process, such as anxiety and fear, so the test card design should pay more attention to the user's psychological feelings and own emotional characteristics [4]. This study attempts to explore the relationship between the IVD test cards and users' emotional needs based on the theory of Kansei Engineering(KE) to provide theoretical reference for future design. The research process is shown in Fig. 1.

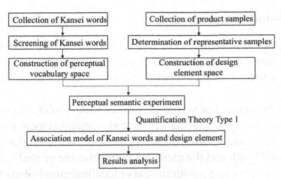

Fig. 1. Research process

2   Kansei Engineering and Related Theories

2.1   Kansei Engineering (KE)

KE is a subject with strong comprehensive attributes and cross attributes, focusing on consumers' own needs and subjective feelings and quantifying them to explore the corresponding product elements [5], which has been widely used in the design field since it was proposed.

2.2   Quantification Theory Type 1 (QT1)

QT1 is a variant of multiple regression analysis. Through mathematical processing, qualitative variables are represented by numerical values [6], so as to determine the influence of qualitative independent variables on quantitative dependent variables. This study will construct the relationship between design elements and perceptual images in order to maximize the degree of positive perceptual images.

3   Selection of Kansei Words and Product Samples

3.1   Identifying Kansei Word Pairs

Through user interviews, shopping website mining, and social network platform research, a total of 68 words describing the perceptual intention of the antigen test cards were collected. Through focus group discussions, the remaining words were grouped and filtered based on the principles of scientificity and similarity [7], and 9 representative perceptual words were extracted and matched with antonyms to form adjective pairs, which covered the descriptions of "performance", "shape", "feeling", and "style".

To reduce the cognitive load of the subsequent subjects [8], the semantic imagery space was further filtered. 10 professionals with design-related experience were invited to fill in the questionnaire, and the most suitable and necessary words were selected from 9 adjective pairs. Finally, 4 groups of adjectives with high scores were got, i.e., "cumbersome - concise", "cold - friendly", "tough - soft", and "restless - relaxed".

3.2 Selecting Product Samples

A total of 52 samples of IVD reagent cards (colloidal gold method) were collected from domestic and international shopping sites, social networking platforms and daily use. The samples were collected to include all kinds of reagent cards of various brands and diseases.

The remaining 46 samples were pre-processed with Adobe Photoshop CC 2018 to remove visual distractions such as logos, QR codes, measurement result markers, pen marks, etc. Since this study focuses on the perception of the product shape, the color [9] factor is not considered, and the elements with color are grayed out. Through focus group discussions, sample images with similar or identical morphology were categorized using an affinity diagram technique, which is also known as KJ [10], to obtain a logical sample classification. The 14 representative sample images finally determined are shown in Table 1.

Table 1. Representative samples

illustration							
sample number	1	2	3	4	5	6	7
illustration							
sample number	8	9	10	11	12	13	14

3.3 Constructing the Space of Product Shape Design Elements

According to the principle of immune colloidal gold technology [11] and the instructions for use of the test kit, it is possible to make a clear division of the structure of the test card, while combining user interviews to understand the product structure that users are concerned about, the design object shape can be decomposed into "external outline", "number of inspection items", "overall aspect ratio", "structure display area and sampling hole" and "surface decoration" by morphological analysis [12]. Among them, the structure display area and the sampling hole are grouped together as the same design element, because they occupy the main body of the inspection card together and the user looks at them almost simultaneously when using.

According to the representative samples, the 5 design elements are then decomposed into 18 design categories. The sample design elements and design categories are shown in Table 2.

Table 2. Product design elements and design categories

design element	design category			
external outline A	rectangle A1	round A2	groove A3	special meaning A4
number of inspection items B	single B1	multiple B2		
overall aspect ratio C	narrow C1	medium C2	wide C3	
structure display area and sampling hole D	rectangle D1	round D2	rectangle + round D3	arch D4
surface decoration E	straight line E1	curve E2	flat dot matrix E3	circular dot matrix E4	surface E5

4 Study of the Correlation Between Kansei Words and Design Elements

4.1 Perceptual Imagery Experiment

The experiment was conducted by means of a questionnaire containing 14 samples, each paired with 4 sets of adjective pairs. The semantic difference (SD) scale [13] consists of 5 orders with negative and positive perceptual words placed at the left and right ends of the interval, respectively, with values ranging from -2 to 2. The scores represent the subjects' perception of the sample pictures. 32 questionnaires were distributed and 30 valid questionnaires were obtained. The subjects all had experience in using the relevant products, including 9 males and 21 females, and 23 of them were engaged in design-related work. Descriptive statistics were analyzed to obtain the mean values of the evaluation results for each sample, which are shown in Table 3.

Table 3. Mean values of the evaluation and design category quantification table

sample	A1	A2	...	E5	cumbersome-concise	cold-friendly	tough-soft	restless-relaxed
1	0	1	...	0	0.6	0.43	0.47	0.43
2	1	0		1	1.43	0.1	0	−0.07
3	1	0		0	−0.37	0.17	−0.13	0.17
4	1	0		1	−0.1	0.3	0.3	0.13
5	0	1		0	−0.23	−0.07	0.17	−0.27
6	0	1		1	−0.97	−0.57	−0.37	−1.1
7	1	0		0	−0.43	−0.97	−1.07	−0.57
8	1	0		0	−0.23	−0.1	0	−0.2
9	0	1		1	0.87	0.37	0.4	0.5
10	0	0		0	−0.37	−0.67	−0.77	−0.43
11	0	0		0	−0.03	1	0.97	0.7
12	0	1		0	0.1	0.47	0.4	0.23
13	0	1		0	0.37	0.43	0.43	0.37
14	1	0		0	−0.77	−0.4	−0.67	−0.47

4.2 Building Mathematical Models

According to QT1, the sample design elements are treated as items, and the subdivided design classes under the same item are called subcategories. The matrix of subcategories composition consists of 0 and 1. Based on this principle, the sample design classes are coded and quantified, see Table 3.

The relationship between product design elements and users' perceptual imagery can be expressed by linear or nonlinear regression models, but in such studies, linear regression models [14] are usually conducted as a premise. Let each of the above design categories be the independent variable and the corresponding mean values of perceptual imagery ratings be the dependent variable, and explore the influence of the independent variable on the dependent variable, a linear mathematical model can be developed. Multiple linear regression analysis was conducted using IBM SPSS Statistics 26.0, and the coefficients of determination R^2 obtained were all close to 1, indicating a high degree of fit of the regression line to the observed values. The coefficient of the influence of design category on perceptual imagery is shown in Table 4. The larger the absolute value of the coefficient, the deeper the influence of the category, and a positive coefficient indicates a positive influence on perceptual imagery. For example, the design categories of straight line E1, curve E2, circular dot matrix E4 and face E5 under surface decoration E have scores of -0.63, 0.4, 0.6 and -0.5 respectively in the "relaxed" perceptual image, which means that the decoration of circular dot matrix will make the detection card the most relaxed, followed by curve decoration, while the decoration of straight line and face form tend to bring serious and uneasy feelings.

Table 4. Relationship between design categories and perceptual imagery

design element	design category	concise	score range	friendly	score range	soft	score range	relaxed	score range
external outline A	round A2	−0.27	2.43	−0.15	1.46	−0.135	1.305	−0.4	0.67
	groove A3	1.53		−1.04		−0.94		−0.8	
	special meaningA4	−0.9		0.42		0.365		−0.13	
number of inspection items B	single B1	1.84	1.84	0.94	0.94	0.77	0.77	1.6	1.6
overall aspect ratio C	narrow C1	−1.53	1.24	0.2	0.22	0.3	0.235	0.2	0.77
	wide C3	−0.29		0.42		0.535		0.97	
structure display area and sampling hole D	rectangle D1	0.34	3.01	−0.57	0.83	−0.4	0.745	−0.1	1.27
	rectangle + roundD3	−1.3		0.01		−0.16		0.37	
	arch D4	−2.67		−0.82		−0.905		−0.9	
surface decoration E	straight line E1	−0.97	1.84	−0.26	0.8	−0.205	1.21	−0.63	1.23
	curve E2	−1.03		0.16		0.37		0.4	
	circular dot matrix E4	0.81		0.48		0.975		0.6	
	surface E5	−0.47		−0.32		−0.235		−0.5	

The magnitude of the effect of items belonging to design categories on perceptual imagery can be measured according to the range of scores for each item [7]. According to the analysis, the largest factor influencing "cumbersome - concise" is 3.01 for "structure display area and sampling holes", the largest factor influencing "cold - friendly" is "1.46 for "external outline", the largest factor influencing "tough - soft" is "1.305 for "external outline", and the largest factor influencing "restless-relaxed" is "1.6 for "number of inspection items".

4.3 Design Strategy

Based on the above data analysis and summarizing the relationship between design elements and perceptual images, the following design strategies can be proposed to guide the design of the test card.

1) From the perspective of emotional design and caring design, the product semantics should be more inclined to affinity and relaxation, and when the external outline has special meaning, the affinity score is the highest. The sample of this experiment is the "HIV Reagent Card", whose shape is derived from the international symbol of AIDS, the "red ribbon", as shown in Fig. 2. The reason for the high score of the sample in terms of affinity may be that the red ribbon logo was designed with care and hope in mind, and the use of its visual elements can convey a similar feeling, so the design of the test card can be based on the design of the care logo for related diseases. In the case of disease detection for domestic pets such as cats and dogs, corresponding morphological features such as cat paws can be added to the outline of the test card to enhance recognition and affinity. Multi-test cards (containing multiple test items) such as the COVID-19, FLUA, FLUB 3-in-1 test card, hepatitis B 5-test card, although providing convenience in use, but the feeling of uneasiness and depression will also increase, but it can be neutralized by the rounded surface decoration design.

Fig. 2. HIV test card sample (left) and HIV international logo (right)

2) The design of test reagent cards should also be as concise as possible. In terms of production, simple disposable medical products are more in line with green design; in terms of use, products with a sense of simplicity and harmony are often more usable. According to the score analysis of "cumbersome-concise ", the results show that the structure display area and the sample addition area should have the same shape, for example, both are square or round; and the arched shape makes the visual sense more crowded and complex due to the combination of straight lines and curves. When the external outline is a notched groove shape, due to the lack of visual elements it looks most simple, but it will look cold and depressing as well.

3) If you want to make the shape more inclined to softness, the design elements should preferably satisfy: the external outline is of special significance type, the surface decoration is rounded dot matrix, the number of inspection items is single, and the structure display area and sampling hole are rounded type.

5   Conclusion

This study takes the IVD reagent card using colloidal gold method as the design object, uses the design method of KE to study the user's perceptual needs, and uses QT1 theory to quantitatively analyze the product modeling characteristics. After multiple linear regression analysis, a correlation model between perceptual imagery and design elements with high credibility is constructed, and design strategies from caring design, green design, ease of use and styling design are summarized to guide the design of testing reagent cards, so that such medical products can pay more attention to users' perceptual needs.

However, there are shortcomings in the study, such as the use of expert rating method to screen adjectives in this experiment, the results may be subjectively influenced by the rating experts. At the same time, the design scheme is only described in textual form, lacking model demonstration and verification. These problems will be improved in the subsequent research and practice.

References

1. Li, Y.H., Zhang, S.Q..: In Vitro diagnostic reagent industry review and outlook. Lab. Med. Clin. **14**, 299–301 (2017)
2. Wu, J.H., Meng, L.: Immunocolloidal gold technology: advances and application. Chin. Agric. Sci. Bull. **35**, 146–151 (2019)
3. Xu, F.P., Huang, H.Y., Chu, S.Z.: China's in vitro diagnostic reagent industry development status, problems and countermeasures. Chin. J. Pharmaceut. **50**, 1367–1373 (2019). https://doi.org/10.16522/j.cnki.cjph.2019.11.023
4. Gao, J., He, X.-M.: Summary of research on the application status of Kansei Engineering in medical product design. Dev. Innov. Mach. Electr. Prod. **35**, 146–149 (2022)
5. Luo, S.J., Pan, Y.H.: Review of theory, key technologies and its application of perceptual image in product design. Chin. J. Mech. Eng. **43**, 8–13 (2007)
6. Faris, J.A.: Quantification Theory. Routledge, Abingdon (2019). https://doi.org/10.4324/978 0367853976
7. Zhang, N.-N., Feng, C., Ji, L., Ren, H.: Kansei Engineering research on visual design elements of automobile digital instrument. Sci. Technol. Eng. **21**, 14976–14981 (2021)
8. Liu, Y.-H., Liu, L.: Modeling design of ceramic liquor bottle based on Kansei Engineering. Packa. Eng. **42**, 330–340 (2021). https://doi.org/10.19554/j.cnki.1001-3563.2021.20.039
9. Xu, J., Sun, S.Q., Zhang, K.J.: Product image form optimization design based on genetical gorithm. Chin. J. Mech. Eng. 53–58+64 (2007)
10. Zhou, J.Y.: Research on campus cultural and creative product design based on KJ method— take Hunan Normal University as an example. Ind. Des. 72–73 (2020)
11. Li, Y.Y., Peng, Y.S., Lin, C.L., Luo, X.Y., et al.: Nanomaterials and biosensing technology for the SARS-CoV-2 detection. J. Inorg. Mater. **38**, 3–31 (2023)
12. Zhou, Z.-Y., Cheng, J.-X., Zhang, X.-Y.: Application of Kansei Engineering in nursing beds design. Packa. Eng. **37**, 98–100+142 (2016). https://doi.org/10.19554/j.cnki.1001-3563.2016. 08.026

13. Llinares, C., Page, A.F.: Differential semantics as a Kansei Engineering tool for analysing the emotional impressions which determine the choice of neighbourhood: the case of Valencia. Spain. Landsc. Urban Plan. **87**, 247–257 (2008). https://doi.org/10.1016/j.landurbplan.2008.06.006
14. Chiu, M.-C., Lin, K.-Z.: Utilizing text mining and Kansei Engineering to support data-driven design automation at conceptual design stage. Adv. Eng. Inform. **38**, 826–839 (2018). https://doi.org/10.1016/j.aei.2018.11.002

I-Health - Designing a Smart Massage Product-Service System for the Sub-health Status of Young People Based on Traditional Chinese Tuina Therapy

Sixiao Zhao and Mickey Mengting Zhang[✉]

Faculty of Humanities and Arts, Macau University of Science and Technology, Macau, China
mtzhang@must.edu.mo, 2220028080@student.must.edu.mo

Abstract. The rapid development of information technologies, artificial intelligence, and the Internet has enabled the emergence of smart products and on-demand e-services as an integrated solution to meet individual user needs. In the medical and health industry, smart product-service systems have been widely applied. Suboptimal health (sub-health) status can be considered an intermediate stage between health and disease, characterized by a range of uncomfortable symptoms such as chronic fatigue, sleep disorders, poor mood, and aches. However, sub-health cannot be identified accurately by medical standards. Tuina therapy, an ancient form of massage from traditional Chinese medicine, can improve these symptoms by focusing on balancing a person's energy flow with various techniques such as kneading, pressing, rolling, and stretching. In this study, we designed a smart massage product-service system based on Tuina therapy for young people suffering from sub-health status. The system integrates traditional Chinese medicine with intelligent technologies, sensors, and connectivity. The product can provide relief to young people who suffer from sub-health but lack the time and energy for long-term medical treatment. This research provides a valuable design case for applying traditional Chinese medicine in a new scenario with smart technologies.

Keywords: Smart product-service system · sub-health status · traditional Chinese medicine · Tuina therapy · intelligent technologies

1 Introduction

Sub-health is a state characterized by disturbances in psychological behaviors, physical characteristics, or medical examination indices, without any typical pathologic features (Wei and Yan 2012). It is considered an intermediate stage between health and disease and afflicts people with various uncomfortable symptoms without diagnosable illnesses (Li et al. 2013). Tuina, a branch of traditional Chinese medical treatment (Ernst 2019), can release sub-health conditions. It is believed to restore the balance and harmony of the body by stimulating the flow of qi, the body's vital energy force, and improving both acute and chronic musculoskeletal conditions, as well as non-musculoskeletal conditions. Tuina therapy is often used in conjunction with acupuncture, moxibustion, fire cupping, Chinese herbalism, tai chi or other Chinese internal martial arts, and qigong (Dorland 2007). Tuina therapy has been applied in the treatment of sub-health symptoms to improve the disturbances in human's psychological and physical condition. It is usually served in the form of hand massage. During the session, a practitioner may use their hands and arms to massage, knead, press, and stretch the body. However, the therapy is limited by human power and time, and there is a lack of massage products incorporating this technique. With the rise of sharing economy and smart product technology, the development of smart product-service systems (SPSS) can enable collaborative consumption of products and services with pro-environmental outcomes. In this context, the current electronic massage products, potential technologies, materials, and Tuina techniques are examined to design and develop an SPSS named i-Health, encompassing user scenario, product design, and user interface design.

2 Literature Review

2.1 Research of Massage Product

Prior medical research has demonstrated that massage can provide numerous benefits, including pain relief, reduced trait anxiety and depression, and temporary reductions in blood pressure, heart rate, and state of anxiety (Moyer et al. 2004). Furthermore, additional testing has revealed an immediate increase and faster recovery periods for muscle performance (Dupuy et al. 2018). Several theories have been proposed regarding the mechanisms of massage therapy, such as enhanced skeletal muscle regrowth and remodeling (Miller et al. 2018), blockage of nociception via the gate control theory (Chen and Michalsen 2017), activation of the parasympathetic nervous system, which can stimulate the release of endorphins and serotonin, prevention of fibrosis (Bove et al. 2016), scar tissue, and increased lymph flow, and improvement in sleep quality (Owais et al. 2018).

The development of massage products has been studied by several researchers. Wang et al. (2011) utilized Kansei Engineering to design massage products that meet the emotional and spiritual needs of consumers, particularly in the case of massage chairs. Shi et al. (2009) investigated the affective experience of massage products, examining aesthetic pleasure, attribution of meaning, and emotional response, particularly for massage chairs. McDonagh et al. (2005) examined massagers that use vibration to relieve muscular strains and pains and promote relaxation, focusing on user attitudes and perceptions to identify areas of dissatisfaction. The authors also highlighted the importance of understanding the differences between consumer and therapist perceptions in order to develop more effective hand-held massagers that meet the needs of all stakeholders. The insights gained from these studies can inform the development of massage products that are more effective and meet the needs of both consumers and therapists.

2.2 Current Massage Product

After examine the previous research, we have classified the general massage products on the market into three different groups for the purposes of this review (Table 1). Each of these groups has its own unique characteristics and features. Hand-held massagers like fascia guns are portable and convenient for targeting specific areas of the body, which uses mechanical vibration to transmit relaxation to deep fascia muscles and reduce muscle tension. While body-carrier devices like shoulder and neck massager can promote blood circulation, relieve muscle tension, and improve the body's condition when used on various massage points. Chair massagers offer a more comprehensive massage experience and can be used for extended periods of time. It utilizes machinery, air bags, electromagnetic components, and electric heating to massage different parts of the body. However, these products have limitations in terms of their effectiveness in treating subhealth conditions, as they typically only provide temporary relief rather than addressing the root cause of the problem. This is where the integration of Tuina therapy and smart technology in the design of massage products can offer a potential solution.

Table 1. Three Types of Current Massage Product

Group	Hand-held Massagers	Body-carrier Massager	Chair Massagers
Name	Fascia gun	Shoulder and neck massager	Shiatsu Neck Back Massager chair
Picture			
Use for	Whole Body	Shoulder and neck	Whole Body
Item Weight	1.85 Kilograms	4.6 Kilograms	9.5 Kilograms
Brand	Raemao	Nekteck	Comfier
Advantages	• Long Battery Life • Powerful & Quiet Deep Massage • Brushless High-torque Super Quiet Motor • LCD Touch Screen • 15 Massage Heads •	• 8 Powerful Deep-Shiatsu Kneading Massage Nodes • Easy and Safe to Use • Adjustable Intensity • Durable and Comfortable Matreial.	• Relax Full Body • Creative 2D/3D Shiatsu Massage • Adjustable Rolling & Spot Massage • Adjustable Compression Massage • Ultimate Comfort
Disadvantages	• The price is high • The volume is large and not easy to carry • The styling products are single	• The massage head is hard • The massage range is limited; • The mute function is poor • The volume is large and not easy to carry • Hands cannot be freed •	• The price of family purchase is high • The volume is too large and not easy to carry • The shape is single

2.3 Tuina Technique

Upon reviewing the literature on massage techniques, it becomes apparent that there are several key techniques that are fundamental to Tuina massage. These techniques include swing, friction, vibration, extrusion, percussion, and sports joints. The swinging manipulation technique involves continuously swinging the palm and wrist joints, such as with the one-finger pushing, and kneading. The friction technique involves creating friction by moving the palm or fingers back and forth in a straight line or in circles, such as with the pushing, rubbing, and wiping. Vibration technique refers to the rhythmic and light continuous action on the human body to create vibrations. The squeezing manipulation technique involves pressing the body with palms, fingers, or other parts of the limbs to make it feel squeezed, such as with pressing, holding, twisting, and stepping. Tapping techniques involve tapping the body surface with the palm, back of the fist, fingers, side of the palm, or a stick to create a tapping sensation, such as with hitting and clapping. Transport joint-moving manipulations refer to performing passive movements on joints, such as with shaking, back method, pulling method, and pulling method (Yu 1985).

2.4 Acupuncture Point of Massage

The following are descriptions of acupuncture points and their indications for therapeutic use (Cheng and Lin 2020). The Zusanli Leg Three Li (足三里)point is located on the anterior and lateral aspect of the calf, 3 cun below the Calf's Nose and slightly more than 1 cun lateral to the tibia, in the interstitial space between two muscles. Although this point primarily controls gastrointestinal and digestive diseases, it can also treat systemic ailments, including bloating, heart and abdominal pain, cold stomach, and vomiting. The Guanyuan Pass Head (關元) point is situated 3 cun below the navel and 2 cun above the pubic bone. It is used for treating conditions such as enuresis, dysmenorrhea, amenorrhea, menstrual disorders, leucorrhea, metrostaxis, uterine prolapse, mounting qi, cold qi entering the abdomen, and lower abdominal pain. The Zhongwan Central Stomach Duct (中脘) point is located at 1 cun below the Upper Stomach Duct, 4 cun above the navel, and between the xiphoid process and the navel. Its indications include various stomach illnesses, food damage with indigestion, difficulty consuming food and drink, indigestion, cold aggregation with qi bind, acute and chronic fright wind, gastritis, stomach ulcer, gastroptosia, and stomach spasms. The Neiguan Inner Pass (內關) point is located below the palm, 2 cun above the wrist, and between two muscles. It is used for treating insomnia, dizziness, fearful throbbing, axillary swelling, elbow spasms, angina pectoris, fullness, distention, and pain in the chest, vomiting, and morning sickness or malign obstruction. The Hegu Union Valley (合谷) point is located at the midpoint of the first metacarpal bone of the palm on the radial side. Its indications include migraines and general headaches, wind injury, coughing, nasal congestion, deep-source nasal congestion, ocular pain, tinnitus, deafness, and wind stroke. The Yanglingquan Yang Mound Spring (陽陵泉) point is situated on the lateral side of the calves, 1 cun below the knee, and in the depression behind the tibia and before the fibula. It can treat pain in the lateral costal area, bitter taste in the mouth, hemiplegia, bisyndrome caused by preponderant cold and numbness in the lower limbs, swelling and pain in the knees, hypertension, and gripping pain in the gallbladder. The Fengchii Wind Pool (風池) point is located behind the mastoid process posterior to the ear, on the lateral border outer face of the large muscle, below naokong Brain Hollow and in the depression in the hairline. Its indications include wind stroke, hemilateral or medial headache, cold-induced febrile diseases without sweating, stiffness of the neck with an inability to turn the head and look back, and crick in the neck. The Yinmen Gate of Abundance (殷門) point is situated in the center of the back of the thigh, at 6 cun below the Support point. It is used to treat lumbar and leg pain, sciatica, and thigh pain. The Mingmen Life Gate (命門) point is located below the fourteenth vertebra, or between the second and third lumbar vertebrae. Its indications include stiffness of the spine with pain in the lumbar region, bi-syndrome caused by preponderant cold in the arms and legs, spasms and tension, and fear and fright with a dizzy head. Lastly, the Dazhui Great Hammer (大椎) point is located in the depression above the first vertebra, or between the first thoracic and seventh cervical vertebrae. Its indications include stiffness of the behind, stiffness of the back along the spine, contracture along the back and arms (Fig. 1).

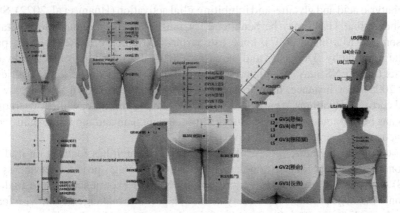

Fig. 1. Acupuncture Point

2.5 Techniques of Massage Product

Electrical muscle stimulation (EMS) is the use of electric impulses to elicit muscle contractions. EMS has been shown to be particularly beneficial prior to exercise and activity due to its ability to activate muscles early (Dupuy et al. 2018). The impulses are generated by a device and delivered through electrodes on the skin in close proximity to the muscles being stimulated, typically using adhesive pads. These impulses mimic the action potential generated by the central nervous system, leading to muscle contraction. EMS has gained increased attention in recent years due to its versatility, as it can be used as a training tool (Babault et al. 2007; Banerjee et al. 2005), a therapeutic tool (Delitto et al. 1988; Lake 1992), or a cosmetic tool. Specifically, it can be utilized as a strength training tool for healthy individuals and athletes, as well as a testing tool for evaluating neural and/or muscular function in vivo. It can also be used as a rehabilitation and preventive tool for individuals who are partially or totally immobilized, such as in physical therapy to prevent muscle atrophy resulting from inactivity or neuromuscular imbalance after musculoskeletal injuries (Palmer et al. 1998).

Transcutaneous electrical nerve stimulation (TENS) is a non-invasive therapeutic technique that utilizes electric current to stimulate nerves for pain management (Johnson 2007). Typically, TENS units consist of two or more conductive gel pads connected to the skin, and the current can be modulated in terms of frequency, pulse width, and intensity. TENS is usually applied at a high frequency (>50 Hz) with an intensity that is below the threshold for motor contraction (sensory intensity) or at a low frequency (<10 Hz) with an intensity that induces motor contraction. Some newer TENS units use a mixed frequency mode to reduce the development of tolerance with repeated use. It is recommended that the stimulation intensity should be strong but comfortable, with greater intensities producing more significant analgesia regardless of frequency (Robinson and Snyder-Mackler 2007). TENS differs from EMS, which utilizes electric current for muscle contraction. TENS has been shown to alleviate both acute and chronic pain by reducing the sensitization of dorsal horn neurons, increasing levels of gamma-aminobutyric acid and glycine, and inhibiting glial activation (Huang et al. 2022). Studies have shown that TENS may be beneficial for managing chronic musculoskeletal pain (Johnson and Martinson 2007), knee osteoarthritis (Maheu et al. 2022), and painful diabetic neuropathy (Dubinsky and Miyasaki 2010). Furthermore, objective evidence suggests that TENS may modulate or suppress pain signals in the brain (Ellrich and Lamp 2005). For instance, high-frequency TENS has been shown to decrease pain-related cortical activations in patients with carpal tunnel syndrome, while low-frequency TENS has been found to reduce shoulder impingement pain and modulate pain-induced brain activation (Kara et al. 2010; Kocyigit et al. 2012).

Based on our literature review, the majority of research has focused on traditional electronic massage products, rather than on smart massage product-service systems (SPSS) that provide users with a more comprehensive experience. While traditional electronic massage products are widely available, portable massage SPSS, with features such as being lighter in weight, capable of simulating manual hand massage techniques, and focusing more on relaxation, have received less attention. However, given the growing trend of meeting users' expectations and needs, further exploration of this area is necessary (McDonagh et al. 2005).

3   i-Health Massage SPSS Design

3.1   i-Health Concept

The i-Health Massage SPSS comprises of two components, the massage product, and the charging station, as illustrated in Fig. 2 and Fig. 3. The design of the i-Health massage product is inspired by the jigsaw puzzle. The jigsaw puzzle is a tiling puzzle that involves fitting interlocking and mosaic-shaped pieces, each of which typically represents a portion of a picture. Previous research has indicated that the design and development of massage products are moving towards increased portability and flexibility (McDonagh et al. 2005). The jigsaw-inspired design allows for greater flexibility and customization of the massage product. It can be used as a single piece for a small area of pain points, or it can be connected with other pieces to cover a larger area of pain points. The i-Health massage SPSS combines TENS and EMS, which offers multiple benefits, including pain relief and muscle strengthening. It can be used after work, exercise, training, or relaxation to reduce tension. Ten acupuncture points, including Zusanli Leg Three Li (足三里), Guanyuan Pass Head (關元), Zhongwan Central Stomach Duct (中脘), Neiguan Inner Pass (內關), Hegu Union Valley (合谷), Yanglingquan Yang Mound Spring (陽陵泉), Fengchii Wind Pool (風池), Yinmen Gate of Abundance (殷門), Mingmen Life Gate (命門), Dazhui Great Hammer (大椎), have been selected based on their effectiveness in relieving muscle pain and stimulating neuromuscular and cellular activity to activate muscle vitality. The selection of these acupuncture points also takes into account sub-health concerns and the effects of i-Health.

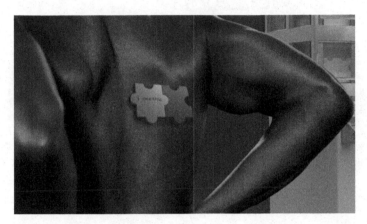

Fig. 2. i-Health Massage

3.2 Components and Materials of i-Health

The i-Health massage SPSS is designed to be user-friendly and convenient. The massage module is lightweight and portable, making it easy to use anywhere and anytime. The control circuit board and chip enable the user to control the smart functions, adjust the intensity of the massage, and choose the massage mode that suits their needs. The battery provides a long-lasting power supply, allowing the user to enjoy the massage for up to 16 h on a single charge. The use of silver wire in the massage module enhances the performance of the product by better conducting intermediate frequency pulse current. The hydrogel layer is an important feature of the product, as it is skin-friendly, washing-friendly, and durable. Its smooth texture and air permeability allow for comfortable, long-term wear without causing skin sensitivity. The wireless communication module in the sharing charging station enables the product to be easily connected, charged, and managed wirelessly, adding to the overall convenience and user-friendliness of the i-Health massage SPSS (Fig. 4).

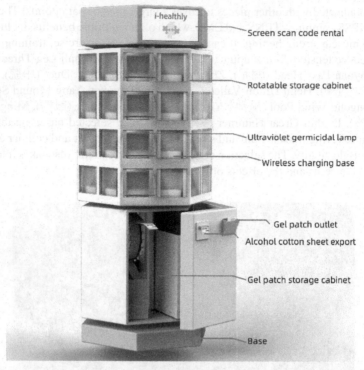

Fig. 3. i-Health Massage SPSS

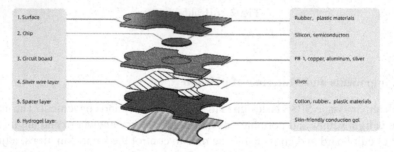

Fig. 4. Massage patch structure diagram

3.3 Massage Mode of i-Health

The i-Health massage SPSS offers users five modes, including kneading, slap, shiatsu, dial-up, and tap, which can be selected through the user interface based on individual needs. Kneading is suitable for treating pain in various parts of the body, particularly the neck, limbs, and localized pain. It facilitates blood circulation, reduces swelling, relieves pain, and reduces spasms. Slap mode primarily targets the shoulders, back, waist, buttocks, and lower limbs, promoting nerve stimulation and tendon relaxation, as well as enhancing blood and Qi flow, while alleviating spasms. Shiatsu mode mainly applies finger pressure and other techniques to acupuncture points, providing a calming and analgesic effect. Dial-up mode is effective in releasing adhesions, promoting blood and Qi flow, relieving spasms and pain, and reducing stenosis. Finally, the tap method is best suited for the head, lower back, or lower limbs, allowing for muscle relaxation and improved circulation, harmonizing Qi and blood flow, and promoting mental refreshment (Fig. 5).

Fig. 5. User Interface Design

4   Discussion

The i-Health product is designed to meet various Product Service System (PSS) attributes, including ease of maintenance, durability, flexibility, and customization. Sundin and Bras (2005) and Williams (2007) argue that ease of maintenance and durability are essential PSS attributes that ensure a longer product lifetime, ease of upgrading, and remanufacturing. In line with these arguments, the i-Health massage product is designed to be durable and easy to maintain, given that it is frequently used and replaced.

Additionally, flexibility and customization are critical PSS attributes in meeting varying user requirements and operational processes (Azarenko et al. 2009; Meier et al. 2010; Ulaga and Reinartz 2011; Tukker 2004). As such, the i-Health design aims to provide flexibility to accommodate different angles and requirements for users with varying pain points. Furthermore, the product is customized to adapt to individual users' needs, ensuring a personalized experience for each user. Overall, the i-Health product's design caters to various PSS attributes, ensuring that it is easy to use, portable, and flexible, while meeting user requirements for maintenance, durability, and customization.

References

Wang, W., Yan, Y.: Suboptimal health: a new health dimension for translational medicine. Clin. Transl. Med. **1**(1), e28 (2012)

Li, G., et al.: Subhealth: definition, criteria for diagnosis and potential prevalence in the central region of China. BMC Public Health **13**(1), 1–8 (2013)

Ernst, E., Ernst, E.: Umbrella terms. In: Alternative Medicine: A Critical Assessment of 150 Modalities, pp. 257–302 (2019)

Dorland, W.: Dorland's medical dictionary for health consumers. Saunders, an imprint of Elsevier (2007)

Hamari, J., Sjöklint, M., Ukkonen, A.: The sharing economy: why people participate in collaborative consumption. J. Am. Soc. Inf. Sci. **67**(9), 2047–2059 (2016)

Prieto, M., Baltas, G., Stan, V.: Car sharing adoption intention in urban areas: what are the key sociodemographic drivers? Transport. Res. Part A: Policy Pract. **101**, 218–227 (2017)

Sutherland, W., Jarrahi, M.H.: The sharing economy and digital platforms: a review and research agenda. Int. J. Inf. Manag. **43**, 328–341 (2018)

Piscicelli, L., Cooper, T., Fisher, T.: The role of values in collaborative consumption: insights from a product-service system for lending and borrowing in the UK. J. Clean. Prod. **97**, 21–29 (2015)

Halen, C.V., Vezzoli, C., Wimmer, R.: Methodology for product service system innovation. Koninklijke Van Gorcum BV, Assen (2005)

Moyer, C.A., Rounds, J., Hannum, J.W.: A meta-analysis of massage therapy research. Psychol. Bull. **130**(1), 3 (2004)

Dupuy, O., Douzi, W., Theurot, D., Bosquet, L., & Dugué, B.: An evidence-based approach for choosing post-exercise recovery techniques to reduce markers of muscle damage, soreness, fatigue, and inflammation: a systematic review with meta-analysis. Front. Physiol. **403** (2018)

Miller, B.F., et al.: Enhanced skeletal muscle regrowth and remodelling in massaged and contralateral non-massaged hindlimb. J. Physiol. **596**(1), 83–103 (2018)

Chen, L., Michalsen, A.: Management of chronic pain using complementary and integrative medicine. Bmj **357** (2017)

Bove, G.M., Harris, M.Y., Zhao, H., Barbe, M.F.: Manual therapy as an effective treatment for fibrosis in a rat model of upper extremity overuse injury. J. Neurol. Sci. **361**, 168–180 (2016)

Owais, S., Chow, C.H., Furtado, M., Frey, B.N., Van Lieshout, R.J.: Non-pharmacological interventions for improving postpartum maternal sleep: a systematic review and meta-analysis. Sleep Med. Rev. **41**, 87–100 (2018)

Wang, Z.Y., Liang, Y.Y., Shi, H.H.: Research on Kansei Engineering and its application in massage chair design. In: Key Engineering Materials, vol. 480, pp. 1014–1017. Trans Tech Publications Ltd. (2011)

Shi, Y., Ying, F., Ying, J.: Affective experience analyse of massage chair. In: 2009 IEEE 10th International Conference on Computer-Aided Industrial Design & Conceptual Design. pp. 1463–1467. IEEE (2009)

McDonagh, D., Wilson, L., Haslam, C., Weightman, D.: Good vibrations: do electrical therapeutic massagers work? Ergonomics **48**(6), 680–691 (2005)

Yu, D.F.: Tuina: Textbooks for Higher Medical Schools. Science and Technology Press, Shanghai (1985)

Cheng, C.Y., Lin, J.G.: Atlas of Acupuncturology. National Research Institute of Chinese Medicine, Taiwan, China (2020)

Babault, N., Cometti, G., Bernardin, M., Pousson, M., Chatard, J.C.: Effects of electromyostimulation training on muscle strength and power of elite rugby players. J. Strength Cond. Res. **21**(2), 431–437 (2007)

Banerjee, P., Caulfield, B., Crowe, L., Clark, A.: Prolonged electrical muscle stimulation exercise improves strength and aerobic capacity in healthy sedentary adults. J. Appl. Physiol. **99**(6), 2307–2311 (2005)

Porcari, J.P., et al.: The effects of neuromuscular electrical stimulation training on abdominal strength, endurance, and selected anthropometric measures. J. Sports Sci. Med. **4**(1), 66 (2005)

Lake, D.A.: Neuromuscular electrical stimulation. an overview and its application in the treatment of sports injuries. Sports Med. **13**(5), 320–336 (1992)

Delitto, A., Rose, S.J., McKowen, J.M., Lehman, R.C., Thomas, J.A., Shively, R.A.: Electrical stimulation versus voluntary exercise in strengthening thigh musculature after anterior cruciate ligament surgery. Phys. Ther. **68**(5), 660–663 (1988)

Johnson, M.: Transcutaneous electrical nerve stimulation: mechanisms, clinical application and evidence. Rev. Pain **1**(1), 7–11 (2007)

Ursache, T., Cretu, A., Petroiu, G., Rotariu, C.: A wireless low-cost device for transcutaneous electrical nerve stimulation. In: 2021 12th International Symposium on Advanced Topics in Electrical Engineering (ATEE), pp. 1–4. IEEE (2021)

Robinson, A.J.: Clinical Electrophysiology: Electrotherapy and Electrophysiologic Testing. Lippincott Williams & Wilkins, Philadelphia (2008)

Huang, J., et al.: Transcutaneous electrical nerve stimulation in rodent models of neuropathic pain: a meta-analysis. Front. Neurosci. **27** (2022)

Johnson, M., Martinson, M.: Efficacy of electrical nerve stimulation for chronic musculoskeletal pain: a meta-analysis of randomized controlled trials. Pain **130**(1–2), 157–165 (2007)

Maheu, E., Soriot-Thomas, S., Noel, E., Ganry, H., Lespessailles, E., Cortet, B.: Wearable transcutaneous electrical nerve stimulation (actiTENS®) is effective and safe for the treatment of knee osteoarthritis pain: a randomized controlled trial versus weak opioids. Therap. Adv. Musculoskel. Dis. **14**, 1759720X211066233 (2022)

Dubinsky, R.M., Miyasaki, J.: Assessment: efficacy of transcutaneous electric nerve stimulation in the treatment of pain in neurologic disorders (an evidence-based review): report of the therapeutics and technology assessment subcommittee of the American academy of neurology. Neurology **74**(2), 173–176 (2010)

Ellrich, J., Lamp, S.: Peripheral nerve stimulation inhibits nociceptive processing: an electrophysiological study in healthy volunteers. Neuromodul. Technol. Neural Interface **8**(4), 225–232 (2005)

Kara, M., et al.: Quantification of the effects of transcutaneous electrical nerve stimulation with functional magnetic resonance imaging: a double-blind randomized placebo-controlled study. Arch. Phys. Med. Rehabil. **91**(8), 1160–1165 (2010)

Kocyigit, F., Akalin, E., Gezer, N.S., Orbay, O., Kocyigit, A., Ada, E.: Functional magnetic resonance imaging of the effects of low-frequency transcutaneous electrical nerve stimulation on central pain modulation: a double-blind, placebo-controlled trial. Clin. J. Pain **28**(7), 581–588 (2012)

Sundin, E., Bras, B.: Making functional sales environmentally and economically beneficial through product remanufacturing. J. Clean. Prod. **13**(9), 913–925 (2005)

Williams, A.: Product service systems in the automobile industry: contribution to system innovation? J. Clean. Prod. **15**(11–12), 1093–1103 (2007)

Evans, S., Partidário, P.J., Lambert, J.: Industrialization as a key element of sustainable product-service solutions. Int. J. Prod. Res. **45**(18–19), 4225–4246 (2007)

Azarenko, A., Roy, R., Shehab, E., Tiwari, A.: Technical product-service systems: some implications for the machine tool industry. J. Manuf. Technol. Manag. **20**(5), 700–722 (2009)

Meier, H., Roy, R., Seliger, G.: Industrial product-service systems—IPS2. CIRP Ann. **59**(2), 607–627 (2010)

Ulaga, W., Reinartz, W.J.: Hybrid offerings: how manufacturing firms combine goods and services successfully. J. Mark. **75**(6), 5–23 (2011)

Tukker, A.: Eight types of product–service system: eight ways to sustainability? experiences from SusProNet. Bus. Strateg. Environ. **13**(4), 246–260 (2004)

Babelt: A Pregnancy Belly Support Belt Connected with an App Designed for Pregnant Women with GDM

Na Zhuo and Zhenyu Cheryl Qian[✉]

Purdue University, West Lafayette, IN 47906, USA
zhuon521@gmail.com

Abstract. Gestational diabetes mellitus, a type of diabetes that develops during pregnancy in women who don't already have diabetes, has a greater impact on the health of pregnant women than is often thought. Research data shows that GDM is caused by hormones produced during pregnancy that can make insulin less effective, which may bring health problems to both the pregnant woman and the baby to be born. There are four main kinds of treatments for pregnant women with GDM to control blood glucose levels: having a special diet in the right amount at right time, keeping regular physical exercise which is moderately intense, monitoring daily blood glucose regularly to ensure it stays in a healthy range and inject insulin if needed. However, pregnant women easily get themselves into trouble during these treatments. Blood glucose measurements cannot always be poked in the same place, as can insulin injections, and pregnant women have limited mobility and often need help from others to complete the process. In addition, pregnant women themselves have some other problems during pregnancy, such as their baby bump getting heavier and heavier, and babies needing regular health data monitoring. This poster proposes a product connected to an App to help pregnant women with GDM to be able to control their blood glucose levels easily and directly during pregnancy while monitoring the health of their baby. This product is in the form of a pregnancy support belt consisting of two belts, the upper belt for different detectors to monitor data and the lower belt for different insulin injectors. Pregnant women can be informed of their own and their baby's health data, receive dietary advice, and set up insulin injections from the App. This design is dedicated to making life healthier and more convenient for pregnant women with GDM.

Keywords: Gestational diabetes mellitus · Wearable design · App design

1 Introduction

Based on data provided by the American Diabetes Association, gestational diabetes mellitus (GDM) affects nearly 10% of pregnancies in the United States annually [1]. GDM, a type of glucose intolerance that is first recognized during pregnancy, poses risks to both pregnant women and their babies. To control blood glucose levels in pregnant

C. Stephanidis et al. (Eds.): HCII 2023, CCIS 1957, pp. 470–477, 2024.
https://doi.org/10.1007/978-3-031-49212-9_58

women with GDM, special diets, moderate exercise, regular blood glucose monitoring, and insulin injections, when needed, are commonly used as main treatments [1]. However, these treatments can be challenging for pregnant women due to limited body mobility and other factors, including pain from frequent injections and poking. In addition to monitoring blood glucose, fetal monitoring is also crucial, accomplished through checking the baby's heart rate and other functions [2]. However, it is impossible for pregnant women to continuously monitor all these data themselves.

Fortunately, the emergence of certain technologies has helped address these challenges. In this study, we propose a pregnancy-supporting belt called Babelt, which utilizes available technologies to develop a product that can alleviate the burden of a pregnant belly and establish a health monitoring system that operates around the clock. Babelt is connected to a mobile app that allows users to easily monitor their health conditions. Key features of the product include 1) real-time monitoring and tracking of blood glucose levels, 2) setting specific injection times with or without alarms, 3) recording insulin injections by time and volume, 4) real-time monitoring and recording of the baby's beats per minute (BPM) with visualization, 5) exercise management, such as setting daily goals with reminders and visualizing progress and other related data, and 6) providing specialized diet suggestions for pregnant women with GDM. Our research aims to design a better experience for pregnant women with GDM, providing them with easy and instant monitoring of their health status and that of their baby, reducing the pain of insulin injections, and offering encouragement and advice on diet and exercise to improve their overall health.

2   Background of the Study

2.1   Self-management of Gestational Diabetes Mellitus

Gestational diabetes mellitus (GDM) is a condition that affects pregnant women and occurs when a hormone produced by the placenta prevents the body from using insulin effectively due to other hormones that make insulin less effective [3]. Although it usually doesn't cause noticeable symptoms, it can pose significant health risks to babies, including excessive birth weight, preterm birth, respiratory distress syndrome, low blood sugar, and an increased risk of type 2 diabetes later in life if left untreated [4]. Daily self-management of diabetes is crucial to achieving positive health outcomes [5].

Gestational diabetes management begins with non-pharmacological measures such as dietary modifications, exercise, and glucose monitoring. The American Diabetes Association (ADA) recommends personalized nutritional counseling by a registered dietitian based on the patient's BMI [6]. Moderate-intensity aerobic exercise for at least 30 min per day, five days a week, or a minimum of 150 min per week is also recommended [6]. Self-monitoring of blood glucose (SMBG) is also essential, with the ADA recommending SMBG three or more times per day for patients using insulin. SMBG should be performed before and one hour after meals and during the night to diagnose and prevent nocturnal hypoglycemia [7].

However, despite these strict rules, self-monitoring and insulin injections are not as simple as they may seem. Frequent injections and finger pricking for blood glucose testing can cause anxiety and fear in patients. In a questionnaire, 14% of patients avoided injections secondary to anxiety, and 42% expressed concern about having to inject more frequently [8]. Fear of injections and pain can also affect adherence to insulin therapy, as a systematic review in 2004 found that only one-third of the prescribed insulin dose was used by young patients, with an estimated adherence rate of 62–64% among patients with type 2 diabetes [9]. These challenges show that diabetes self-management based on existing modalities is difficult to accomplish.

2.2 Opportunity Area

Continuous Glucose Monitoring

Blood glucose testing is a routine and necessary part of diabetes management, but the current method of fingertip blood testing has limitations. This method can only be performed up to seven times a day and only provides a snapshot of blood glucose at a single point in time, which may not reflect the changes in blood glucose levels throughout the day.

Continuous glucose monitoring (CGM) devices have been developed to overcome these limitations. CGM devices use a miniature sensor that is usually attached to the skin to continuously monitor blood glucose levels in the tissue fluid. This technology allows for real-time monitoring of blood glucose trends and levels around the clock and provides access to a full picture of the changes in blood glucose levels. The CGM device sends this data to an app, which can be used to improve health outcomes and prevent dangerous situations. Compared to the traditional fingertip blood test, the CGM device is painless and does not require frequent blood sampling. Instead, micro-sensor electrodes are used to intervene under the skin [10]. The use of CGM devices represents a significant advancement in diabetes management technology and offers a more effective and convenient approach to blood glucose monitoring.

Microneedle Injection

Subcutaneous injections are the most commonly used method for administering insulin, however, their usage is hindered by several obstacles such as potential pain, patient avoidance of injections due to injection-related anxiety or phobias, concerns about the frequency of injections, and the negative impact on quality of life. These issues may impede patient adherence to treatment, ultimately leading to poor glycemic control [11].

Recent advancements in the use of micron-scale needles have demonstrated promising results in increasing skin permeability to transdermal delivery, especially for macromolecules. Hollow microneedles have been developed and shown to successfully microinject insulin into diabetic rats [12]. The use of microneedles offers a viable solution to address patient concerns and ensure a painless experience for those who require frequent injections. Innovative insulin-specific injections, such as the i-Port Advance injection port, are already available to provide a comfortable yet reliable method for administering multiple daily subcutaneous injections over three days without puncturing the skin for each dose. Moreover, patients can continue their daily activities without having to remove the i-Port Advance [11]. In this way, pain-free and controlled insulin injections are possible.

3 User Experience Research

To gain a deeper understanding of the challenges pregnant women with gestational diabetes mellitus (GDM) face during pregnancy and childbirth, and to avoid design bias, I conducted an authorized interview with a 49-year-old woman who was diagnosed with GDM during her pregnancy two decades ago. The interviewee had to endure a higher level of discomfort than the average person during her pregnancy, including daily fingertip blood collection to monitor her blood glucose levels, adherence to a special diet, and regular exercise. Additionally, the interview yielded several other user needs. The following key insights were identified:

- One of the primary pain points was the frequent finger pokes required to check blood glucose levels, which were found to be both annoying and painful.
- Another challenge identified was the difficulty of remembering to inject insulin 10 min prior to meals, especially while eating outside.
- Additionally, the limited and unappetizing food options available for GDM patients made meal planning challenging.
- The growing belly during pregnancy was found to be a deterrent for physical exercise, and participants expressed reluctance to go to the hospital for weekly pregnancy tests.

Based on the key requirements obtained from the interview, the design objectives of the product aimed to address several areas of concern for pregnant women with GDM. These objectives include reducing the physical burden of the growing belly, providing guidance on appropriate dietary choices, and encouraging regular exercise. Furthermore, the product should enable continuous monitoring of blood glucose levels, mitigating the need for frequent and painful fingertip blood collection, and aid in setting reminders for insulin injections, both of which we have solved with the new technology mentioned above. Additionally, the product should allow for daily monitoring of fetal well-being, with appropriate alerts and warnings when necessary. These design objectives have been informed by the findings obtained through the interview process and serve as a foundation for developing a product that meets the needs of pregnant women with GDM.

4 Final Design

Based on the findings from the collected data and user interviews, the product design process commenced with a focus on form. The NewYork-Presbyterian website recommends the belly area, at least 2 inches (5.1 cm) from the belly button, as the optimal injection site for GDM due to its consistent insulin absorption. Other potential injection sites include the back of the upper arms and upper buttocks [13]. Figure 1 shows the ideal injection area, which coincides with the location covered by pregnancy support belts (see Fig. 2) that pregnant women wear for numerous benefits such as easing exercise, reducing the discomfort of a heavy belly, and mitigating the risk of falls [14]. As such, the decision was made to integrate continuous glucose monitoring detectors, insulin syringes, and pregnancy support belts, with data displayed through a mobile app. The product is named Babelt, with the intention of serving as a supporting belt for a safe and secure birth of the baby.

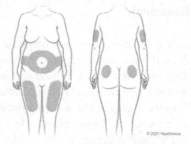

Fig. 1. The ideal injection areas are around the belly, the back of the upper arms and the upper buttocks.

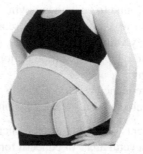

Fig. 2. Pregnancy support belts wrap around the belly to help support the lower back, pelvis, hips, and abdomen during pregnancy.

4.1 Product Design

After establishing the form of the Babelt, attention was turned towards refining the details of its design (see Fig. 3). To accommodate the mobility of pregnant women, a snap has been incorporated into the back of the Babelt to facilitate easy wear and removal. Furthermore, the length of the upper and lower straps can be adjusted using a side wheel situated on the side of the Babelt, ensuring that it can be used as the pregnancy progresses and the belly expands. The body of the belt has been crafted from high-quality silicon, which endows it with excellent flexibility and ease of cleaning. The careful selection of materials ensures that the Babelt is both durable and comfortable to wear.

The Babelt incorporates different holes on the upper strap, each specifically designed to hold various types of detectors and sensors. Among these is the Continuous Glucose Monitoring (CDM) detector, which continuously tracks and displays the blood glucose level of pregnant women with GDM through the mobile app. Additionally, the baby's Beats Per Minute (BPM) detector continuously monitors the baby's activity status and alerts the user if any unusual movements are detected. Furthermore, the BPM data is continuously uploaded to the mobile app for visualization. A motion sensor is also integrated into the Babelt, which records the wearer's number of steps and activities, and syncs the data with the app for analysis.

The lower strap of the Babelt features four holes for insulin injection. These holes enable the user to adjust the position of the insulin syringe at regular intervals, as repeated injections on the same body part can lead to discomfort and complications. The elasticity

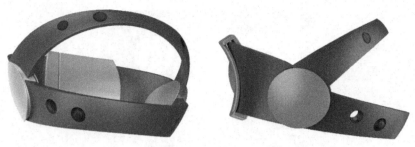

Fig. 3. The perspective view and side view of Babelt shows the shape and composition of the product.

and toughness of the material used to make the Babelt ensure that all detectors, sensors, and syringes are securely held in their respective positions.

4.2 App Design

As previously mentioned, the collected data from the various detectors and sensors are synchronized and visualized on the mobile application interface. The primary functionalities of the app are comprised of the following four modules.

Blood glucose related module (see Fig. 4). This module displays the real-time glucose levels of the pregnant woman. The data is presented in a clear and easy-to-understand manner and can be viewed in various forms. Moreover, the application provides a comprehensive record of all insulin injections for pregnant women with GDM, which includes an option to pre-set the time and dosage of automatic injections. Alternatively, manual injection is also available and can be paired with an alarm to avoid oversight. This feature not only assists with insulin dosage accuracy but also promotes a sense of control and accountability for the user.

Baby activity monitoring module (see Fig. 5). This module continuously monitors the baby's activity status and alerts the user to take necessary actions in case of any anomaly. It also allows users to record their baby's heartbeat as a keepsake.

Exercise management module (see Fig. 5). This module records and analyzes daily steps and activities, displaying the data in a comprehensive manner to track physical activity progress. Users can set an alarm to remind themselves to exercise.

Dietary advice module (see Fig. 5). This module provides customized nutritional recommendations with recipes and nutrition information for pregnant women with GDM, based on their current blood glucose levels. Users can easily navigate between menus for tailored food choices.

Fig. 4. Representative interfaces for blood glucose monitoring and insulin injection.

Fig. 5. Representative interfaces for BPM monitoring, exercise management, diet suggestion.

5   Conclusion

In conclusion, the Babelt is an innovative wearable device designed to help pregnant women with gestational diabetes manage their health more effectively. By combining continuous glucose monitoring detectors, insulin syringes, and pregnancy support belts with an app that provides real-time feedback, personalized dietary advice, and exercise management, the Babelt aims to improve the health outcomes for both mother and baby. With its user-friendly interface and comprehensive features, the Babelt has the potential to revolutionize the way we manage gestational diabetes during pregnancy. Further research is needed to evaluate its efficacy and usability, but the initial result is promising.

References

1. Gestational Diabetes - Symptoms, Treatments | ADA. https://diabetes.org/diabetes/gestational-diabetes. Accessed 16 Mar 2023
2. Default - Stanford Medicine Children's Health. https://www.stanfordchildrens.org/en/topic/default?id=fetal-monitoring-90-P02448. Accessed 16 Mar 2023
3. Gestational Diabetes Mellitus (GDM). https://www.hopkinsmedicine.org/health/conditions-and-diseases/diabetes/gestational-diabetes. Accessed 16 Mar 2023
4. What are the warning signs of gestational diabetes? http://www.riversideonline.com/patients-and-visitors/healthy-you-blog/blog/w/what-are-the-warning-signs-of-gestational-diabetes. Accessed 16 Mar 2023
5. Beckerle, C.M., Lavin, M.A.: Association of self-efficacy and self-care with glycemic control in diabetes. Diabetes Spectrum. 26, 172–178 (2013). https://doi.org/10.2337/diaspect.26.3.172
6. Quintanilla Rodriguez, B.S., Mahdy, H.: Gestational diabetes. In: StatPearls. StatPearls Publishing, Treasure Island (2022)
7. Negrato, C.A., Zajdenverg, L.: Self-monitoring of blood glucose during pregnancy: indications and limitations. Diabetol. Metab. Syndr. 4, 54 (2012). https://doi.org/10.1186/1758-5996-4-54
8. Zambanini, A., Newson, R.B., Maisey, M., Feher, M.D.: Injection related anxiety in insulin-treated diabetes. Diabetes Res. Clin. Pract. 46, 239–246 (1999). https://doi.org/10.1016/S0168-8227(99)00099-6
9. Farsaei, S., Radfar, M., Heydari, Z., Abbasi, F., Qorbani, M.: Insulin adherence in patients with diabetes: risk factors for injection omission. Prim. Care Diabetes 8, 338–345 (2014). https://doi.org/10.1016/j.pcd.2014.03.001
10. Meiqi: Thinking Smaller to Manage Diabetes with Continuous Glucose Monitoring Devices (CGM) | Analog Devices. https://www.analog.com/en/signals/articles/improving-quality-of-life-for-diabetics-with-cgm.html. Accessed 17 Mar 2023
11. Khan, A.M., Alswat, K.A.: Benefits of using the i-port system on insulin-treated patients. Diabetes Spectr. 32, 30–35 (2019). https://doi.org/10.2337/ds18-0015
12. Prausnitz, M.R.: Microneedles for transdermal drug delivery. Adv. Drug Deliv. Rev. 56, 581–587 (2004). https://doi.org/10.1016/j.addr.2003.10.023
13. Insulin Injection Areas For Gestational Diabetes | NYP. https://www.nyp.org/healthlibrary/multimedia/insulin-injection-areas-for-gestational-diabetes. Accessed 17 Mar 2023
14. How Belly Bands And Belts Help Relieve Pregnancy's Discomfort | Premier Health. https://www.premierhealth.com/your-health/articles/women-wisdom-wellness-/how-belly-bands-and-belts-help-relieve-pregnancy-s-discomfort. Accessed 17 Mar 2023

User Experience Design for Cultural Heritage

Reviving Events, Historical Figures and Artefacts in the Context of a Physical Museum Exhibition

Antonis Chatziantoniou[1], Vassiliki Neroutsou[1], Michalis Sifakis[1],
Emmanouil Zidianakis[1], Nikolaos Menelaos Stivaktakis[1], Eirini Kontaki[1],
Andreas Pattakos[1], Stavroula Ntoa[1], Nikolaos Partarakis[1(✉)], Margherita Antona[1],
and Constantine Stephanidis[1,2]

[1] Institute of Computer Science, Foundation for Research and Technology—Hellas (FORTH),
70013 Heraklion, Crete, Greece
{hatjiant,vaner,misi,zidian,nstivaktak,anpattakos,stant,
partarak,antona,cs}@ics.forth.gr
[2] Computer Science Department, School of Sciences and Engineering, University of Crete,
70013 Heraklion, Crete, Greece

Abstract. In this work, we present our approach towards reviving events, historical figures and artefacts in the context of a physical museum exhibition organized by the National Historical Museum in the Old Parliament House as part of the celebration of 200 years since the beginning of the Greek Revolution. In this context, several interactive systems were created to accompany the museum exhibits aiming at augmenting the museum visiting experience through an interactive dialogue with objects, places, persons and events.

Keywords: Interactive systems · interactive storytelling · interactive museum installation · digital information systems

1 Introduction

The central anniversary exhibition highlighted the ideas, causes, persons, events and results of the Greek War of Independence, as they were formed through conflicts and compositions of different interests and traditions. The exhibition has been enriched with a series of interactive systems designed and implemented by ICS-FORTH to serve the needs of the exhibition.

The systems focus on several topics in the exhibition:

- The Chart of Rigas, where a large interactive view of the Chart allows visitors to explore the complex content of this landmark work of Rigas Feraios.
- The Athens Bazaar, an excellent watercolour by the traveller Edward Dodwell, depicting the inhabitants of the city in the early 19th century, is presented on a touch screen and offers information about society at the time.
- Weapons of the Revolution, a "smart" interactive showcase of relics of the Revolution.

© The Author(s), under exclusive license to Springer Nature Switzerland AG 2024
C. Stephanidis et al. (Eds.): HCII 2023, CCIS 1957, pp. 481–488, 2024.
https://doi.org/10.1007/978-3-031-49212-9_59

- The Press of the Revolution, a system that presents on a touch screen articles about the Revolution from Greek and Foreign Newspapers of the 1820s.
- The Chronology of the Struggle unfolds in two large interactive touch projections and presents events, persons and places of the Revolution.

2 Background and Related Work

The evolution of interactive ICT technology [1, 2] has provided today a plethora of new applications of Virtual and Augmented Reality (VR) [3–6]. At the same time, MR presents real and virtual world objects together on a single display [7, 8]. Recent and current research activities on Virtual Museums [9] are exploiting the aforementioned technical progress and have identified new technological methods and development tools [10, 11].

In this context, CH institutions have identified the potential of increasing their appeal and enhance their visitor's engagement through interactive installations that include some form of public information displays [12]. In addition to improving the aesthetic experience, Mixed Reality (MR) environments positively influence visitor experience, thus favoring the probability of revisiting a specific attraction [13, 14]. Apart from providing an enjoyable experience, MR installations can facilitate cultural awareness, historical reconstruction and heritage awareness. State-of-the-art approaches are not limited to installations in indoor spaces [15, 16], but can also involve vehicles that act as portable kiosks [17].

2.1 New Museology and Immersive Cultural Experiences

Today in the post-COVID era Cultural Heritage Institutions seek new ways to attract and engage new visitors [18]. One of the ways to obtain a competitive advantage in this era is to implement strategies that have been proposed a long time before the pandemic such as investing and implementing interactive experiences on-site [19, 20]. In the context of the new museology [21], telling stories through immersive cultural experiences has been proposed since it provides a feeling of being inside or part of the story [22]. Modern technology provides additional benefits to the museum storyline since the visitor is able of exploring a virtual world, perhaps from the viewpoint of one of the characters in the story [23]. Furthermore, through user immersion, a "sense of place" and a "sense of time" contributes to the creation of memorable moments that bind the audience to the story. Examples of engaging storytelling experiences include (a) exploring collections, creating virtual paths, and making links between artefacts [24]; (b) exploring narratives and through them digital collections linked with them [25]; and (c) experiencing interactive stories authored on top of museum collections [26].

3 Overview of Interactive Experiences

The basic storyline created by the museum evolves in three axes. The first regards the presentation of the events of the revolution, the second dives into the social aspects of living under the Ottoman rule and the third is on providing stories on great personalities of the revolution through their tangible remains that are exhibited in the museum (their weapons). Information on the first axis is transmitted through a map of the key location and a timeline of key events accompanied by testimonies recorded on the printed press of the time. The second axis is transmitted through analysing the social structure through a painting of the Athens bazaar of the time. The third axis is presented by linking the weapons of the revolution with audiovisual story production. In this section, we analyse each of the systems individually.

3.1 Chart of Greece

The interactive system "Chart of Greece" has a central role in the subsection "Modern Greek Enlightenment" which features the importance of the Age of Enlightenment and its influence in the Greek War of Independence (1821). The interactive system presents the life of Rigas Velestinlis who published the Chart in Vienna (1797). It also presents the impact of his work, his associates, the symbols, the historic places and the coins depicted on the Chart. A special mention is made of the French Revolution and its influence on Rigas' ideas.

The interactive system was implemented in two versions: The first one, to be installed in the exhibition spaces of the Old Parliament Building, comprises an oversized projection with a touch-screen and users can interact both with touch and through an augmented physical object (see Fig. 1). The second version is simpler, for the system to be presented through a single touch screen so that it can travel to different cities for temporary or long-term exhibitions.

Fig. 1. The Chart of Greece

3.2 The Athens Bazaar

The Athens Bazaar presents a watercolor drawing from the early 19th century. Users interact via a touch screen. The system was installed both in the museum and in regional exhibitions organized by the museum. The drawing depicts the inhabitants of the city in the early 19th century. Figures revive when interacted by the visitor to present information on the social context of the period including trade and professions, traditional crafts, places of social activity and historical figures (see Fig. 2).

Fig. 2. Edward Dodwell: The Bazaar at Athens

3.3 Weapons of the Revolution

The Weapons of the Revolution is an Interactive Showcase that presents historical weapons and other relics of the Revolution. The system comprises a physical showcase and a projection screen. When a visitor touches the glass of the showcase over a

Fig. 3. Weapons of the Revolution

certain object, a multimedia presentation in regard to that object is shown on the screen thus extending and enhancing the provided information (see Fig. 3).

3.4 The Press of the Revolution

The Press of the Revolution is a Historical Texts Anthology that presents selected articles from Greek and English language newspapers dating from the early 19th century. Users interact via a touch screen for the selection of articles (see Fig. 4).

Fig. 4. The Press of the Revolution

3.5 The Chronology of the Struggle

This is an interactive timeline application that present historic information in the form of an information stream with which the user can interact to extract information. Several categorizations are available to support information filtering. An indicative screenshot of the system in its operational mode is presented in Fig. 5.

Fig. 5. The Chronology of the Struggle

4   Conclusion

In this paper, we presented a number of technologies integrated in a museum exhibition organized by the National Historical Museum in the Old Parliament House as part of the celebration of 200 years since the beginning of the Greek Revolution. These technologies were carefully selected to augment visitor experience per thematic area-type of exhibit thus allowing both interactive presentation of information on historic artefacts and intuitive touch-based information retrieval.

Acknowledgment. The authors would like to thank the National Historical Museum in the Old Parliament House for their valuable collaboration and contribution to the success of this work.

References

1. Carmigniani, J., Furht, B.: Augmented reality: an overview. Handbook of Augmented Reality, pp. 3–46 (2011)
2. Papagiannakis, G., Singh, G., Magnenat-Thalmann, N.: A survey of mobile and wireless technologies for augmented reality systems. Comput. Animation Virtual Worlds **19**(1), 3–22 (2008)
3. Cavallo, M., Rhodes, G. A., Forbes, A. G.: Riverwalk: incorporating historical photographs in public outdoor augmented reality experiences. In: 2016 IEEE International Symposium on Mixed and Augmented Reality (ISMAR-Adjunct), pp. 160–165. IEEE (2016)
4. Rainio, K., Honkamaa, P., Spilling, K.: Presenting historical photos using augmented reality. Area **15**, 11–12 (2015)
5. Sauter, L., Rossetto, L., Schuldt, H.:. Exploring cultural heritage in augmented reality with gofind!. In: 2018 IEEE International Conference on Artificial Intelligence and Virtual Reality (AIVR), pp. 187–188. IEEE (2018)

6. Jingen Liang, L., Elliot, S.: A systematic review of augmented reality tourism research: what is now and what is next? Tour. Hosp. Res. **21**(1), 15–30 (2021)
7. Milgram, P., Kishino, F.: A taxonomy of mixed reality visual displays. IEICE Trans. Inf. Syst. **E77-D**(12), 1321–1329 (1994)
8. Hughes, C.E., Stapleton, C.B., Hughes, D.E., Smith, E.: Mixed reality in education, entertainment and training: an interdisciplinary approach. IEEE Comput. Graphics Appl. **26**(6), 24–30 (2005)
9. Examples Virtual Museums. http://www.v-must.net/virtual-museums. Accessed 15 Feb 2015
10. Zidianakis, E., et al.: The invisible museum: a user-centric platform for creating virtual 3D exhibitions with VR support. Electronics **10**(3), 363 (2021)
11. Zidianakis, E., et al.: Web-based authoring tool for virtual exhibitions. In: HCI International 2022–Late Breaking Posters: 24th International Conference on Human-Computer Interaction, HCII 2022, Virtual Event, June 26–July 1, 2022, Proceedings, Part I, pp. 378–385. Springer, Cham (2022). https://doi.org/10.1007/978-3-031-19679-9_48
12. Partarakis, N., et al.: Digital Cultural Heritage Experience in Ambient Intelligence, pp. 473–505. Springer, Cham (2017).https://doi.org/10.1007/978-3-319-49607-8_19
13. Timothy Jung, M., Dieck, C., Lee, H., Chung, N.: Effects of virtual reality and augmented reality on visitor experiences in museum. In: Inversini, A., Schegg, R. (eds.) Information and Communication Technologies in Tourism 2016, pp. 621–635. Springer, Cham (2016). https://doi.org/10.1007/978-3-319-28231-2_45
14. Carre, A.L., et al.: Mixed-reality demonstration and training of glassblowing. Heritage **5**(1), 103–128 (2022)
15. Grammenos, D., et al.: Macedonia from fragments to pixels: a permanent exhibition of interactive systems at the archaeological museum of thessaloniki. In: Ioannides, M., Fritsch, D., Leissner, J., Davies, R., Remondino, F., Caffo, R. (eds.) Progress in Cultural Heritage Preservation, pp. 602–609. Springer Berlin Heidelberg, Berlin, Heidelberg (2012). https://doi.org/10.1007/978-3-642-34234-9_62
16. Partarakis, N., et al.: Digital Heritage Technology at the Archaeological Museum of Heraklion. In: Stephanidis, C. (ed.) HCI 2018. CCIS, vol. 852, pp. 196–203. Springer, Cham (2018). https://doi.org/10.1007/978-3-319-92285-0_28
17. Zidianakis, E., et al.: Turning an Electric Cargo Vehicle into a Portable Interactive Information Kiosk. In: Stephanidis, C. (ed.) HCI 2016. CCIS, vol. 618, pp. 463–469. Springer, Cham (2016). https://doi.org/10.1007/978-3-319-40542-1_75
18. Hussain, Z.: Paradigm of technological convergence and digital transformation: the challenges of CH sectors in the global COVID-19 pandemic and commencing resilience-based structure for the post-COVID-19 era. Digital Appl. Archaeol. Cult. Heritage **21**, e00182 (2021)
19. Tscheu, F., Buhalis, D.: Augmented reality at cultural heritage sites. In: Inversini, A., Schegg, R. (eds.) Information and Communication Technologies in Tourism 2016, pp. 607–619. Springer International Publishing, Cham (2016). https://doi.org/10.1007/978-3-319-28231-2_44
20. Bozzelli, G., et al.: An integrated VR/AR framework for user-centric interactive experience of cultural heritage: the ArkaeVision project. Digital Appl. Archaeol. Cult. Heritage **15**, e00124 (2019)
21. Vergo, P.: New Museology. Reaktion Books (1997)
22. Stogner, M.B.: The immersive cultural museum experience – creating context and story with new media technology. Int. J. Incl. Mus. **3**(3), 117–130 (2011). https://doi.org/10.18848/1835-2014/CGP/v03i03/44339
23. Mulholland, P., Collins, T.: Using digital narratives to support the collaborative learning and exploration of cultural heritage. In: Proceedings of 13th International Workshop on Database and Expert Systems Applications, pp 527–531. IEEE (2002)

24. Clough, P., Ford, N., Stevenson, M.: Personalizing access to cultural heritage collections using pathways. In: International Workshop on Personalized Access to Cultural Heritage (2011)
25. De Polo, A.: Digital environment for cultural interfaces: promoting heritage education and research. In: Proceedings of Museums and The Web 2011. Arch Mus Inform., Toronto (2011)
26. Pujol, L., Roussou, M., Poulou, S., Balet, O., Vayanou, M., Ioannidis, Y.: Personalizing interactive digital storytelling in archaeological museums: the CHESS project. In: 40th Annual Conference of Computer Applications and Quantitative Methods in Archaeology. Amsterdam University Press (2012)

A Mobile Tour Guide with Localization Features and AR Support

Michalis Foukarakis[1], Orestis Faltakas[1], Giannis Frantzeskakis[1],
Emmanouil Ntafotis[1], Emmanouil Zidianakis[1], Eirini Kontaki[1], Constantina Manoli[1],
Stavroula Ntoa[1], Nikolaos Partarakis[1(✉)], and Constantine Stephanidis[1,2]

[1] Institute of Computer Science, Foundation for Research and Technology—Hellas (FORTH),
70013 Heraklion, Crete, Greece
{foukas,faltakas,giannisf,ntafotis,zidian,ekontaki,cmanoli,
stant,partarak,cs}@ics.forth.gr
[2] Computer Science Department, School of Sciences and Engineering, University of Crete,
70013 Heraklion, Crete, Greece

Abstract. In this paper, we present an interactive guided tour of the House-Museum of Eleftherios Venizelos located in the city of Chania, Crete, Greece. The mobile application is using a mixture of Bluetooth beacons and Augmented Reality (AR) to expand the museum experience both while visiting the museum and when planning for a museum visit. In terms of tour personalisation, several options are provided including short and long tours and audience-specific tours for younger generations.

Keywords: Mobile tour guide · AR · Mobile localization

1 Introduction

For the past three decades, tourism research has endeavoured to describe sustainability in the field. Through this effort, researchers were able to formulate the concept of sustainable tourism and have it show positive results by establishing a theoretical foundation and expanding the base of quantitative studies. Sustainability in tourism has been an active research field for the past three decades [1–5]. At the same time, the emergence of mobile information technology as a commodity in our daily life has provided new opportunities for its exploration in the domain of tourism.

The role of mobile technology in tourism has been emphasized and conceptualized under the term smart tourism [6–9]. Modern high-power mobile devices and mobile internet services allowed the further penetration of mobile technology into daily life [10]. As a result, the importance of ICT in tourism was acknowledged [11, 12].

This work builds on the technical advancement in mobile technologies and exploits Bluetooth localization of mobile devices and RGB-based feature recognition for AR augmentation to develop a mobile tour guide that can supplement the museum visiting experience through mobile location detection and museum exhibit recognition.

© The Author(s), under exclusive license to Springer Nature Switzerland AG 2024
C. Stephanidis et al. (Eds.): HCII 2023, CCIS 1957, pp. 489–496, 2024.
https://doi.org/10.1007/978-3-031-49212-9_60

2   Background and Related Work

The evolution of mobile tourism applications and services generated a new trend of mobile tour guides with one of its applications being in the domain of museums focusing both on the tangible and intangible cultural heritage dimensions [13, 14]. Those approaches facilitate mobile technology in standalone mode or in combination with stationery ICT technology to provide various forms of mixed reality experiences [15]. Museum tour guides explore mobile technologies to enhance the museum visiting experience and over the years several different approaches have been proposed including ones that blend virtual humans in the physical space [16–19] and approaches targeted to the provision of cultural information to people with disabilities [20, 21].

In this research work, we implement a cost-effective localization feature for mobile tour guides based on the combination of AR-based scene feature detection and Bluetooth beacons. Bluetooth beacons are used for a rough estimation of the location of the mobile device (e.g. the room it is in) while AR-based localization provides fine-tuning based on the detected features. Together they implement an efficient yet cost-effective localisation approach validated in the context of a museum installation. Among these mobile-AR based tour guides have received a wide attention. From these we can distinguish two main categories. The first category is using AR-based recognition from the mobile device's camera for localization [22–24] and the second is using AR-based recognition for artefact/point of interest recognition [25–30].

3   Overview of the Tour Guide

The Venizelos Museum mobile app provides a tour guide experience for visitors of the Museum-Residence of Eleftherios Venizelos in Chania, Crete [31]. Users can select among three different tours, including a complete tour of the premises and a tour focused on children. The application suggests the next exhibit to visit according to the selected tour but also allows the user to freely scan any exhibit's QR code to view information about it. The details view of each exhibit allows the visitor to view photographs of the exhibit, locate it on the map and read or listen to an extensive description of the item.

Detailed maps of every floor of the museum along with location markers of every exhibit are available, facilitating navigation. The app also communicates with Bluetooth beacons placed around the museum to display on the map the room where the visitor is currently located. If the user has started a tour, the map will only show the exhibits included in the tour, otherwise, the map will display the markers for all the exhibits.

Several exhibits have been enhanced with Augmented Reality features, indicated by physical AR signs next to them. Scanning their QR code or navigating to their details screen through the app enables an AR button that turns on the device's camera to outset the exhibit's AR features. Some of the exhibits come to life and start moving, while others show an animation, video or audio related to the exhibit.

The application is multiplatform and runs on iOS and Android phones and tablets. On iOS, it is written in the Swift language [32], using the latest SwiftUI framework [33]. Location beacon communication is achieved using Apple's iBeacon protocol [34], while Augmented Reality features are powered by the RealityKit framework [35]. On Android, it is written in Kotlin [36], using standard Android mobile development practices. Augmented reality features are powered by the AR Core framework [37]. Both versions of the app share a common JSON data source containing information on exhibits, tours and localized strings in four different languages (Greek, English, German, and French).

4 UI Overview

From the home page of the application, the user has the option to get information about the museum itself or get started with one of the available tours. Among those, the provided variations are long or short, tours that are adapted to younger audiences and free exploration (see Fig. 1, a). Each tour is comprised of several information spots (see Fig. 1, b). Each information point is linked to multimedia information (see Fig. 1, c). While on the tour information points are visualised on the building's map with the option of filtering them based on the room they are on the floor (see Fig. 1 c, 1 e, 1 f). To support offline visits to the museum this functionality is available both onsite and offsite. When offsite, users can browse information points virtually through the digital map and get more information about what's available for them to explore.

The activation of information spots is accomplished either by selecting them through the map or by scanning their respective QR code. Points of interest with AR content can be also located through scanning of the room using the camera of the mobile device. Further information is provided by linking the application with the Bluetooth beacons. Using these beacons the application can localise itself within the museum and provide information when entering or leaving a museum room.

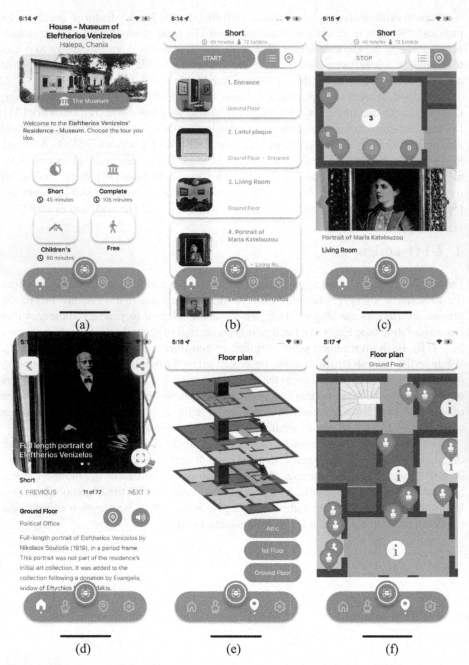

Fig. 1. (a) Mobile App home page, (b) Create personalised route, (c) Preview the route on your mobile phone, (d) On-site AR information, (e) Information point details, (f) Accessibility options.

5 Evaluation

The application has been evaluated following an expert-based evaluation with usability and domain experts, namely museum curators. More specifically, evaluation was pursued through the heuristic evaluation approach, according to which a small number of evaluators assess the user interface of the application against well-established principles of usable design, the heuristics [38–41]. The goal of the evaluation is to identify any potential roadblocks or areas for improvement of the user experience, identifying for each problem the usability principle that is violated. A total of five experts assessed the system across three iterations; in each iteration, the evaluators carefully examined the interface and reported the problems identified, while after the evaluation the interface was updated based on the recommendations provided.

Once the system was deemed acceptable in terms of usability, it was installed at the museum, where it has been used until today by more than 2,000 visitors. This section summarizes findings from the expert-based evaluation, as well as from in situ audits observing the system in action, outlining lessons learned that may be useful for designers of AR museum experiences.

More specifically, the following user experience issues we identified:

- User localization with beacons requires extensive testing to avoid erroneous recognition, which then causes serious problems for the UX.
- It is important to be able to correctly identify the user's location and whereabouts in the museum and to provide information through the mobile guide, correctly indicating which exhibits the user has already visited and which are pending to see.
- Museum maps displayed on mobile phone screens should present information gradually, depending on the zoom level, to avoid information 'pollution' resulting in poor usability.
- Users should be able to deviate from a selected guided tour (e.g. to see an exhibit that seems interesting and get information about it) and resume the tour at their own convenience, continuing where they left off. In our application, this was supported by scanning the QR code next to the exhibit of interest and then selecting the guided tour to resume.
- Information about the museum exhibits should be available both on the map and as a list (e.g. list of exhibits available in a guided tour) to support different navigation modalities and user preferences.
- Museum exhibits placed in a glass display case may cause problems with the feature detection algorithms used in AR. In our approach, this was bypassed by utilizing QR codes placed in close proximity to the exhibit, outside its display case, which acted as anchors for determining the correct location to display the AR objects.
- The AR viewing experience should afford sudden movements of the camera made by users trying to initiate the AR mode, ensuring to the best possible extent that the AR object is not displaced from the user's screen.
- In the case that only specific museum exhibits are augmented with AR, this should be clearly annotated not only in the mobile AR application, but also through a physical sign in the museum. Otherwise, visitors may miss the AR experience or try to initiate AR in exhibits not supporting it, thus creating frustration for visitors. In addition,

in situ observations revealed that to launch the camera for AR, users sometimes pressed the "Scan QR" button always available in the app's main menu instead of the dedicated AR button shown only on the AR-powered exhibit's details screen.

6 Conclusion

In this paper, we provided an overview of a museum tour guide application that provides alternative visiting modes to support seamless information provision to various audiences and visiting periods both offsite and onsite. For user localization, a mixture of Bluetooth beacons and RGB image feature extraction is employed to provide targeted information on the location the user is in the museum and specific exhibits that through QR codes provide information blended with AR features. The application is currently available both for android and iOS-based devices through the respective app stores [42, 43].

Acknowledgement. This project was funded by the European Regional Development Fund, Regional Programme Crete 2014–2022, under a public tender by the National Research Foundation "Eleftherios K. Venizelos".

References

1. Moscardo, G., Murphy, L.: There is no such thing as sustainable tourism: re-conceptualizing tourism as a tool for sustainability. Sustainability **6**, 2538–2561 (2014)
2. Montaño-Vallef, A.: Sustainability strategy as a source of competitive advantages in the tourism industry. a model for the integration of natural resources. Eur. J. Tour. Res. **14**, 106–109 (2016)
3. Klemm, M.: Sustainable tourism development. Tour. Manag. **13**, 169–180 (1992)
4. Mak, J., Moncur, J.E.T.: Sustainable tourism development: managing hawaii's "unique" touristic resource—Hanauma bay. J. Travel Res. **33**, 51–57 (1995)
5. Camargo, B.A., Gretzel, U.: What do tourism students know about sustainability and sustainable tourism? an exploratory study of Latin American students. J. Teach. Travel Tour. **17**, 1–17 (2017)
6. Gretzel, U., Sigala, M., Xiang, Z., Koo, C.: Smart tourism: foundations and developments. Electron. Mark. **25**, 179–188 (2015)
7. Koo, C., Park, J., Lee, J.N.: Smart tourism: traveler, business, and organizational perspectives. Inf. Manag. **54**, 683–686 (2017)
8. Werthner, H., Koo, C., Gretzel, U., Lamsfus, C.: Special issue on smart tourism systems: convergence of information technologies, business models, and experiences. Comput. Hum. Behav. **50**, 556–557 (2015)
9. Li, Y., Hu, C., Huang, C., Duan, L.: The concept of smart tourism in the context of tourism information services. Tour. Manag. **58**, 293–300 (2017)
10. Neuhofer, B., Buhalis, D., Ladkin, A.: A typology of technology-enhanced tourism experiences. Int. J. Tour. Res. **16**, 340–350 (2014)
11. Ali, A., Frew, A.J.: ICT and sustainable tourism development: an innovative perspective. J. Hosp. Tour. Technol. **5**, 2–16 (2014)
12. Stockdale, R.: Managing customer relationships in the self-service environment of e-tourism. J. Vacat. Mark. **13**, 205–219 (2007)

13. Partarakis, N., et al.: Digital cultural heritage experience in ambient intelligence, pp. 473–505. Springer, Cham (2017).https://doi.org/10.1007/978-3-319-49607-8_19
14. Partarakis, N., Zabulis, X., Antona, M., Stephanidis, C.: Transforming heritage crafts to engaging digital experiences. In: Liarokapis, F., Voulodimos, A., Doulamis, N., Doulamis, A. (eds.) Visual Computing for Cultural Heritage. SSCC, pp. 245–262. Springer, Cham (2020). https://doi.org/10.1007/978-3-030-37191-3_13
15. Partarakis, N., Antona, M., Zidianakis, E., Stephanidis, C.: Adaptation and content personalization in the context of multi user museum exhibits. In: AVI* CH, pp. 5–10 (2016)
16. Ringas, C., et al.: Traditional craft training and demonstration in museums. Heritage **5**(1), 431–459 (2022)
17. Hauser, H., et al.: Multimodal narratives for the presentation of silk heritage in the museum. Heritage **5**(1), 461–487 (2022)
18. Partarakis, N., Antona, M., Stephanidis, C.: Adaptable, personalizable and multi user museum exhibits. In: England, D., Schiphorst, T., Bryan-Kinns, N. (eds.) Curating the Digital. SSCC, pp. 167–179. Springer, Cham (2016). https://doi.org/10.1007/978-3-319-28722-5_11
19. Partarakis, N., et al.: An approach to enhancing contemporary handmade products with historic narratives. Int. J. Intang. Herit **16**, 124–141 (2021)
20. Partarakis, N., et al.: Supporting sign language narrations in the museum. Heritage **5**(1), 1–20 (2022)
21. Kosmopoulos, D., et al.: Museum guidance in sign language: the signguide project. In: Proceedings of the 15th International Conference on PErvasive Technologies Related to Assistive Environments, pp. 646–652 (2022)
22. Seo, B.-K., Kim, K., Park, J.-I.: Augmented reality-based on-site tour guide: a study in Gyeongbokgung. In: Koch, R., Huang, F. (eds.) ACCV 2010. LNCS, vol. 6469, pp. 276–285. Springer, Heidelberg (2011). https://doi.org/10.1007/978-3-642-22819-3_28
23. Harley, J.M., Lajoie, S.P., Tressel, T., Jarrell, A.: Fostering positive emotions and history knowledge with location-based augmented reality and tour-guide prompts. Learn. Instr. **70**, 101163 (2020)
24. Wijesuriya, M.U.E., Mendis, S.U., Bandara, B.E.S., Mahawattage, K.P., Walgampaya, N., De Silva, D.: Interactive mobile based tour guide. In: Proceedings of the SAITM Research Symposium on Engineering Advancements (RSEA), April, vol. 27, pp. 53–56 (2013)
25. Koo, S., Kim, J., Kim, C., Kim, J., Cha, H.S.: Development of an augmented reality tour guide for a cultural heritage site. J. Comput. Cultural Heritage (JOCCH) **12**(4), 1–24 (2019)
26. Thennakoon, M.S.B.W.T.M.P.S.B., Rajarathna, R.D.T.N., Jayawickrama, S.P.B., Kumara, M.P.D.S.M., Imbulpitiya, A.M., Kodagoda, N.: TOURGURU: tour guide mobile application for tourists. In: 2019 International Conference on Advancements in Computing (ICAC), pp. 133–138. IEEE (2019)
27. Choi, H., Han, G.C., Kim, I.J.: Smart booklet: tour guide system with mobile augmented reality. In: 2014 IEEE International Conference on Consumer Electronics (ICCE), pp. 353–354. IEEE (2014)
28. Shin, C., Kim, H., Kang, C., Jang, Y., Choi, A., Woo, W.: Unified context-aware augmented reality application framework for user-driven tour guides. In: 2010 International Symposium on Ubiquitous Virtual Reality, pp. 52–55. IEEE (2010)
29. Mohammed-Amin, R.K., Levy, R.M., Boyd, J.E.: Mobile augmented reality for interpretation of archaeological sites. In: Proceedings of the Second International ACM Workshop on Personalized Access to Cultural Heritage, pp. 11–14 (2012)
30. Jing, C., Junwei, G., Yongtian, W.: Mobile augmented reality system for personal museum tour guide applications (2011)
31. Museum-Venizelos Residence. https://www.venizelos-foundation.gr/en/museums/museum-venizelos-residence/. Accessed 02 Jun 2013

32. Swift. https://developer.apple.com/swift/. Accessed 02 Jun 2013
33. SwiftUI. https://developer.apple.com/documentation/swiftui. Accessed 02 Jun 2013
34. Ibeacon. https://developer.apple.com/ibeacon/. Accessed 02 Jun 2013
35. RealityKit. https://developer.apple.com/documentation/realitykit/. Accessed 02 Jun 2013
36. Kotlin. https://kotlinlang.org/. Accessed 02 Jun 2013
37. ARCore. https://developers.google.com/ar. Accessed 02 Jun 2013
38. Nielsen, J., Molich, R.: Heuristic evaluation of user interfaces. In: Proceedings of the SIGCHI Conference on Human Factors in Computing Systems, pp. 249–256 (1990)
39. Gómez, R.Y., Caballero, D.C., Sevillano, J.-L.: Heuristic evaluation on mobile interfaces: a new checklist. Sci. World J. **2014**, 1–19 (2014). https://doi.org/10.1155/2014/434326
40. Joyce, G., Lilley, M., Barker, T., Jefferies, A.: Mobile application usability: heuristic evaluation and evaluation of heuristics. In: Advances in Human Factors, Software, and Systems Engineering: Proceedings of the AHFE 2016 International Conference on Human Factors, Software, and Systems Engineering, July 27–31, 2016, Walt Disney World®, Florida, USA, pp. 77–86. Springer, Cham (2016). https://doi.org/10.1007/978-3-319-41935-0_8
41. Gale, N., Mirza-Babaei, P., Pedersen, I.: Heuristic guidelines for playful wearable augmented reality applications. In: Proceedings of the 2015 Annual Symposium on Computer-Human Interaction in Play, pp. 529–534 (2015)
42. Museum Venizelos mobile app for iOS devices. https://apps.apple.com/app/venizelosguide/id1607299997. Accessed 09 Feb 2023
43. Museum Venizelos mobile app for iOS devices. https://play.google.com/store/apps/details?id=com.userfaltakas.venizelosmuseumguide. Accessed 09 Feb 2023

The Virtual Environment as a Setting for Culture Heritage Mediation

Ben Maallem Héla[✉]

Higher Institute of Arts and Crafts, University of Gabes, Gabes, Tunisia
hela.benmalem@isamgb.u-gabes.tn

Abstract. The fully immersive virtual reality experience leads to living new cognitive and scientific experiences giving an additional dimension and value to the public. New paths of reflection around valorization and mediation of heritage are crossed. The 360°VR Videos seem to offer innovative solutions to facilitate the involvement of communities in the definition and valorization of their inheritance. The main purpose of this paper is to study virtual reality devices and techniques in the context of heritage mediation. We propose to understand the nature of the mediations implemented and their potential uses for culture heritage mediation. Furthermore, we highlight the mechanisms of immersive storytelling in 360° video and the influence they have on the audience's perception, particularly the sense of presence.

Keywords: Virtual environment · 360° videos in VR · Culture Heritage · Mediation · Public · Valorization · Immersive storytelling

1 Introduction

The monumental and patrimonial richness, and the diversity of the cultural offer, can constitute the main motivations for the designers and researchers to promote and enhance the culture through digital technologies.

We are assisting in a revolution in the approaches and modalities of creation. The use of virtual reality technology, more specifically the 360° VR videos, in the reconstruction of cultural heritage has demolished the frontal relationship with museums and monumental sites. The advantage of these technological tools consists not only in the fact that they make it easier to conserve and safeguard information relating to heritage elements but also in the opportunities they offer to access and valorize this information.

We can identify that these new digital tools seem to provide innovative opportunities to facilitate the engagement of communities in the definition of their heritage. We wonder how and in which way the virtual environment can be considered a medium for cultural heritage mediation. What changes the perception of the public? Indeed, immersive virtual reality, as a new medium, offers new approaches to producing and telling a story about a heritage or monumental site. The storytelling in VR or "immersive storytelling" questions today the conventional narrative mechanisms to offer new immersive stories.

C. Stephanidis et al. (Eds.): HCII 2023, CCIS 1957, pp. 497–505, 2024.
https://doi.org/10.1007/978-3-031-49212-9_61

The main contribution of the paper is to investigate the technique of 360° VR video, which is based on immersive storytelling. We wonder if this technique contributes to the immersion of the user in the preservation and valorization of cultural heritage. The approaches introduced are tested in the context of a case study on the preservation of the tradition of olive oil extraction (the case of the traditional oil mill in the ancient region of Matmata - South Tunisia). Indeed, this article questions the immersive narrative mechanisms implemented and the influence they have on the perception of the public, particularly the feeling of presence.

2   Concepts and Approaches

2.1   Culture Heritage

Traditionally, the term "cultural heritage" refers to tangible heritage. However, in the last decades of the century, the meaning of the term has been extended to include intangible heritage. Cultural heritage as introduced by UNESCO [17] includes tangible heritage (TCH): (artworks, monuments, buildings, archaeological sites, cultural landscapes, and museums that are distinguished by their diverse values, as well as symbolic, historical, artistic, aesthetic, ethnological or anthropological, scientific, and social meanings) and intangible cultural heritage (ICH) embedded in cultural and natural heritage artifacts (oral traditions, songs, artistic expressions, social practices, cultural events, knowledge and practices related to nature and the universe).

2.2   Mediation

The notion of mediation has considerably evolved and it has taken various orientations according to the cultural field in which it is applied and according to the actors who practice it, and the researchers who observe it. Today in the Sciences of Information and Communication (SIC), it is rather to be understood as all the forms of intervention to cultural character organized to the attention of the visitors [6]. The digital mediation of cultural heritage is a form of heritage mediation that takes part in cultural mediation at a wider dimension. It refers to the use of digital technologies to facilitate access, comprehension, and valorization of cultural heritage for the wide public. It covers a very large field of practices and actions within which digital technologies occupy a more or less central place.

2.3   Technical Approach and Tools

In the paper entitled "Visiting Heritage Sites in AR and VR" [10], the authors tried to examine and explore the potential of augmented reality (AR) and virtual reality (VR) technologies that have been developed for heritage sites. They also examine the user experience of these two applications and the role of these technologies in preserving and communicating cultural heritage for future generations. Indeed, different methods and techniques of communication and digital preservation are being developed.

The devices of digital mediation of the heritage can be classified in multiple ways, according to not only the technology, which they use but also regarding the use of the technology and the intention of mediation in which they are involved. We can point out, among others, the following non-exhaustive examples:

- The 3D Reconstitution Technology: the creation of 3D models is one of the key elements of Virtual Reality applied to cultural heritage. This three-dimensional representation has opened up new possibilities for mediation. Heritage sights can be digitalized in 3D using such technologies as photogrammetry, laser scanning, or 3D scanners [8, 11, 13].
- Augmented Reality (AR) is another technique, which can be used to enhance heritage site visits. AR offers visitors additional information about heritage sites or reconstructions of lost structures. In "augmented reality in culture Heritage" [2], Boboc, R and al. Present a comprehensive review of the use of augmented reality in cultural heritage by examining a series of applications and case studies published on the Scopus and Clarivate Web of Science databases over 9 years (2012–2021). The authors discuss the benefits and challenges of using augmented reality in this context and suggest future directions for research in this area.
- 360-degree VR video is a technique providing a fully immersive experience that allows users to interact with and explore a virtual environment in a way that simulates a real-world experience [19]. This technology has the potential to enhance users' sense of presence and engagement, particularly in the context of tourism and cultural heritage. These videos can be shot with special cameras and allow visitors to move freely in the virtual environment.
- Interactive virtual tours: may be a useful tool in the context of cultural heritage, offering the general public access to heritage while encouraging visitor participation and engagement via an interactive and immersive experience. According to Aznoora Osman and al. [1], interactive virtual tours refer to virtual environments that enable users to navigate, explore, and interact with virtual objects or scenes in real-time. Indeed, visitors can interact with 3D models, interactive maps, videos, and images to better understand the history and significance of sites.

In other words, VR offers many possibilities for the preservation, promotion, and mediation of cultural heritage while making it more accessible and interactive. In this paper, we will only look at the technique of 360° VR video in VR, which is based on immersive storytelling.

3   The 360° VR Video in the Context of Cultural Heritage

Some definitions of Virtual Reality highlight the subjective and experiential nature of presence [3, 4] in virtual environments and emphasize the importance of immersion, engagement, and interaction with the virtual world in a natural and intuitive way [15].

Overall, the concept of presence is a key concept for the evaluation of virtual reality experiences, especially in relation to the cognitive and emotional aspects that contribute to the perception of the virtual environment. To communicate and preserve a cultural heritage it is important to have access to the experience of the community and the key people involved in this heritage. In the case of this work, we have used a case study to explore the techniques of immersive storytelling in the context of heritage valorization.

3.1 Methodological Approach and Tools

The 360° video in VR is getting more and more popular in the field of tourism and cultural heritage. Maud C. & Chris I. [9], and Wimmer, J. et al., [18] state that the combination of 360° video with immersive storytelling, forms an approach that allows to the creation of captivating and engaging immersive virtual experiences. One of the main advantages of this technology is to allow users to move around the environment at 360° and explore, for example, the interior of a historical building, walk around a statue or monument, admire a picturesque landscape, discover a story, a plot, characters, etc. The 360° video can be also associated with interactive elements, such as interactive menus, contextual information, historical details, dialogues, three-dimensional sounds, and special effects; to create a significant immersive experience.

To film the environment at 360° it was necessary to use specific cameras called 360 cameras. We can mention here, as a non-exhaustive reference: (Samsung Gear, the Kandao Obsidian I 8K, the Insta 360, the insta 360 One X, One X2 or OneX3, etc. (Fig. 1). Indeed, these cameras produce an immersive video format where the user chooses his point of view and chooses the type of experience he wants to conduct in space, defined by a sphere around him.

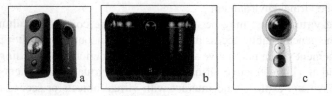

Fig. 1. (a) Insta 360 one x2 (b) Kandao Obsidian S, (c) Samsung Gear

The realization of a video in 360° requires three steps:

- The pre-production stage in filming 360° videos involves planning and preparation before the filming takes place. This stage involved these main steps:

- Concept Development: This involves coming up with the idea for the 360° video, including the story, the message, and the target audience. It also involves determining the goals and objectives of the video (the case of cultural Heritage).
- Scriptwriting: Once the concept is developed, the next step is to write a script. The script should include a detailed storyboard that outlines the camera angles, movement, and action.
- Location Scouting: This involves identifying potential locations for filming and determining whether they are suitable for 360° video. Factors to consider include technical planner: camera placement, lighting, audio recording, and the availability of power sources. Indeed, before filming it will be rather to plan some shots, to think about the

story we want to tell and the specific scenes we need to capture. Consider the location and any obstacles that might affect the filming. (Fig. 2).

- Casting: If actors are required, the casting process involves selecting individuals who are suitable for the roles. This involves also planning the look and feel of the video, including the costumes, props, and sets.

Overall, the pre-production stage is crucial to the success of a 360° video. A well-planned and executed pre-production stage can help ensure a smooth and efficient filming process and a high-quality final product.

- The Second step is production. Once everything is set up (we will need to set up the camera in the location we want to film, and make sure it is properly calibrated and configured), it is time to start filming. Because we are capturing a 360° view, we will need to think carefully about camera placement and movement to ensure the capturing of the action from all angles. In addition, as we are filming, it is important to monitor the footage in real-time to ensure everything is being captured correctly. This can be done using a VR headset or other specialized equipment (phone with a specific application for the camera).
- The Third step is Post-production. Once filming is complete, the footage will need to be stitched together using specialized software. This process takes the separate images captured by the camera and combines them into a single, seamless video. Here we can also apply effects like horizon correction and improve stitching quality with specific software (our case insta360 studio, Fig. 3). After, we can edit the video just like any other video production. This includes adding effects, transitions, and sound effects with specific software (Final cut, Davinci resolve, adobe premiere pro, etc.). Once the video is complete, it can be exported in a variety of formats depending on where it will be displayed (The structure of the video is designed and presented for a Head Mounted Display (oculus RiftS). The link to the video is provided online [16]). Overall, producing 360° video requires careful planning and execution to capture the immersive experience that this medium offers. Where the classic format offers broadcasting on a flat screen, thus inducing a certain distance with the user, the 360 video offers a 360-degree vision, made by the combination in post-production of the different shots, respecting the specific methodology of 360 video editing.

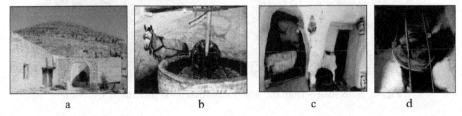

a   b   c   d

Fig. 2. (a) the porch of the oil mill, (b,c) the Inside of the oil mill (d) the pressing machine.

Fig. 3. Stitching Step on insta360 studio.

3.2 VR Storytelling

Digital approaches applied to the preservation and enhancement of a community's cultural heritage must take into consideration some elementary details related to the history and cultural significance of that heritage. Indeed, interactive digital storytelling systems provide users with an immersive experience by allowing them to control the events and elements of the story and interact with the narrative environment.

Dooley [5] claims that this emerging medium requires a new "screen grammar" which refers to the rules and conventions of this particular visual storytelling in order to tell stories and engage audiences. This means that filmmakers need to carefully consider how to guide the audience's attention and tell a cohesive story.

Our video has been recorded by Insta360 one x2 Camera. The sound and the voice-over of the storytelling were recorded separately with Zoom H3-VR virtual reality audio recorder. We elected not to perform any specialization of the sound and chose to present sounds in a binaural way. We ensured as much as possible, the guidelines of the storytelling (on the left side, in front of you, etc.) [12]. In fact, to orient the users, storytelling still has the main and the utmost unique guidance for them. The visitors could be transported back in time more than 300 years to a specific place. The main actor heads toward a deep underground hole called the amazing traditional winepress or the stone press whose builders. They could then explore the environment and interact with virtual sounds and characters to learn more about this traditional method of pressing olive (Fig. 4).

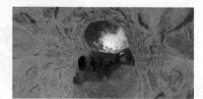

Fig. 4. Screenshots from the 360°video, extended panoramic overview

Overall, storytelling in virtual reality provides a powerful way for visitors to be engaged in a new and exciting way. Maud Ceuterick & Chris Ingraham [9] (2021), highlight that by creating immersive and personalized experiences, history can be more accessible and engaging to a wider audience. Then, Visitors can experience cultural heritage in a more meaningful way, and gain a deeper appreciation for the importance of cultural heritage objects. Interactive storytelling is another powerful approach that cultural heritage institutions can use in virtual reality exhibits [14]. By allowing visitors to make choices and interact with virtual characters (learn about their perspectives and experiences, objects, sounds, etc.). Visitors could play, for example, the role of a historical figure and make decisions that affect the outcome of the story.

3.3 The Immersive Binaural Sound

Immersive binaural sound is a crucial component of immersive storytelling. It is often used to create a realistic atmosphere and enhance immersion in the story or virtual environment. This technology produces a 3D sound experience for the users. It is designed to simulate the way that our ears perceive sound in the real world, by using special microphones that capture sounds from different positions and by using algorithms to process those sounds and play them back through the headsets. Binaural sound can also create a sense of spatial awareness that is crucial for immersion. Besides, it also can be used to provide audio cues or to direct the user's attention to important elements and this is what makes it an essential element of the story or the virtual environment of the story.

3.4 Point of View and Sense of Presence

Immersive video in 360° can greatly enhance the experience of cultural heritage sites for visitors. By creating experiences that enhance empathy and emotional connection with cultural heritage sites, visitors may be more interested in appreciating and caring for these sites, leading to greater preservation efforts.

In fact, this immersive technology aims to submerge the spectator in the space of the story. In the historical and archaeological mediation, the use of immersive techniques requires questioning the point of view that the narration seeks to develop and thus the place given to the spectator in the visit that we have proposed to him [7]. It seems to be relevant to highlight the human stories behind cultural heritage sites, such as the daily lives of people who lived in a historic building or the cultural significance of a particular artifact (the case of the oil mill).

By sharing these stories through immersive video, visitors can develop a deeper emotional connection to the site and a greater appreciation for its cultural significance.

4 Conclusion

Storytelling is at the center of the development of VR technologies. It allows a new extension of artistic expression in order to make the public live through new experiences. Thus, thanks to VR, we can submerge the user in a parallel world or allow him to transpose himself into situations in which he could not live in normal times. We can see below here some relevant points that summarize the new values offered by VR applied to cultural heritage:

- The user observes and establishes an emotional connection with the space just through his presence in the VR world.
- The strong sense of presence in the Virtual world breaks the distance between the space - the user - and the reality.
- Associated with an immersive narration (storytelling), the user can be integrated into VR environments, which project him into an unexpected immersive experience.
- The user observe-Interact in Virtual Environments.
- The user is not passive, he operates an active perception. The sensorimotor theories of perception have developed in opposition to a linear and sequential conception of the perceptive process.

Such a conception of perception has a fundamental implication on the definitions of immersion in virtual environments, such as cultural, architectural, and archaeological heritage: the process of interaction is already at the center of the phenomenon of immersion.

References

1. Aznoora, O., Abdul Wahab, N., Ismail, M.H.: Development and evaluation of an interactive 360° virtual tour for tourist destinations. J. Inf. Technol. Impact **9**(3), 173–182 (2009)
2. Boboc, R., Băutu , E.; Gîrbacia, F.; Popovici, N.; Popovici, D.-M.: Augmented reality in cultural heritage: an overview of the last decade of applications. Appl. Sci. **12**, 9859 (2022). https://doi.org/10.3390/app12199859
3. Cecotti, H.: Cultural heritage in fully immersive virtual reality. Virtual Worlds **1**, 82–102 (2022). https://doi.org/10.3390/virtualworlds1010006
4. Cummings, J.J., Bailenson, J.N.: How immersive is enough? a meta-analysis of the effect of immersive technology on user presence. Media Psychol. **19**(2), 272–309 (2016). https://doi.org/10.1080/15213269.2015.1015740
5. Dooley, K.: Storytelling with virtual reality in 360- degrees: a new screen grammar. Stud. Australas. Cinema **11**(3), 161–171 (2017). https://doi.org/10.1080/17503175.2017.1387357
6. Jacobi, Daniel. La communication scientifique. Discours, figures, modèles. Presses universitaires de Grenoble. Communication, médias et sociétés. Grenoble, (1999)
7. Laurent, L., Jean-Michel, G., Marquet, M., Victor Yvin, Pacôme Gérard et Pascal Magontier: Les enjeux de la narration dans l'immersion 3D archéologique », *In Situ* [En ligne], 42 | 2020, mis en ligne le 12 juin 2020, consulté le 12 janvier (2023). http://journals.openedition.org/insitu/27623. https://doi.org/10.4000/insitu.27623
8. Lenzi, S.: 3D Acquisition techniques and accuracy in cultural heritage documentation: an overview. In: Ferdani, D., Demetrescu, E., Cavalieri, M., Pace, G. (eds.) 3D Modelling and Visualization in Field Archaeology. From Survey to Interpretation of The Past Using Digital Technologies, pp. 13–24. Archaeopress Publishing Ltd. ISBN: 9781789690652. (2019)
9. Ceuterick, M., Ingraham, C.: Immersive storytelling and affective ethnography in virtual reality. Rev. Commun. **21**(1), 9–22 (2021). https://doi.org/10.1080/15358593.2021.1881610
10. Pervolarakis, Z., et al.: Visiting heritage sites in AR and VR. Heritage **6**(3), 2489–2502 (2023). https://doi.org/10.3390/heritage6030131
11. Remondino, F.: Heritage recording and 3D modeling with photogrammetry and 3D scanning. Remote Sens. **3**(6), 1104–1138 (2011). https://doi.org/10.3390/rs3061104
12. Rizvic, N., et al.: Guidelines for interactive digital storytelling presentations of cultural heritage. In: 2017 9th International Conference on Virtual Worlds and Games for Serious Applications (VS-Games), vol. 00, pp. 253–259. IEEE (2017). https://doi.org/10.1109/VS-GAMES.2017.8056593

13. Simou, S., Baba, K., Nounah, A.: The integration of 3D technology for the conservation and restoration of ruined archaeological artifacts. Hist. Sci. Technol. **12**(1), 150–168 (2022). https://doi.org/10.32703/2415-7422-2022-12-1-150-168

14. Škola, F., et al.: Virtual reality with 360-video storytelling in cultural heritage: study of presence, engagement, and immersion. Appl. Sci. **10**(23), 8656 (2020). https://doi.org/10. 3390/app10238656

15. Slater, M., Steed, A.: A virtual presence counter. Presence Teleoperators Virtual Environ. **9**(5), 413–434 (2000). https://doi.org/10.1162/105474600566925

16. The tradionnal oil mil of matmata « Andour »: https://www.youtube.com/watch?v=PpYk0B uAMhQ&t=25s

17. UNESCO for cultural statistics (2009). https://uis.unesco.org/fr/glossary-term/patrimoine-cul turel. Accessed 05 Feb 2023

18. Wimmer, J., Elmezeny, A., Edenhofer, N.: Immersive storytelling in 360-degree videos: an analysis of interplay between narrative and technical immersion. J. Virtual Worlds Res. **11**(1), 1–20 (2018). https://doi.org/10.4101/jvwr.v11i1.7298

19. Zeng, Y., Liu, L., Xu, R.: The effects of a virtual reality tourism experience on tourist's cultural dissemination behavior. Tourism and Hospitality **3**(1), 314–329 (2022). https://doi. org/10.3390/tourhosp3010021

Research on Construction of Cantonese Cultural Design Resource Library

Jiayan Huang[(⊠)] [iD] and Xumin Wu

Wuhan University of Technology, 430000 Wuhan, People's Republic of China
710867217@qq.com

Abstract. Intending to excavate and organize representative Cantonese cultural resources, the author proposes a method and process for constructing Cantonese cultural design resources based on creative design. This essay begins by thoroughly surveying the needs of dialect designers to set clear design objectives. The second section describes how Cantonese cultural knowledge is organized and categorized, creating a classifiable system geared toward Cantonese creative designs. Additionally, the dialectal culture monomer resources are further designed and translated to identify the knowledge framework of cultural design monomer information. Finally, the Cantonese cultural design-resource-library is constructed by combining the user requirements, the knowledge classification system of Cantonese culture, and the cultural monomer knowledge framework. The Cantonese cultural design resource library is a valuable resource for designers to improve efficiency and elevate the standard of design within Cantonese culture, promoting the inheritance of Cantonese culture.

Keywords: Dialect culture · Cantonese · Design-resource-library · Culture creative · Classification

1 Current status of Dialect Culture Resource Library

Currently, there are two main areas focusing on the theoretical investigation and practical research of dialect culture resource databases. The first area of focus is on the collection and documentation of dialect data, such as audible corpus, vocabulary, and other linguistic data from various regions. Normally this data is usually preserved in text and audio formats. Examples of such databases include the "Chinese Language Resource Noise Database," "Tianjin Dialect Speech File Resource Database," and "Hong Kong Cantonese Oral Corpus" [1], all of which are used to safeguard valuable dialect data. The second area of interest in the application of dialects uses digital technology to achieve speech recognition and synthesis. For instance, the XunFei Input Method has realized the recognition of 23 dialects through intelligent speech technology. Based on current research, Most studies in dialect resource libraries have primarily concentrated on linguistics and computers. Aiming to collect, preserve, and apply dialect ontology knowledge. However, they lack the collection of dialect using contexts, cultural connotations, and spiritual characteristics, which makes it challenging to support the creative

C. Stephanidis et al. (Eds.): HCII 2023, CCIS 1957, pp. 506–512, 2024.
https://doi.org/10.1007/978-3-031-49212-9_62

design of dialect culture. With the knowledge gathered from previous research, this paper proposes an original method to construct a resource library for Cantonese cultural design. Furthermore, it establishes a comprehensive and professional principle for collecting Cantonese cultural design resources, a system for classifying knowledge, as well as defining dialect cultural monomer information. Therefore, creative designers can have easy and convenient access to these access design materials and cultural knowledge, ultimately promoting Cantonese culture's creative design and development.

2   Product Positioning and Requirements Analysis

The purpose of constructing the Cantonese Cultural Design Resource Library is to explore and collect cultural design resources that embody the unique characteristics of the Cantonese region. Additionally, it aims to organize dialectal cultural knowledge systematically and scientifically from the creative design perspective. The primary users of this library are creative designers. To facilitate designers in obtaining and utilizing Cantonese cultural design resources for enhanced dialect visual design, this study analyzes the needs of designers based on relevant literature and case studies in dialect creative design.

The identified needs of dialect creative designers include:

1. Obtaining representative dialect cultural elements: During the research and analysis phase, designers aim to acquire dialect cultural elements that best exemplify the distinctive features of Cantonese culture, focusing on a specific theme or cultural phenomena. These cultural elements should be intuitive and easily understandable while possessing a compelling narrative and cultural value, evoking emotional resonance in viewers, and prompting contemplation on culture.
2. Acquiring the characteristics of cultural elements: Designers must also comprehend the characteristics of dialect cultural elements to proceed with the design creation. These attributes can be presented in the form of text, images, audio, and video.
3. Accessing Design Case: In the design conception stage, designers require relevant design cases aligned with their design goals and positioning to derive inspiration.

The purpose of constructing the Cantonese cultural design resource library is to facilitate designers in accessing the most representative dialect cultural elements of Cantonese culture and their corresponding characteristics. Additionally, the library aims to offer diverse dialect design cases across various design types. As a result, the construction process of the Cantonese Cultural Design Resource Library is illustrated in Fig. 1.

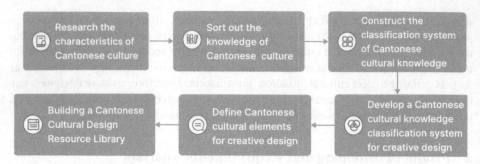

Fig. 1. Construction Process of Cantonese Cultural Design Resource Database

3   A Study on Classification of Cantonese Cultural Design Resources

3.1   Dialect Cultural Knowledge Classification

Within the context of this essay, the term Dialect Culture refers to three elements: dialect usage, dialect phenomena, and the dialect itself, which hold cultural significance and value[2]. According to this definition, dialect culture can be divided into three parts. The first part is dialect ontology knowledge, which includes pronunciation, vocabulary, and grammar. The second part consists of dialect phenomena that hold cultural significance, referring to the expression of local namesake through dialect, including architecture, common tools, clothing, diet, etc. Finally, the third part is dialect folk customs and art with cultural value, such as blessing and tabooed words, proverbs, sacrificial worship, and other folk activities. This includes dialect literature and art, such as folk songs, local music, local drama, and story legends [3].

3.2   A Classification System of Cantonese Cultural Knowledge

The Cantonese is a significant part of Guang Fu culture, and Guangzhou is the center of this culture[4]. So, this paper focuses on the Cantonese culture in Guangzhou. The author classifies it into three categories based on the linguistic circles' classification method. These categories include 1) Cantonese ontology knowledge [5]; 2) Cantonese phenomenon with cultural value and significance [6]; 3) Cantonese folk customs or art with cultural value and significance [7]. To establish the classification system of Cantonese cultural knowledge, this essay extensively researched and analyzed various literary works, such as Annals of Guangzhou Dialects, Guangzhou Folklore Ethnography, and List of Guangzhou Language Intangible Cultural Heritage.

3.3   The Classification System of Cantonese Cultural Knowledge for Creative Design

The previous categorization of Cantonese cultural knowledge focused on linguistic aspects. Regarding the design resource library, it is important to classify and organize cultural knowledge from a creative design perspective. Cantonese culture contains a wealth of cultural information, and this study aims to select culturally representative elements suitable for design creation [8]. Firstly, this paper provides guidelines for collecting Cantonese elements that apply to creative design requirements by analyzing literature and design cases. In addition, distinctive and design-relevant Cantonese cultural elements are identified based on these guidelines and the frequency of cultural element occurrence. Finally, an oriented classification system of Cantonese cultural knowledge for creative design is constructed, as shown in Fig. 2.

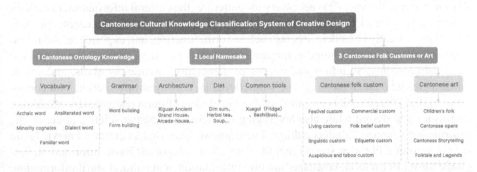

Fig. 2. Cantonese Cultural Knowledge Classification System of Creative Design

Principles for collecting Cantonese cultural monomers based on creative design requirements are as follows:

1. Reflect the Cantonese region's unique historical, traditional, and humanistic characteristics, promote cultural identity, and enhance social cohesion in the Cantonese area.
2. Highlight Cantonese culture's independence and distinctive traits, incorporating elements that showcase the people's unique personality while reflecting the local customs, seasonal traditions, climate, scenery, and traces of daily life in the Cantonese region from the past and present.
3. Embody the unique linguistic features of Cantonese, including its distinct pronunciation system, peculiar vocabulary, and unique written expression system.
4. Facilitate dialect design creation: widely accepted, evoking emotional resonance and cultural identification, also allowing for creative exploration in both visual and auditory aspects.

4 A Study on the Classification of Cultural Monolithic Knowledge of Cantonese

4.1 A Study on the Classification of Dialect Culture Monolithic Knowledge

Dialect culture is a subset of language culture. In this regard this essay categorizes dialect cultural knowledge into three aspects: 1) Dialect ontology information, including pronunciation, phonogram, text, and semantics; 2) behavioral layer content, encompassing language usage and life situation associated with it; 3) Intrinsic cultural and spiritual essence of the dialect, which includes the historical and cultural background and the dominant collective spirit or folk psychology. These deeper aspects constitute the essence of dialect culture [9].

4.2 A Study on the Classification of Dialect Culture Monolithic Knowledge in Design Resource Library

The above framework is based on linguistic perspectives. However, while applying in design resource libraries, it is necessary to reinterpret the cultural information in dialects within the framework to meet creative design requirements. In design research, the study of objects typically considers aspects such as form, function, and experience. Additionally, dialects are often regarded as linguistic symbols, consisting of signifiers (form) and signified (content). Signifiers encompass pronunciation, written symbols, and so on, while signified refer to the language's functionality, conveyed information, and connotations [10]. Therefore, it is essential to integrate dialect cultural resources by combining linguistics and design while also leveraging the field of computer science to enrich the information sources of dialect culture. The framework for dialect cultural knowledge in design resource libraries should include four main categories: basic information, language form information, language function information, and cultural spirit information, as illustrated in Fig. 3.

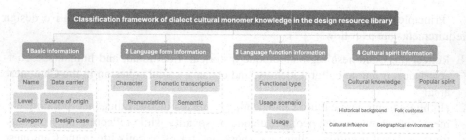

Fig. 3. Classification framework of dialect cultural monomer knowledge in the design resource library

5 Design Resource Library Application Instances

According to the method described above, the author developed a website for the Cantonese culture design resource library. By combining videos, audio, images, and texts, the system provides a three-dimensional presentation of the core aspects of Cantonese culture, including dialect itself, local phenomena expressed in dialect, dialect customs, and art. The main interface of the design resource library includes a homepage, dimensions for displaying resource attributes and distinctive cultures, a design case library, a search results interface, and a cultural resource display interface. Functionally, the system covers keyword search, multimedia storage, and playback, resource content management, import and export of content, resource statistics, and more. The system's information architecture is shown in Fig. 4.

The homepage of the design resource library presents an overview, resource statistics, keyword search, and culture type screening function. Additionally, the overview provides a comprehensive introduction to Cantonese culture. Moreover, the Resource statistics section displays the number of available design resources. Users can use keyword search to access relevant cultural resource information. Furthermore, on the search results page, users can filter resources based on cultural type, functionality, and format, enhancing the efficiency of their search. Lastly, users can conveniently filter materials based on different cultural types and easily access detailed information.

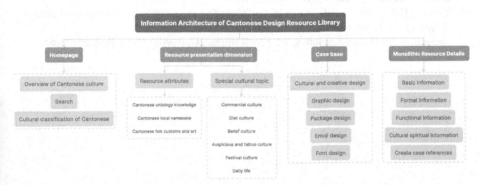

Fig. 4. Information Architecture of Cantonese Design Resource Library

6   Conclusion

Dialect is not only part of the culture but also the carrier of cultural information. It contains rich cultural knowledge and is an important source of inspiration for cultural creative design. This paper focuses on Cantonese culture and proposes a method for constructing a design resource library tailored to the needs of the creative design field. The library includes a classification framework and collection principles specific to Cantonese culture. This resource library facilitates easy access to comprehensive, professional, and diverse design resources for creative designers by addressing the lack of standardized and targeted Cantonese cultural knowledge. It aims to enhance the efficiency and quality of dialect cultural creative design while promoting the inheritance of Cantonese culture.

References

1. Gala, T.: Review the construction and research status of the dialect database. Librar. J. Fujian **01**,13–16+57 (2020)
2. Lining, W., Jianqiao, K.: Thoughts on current situation of Chinese dialect cultural protection. Chinese J. Lang. Policy Plann. **7**(4), 76–85 (2022)
3. Lining, W.: Behind the popularity of dialect culture. Guangming Daily (2021)

4. Kequn, W.: The characteristics and influence of Cantonese culture. J. Guangzhou Inst. Soc. **9**(2), 80–82 (2011)
5. Jie, W.: A short description of the substance of Guangfu culture. Soc. Sci. Hunan **187**(03), 176–179 (2018)
6. Chorography compile committee of Guangzhou.: Annals of Guangzhou (dialect choreography). Guangzhou Press (2000)
7. Chorography compile committee of Guangzhou.: Annals of Guangzhou (Folkloristic Ethnology). Guangzhou Press (2000)
8. Cuiting, K., Dihu, X., Hui, L.: Repository construction of Hunan culture creative product design. Packag. Eng. **38**(04), 161–165 (2016)
9. Tao, H.: The characteristics, values and safeguarding tactics of linguistic cultural heritage. J. Renmin Univ. China **130**(04), 27–33 (2008)
10. Hengchun, X.: Design Semiotics, 4th edn. Tsinghua University Press, Beijing (2008)

Automatic Transcription of Greek Folk Dance Videos to Labanotation Based on Autoencoders

Georgios Loupas[1($\boxtimes$)], Theodora Pistola[1], Sotiris Diplaris[1],
Christos Stentoumis[2], Konstantinos Ioannidis[1], Stefanos Vrochidis[1],
and Ioannis Kompatsiaris[1]

[1] Information Technologies Institute - CERTH, Thessaloniki, Greece
{loupgeor,tpistola,diplaris,kioannid,stefanos,ikom}@iti.gr
[2] up2metric P.C., Athens, Greece
christos@up2metric.com

Abstract. We're creating an automatic system, based on autoencoders, to transcribe dance videos into labanotation [1], a movement notation system. Manual labanotation generation is a time-consuming process that requires specialized knowledge. Our system aims to save time and provide a valuable tool for choreographers, dancers, and anyone interested in documenting body movement. Our system analyzes RGB videos of dancers, isolates their movements, and generates labanotation as an image. The process involves extracting the 3D skeleton, segmenting movements, identifying them, and mapping them to Laban symbols. In our research, we focus on segmenting the movements of the dancer's lower body. We calculate the angles of the legs and use them as features to train an autoencoder. This approach, inspired by [2], has not been previously explored for human movement segmentation. Human movement segmentation remains a hard problem due to the temporal complexity among the high-dimensional motion features. Our work aims to automatically generate labanotation for Greek folk dances, contributing to the preservation and transmission of dance-related Intangible Cultural Heritage (ICH). The system is integrated into the CHROMATA online platform [3], which offers AI tools for analyzing, classifying, and annotating ICH content. This integration assists designers in creating immersive experiences based on ICH.

Keywords: Autoencoders · Labanotation · Folk Dances

1 Introduction

The segmentation of human motion is a complex problem. Segmenting and understanding human steps has numerous applications, such as choreography analysis and automatic notation in Labanotation. In this study, we tackle the problem of segmentation using an unsupervised approach. Unlike supervised

C. Stephanidis et al. (Eds.): HCII 2023, CCIS 1957, pp. 513–521, 2024.
https://doi.org/10.1007/978-3-031-49212-9_63

methods, unsupervised methods do not require a large amount of annotated data. The lack of annotated data for training algorithms in generating Labanotation highlights the importance of approaching the problem in an unsupervised manner.

2   Related Work

Signal segmentation techniques find applications in various domains and problems involving the analysis of sequential data. Some of the areas where these techniques are used include speech processing, time series data, computer vision, bioinformatics, sensor data analysis, and medical signal processing.

2.1   Human Movement Segmentation

Motion segmentation has the ability to partition lengthy sequences of high-dimensional human motion data into fragments that are semantically independent in nature. This technique finds application in various domains, including gesture recognition, primitive modeling, action recognition, robotics, and human movement recognition [4]. Manual segmentation of motion capture data is a time-consuming and demanding task, as noted by previous research [5]. Traditional methods of human motion segmentation have predominantly concentrated on features associated with periodicity or angular velocity [6]. However, these features only capture elementary aspects of motion sequences and are limited in their ability to effectively segment complex motion patterns [7]. To address this limitation and extract higher-level feature information, researchers have proposed automated segmentation algorithms based on Kernel Principal Component Analysis (KPCA) and Probabilistic Principal Component Analysis (PPCA) [8] or Short-Term Principal Component Analysis (ST-PCA) [9] for analyzing high-dimensional time series data in motion capture. Machine learning techniques, including kernel k-means and spectral clustering, have also been applied to motion segmentation [10,11]. An alternative approach introduced by Li et al. involves Temporal Subspace Clustering (TSC) [12]. Lin et al. have proposed an optimal control strategy based on reverse optimization criteria and residual estimation for determining segmentation points [13]. To improve segmentation effectiveness, a low-level time segmentation algorithm utilizing cosine distance has been developed [14]. Furthermore, researchers have explored Hierarchical Aligned Cluster Analysis (HACA) as a temporal clustering method for motion segmentation [15]. Lastly, rhythm-based segmentation has been proposed from a dance rhythm/beat perspective [16,17].

2.2   Automatic Labanotation Generation

Regarding the automated extraction of Laban notation, some techniques focus on spatial analysis of movements [17–20] for automated extraction of Laban notation. They involve motion segmentation to divide the motion into elemental movements and spatial analysis to map them to Laban symbols. However, these rule-based techniques have limitations in capturing the complexities of human body movements. In other methods, movements and their Laban symbols are recognized by comparing them to standard basic movements in a motion library, using Euclidean distance and Dynamic Time Warping (DTW) [21].

More recent techniques employ Hidden Markov Models (HMMs) for labeling the lower extremities and Extra-Trees for the upper extremities [22]. Others utilize the dynamics of machine learning to train algorithms such as Neural Networks and Extreme Learning Machines (ELMs) [23], Recursive Neural Networks [24,25], as well as seq2seq models with and without attention mechanisms [26,27]. These approaches yield improved results compared to simple spatial analysis methods mentioned earlier but necessitate an adequate amount of training data.

3 Methodology

Our approach uses autoencoders to compare similarity in the latent space between successive frames, determining segmentation points in a 3D skeleton pose sequence. We extract motion information from knee-crotch angles, resulting in a time series of 2 variables.

The time series is divided into smaller chunks using a sliding window and fed into the autoencoder to obtain latent representations. This sliding window is continuously shifted with a constant stride until reaching the end of the signal.

Thus, essentially each time point is represented as a vector in the latent space, and due to the sliding window, temporal information is embedded. The autoencoder, in this context, acts as a feature extractor.

Given the latent representations, our algorithm then utilizes the concept that frames within a segment are expected to display a greater similarity compared to frames across different segments. The similarity between two feature vectors, z_i and z_j, is given by:

$$G(i,j) = \frac{z_i \cdot z_j}{\|z_i\| \|z_j\|} \qquad (1)$$

So the self-similarity matrix is computed, and starting from a frame, the cosine similarity is taken into account with each subsequent frame until it reaches a minimum value. Since the similarity measure can be noisy and may exhibit several minimal points, an adaptive threshold is applied, so that a point is considered as a segment boundary only when it has a minimum and its value is lower than the threshold.

In our method, two autoencoder architectures were employed. A 1D convolutional autoencoder (CAE) was used as well as a full connected self-expressive autoencoder (SEA). The 1D CAE functions as a feature extractor that encapsulates the temporal information.

The SEA receives the representations generated by the 1D CAE as input and is trained to simultaneously minimize the mean squared error (MSE) and the self-expressive loss.

$$\text{Loss} = \|X - \hat{\underline{X}}\| + \|X - \hat{X}\| \qquad (2)$$

where $\hat{X}$ is the direct reconstruction and $\underline{\hat{X}}$ is the self-expressed reconstruction. This objective aims to bring representations expressing similar segments of the signal closer in the latent space while pushing apart dissimilar representations.

4 Experiments and Results

The data used in this study obtained from the Dance DB[1] and consists of 10 motion capture files of greek dances in BVH format of varying durations. From each BVH file, the three-dimensional coordinates of the joints were extracted. Each file was sampled to have a frame rate of 30 fps. To handle occasional sudden variations in joint coordinates, a median filter was used to eliminate outliers within the mostly noise-free data.

This study focuses on segmenting leg movements by extracting informative features such as knee and crotch angles, thus each leg sequence is represented as a time series with two variables. Separate experiments were conducted for the right and left leg due to different segmentation intervals. Due to the limited availability of annotated data and the difficulty of manual annotation, a rule-based algorithm was developed for motion segmentation, that detects motion changes using the minima of kinetic energy in the relevant limb. The rule-based algorithm, through observation, effectively identifies logical segments of movements by detecting changes that minimize the kinetic energy of the legs. While it serves as a suitable ground truth for evaluating accuracy, it may have limitations with complex and smooth movements.

Two experiments were conducted: one with noise-free signals and another with synthetic noise introduced in the skeletons. Segmentation results were obtained based on autoencoder representations as well as the characteristics of the original time series. The second experiment involved training autoencoders to denoise the signal and improve segmentation in the presence of synthetic noise. A comparison was made with the rule-based algorithm applied to the noisy signal, revealing its weaknesses in over-segmentation. The synthetic noise induced local minima in kinetic energy, potentially causing over-segmentation and exposing the weakness of the rule-based algorithm. However, the displacement information of each leg during movement was preserved, such as forward steps remaining predominantly forward with minimal alterations.

In the experiments, different window sizes, specifically 8, 16, and 32 frames, were considered, with a stride value set to one. The adaptive threshold for the i-th row is determined as the mean of the similarity values in the i-th row, specifically from the i-th column to the (i+96)-th column. This implies that, for a given frame, the adaptive threshold is computed as the average of the similarity values across subsequent frames up to a duration of approximately 3 s, or 96 frames, in the similarity matrix.

---

[1] http://dancedb.cs.ucy.ac.cy, the Dance Motion Capture Database of the University of Cyprus.

The evaluation metrics used were Recall, Precision, F1-score, and R-value [28], with a tolerance of 16 frames. The R-value is a metric that takes into account the over-segmentation that can lead to increased recall values, providing a more robust quantification of segmentation performance.

The 1D CAE consists of three 1d convolutional layers with max pooling and batch normalization and then a fully connected layer to produce the final encoding. The first layer has 32 filters, followed by a layer with 16 filters, and a final layer with 8 filters. Each layer uses a kernel size of 3 and a stride of 1.

Two layers were used as encoders of the SEA: the first layer has double the dimensions of the input, and the second layer has the same dimensions as the input representations. This configuration allows for a nonlinear transformation in the initial space of representations generated by the 1D CAE.

Training was performed using the Adam optimizer with a learning rate of 0.001. The models were trained until convergence, with early stopping applied after 20 epochs. A leave-one-out methodology was employed to train the autoencoders so we can evaluate the generalization capabilities of the learned representations. For our experiments, we used a NVIDIA GeForce RTX 3090 GPU.

The following results pertain to the average of the segmentation outcomes for both legs (Table 1).

Table 1. Performance of the time series representation and the autoencoder latent representations in noiseless conditions.

Method	Window Size	Recall	Precision	F1	R-Value
Initial features	-	**0.67**	0.62	**0.65**	0.69
CAE	8	0.63	0.65	0.64	0.69
SEA	8	0.64	**0.66**	**0.65**	**0.70**
CAE	16	0.59	0.63	0.61	0.67
SEA	16	0.60	0.63	0.61	0.67
CAE	32	0.52	**0.66**	0.58	0.64
SEA	32	0.55	**0.66**	0.60	0.66

In noiseless case, the algorithm applied to the initial time series has higher recall, while autoencoders achieve higher precision and similar F1 scores. R-value, indicating segmentation stability, is similar for both cases, suggesting comparable performance. Larger window sizes (e.g., 32) result in decreased performance, indicating difficulty in capturing fast-paced changes (Table 2).

We observe that the rule-based algorithm performs poorly under noisy conditions, with over-segmentation and low R-value. Autoencoders achieve higher recall and outperform in all metrics. This demonstrates that the learned representations likely contain substantial information that makes them more resilient to noise. Increasing window size also leads to decreased performance.

Table 2. Performance of the rule-based algorithm, the time series representation and the autoencoder latent representations in noise conditions.

Method	Window Size	Recall	Precision	F1	R-Value
Rule-based	-	0.69	0.37	0.46	0.27
Initial features	-	0.57	0.61	0.59	0.65
CAE	8	**0.72**	0.62	**0.67**	0.69
SEA	8	0.67	**0.65**	0.66	**0.71**
CAE	16	0.66	0.61	0.63	0.67
SEA	16	0.69	0.62	0.65	0.68
CAE	32	0.57	0.61	0.59	0.66
SEA	32	0.62	0.62	0.62	0.68

A qualitative comparison of the generated Labanotation using the mentioned methods in relation to the ground truth is shown below. It can be observed that the networks manage to be more resilient to noise (Fig. 1).

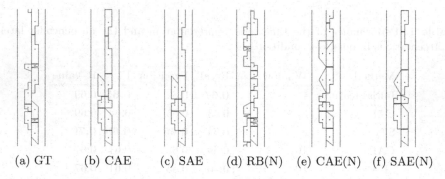

(a) GT   (b) CAE   (c) SAE   (d) RB(N)   (e) CAE(N)   (f) SAE(N)

Fig. 1. Comparison of Labanotation Generation outputs, where GT refers to the Ground Truth, RB to the Rule-based algorithm and (N) refers to noisy experiments

5   Conclusions and Future Work

Autoencoders seems to be effective for unsupervised motion segmentation, even in noisy conditions. The dynamics of the latent representations were observed, indicating potential for improvement with more complex architectures and additional cost functions. Proper motion segmentation is crucial for analyzing motion and transform it to labanotation where annotated data for training supervised techniques is not readily available. The use of autoencoders for denoising and segmenting motion could enhance also the results of rule-based algorithms in generating labanotation, yielding reliable outcomes regardless of the available data. In the future, we aim to explore more complex architectures. One idea is to employ transformer models, training them in a self-supervised manner using available non-labeled mocap files. Subsequently, fine-tuning could be performed on a small set of annotated data for labanotation generation, leading to improved performance.

Acknowledgments. This research has been co-financed by the European Union and Greek national funds through the Operational Program Competitiveness, Entrepreneurship and Innovation, under the call RESEARCH-CREATE-INNOVATE (project code: T2EDK-01856).

References

1. Hutchinson, A., Guest, A.H., Hutchinson, W.A.: Labanotation: or, Kinetography Laban: the System of Analyzing and Recording Movement, no. 27. Taylor & Francis (1977)
2. Bhati, S., Villalba, J., Żelasko, P., Dehak, N.: Self-expressing autoencoders for unsupervised spoken term discovery, pp. 4876–4880. https://doi.org/10.21437/Interspeech.2020-3000
3. Pistola, T., et al.: Creating immersive experiences based on intangible cultural heritage, pp. 17–24 (2021). https://doi.org/10.1109/ICIR51845.2021.00012
4. Lin, J.F.-S., Karg, M., Kulić, D.: Movement primitive segmentation for human motion modeling: a framework for analysis. IEEE Trans. Hum. Mach. Syst. **46**(3), 325–339 (2016). https://doi.org/10.1109/THMS.2015.2493536
5. Xia, G., Sun, H., Feng, L., Zhang, G., Liu, Y.: Human motion segmentation via robust kernel sparse subspace clustering. IEEE Trans. Image Process. **27**(1), 135–150 (2018). https://doi.org/10.1109/TIP.2017.2738562
6. Okada, N., Iwamoto, N., Fukusato, T., Morishima, S.: Dance motion segmentation method based on choreographic primitives. In: GRAPP 2015–10th International Conference on Computer Graphics Theory and Applications, VISIGRAPP, Proceedings, pp. 332–339 (2015). https://doi.org/10.5220/0005304303320339
7. Wang, Y., Lin, X., Wu, L., Zhang, W., Zhang, Q., Huang, X.: Robust subspace clustering for multi-view data by exploiting correlation consensus. IEEE Trans. Image Process. **24**(11), 3939–3949 (2015). https://doi.org/10.1109/TIP.2015.2457339
8. Chen, S.-X., Chen, S., Li, J.-W., Chen, X.: A hybrid P/KPCA-based approach for motion capture data automatic segmentation. J. Comp. Methods Sci. Eng. **16**(2), 197–206 (2016). https://doi.org/10.3233/JCM-160610
9. xu, J., Takagi, K., Yoneyama, A.: Three-dimensional image information media: beat induction from motion capture data using short-term principal component analysis. J. Inst. Image Inf. Telev. Eng. **64**, 577–583 (2010). https://doi.org/10.3169/itej.64.577
10. Zhou, F., De la Torre, F., Hodgins, J.K.: Aligned cluster analysis for temporal segmentation of human motion. In: 2008 8th IEEE International Conference on Automatic Face & Gesture Recognition, Amsterdam, Netherlands, pp 1–7 (2008). https://doi.org/10.1109/AFGR.2008.4813468
11. Wang, W., Shen, J., Porikli, F., Yang, R.: Semi-supervised video object segmentation with super-trajectories. IEEE Trans. Pattern Anal. Mach. Intell. **41**(4), 985–998 (2019). https://doi.org/10.1109/TPAMI.2018.2819173

12. Li, S., Li, K., Fu, Y.: Temporal subspace clustering for human motion segmentation. In: 2015 IEEE International Conference on Computer Vision (ICCV), Santiago, Chile, pp. 4453–4461 (2015). https://doi.org/10.1109/ICCV.2015.506

13. Lin, J.F.-S., Bonnet, V., Panchea, A.M., Ramdani, N., Venture, G., Kulić, D.: Human motion segmentation using cost weights recovered from inverse optimal control. In: 2016 IEEE-RAS 16th International Conference on Humanoid Robots (Humanoids), Cancun, Mexico, pp. 1107–1113 (2016). https://doi.org/10.1109/HUMANOIDS.2016.7803409

14. Yang, Y., Chen, J., Zhan, Y., Wang, X., Wang, J., Liu, Z.: Low level segmentation of motion capture data based on cosine distance. In: 2015 3rd International Conference on Computer, Information and Application, Yeosu, Korea (South), pp. 26–28 (2015). https://doi.org/10.1109/CIA.2015.14

15. Zhou, F., De la Torre, F., Hodgins, J.K.: Hierarchical aligned cluster analysis for temporal clustering of human motion. IEEE Trans. Pattern Anal. Mach. Intell. **35**(3), 582–596 (2013). https://doi.org/10.1109/TPAMI.2012.137

16. Chu, W.-T., Tsai, S.-Y.: Rhythm of motion extraction and rhythm-based cross-media alignment for dance videos. IEEE Trans. Multimedia **14**(1), 129–141 (2012). https://doi.org/10.1109/TMM.2011.2172401

17. Cui, C., Li, J., Du, D., Wang, H., Tu, P., Cao, T.: The method of dance movement segmentation and labanotation generation based on rhythm. IEEE Access **9**, 31213–31224 (2021). https://doi.org/10.1109/ACCESS.2021.3060103

18. Guo, H., Miao, Z., Zhu, F., Zhang, C., Li, S.: Automatic labanotation generation based on human motion capture data. In: Li, S., Liu, C., Wang, Y. (eds.) CCPR 2014. CCIS, vol. 483, pp. 426–435. Springer, Heidelberg (2014). https://doi.org/10.1007/978-3-662-45646-0_44

19. Wang, J., Miao, Z., Guo, H., Zhou, Z., Wu, H.: Using automatic generation of Labanotation to protect folk dance. J. Electron. Imaging **26**(1), 01102 (2017)

20. Ikeuchi, K., Ma, Z., Yan, Z., Kudoh, S., Nakamura, M.: Describing upper-body motions based on labanotation for learning-from-observation robots. Int. J. Comput. Vision **126**(12), 1415–1429 (2018)

21. Zhou, Z., Miao, Z., Wang, J.: A system for automatic generation of labanotation from motion capture data. In: 2016 IEEE 13th International Conference on Signal Processing (ICSP), pp. 1031–1034. IEEE, November 2016

22. Li, M., Miao, Z., Ma, C.: Dance movement learning for labanotation generation based on motion-captured data. IEEE Access **7**, 161561–161572 (2019)

23. Zhang, X., Miao, Z., Zhang, Q.: Automatic generation of Labanotation based on extreme learning machine with skeleton topology feature. In: 2018 14th IEEE International Conference on Signal Processing (ICSP), pp. 510–515. IEEE, August 2018

24. Zhang, X., Miao, Z., Yang, X., Zhang, Q.: An efficient method for automatic generation of labanotation based on bi-directional LSTM. J. Phys. Conf. Ser. **1229**(1), 012031 (2019)

25. Hao, S., Miao, Z., Wang, J., Xu, W., Zhang, Q.: Labanotation generation based on bidirectional gated recurrent units with joint and line features. In: 2019 IEEE International Conference on Image Processing (ICIP), pp. 4265–4269. IEEE, September 2019

26. Li, M., Miao, Z., Ma, C.: Sequence-to-sequence labanotation generation based on motion capture data. In: ICASSP 2020–2020 IEEE International Conference on Acoustics, Speech and Signal Processing (ICASSP), pp. 4517–4521. IEEE, May 2020

27. Li, M., Miao, Z., Xu, W.: A CRNN-based attention-seq2seq model with fusion feature for automatic Labanotation generation. Neurocomputing **454**, 430–440 (2021)
28. Räsänen, O., Laine, U., Altosaar, T.: An improved speech segmentation quality measure: the R-value. In: Proceedings of the Annual Conference of the International Speech Communication Association, INTERSPEECH, pp. 1851–1854 (2009). https://doi.org/10.21437/Interspeech.2009-538

How Do Historians Interact with Digital Cultural Collections? A Study on Search and Selection Behavior

Anna Neovesky[✉]

Technical University Darmstadt Coding Friends UG, Berlin, Germany
anna@coding-friends.com

Abstract. This paper aims to examine the search and information behavior of historians. The central question is, how historians achieve relevant results when they are using retrieval systems for their research and how they interact with these systems, especially when using digital source collections. Since problem-oriented information needs are predominant in academic research, a qualitative study on search and selection behavior was carried out. The results indicate that approaches are targeted-oriented and that scholars heavily rely on extended search functionalities and categorizations. Scholars arrive at relevant results through individually developed strategies and with a high degree of willingness to make use of the available options, even at the cost of a large amount of time. Transparency and quality can be identified as central topics in several steps of search and result evaluation. Hence, it is necessary that they are better addressed by digital cultural collections and further information systems.

Keywords: Search behaviour · Selection behaviour · Digital literacy · Problem-oriented search

1 Searching and Selecting Information as Part of the Research Process

Both information search and the interaction with search systems play a crucial part in the everyday tasks of anyone working in research, also for historians. While certain systems and collections – such as search engines and library catalogs – are used by scholars of all disciplines, historians rely especially on historical sources. Written sources, such as manuscripts, charters, diaries or inscriptions, are available in an increasing number of digital cultural collections – such as primary source editions, thematic catalogs, and other scientific materials. First born-digital collections are already being created as purely digitally available publications.

But the digital provision not only facilitates access, it also means an obligation for the providing institutions to supply effective and sustainable access for users. The functionalities of the collections as well as the quality of their content determine which information can be found and used. This requires – especially for the historical discipline – a design that considers both the aspects of the scholarly work process, source

C. Stephanidis et al. (Eds.): HCII 2023, CCIS 1957, pp. 522–527, 2024.
https://doi.org/10.1007/978-3-031-49212-9_64

criticism and its digital transformation, and the specific needs and procedures of the users [1].

Search in an academic context particularly attaches great importance to cognitive interest, evidence, analysis, interpretation and source criticism. [2, 3] In history, especially the latter is particularly strongly formulated and formalized in a methodical tradition of academic work and quality assurance. The digitalization had and has a substituting, transforming and enabling impact on all aspects of academic work and scholarly information practices. [4] For collections of historical sources, materiality, reproducibility and a new concept of authenticity play a key role. On that basis, Fickers pleaded for a "new digital historicism" that addresses tools criticism and search literacy as further relevant skills besides source criticism. [5] These play an important role in the selection of search systems as well as in the evaluation and selection of information and search results.

2 The Need for A domain-Specific View on the Search Process and on System Interaction

Problem-oriented information needs [6] are predominant in academic research [7]. Thus, the search process and the interaction with the system must be considered in the context of prior knowledge, systems, and dynamic, iterative aspects of search [8]. Therefore, a domain-specific view is necessary. Moreover, depending on the field, different types of specific collections are used: Particularly relevant for scholars are archives, (university) library catalogs, journal databases and digital libraries as well as digital cultural collections. [7] All these collections have unique characteristics regarding interfaces, functionalities and quality criteria.

While numerous studies deal with search strategies and selection behavior, addressing both the system and the user side, studies that deal with searching the web and specifically library catalogs predominate. Where subject-specific collections are evaluated, the focus lies primarily on functionalities, detached from concrete research questions and user needs. Qualitative investigations with a focus on specific disciplines and their particular content-related and methodological needs are missing.

3 Search and Selection Behavior of Historians

3.1 A Qualitative Study on Search and Selection Behavior

To address the need for a domain-specific view that observes the information search in the light of common methods and resources, seven historians focusing on the middle ages and early modern history where selected as participants of this qualitative study. In the qualitative interviews and observations, the participants were questioned on their usage of collections and preferred and applied approaches of search, evaluation and selection. They described concrete approaches and problems from their scholarly work. The interviews were were conducted as expert interviews [9] and analysed using qualitative content analysis. This methods allows to develop topics and statements based on the empirical material. [10] The results of the qualitative study were contextualized with studies on the search and selection behavior of scientists and compared with log file analyses of the repositories being mentioned by the historians [11].

3.2 Specific Domains, Specific Needs – Main Findings of the Study

All participants described and reflected on their approaches to searching for information related to their research. They contextualized them in their field of study, together with describing and demonstrating them based on current or recent information seeking endeavors.

Collections of regesta (brief descriptions of mostly royal documents), OPACs, source editions, and encyclopedias were named by almost all participants. The utilization of physical locations like libraries was little discussed, as well as non-academic resources. Mainly people with very specific questions (e.g., in the context of a dissertation or book project) use specific collections also on site. More pronounced digital skills of the scholars lead to a more extensive use of data. Also, the perception of digital and printed representations differ depending on habits and on which representation is used more regularly. Noticeable, all scholars described the use of one or two, usually highly specialized, collection in considerate depth. Thus, the topics scholars are researching highly predetermine what is used and lead to a high degree of specialization when it comes to certain resources.

Regarding the search interface, priority is given to search with extended functionalities, categorizations and filtering options. A log analysis of one of the most frequently named source collection, the Regesta Imperii, supports this pattern, as around 40% of the queries where entered using the extended search interface. [12] This is a significant difference to other resources and also library catalogs.

Five participants describe how they – depending on what is offered by the specific collection – use the index, volumes, author names, topics and periods to restrict their initial search results. The skimming and refinement of search results can be viewed as one of the central patterns described. Larger result sets are not perceived as a problem. Challenges are mainly mentioned regarding the quality of interface and content, especially when the scholars were very familiar with a collection. Wishes were more general, for example with regard to search functions (better support of combined terms, full text search, translation of content).

All respondents reflect on their approach (for example, by evaluating it or naming important aspects). Nevertheless, they primarily use initially offered and directly visible functionalities, even if these are otherwise criticized. One example is the sorting of the search results. While chronology is preferred, relevance is perceived critically by all participants who point out that it is best assessed by the users themselves. However, in most collections discussed in the demonstrations of search approaches, relevance was the initial setting. But in all cases it was used regardless the disapproval. This highlights the importance of which functions and informations get placed prominently.

Criteria that the users name for the selection of results are especially the period the information refers to, its reputation, and if they assume the information is interesting. This results in a need for an overview of the available content of the collections and the collection criteria. Criticism relates to (misleading) categories, insufficient topicality, and insufficient or inconsistent preparation (depth of indexing) of content or data.

While there is a wide range of digital resources used, researchers have close ties to specific collections. Through long-term research topics and long-term usage of specific collections, they have in-depth prior knowledge about the subjects as well as the collections. Scholars are willing to use the offered functionalities even by investing a lot of time, such as when reviewing, evaluating, and trimming down larger result sets. The approaches are also characterized by a need for autonomy over the organization of results and for an overview of the content and the processing of the material. Looking at the search strategy and the choice of search terms, three overarching characteristics can be noted, although the concrete approach varies from person to person:

- The search approaches are targeted-oriented (regarding collection, approach, and functionalities).
- Using structures and going through search results is a widespread technique.
- The search for persons is an important entry point.

The findings suggest that research subjects, experiences, and subject-specific knowledge have a great influence on the choice of repositories used for research. Furthermore, they also influence expectations, preferences, and usage of functionalities, especially regarding filtering and keywords. Content-related functionalities and extended search and filtering functionalities play a significantly more important role in digital cultural collections than for other (academic) search systems. Quality and transparency are even more critical in a discipline such as history, where the methodological focus is on source criticism. Hence, they must be made clear in terms of content, but also in terms of functionalities and systems, to best support source and tool criticism and quality-assured scholarly work.

3.3 Implications for the Design of Digital Cultural Collections

The role of quality and transparency, and the importance of categories, structures and detailed inspection of results thus directly result in requirements for the design of digital cultural collections. They must enable the verifiability and transparency of content and functions. This includes the use of open-source software, comprehensible documentation of frameworks and algorithms used, as well as technical decisions, such as settings for ranking results or displaying results. Instances that guarantee or critically evaluate the quality of collections and tools (review platforms, review journals) can play a role here, as in the case of book publications.

Essential requirements concern criteria that generally apply to research data and content, such as the FAIR principles for scientific data [13], but also qualitative aspects that consider the collection and the content. The main requirements are: findability and accessibility of the collection, content relevance of the collection (outlined by the collection criteria), content relevance of individual objects in the collection (presented through contextualizing information), transparent functionalities (self-explanatory, named), context (who is responsible for what is offered) and sustainability (license, data, infrastructure, documentation).

It is particularly important to consider which functions and presentation methods are initially chosen. In spite of critical use, the accesses that are initially provided get primarily used. This applies not only to search but to all aspects of the interface.

4 Synopsis and Outlook

In conclusion, scholars arrive at relevant results through individually developed strategies and with a high degree of willingness to make use of the available options, even at the cost of a large amount of time – for example, when sifting through large quantities of results or through restrictions and reformulations of the search query. At the same time, scholars often search in a targeted manner, i.e. they already have ideas and expectations regarding suitable entry points, used collections or required results. They differ from other domains primarily in terms of long-term topics, in-depth prior knowledge and methodological self-understanding.

However, the topics of transparency (and thus a parameter that is essentially aimed at the trustworthiness of resources) and quality are also topics that concern web search in general. Factors of quality, credibility, and competencies play a even more prominent role when addressing AI-supported tools, especially generative AI and AI-chatbots. Natural-language search and information acquisition is at first a logical and anticipated step in the further development of search systems. [14] The change of the presentation from a result list to formulated, answers in natural language, implies a change in output, interaction, and perception and leads to new expectations of users. Answers that are returned as formulated text are more detached from the various contents from which they are generated, which makes the questions of quality, transparency, and truthfulness even more pressing. It also raises new questions about copyright and the value of text production.

ChatGPT and other AI-based tools are ultimately a good example to teach and learn the necessity and application of source and tool criticism and search competence. So, gaining search competence, information competence and source competence remains one of the great desiderata of the information age. Since this is directly linked to the subject or domain-specific content of information needs, they must be conveyed in a content-related context, grounded in the respective domains.

References

1. Haber, F.: Digital Past, Munich (2011)
2. Fickers, A.: Towards a New Digital Historicism? Doing History in the Age of Abundance. View J. Eur. Television History Culture 1(1), 19–26 (2012)
3. Blümm, S.E., Funk, S.E., Söring, S.: Die Infrastruktur-Angebote von DARIAH-DE und TextGrid, Information – Wissenschaft & Praxis 66/5–6 (2015), pp. 304–312
4. Katerbow et al.: Digitaler Wandel in den Wissenschaften 2020
5. Universität Luxemburg (Ed.): Digitale Hermeneutik - Ein Update für das kritische Denken in den Geisteswissenschaften. In: science.lu (2018)
6. Frants, V., Shapiro, J., Voiskunskii, V.: Automated Information Retrieval: Theory and Methods (= Library and Information Science 97), San Diego (1997)
7. Warwick, C.: Studying Users in Digital Humanities, in: Digital Humanities in Practice. In: Warwick, C., Terras, M., Nyhan, J., Cambridge (2012)
8. Wilson, T.D.: Models in Information Behavior Research, The Journal of Documentation 55/3 (1999), pp. 249–270, Belkin, N.J., Marchetti, P.G., Cool, C.: BRAQUE: Design of an Interface to Support User Interaction in Information Retrieval, Information Processing and Management 29/3 (1993), pp. 325–344

9. Gläser, J., Laudel, G.: Experteninterviews und qualitative Inhaltsanalyse [Expert interviews and qualitative content analysis], Wiesbaden (2010)
10. Mayring, P.: Qualitative Inhaltsanalyse. Grundlagen und Techniken [Qualitative content analysis. Foundations and techniques], Weinheim (2015)
11. Neovesky, A.: Suche und Relevanz in digitalen wissenschaftlichen Sammlungen – Eine Untersuchung zu Suchstrategien, Auswahlverhalten und Digital Literacy von Historiker*innen, Darmstadt (2023), especially pp. 155–298
12. Schrade, T. Andreas, K.: From Charter Data to Charter Presentation: Thinking about Web Usability in the Regesta Imperii Online, Digital Diplomatics 2013. What is Diplomatics in the Digital Environment? (2013)
13. GO FAIR Homepage. https://www.go-fair.org/fair-principles. Accessed 21 June 2023
14. Lewandowski, D.: Understanding Search Engines. Berlin, Heidelberg (2021), pp. 275–277

ICT and Augmented Reality in Baños de Agua Santa-Ecuador, Tourist Attractions Generation

Jose A. Oleas-Orozco[✉], Patricia Jara-Garzón, Franklin Castillo, and Paulina Amaluisa

Universidad Indoamérica, Ambato, Ecuador
joleas@indoamerica.edu.ec

Abstract. Tourism in Ecuadorian context contributes to 2% GDP's country, it has great potential for growth and exploitation thanks to geographical, natural, cultural, heritage and social factors, among others. These resources are very attractive for internal and external tourism. Baños de Agua Santa, is one of main destinations for local tourists and visitors. Its geographical location, climate and volcanic, mountainous and fluvial landforms have made the place a great interest tourist center. The natural attractions have given way to inhabitant's initiative for man-made tourist attractions creation, a category part of World Tourism Organization UNWTO classification". In this way, "Dinosaurs Park" analysis is presented, a theme park, man-made tourist place, which is mainly supported on ICT use, multimedia, offline web APPs and augmented reality AR, for playful learning experiences generation about prehistoric species not native from the area. The AR Through a mixed, quantitative and qualitative approach, information has been obtained on theme park visitors use and satisfaction showing over 90% of positive ratings. The AR applied in theme park, through mobile devices, shows information about prehistoric species, generating entertainment family experiences and significant knowledge in visitors. The results highlight the place's positive economic benefits since the post-pandemic economic reactivation.

Keywords: ICT · Augmented Reality · Tourism · Man-Made attractions

1 Introduction

For Latin American countries, tourism is an important contribution to their economy [1]. In Ecuadorian scenario, the impulse towards tourist activity has been highlighted with projects that underline its geographical regions, flora, fauna, natural, patrimonial and cultural wealth in UNESCO declaration [2]. Likewise, it can be emphasized that tourist area contributes to 2% of Ecuadorian GDP [3], where its contribution to work generation stands out, for each direct job it produces 3 to 6 indirect jobs [4, 5]. For CELAC [6]:

The group of countries with the lowest contributions in this area of the region includes Bolivia (Plurinational State of), Ecuador, Colombia and Paraguay, where the contribution of tourism to GDP ranges from 6 to 4%, and employment between 6 and 5%, with Paraguay showing the lowest figures.

C. Stephanidis et al. (Eds.): HCII 2023, CCIS 1957, pp. 528–536, 2024.
https://doi.org/10.1007/978-3-031-49212-9_65

In this way, tourism is positioned as an economy engine still growing [7]. However, tourism sector activities were affected by the quarantine produced by the COVID-19 virus, with data at the regional level at a detriment of 0.7 of GDP [6]. Thus, "Tourism is one of the sectors most affected by the coronavirus disease (COVID-19) pandemic, which has impacted economies, livelihoods, public services and opportunities on all continents." [8].

ICT, Augmented Reality AR and Tourism. Among the proposals for globally tourism reactivation, the United Nations has proposed a series of phases, in which the following stand out:

PROMOTION OF INNOVATION AND DIGITALIZATION OF TOURISM ECOSYSTEM. Recovery packages and future development of tourism could make the most of technology use in tourism ecosystem, promote digitization to create innovative solutions and invest in digital skills, particularly for those without a job temporarily and those looking for work. [8]

Thanks to development and advancement of Information and Communication Technologies ICT, information and knowledge in quality and quantity, has had a considerable improvement, eliminating barriers of distance and time [9]. Their constant evolution is present in every aspect of society [10], they facilitate creation, access, communication, manipulation and information transmission [11].

In global information age, social networks, mobile devices applications APP, multimedia, video games, AR augmented reality, among others, are part of ICT. The usefulness of these has been documented in several investigations, as a tool for educational content dissemination [12–14], for inclusive environments generation in special education [15, 16] and inclusive tourism [17], to mention a few. Tourism covers social and economic areas, it finds affinity with ICT use, to improve procedures and innovations of its activity [18]. The ICT benefits in tourism have been documented, at a regional level, in hotel projects about its versatility in data processing [19] and its usefulness within the promotion of attractions and resources [20–22].

AR Augmented Reality is defined as a new and broad field of ICT within virtual reality [23]. In addition, augmented reality is a form of technology produced and developed by superimposing images on objects via computers [24]. Similarly, it can be noted, "While the real situation of virtual reality environment is transferred to the virtual world, the augmented reality environment is enriched with data from the digital environment transmitted to the real world" [25].

This way, is necessary to mention AR as part of ICT contribution inside tourism. Its benefits have been demonstrated in urban heritage terms, helping the tourist experience [26]. Similarly, its great utility has been documented in applications in museums, accommodation, transportation, food and beverage services [25, 27, 28]. Likewise, within mobile devices at specific projects on AR implementation, in APP development for tourism in European cities [29, 30].

Baños de Agua Santa Tourism. Regarding internal tourism, cities that are located as preferential destinations for visitors are: Guayaquil, Baños, Atacames, Quito, Salinas, Esmeraldas among others [4]. The Baños de Agua Santa city, thanks to its geographical position as a connection to Ecuadorian Amazon, is positioned as a destination that stands out within the productive axis of tourism in Tungurahua province. Baños and its Lligua, Río Verde, Ulba and Río Negro parishes are located on the limits of the Pastaza river basin, extending its benefit to other parts of the province, as a nucleus of tourist activities characterized by the provision of defined tourist services and products and specialized [3, 31]. Likewise, Baños de Agua Santa is one of the cantons with the highest concentration of natural tourist attractions compared to the regional total [32], with data from 2015, canton´s rural parishes showed an occupation of their economically active population to tourism of 5% in tourist area, since its main activity was framed in agricultural activities [33, 34]. However, in recent years thanks to its natural attraction's potential, man-made attractions have seen a considerable increase in parish economic activity.

In tourist attractions and resources context, tourist attraction definition can be pointed out:

(…) tourist attraction Almighty God creation, which is tangible, the state of nature as flora and fauna; tourist attraction of the human masterpiece that is intangible, such as museums, historical relics, ancient heritage, cultural arts and entertainment venues. Other tourist attractions were made as a mixture of natural and man-made state. [35]

Therefore, regarding tourist attractions classification, Sancho [36] is taken, based on Swarbrooke [37], mentioned in Moreno [38], for tourist attractions in which it is located in:

• Natural
• Man-made, not designed with the intent to attract visitors.
• Man-made, designed with the intent to attract visitors
• Special events

Within these tourist typologies, specifically those "Man-made, designed with the intention of attracting visitors, are theme parks, a category in which this analysis is framed. Within Baños de Agua Santa canton, on Santa Rosa de Runtún route, there are several artificial tourist attractions that are shown in the following Table 1 (Fig. 1):

Dinosaurios Park theme park, a tourist attraction enters the category "Man-made, designed with the intent to attract visitors" [38], supports its tourist experience in interactivity with Augmented Reality through an offline APP (Fig. 2).

Within an approximate two hectares area, there are several artificial blocks in the shape of prehistoric animals from the Jurassic and Cretaceous periods, which serve as an initial attraction for the place tourist experience (Fig. 3).

Likewise, located along theme park surface there are 30 QR modules, which through "Dinosaurs Park" APP displays virtual 3D prehistoric animations species that can be photographed together with visitors (Fig. 4).

Table 1. Touristic Attractions, Santa Rosa de Runtún

Man-made, designed with the intent to attract visitors	Latitude	Longitude	Altitude
Hanan Park	−1,4149959	−78,4159257	2.412,02
Casa del Árbol	−1,418484	−78,4255811	2.587,31
Criadero de Ciervos	−1,4158811	−78,4218409	2.454,15
Mirador del volcán	−1,4113862	−78,4183457	2.344,29
Orquideario "Los Corazones"	−1,4111737	−78,4160227	2.331,44
AnimalPark Parque Temático	−1,4104667	−78,4165571	2.332,62
La mano de la Pachamama	−1,4137831	−78,4145652	2.400,69
El molino	−1,4128125	−78,4146755	2.387,45
Columpio Fantasías de Volar	−1,408075	−78,4244178	2.423,32
RuntunPark /Dolinda	−1,4112989	−78,4157777	2.331,51
Paintball Baños de Agua Santa	−1,4054282	−78,414136	2.235,55
Dinosaurios Park	−1,4014572	−78,4116419	2.129,12
Mirador Bellavista	−1,3993408	−78,4133983	2.076,29
Café Giratorio	−1,3993408	−78,4133983	2.076,29
Sacha 360	−1,3993408	−78,4133983	2.076,29
Café del Cielo	−1,4046999	−78,417727	2.191,63
Pumamaqui Boutique Gastro Bar	−1,415996	−78,4219759	2.458,58

The APP installed on mobile device provides the services of:

- Augmented reality QR reading showing virtual prehistoric species.
- Linking of AR animations with the camera to capture images.
- Basic species auditory information, environment, location and temporal dating (Fig. 5).

The natural tropical environment of the area, the artificial constructions and the augmented reality provide a different experience, which is shared through social networks by tourists. In the same way, the artificial tourist attraction provides 15 direct jobs with an influx to the theme park and more than 30 indirect jobs that involve tourism, transportation and food agencies in the area. Regarding the influx of tourists, this is detailed in the following Table 2:

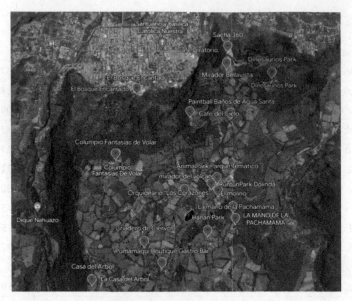

Fig. 1. Image 1. Artificial tourist attractions Geolocation map

Fig. 2. Image 2 Constructions of prehistoric species shape in Dinosaur Park

As an interviews result carried out with 50 tourists, inside the theme park, they showed:

- 90% of positive evaluations, shows a tendency to recommend other people to visit the place.
- 95% of people were pleased with the experience of using the APP.
- 85% of people rated the animations and information provided by the AR APP with positive reviews.
- 90% of the tourists highlighted AR APP interaction, mainly with children.

Fig. 3. Imagen 3. APP screen & AR QR activation codes

Fig. 4. Imagen 4. AR Tridimensional animations

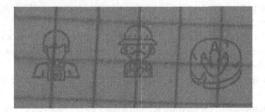

Fig. 5. Imagen 5. APP buttons. Photographic Camera, Audio information and Exit

Table 2. Tourist fluctuation

Fluctuation-local and foreign tourists (Monday-Friday)	Fluctuation-local and foreign tourists (Saturday y Sunday)	Fluctuation-local and foreign tourists (holydays)
50–100	700–1000	1000–2000

Conclusions. Baños de Agua Santa city inhabitants private initiatives, have been able to take advantage of natural attraction of its geolocation, which with creativity have been able to contribute to the sector economy in tourism field, in locations that had different uses and hardly provided more benefit to their owners. On the other hand, Augmented Reality applications offer a different way of interaction between ICT and people, showing in a playful and attractive way information from realities far away from the place where they are located. RA APPs provide an unusual tourist offer, from which service operators can benefit as a novel resource. Likewise, Augmented Reality has great potential to be a technological tool to support tourist experiences.

References

1. Castillo Montesdeoca, E., Martínez Roget, F., Vázquez Rozas, E.: El turismo en Ecuador. Nuevas tendencias en el turismo sostenible y contribución al crecimiento económico. Revista Galega de Economía. **24**(2), 69–88 (2015)
2. de Turismo, M.: Ministerio de Turismo (2015). https://www.turismo.gob.ec/wp-content/upl oads/2015/05/Documento-Proyecto-Ecuador-Potencia-Tur%C3%ADstica.pdf. Accessed 10 junio 2022
3. Santamaría-Freire, E.J. López-Pérez, S.A.: Beneficio social de la actividad turística en Ecuador. Revista Venezolana de Gerencia. **24**(86), 417–484 (2019)
4. Guzmán Barquet, E.: El turismo interno como alternativa creciente de desarrollo turístico del Ecuador. TURYDES: Revista sobre Turismo y Desarrollo local sostenible. **7**, 17 (2014)
5. Chen Mok, S., García Cousin, K.: Puntarenas y el turismo: "Qué ha psado con la "Perla del pacífico"?" InterSedes. **8**(15), 109–131 (2011)
6. Comisión Económica para América Latina y el Caribe (CEPAL): Evaluación de los efectos e impactos de la pandemia de COVID-19 sobre el turismo en América Latina y el Caribe. Aplicación de la metodología para la evaluación de desastres (DaLA). Publicación de las Naciones Unidas, Santiago (2020)
7. Orgaz Agüera, F., Moral Cuadra, S.: El turismo como motor potencial para el desarrollo económico de zonas fronterizas en vías de desarrollo. Un estudio de caso. El Periplo Sustentable. **31**, 1-17 (2016)
8. Unidas, N.: Informe de políticas: La COVID-19 y la transformación del turismo. Naciones Unidas (2020)
9. Jimenez, R., Armando, M.: Desarrollo tecnológico y su impacto en el proceso de globalización económica: Retos y oportunidades para los países en desarrollo en el marco de la era del acceso. Visión Gerencial **1**, 123–150 (2013)
10. Gregorio Pachón, M.: Impacto de las Tic's en el sector Turistico. Universidad de Valladolid, Valladolid (2014)
11. Cámpora Espí, E.: Estudio del impacto de las TIC en el turismo: análisis de su influencia en los habitantes de la ciudad de Gandía durante la planificación de un viaje. Universidad Politecnica de Valencia, Valencia (2013)

12. Oleas-Orozco, J.A., Castillo, F., Saá-Tapia, F., Barrera-Urbina, P.: ICT as a resource for the professional training of drivers. Education and training school for professional drivers, Pelileo-Ecuador. In: Stephanidis, C., Antona, M., Ntoa, S., Salvendy, G. (eds.) HCI International 2022, pp. 399–412. Springer Nature Switzerland, Cham (2022). https://doi.org/10.1007/978-3-031-19682-9_51
13. Navas, E., Oleas, J., Zambrano, M.: Augmented reality to facilitate the process of teaching - learning in school textbooks. In: 2021 Fifth World Conference on Smart Trends in Systems Security and Sustainability (WorldS4), pp. 316–321 (2021)
14. Oleas-Orozco, J., Padilla, N., Cayambe, Á.: Multimedia en la enseñanza de vocabulario de idiomas," in Aportes de ingeniería para desarrollo regional, pp. 421–427. Universidad Técnica del Norte, Ibarra (2017)
15. Jadán-Guerrero, J., Arias-Flores, H., Altamirano, I.: Q'inqu: inclusive board game for the integration of people with disabilities. In: Botto-Tobar, Miguel, et al. (eds.) Applied Technologies. CCIS, vol. 1193, pp. 85–94. Springer, Cham (2019). https://doi.org/10.1007/978-3-030-42517-3_7
16. Oleas-Orozco, J.A., Mena, A., Ripalda, D.: Hearing loss, mobile applications and inclusive social environments: approach to learning sign language for children without disabilities. In: Intelligent Human Systems Integration (IHSI 2022) Integrating People and Intelligent Systems, Venecia (2022)
17. Rodríguez Moreno, D.C.: Tecnologías de Iinformación y comunicación para el turismo inclusive. Revista Facultad de Ciencias Económicas. 16(1), 125–146 (2018)
18. Charne, U.: Turismo y nuevas tecnologías: el desafío de las instituciones educativas. In: XII Jornadas Nacionales y VI Simposio de Investigación-Acción en Turismo: el turismo y los nuevos paradigmas educativos, Mar del Plata (2014)
19. Oliveros Contreras, D., Martínez, G.M.: Efecto de las TIC sobre la gestión de las empresas hoteleras afiliadas a Cotelco de Bucaramanga Santander, Colombia. Revista EAN. 83, 15–30 (2017)
20. Minda, J.C., Ortíz, D.V., Palomeque, T.V.: Promoción turística a Través de las TIC's en el cantón Antonio Ante – Provincia de Imbabura. Tierra Infinita. 7, 45–58 (2021)
21. Tafur Avilés, G., Vélez Barros, C., Alejo Machado, O., Zumba Córdova, M., Jacome Tapia, J.: Desarrollo tecnológico del sector turístico en la ciudad de Guayaquil (Ecuador). Revista Espacios. 39(44), 3 (2018)
22. Brunett, A.L.L., Masache, E.V., Brunett, A.H.L.: Turismo 2.0 como herramienta para promocionar los atractivos culturales de Guayaquil. INNOVA Res. J. 2(6), 154–163 (2017). https://doi.org/10.33890/innova.v2.n6.2017.299
23. Pagani, A., Henriques, J., Stricker, D.: Sensors for location-based augmented reality the example of Galileo and Egnos. In: The International Archives of the Photogrammetry, Remote Sensing and Spatial Information Sciences, Prague (2016)
24. Jacob, J., da Silva, H., Coelho, A., Rodrigues, R.: Towards location-based augmented reality games. Procedia Comput. Sci. 15, 318–319 (2012). https://doi.org/10.1016/j.procs.2012.10.093
25. Özkul, E., Kumlu, S.T.: Augments reality applications in tourism. Int. J. Contemp. Tour. Res. 3(2), 107–122 (2019)
26. Jung, T., Han, D.-I.: Augmented Reality (AR) in urban heritage tourism. e-Rev. Tour. Res. 5, 1–6 (2014)
27. Ferrari, S., Gilli, M.: From the Museums of Objects to the Virtual Museums; An Opportunity for Local Tourism Development1, in New Business Opportunities in the Growing E-Tourism Industry, pp. 255–272. Pennsylvania (USA), IGI Global Publication, Hershey (2015)
28. Cranmer, E.E., ClaudiaDieck, M., Jung, T.: How can tourist attractions profit from augmented reality? In: TimothyJung, M., Dieck, C. (eds.) Augmented Reality and Virtual Reality. PI, pp. 21–32. Springer, Cham (2018). https://doi.org/10.1007/978-3-319-64027-3_2

29. Han, D.-I., Jung, T., Gibson, A.: Dublin AR: implementing augmented reality in tourism. In: Xiang, Z., Tussyadiah, I. (eds.) Information and Communication Technologies in Tourism 2014, pp. 511–523. Springer, Cham (2013). https://doi.org/10.1007/978-3-319-03973-2_37

30. Cibilić, I., Poslončec-Petrić, V., Tominić, K.: Implementing augmented reality in tourism. Proc. ICA **4**, 1–5 (2021). https://doi.org/10.5194/ica-proc-4-21-2021

31. de Tungurahua, G.P.: Sistema Nacional de Información SNI (2015). https://app.sni.gob.ec/sni-link/sni/PORTAL_SNI/data_sigad_plus/sigadplusdocumentofinal/1860000130001_P LAN%20DE%20ORDENAMIENTO%20TERRITORIAL%20TUNGURAHUA%202015-2016_11-05-2016_08-30-43.pdf. Accessed 01 Febrero 2023

32. Instituto Geográfico Militar, Atlas turístico del Ecuador: cuatro mundos para descubrir, Quito: Instituto Geográfico Militar (2020)

33. GAD Parroquial Ulba, "Diagnóstico de la parroquia rural de Ulba. Actualización del plan de desarrollo y ordenamiento territorial (2015–2019), 15 Agosto 2015. https://app.sni.gob.ec/sni-link/sni/PORTAL_SNI/data_sigad_plus/sigadplusdocumentofinal/1865019340001_P DOT%20ULBA_01-07-2016_16-31-11.pdf. Accessed Febrero 2023

34. GAD Municipal Baños de agua Santa, "Plan de Desarrollo y Ordenamiento Territorial 2019–2023 (2019). https://municipiobanos.gob.ec/banos/images/LOTAIP2020/agosto2020/PDOT_2019-2023.pdf. Accessed Enero 2023

35. Erislan: Tourist attraction and the uniqueness of resources on tourist destination in West Java, Indonesia. Rev. Integr. Bus. Econ. Res. **5**(1), 251–266 (2016)

36. Sancho, A.: Introducción al turismo. Organización Mundial del Turismo, Madrid (1998)

37. Swarbrooke, J.: The Development and Management of Visitor Attractions. Routledge, Oxford (2002)

38. Navarro, D.: Recursos turísticos y atractivos turísticos: conceptualización, clasificación y valoración. Cuadernos de Turismo **35**, 335–357 (2015)

Factors Influencing the Use of a Mobile Recommender System in Tourism: A Social Cognitive Theory Perspective

Panca O. Hadi Putra[1]([✉]), Achmad Nizar Hidayanto[1], Mufti Mahmud[2],
Kongkiti Phusavat[3], Bricen Sarido Simamora[1], Dzaky Abdi Al Jabbar[1],
Muhammad Nur Faiz Habibullah[1], and Prissy Azzahra[1]

[1] Universitas Indonesia, Depok, West Java 16424, Indonesia
hadiputra@cs.ui.ac.id
[2] Nottingham Trent University, Nottingham NG1 4FQ, UK
[3] Kasetsart University, 10900, Krung Thep Maha Nakhon, Thailand

Abstract. The growth of circulating information in tourism often makes tourists
have difficulties in choosing tourist attractions. These difficulties may be due to
information overload or inaccurate information. To overcome this, tourists typically use mobile recommender applications such as TripAdvisor and Google Trips
to get recommendations for suitable tourist attractions. This study aims to determine what factors influence the use of a mobile recommender system in tourism,
from the perspective of Social Cognitive Theory. In the context of this theory,
there are three factors that need to be examined, namely the Technical Environment, Social Environment, and Person. Data were collected through an online
questionnaire from 213 valid respondents and analyzed using partial least squares
structural equation modelling technique (PLS-SEM). The results indicate that
critical mass, peer influence, external influence, subjective norm, perceived credibility, subjective norm, outcome expectation, and self-efficacy have a significant
effect on the use of mobile recommender systems in tourism, with self-efficacy
having the biggest influence.

Keywords: Mobile Recommender System · Tourism · Social Cognitive Theory ·
PLS-SEM

1 Introduction

The advancement of the tourism industry is closely related to the development of information technology. Tourism is one of the largest information-based industries in the world,
but the sheer number and diversity of tourist information and interests often confuse
tourists (Gavalas et al. 2014). To overcome the information overload faced by tourists, it
is necessary to implement a mobile recommendation system. The mobile recommender
system is an information filtering system that aims to provide recommendations for
something the user wants (Gavalas et al. 2014). The mobile recommender system is a
technology that can overcome information overload (Ricci 2010). The development of a

C. Stephanidis et al. (Eds.): HCII 2023, CCIS 1957, pp. 537–547, 2024.
https://doi.org/10.1007/978-3-031-49212-9_66

mobile recommendation system for tourism can reduce information overload and make it easier to find appropriate information for tourists (Gavalas et al. 2014). Several mobile recommendation systems in the tourism sector have developed to date in the form of websites and mobile applications that can be accessed anytime and anywhere. Examples of mobile recommender systems in the world of tourism are Traveloka and TripAdvisor. With the mobile recommender system, tourists can get travel recommendations easily, as well as get recommendations that are in accordance with the resulting personalization.

In previous studies, the types and architectural classifications of mobile recommender systems for tourism have been investigated. Research conducted by Gavalas et al. (2014) shows that there are five types of services currently provided in the mobile recommender system in tourism. The five services are 1) attractions or points of interests (POIs) recommendations, 2) tourist services recommendations, 3) collaborative user-generated content and social networking services for tourists, 4) routes and tours recommendations, and 5) personalized multiple-days tour planning. Furthermore, research conducted by Modsching et al. (2008) showed that location-based mobile recommender systems can be effective in supporting tourism. The research tested several methods to see the effectiveness of these methods in encouraging users to visit tourist attractions. Based on this, there is still an opportunity to conduct research on factors that might encourage mobile recommender system users to travel based on the recommendations obtained. If the development of a mobile recommender system can determine the factors that need to be emphasized, then the use of a mobile recommender system will be increasingly useful in tourism. Therefore, this study aims to determine the factors that influence the use of mobile recommender systems in tourism.

This study uses social cognitive theory to model the habits of mobile recommender system users in tourism. Social cognitive theory has been widely accepted to model individual behavior by explaining the relationship between personal cognition, environmental influences, and behavioral outcomes in using a technology (Carillo 2010).

2 Literature Review

2.1 Mobile Recommender System

Recommender system (RS) is a means or tool used to find information. The recommender system was created as a solution to the problem of information overload, which is when a user is given too much information before making a decision, so that the user takes a lot of time to process that information. A recommender system personalizes information provided to users according to the user's wishes by using a special algorithm (Ricci 2010). The mobile recommender system is an implementation of a recommender system that runs in an application on a smart device, for example on a smart phone or tablet. With a recommender system in this form, users can access the information they need anytime and anywhere. This is generated through the process of developing mobile computing in supporting everyday life. At present, mobile recommender systems are used in various industries, for example in e-commerce or tourism (Gavalas et al. 2014).

There are several techniques that can be used in developing a mobile recommender system. These techniques include demographic recommender systems, context-based recommender systems, collaborative filtering recommender systems, knowledge-based recommender systems, and utility-based recommender systems. Although there are several types of techniques, applications in the real world generally use a mixture of these techniques (Barranco et al. 2012).

2.2 Mobile Recommender System Adoption in Tourism

Tourism is a combination of industrial activities and services such as means of transportation, accommodation and entertainment venues, sports centers, restaurants, shops etc. Tourism is one of the world's largest information-based industries. Tourism development is inseparable from technological developments that provide many changes and conveniences in the tourism industry.

Utilization of information technology in tourism activities is called electronic tourism (e-tourism), which is a form of digitalization of tourism (Kazandzhieva and Santana 2019). The trend of global tourism that is increasingly open to new technologies, even more so in the development of digital technology has led to an increase in interest in the field of e-tourism (Buhalis and Licata 2002).

One of the digital technologies currently being developed in e-tourism is the mobile recommender system. The mobile recommender system makes it easier for users to do tourism because it can increase the use of e-tourism in providing more effective information (Ricci 2010). One example of a mobile recommender system in tourism, namely TripAdvisor, is a system that aims to suggest trips, locations and activities for each user and contains certain information to be reviewed, commented on and assessed by other users to assist in the decision-making process in making travel trips.

2.3 Social Cognitive Theory

Social Cognitive Theory (SCT) is a theory developed by Bandura (1977). SCT is a widely accepted theory that models individual behavior by explaining the relationship between personal cognition, environmental influences, and behavioral outcomes (Carillo 2010). SCT has been widely accepted and applied in the information systems (IS) literature (Compeau and Higgins 1995; Carillo 2010; Middleton et al. 2019). Recent studies applied SCT in various contexts such as live streaming games (Lim et al. 2020), omnichannel service usage (Sun et al. 2020), and mobile learning (Almogren and Aljammaz 2022).

The premise of SCT is that human behavior originates from personal interactions (e.g. values, self-efficacy, outcome expectations), environment (e.g. others' behavior, feedback) and behavior (e.g. factors of prior behavior, which called triadic reciprocal causal (Bandura 1977). SCT argues that human behavior is intentionally driven by a person's recognized goals and regulated by exercising some control over internal cognition and action as well as external sources of influence. Many studies have used SCT as a theoretical background for predicting diverse human behavior.

3 Research Model

This research is based on Social Cognitive Theory that is divided into three different groups, namely the Technical Environment, Social Environment, and Person. According to Bandura (1977), a person's behavior can be influenced through his ability to learn through observation. Basically, the Technical Environment includes all technical matters and how satisfactory the results of the use are according to the user. The Social Environment can influence behavior based on recommendations or usage trends based on other users or those closest to them. Finally, humans or Persons include things that come from within the user and the independence of the user in getting the appropriate results. The research model to determine the factors that influence the use of a mobile recommender system in tourism is modeled in Fig. 1.

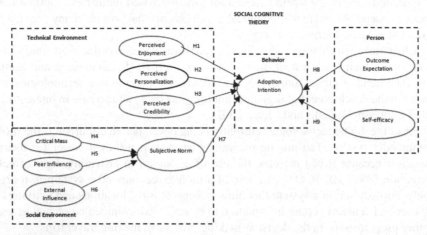

Fig. 1. Proposed research model.

The Technical Environment can affect the Behavior of users in using a technology (Bang and Wojdynski 2016). The technical environment describes perceived enjoyment, perceived personalization, and perceived credibility. Perceived enjoyment is the satisfaction the user gets after carrying out an activity (Ayeh et al. 2013). The more satisfying the tourism recommendations provided by the mobile recommender system, the more likely it is for users to use the mobile recommender system (Childers et al. 2001). Perceived personalization is the adjustment between information about individuals, such as demographic information, browsing history, and brand preferences with recommendations (Bang and Wojdynski 2016). A mobile recommender system that operates in the tourism sector can improve personalization by analyzing destinations that have seen pages in the application used. In this way, the recommendations given will adjust to the user's habits in making decisions, so that users will have more confidence in the mobile recommender system's ability to make recommendations and will continue to use them (Komiak and Benbasat 2006). Perceived credibility, namely the credibility of a source can determine the next action to be taken by the user (Li and Suh 2015). The higher the credibility of the recommendations provided, the more likely it is that these recommendations can increase the user's desire to use the mobile recommender system application continuously. Thus, we hypothesize that:

H1. Perceived Enjoyment influences the desire to use (Adoption Intention) mobile recommender systems in tourism.

H2. Adjustment of information (Perceived Personalization) affects the desire to use (Adoption Intention) mobile recommender system in tourism.

H3. The credibility of the recommended information (Perceived Credibility) influences the desire to use (Adoption Intention) mobile recommender system in tourism.

Critical mass illustrates that in the concept of collaborative consumption, a platform must be able to provide a sufficient variety of choices to embrace their potential consumers (Störby and Strömbladh 2015). A platform is expected to have a variety of features and have the availability of sufficient product/service units to survive in the long term. Meanwhile, peer influence is the influence of one or more peers on someone to carry out activities or actions so that person can be accepted by their network.

Subjective norm is a person's perception of social pressure to perform or not perform behavior (Zhuang et al. 2021). In this theory a person's behavior depends on intention, then the intention to behave depends on attitude and subjective norms. Subjective norms are social influences that influence a person to behave. A person will have a desire for an object or behavior if he is influenced by the people around him to do it or believes that the environment or the people around him support what he is doing. Based on this analysis, we develop the following hypotheses:

H4. Critical mass influences subjective norms in the social environment.

H5. Peer influence affects the subjective norm in the social environment.

H6. External influence affects the subjective norm in the social environment.

Based on theory of reasoned action (TRA) and theory of planned behavior (TPB), subjective norms directly determine behavioral intentions (Ajzen 1991; Ajzen and Fishbein 1975). The more subjective norms are formed, the higher the social pressure that drives the user's intention to continue using the mobile recommender system. Based on this analysis, we develop the following hypotheses:

H7. Subjective norms affect the user's intention to adopt a mobile recommender system in tourism.

In the research model, the person is meant as a person or user who makes decisions. In decision making, there are two variables that can influence, namely outcome expectation and self-efficacy. Self-efficacy is an individual's belief in their ability to be successful in carrying out certain activities (Wang and Xu 2015). Self-efficacy can influence the decision-making process in several ways. Among other things, self-efficacy can increase or decrease one's motivation. One's belief in self-efficacy can be influenced by personal achievements as long as these achievements can produce a sense of accomplishment in an individual (Bandura 1997). Furthermore, self-efficacy also helps regulate the way humans act through four important aspects, namely cognitively, motivationally, emotionally, and in the process of choosing (Bandura 2010). In this research, self-efficacy is meant as a person's level of confidence in his ability to make decisions according to the travel recommendations that have been given by the mobile recommender system he has used.

Result expectation or outcome expectation is defined as the expected consequence of one's own behavior (Compeau and Higgins 1995). Expected results can affect a person's motivation in carrying out an activity because the individual believes that a certain sequence of activities can provide results that are in accordance with expectations (Bandura 1977). Based on this analysis, we develop the following hypotheses:

H8. Outcome Expectation affects the user's intention to adopt the mobile recommender system in tourism.

H9. Self-efficacy influences the user's intention to adopt the mobile recommender system in tourism.

4   Methodology

This research uses measurements based on survey instruments that have been validated in previous studies. The survey consists of several questions that can be grouped into three parts, namely opening questions, demography, and statements about the influence of the mobile recommender system on tourism. The demographics section contains questions about age, mobile phone number, gender, domicile, occupation, and monthly income. The statement section about the influence of the mobile recommender system consists of statements compiled based on variables and indicators that have been determined referring to research journals that have been conducted previously. In this section, each statement is stated on a scale of one to five, namely (1) Strongly disagree; (2) Disagree; (3) Ordinary; (4) Agree; and (5) Strongly agree.

Data collection was carried out using an online questionnaire created on Google Form. Questionnaires were distributed using social media such as LINE, Instagram, and WhatsApp. To attract respondents, a total prize of IDR 200,000 was offered for five lucky respondents. The method used to analyze the data was partial least squares structural equation modeling (PLS-SEM) using the SmartPLS software (Hair et al. 2019).

5   Results and Discussion

5.1   Respondent Demographics

The number of valid respondents from the results of distributing questionnaires was 213 people. The demographics of the respondents are summarized as follows. Most respondents used applications for tourism, namely Instagram (41%) and Traveloka (46.2%), the rest used applications such as TripAdvisor (6%), Google Trips (1.2%), Tiket.com (1.6%), and others (3.9%). Monthly frequency of using the mobile recommender system application is 1–3 times (68.1%) the most chosen, the rest choose > 9 times (4.8%), 7–9 times (2%), 4 - 6 times (8%), and never (17.1%). Survey respondents consisted of men (53%) and women (47%). Most survey respondents were in the age range of 16–20 years (51.6%), the remaining 21–25 years (40.5%), 26–30 years (4.2%), 31–35 years (2.8%), and >35 years (0.9%). Most of the respondents work as students (86%), the rest are civil servants (2.8%), self-employed (2.8%), private employees (4.2%), not working (1.4%), and others (2.8%). Respondents came from Jakarta (45.6%), Bogor (5.1%), Depok (19.5%), Tangerang (7.9%), Bekasi (2.3%), Pekanbaru (1.9%), South Tangerang (1.9%), Medan (1.4%), and others (14.4%). Respondents have the most income/allowance per month in rupiah of IDR 1,000,000 - IDR 5,000,000 (65.6%), the rest choose < IDR 1,000,000 (22.3%), IDR 5,000,000 - IDR 10,000,000 (4.7%), IDR 10,000,000 - IDR 15,000,000 (4.7%), and >15,000,000 (2.8%).

5.2 Measurement Model Assessment

Measurement model testing is carried out using confirmatory factor analysis which is used to test the validity and reliability of the variables that will be used in the structural model testing stage. The validity test was carried out by analyzing the loading factor value and the average variance extracted (AVE) value. Meanwhile, the reliability test was carried out by analyzing the Cronbach alpha value and the composite reliability value. A variable can be said to be valid if the composite reliability value and Cronbach alpha value exceeds 0.7 and the loading factor value is more than 0.6.

Table 1. Values of loading factors, CA, CR, and AVE.

Constructs	Variables	Loading Factors (>0.60)	Cronbach Alpha (CA) (>0.7)	Composite Reliability (CR) (>0.7)	Average Variance Extracted (AVE) (>0.5)
Perceived enjoyment	PE1	0.888	0.803	0.884	0.718
	PE2	0.842			
	PE3	0.812			
Perceived personalization	PP1	0.805	0.780	0.871	0.694
	PP2	0.872			
	PP3	0.820			
Perceived credibility	PC1	0.852	0.846	0.907	0.764
	PC2	0.871			
	PC3	0.899			
Subjective norm	SN1	0.814	0.799	0.882	0.714
	SN2	0.870			
	SN3	0.849			
Critical Mass	CM1	0.831	0.825	0.896	0.741
	CM2	0.814			
	CM3	0.871			
Peer Influence	PI1	0.831	0.860	0.905	0.704
	PI2	0.814			
	PI3	0.886			
	PI4	0.822			
External influence	EI1	0.862	0.730	0.847	0.650
	EI2	0.778			
	EI3	0.775			

(continued)

Table 1. (*continued*)

Constructs	Variables	Loading Factors (>0.60)	Cronbach Alpha (CA) (>0.7)	Composite Reliability (CR) (>0.7)	Average Variance Extracted (AVE) (>0.5)
Outcome expectation	OE1	0.790	0.754	0.859	0.670
	OE2	0.829			
	OE3	0.836			
Self Efficacy	SE2	0.858	0.706	0.871	0.772
	SE3	0.899			
Adoption Intention	AI1	0.905	0.860	0.914	0.781
	AI2	0.882			
	AI3	0.863			

Based on the calculation results above (see Table 1), all variables have loading factor values above 0.6 with the highest loading factor value being AI1 with a value of 0.905 and the lowest loading factor value being EI3 with a value of 0.775. From the results of these calculations, all variables are considered valid. Next is the discriminant validity test that aims to measure the compatibility between constructs. This analysis can be seen through the Fornell-Larcker criterion and cross loadings. A value can be said to be ideal if the variable has a value of AVE latent construct greater than the correlation power of two other variables. Based on the results of the discriminant validity test, we all variables have a value of the AVE latent construct greater than the correlation of the other two variables. It can be concluded that this research model has met discriminant validity values.

5.3 Structural Model Assessment

Hypothesis testing is done by comparing the p-value at the 5% significance level. Therefore, if the p-value test results have a value above 0.05, then the hypothesis will be rejected. The test was carried out using the two-tailed test type. The test results can be seen in Table 2.

Table 2. Table Hasil Uji *Structural Model*

Hypotheses	Path	T-values	P-values	Result
H1	Perceived Enjoyment -> Adoption Intention	1.832	0.067	Rejected
H2	Perceived Personalization -> Adoption Intention	0.161	0.872	Rejected
H3	Perceived Credibility -> Adoption Intention	2.316	0.021	Accepted
H4	Critical Mass -> Subjective Norm	3.092	0.002	Accepted

(*continued*)

Table 2. (*continued*)

Hypotheses	Path	T-values	P-values	Result
H5	Peer Influence -> Subjective Norm	2.980	0.003	Accepted
H6	External Influence -> Subjective Norm	3.490	0.000	Accepted
H7	Subjective Norm -> Adoption Intention	1.989	0.047	Accepted
H8	Outcome Expectation -> Adoption Intention	2.266	0.023	Accepted
H9	Self-efficacy -> Adoption Intention	3.889	0.000	Accepted

The results of hypothesis testing show that two of the nine hypotheses are rejected. The hypothesis that was rejected was H1 (perceived enjoyment affects adoption intention) and H2 (perceived enjoyment influences adoption intention). Both hypotheses were rejected because the resulting p-value was more than 0.05, while the other seven hypotheses, namely H3, H4, H5, H6, H7, H8 and H9, were accepted because the p-value was lower than 0.05.

5.4 Discussion and Implications

By using social cognitive theory, this research has identified models and factors for using a mobile recommender system for tourism. This theory models individual behavior by explaining the relationship between personal cognition, environmental influences, and behavioral outcomes in using a technology. The results of the analysis that have been discussed in the previous sub-section prove that personal cognition, environmental influences, and behavioral results have an effect on using the mobile recommender system.

This research was conducted to find out what factors influence the use of a mobile recommender system in tourism. Based on the calculations that have been done, the strongest predictor is self-efficacy that influences adoption intention. This research has succeeded in identifying the model along with the driving factors for tourists to accept the recommendations provided by the mobile recommender system.

These results indicate that critical mass, peer influence, and external influences affect subjective norms in the social environment. The constructs that influence adoption intention are perceived credibility, self-efficacy, outcome expectations, and subjective norms. This shows that the user's decision to accept the mobile recommendation system recommendation is influenced by internal motivation that comes from knowledge and belief in one's own decisions, and external factors that come from other users around them. However, self-satisfaction and trust in the mobile recommender system did not affect the decision-making process. Based on the research gap that was defined at the beginning of this research, it can be said that these factors need to be considered in giving recommendations on the mobile recommender system so that the recommendations can be well received by tourists.

6 Conclusions

This research aims to determine the factors that influence the use of a mobile recommender system in tourism using social cognitive theory. Based on the research results, it can be concluded that the credibility of the recommended information (perceived credibility) has proven to have a significant effect on the intention to adopt mobile recommender system in tourism. However, for perceived enjoyment and perceived personalization in the mobile recommender system for tourism, there is not enough evidence to show that they have a significant influence on adoption intention. Critical mass, peer influence, and external influence are proven to have significant effects on social subjective norm, which significantly influence the intention to adopt the mobile recommender system for tourism. Then, the outcome expectation and self-efficacy are proven to significantly influence the adoption intention of the mobile recommender system for tourism.

Acknowledgement. This research is supported by Universitas Indonesia through PUTI Q1 research grant number NKB- 295/UN2.RST/HKP.05.00/2023.

References

Almogren, A.S., Aljammaz, N.A.: The integrated social cognitive theory with the TAM model: the impact of M-learning in King Saud University art education. Front. Psychol. **13**, 1050532 (2022)

Ayeh, J.K., Au, N., Law, R.: Do we believe in TripAdvisor? Examining credibility perceptions and online travelers' attitude toward using user-generated content. J. Travel Res. **52**(4), 437–452 (2013)

Ajzen, I.: The theory of planned behavior. Organ. Behav. Hum. Decis. Process. **50**(2), 179–211 (1991)

Ajzen, I., Fishbein, M.: A Bayesian analysis of attribution processes. Psychol. Bull. **82**(2), 261 (1975)

Bandura, A.: Self-efficacy: towards a unifying theory of behavioral change. Psychol. Rev. **84**(2), 191–215 (1977)

Bandura, A.: Self-Efficacy. The Corsini Encyclopedia of Psychology. John Wiley & Sons, London (2010). https://doi.org/10.1002/9780470479216.corpsy0836

Bang, H., Wojdynski, B.W.: Tracking users' visual attention and responses to personalized advertising based on task cognitive demand. Comput. Hum. Behav. **55**, 867–876 (2016)

Barranco, M.J., Noguera, J.M., Castro, J., Martínez, L.: A context-aware mobile recommender system based on location and trajectory. In: Casillas, J., Martínez-López, F., Corchado Rodríguez, J. (eds.) Management Intelligent Systems. Advances in Intelligent Systems and Computing, vol. 171, pp. 153–162. Springer, Berlin, Heidelberg (2012). https://doi.org/10.1007/978-3-642-30864-2_15

Buhalis, D., Licata, M.: The future eTourism intermediaries. Tour. Manage. **23**(3), 207–220 (2002)

Carillo, K.D.: Social cognitive theory in IS research – literature review, criticism, and research agenda. In: Prasad, S.K., Vin, H.M., Sahni, S., Jaiswal, M.P., Thipakorn, B. (eds.) Information Systems, Technology and Management. CCIS, vol. 54, pp. 20–31. Springer, Heidelberg (2010). https://doi.org/10.1007/978-3-642-12035-0_4

Childers, T.L., Carr, C.L., Peck, J., Carson, S.: Hedonic and utilitarian motivations for online retail shopping behavior. J. Retail. **77**(4), 511–535 (2001)

Compeau, D.R., Higgins, C.A.: Application of social cognitive theory to training for computer skills. Inf. Syst. Res. **6**(2), 118–143 (1995)

Gavalas, D., Konstantopoulos, C., Mastakas, K., Pantziou, G.: Mobile recommender systems in tourism. J. Netw. Comput. Appl. **39**, 319–333 (2014). https://doi.org/10.1016/j.jnca.2013.04.006

Hair, J.F., Risher, J.J., Sarstedt, M., Ringle, C.M.: When to use and how to report the results of PLS-SEM. Eur. Bus. Rev. **31**(1), 2–24 (2019)

Kazandzhieva, V., Santana, H.: E-tourism: definition, development and conceptual framework. Tour. Int. Interdiscip. J. **67**(4), 332–350 (2019)

Komiak, B.: The effects of personalization and familiarity on trust and adoption of recommendation agents. MIS Q **30**(4), 941 (2006). https://doi.org/10.2307/25148760

Li, R., Suh, A.: Factors influencing information credibility on social media platforms: evidence from Facebook pages. Procedia Comput. Sci. **72**, 314–328 (2015)

Lim, J.S., Choe, M.J., Zhang, J., Noh, G.Y.: The role of wishful identification, emotional engagement, and parasocial relationships in repeated viewing of live-streaming games: a social cognitive theory perspective. Comput. Hum. Behav. **108**, 106327 (2020)

Middleton, L., Hall, H., Raeside, R.: Applications and applicability of social cognitive theory in information science research. J. Librariansh. Inf. Sci. **51**(4), 927–937 (2019)

Modsching, M., Kramer, R., Hagen, K., Gretzel, U.: Using location-based tracking data to analyze the movements of city tourists. Inf. Technol. Tour. **10**(1), 31–42 (2008). https://doi.org/10.3727/109830508785059011

Ricci, F.: Mobile recommender systems. Inf. Technol. Tour. **12**(3), 205–231 (2010). https://doi.org/10.3727/109830511x12978702284390

Sun, Y., Yang, C., Shen, X.L., Wang, N.: When digitalized customers meet digitalized services: a digitalized social cognitive perspective of omnichannel service usage. Int. J. Inf. Manage. **54**, 102200 (2020)

Darhult Störby, A., Strömbladh, J.: There is something about collaborative lifestyles: a study on motivational factors for participation in collaborative lifestyles (2015)

Wang, S., Xu, H.: Influence of place-based senses of distinctiveness, continuity, self-esteem and self-efficacy on residents' attitudes toward tourism. Tour. Manage. **47**, 241–250 (2015)

Zhuang, X., Hou, X., Feng, Z., Lin, Z., Li, J.: Subjective norms, attitudes, and intentions of AR technology use in tourism experience: the moderating effect of millennials. Leis. Stud. **40**(3), 392–406 (2021)

Up Start–Creative Industries. Assemblage for Immigrant Integration and Creative Heritage Preservation

Paula Reaes Pinto[1] , António Gorgel Pinto[2]([✉]) , and Paulo Simões Rodrigues[1]

[1] CHAIA/University of Évora, Évora, Portugal
{pmrp,psr}@uevora.pt
[2] UNIDCOM-IADE/Universidade Europeia, Lisbon, Portugal
antonio.gorgel@universidadeeuropeia.pt

Abstract. The Up Start-Creative Industries is the result of a collaboration between the Aga Khan Foundation and the University of Évora (UÉ), financed by the Portugal Social Innovation program. It focuses on a synergy founded in design for social innovation, heritage, and management. Within this collaboration, the UÉ has been conducting research on constructing an alternative economic model based on socio-cultural innovation and creative ways with disenfranchised individuals. The hypothesis advanced by the Up Start initiative is based on the possibility of leveraging participants' income and improving living conditions for the communities involved – migrant groups from the Lisbon metropolitan area – through the development of cultural and creative industries, beginning with the identification and mapping of methods, arts, and crafts created by migrants from their cultural heritage.

The paper is composed of three parts: the first part critically analyses the network of interactions between all actors involved in the project, the creation of the Bandim cooperative, and the production of handicrafts, in the light of the concept of assemblage, by the philosophers Deleuze and Guattari; the second part investigates how the preservation of cultural heritage is a key factor for the development of an alternative form of entrepreneurship of disenfranchised people; and the third and last part makes a critical reflection on how Human-Computer Interaction (HCI) and e-commerce can improve communication, access to information, collaboration, and economic sustainability of social and cultural projects such as the Bandim cooperative.

Keywords: Social design · Cultural entrepreneurship · E-commerce

1 Integrating Migrants Through Design, Heritage, and Entrepreneurship

The Up Start is a collaboration project of the Aga Khan Foundation with the University of Évora (UÉ), supported by the Portugal Social Innovation program, which focuses on a synergy rooted in design for social innovation, heritage, and management. Within

C. Stephanidis et al. (Eds.): HCII 2023, CCIS 1957, pp. 548–555, 2024.
https://doi.org/10.1007/978-3-031-49212-9_67

this partnership, the UÉ has been developing research whose central question is creating an alternative economic model based on socio-cultural innovation and creative methods with disenfranchised people. Starting from the identification and mapping of methods, arts, and crafts created by migrants from their cultural heritage, the hypothesis raised by the Up Start initiative is based on the possibility of leveraging the participants' income and enhancing living conditions for the communities engaged – migrant groups from the Lisbon metropolitan area, through the development of cultural and creative industries.

At the root of the problem is the socioeconomic exclusion of underprivileged immigrants living on Lisbon's outskirts. Since the Portuguese overseas territories in Africa gained independence in the 1970s, immigration in Portugal has earned an unfavorable reputation. The problem's scale grew with more immigrant entrances emerging in the 1980s, mainly from Brazil and Asia. Following Portugal's entry into the European Economic Community in 1986, other immigrants arrived from Russia, Ukraine, and Moldavia [2].

Integrating into society is difficult for many immigrants, particularly in finding employment. Entrepreneurship can be a solution in these circumstances because the host communities have local resources and opportunities to facilitate integration. Among the most meaningful resources immigrants possess are age, family, experience, language proficiency, and cultural influences from ethnic opportunities and the immigrant flow. In this context, cultural and creative industries are well-positioned to support immigrant entrepreneurs' business ventures [3].

In light of this sociocultural fabric, promoting the welfare and removing barriers to employment and inclusion can be accomplished by integrating migrants and refugees using cultural and creative processes. Through cultural heterogeneity, creativity, and skills, the cultural and creative industries produce innovation and add economic and social value [4]. Cultural and creative industries typically operate in flexible contexts where people's involvement in various events increases their propensity to change their mindsets, which can also be crucial for valuing their citizenship.

The Up Start initiative offered the chance to improve immigrants' integration and foster their creativity to produce goods that reflect their history and a hybrid culture due to life experiences between their place of origin and Portugal. Using this process, each immigrant artisan who joined the project had their brand created with a specific visual identity design. In turn, it integrates the mother brand and now cooperative Bandim (see Fig. 1), which was co-designed with the first beneficiaries of the project, representing a multi-brand platform and a network of artisans where people of various nationalities work, receive continuous training and support for the exhibition and commercialization of their products and generate their income. Several artists, designers, and stakeholders have collaborated with Bandim in workshops and exhibitions: artists/designers from the UÉ, the artisans/designers Renato Imbroisi and Cristiana Barretto, the A Vida Portuguesa more-than-a-shop project, among others.

2   An Assemblage of Relationships, Interactions, and Crafts

This network of relationships and interactions can be understood as an *assemblage*, as developed by Deleuze and Guattari in their book *A Thousand Plateaus: Capitalism and Schizophrenia* [1], which explores the interconnectedness of all things and how these connections can be harnessed for creative purposes. Within the Up Start and the Bandim large system, the added value is that it connects the participants involved and the objects they produce, the structures on which they are based, including social formations, political systems, and individual subjectivities.

The concept of *assemblage* is rooted in the French word *agencement* employed by Deleuze and Guattari. Le Robert dictionary [5] states that the French word *agencement* derives from the verb *agencer*, which means "to arrange, to lay out, to piece together." This definition of *agencement* is "a construction, an arrangement, or a layout." Thus, for Deleuze and Guattari [1], the concept of *assemblage* is a process of arranging or layout diverse elements based on a relational understanding of the social fabric, according to which human action is originated from interdependent dynamic interconnections between human and more than human realms. In this way, the components of an *assemblage* are constituted by external relations that make possible the constant reconfiguration of it.

Assemblages are dynamic arrangements or formations that bring together various elements, conditions, and agents which are distinguished by three characteristics: their conditions, their components, and their actors, which Deleuze and Guattari [1] refer to as the *abstract machine*, the *concrete assemblage*, and the *personae*.

2.1 Conditions – *Abstract Machine*

The underlying policies, frameworks, and organizing ideas that guide an *assemblage's* operation are referred to as its conditions. Deleuze and Guattari refer to this feature as the *abstract machine*, which embodies the collection of abstract relations and possibilities that define an *assemblage's* potential or virtuality. It includes the abstract tendencies, codes, and processes that govern how the *assemblage* functions and changes. The *abstract machine* is flexible and open to constant reconfiguration as well as potential connections with other *assemblages*.

2.2 Elements – *Concrete Assemblage*

The real parts or things that combine to make up an *assemblage* are called their elements. Depending on the context, these components can be human or nonhuman, tangible or immaterial, and have various characteristics. They can be material things, social structures, discourses, technological innovations, ideas, or even affects and desires. The parts come together and interact within a particular physical and chronological context in the *concrete assemblage*, which is their palpable manifestation or actualization. The *concrete assemblage*, which incorporates the *assemblage's* components in a specific arrangement, is the realized or manifested form of the *assemblage*.

2.3 Agents – *Personae*

The agents of an *assemblage* are the actors or subjects who contribute to its construction and operation. Deleuze and Guattari refer to these agents as *personae*. Individuals, groups, organizations, or even non-human entities having agency within the *assemblage* are examples of *personae*. They have the ability to act and affect the *assemblage*, helping it to function and transform. *Personae* may include animals, robots, institutions, or even abstract forces in addition to human players. Each *personae* contributes to the *assemblage*, its own wants, ambitions, and capacities, impacting its dynamics and contributing to its overall becoming [1].

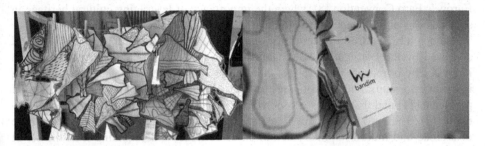

Fig. 1. Bandim branding and products in a Lisbon shop, 2022.

2.4 Bandim *Assemblage*

An *assemblage*, such as the cooperative Bandim that brings together people with different cultures and know-how, crafts, and small businesses, is a collection that forms a functional whole in its multiplicity nature. It is an active and dynamic entity that is constantly in the process of assembling and disassembling itself. Bandim is a platform that addresses issues such as immigration, politics, cultural heritage, willingness to give immigrants a voice, search for newcomer integration into new culture, workshops, exhibitions, and dialogue with potential immigrant participants to listen to their needs in participating in the project, among others, which brought us together and compelled us to assemble. In this sense, Bandim is an *assemblage* that is not simply a material entity but a complex network of relationships and interactions constantly evolving and adapting to its environment. As Ezio Manzini [6] states, social innovation "is based on collaboration and because it regenerates the commons is critical for dominant ideas and practices, and what it proposes could constitute concrete steps towards social and environmental sustainability."

3 An Alternate Form of Entrepreneurship and Creative Heritage Preservation

Regarding the focus on including immigrants living in Portugal, a particular issue of the Up Start project is the objective of representing an alternative form of entrepreneurship and creative heritage preservation. The Bandim cooperative constitutes a social assemblage centered on co-designing innovative forms of entrepreneurship with various stakeholders and participants, aiming to boost Lisbon's sustainable sociocultural development.

A key component of how communities represent themselves is through their cultural heritage, which defines who belongs within them [7]. In addition to fostering economic sustainability, the Up Start project aims to support immigrants' societal integration, specifically through valorizing their heritage, so that their social and cultural identities aren't a variable of exclusion in communities of destination but rather of inclusion. It plans to do this by basing its decisions on the guidelines outlined in the Council of Europe's Faro Convention [8], where the importance of leveraging cultural heritage in societies was highlighted by its significance.

Adopted by the Committee of Ministers of the Council of Europe in 2005 [9] and approved by the Portuguese parliament in 2008 [10], the so-called Faro Convention innovates by proposing the idea that cultural heritage can be a means of empowering individuals, groups, and communities to find solutions to social, political and cultural problems [11] and that heritage-based activities can contribute to sustainable development [12]. The Faro Convention does so, firstly, by placing human values at the base of a broad and multidisciplinary definition of heritage, understanding it as the set of resources inherited from the past, regardless of how they are manifested in the present, which individuals, groups and communities identify as the expression of their values, beliefs, knowledge, and traditions (Article 2). Secondly, by establishing that the main goal of heritage conservation and its sustainable use is human development and quality of life; by establishing that the conservation of heritage and its sustainable use has human development and quality of life as its main goal and that heritage has a role in building a more sustainable, peaceful, and democratic society, as well as in the promotion of cultural diversity (Article 1). Finally, when considering that heritage can be used as a resource for sustainable development and a life with quality in societies in constant evolution (Article 2); that all individuals, groups, and communities have the right to benefit from cultural heritage and also to contribute to its enrichment (Article 4); that heritage can be a resource for economic, political, social and cultural development (Articles 8 and 10); that it is possible to exploit the potential of materials, techniques, and skills based on tradition in contemporary applications (Article 9); and that it should promote high-quality work through systems of professional qualifications and accreditation of individuals, businesses and institutions (Article 9). This means that heritage stems from the signification and re-signification of past resources. These resources only become heritage when establishing socio-cultural relationships with or between individuals and become devices for creating memories and identities.

It is precisely this broad conceptualization of heritage that the UpStart project puts into practice. It started by creating a professional qualification and accreditation system, identifying individuals from migrant communities with artistic skills, providing their development through technical and artistic training, and supporting their commercialization through associations such as Bandim. The qualification process consisted of providing project participants with the necessary skills to explore the potential of applying materials, techniques, and traditional know-how brought by migrants, as well as their memories or aspects of their cultural identity, to contemporary uses, including the creation of new products. The main goal is to provide migrant individuals with skills that can be a means of sustainability and, consequently, of social and economic integration that does not imply the total loss of their memories and their original identity. On the contrary, being possible to have a means of sustainability and integration based on traditions and cultural identities of origin, migrant individuals will be able to contribute to a more humanized, peaceful, democratic and culturally diversified society. In this way, they benefit from and, at the same time, by developing new activities and creating new products, they enrich cultural heritage.

4   Enhancing Sociocultural Support Through HCI and e-commerce

Another critical dimension of the research is related to the importance of Human-Computer Interaction (HCI) and e-commerce to social and cultural projects like Bandim and how its beneficiaries and stakeholders can enhance communication, improve access to information, facilitate collaboration, and transform the way individuals and organizations interact and conduct transactions, which is a key aspect for the project's economic sustainability. This part of the project is being developed in collaboration with the Bachelor of Computer Engineering and Business Informatics from IADE–Universidade Europeia (Lisbon, Portugal), where students are developing an e-commerce website for Bandim.

The complete satisfaction and fulfillment that users may feel when interacting with an e-commerce website during their online buying experience is called the e-commerce user experience. Usability, functionality, design, and the emotional reaction triggered among users are essential qualities to consider in this context. A satisfying online shopping experience is essential for attracting customers, fostering trust, and promoting return business. Usability is crucial in e-commerce to enhance user experience, increase interaction, and build customer satisfaction. Also relevant is the need for clear and intuitive navigation, streamlined checkout processes, informative product descriptions, and responsive design to create a positive user experience in online shopping [13].

This enhanced access to information provided by HCI and e-commerce enables social institutions to disseminate information and products more widely and easily. Users can access the information they need to enter the project realm through a specific website with an online database of Bandim products for commercialization. Parallel to the commercial approach, the website will also include a more ethnographic dimension with cultural resources, research findings, and institutional support for participants. This use of HCI in the Upstart project is a powerful tool to bridge information gaps and empower individuals with valuable resources.

The Bandim e-commerce platform aims to expand market reach not just in Lisbon but to other important cities and establish a significant global network of supporters. E-commerce has revolutionized how social institutions, including businesses, nonprofits, and government agencies, engage with their target audiences. Retailers gained plenty of expertise with digitalization, namely after the Covid-19 epidemic, in which e-commerce and retail played a crucial role in the economy and society [14]. By leveraging online marketplaces, organizations can reach customers beyond geographical boundaries, extending their market reach globally. Taking into consideration that Bandim is a cooperative organization available to immigrants, the website will also be a powerful way of spreading the whole project dynamics to the participants' countries of origin, which can be a way of valuing local heritage and know-how and engaging people in a pro-active attitude of establishing their craft businesses without the need of migration. Also important in this context is integrating efficient transactions and services within the Bandim e-commerce platform, which consolidates safe currency transactions and service delivery, making processes more efficient for immigrants and social organizations.

Other opportunities may flourish through HCI collaborative work environments. The Bandim website, with integrated e-commerce, can leverage collaborative work environments globally, enabling social institutions to engage in remote collaboration and knowledge sharing. Thus, shortly, the project aims the development of virtual workspaces, international initiatives, and online resource sharing to facilitate teamwork and cooperation among immigrants and locals within their communities.

5 Conclusion

Inspired by the *assemblage* concept developed by Deleuze and Guattari, the Up Start project, particularly the Bandim cooperative, emphasizes the diverse and dynamic aspects of social, cultural, and material formations. This *assemblage* approach is formed by the interaction of conditions, elements, and agents and is neither fixed nor predefined. It is constantly changing, molded by their *abstract machines*, realized in *concrete assemblages*, and enacted by *personae*. This paradigm provides a wide range of linkages, interactions, and possibilities, stressing *assemblages'* rhizomatic and non-hierarchical nature. All these dynamic arrangements or formations are strengthened by the efforts for social and economic integration of the communities involved in the project by enhancing their cultural heritage. In this regard, the Bandim *assemblage* cooperative is creative and fruitful. A fruitful *assemblage* produces new ways of expression, new geographical or spatial organizations, institutions, behaviors, or realizations. All this expanded process is anchored in the HCI and e-commerce of the Bandim cooperative to ensure the project's economic sustainability.

The website will also effectively communicate the project dynamics to the participants' home countries. It can be a way to value local heritage and know-how and engage people proactively in establishing their craft businesses without the need for migration. Bandim is a cooperative organization open to immigrants whose website with integrated e-commerce has the potential to take advantage of teamwork environments in a global setting, allowing social institutions to collaborate remotely and share knowledge. As a result, the project hopes to create virtual workspaces, global initiatives, and online resource sharing to encourage collaboration and teamwork between locals and immigrants in their communities. Bandim will create a new reality through various interconnections, many of which will be unanticipated.

References

1. Deleuze, G., Guattari, F.: A thousand plateaus: capitalism and schizophrenia. University of Minnesota Press (1987)
2. Peixoto, J.: Strong market, weak state: the case of recent foreign immigration in Portugal. J. Ethn. Migr. Stud. **28**(3), 483–497 (2010)

3. Oliveira, C.R.: Empresários de origem cabo-verdiana em Portugal: estratégias de mobilidade ou situações de sobrevivência material temporária? In: Oficina do CES, p. 243 (2006)
4. Gustafson, C., Lazzaro, E.: The innovative response of cultural and creative industries to major European societal challenges: toward a knowledge and competence base. Sustainability **13**, 13267 (2021)
5. Le Robert Dico en ligne. https://dictionnaire.lerobert.com/definition/agencement. Accessed 13 June 2023
6. Manzini, E.: Politics of the Everyday. Bloomsbury, New York (2019)
7. Rose, D. V: Património cultural em conflito: da violência à reparação. In: Jerónimo, Miguel Bandeira; Rossa, Walter (coord.), Patrimónios Contestados. Lisboa: Público (2029)
8. Council of Europe: Council of Europe framework convention on the value of cultural heritage for society. In: Council of Europe Treaty Series, No. 199 (2005). https://rm.coe.int/168008 3746. Accessed 13 June 2023
9. Conselho da Europa: A Convenção de Faro: Património cultural, um caminho para o futuro. Ministério da Cultura, Direção Geral do Património, Lisboa (2021). https://rm.coe.int/a-con vencao-de-faro-patrimonio-cultural-um-caminho-para-o-futuro-/1680a3e95e. Accessed 13 June 2023
10. Diário da República: 1ª série, no. 177, 12 setembro, pp. 6640–6651 (2008)
11. Colomer, L.: Exploring participatory heritage governance after the EU faro convention. J. Cult. Herit. Manage. Sustain. Dev. (2021). https://doi.org/10.1108/JCHMSD-03-2021-0041/ full/html. Accessed 13 June 2023
12. Fairclough, G., et al.: The faro convention, a new paradigm for socially – and culturally – sustainable heritage action? In: Kyrrypa/Cultura. S.l., no. 8, pp. 9–19, march 2015. https:// journals.cultcenter.net/index.php/culture/article/view/111. Accessed 13 June 2023
13. Nielsen, J., Snyder, C., Molich, R., Farrell, S.E.: E-commerce user experience (2001). https:// openlibrary.org/books/OL3658534M/E-commerce_user_experience. Accessed 13 June 2023
14. Cassetti, L.: A word from e-commerce Europe. European e-commerce report (2022). https:// ecommerce-europe.eu/wp-content/uploads/2022/06/CMI2022_FullVersion_LIGHT_v2.pdf. Accessed 13 June 2023

COVID-Free Interaction with Public Displays

Antonis Chatziantoniou[1], Nikolaos Menelaos Stivaktakis[1], Michalis Sifakis[1],
Emmanouil Zidianakis[1], George Margetis[1(✉)], George Paparoulis[1],
Nikolaos Partarakis[1], and Constantine Stephanidis[1,2]

[1] Institute of Computer Science, Foundation for Research and Technology—Hellas (FORTH),
70013 Heraklion, Crete, Greece
{hatjiant,nstivaktak,misi,zidian,gmarget,groulis,partarak,
cs}@ics.forth.gr
[2] Computer Science Department, School of Sciences and Engineering, University of Crete,
70013 Heraklion, Crete, Greece

Abstract. In response to the COVID-19 pandemic, there has been a need to reassess and adapt interaction modalities to prioritize hygiene and safety. Contactless interaction has emerged as a potentially effective approach for applications on publicly available interactive systems. This paper introduces an interactive system designed for contactless interaction with publicly accessible information displays. The system was implemented and deployed in a busy bank branch in Greece, catering to a high volume of users. Its goal is to provide a safe and hygienic way for users to engage with interactive information displays. By enabling contactless interaction, the system addresses the concerns and precautions associated with the pandemic, while maintaining a high level of accessibility and user engagement.

Keywords: Information displays · interactive information system · touchless interaction · interaction paradigms

1 Introduction

The abundance of interactive installations addressing the public for providing information regarding diverse application domains testifies that it is a good practice that has been followed for many years. A prominent category of such systems is interactive kiosks through which people can get information, but also conduct transactions varying from bill payment to organizing a sightseeing trip in a destination. The most common interaction modality provided by such systems is touch, as it has become a de facto standard due to its popularity. However, with the proliferation of IoT and the advent of ubiquitous computing, novel interactive public systems have emerged providing enriched interplay with the users and enabling diverse natural ways of interaction, appropriately designed as per the context of use [1–3].

Since the COVID-19 pandemic's outbreak, social distancing and extended hygiene rules have become important in our life. Even after the World Health Organization International Health Regulations Emergency Committee officially concurred that the

C. Stephanidis et al. (Eds.): HCII 2023, CCIS 1957, pp. 556–563, 2024.
https://doi.org/10.1007/978-3-031-49212-9_68

public health emergency of international concern should end (May 2023)[1], numerous practices that individuals adopted during the pandemic continue to persist. In this respect, considering that publicly available devices used by numerous people should be used in as much as possible contactless manner, a considerable number of interaction approaches emerged trying to address this concern [4–6].

This work has been developed under a commission by a large Bank in Greece, the Piraeus Bank, aiming to develop a temporary interactive installation at their seminal e-Branch at St. Titus Square in Heraklion, related to the cultural heritage and tourism product of the island of Crete. The system was successfully installed at the e-Branch premises in July 2020, encouraging customers to (re)discover Crete while highlighting three pivotal elements of the island: the sea, the land, and the people of Crete.

Aiming to facilitate contactless interaction with the interactive installation, user interaction is achieved through an innovative augmented physical object operated via close-distance gestures rather than touch. More specifically, the interaction controller is a three-part showcase made of glass, where each part is specifically dedicated to showcasing a distinct key element of the island. When a user selects a particular part, by placing their hand over the appropriate showcase compartment, it becomes illuminated, triggering the display of corresponding images on two large screens. It is worth noticing the images displayed are courtesy of the Region of Crete.

The design and implementation of this work took place during the COVID-19 pandemic, mandating contactless interaction as the only interaction option. This objective was achieved through the incorporation of specially developed IoT sensors, which were meticulously designed and integrated into the system to support the seamless and touch-free engagement of users.

This paper is structured as follows. Section 2 provides insights into background and related work. Section 3 introduces the methodology employed for the design and implementation of the syste. Section 4 presents the system in more detail. Finally, Sect. 5 concludes this work and discusses future extensions.

2 Background and Related Work

Since the outbreak of the pandemic, social interaction with public displays has been put under scrutiny due to the shortage of empirical evidence regarding the potential for contamination in such interactions. Research on medical facilities has shown that the air and surfaces are locations where the virus can be traced and thus are susceptible to contaminating others [7–10]. Although the main COVID-19 transmission route is aerial, via exposure to droplets and aerosols contaminated with the virus [11], coronavirus has been also found in solid surfaces [12, 13]. For example, research results from devices daily in use have shown that random ATM checks returned a positive result for COVID-19 [14]. At the same time, another associated risk was identified in cash bills used for financial transactions [15, 16].

---

[1] https://www.who.int/news/item/05-05-2023-statement-on-the-fifteenth-meeting-of-the-international-health-regulations-(2005)-emergency-committee-regarding-the-coronavirus-disease-(covid-19)-pandemic.

The risks associated with the interaction with public displays have reduced the usage of ATMs during the pandemic and can inherently affect any form of interaction in public that is based on some form of physical contact (e.g. public touch screens, buttons, keypads, etc.).

In the past decades, several solutions have been proposed to support touchless interaction with information systems, including computer vision approaches (e.g. [3]), approaches based on commercial devices such as depth sensors (e.g. [17]), and IR-based technologies (e.g. [18]). Based on these technologies, several interaction methods were implemented including touch, hand gestures, body movement, interaction with objects, etc. [19–23]. All the aforementioned technologies have been proven to be adequate for various interaction scenarios, but pose limitations when employed in public spaces mainly due to instability in illumination and infrared radiation. At the same time, several interaction-related challenges emerge, such as discovering the interactivity of systems, performing the correct interaction gesture, and being engaged by the system and its content in a given social setting [24].

Motivated by the above shortcomings, this work is providing a method and technical implementation of a remote, cost-efficient, and contactless interaction paradigm for public displays, aiming to address existing interaction challenges by employing a small set of simple interaction gestures to achieve discoverability and learnability.

3   System Design and Interaction Implementation

The design process followed was iterative, spanning three directions: user interface design, interaction design, and industrial design. With regard to the latter, the design of the enclosure of the system was conducted in 3D using CAD software to allow the team to assess its affordances and usability, present to the clients how the design will fit into their space, and of course, simplify the production by providing schematics and accurate dimensions to the construction team. Figure 1 presents the design of the main part of the system through which user interaction is provided. Three glass displays are visualized each one presenting parts from the natural landscape of Crete.

Interaction design embraced a straightforward approach, utilizing hover gestures over three designated hotspots placed in front of each display. In more detail, when a user hovers their hand over a display, the system provides feedback by illuminating the corresponding display. In parallel, a signal is generated triggering the execution of the system action associated with that particular display. The overview of the design of the installation is shown in Fig. 2.

For the realization of the contactless interaction, infrared sonars are placed on top of the display in a position appropriately selected to cover only the range of the specific display. All sensors are wired up to an Arduino board which in turn hosts the control software which transmits the reading to the computer hosting the interactive application through a USB serial port.

Finally, user interface design employed a minimalis approach as well, prioritizing the presentation of images accompanied by concise and informative texts.

Fig. 1. Design of the interactive displays.

Fig. 2. Overview of the design of the installation

4   Application

The proposed interactive system offers an alternative to traditional information kiosks typically found in museums for browsing item collections. Instead of navigating through complex menus, visitors can browse all the available artifacts effortlessly. More specifically, the metaphor of a flipping book organized in three main categories was adopted, with each category corresponding to a display showcase.

To delve into a specific information category, users simply hover their hand over the respective glass case, causing the virtual book to open to the pertinent category, enabling them to start exploring the content therein. In order to do so, they use the same interaction modality, hovering their hands over the glass cases. When the rightmost glass case is hovered over, a "next" action is performed, whereas hovering over the leftmost case triggers a "previous" action. Accordingly, the system showcases on the lateral display panels the next or previous information item of the selected category.

Furthermore, when users desire to activate an interactive element presented they can hover their hand over the middle glass case initiating the "select" action. With this simplified gesture vocabulary, visitors can seamlessly browse the entire collection of the interactive system. Figure 3 presents an example of a person interacting with the display hovering over the rightmost glass case, thus triggering a "next" action. Correspondingly, the virtual book displayed on the screens flips to the next page.. A close-up of this contact-free interaction can be seen in Fig. 4.

Fig. 3. Example of user interaction with the system

Fig. 4. Close-up view of the interaction

5   Conclusion

In this paper, we proposed a technical solution that effectively caters to touchless interaction requirements in simple scenarios without the need for high-end equipment. The interactive installation, which was developed for the Piraeus Bank e-Branch in Heraklion, Crete, provides a contactless and engaging method for users to explore information related to the cultural heritage and tourism offerings of the island. By utilizing close distance gesture interaction and custom-built IoT sensors, the system allows users to navigate through different information categories by hovering their hands over glass displays, each associated with a particular content category, this eliminating the need for physical touch. Furthermore, a simple and intuitive paradigm was adopted, reminiscent of a flipping book, enabling the users to navigate content in a straightforward manner. The use of infrared sonars and an Arduino board facilitated contactless interaction, transmitting user actions to the interactive application running on a computer.

The design and implementation of the interactive installation took into consideration the challenges imposed by the COVID-19 pandemic, prioritizing contactless interaction to ensure the safety and well-being of users. By providing an alternative to traditional information kiosks, the system offers a novel and engaging way for visitors to interact with the cultural heritage and tourism information of Crete.

Overall, the developed system, which has been available to the public since July 2020 until today, demonstrates the feasibility and effectiveness of contactless interaction in public displays, opening up possibilities for future applications in various domains where public health and safety are paramount considerations.

Future work will focus on user-based in situ studies, aiming to assess the usability of the described system, user engagement, as well as the discoverability and learnability of the interaction modality.

Acknowledgment. The authors thank Piraeus Bank for their support and collaboration in this research work's context.

References

1. Birliraki, C., et al.: Interactive edutainment: a technologically enhanced theme park. In: Stephanidis, C. (ed.) HCI International 2019 - Posters. Communications in Computer and Information Science, vol. 1034, pp. 549–559. Springer, Cham (2019). https://doi.org/10.1007/978-3-030-23525-3_75
2. Partarakis, N., et al.: Interactive city information point: your guide to Heraklion city. In: Stephanidis, C. (ed.) HCI International 2018 – Posters' Extended Abstracts. Communications in Computer and Information Science, vol. 852, pp. 204–212. Springer, Cham (2018). https://doi.org/10.1007/978-3-319-92285-0_29
3. Margetis, G., et al.: Enhancing education through natural interaction with physical paper. Univ. Access Inf. Soc. **14**, 427–447 (2015)
4. Li, M., Yin, D., Qiu, H., Bai, B.: Examining the effects of AI contactless services on customer psychological safety, perceived value, and hospitality service quality during the COVID-19 pandemic. J. Hosp. Market. Manag. **31**(1), 24–48 (2022)
5. Kumar, S.S., Dashtipour, K., Abbasi, Q.H., Imran, M.A., Ahmad, W.: A review on wearable and contactless sensing for COVID-19 with policy challenges. Front. Commun. Netw. **2**, 636293 (2021)
6. O'Leary, D.E.: Evolving information systems and technology research issues for COVID-19 and other pandemics. J. Organ. Comput. Electron. Commer. **30**(1), 1–8 (2020)
7. Razzini, K., et al.: SARS-CoV-2 RNA detection in the air and on surfaces in the COVID-19 ward of a hospital in Milan Italy. Sci. Total Environ. **742**, 140540 (2020)
8. Ben-Shmuel, A., et al.: Detection and infectivity potential of severe acute respiratory syndrome coronavirus 2 (SARS-CoV-2) environmental contamination in isolation units and quarantine facilities. Clin. Microbiol. Infect. **26**(12), 1658–1662 (2020)
9. Butot, S., Baert, L., Zuber, S.: Assessment of antiviral coatings for high-touch surfaces by using human coronaviruses HCoV-229E and SARS-CoV-2. Appl. Environ. Microbiol. **87**(19), e01098-e1121 (2021)
10. Kanamori, H., Weber, D.J., Rutala, W.A.: The role of the healthcare surface environment in SARS-CoV-2 transmission and potential control measures. Clin. Infect. Dis. **28**, ciaa1467 (2020)
11. Lu, R., et al.: Genomic characterisation and epidemiology of 2019 novel coronavirus: implications for virus origins and receptor binding. Lancet (2020). https://doi.org/10.1016/S0140-6736(20)30251-8
12. Orenes-Piñero, E., Baño, F., Navas-Carrillo, D.: Evidences of SARS-CoV-2 virus air transmission indoors using several untouched surfaces: a pilot study. Sci. Total Environ. **751**, 142317 (2021)
13. Elbadawy, H.M., et al.: The detection of SARS-CoV-2 in outpatient clinics and public facilities during the COVID-19 pandemic. J. Med. Virol. **93**(5), 2955–2961 (2021)
14. Górny, R.L., Stobnicka-Kupiec, A., Gołofit-Szymczak, M., Cyprowski, M., Ławniczek-Wałczyk, A.: Viral, bacterial, and fungal contamination of automated teller machines (ATMs). Ann. Agric. Environ. Med. **29**(3), 383 (2022)
15. Tamele, B., Zamora-Pérez, A., Litardi, C., Howes, J., Steinmann, E., Todt, D.: Catch me (if you can): assessing the risk of SARS-CoV-2 transmission via euro cash. ECB Occasional Paper, (2021/259) (2021)

16. Pal, R., Bhadada, S.K.: Cash, currency and COVID-19. Postgrad. Med. J. **96**(1137), 427–428 (2020)
17. Grammenos, D., Margetis, G., Koutlemanis, P., Zabulis, X.: 53.090 Virtual Rusks = 510 real smiles using a fun Exergame installation for advertising traditional food products. In: Nijholt, A., Romão, T., Reidsma, D. (eds.) Advances in Computer Entertainment. Lecture Notes in Computer Science, vol. 7624, pp. 214–229. Springer, Heidelberg (2012). https://doi.org/10.1007/978-3-642-34292-9_15
18. Marin, G., Dominio, F., Zanuttigh, P.: Hand gesture recognition with leap motion and kinect devices. In 2014 IEEE International Conference on Image Processing (ICIP), pp. 1565–1569. IEEE (2014)
19. Partarakis, N., Antona, M., Stephanidis, C.: Adaptable, personalizable and multi user museum exhibits. Curat. Digit.: Space Art Interact., 167–179 (2016)
20. Zidianakis, E., Partarakis, N., Antona, M., Stephanidis, C.: Building a sensory infrastructure to support interaction and monitoring in ambient intelligence environments. In: Streitz, N., Markopoulos, P. (eds.) Distributed, Ambient, and Pervasive Interactions. Lecture Notes in Computer Science, vol. 8530, pp. 519–529. Springer, Cham (2014). https://doi.org/10.1007/978-3-319-07788-8_48
21. Grammenos, D., et al.: Rapid Prototyping of an AmI-augmented office environment demonstrator. In: Jacko, J.A. (ed.) Human-Computer Interaction. Ambient, Ubiquitous and Intelligent Interaction. Lecture Notes in Computer Science, vol. 5612, pp. 397–406. Springer, Heidelberg (2009). https://doi.org/10.1007/978-3-642-02580-8_43
22. Zidianakis, E., et al.: Employing ambient intelligence technologies to adapt games to children's playing maturity. In: Antona, M., Stephanidis, C. (eds.) Universal Access in Human-Computer Interaction. Access to Learning, Health and Well-Being. Lecture Notes in Computer Science, vol. 9177, pp. 577–589. Springer, Cham (2015). https://doi.org/10.1007/978-3-319-20684-4_56
23. Ntoa, S., Birliraki, C., Drossis, G., Margetis, G., Adami, I., Stephanidis, C.: UX design of a big data visualization application supporting gesture-based interaction with a large display. In: Yamamoto, S. (ed.) Human Interface and the Management of Information: Information, Knowledge and Interaction Design. Lecture Notes in Computer Science, vol. 10273, pp. 248–265. Springer, Cham (2017). https://doi.org/10.1007/978-3-319-58521-5_20
24. Hardy, J., Rukzio, E., Davies, N.: Real world responses to interactive gesture based public displays. In: Proceedings of the 10th International Conference on Mobile and Ubiquitous Multimedia, pp. 33–39 (2011)

Interactive Media and Local Art Centered Mobile Modular Museum Design

Liyuan Zhai(✉)

Xiamen University, Xiamen, China
1971426734@qq.com

Abstract. The core function of museums is to store cultural and natural relics. However, the disadvantages of traditional museums, have been unable to meet the diversified needs of people such as uniform layout, lack of affinity and insufficient connections between disparate regions. Correspondingly, the emergence of portable miniature museums has become an effective solution. As a modular, lightweight and environmentally friendly detachable-type mobile museum, compared with the general museum and exhibition space, this fresh museum with a high degree of flexibility and versatility in site planning, target audience, overall layout and material application, which capable of offering comprehensive and aesthetic experience. This project gives priority to explore how to improve the feelings of participants in the venue and encourages users to actively immerse themselves in the created environment. Additionally, this paper uses a method different from the traditional popularization of intangible cultural heritage, adopts the movable modular building as the exhibition venue, and through the digital interactive design, makes the southern Fujian culture break through the regional, space and time limitations, creates a cultural atmosphere for the whole people to view the exhibition, and arouses the audience's emotional identification and protection awareness of intangible historical remains. By constructing a diversified perceptual structure, visitors are competent to gain a panoramic cognition and profound thinking of southern Fujian culture in the limited exhibition space, excavate and interpret the diversity value of cultural heritage, and enshrine new vitality in the cultural heritage.

Keywords: Portable Miniature Museums · Immersive Experience · Intangible Cultural Heritage

1 Introduction

Museums, as tangible cultural symbols, play a crucial role in preserving cultural and natural heritage for future generations and providing valuable artifacts for scientific and historical research. However, traditional museum structures, as exhibition mediums, often focus on specific regions or periods, limiting their ability to showcase the diversity and interconnectedness of different cultures and histories. Additionally, most exhibits are presented to visitors through labels and descriptions, lacking innovative and diverse display formats. Moreover, the lack of change in exhibits over time reduces the likelihood of repeat visits, making it challenging for visitors to have new and engaging experiences. These factors result in a passive mode of museum visitation, making it difficult to meet the diverse needs of people.

In this context, portable micro-museums, as a novel form of mobile museums, can effectively address some of the limitations of traditional museums. Compared to traditional museums, portable micro-museums offer higher flexibility and multifunctionality. Firstly, in terms of site planning, portable micro-museums can be relocated at any time according to exhibition needs, unrestricted by venue limitations, providing visitors with a more convenient exhibition experience. Secondly, in terms of target audience, the exhibit content of portable micro-museums can be adjusted based on the needs and interests of different visitor groups, enabling better dissemination and showcasing of culture, thereby arousing emotional identification and awareness of intangible cultural heritage among visitors.

Considering the multifunctionality of portable micro-museums, the digital media age offers more possibilities and development paths for museum exhibitions. Visitors are no longer passive recipients of meticulously curated knowledge but engage in comprehensive sensory experiences, intellectual stimulation, aesthetic enjoyment, and social interaction. Through such experiences, visitors can learn, question, reflect, relax, and find sensory pleasure, as well as new social relationships, lasting impressions, or profound memories of the past. Different combinations and forms of digital exhibitions can bring different paths and effects to the content, narrative, and emotional expression of museums. Proper interactive effects not only promote the development of museum exhibitions and provide a good interactive experience but also fully leverage the advantages of museums in knowledge dissemination, public education, and cultural heritage preservation.

Compared to the established visiting experiences of traditional museums, this project emphasizes visitors' construction of their own history, culture, and self within the narrative. By creating personalized and captivating experiences, visitors are more likely to form emotional connections with heritage and become more aware of the necessity to protect it. The museum experience of this project goes beyond traditional artifact display and focuses on establishing emotional connections between visitors and cultural heritage. Through immersive technologies, visitors are transported to different times and places, allowing them to experience intangible cultural heritage in more compelling and interactive ways.

2 Design Concept

When designing this museum, inspiration was drawn from the distinctive architecture of the Minnan region, aiming to create a modern exhibition space. Historical buildings and sites, once bearing cultural memories as the most characteristic material heritage, have gradually disappeared in the process of urban transformation with the emergence of high-rise buildings, leading to profound changes in urban landscapes and cultural ambiance. The author hopes that visitors can not only gain knowledge of historical culture but also enjoy the pleasure of exhibition in this place that showcases modern aesthetics. In the spatial design, this project primarily incorporates the element of "yanwei ridge," which is a unique feature of the region's architecture. By employing diagonal symmetry enhancement techniques, the traditional yanwei ridge form is integrated with modern geometric elements. This approach not only preserves its original characteristics but also, from the perspective of visitors, positions the yanwei ridge as an important carrier of spatial narrative. The design rises from the ground and returns to the ground, creating the optimal display method, allowing viewers to deeply appreciate the creative regeneration of the yanwei ridge within the uplifting modern form

To showcase the combination of modern and traditional culture, this project utilizes modern technology to exhibit traditional elements of flower tiles and earthen buildings. When these traditional materials are incorporated or highlighted as part of the architectural composition, they transcend their physical nature and acquire meanings and sublimation that can evoke emotions and perceptions beyond themselves

This museum encapsulates architectural details from past to present, serving as a gateway for people to connect with the past, present, and future the moment they step into this unique museum. Inside the museum, they can witness the presentation of architectural exhibits from different periods, where people in the present construct their future by looking back. Minnan's architecture, in essence, is a museum with the concept of time as its theme

3 Design Strategies Based on Cognitive Experience

Cognition is closely related to users' perception, attention, memory, and thinking. In the context of interactive narrative presentations, users' cognitive processes involve four components: information acquisition, information processing, information output, and memory formation of the presented content. This article aims to establish a multi-role cognitive model, facilitate information transmission through multiple sensory channels, and design adaptive expressions for various types of content, all from the perspective of cognitive experience.

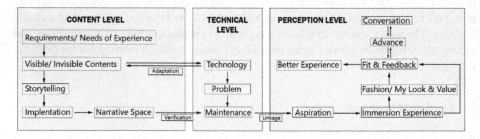

Fig. 1. Museum interactive experience design model.

3.1 Transmission of Multi-Sensory Information Channels

The foundation of a museum experience is the perceptual interaction between individuals and the material properties of objects [1]. The attributes of objects have an impact on the audience by triggering associations of perception, emotion, sensation, cognition, and memory. This influence not only shapes the audience's experience but also becomes an integral part of the materiality [2]. This project employs a multi-sensory cognitive approach to guide the audience in forming emotional connections with the physical attributes of objects, thus shaping unique personal experiences and creating a contextual experiential space based on multi-dimensional perception.

This project focuses on the Minnan architectural culture and takes three unique architectural forms as subplots to embark on a cultural journey.

Firstly, in the introduction section about Tulou (earthen buildings), empathy is evoked through a change in perspective, with time serving as the narrative thread. The audience can imagine themselves in the displayed era and understand the reasons behind the formation of this architectural form from a macro perspective. Additionally, the buildings are personified and interact with the audience, eliciting empathetic concern and guiding individuals to respond emotionally [6].

In the introduction section about Minnan decorative tiles, the audience's perception is linked through somatosensory interaction, which identifies three directly related sensory modalities: visual, tactile, and auditory. By transforming cultural stories into perceptible physical properties, the narrative guides the audience's emotional response, outlining the perceptual attributes of emotional affordance [4]. Visual and tactile modalities serve as the primary forms of emotional affordance. In this museum, the audience can intuitively experience the detailed parts of the architecture through three-dimensional interactive displays. As they pull out tiles from the grids, auditory elements accompany the experience. The displayed physical tiles occupy a central position, providing a stronger visual impact.

As the core of the exhibition, the introduction of the "swallowtail ridge" mainly utilizes 3D imaging technology and interactive mechanisms with immersive domes. After entering the exhibition space, the audience is guided by the upward-curving shape of the swallowtail ridge, following the changes in the display screen and moving their viewing perspective accordingly. Through somatosensory interaction, interactive mechanisms such as body leaning and screen control through shifting are triggered. Immersive 3D imaging technology transforms two-dimensional objects into three-dimensional forms, activating the audience to make movements in response to the operational mechanism, thus stimulating the audience's subjective agency with a sense of motion and responsiveness.

Interactive design transforms architecture from static artwork into a sensory experiential process connected to individuals. Essentially, it establishes a bidirectional communication bridge between exhibits and the audience, guiding and stimulating "communication and feedback," creating a mechanism for the audience to experience across time and space. Through the transmission of multi-sensory information, the cognitive experience dimension of users during the visit is expanded. By increasing cognitive channels and shifting the cognitive load from a single sensory channel, users can more comprehensively and effortlessly access information in interactive narrative digital displays, enriching their experience.

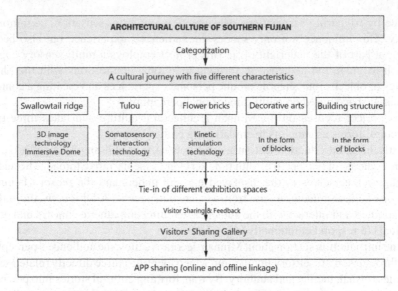

Fig. 2. Interactive experience design process diagram.

4 Emotional Experience-Based Design Strategies

When it comes to the emotional experience of traditional architecture, there are three main aspects: promoting social interaction during exhibitions, fostering a sense of belonging and identification, and mapping inner emotions. In interactive narrative digital displays, these aspects can be achieved through facilitating offline social interactions, creating online communities, and establishing immersive contexts.

4.1 Building Online Communities to Foster Group Belonging

The majority of the audience for the mobile museum consists of local residents who share the same language system and customs, and most of them hold similar notions about architectural craftsmanship. By creating an online community based on these character-istics, a local circle with its own regional attributes can be formed. The establishment of a digital community extends offline interactions to the online realm, facilitating a sense of belonging and identification among local audiences through the production and circulation of community-generated digital content.

Field research conducted on existing museums revealed that while interactive engagement among visitors and their companions can be fostered during offline exhibi-tions, there is a lack of linkage between visitors entering the museum at different times or in different batches. This overlooks the potential for attracting repeat visits from users and hampers content innovation and re-creation.

Therefore, for this project, creating a network-based user-generated content (UGC) community through a dedicated website and social media platforms can encourage audi-ence engagement with the socially-oriented content presented in the digital displays. This strengthens the significance of the exhibit's content through public contributions, allowing the public to gain a deeper understanding and broader perspective on the related material culture and history.

4.2 Creating Immersive Contexts to Foster Emotional Engagement

Context is composed of all tangible and intangible information [5]. The impact of context on emotional experiences can be achieved through two aspects: first, by utilizing context perception to simulate real scenarios and create a natural emotional immersion; second, by employing the concept of "situation" as proposed by Dewey in psychology, known as "reconstructive memory," to construct immersive contexts [3]. The generation of emotions can be facilitated through context perception and imagination, promoting recollection and empathy.

Moreover, viewers will engage in cognitive imagination to construct immersive experiential contexts through "reconstructive memory." Human memory evolves with time and scenes, and memories are closely associated with emotions. Contextual participation influences users' emotional experiences in interactive narrative digital exhibitions.

5 Conclusion

This paper primarily focused on the research of interactive narrative design in digital exhibitions of mobile museums. Through analysis and investigation, the predicaments faced by contemporary museums were identified. The categorization of display content, handling methods of display content, and user behavior patterns in the digital presentation of traditional architecture were summarized. By combining the analysis of traditional architecture, a model for constructing narratives in digital exhibitions was established, clarifying the current public perception and emotional connection to traditional architecture, as well as user needs and experiential dimensions. Interactive narrative design principles for digital exhibitions were proposed, and corresponding display strategies were designed based on different experiential dimensions.

The trend in the development of contemporary museums emphasizes that exhibitions are not solely about displaying objects but also about providing opportunities for public experiences with the users at the center. This project showcases not only the rich and diverse intangible cultural heritage but also injects new vitality into it through innovative technologies and interactive designs. By offering visitors unique immersive experiences, this project promotes cultural heritage in a striking and memorable way, making it more accessible to a broader audience. By highlighting the importance of cultural exchange and understanding, this project strives to raise awareness about the significance of preserving cultural heritage and its diversity. By emphasizing the value of cultural heritage, it aims to inspire visitors to become advocates for its preservation and continuation. The project aims to bring the past to life and connect it with the present, fostering a deeper appreciation of cultural heritage and its profound impact on our collective human history.

References

1. Dudley, S.: Museum materialities: objects. Sense Feeling J. **2**(5), 99–110 (2016)

570   L. Zhai

2. Dudley, S.: Museum objects: experiencing the properties of Things. In: Editor, F., Editor, S. (eds.) CONFERENCE 2016, LNCS, vol. 9999, pp. 1–13. Springer, Heidelberg (2016)
3. Deng, Z., Xu, L., Zhu, Q., Gu, J.: Research on Dialogue Content of Visitors in Natural Museums. Book title. 2nd edn. Publisher, Location (1999)
4. Gibson, J.: The Ecological Approach to Visual Perception. In: 9th International Proceedings on Proceedings, pp. 1–2. Publisher, Location (2010)
5. He, L., Yang, X.: Analysis of the current situation of smart museum construction in China. Chinese Museum **03**, 116–126 (2018)
6. Maibom, H.: Self-Simulation and Empathy. In: Roughley, N., Schramme, T. (eds.) Forms of Fellow Feeling: Empathy, Sympathy, Concern and Moral Agency, pp. 109–132. Cambridge: Cambridge University Press (2018)

Author Index

Printed in the United States
by Baker & Taylor Publisher Services